In Her Nature

Also by Rachel Hewitt

A Revolution of Feeling

Map of a Nation

In Her Nature

How Women Break Boundaries in the Great Outdoors

RACHEL HEWITT

Chatto & Windus
LONDON

1 3 5 7 9 10 8 6 4 2

Chatto & Windus, an imprint of Vintage, is part of the Penguin Random House group of companies whose addresses can be found at global.penguinrandomhouse.com

First published by Chatto & Windus in 2023

Maps by Bill Donohoe

penguin.co.uk/vintage

Typeset in 12/14.75 pt Dante MT Std by Jouve (UK), Milton Keynes
Printed and bound in Great Britain by Clays Ltd, Elcograf S.p.A.

The authorised representative in the EEA is Penguin Random House Ireland, Morrison Chambers, 32 Nassau Street, Dublin D02 YH68

A CIP catalogue record for this book is available from the British Library

HB ISBN 9781784742898

In memory of:

Josie Camus

Nick Hewitt

Bethany Jane Skinner

Willy Brown

Ian Newbon

Pete Newbon

And for my girls, Molly, Martha and Esme

Contents

Introduction 1

PART ONE: FREEDOM

1. Running like a girl 19
2. The high life 39
3. The mountains have room for all 61
4. Why can't you just run faster? 97
5. In the mountains, there you feel free 129

PART TWO: LOSS

6. Lockdown 171
7. Separation anxiety 199
8. Frozen out 229

PART THREE: RECOVERY

9. Risk management 267
10. Resistance training 303
11. Recovery run 337

Afterword 377
Acknowledgements 379
List of illustrations 385
Bibliography 387
Notes 447
Index 497

Introduction

In April 2018, I visit a running shop to buy a new pair of shoes. The store's three walls are covered in shelves displaying brightly coloured trainers – road-running trainers with soles built from hollow pods that compress as they strike the ground and bounce back propulsively; narrow, fell-running shoes with sharp toothy 'lugs' across the bottom to cling to mud and peat. There are ultra-running shoes with thick, mattressed soles to cushion the feet after 50, 100, even 200 miles; and plimsoles with spikes protruding from the front, to grip the rubber of athletics tracks. There are shoes for pretty much every distance and every type of ground cover. But they are almost all for men. The shop has only four types of running shoe made specifically for women.

Women's bodies need different shoes from men. Because of our wider hips, women have a larger 'Q angle' – the angle between a vertical line running through the kneecap and a diagonal line tracking from the kneecap to the hip – meaning that female runners are more likely to run 'knock-kneed'. So shoes designed specifically for women are often shaped to encourage the foot and knee outwards, to mitigate this tendency. The proportions of women's feet are also different to men's: wider at the forefoot and narrower at the heel, meaning that when women wear men's running shoes, we often find them too tight at the front and too loose at the back. And women are, on average, lighter than men, so the cushioning on men's running shoes may not properly compress and spring back under a female runner's weight.

I ask the shop assistant why they stock so few shoes for women.

'It's the numbers,' he replies, flicking a wing of hair off his forehead. 'Men have been running since, like, ancient Greece. But women only started around 1975. There are lots of women running now but it's a really recent thing. So kit designers are playing catch-up. Whereas they've been designing for men for hundreds of years.'

Hmm, sounds plausible. I nod, smile, pay for a pair of trainers and leave.

A few weeks later, while I'm out running, I think about the shop assistant's claim that 'women only started running around 1975'. Even if he was referring only to running as a sport or weekend pursuit, this surely can't be true? Running, in its most basic form, is a pretty natural human activity. Young children have to be socialised *not* to run and are taught to walk instead, along school corridors and busy pavements.

I decide to look deeper into the notion that women have only really taken to running since the mid 1970s, for roughly as long as I have been alive. But women don't feature much in bestselling books about running. Covers overwhelmingly bear silhouettes of sleek and honed men's physiques, posed in the muscular right-angles of running 'flight', and women are often invisible inside these books too. One writer claims that 'the body-fat ratio' of the 'average fit person' is 15 per cent. But he means the average *male* 'fit person'. The average fit woman's body fat percentage is 21–4 per cent.[1]

In one memoir I read about female runners through a heterosexual man's eyes – as 'pretty girls' whom it's 'pretty wonderful to watch' – but there is nothing about women's own achievements or what running means to us. Another book claims to explore 'how running makes us human', but when the author lists all the reasons that people run, he doesn't mention motivations that I recognise – such as needing to find myself again after having children – and I suspect that many of these writers are really interested in 'how running makes us men'.[2]

Women are not entirely absent from the sports shelves of bookshops. Recently books about 'running like a girl' have been written by authors such as Bella Mackie, Anna McNuff, Alexandra Heminsley and Rosie Swale Pope. But women's writings aren't always given equal credence or visibility. 'Look at any list of the greatest sports books of all time and you will struggle to find a female protagonist represented,' writes Emma John in an article that demands: 'Where are all the great books about women in sport?' Mixed-sex anthologies about sport, the outdoors and the natural world are routinely male-dominated. Even *Granta* magazine's landmark 'New Nature Writing' volume included only two women to seventeen men (despite the (male) editor's pledge that he wanted it to offer an alternative to the 'conventional nature writer' who is 'a certain kind of man, and it would always be a man: bearded, badly dressed, ascetic, misanthropic'). And this male bias continues across other forms of publications, including websites and blogs. One site I encounter makes a similar claim to the man in the shop and tells me that 'women didn't run before 1974'.[3]

I widen my search and start looking for women in the outdoors more generally – female hikers, mountaineers, rock climbers. There seems to be a benchmark here too for when women first entered outdoor sport. A blog post suggests that women's long-distance walking started in 1955, when Emma Gatewood became the first woman to hike the entire Appalachian Trail. One scholar reports that 'few women were . . . climbing' mountains in the nineteenth century and another claims that 'women's historic role [in sport] was that of handkerchief-fluttering spectators'.[4] It is even harder to find any mention of either early BAME sportswomen, women athletes with disabilities, and/or those from working-class backgrounds. After a number of Google searches, I read about Sophia Danenberg, the first Black woman to climb Everest (in 2006); Bachendri Pal, the first Indian woman to climb Everest (in 1984); and Junko Tabei from Japan, who became the first woman to reach the summit of Everest (in 1975). But I cannot easily find available information about any BAME female climbers before the 1970s. Blogs and articles about the history of disability in sport rarely cover a time before archer Neroli Fairhall became the first paraplegic competitor in the (1984) Olympic Games.

This initial research leaves me with the impression that, before the 1970s, women were basically absent from the sporting world. Perhaps the man in the running shop was right after all?

Then, while I'm continuing to look online, I come across a collection of digitised photographs, taken in the 1880s and 1890s, by the glamorously named Lizzie Le Blond.

I discover that Lizzie – born Elizabeth Hawkins-Whitshed – was a highly respected 'lady mountaineer', who recorded the challenges she set herself in thousands of photographs of the mountains, valleys and lakes in the Upper Engadin region of the Swiss Alps. Her photographs are not just of solitary mountain scenes: she also captured the people with whom she climbed, hiked, skated, tobogganed, played tennis and bicycled. Everywhere in her photographs there are women. Le Blond photographed sportswomen racing skeleton sledges down the notoriously fast Cresta Run and through the snowed-in streets of St Moritz. She photographed female athletes cycling across Switzerland, Italy and France. She photographed women figure-skating, curling, playing 'bandy'; women competing in singles and doubles tennis matches. Women roped together, peering down crevasses and scrambling up ridges and hiking through forest trails. And she wrote about women taking part in 'hare and hounds' competitive running events. These are no handkerchief-fluttering spectators.

Lizzie's photograph of two women tobogganing on the Cresta Run in St Moritz

Women playing bandy, a form of ice hockey, in 1890s Switzerland, likely photographed by Lizzie's friend Tony Dod

I immediately want to know more. I read a few potted biographies of Lizzie Le Blond – I learn that she was 'the best-known woman mountain climber of her time', 'among the world's first three female film-makers', responsible for 'thousands of photographs', the first president of the Ladies' Alpine Club, 'often profiled in women's magazines' and author of '69 works in 220 publications in 3 languages' – and wonder why it is that she is not better known.[5]

Lizzie's photographs send a jolt through me. They make me realise that, deep down, I too had somehow subscribed to a version of women's sporting history not dissimilar to that described by the man in the shop. I'd bought into a stereotype that Victorian women were 'Angels in the House', reluctant to show an ankle, not racing around the hills with flushed and sweaty cheeks. In an instant, Lizzie's images demolish these stereotypes. They show me women engaging in both solitary and organised outdoor pursuits. It is a history that seems to have been lost. What happened, I wonder, to cause these early sportswomen to be so obscured from our view of the past? What determined that their stories would largely disappear from public memory?

Reading further into her life, I learn that Lizzie was among a number of women who stopped participating in sport and other outdoor pursuits near the start of the twentieth century. Around this time, French aristocrat Baron Pierre de Coubertin, founder of the modern Olympic Games and the International Olympic Committee, declared women's sport to be 'against the laws of nature'. His physical ideal was an adult man. The twentieth-century, modern Olympic spirit was defined as the 'exaltation of male athleticism . . . with the applause of women as the reward'.[6] And it strikes me that the most famous icons of early twentieth-century sport and adventure are similarly male-dominated: the Everest expeditions, *Chariots of Fire*, Shackleton in Antarctica, Baden-Powell and his boy scouts, the attempts at the four-minute mile. Where did all the women, such as the ones in Lizzie's photographs, go?

I wonder what motivated powerful and influential men such as Pierre de Coubertin to make women so unwelcome in the world of sport, and what effect that exclusion had on individual women, and on women in society more generally. Could Lizzie Le Blond's descent into historical obscurity have been a result of this systematic marginalisation of women from organised sport and outdoor spaces? After delving deeper I decide to write a book about Lizzie and how she and other women of her generation found – and lost – their own freedoms through outdoor sports.

Then, while I'm in the middle of my research, I am upended. In the space of five months, I lose five members of my family.

My father had been unwell for most of his adult life, with an addiction to alcohol that meant I rarely phoned him after six in the evening, dreading the slurring and repetitions.

One evening around eighteen months earlier, he'd sent me a text asking if he could speak to me that evening. I knew, even before he called, what was wrong. Finally, his body had given up.

Over the next year, Dad was proud to be placed on the liver transplant list, a recognition of his genuine efforts to claw back health by eliminating salt, joining a gym and staying off the booze. During this time, he received a number of TACE (transarterial chemoembolisation) procedures – injections of chemotherapy medicine straight into his liver tumours to suffocate their blood supply. But in early 2019, almost exactly a year after they'd found the first tumour, a new one is detected: belligerent, fast-growing.

'I'm sorry I had to give you such a large dose,' the radiologist apologises after administering another TACE injection. Within a few weeks, my dad is vomiting grainy black blood. His stomach balloons above the height of his small yellow head, which rests on three understuffed hospital pillows. Dad's liver is entering the final stage of what I will learn from his death certificate is called 'Decompensated Cirrhosis' – when its damage fatally outweighs its function. He dies, on his own, in the liver ward, at two in the morning on 1 March that year.

Just days before Dad died I'd been on a train en route to visit him in hospital when my phone had vibrated with a call from my mother. 'I've got some very distressing news and it's not about your father,' she said. 'Bethany was pulled from the sea in the early hours of Sunday morning. It's not certain she's going to die, but . . .'

Bethany is my young cousin: a glorious whirlwind of bleached dreadlocks, piercings, mandalas and zest. So alive. Twirling across my Facebook timeline in haphazard videos of laughing, smooching young women. Somehow – and what happened that night will probably never be clear – after leaving a nightclub on the coast with her boyfriend, who had been arguing with her, she ends up in the sea, alone, unable to swim. It is a winter sea at high tide – bitter and violent – with waves up to fifteen metres high. Her boyfriend reportedly tries, but fails, to save her and a lifeboat is called. By the time it reaches Bethany, she has been in the water for nearly half an hour, thrown repeatedly against the pier. Somehow, she is resuscitated and taken to hospital. Over the next few days, while my father is dying in a hospital in Nottingham, machines keep my young cousin alive. But then all the tests show that she is not really alive. When the machines are turned off, she dies quickly. She is just twenty-two years old.

Months later, my uncle passes away – a shock to everyone except himself. Living in my ninety-five-year-old grandmother's attic, he had not told anyone about his cancer, and the first she knows is when an ambulance arrives, and he is carried down to hospital, to die.

Everyone is so very sad. My mother and I are like some kind of early Christian diptych of mourning, each of us imploring the other for relief. But I cannot be – have never been – what my mother seems to want, and I cannot seem to give her what she appears to want now. This becomes too painful for us both.

I temporarily halt our contact. Within months, the estrangement between us becomes permanent and necessary. Another loss to add to the year's toll. Or maybe it is the reinscription of a loss or absence that has always been there.

I had not expected grief to be so physical. I usually run pretty much every day, but now I cannot manage it. On my first outing following Dad's and Bethany's deaths I have to stop after four kilometres. Thinking about my decimated family makes me sob. It tightens my throat and chest and makes it impossible to breathe.

But, over the next few months, I gradually start to move again.

In August, five months after Dad died, I have my first really good run of the summer. Around 6 p.m. I set off on one of my favourite local routes: five miles on a soft path around muddy fields and an empty golf course, and then home via a ragged piece of common land. I feel strong and calm throughout. I speed up in the final mile or so to arrive home breathing hard, bare skin thrumming against the warm evening air. I have a shower, wrap my hair in a towel, pull on yoga pants and a sweatshirt and go downstairs to the kitchen, where I boil a kettle for spaghetti, chop cauliflower, garlic, chilli and rosemary, toss them in oil and lemon juice and put them in the oven. While the spaghetti roils on the hob and the cauliflower roasts, I pour a glass of wine, pick up my phone and scroll through Twitter, Facebook and, finally, my emails.

There are messages from work – the daily round-up of 'university in the news' stories; an agenda for an upcoming meeting – and marketing shots from sportswear shops and a race entry website. There are also two emails whose subject lines I cannot fathom: 'Emergency

W. Brown Please Read'. I do not recognise the sender's name; it looks like junk. But my much-loved stepfather's name is Willy Brown, which surely cannot be coincidence. I open one of the emails. 'Please can you phone Willy's phone my sister has it Willy is very very poorly, sorry to email we cannot get your number.' In the moment, I do not understand what it is asking of me. I do not understand what information it is imparting.

I open the second email, which is more coherent. 'Willy has been airlifted to hospital, they think he has had multiple clots. I am so sorry.' It is from the daughter of my stepfather's second wife (my step-stepsister, I suppose. I have never met her; it's complicated).

In the event, my stepfather isn't airlifted to hospital – he dies in an ambulance on the driveway of his home in a village ten miles south of Cambridge, having developed a pain in his leg while gardening. That is it, I think. Now I have no real family at all.

The night Willy dies, I don't know what to do with myself. I send an email to my boss requesting yet another period of compassionate leave. I think I might go to Cambridgeshire to see Willy's wife, but I've missed the last train and I don't like driving in the dark. I think I might pull on my trainers and head torch and go out, for a walk or a run, by the river, to the black fields between York and Bishopthorpe. I think I might go to the moors in the morning.

Instead, I go to bed and stay there, more or less, for two weeks. There I fantasise about coasting: about lifting my feet from a bike's pedals and freewheeling. About running down a hill, arms unfurled. About my body's buoyancy in water. In bed, I starfish across the sheets, trying to recreate that feeling of ease after hard work, of floating.

At first, I think I will never run again. It seems unimaginable. I cannot even stand up straight. In those weeks I shuffle between the bed and the sofa. My eyes only open halfway. I am heavy and slow and I do not want food or drink.

At night, not being able to bear proximity to another living body, I leave my husband Pete asleep in our bed, go downstairs and watch property and house design programmes. A woman purchases a derelict Victorian milking parlour in south London and sees in it the potential for a Parisian hidden courtyard or the secret garden of a Moroccan riad. In the early hours of the mornings, I scour Rightmove for ruined dairies and small plots of old industrial land in London.

On 4 August, I am supposed to be running a marathon: my fourteenth. I would usually spend the days immediately before and after exchanging tips and debriefing with fellow runners on the race company's Facebook page. But I lie in bed, staring at the window or sleeping. I do not open my computer or turn on my phone. I let the battery of my sports watch run down. Its assessment of my current fitness level changes from 'maintaining', to 'recovery', to 'detraining'. Finally, it switches itself off. I do not recharge it.

Years ago, I remember reading an article about a kind of 'map of mourning'. Clinical psychologist Susan Silk and mediator Barry Goldman devised a 'ring theory' of grief, in which they placed friends and family members in concentric circles, according to their proximity to the deceased – like contour lines on a mountain. People most affected by the death occupy the smallest circle, in the centre, at the summit. 'In each larger ring put the next closest people,' instruct Silk and Goldman. 'Parents and children [of the deceased] before more distant relatives. Intimate friends in smaller rings, less intimate friends in larger ones.' The rings then serve as guides for how people affected by a death might offer and seek support: 'Comfort IN, dump OUT'.[7] Mourners should not burden those who are closer to the centre, higher up the mountain. If they need support, they should seek it from those in wider circles, lower contour lines; at a greater distance from the eye of the storm, further down the mountain. The few individuals right at the top lean on others beneath them, as they attempt their slow and careful descent.

Right now, I do not know my place on this map of grief. Willy is the family member to whom I've been closest for most of my life, even after he and my mother divorced – but there is no official name for the relationship between a stepfather and stepdaughter after the 'step' between them has been dissolved. I'm not sure that I even count as a relative any more.

At Willy's funeral, I do not know where to sit. When we arrive, there are not enough places to allow me to be together with my husband and three young daughters. It is August when Willy dies and friends are on holiday and very few people offer condolences. Even when people do contact me, I am offended at the muted, insufficient nature of their messages: 'Sorry for your loss,' 'so sad', 'life is so hard sometimes'. I cannot bring myself to politely 'like' these comments on Facebook. Only the most exaggerated expressions of sympathy seem fitting: the friends who club together to send extravagant care packages – a caravan of parcels of books, magazines, cashmere socks, gin, biscuits; bags of entertainment for my children; moisturiser, pillow spray, bubble bath; pyjamas that I will not take off for days.

Then, over the next weeks and months, I realise I need to be outdoors, to rebuild the strength and health that have been eroded by grief.

But the world beyond my house appears to have changed during my absence. It now seems full of dangers and threats I had not previously noticed. One evening in the early autumn, about six weeks after Willy's death, I jog down to the river, past a buckling picnic bench around which three teenage boys sit, legs splayed, rolling cigarettes. As I run, one calls out, 'Give us a smile!' I mutter 'Fuck off' under my breath. Then I stop running and I walk back to them. Fuck it.

'I'm not here to entertain you,' I say. 'Do you have any idea what it's like to not be able to run down the street in peace?'

A boy stands. He is almost a foot taller than me, and his baggy sweatshirt hangs in pleats from his muscular shoulders. 'How dare you talk to us like that?' he says. 'Do you think you're better than us? Do you think you're too good to smile for us?' I start walking away, and he follows me, shouting, 'Fucking bitch!'

The next day, I am pedalling along the cycle path that borders our road, and a car tries to overtake me. We are both heading in the direction of a traffic island and, unable to overtake in time, the driver violently swerves his car back towards the cycle lane, beeping. He comes so close that if I lift my hand from the handlebars, I could touch his passenger window. I raise my middle finger – fuck OFF – and ride on, and a little way ahead the traffic lights turn to red and we come to a halt beside one another. The driver lowers the passenger window, and he shouts at me, 'Fucking bitch!'

Later, I am at the train station, buying coffee and a croissant for my journey. I hand over my reusable travel mug to the barista, and a man standing in the queue behind me speaks: 'Oh, look at you, Miss Goody-Two-Shoes, trying to save the world.' I, and the female barista, say nothing. On the train, I find my reserved window seat, squeeze past my neighbour's reluctantly slanted knees, and slot myself into my chair. I put in earplugs, fold down the table and slide my croissant out from its paper bag. My neighbour has his arms outspread on both armrests, including the shared one in between us, and I have to pull the croissant apart with my elbows clamped to my ribs. He taps me on the shoulder and I remove my earplugs, and he says: 'You should really think about going low-carb, y'know.' FUCK OFF.

A month or so later, I am taking part in a long-distance trail-running race and am jogging along a narrow muddy footpath when I hear footsteps behind me. A man is coming up quickly and his eyes are focused on the few metres in front of his feet. But then he detours onto a rough track veering away from the main trail. Realising his mistake, he swears loudly and doubles back to rejoin the route. I turn to smile in anticipated greeting as he accelerates towards me. Eyes still low and ahead, he overtakes me and, as he does so, he places one hand on each of my shoulders and pushes me backwards off the path – as if I am a gate or a recalcitrant tree branch, needing to be swung out of his way. I stagger to keep my balance in the ditch and shout 'Fuck off!' after him. He doesn't look up. I make my way back onto the path, shaking with rage. A woman comes up behind. 'He was in a hurry,' she says, rolling her eyes. I tut in agreement.

These encounters are part of the fabric of ordinary life. Usually I'd probably forget about them after a couple of hours. But now, I tear up. I cannot bear any more attempts to make me feel like I do not belong. I need to be outdoors, I need to run. It is the only way I can feel like I have a place again, in the world and in my own body. However, I'm increasingly scared to go outside.

When I originally encountered Lizzie Le Blond and pored over her images of outdoor sportswomen – women on lakes, hills, mountains, courts, rinks, pitches, footpaths, bridleways and roads – I'd felt intellectually affronted that such women had been sidelined from narratives about the history of sport. But after my family bereavements, the book I'm researching takes on a more personal and present-day significance. I start viewing the world through a lens of grief. All I can see is how women are repeatedly deprived of opportunities to be free in the world outside, and how that, in turns, leads to further losses for us – of the ability to feel strong, comfortable and at home in our own bodies and minds, to move around the world with confidence and ease, to be fully accommodated in the public sphere of work and politics.

The harassment and discomfort I experience outdoors has knock-on consequences elsewhere. I become more timid about raising my hand in meetings and research seminars; more afraid to speak to strangers; more reluctant to exit the front door without a full shield of make-up. When the world outside the house starts to feel hostile to women, it affects far more than our running and sport.

The book I'm writing starts to shift and expand. Originally, I had wanted to investigate whether the years around the start of the twentieth century were a historical turning point in which women were pushed out of such sports – and whether this departure was coerced by men such as de Coubertin and the institutions they represented. But now I am starting to wonder if there is any relationship between early sportswomen's stories and my own recent experiences of street harassment. I scribble a question in my notebook: *Are we living through a period in which women worldwide are being driven out of the outdoors?* I think back to the first questions that Lizzie Le Blond's photographs prompted in me. A few months ago these queries were mainly academic, but now they're much more personal. I still want to unearth the stories of Lizzie's generation of *fin-de-siècle* female athletes, but I now also want to understand the constraints that women of other periods and places negotiate in order to feel free and strong outdoors. I want to delve into the obstacles that sometimes seem insurmountable and prevent us from going outside at all. I want to learn from women who have experienced exclusion from outdoor activities; to understand the different types of barrier and hostility that they have faced historically and how they have fought back against attempts to limit them. I want to learn about women of the nineteenth and early twentieth centuries *and* today.

Ultimately, I am desperate to find out how women, past and present, have resisted and recovered from attempts to intimidate us outdoors. I need to find a way to recover from my own griefs: from the loss of so many loved ones, and the loss of my ability to move freely outside.

This is a story which does not just lie in books, libraries and archives, but on moors and mountains too. In the telling of it, I realise I will need to run as well as to read and write.

De Coubertin had decreed that being free and active and powerful outdoors was not in women's nature, but I know that's not true. I want to enter the worlds captured by Lizzie in her photographs; to learn how women staked a claim to the world beyond the home by discovering previously untapped strengths out of doors. And to see how different the natural world looks when we view it through the eyes of women rather than the men who traditionally dominate sport and nature-writing. I want to step into *her* nature.

PART ONE

Freedom

I.

Running like a girl

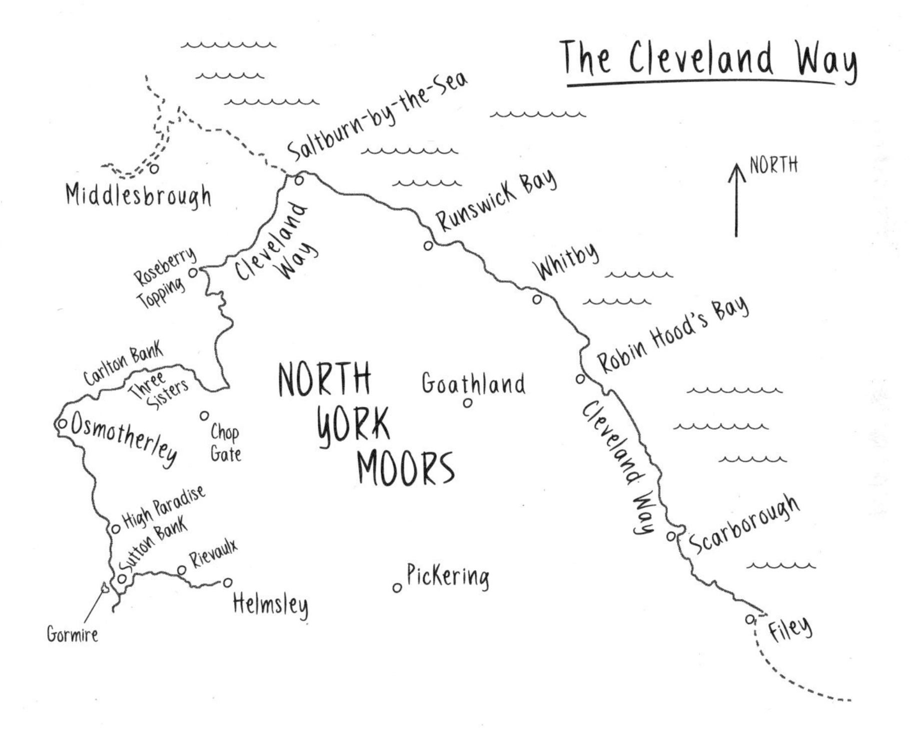

Every run I do is saved on my running watch and transferred to its manufacturer's database, Garmin Connect, where the information is translated into graphs. These graphs are designed to show change, mostly: a decrease in my resting heart-rate, or improvement of my 'VO2 max' (the rate at which my body takes in oxygen during exercise, which can indicate levels of fitness and endurance). But each run's dataset is also overlain by personal memories, which do not show up on this app: the stiles I clambered over, and the bushes I crouched in to urinate; the burst of endorphins that made my arms tingle; the rush of fear when a strange man leaped out in front of me. My watch's database is a type of autobiographical resource – 'My Life in Running'. It shows that running is both bellwether and bolster to my wellbeing. If I am running less, usually there is something wrong, and the missed runs make the unhappiness worse.

After Willy dies, Garmin records that I do not run at all for two weeks, which feels like an unimaginably long time when I am used to running every day. Finally, I attempt a brief run from the gym, where I leave my three daughters in sports classes and Pete lifting weights. I jog down the hill to a piece of common land, where cattle are grazing far off in the opposite corner, and onto a public right of way at the other end, bordered by twelve-foot wire fences.

Here, my legs slow and stop. I usually enjoy being distracted while I'm running: I like to mull over recipes for dinner or imagine shades of paint on a garden trellis. But now the balance is off. I am being distracted from running by grief; it is taking up too much of my bandwidth, ticking over in the background, slowing me down – as when my laptop can't cope with my requests because of updates or malware invisibly taking up its resources. My computer flags its distress with the spinning wait cursor, and this is how I feel too: like a ball or pinwheel, spiralling with rage, disbelief and sadness. On top of all of this, running is just too much extra work.

I walk home slowly, past children picking blackberries from brambles growing up against the fences, go back indoors, and climb back under the bedcovers.

Three days later, I get up again and drive to Sutton Bank Visitors' Centre, a neat, low stone building on the western brink of the North York Moors National Park. I plan to follow a route I know well: a short version of a trail marathon I ran the previous year. I start by running along a section of the Cleveland Way long-distance footpath, along the top verge of the moors. Cleveland is the name of an old administrative county formed around the estuary of the River Tees, and straddling County Durham and North Yorkshire. It means, literally, 'Cliff-land', and it is indeed a land of cliffs, from the coastal type in the east, to the inland limestone escarpments that outline the northern and western borders of the moors, at places such as Highcliff Nab and Roulston Scar. As I run, I look down over one of these inland cliffs to the settlements below: Sutton-under-Whitestonecliffe, Thirlby, Boltby. Another village may, or may not, be down there too, submerged beneath Gormire – a lake which is not visibly fed by, nor discharges into, any overground rivers or streams, and seems to have emerged in the landscape miraculously, fully formed.

I cannot run for long. My stomach aches, as if I have been struck by a bowling ball. I half-stagger, half-trot, along the cliff edge – the way I run in dreams when I am being chased, or impeded from reaching a loved, lost person. The path passes through a small wood and then sidles alongside a farm called High Paradise until it reaches a crossroads. If I were to turn left here, the Cleveland Way would take me north along the old Hambleton Drove Road – one of the oldest roads in England, used in the eighteenth century by Scottish drovers manoeuvring tens of thousands of Galloway and West Highland cattle down to market – to a village called Osmotherley.

But I do not turn left, and instead I leave the Cleveland Way and continue dead ahead, cutting across open moor that is purpling into rust as late summer turns to early autumn. From the moorland, I drop down through green forests and farmland and wind up in the ruins of Rievaulx Abbey. Here I buy a fizzy apple drink at the tea-rooms and take it to the garden, before the sensory overload of barking dogs and squabbling children drives me out. The four miles back to my starting point at Sutton Bank take me on steep slopes through lush firs, and small lakes reflecting blue skies. They make me think of Switzerland, or how I imagine it to be. I get into the car and drive back to cuddle with my children on the sofa before bedtime.

Though it has not been a remarkable day – my running has been slow and clumsy – the excursion has got me out of bed, got me moving again, and persuaded my body back into some basic routines. Grief has turned my body into a residence I no longer recognise. But I hope that I will be able to run my way back home eventually.

I hope that running will help me recover, because I have found it to be true before.

In October 2015, we – Pete and I, our three girls and our small black cat Mattie – moved from London to the north of England – to York. We moved partly to be closer to Pete's university job, and partly because I wanted to leave the south. My closest friend, Josie, whom I'd known since childhood, had just died of cancer at the age of thirty-five. It seemed less hazardous to flee the places I associated with her, and to start again, than to stay in a city where her absence would daily trip me up.

In the immediate wake of Josie's death, I picked fights with other old, loved friends. I cropped my hair short and I drank a lot. When my work contract came up for renewal, I handed in my notice. We put our house on the market, accepted an offer within a week and bought a run-down ex-bed-and-breakfast on a busy main road, a little way outside York's city walls. In London, we had known most of our neighbours by name, and we left with promises to return to the street's twice-yearly parties. Our new house had no neighbours and no street parties. We hired builders, who ripped out supporting walls and bathrooms and the kitchen, and left us with an ancient toilet plumbed into the shed and a makeshift cooking area on the half-turn of the stairs where, every evening, I scoured inches of dust from an electric two-ring hob to heat up baked beans for the kids.

I regretted the move within a week. Our double buggy didn't fit through any of the doorways in the small medieval city. I was used to the anonymity and indifference of London's crowds and was startled by passers-by who stopped me on the pavements to tell me that I 'have my hands full' with my three small children. Mattie, the cat we brought with us from London, was soon run over and killed on the busy road in front of the house.

On the day we arrived in York, it started raining and it did not stop for four months. The river, which runs through the city centre, flooded. At first, it submerged the riverside cycle lane, and then the rain kept falling and the waters continued to rise until, in the old city, cars crossed a bridge at the same height as a boat that floated aloft on the water beside them. Rain gushed from our house's guttering down the drainpipes and engulfed the cellar. Our road flooded at both ends until there was no way in and no way out.

Not understanding then the rivers and geography of Yorkshire, I had no idea where all this water was coming from, so it was easy to fantasise that it originated inside me: a deluge of sadness. When the floodwaters finally receded, leaving a sticky coating of sludge through the city, I decided I needed to find something to reorient me up here in the north; to introduce me to the Yorkshire that lay outside the city walls. I remembered how much I had loved hiking as a teenager and told a friend how much I wished I could take it up again – but I lamented that, now I had children, there was no time. 'What about trail running?' she suggested. 'It's like hiking, but quicker.'

So that winter, I downloaded a beginner's trail-running plan from the internet. Garmin's database reminds me now that, in those early weeks, I began by jogging for just two kilometres at a time, or three: a short trudge along the river path and back. It wasn't particularly pleasant at first. My legs didn't propel my body weight with the elastic, effortless motion that other runners seemed to possess; instead, they felt like weights themselves, which I had to drag across the ground. I kicked rocks and stumbled, clutching for handholds in the air. I was embarrassed by the swollen redness of my face, and how the soft edges of my thighs audibly rubbed together in my leggings. Running was messy and I seemed to leak constantly: urine from the prolapse that was a legacy of multiple childbirths; sweat prickling into beads across my cheeks and back and pooling between my breasts. And I was scared all the time: of breaking an ankle, of getting lost, of developing hypothermia; of having a heart attack; of being raped and murdered.

But there was joy, too, right from the beginning, and the joy was just enough to outweigh the discomforts. The initial stiffness in my legs soon receded and running started to feel more like the sort of light, scampering motion that my children enjoyed; more like playing than trudging. On odd occasions when I ran fast, a small explosion seemed to take place in my brain, flooding my system with a galaxy of happiness, making me smile and run even faster, and reminding me of dancing in nightclubs when I was younger. The fear did not entirely go, but I came to think that death was not so likely an outcome of a 5K trot around the park. And I loved spending more time outdoors. The rest of my life revolved around being enclosed: all our shopping was done online; I took my children to playgroups in the car and my working life was entirely spent in classrooms, lecture theatres, libraries and my office. Running was the only time in the week that I got to breathe cool air and stretch my limbs in damp riverside grass. And so, I persevered.

By the following spring, Easter 2016, I was able to run for an hour. During a weekend excursion in a cottage on the edge of the Yorkshire Dales National Park, I jogged up a rocky track to a cairn at the top of the nearby peak, then plunged down a steep funnel cut into the hillside to a reservoir and dam, before curving home on a gently declining path with a sharp uphill coda. Over the next year, I was able to spend even more time on my feet and I started plotting more elaborate routes. Local bus schedules and train timetables were like passwords that opened up places such as the twelfth-century spa town of Knaresborough, where I ran along a tree-lined cycle path before dropping down to the densely wooded gorge that collars the river. My feet jack-knifed in claggy mud, my cheeks grew sticky with effort, and I ran the final descent, arms outstretched and whooping like a child mimicking a plane.

One day I ran up the steep ascent of Roseberry Topping – a hill once thought to be the region's highest, and which, because of a partial collapse in 1912 of the shale and clay underlying its hard sandstone cap, now resembles Hokusai's Great Wave. (Rather hyperbolically, it is known as Yorkshire's Matterhorn, though my children think Roseberry Topping sounds more like a type of dessert, such as Angel Delight.) By 2017, I'd started signing up for races. I didn't think it was likely that I would ever win anything – I didn't really care one way or another – but I craved adventure, to discover new routes, to have an excuse to range across Yorkshire's national parks for whole days at a time, as I used to do as a hiking teenager.

And I was still lonely, having lost my London friends and neighbours. I began eavesdropping on the sidelines of a Facebook group run by 'Hardmoors', a company which organises off-road trail races on the North York Moors. In March I took the plunge and signed up for my first trail race: a marathon taking place along the Cleveland Way later that year, in October, which would begin and end in Osmotherley, on the western border of the moors. I enrolled in some shorter events in the meantime, as preparation.

That summer, I travelled to the Lake District for one of those training runs – a half-marathon taking place the following day. In trail races – which are run off-road in the countryside, with the aim of taking runners on adventures through a variety of scenery, ground cover and ascent – distances are not precise. When run on roads, a half-marathon should be exactly 13.1 miles; but because trail-runners and race directors tend to care more about beautiful routes than about bettering their 'personal best' speeds (PBs) (or 'personal records' (PRs)) over precisely measured courses, the length of 'trail halves' can vary, between around 12 and 16 miles. There was also a full marathon on offer that day (which is 26.2 miles on road but can be anything from 25 to about 32 miles on trail) and, a month later, an 'ultra' too. An ultra-marathon is any run in excess of marathon distance and some people use the term to refer to any event longer than 26.2 miles, while many insist that a *proper* 'ultra' has to be over thirty miles. There is no upper limit though, and, at the time of writing, the longest ultra in the world – the 'Self-Transcendence' race, in which runners cover 5,649 laps around one single city block in Queens, New York, within a time limit of fifty-two days – is 3,100 miles.

I arrived at my accommodation at Coniston Coppermines in the early afternoon – a youth hostel in a low, white-washed cottage, nestling high up above the village of Coniston in the crook of the hills of Brim Fell, Raven Tor and the Coniston Fells. Most of the hostel's residents were there to run. As I heaved my backpack through the front door, it swung wide open and a surge of air rushed in. The gust shaped itself into a woman, and as she ran past me into the hallway, she stopped and turned.

'Hi,' she exhaled.

Her lower legs were a camouflage of silt and bogwater, and neon markings on her shoes glinted through thick black peat, studded with scree. A few stems of wet hair clung to her face around a wide, buff hairband, and dripped water into rivulets of sweat beside her nose. As she bent to pick out her laces from the mud, a man emerged from the stairwell. He too was dressed in shorts and T-shirt, but he was bright and clean and holding a baby, perhaps six months old. As he approached her, she wiped her hands on her thighs and took the child from him, pressing it between one arm and the front of her tight running backpack.

'How was it?' he asked.

'Yeah, brilliant,' she replied. 'I got about thirty miles in. It's slippy though. Have a good run!' she called out as he broke into a jog, pushing through the door and out onto the fells.

Over the communal dinner at the hostel that night, everyone around the table, apart from me, was running the marathon and most were signed up for the ultra-marathon too. While eating, they compared notes, casually listing the races they'd completed, the long-distance footpaths they'd covered, the injuries they'd sustained, the kit they most prized. The running woman I'd encountered earlier, who was now showered and free of mud, turned to me and asked: 'Are you running tomorrow?'

'Yes. Just the half-marathon though,' I replied. 'I honestly can't imagine running any further. I just can't imagine what it's like to run the distances you're talking about. Anything more than, I dunno, twenty miles seems just . . . silly. Silly distances. Mad. Crazy!'

Nobody said anything. The running woman took a mouthful of dinner and turned back to her husband.

I still hear myself now and cringe. I knew then so little about why people run – about why women run.

Five months later, it was the night before the Hardmoors Osmotherley Marathon. I laid out my kit on my bed: not just my clothes and shoes, but tape to stick onto my back, behind the clasps of my bra to stop it rubbing my skin raw; pieces of kitchen roll to wipe my nose (which drips in cold winds); incontinence pads (unwrapped and put into biodegradable freezer bags, so that, when I have to change a pad behind a tree, there is less packaging to negotiate, and a ready-made disposal bag to boot); and food – energy gels, ginger biscuits, jelly babies, KitKats, salt tablets, flapjacks and malt loaf.

There is an attraction in short runs, in leaving the house unencumbered by anything other than a front door key. I found it especially liberating after my daughters were born, to be able to leave the house so weightlessly and glide through space in Lycra, instead of struggling with bags of nappies, milk, snacks, toys and changes of children's clothes stuffed into the basket underneath our enormous buggy. But I came to realise that long-distance running offered a different attraction to those lithe, thirty-minute outings. It used the same skills required for planning a day trip with young children, but with one crucial difference. When I pack for a day out running, I do not have to think about anybody else's requirements or desires, other than my own.

Between my introduction to trail running in late 2015 and the Osmotherley Marathon in October 2017, I got to know myself, and the way my body responds to exertion over many hours. I became conscious of the 'tells' through which my body communicates its needs. I learned that if I can be breezy and cheerful, then I have eaten and drunk enough for the moment. But boredom, irritability, a premature hankering for the finish line, and even tears, all require me to take action – a gulp of coke, a handful of jelly babies, a flapjack, a salt tablet. I learned that nausea often means hunger rather than gluttony, and that I cannot eat only sugar, which over time roils my stomach and felts my teeth. I need to take in more substantial food too: sandwiches, crisps, pork pies, salted potatoes, buttered fruit loaf and, in the later stages of a really long run, citrus – orange slices, juice, Calippo ice lollies. I learned to pay greater attention to my heart-rate, to make more effort to keep it low, to stop sweat saturating my T-shirt on steep climbs and chilling my skin as darkness falls and the air cools. I became aware of the way my left foot rocks fractionally from side to side inside its shoe on loose, stony paths, gradually abrading the skin on the outer edge of my big toe and eventually needing to be protected with tape. I discovered how a brisk wind can bring in, or brush aside, cloud cover in minutes, swapping hot sun for dense rain, and vice versa, and requiring the repeated interchange of waterproofs and sunscreen. And I learned to pace myself: to find the balance between moving swiftly enough to keep alert and engaged, but not so fast as to exhaust my reserves.

In an essay from 1980 called 'Throwing Like a Girl', the philosopher Iris Marion Young wrote about differences between men and women's experiences of participating in sport. She describes how men generally possess enough knowledge of their physical capabilities so that, when they go to catch a ball, their minds and bodies work together – they think *through* their bodies – to bring that desire to fruition almost instantaneously. But from a young age, girls and women are encouraged to see ourselves through the eyes of others: as physical objects and in comparison to external standards of beauty and perfection. Young describes how this leaves many girls and women with a split consciousness. We act at the same time as being aware of how we look while we're acting: 'the body frequently is both subject and object for itself at the same time'. This means that when we want to catch a ball, there can be an interruption between desire and action. We do not think entirely through our bodies, but rather we tend to think about our intention and then consider our body as an instrument to attain it, 'a fragile encumbrance, rather than the medium for the enactment of our aims'.[1] Our bodies can feel like unwieldy appendages that get in the way of realising our wishes and let us down.

In long-distance running, I found – and continue to find – a way to combat this split consciousness; to know and inhabit my body as a mass of sensations and needs felt inwardly: to exist *through* my body, not apart from and despite it. Running shows me the rise and fall of the landscape, not viewed at a distance through a phone camera lens, taking snaps for social media, but felt internally, as exhaustion, elation, contentment, hunger, thirst, nausea, pleasure and pain. And the more time I spend running, the more its effects extend into the rest of my life. I'd previously thought of running as the absolute opposite to my sedentary day job – an escape – and I'd considered the moors and mountains as very different spaces to my usual habitat of streets, offices, shops and libraries. But I have come to realise that there isn't really a clear-cut opposition between these two worlds.

The way I move when I am running influences how I move more generally through my life. Experiencing free movement and a sense of physical power on the trail makes me hungry for other forms of liberation and authority in my day-to-day existence. I am sure that it is because of running that I have become better able to recognise and act on my own desires. Bit by bit I have stopped putting on make-up because of the way it clogs my skin, even though I am scared of being thought of as ugly and old. I have stopped wearing heels because of the tightness they cause in my calves, and I have started wearing stretchy clothes with comfortable, elastic waistbands, even though I hate the idea of seeming short and fat and 'frumpy'. I now eat three full meals every day, even though I worry about not being 'perfectly thin'. I no longer drink wine, as it gives me headaches and makes me tired, even though I am anxious that I may not be effervescent and fun company with others. I have learned to urinate outside in bushes during races, even though I was initially bothered by being seen by passers-by and considered disgusting. I took up weight-training and love feeling stronger, even though, when I was younger, I had wanted to be slight and fragile-looking. I have stopped faking orgasms, even though I have always been nervous of articulating my own sexual preferences.

I have never liked approaching strangers – feeling self-conscious about the sound of my own voice, worrying that I would trip over my words, or that my southern accent would stand out in the north – but I now know there are some questions I need to ask simply in order to get around: where to pick up a footpath, or when the next bus departs, or how long a café stays open. I have realised that I have spent my life moving around the world apologetically, trying not to invite attention or ridicule – even though those attempts to remain inconspicuous have caused me problems and discomfort. Running shows me a way of moving around public space with much less self-consciousness and more of a sense of belonging – entitlement, even.

Because of running, I can recognise what I need and I do what is necessary to obtain it.

On the day of the Osmotherley marathon, in October 2017, I woke in the youth hostel to the sound of heavy rain tumbling into the waterfall outside the dormitory window. Race registration was taking place in the village hall. I opened the door and was met by air already fetid with sweat and mud; 120 runners were queuing at tables around the room, collecting race numbers, filling out emergency contact details, proving possession of compulsory kit, lining up outside toilets.

At five to nine, the hum of chatter stopped. One of the race directors, a softly spoken giant of a man called Jon, read out a briefing and the other director, Shirley, handed out plaques to runners who'd clocked up a thousand miles over previous races. We then traipsed out of the hall and up the steep road leading north to the junction where the Cleveland Way departs from the village. I stood towards the back of the pack of runners, Jon blew a whistle and we were off, all of us plodding along a wide trail, a rutted field and into a wood where the path veers sharply and unevenly upwards. In recces I'd tried to jog up this rising track, but today the runners surrounding me slowed to a fast stride. 'That's the idea!' a voice coming up beside me exclaimed. 'You've got a good pace on you!'

Three women emerged out of the pack to my right. 'This is my first marathon,' I blurted out. 'Do you have any advice?'

'Marathon? This isn't a marathon!' cried the first woman. 'This is an ultra! It's twenty-nine miles!'

Twenty-nine miles. Nine miles further than I had ever run before. Why hadn't I read the race instructions properly?

'Is this the longest that you've run before too?' I asked hopefully.

'Ha, no!' she laughed. 'I did the Hardmoors 110 – which is really 112 miles – five months ago. I puked pretty much the whole way round! And I'm training for the Spine Race.'

The Spine Race, she told me, is a nonstop run along the 268-mile course of the Pennine Way long-distance footpath, undertaken in the depths of northern Britain's winter, when two-thirds of the seven-day time limit are spent in darkness.

'So today is good training,' she continued. 'I'll probably run a similar distance tomorrow too, but with a much heavier pack. I'm Harriet, by the way. And this is Kate, and Jayne.'

Kate's phone started to ring. She pulled it out of a pocket in her running pack, looked at its screen, and tutted: 'It's work.'

'Kate's a farmer,' Harriet explained. 'She did worry that she might have to deal with some work logistics during today's run. Anyway, you'll have a great time. You'll soon be doing longer distances. We're all doing a fifty-five-mile race together in March, so if you want some training buddies, you should come along on some of our weekend runs.' Kate gave a thumbs-up. Fifty-five miles, 110 miles, 268 miles . . . These distances seemed like a fantasy.

Harriet strode past me and disappeared out of sight. Jayne and I introduced ourselves while Kate negotiated on the phone with potato distributors. We ran up along the clearly marked, wide paths of the Cleveland Way, into a wood and out the other side, past an Ordnance Survey trig point, through a gate and onto the sloping expanse of Scarth Wood Moor. After four miles through a forest and fields, the path dipped down into an agricultural hamlet called Scugdale and then rose steeply up again, onto Carlton Bank, a long heather-strewn ridge that forms a run-up onto three distinct, sharply rising, sharply falling hills – Cringle Moor, Cold Moor and Hasty Bank – known locally as the 'Three Sisters'. This is part of a pattern across the world – a tendency to imagine closely spaced peaks as an intimate, forbidding, powerful group of women, with hints of malevolence. There are Three Sisters in Oregon, Scotland's Glencoe and Alberta in Canada. In northern Norway there are Seven Sisters which, in folklore, were female trolls who were turned to stone as they ran down the coast, fleeing from male suitors. Mountains and women have historically been something for men to try to conquer; and such female names for geographical landmarks signify both the acquisitive nature of men's desires and their female targets' tendency to strongly resist.

After crossing Yorkshire's Three Sisters, the race course turned south and we all ran for a couple of miles along the moorland ridge of Hasty Bank, before dropping down, first into fields and then into a small village called Chop Gate (or *Chop Yat*, as Kate said it). Here I used the public loos and grabbed a cup of warm, flat coke and a flapjack at the checkpoint, and began to chat cheerily with the marshals – but neither Kate or Jayne seemed to want to hang around and were already jogging out of the car park. After I had sprinted to catch them up, we immediately set off steeply uphill again, trudging for ten minutes or so up Wether Hill until we reached the ridge at the top, which turns to head northwards, back to close the loop and rejoin the Cleveland Way at the point where, a few hours earlier, we'd been steeling ourselves to begin crossing the Three Sisters. But now we turned the other way and followed our outgoing route in reverse: back along Carlton Bank, down into Scugdale, through the wood and up a series of steps that, in the morning, I'd barely noticed descending, but now stretched up in front of me like a biblical ladder. A familiar needling pain was beginning in my right knee, and I stopped momentarily to stretch out my thigh muscles, flex my ankles and catch my breath. When I finally emerged from the wood, panting and sweaty, a marshal pointed me up along the road: the old Hambleton Drove Road, which rises up above a reservoir glinting through gaps in the surrounding trees.

Here I left Kate and Jayne and felt strong enough – despite my knee; despite the fact that I'd been moving nonstop for nearly seven hours – to run, not walk, up the gently inclining footpath. A mile or so later, at an old drovers' inn called Chequers, my sports watch clocked 26.2 miles: the official distance of a marathon. There were still three miles to cover before the end, but I whooped to myself, pumped an arm ('Yesssss!') and took a selfie.

Now I knew I would finish.

Forty-five minutes later, after careering happily downhill from the drove road, across a beck and hauling myself inelegantly up the handrails that ascended the other side, I completed the race. I ran into the village hall, 7 hours, 41 minutes and 22 seconds after setting off that morning. Once I'd collected my finisher's medal and T-shirt, I spotted Harriet bearing a cup of hot, sweet tea and a slice of fruit loaf for me.

'You're buzzing!' she exclaimed with satisfaction.

I was.

After Josie's death in 2014 and our move to York the following year, the exercise schedule that had taken me from short jogs along the river path, to running my first marathon in 2017, helped me find a new home: greater comfort in my own body and in the world at large.

I think that is why I have this hope now: that running will help me to live with these new griefs, the terrible devastation that has ripped through my family and the wider sense of dispossession that has come with it and is related to living in the world as a woman. I set myself a challenge – a programme of hill reps, interval training, tempo runs, long runs, recovery runs, resistance training and stretching to bring me back fitter, faster, stronger. I reckon that a year sounds like enough time to bring about this change, my recovery from grief.

I search race entry websites and start making a shortlist of races taking place at roughly this time next year. My target will need to be a race that's longer than I've ever run before, to mirror the task of endurance before me. I see a listing for the West Highland Way run: a ninety-five-mile race along the entire route of the long-distance footpath from Milngavie (outside Glasgow) to Fort William, at the foot of Ben Nevis, Britain's highest mountain. The race is run nonstop, with a thirty-five-hour time limit, and it will take place on 20 June 2020, close to the longest day of the year and eleven months after my stepdad's death. It is a trail that I have covered before, hiking a long time ago in my teens, before all this loss and sadness. It seems perfect. I write the date in my diary, download a '100-mile-ultra training plan' from the internet, and cross my fingers that my entry in the ballot will be successful. With a new sense of structure and progression, there seems to be hope again. I instantly feel better.

As I go to shut my laptop, I catch sight of an advert for a different race: the Lyke Wake Challenge. The strange name rings a bell. After I'd got home from that first marathon, in Osmotherley in 2017, I'd sent some photographs taken during the race to Willy. One was of a signpost bearing the outline of a black coffin, to which he'd replied, excitedly: 'Aha! *Lyke Wake!*'

I'd never heard those weird words before, but now here they are again.

I click on the link and learn that the Lyke Wake race, held annually on the nearest Saturday to 10 July, was originally part of the Osmotherley Summer Games, and then later became an independent running 'challenge'. It takes place on a forty-mile footpath called the Lyke Wake Walk, which spools more or less horizontally across the entire width of the North York Moors, from Osmotherley in the west, finishing at Ravenscar in the east, at the sea. The walk was named after the 'Lyke Wake Dirge', a

Cleveland folk song from the Middle Ages. (*Lyke* means corpse, and *wake* being the ritual of watching over the corpse between the deceased's death and funeral.) Rather terrifyingly the 'Lyke Wake Dirge' describes the trials that the soul undergoes in that period between death and burial, comparing that transition to a crossing of a 'whinny' (thorny) moor:

When thoo fra hence away art passed,	*(When you have passed away from here,*
Ivvery neet an all,	*Every night and all,*
Ti Whinny Moor thoo cums at last,	*To Whinny Moor you come at last,*
An Christ tak up thy saul.	*And Christ takes up your soul.)*

According to the dirge, the moor crossing that immediately follows death involves a series of tests. If, while alive, the dead person had ever charitably given away 'hosen and shoon' (socks and shoes), 'meat or drink' or 'siller an' gawd' (silver and gold), then after death their soul is equipped with strong footwear, hearty sustenance and safe footholds, to allow them to cross the whinny moor unscathed, until 'Christ tak up thy saul'. However, if they had been mean and held onto their possessions during life, then in death they are forced to walk across the moor barefoot, pricked 'to the bare bane' by thorns, consumed by fire and deprived of footholds at the 'Brig o' Dread'. They would then *'doon tumm'l tiwards Hell fleeames'*.

The forty-mile Lyke Wake crossing was devised as a walk by local farmer and writer Bill Cowley in 1955. At three in the morning, the lonely heather had reminded Cowley of the dirge's hazardous moorland and, by the end of the arduous route, twenty-three hours after setting off and feeling like a corpse or 'lyke' who had gone through purgatory himself, Cowley had drily adopted the dirge's name for his new footpath.

The traditional Christian funeral oration, Psalm 23, conceives of a life lived in the 'shadow of death' as a walk through a valley, but as the shadow of death falls upon me now, it seems to me that recovery from grief may be more like an ultra-marathon across an exposed hill-top. I think about the hazards of the moor: the peat bogs whose black, crumbly surfaces might hold firm or give way without warning to swallow a leg thigh-deep; the roaks, or hill fogs, that can suddenly wall up before your eyes. Ticks that might burrow into the folds behind your knees, imparting fatal Lyme disease. Adders lazing beneath gorse on warm stone paths.

Such hidden dangers resonate with my earlier experience of grief five years ago, after my dear friend's death in 2014, when there were some days and nights in which memories of her unexpectedly stung the whole surface of my consciousness. Yet on other days, I felt oddly cocooned from it all, and able to carry on as normal. I realised, then, that grief is a surprisingly physical experience, much more like illness than I had anticipated, and unpredictable. It strikes me that a moor crossing is not just a fitting metaphor for the soul's travails after death, but an appropriate path for my journey as I learn to recover, write and run my way through grief. It is a metaphor made literal: as part of my training plan to run the West Highland Way, I will be spending most of the next year running across Yorkshire's moors.

Apt, too, is the fact that the Lyke Wake Walk begins just outside Osmotherley. According to local folklore, Osmotherley's place name is a contraction of 'Where Osmund's Mother Lies' (or 'Oswald-with-his-mother-lay'). The legend describes how the mother of a villager named Osmund (or Oswald) went to collect firewood one bitter winter's afternoon and did not return. Her son went out to search for her, and found her lying on the ground, close to death, having fallen. Unable to carry her back to safety, he lay down beside her in the snow, and there they died together.

The Osmotherley legend is rooted in the ties that bind us to our mothers. I think about my own mother, who seemed to me to be lacking in ties, either to her own mother or to a fixed home, and who repeatedly moved house in search of the 'motherland' that eluded her. I think I inherited those missing roots and, maybe that's why, in the wake of estrangement from my biological mother, I'm looking for foremothers elsewhere. In a world in which I've come to feel dispossessed from family, home or physical ease, I am looking to pioneering women who found freedom outdoors for the reassurance and belonging which I need.

2.

The high life

I start my research by looking for my running foremothers in the nineteenth century, in an era before Pierre de Coubertin declared women's sport to be unnatural.

But my search for historical trail-running women, specifically, meets an early hurdle. Running and most outdoor sport, was not always as clearly defined and specialised as it is now. Today, sky running, fell running, trail running, cross-country, track, athletics and road running are all distinct disciplines, with their own separate events, clubs, competitions and constituencies. Running is often considered a very different pursuit to hiking or rock-climbing. For much of the nineteenth century, however, the boundaries were far less obvious. Running was rarely a discrete activity, a form of motion practised on its own – people did not tend to 'go for a run'; it was usually one element of an array of different pastimes.

In September 1858, Mariana Fox Tuckett wrote in her diary about a blissful day on holiday in Cornwall in which she scrambled on rocks, went on a long hike and turned down a carriage ride to 'walk (& run)' twenty-odd miles with her cousin Helen.[1] Outdoor adventures frequently began or ended with carriage or horse rides. In between, participants rambled, sprinted, jogged, scrambled and climbed – sometimes all in the same excursion. And often they used the term 'mountaineering' to describe this hybrid form of outdoor exploration, in which both men and women ranged widely, on foot, hands, hooves and wheels, over hills, cliffs, moors and mountains. So, instead of searching specifically for foremothers who were purely runners, I decide instead to look for my antecedents among historical female *mountaineers*.

I look again at the images taken by Lizzie Le Blond of her cohort of intrepid outdoor women. I wish I could bring those monochrome and sepia women back to life, to learn what the outdoors meant to them. I wonder how Lizzie came to be in the mountains in the first place: what were the circumstances that saw her entering the hills for recreational purposes, and what did she find there? Were there any hints that, within two decades, athletic women were to be so vilified and excluded?

I turn first to Lizzie's autobiography, published in 1928, six years before her death. Its strangely bland title – *Day In, Day Out* – belies the varied, energetic nature of her life, but in the initial pages, she describes her first joyful, proper visit to the mountains. It was in late June 1881, when she was twenty-one, that she 'set out and saw for the first time those glacier-clad Alpine ranges which were to mean so much to [her] for the rest of [her] life'. Lizzie had been suffering from suspected tuberculosis for the last few years. It was a disease that was then widely thought to be hereditary, and treatment for it was largely palliative – a 'change of air' to help the lungs. Earlier that month, a 'dear old friend and doctor' had 'ordered [Lizzie] to Switzerland' for the clear, clean air after a social season of 'balls, dinners, etc., in quick succession [had] proved too much' for her.[2] There she initially discovered that altitude and strenuous physical exercise seemed to alleviate her symptoms, but mountaineering would become so much more than that to her: it would offer an education, a social experiment, an alternative family and opportunities for hard work, respect and fame.

When Lizzie first started mountaineering, its most visible participants were from social groups similar to her own: the wealthy, white, upper and upper-middle classes – those with disposable income, personal connections and the luxury of free time in which to indulge in leisure activities, exploration and adventurism. Today, outdoor activities are far more accessible to all, aided by initiatives such as the Outward Bound Trust's diversity team, the walking communities Black Girls Hike, Wanderlust Women and Bonnie Boots (a Glaswegian hiking group for BAME women), organisations for hikers with disabilities (such as the Disabled Ramblers and British Blind Sport) and groups concerned about social inequality, such as Carers Stepping Out and the Horton Women's Holiday Centre (a cooperative non-profit in the Yorkshire Dales offering affordable holidays to women and children). Because of the diversity of its participants, today the 'great outdoors' is not associated with a uniform, universal set of meanings and practices: hiking, climbing and running mean different things to different people, and different demographics have widely varying experiences of sport in rural settings. And actually the same could also be said of the nineteenth century. Even though books, newspaper articles – and, later, photographs and cine films – focused on the upper and middle classes, early sporting communities nevertheless included a wide range of participants, for whom the outdoors held a range of different associations, even if some of those enthusiasts' experiences were far less frequently recorded and publicised and have therefore been largely forgotten.

Lizzie had been to Switzerland on another occasion before her life-changing visit of June 1881 – probably the previous year. The sights had then seemed underwhelming: the Jungfrau mountain had appeared 'nothing more than a far-off vision of glittering snows on which none but the foot of folly could ever wish to tread', and she had not been much moved by the Alps generally. She had even spoken scornfully of mountaineers as 'wicked' and risking their lives 'for nothing'. And in 1881, when Lizzie travelled with a friend ('Miss H') to the low-lying village of Interlaken, and then on to Montreux, it seemed again that Switzerland, despite its fine air, would in other ways disappoint her. But then some new visitors arrived at her hotel – 'a party of young people' who told her to 'venture farther afield' – and she 'determined to take the management of my health into my own hands' and make the fifty-mile journey and 2,000-foot ascent from Montreux to the higher mountain resort of Chamonix. Lizzie stayed there for several weeks and her health began to improve. 'The fresh mountain air seemed to put new life into me,' she wrote, and 'in a few days I could leave my sofa and sit out in the pine woods'. Two more friends joined her and, after dipping their toes into the joys of outdoor leisure with a few short carriage drives, and horse rides, they all bought alpenstocks – tall walking sticks with sharp chamois-horned tips – and started climbing.[3]

First, Lizzie and her friends rambled to the Mer de Glace, France's largest glacier, on the northern slopes of Mont Blanc. Then they crossed the nearby Le Mauvais Pas, a perilous rocky passage, and next went up Le Brévent, a mountain of medium height, via a steep, zigzagging path now known as the Vertical Kilometre. Lizzie and her friends paid for records of each expedition to be charred into their alpenstocks. The sought-after mountain guides they had hired to show them routes and techniques, Jean-Pierre Balmat and Alphonse Charlet, were impressed by the young women's determination and enthusiasm, and suggested more ambitious trips – perhaps even to the Pierre Pointue, the lookout point over the Bossons Glacier, just over a third of the way up the north face of Mont Blanc, western Europe's highest mountain.[4]

The very same evening that Balmat and Charlet raised this possibility, Lizzie and her friends met a young woman in their hotel who had just climbed Mont Blanc as far as the Grands Mulets Hut, a mountain refuge lying 3,000 feet higher than the Pierre Pointue. 'We gazed enthralled at one so brave,' Lizzie recalled, though she could not imagine herself climbing so high.[5]

Nevertheless, on a clear-skied morning soon afterwards, on Monday 25 July 1881, Lizzie's maid helped her to put on riding clothes – the closest she had to proper mountaineering garb – and 'with high-heeled buttoned boots and shady hats', she and her group set off up the first slopes of Mont Blanc, hoping to make it as far as the Pierre Pointue. After around three hours of continuous climbing on foot, Balmat and Charlet mentioned that they were carrying a rope and raised the tantalising possibility that Lizzie herself could be up to the Grands Mulets, far beyond the Pierre Pointue, in a couple of hours, if she wished. Two members of her party decided to stay put, but Lizzie and a female friend pressed on with their guides, the party of four walking in a line, tied together with rope like beads on a string. In their high-heeled riding boots and long skirts – and with next-to-no previous mountaineering experience – the women scrambled across treacherous glaciers and ladder bridges laid over deep crevasses. By the early evening they had 'clambered to the top of the rocky pinnacles behind the hut' to watch the sunset. 'Our boots were pulp, our stockings wet sponges, [and] our skirts sodden,' wrote Lizzie, exhilarated, but the guides had spare dry footwear – though not the most suitable – and the women made the twilight descent in 'enormous felt slippers that dropped off at every step'.[6]

Once down safely, Lizzie and her friend each received a 'Certificat d'Ascension aux Grands-Mulets'. The expedition was reported in the British press a month later, which described how Lizzie, 'who left England in such bad health a short time ago, is almost, if not completely, recovered' and 'found herself able to make the ascent of Mount Blanc as far as the Grands Mulets – no light task even for a vigorous woman'.[7]

During that summer of 1881, Lizzie had found something transformative. In the mountains she discovered opportunities for physical, intellectual and aesthetic experiences she had never before encountered. Climbing called upon strengths she did not know she possessed – self-control, level-headedness, decision-making and 'staying power'.[8]

She had arrived in Chamonix as a deeply unwell young woman. Through mountaineering, she came to understand how her ill health was not a physical accident, but an indictment of her society and its treatment of women. And the mountains did not just shine a light on Lizzie's problems; they also offered a solution. In such outdoor pursuits Lizzie saw the possibility of a brand new and healthier way of living, in which women might find a better place in the world.

What she had discovered was by no means a readymade feminist utopia, however. Lizzie's 'Certificat d'Ascension aux Grands-Mulets' survives to this day in the archives of the Alpine Club in London (the world's first mountaineering club, which remained a largely men-only establishment until 1975). The certificate is illustrated with a lithograph of a party of twelve climbers – all men – and its generic phrasing, in which the climber was assumed to be an 'M', short for

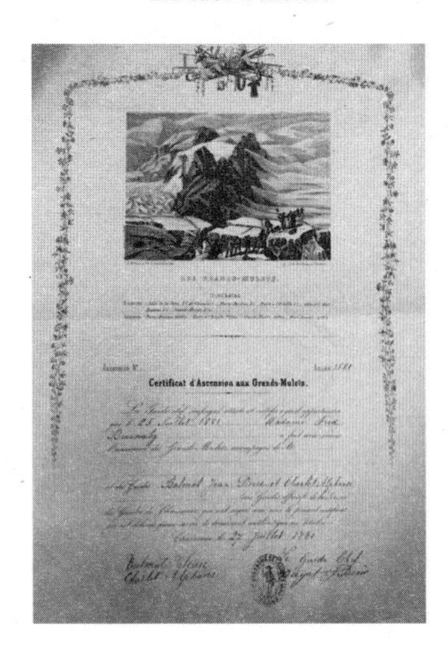
Certificat d'Ascension aux Grands-Mulets.

Lizzie's certificate for climbing to the Grands Mulets refuge on Mont Blanc, 25 July 1881

'Monsieur', shows that the mountaineering world was fundamentally shaped around men.[9]

What we look for, what we find and how we behave outdoors often depend on who we are, and how we are treated in the world. The meanings that we find in the natural environment are shaped not just by our sex and gender, but also by factors such as age, race, social class, ethnicity, nationality and language. As I dig a little deeper into Lizzie Le Blond's background, I see that the importance that outdoor adventure came to hold in her life was a reaction to the upper-class Anglo-Irish society in which she had been brought up – and, specifically, its attitude towards women.

Both of Lizzie's parents came from dynasties of wealthy Irish 'Protestant Ascendancy' landowners. Her early childhood was spent on her family's large estate of Killincarrick, lying between the villages of Delgany and Greystones, about eighteen miles south of Dublin. The Irish Sea unfurled to the east. To the west, the Wicklow Mountains rose up into what Lizzie described as 'some of the most beautiful scenery of Co. Wicklow, and indeed of Ireland'.[10]

The estate had come into Lizzie's family through her

great-grandfather James, a decorated admiral with the Royal Navy and an absentee landlord, who spent most of his time in England while agents oversaw his Irish lands. Lizzie's relationship to Killincarrick would forever be shaped by the terms of James's marriage settlement which, back in the late eighteenth century, had decreed that the lands and his title of baronet would be passed down only to 'heirs male'. Women were not usually considered viable heirs, because landed aristocrats wanted to keep estates intact within their families, and patriarchal marriage laws dictated that women's property would transfer to their husbands and thus out of the original family bloodline. Male-preference primogeniture – the practice through which property passed only through men – was particularly rigidly pursued in Ireland, where it was vanishingly rare that daughters were allowed to inherit and control lands in their own right. When in 1827 a list was made of ninety-five major estates in County Wicklow, only one of them was under a woman's control. As it happens, this was the neighbouring estate to Killincarrick, Bromley Park, which was overseen by the landowner Lady Harriet Daly, whose example may have been influential in young Lizzie's development. In historian Donald Harman Akenson's words, upper-class women were 'not seen as being of positive economic value' in mid nineteenth-century Ireland, which was like 'Jane Austen's world on steroids'.[11]

In Ireland, primogeniture was frequently coupled to an inheritance practice known as 'strict settlement', in which even male heirs did not wield absolute power over their inherited property, but instead had the status of 'life tenants'. They benefitted from the estate's profits, which were doled out by trustees, but they were often unable to make major decisions such as selling off portions of land, because the estates were perpetually 'entailed' to succeeding generations in order to protect property from profligate heirs who might otherwise fritter it away in gambling dens. These conventions meant that women often felt particularly alienated from landed estates. Unable to inherit and charged with the responsibility of producing male heirs to act only as place-holders in the succession, many upper-class women experienced their families' estates as poisoned chalices, burdens with few direct benefits, and reminders of the low regard and limited prospects on offer to them. Lizzie described herself as having had a 'simple outdoor . . . girlhood'. But in both girlhood and adulthood, the aristocracy's treatment of women like her made her relationship with the land far from simple.[12]

Hostility to aristocratic landlordism came from numerous quarters, particularly from tenant farmers who worked land they were prevented from owning and struggled with exorbitant rents inflicted by unsympathetic agents acting for absentee landlords. From the 1840s, the potato famine – in which around a million people died and double that number were forced to leave Ireland as refugees – saw the intensification of hostility to landlords and to the British government, and a rise in nationalism and republicanism in Ireland. Upper-class Protestant women, such as the ones in Lizzie's family, did not suffer under Ascendancy landowning practices in the way that victims of the Great Hunger suffered. However, many of these women were nevertheless damaged by the sexist injustice of those legal strictures, and a couple of years before Lizzie's birth, her family was rocked by distressing events rooted in aristocratic female misery.

Shortly after Christmas 1857, Lizzie's twenty-two-year-old aunt, Eliza, gave birth to her first child, a boy. The baby was born at a mansion called Kinnaird House, which Lizzie's grandparents Pippy and Mimmy had been leasing for the last four years; nestling in forests dense with deer and hares, near the small town of Dunkeld in Scotland. Eliza's son, christened William John Arthur Charles James Cavendish-Bentinck, became known to everyone as 'Dartch' or 'Dartchie' (in what was perhaps a child's mangling of 'Arthur Charles' or 'Archie'). Four days after Dartchie's birth, the local doctor rode down to Kinnaird and pronounced young Eliza's increasingly disturbed behaviour as 'puerperal mania', a precursor of what we might today call postpartum psychosis.[13] Ten years earlier, a London obstetrician, James Reid, had described a patient's symptoms:

> talking becomes almost incessant, and generally on one particular subject, such as imaginary wrongs done to her by her dearest friends;

> a total negligence of, and often strong aversion to her child and husband are evinced; explosions of anger occur, with vociferations and violent gesticulations; and although the patient may have been remarkable previously for her correct, modest demeanour, and attention to her religious duties, most awful oaths and imprecations are uttered, and language used which astonishes her friends.[14]

In the most severe cases of puerperal mania, women threatened violence towards their babies or themselves. The Scottish physician John Batty Tuke, who was appointed to the Royal Edinburgh Asylum five years after Eliza's suffering, warned that in no other mental disorder was 'the suicidal tendency so well marked', and that 'attempts were most determined, a loathing of life and intense desire to get rid of it being the actuating motives'.[15]

On the evening of 4 January 1858 – eight days after giving birth to Dartchie, and four days after developing symptoms – Eliza died at Kinnaird, almost certainly by suicide. She was buried six miles away, in the churchyard of the austere white Presbyterian kirk at Little Dunkeld, where the Tay noisily encircles a small island. Nineteenth-century families often tried to suppress publicity around cases of puerperal insanity and suicide, and Eliza's grave at Little Dunkeld was given no headstone or memorial. The few death notices that were published were curt and gave no details about the cause of death.[16]

In Eliza's day, some degree of puerperal insanity was considered a potential side effect of childbirth for all women. The condition was thought to be partly hereditary, but the main triggers were observed to lie in women's social environments. In poorer female patients, physicians noted the strains caused by poverty; and in bourgeois young women, doctors lamented that 'fashionable manners' were inducing 'debility', cultivating their minds 'at the expense of their physical strength' and leading to feelings of uselessness. Across all classes of patients, physicians worried that puerperal mania was a symptom of women's discontent with the limitations of their lives. The physician Robert Boyd pointed out that patients' violence and frustration were as frequently directed towards husbands as to babies, and treatment plans recommended quarantining women away from their families.[17]

In the nineteenth century, 'puerperal mania' exemplified how, by denying them opportunities for education, work, independence and self-worth, society could literally make women sick. In Lizzie's family, the redundancy foisted upon women was at least partly exerted through male-biased aristocratic conventions around land. The harmful nature of these practices affected upper-class men too, who were not immune to feelings of uselessness. They could suffer from overwork, anxiety and poor mental health when managing their responsibilities as landowners, as Eliza's older brother – Lizzie's father – discovered.

Just three and a half years after Eliza's death, when baby Lizzie was days away from turning one, Lizzie's father Vin (short for St Vincent Bentinck Hawkins-Whitshed) became heir to Killincarrick when his older brother died unexpectedly. Vin took his new responsibilities very seriously, throwing himself into roles that cemented male landowners' authority in their local communities, including becoming high sheriff and occupying figurehead roles at the Royal Irish Academy in Dublin and at agricultural shows. With his father's help, Vin renovated the Killincarrick estate, commissioning pleasure gardens directly overlooking the sea and a pristine white mansion, linked by a modern road with Delgany's new railway station. The two men reformed the estate's drainage and built a large farmstead with steam-powered sawmills and cottages for its workers.[18]

Vin, however, seems to have found these new roles overwhelming. Throughout Lizzie's early childhood the family took lengthy breaks so he could recuperate at his parents' estate in Scotland. During these times, Lizzie played at Kinnaird with her cousin Dartchie – paddling in the Tay, building dens in the forest, trailing the gamekeeper, clamouring to be taught how to shoot rabbits and carving their initials into a silver birch tree near a 'gate made from the jaw-bones of a whale' (which still today arches above a spring at the entrance to the grounds).[19] It was likely Lizzie's first experience of how outdoor adventure could be an escape from, and cure for, the stressors of everyday life.

When Lizzie was seven, her father's health began to deteriorate significantly. First, there was an incident in the grounds of Killincarrick in which Vin accidentally shot his brother-in-law in the leg, leading to its amputation. This plunged Vin into what a local reporter described as 'much pain and distress'. Three years later, on the death of his father Pippy from 'disease of the bladder and prostate', Vin inherited the estate and the title 'Sir St Vincent Bentinck Hawkins-Whitshed, 3rd Baronet'.[20] Though the papers reported that the 3rd Baronet was in the 'prime of life', the opposite was true. Vin was experiencing a catastrophic breakdown, he stopped eating and on 9 March 1871, died from 'nervous exhaustion'.[21]

Eleven-year-old Lizzie was now sole heir to Killincarrick House and lands totalling around 2,000 acres in counties Wicklow, Dublin and Meath, worth somewhere between £6,000 and £10,000 a year (the equivalent of around £375,000 to £625,000 today), and she was made a ward of the Court of Chancery.[22] But, as a girl, she likely did not anticipate any real power or say in the estate's management, other than receiving an annual allowance, and an expectation to marry and produce a male heir. She may have seen enough damage in her family's history to be wary of the prospect of a lifelong bind to Killincarrick.

Lizzie's teenagehood reinscribed her basic redundancy in the aristocratic scheme – but it also offered the first glimpses of escape. After Vin's death, Lizzie embarked on what she described as a 'sheltered' adolescence in which, as a girl, her education was largely neglected, and she spent most of her time playing with her mother's dogs in Killincarrick's grounds, with occasional trips to England, where she learned to ride a horse and saw 'something of my father's people'. Katharine Tynan, who later became a well-known novelist and poet, had friends in common with young Lizzie. Tynan mourned the empty lives of 'thousands of daughters of the Protestant gentle-folk of the English and Irish country', who were 'enclosed in a walled garden of life [and] wanted the world hungrily'. Some of those girls – including Frances Wynne, a mutual friend of Lizzie and Katharine – looked to adventurous female role models. Wynne corresponded with 'Mrs Rae, the wife of the Arctic explorer' John Rae, and with the daredevil celebrity Violet Fane.[23]

By her late teens, Lizzie also seems to have been yearning for a different life, possibly supported by her mother, Anne Alicia Hawkins-Whitshed (née Handcock, and generally called 'Alice'), who read out loud to her daughter Edward Whymper's bestselling mountaineering memoir *Scrambles Amongst the Alps*.[24] Then, on the cusp of turning eighteen, Lizzie met a man who seemed to embody the spirit of adventure she craved.

In the spring of 1878, Lizzie took part in London society for the first time. Her debutante season was part of a calendar of flashy parties at palaces and grand private residences in the capital, designed to motivate the landowning classes to leave their country estates and network in London. It was also a marketplace in which young women were displayed like livestock to eligible bachelors.

At a party presided over by Queen Victoria in May, Lizzie was introduced to Captain Frederick Gustavus Burnaby, an officer with the British Army, who strode into the room like a figure from 'the age of Romance', according to one of his friends. Fred was 'six feet four in stockings', with a 46-inch chest, and was rumoured to be the strongest man in the army: it was said he could lift a 120lb dumb-bell above his head with one hand and, more improbably, carry a small pony under each arm. He spoke seven languages fluently and had ridden on horseback across central Asia in winter, from St Petersburg to Khiva (now in Uzbekistan), nearly losing both hands to frostbite. He had published an account of his travels as *A Ride to Khiva*, which had become a bestseller and turned him into a celebrity. Lizzie had read it and had reportedly 'become inamoured of the gallant' officer.[25]

By August 1878, Lizzie and Fred were engaged. Ireland's Court of Chancery began drawing up a marriage settlement, granting Fred £1,000 a year from Lizzie's estate, but largely preserving her family's lands separate and intact for any male child resulting from the marriage.[26]

To Lizzie, Fred's attractions were likely manifold. A husband offered the chance to produce an heir and quickly discharge her responsibility to her family's estate. Once that duty had been done, Lizzie may have hoped for a new life of travel with him, uncoupled from the binds of hereditary land, with broader horizons than she – as an aristocratic woman – may otherwise have dared to anticipate. Her engagement to Fred also occurred at a time when groups such as the Irish National Land League were starting to rally against hereditary landowning conventions, leading to the Irish Land War of 1879–82. Within a couple of years, large public meetings and demonstrations against rural landlordism would occur across County Wicklow, in which 'gentlemen's demesnes' would be broken into and property, such as game, taken; angry protests at the widespread hunger and impoverishment of the 1840s onwards.[27] It would be understandable if Lizzie's desire to leave Killincarrick, and Ireland in general, intensified in this period. Fred may have represented a means to escape.

Burnaby's meeting with Lizzie also occurred at a fortuitous time for him. The prospect of a wife had been previously quashed by his regimental colonel, who disapproved of soldiers marrying, but in the spring of 1878 Fred was toying with the idea of retiring from the army and pursuing a new career in politics, in which a wealthy wife was a positive asset.[28]

It took nine months to finalise the paperwork for Lizzie and Fred's marriage settlement, and on 25 June 1879, they were married at St Peter's Church, Onslow Gardens, South Kensington. Some surprise at the 'match' was expressed by members of the public. Fred towered over Lizzie, who was 'below the medium height'. He was thirty-seven and she a day shy of nineteen, extremely slight, and with what newspapers called 'a piquant beauty': dark straight brows over hooded eyes that shifted easily between amusement and boredom, a small thin mouth, and dark hair pulled severely up onto her crown, until it looked almost cropped. Lizzie's cousin Dartchie – who was about to become the 6th Duke of Portland – gave her away. A reception for over 400 people was held at Bailey's Hotel in Kensington, where wedding presents (including a bejewelled gun from Don

Carlos, the pretender to the Spanish throne) were ostentatiously displayed, and guests ascended a five-storey staircase whose bannisters had been interwoven with evergreens and perfumed flowers, resembling a Swiss mountain path in springtime.[29]

The newlyweds honeymooned in the spa town of Bad Homburg, just outside Frankfurt, at the foot of the craggy, wooded highland Taunus range. On their return, they set up home at 29 Emperor's Gate, a grand Kensington townhouse, where they were joined by Lizzie's mother and six servants, including a French chef and a butler from Leipzig.[30]

In marrying Fred, Lizzie was doubtless expecting an adventurous life, so their first excursions must have been a disappointment. He took her, not to the Balkans or the Middle East, but on a round of London society events and to a series of staid dinners and Conservative Party garden parties, which aimed at boosting Fred's fledgling political career. There she met 'most alarming' celebrities, including the novelist George Eliot, who, she worried, 'must have found me a bore'.[31]

In mid October 1879, Lizzie finally got a taste of the excitement she hoped for – although by this stage she was already a couple of months pregnant. She and Fred travelled to France, then took the Paris–Lyons–Méditerranée railway to Marseilles, from where they would embark on a scheduled crossing of the Mediterranean to Algiers. The north African city had become a fashionable winter holiday destination for wealthy British tourists, who found the weather of the French Riviera, ravaged by the northerly mistral wind, too unpredictable.[32]

It was an unseasonably early winter on the continent and, as the couple travelled towards Marseilles, their train ground to a halt in deep snow. Lizzie became hypothermic. There then followed the crossing to Algeria – a voyage of around forty hours. 'By the time we were installed in our hotel at Algiers,' Lizzie remembered many years later, 'I was down with congestion of the lungs and had so sharp an attack that I bear traces of it to this day.'[33]

The trip may have been designed simply as a winter sun vacation for the couple or as a rest-cure for the pregnant Lizzie – but their north Africa expedition may have had more public significance. Earlier in the year, the French minister of public works had established a commission to explore the possibility of constructing a new railway across Africa, to remedy widespread anxiety in France that, as historical geographer Mike Heffernan puts it, France's 'colonial influence in Africa was limited by the geographical distance that separated French colonies in North and West Africa'. The railway – its route passing through Algeria – would allow troops, military equipment and trading commodities to be transported between settlements. This triggered anxieties in London about protecting access to the Suez Canal, and fears that the French railway would threaten wider British interests.[34]

Fred had long been interested in north Africa – he had reported from Egypt and Sudan for *The Times* newspaper in the mid 1870s – and during the period of his and Lizzie's holiday in Algeria, *The Times* published numerous accounts of France's trans-Saharan railway plans, which showed especial interest in a proposed line from Algiers to Constantine. It seems likely that Fred was the author – and that Lizzie had also intended to participate in intelligence-gathering missions. That same winter, a pair of British newlyweds called Henry and Alice Colvile were scoping out the western course of the potential French railway, from Algiers to Tangier, with Alice travelling some of the journey in disguise as a 'lady of the [Moroccan] Sultan's harem' and Henry as 'her escort'. Henry held his wife's presence responsible for helping him to glean information about the railway, for who 'could suspect such an innocent-looking newly married couple of any serious designs?' he wrote in his report of their trip.[35] Henry and Alice were friends with Lizzie and Fred, and it seems very possible that the latter couple had planned to do exactly the same, using their romantic holiday as a smokescreen for undercover reportage.

But sadly Lizzie did not get to play the spy, and instead she spent the entire winter in bad health. While Fred was likely off scouting out the railway, she remained indoors, sick, frustrated and resentful, enduring her first pregnancy, and tended to by her mother, who had travelled out to Algiers to care for her.

In the second week of January 1880, Lizzie and Fred reunited with the Colviles and all four returned by steamer to Marseilles, no doubt with Henry and Alice regaling an envious Lizzie about their adventures. From there, the Colviles headed to their 'native fog' in London while Fred and Lizzie went on to the French Riviera resort of Hyères. When a general election was called in March, Fred raced back to Britain, where he unsuccessfully contested a seat in Birmingham.[36]

Lizzie, meanwhile, remained in France, growing larger and larger, until she had no choice but to go home and face motherhood. On 10 May 1880, she gave birth to a son, Harry Arthur Gustavus St Vincent Burnaby. She re-entered London society very soon afterwards, attending a ball within six weeks of Harry's birth. But she was in the middle of an emotional crisis, and the social events that she initially hoped would return her to herself again did the opposite; they became, in her words, 'too much'.[37] She would soon flee her domestic set-up, forever.

What went wrong? In new motherhood the future can suddenly appear mapped out and frighteningly inflexible. Did Lizzie have a vision of the impending years, in which, far from freeing her from her estate, the birth of an heir actually tied her closer to it, and put the independent adventures she desired even further out of reach? Perhaps childbirth traumatised Lizzie and damaged her physically: she would not have any more children. Her husband, too, seems to have been at the very least a disappointment, and perhaps worse.

According to the writer Wilfrid Scawen Blunt, Fred was 'a dull heavy fellow . . . with a dash of cunning and more than a dash of brutality'. A female writer would later speculate that 'his persistent recklessness must have made [Lizzie] unhappy'. Decades later, when she came to write about her early life, Lizzie dodged the question of what went wrong in her first marriage – and instead she told a story about an anonymous young woman whose bullying husband 'could not make [her] happy'.[38] In a foray into fiction, a novel she called *The Story of an Alpine Winter* and published in 1907, Lizzie devised a character called Rosamond Whitchurch – a name strikingly similar to

Lizzie's own maiden name, Whitshed – who 'separated from a husband who had rendered her life quite intolerable'.[39] Lizzie had grown up with cautionary evidence of how her aunt's and father's lives had been destroyed by aristocratic family duties and, following Harry's birth, she may well have been terrified that the same fate was facing her too.

The fictional Rosamond Whitchurch fled her marriage for a 'rest-cure' in the Alps. And Lizzie did the same. In the summer of Harry's birth, she left her baby son in the care of her mother and Fred and headed for her first visit to the mountains of Switzerland. After a frustrating and disappointing holiday 'season' – peak periods for travel and leisure shared the same terminology as the calendar of city-based upper-class society events known as 'The Season', largely because the same people populated both – Lizzie retreated for the winter of 1880/81 to Menton. But 'still I was not satisfied', she wrote, and 'lost several pounds'. Next she travelled to Meran, 'a beautiful little town in the Tyrol', and stayed for two months, but she knew that 'the place did not suit me'.[40] By April 1881, she was back in London, still unsettled.

That summer, Lizzie met a woman who had forged quite a different path, showing how aristocratic land and status could offer freedom, utility and privilege to wealthy women – rather than constraint and spiralling madness.

Angela Burdett-Coutts was 'the richest heiress in all England'. She possessed complete control over her finances, which she'd inherited from her grandfather Thomas Coutts's banking fortune. Angela's money immunised her against much social criticism and allowed her to map her own route through life. She had been inundated with marriage proposals but had turned them all down in favour of a close friendship with her companion, Hannah Brown. She sought the philanthropical advice of novelist Charles Dickens, and together they established Urania Cottage, a refuge in west London for homeless and prostituted women. Angela supported 'ragged schools' – charitable schools for destitute children – and built and endowed more educational establishments, including a home for female art students and a sewing academy for adult women. She devised a scheme to improve sanitation in Westminster slums; sent aid to districts in Ireland that were still suffering from the famine's effects; patronised the London Society for the Prevention of Cruelty to Children; and was president of the Royal Society for the Prevention of Cruelty to Animals (RSPCA). She also gave huge sums to the Church of England to build churches and set up temperance societies and self-help associations.[41]

When Lizzie first met Angela Burdett-Coutts at a dinner, Angela was sixty-seven years old and had just married her twenty-nine-year-old American secretary, William Ashmead Bartlett – whose childhood education she had once funded and who, when they married, took her surname. She and William had been working together on a parliamentary act to defend public access to common land, and keep Hampstead Heath and adjacent land 'open, unenclosed and unbuilt on'. Her inheritance of the Coutts estate was dependent on Angela *not* marrying a foreigner and so, overnight, she lost three-fifths of her fortune and created a huge scandal (Queen Victoria referred to the union as 'the *mad* marriage'). Angela remained seemingly unconcerned, however, insulated by her remaining wealth and devotion to her projects.[42]

The late nineteenth century saw the emergence of an upper-class strand of women's rights activism, sometimes referred to as 'imperial feminism'. As historian Barbara Caine describes it, 'bourgeois women shared a self-image of themselves as the rightful citizens of an imperial nation'. Campaigners fought specifically for the right of elite women to enjoy the same privileges as male landowners, community figureheads and politicians. During the Irish Land War, for instance, the conservative periodical *The Englishwoman's Review* – its full name was *The Englishwoman's Review of Social and Industrial Questions* – called for the erosion of male-preference primogeniture and argued that allowing women to inherit estates was in 'Britain's national self-interest', because women were equally competent as leaders and managers as men and would successfully defend land-owning interests against the agitators. (Today, the pressure group Daughters' Rights continues the campaign against patrilineal inheritance and the unequal privileging of aristocratic sons over daughters, especially in the ability to play a full role in the life of the nation. For instance, Britain's House of Lords still reserves ninety-two seats for 'hereditary peers', all of whom are men.)[43]

Some women saw the importance of outdoor activities precisely in the context of imperial feminism. Historian Malcolm Craig describes how the nineteenth-century traveller Elizabeth Sarah Mazuchelli linked mountaineering to empire-building. Mountaineering could be seen as a good pursuit for ambitious upper-class women because it allowed them to exercise leadership skills that they were denied elsewhere, and it proved their suitability for government.[44]

Both Angela and Lizzie Le Blond would have been aware of such discussions, which gave voice to many of their own experiences and beliefs.

Less than a month after meeting Angela Burdett-Coutts, Lizzie was spurred into leaving Fred and Harry once again, and taking that second – and life-changing – trip to the mountains, during which she climbed to the Grands Mulets Hut.

At first, Lizzie's departure did not constitute a decisive end to her marriage: Fred came to Geneva to meet her at the end of her holiday, and together they went to the thermal spa towns of Aix-les-Bains and Allevard-les-Bains. But it marked the beginning of the end and, by July the following year, Fred had moved out of their home on Emperor's Gate. Newspapers reported that 'Mrs Burnaby' would from now on 'live abroad', alone. Much of the responsibility for Harry's care was left permanently to Lizzie's mother, Alice.[45]

Lizzie would present this turning point in her life as necessitated by 'delicate health': a flare-up of tuberculosis exacerbated by the strain on her lungs a few years earlier. However, there is no real evidence that she suffered from consumption. Throughout her life she repeatedly used ill health as shorthand (and cover) for acute unhappiness. Her escape to the mountains was an attempt to find an alternative lifestyle that would be more conducive to her physical and emotional health. Years after, Lizzie published a book called *High Life and Towers of Silence*, in which she argued that the 'high life' of mountaineering was a healthier substitute for high society balls, palace parties and elite marriages, and later she would comment that she owed a 'supreme debt of gratitude to the mountains for knocking from me the shackles of conventionality'.[46]

At first glance, I take Lizzie's reference to bucking convention to mean that, by turning to the mountains to escape her life as wife, mother and aristocratic place-holder, she was an outlier in her society. But then I remember that, in the mountains, Lizzie was rarely alone: even in those first excursions to Switzerland, she was accompanied by female friends. So the truth, it seems, is a little more complicated – and surprising to someone like me, who, not so long ago, lazily assumed that nineteenth-century women were, for the most part, confined indoors.

3.

The mountains have room for all

I expand my search for women in the mountains beyond Lizzie herself. I want to look at when outdoor activities took off as a more widespread leisure phenomenon – for instance, when it became commonplace *to go for a walk* – and whether women were keen to participate from the start. I want also to understand the ideas that women attached to the outdoors. Did these differ from the nineteenth-century guidebooks, travel writing and nature poetry that were published and produced by men? And was the world of mountaineering that Lizzie entered in 1881 accommodating and welcoming to women; or did female climbers face an uphill battle in pursuit of their ventures? Was Lizzie really an outlier, forging her rare talent in the face of male hostility and aggression – or was she assisted by a wider adventure community who accepted and even encouraged women? If nineteenth-century outdoor leisure was indeed characterised by discrimination and exclusion, then was it chiefly levelled at women – or were other demographic groups similarly affected?

I am interested in uncovering what happened to cause Lizzie, and numerous women like her, to have exited the public face of elite outdoor sport around the turn of the century. I hope this might help me to understand the factors that still deter women from the outdoors and from sport today, and so to better understand my own discomfort in the world at large at this moment in time.

In order to understand that *fin-de-siècle* departure of women from the mountains, I first need to find out how many women were present in those outdoor adventure communities prior to that turning point. When women's visibility in sport started waning in the early twentieth century, was this simply an intensification of a dynamic that had always been present: the strengthening of a sense that women had always been unwelcome in what was fundamentally a man's world? Or was the exodus of women from outdoor sport and leisure something startling and new? Did it overturn the comfort, belonging and freedom of large numbers of athletic women who had hitherto assumed their presence outdoors was accepted and ensured for the long term?

I dive into researching the origins of the outdoor leisure movement. I soon realise that, in her desire to find an alternative lifestyle, Lizzie was representative of many of the first ramblers and mountaineers, who were also looking for new ways of life. But not all of those earliest enthusiasts shared the same specific goal as Lizzie, which was an escape from the sexist practices of the landed aristocracy.

When rambling and mountaineering became recognisable leisure activities – around the beginning of the nineteenth century – the 'great outdoors' was attractive to most of its enthusiasts, not as an escape from the patriarchal mores of the upper classes, but because it offered respite from the new cities that were mushrooming across Britain, Europe and North America, with their cramped living quarters, polluted air, crushing crowds and regimented timetables. In Australia and New Zealand, industrialisation and urbanisation would happen later, from the end of the nineteenth century, and later still in Latin America, Africa and Asia – giving rise to much more recent outdoor sports industries in those regions. Because I want to explore the apparent disappearance of sporting women at the turn of the twentieth century, my focus is mainly on the countries in which outdoor leisure had been firmly established as a mass phenomenon by that point – namely in Europe and North America.

The mass migration of people from the countryside to cities over the nineteenth century profoundly changed those nations, not just in their topographical appearance, but in their practices and beliefs – including their attitudes towards outdoor space. Between 1800 and 1900 in New York City, for instance, the population rocketed from 60,000 to around 3.5 million, and it became the busiest port and one of the wealthiest cities in the world, with similar explosions happening in Philadelphia and Chicago, whose populations increased nearly tenfold between 1837 and 1850. The 1850s gold rush in Victoria,

Australia, grew the state's population by over 450 per cent, and the population of its capital city Melbourne increased sixfold in that decade and twentyfold between 1851 and 1901. In 1801, London's population was 1 million, but by 1851 it was nearly 2.5 million. At the start of the nineteenth century, 70 to 80 per cent of the population of England and Wales were living in small towns, villages, hamlets and other rural settlements, but by 1851 this number had shrunk to 44 per cent as people moved en masse to cities like Birmingham, Bradford, Liverpool, Manchester, Sheffield and Leeds – and the rural population continued to diminish even further, to just 20 per cent by 1911. There were similar trends in cities across continental Europe. Between 1800 and 1914, the populations of Paris, Berlin and Vienna increased by 631 per cent, 1,935 per cent and 830 per cent respectively.[1]

The new urban lifestyle was, in large part, driven by changes in work and production, as cottage industries were replaced by intensive communal workplaces such as factories, warehouses and offices. Urbanisation tends to be linked to higher levels of economic activity, higher wages and, in some instances, to better living standards – but it also leads to much higher levels of inequality. Urbanisation had passionate critics who worried that, as epidemiologist William Farr put to the House of Commons in 1840, 'the aggregation of mankind in towns [might be] disastrous' once population density breached certain levels. The population density in both industrial and residential areas of the new cities caused environmental and health catastrophes that the nineteenth-century reformer Hector Gavin listed as ranging from 'the want of ventilation and consequent impurity of the air; to the defective state of paving, drainage, and sewage; to the filthy state of the dwellings of the poor and of their immediate neighbourhood; to the *concentration* of unhealthy and putrescent emanations from narrow streets, courts and alleys; to the crowded and unhealthy state of workshops, and to the injurious occupations which are carried on in them'.[2]

Life expectancy plummeted as typhoid, cholera, tuberculosis and malnutrition raged through the urban population, especially among the poorest. The harms could be psychological too: patients with 'shattered nerves' complained of incessant noise and danger on the streets. There was not a clear-cut distinction between physical and emotional symptoms: both were considered to be intertwined responses to an unhealthy society. For many people across the urbanising world, the ensuing search for wellness in these new societies was a form of social critique, articulating how bodies and minds were suffering alike in nineteenth-century industrial cities. 'Public health' emerged as an idea that suggested that wellbeing was not only the concern of the individual but a manifestation of how people were treated by their society – and that it was therefore the state's responsibility to tackle.

It strikes me how many contemporary memoirs feature their authors turning to the natural world as salve for personal bereavements, including Helen Macdonald and Charlie Gilmour who, in *H is for Hawk* and *Featherhood* respectively, both look to birdlife to help with grief. Perhaps in individual experiences of bereavement – the losses of family members, friends, partners – we catch a glimpse of broader, societal forms of mourning. I wonder if we are prone to turning to nature when we are grieving because we hope that the natural world might comfort us for personal losses, but that it also might heal more chronic, existential forms of deficiency; the things we lack because we are deprived of them by our societies, rather than because of the death of loved ones. Do we see in the natural world a more nourishing way of life that we have lost – perhaps because of the dispossessions involved in industrialisation, urbanisation, capitalism or patriarchy – and do we look to nature for the possibility of finding such sustenance again?

City-dwellers looked for correctives to everything that had been lost during urbanisation. Throughout the nineteenth century (and after), many found antidotes beyond industrial confines, in spaces and activities that did not typically feature in their day-to-day lives, such as forest footpaths or backcountry camping. In America, Henry David Thoreau described how walking outdoors was respite from the 'moral insensibility of my neighbors who confine themselves to shops and offices the whole day for weeks and months, ay, and years almost together'. Travel writer James Hingston, editor of

Australia's first tourist guidebook, in 1868, depicted outdoor adventure as an 'escape from civilisation' and its 'conventionalities'.[3]

Sometimes curative natural spaces were preserved *within* cities. After a successful campaign in Britain in the 1840s for a 'half-day holiday on Saturdays' to be given to 'people employed in warehouses etc.', protesters agitated for 'Public Walks or Open Spaces' where workers 'among the middle or humbler classes' could spend their new 'week-ends' finding amusement and refreshment. On 22 August 1846, the first three public parks in Britain – and some of the first in the world – opened in Manchester and Salford. In the United States, city planners constructed networks of paths for walking in cemeteries and greenways beside canals, and the 1850s saw the building of parks such as New York City's Central Park. Lucy Larcom from New England reflected on how such spaces counteracted the detriments of her usual industrial lifestyle: 'No matter if we must get up at five the next morning and go back to our humdrum toil, we should have the roses to take with us for company, and the sweet air of the woodland which lingered about them would scent our thoughts all day and make us forget the oily smell of the machinery.'[4]

The history of outdoor pursuits, from its beginnings to the present, is marked by a belief that immersion in the natural world offers respite from our day-to-day routines, and sometimes inspires us to make permanent and dramatic changes in our lives.

From the late eighteenth century onwards, pioneers, rebels and mavericks of the leisured classes increasingly embraced sport and adventurism. The history of Lizzie's newfound passion, mountaineering, for instance, evolved across three fairly distinct periods: the years of early urbanisation from the 1780s to the 1850s, which saw the birth of recreational mountaineering. This was followed in the 1850s and 1860s by what has been called the 'Golden Age of Alpinism'. After that there came the expansion and consolidation of a mass tourist industry from the late nineteenth century onwards, and the onset of cheap package tours. Each stage saw an increase – sometimes steady, sometimes explosive – in the number of people turning to the outdoors to seek adventure or escape from their daily lives.

Up until around 1850, mountaineering and rambling were mostly the pursuits of unconventional individuals, rather than mainstream activities. Many – but not all – of these early enthusiasts were moneyed and independent, in control of their own time and energy. In these decades, there were some mass crazes concerning the outdoors – such as the fashion for identifying 'picturesque' viewpoints, capturing 'prospects' with viewing equipment such as 'Claude glasses' and visiting stately homes with grounds designed by landscape gardeners – but aficionados nevertheless tended to venture into the great outdoors alone, or in intimate groups of family or friends, or with the help of local guides, rather than in large package excursions. There were still very few outdoor clubs, agencies, organised tours or mountaineering guidebooks; nor was there accommodation or transport specifically aimed at bustling parties of hundreds of adventurous souls. From the 1810s, some guidebooks included advice for 'pedestrians' and wanderers: Wordsworth's 1810 *Guide to the Lakes*, for example, was clearly written from a walker's point of view. But, when devising routes or choosing locations for outdoor excursions, ramblers and mountaineers couldn't assume that advice would be readily accessible in tourist literature. They often had to make their way alone, drawing upon books designed for very different purposes, such as 'road books' (directories of roads between towns and inns, including stagecoach times), topographical and antiquarian publications, geological maps, travel writing and guides to military surveying. In the hills, they did not expect to encounter coachloads of other tourists, but to spend the day largely in solitude, or with their companions, except for encounters with the 'rustic' permanent inhabitants of rural settlements. The poet Samuel Taylor Coleridge declared that, when rambling, 'every man [is] his own path-maker'.[5]

For many of these early 'explorers', their relative uniqueness – their solitude in the wilderness – was an important part of the attraction of outdoor leisure. Rambling and mountaineering allowed them to distinguish themselves from the city-bound masses.

It was an opportunity to gain perspective on their day-to-day lives, and to consider changes that might be necessary for better emotional and physical health. Long-distance walks and climbs often required people to camp, for which they had to weigh up which of the trappings of contemporary comfort were really essential and which could be jettisoned. Australian historian Bill Garner points out that early camping also required people to experiment with their usual domestic roles and to adjust preconceived ideas about who did the cooking, repairs, navigation and packing.[6] Everyone was expected to chip in with everything and, from the very beginning of outdoor leisure, both men and women saw the chance to alter and expand conventional gender stereotypes. Outdoor communities could also provide opportunities for new, and sometimes even transgressive, kinds of relationship.

Nevertheless, despite the profound importance that outdoor leisure possessed for its first devotees, their numbers were relatively small. In the early 1850s it was still possible to claim that, as British mountaineer and solicitor Charles Edward Mathews put it in a potted history of 'the growth of mountaineering', the men and women 'who practised climbing for its own sake were so few that they might be counted on the fingers of one hand'. But, in that decade, things started to shift. Mathews reported how a 'craze for Alpine adventure' took hold and subjected the European mountains to a scramble for first recorded ascents, in which 'Englishmen . . . Germans, Italians, Swiss, and Frenchmen, claimed some share in the honour and the spoil'.[7] Outdoor enthusiasts in the 1850s reported feeling like pioneers, riding a surge of public interest in mountaineering, racking up first ascents of previously untrodden summits and basking in widespread adulation.

In this mid-century decade, many travellers were searching for the same 'sweet spot': locations where visitors could benefit from the improved facilities and infrastructure that were the result of fifty years of slow growth of the tourist industry, but with the solitude, quiet and exclusivity that preceded the arrival of the masses. Such places could only remain sweet for a very brief window of time. As the century pivoted into its second half, the Golden Age Alpinists were joined by tens of thousands of fellow tourists, and it was no longer possible to sustain a fantasy of being alone in the hills.

As this suggests, during the second half of the nineteenth century a large-scale outdoor tourist industry coalesced across Europe and North America. (Outdoor leisure similarly took off in Australasia towards the end of the century.) This was the context in which Lizzie started mountaineering: when she made those first trips into the Alps in the 1880s, her expeditions were facilitated by a fairly recent explosion in the availability of guidebooks, literature describing the pleasures and pioneers of rambling and climbing, and dedicated tourist accommodation and transport networks. One of the most incontrovertible markers of this shift, from outdoor leisure as a pursuit of eccentric individuals to a mass-market activity, was the travel agent Thomas Cook's inaugural package tour to Switzerland in the summer of 1863, offering 'cheap tickets to Mont Blanc'.[8]

By 1884, it was estimated that 'some 13,000 strangers' were visiting Chamonix each year. Karl Baedeker's Swiss *Handbook for Travellers* went through eight new editions between 1872 and 1889, each one substantially revised to keep pace with the new hotels and public transport routes that emerged year on year. New guidebooks were being published all the time. In 1873, the mountaineer, explorer and Egyptologist Amelia Edwards held John Ball's *Alpine Guide* responsible for widely opening up 'the Eastern Alps', including the south-eastern Tyrol and Dolomites, regions that had once been 'scarcely known even by name'.[9]

Transport networks had been improving for a while, in tandem with the swelling of cities across developed nations. In Britain, some 22,000 miles of roads were built between 1750 and 1815, and in France and Italy, public works engineers improved roads in the early 1800s as part of Napoleon's programme of international conquest and centralisation. Similar projects followed in Switzerland. Better roads meant that people could travel further and more comfortably, first in privately owned carriages and then also on public transport, such as stagecoach services, which increased eightfold in Britain between

1790 and 1836, and omnibuses, which were serving around 120,000 passengers per day in Philadelphia by 1858.[10]

Improved transport drove outdoor tourism in two major ways. More roads and services allowed larger numbers of North American and European citizens to leave cities and be transported faster, and more cheaply, comfortably and frequently, to a wider range of rural locations to hike, run and climb. And, secondly, as historian Silas Chamberlin points out, public transport drove not just logistics but also the *desire* to participate in outdoor activities – albeit in a slightly contradictory manner. Pedestrian activities such as rambling and mountaineering were arguably part of a backlash against the very accessibility of public transport that made them more possible. Strenuous physical pursuits became attractive as counterpoints to a modern world in which people were more and more reliant on public transport. It is notable that citizens only started choosing to hike long distances for fun once walking had stopped being an unavoidable chore, while many loved rambling because it seemed like an idealised return to a pre-industrial world without trains and omnibuses. Nevertheless, most ramblers, mountaineers and runners weren't purists, and they were still content to use those trains and omnibuses to travel to their outdoor playgrounds.[11]

As the century wore on, women were increasingly recognised and catered for as a distinct constituency of outdoor tourism. In the 1850s, two middle-aged British women, Eliza Cole and Jane Freshfield, who rambled with their lawyer husbands around the valleys and 'by-ways and higher passes of the Alps', had complained about the belittling inaccuracy of John Murray's bestselling *Handbook for Switzerland*, which claimed that the Gries Pass, between Valais in Switzerland and Formazza in Italy, 'is not a pass for ladies'.[12] But by the 1880s, guidebook writers were acknowledging a significant market of female outdoors enthusiasts, and were showing them greater respect. In 1883, the tenth edition of Baedeker's Swiss *Handbook* added a new comment – deviating from the text of earlier editions – noting that, with regard to 'mountaineering ambition', 'ladies now *frequently* vie with the stronger sex in their deeds of daring'. By the sixteenth

Women and guides on the Mer de Glace, a glacier in the Chamonix valley, around 1886

edition in 1895, the generic pronouns 'he' and 'himself', which had specified a male readership throughout earlier issues, were being omitted and replaced by gender-neutral references to 'the traveller' or 'the pedestrian'.[13]

Businesses catering for mountain tourists recognised the specific requirements of female travellers. In Chamonix, a system was set up to ensure that mountain guides found roughly equal amounts of employment, by allocating them to tourists on a rota system. Male mountaineers complained about being unable to select their favourite guides, but the system was partly devised to reduce the heckling of tourists – whose 'bedroom doors used to be besieged by guides, clamouring to take them' – which the Chamonix Compagnie des Guides acknowledged could be particularly intimidating for women. And, knowing that lone female mountaineers might feel vulnerable with a team of unfamiliar men in remote locations, the Compagnie also allowed women to bypass the rota system and employ known men with whom they felt comfortable.[14]

Women were also becoming better served in terms of kit and equipment. Many excursions started with a horse or mule ride, until paths became too steep and rocky for the animals to climb, but it had been a common complaint among women venturers in earlier decades that side-saddles were in short supply. Eliza Cole, for example, had been irritated at having to fashion one out of hay, cloth and stirrups, noting how there was 'little provision for the wants of lady-riders'. (She wished she'd followed the example of her friend Emma King, who had recently obtained a portable side-saddle 'which folded into a compact waterproof case, and could be adapted with equal facility to horse, mule, or donkey', inspiring 'the proudest feeling of independence' among female users.) Jane Freshfield had further noted that women were faced not only with difficulties in sourcing their own riding equipment, but their children's too. But by the 1870s, organisations such as the Norwegian Tourist Association (Den Norske Turistförening) began tackling the widespread lack of women-friendly saddles by allocating funds to supply these in the Haukelifjell mountain areas. The Club Alpin Française also obtained side-saddles for women members, and widened paths for mules and ponies, which women were more likely than men to ride, thus allowing *'aux dames . . . de faire cette promenade sans fatigue'*.[15]

An important driver of the outdoor leisure industry, which particularly boosted women's participation from the mid nineteenth century, was health tourism. The natural world had been tapped for medical cures since ancient times. In Europe, thermal spas had long been used to treat maladies, and for over 10,000 years Indigenous tribes in North America had regarded hot springs as sacred places with healing powers. Enthusiasm for such practices was renewed in the eighteenth century: European travellers to the United States flocked to the springs of Pennsylvania and Virginia, and spas, baths and hotels were built around springs on the European continent, at places such as Karlsbad and Vichy. Until the mid nineteenth century, physicians had mostly advised invalids to travel to the warmer climates of the Mediterranean, but from the 1840s, medics were swayed by the belief that less-oxygenated mountain air might help patients with tuberculosis and other lung complaints. In 1842, Dr John Davy wondered if 'alpine people rarely had tubercles because of the greater respiratory activity occasioned by a rarefied atmosphere'. Mountains also offered the added benefits of mineral springs and 'milk cures', in which milk from herb-fed goats, cows, asses, horses and even women was used to treat tuberculosis and gout. Before the discovery in 1882 of the highly infectious bacillus bacteria that cause tuberculosis, the disease was thought to be hereditary, and no harm was anticipated from cramming invalids and tourists together in treatment centres, spas and hotels.[16]

Among the treatments on offer, TB sanatoria explicitly provided outdoor leisure activities, including regimes of graded hikes. Those activities soon took on a life of their own outside sanatoria and helped to accelerate the outdoor recreation movement. For example, Hugo Richter, one of the first two visitors to a sanatorium in Davos, went on to set up the Davos Kurverein (tourist organisation) and a local branch of the Swiss Alpine Club. It was a woman – British tourist and one-time patient Elizabeth MacMorland – who played a large part in popularising the Swiss village of Davos as 'a new Alpine resort for sick and sound in summer and winter', through the publication of her book *Davos-Platz* in 1878.[17]

Because of this overlap between health tourism and outdoor leisure – reinforcing the conventional belief that activities like hiking offered respite from the harms of industrial society – it remained typical for ramblers and mountaineers to justify their pursuits using theories of disease and cure well into the next century. (This is still prevalent in the present day: for example, the widely accepted belief that there is a 'nature cure' for depression and other illnesses.) Certainly, in the 1880s, the references that Lizzie Le Blond made to mountaineering 'for health' were common shorthand for the idea that immersion in nature could remedy, not just personal trauma, but also the physical and psychological injuries that were inflicted by modern life – and it was an idea that was considered particularly relevant to women, because female minds and bodies were seen to be suffering in distinct ways in late nineteenth-century Western societies.

Indeed, many of the ills of modern industrial living were observed to be affecting women specifically. In one study in nineteenth-century America, serious anaemia was diagnosed in 70 per cent of urban working women and was thought to be caused by poor nutrition and to lead to contracted pelvises that made childbirth more dangerous. British medical officer John Simon warned that 'the extensive factory employment of female labour is a sure source of very large infantile mortality' – caused, in great part, by feeding babies adulterated, unsanitary bottled milk which lowered surviving infants' resistance to illnesses such as tuberculosis, measles, typhus and whooping cough.[18] Tuberculosis afflicted all classes, but it was particularly correlated to industrialised cities in which overcrowded and poorly ventilated working and living quarters ensured rapid transmission – and it seemed to disproportionately affect young women, which was thought to be linked to childbirth's depletion of women's immune systems. 'Female nervous exhaustion' was identified as a modern condition and was considered to be exacerbated by women's domestic responsibilities and the constitutionally 'highly strung nerve centres' of 'delicate, decorative, and fundamentally idle' middle- and upper-class wives – just as Lizzie's young aunt Eliza had experienced in the 1850s, before most likely taking her own life shortly after childbirth.[19]

Even though women of all classes were considered distinctly vulnerable to the harms of industrialisation, relatively few could afford to retreat to the mountains for rest-cures, like Lizzie. But those who could take such expensive trips found an industry increasingly prepared to make accommodations for their sex. Resorts such as Aix-les-Bains, Lourdes and Sedan in France provided *chaises-à-porteurs* or sedan chairs – elevated litters, chairs or boxes suspended on long rods, which were carried by two porters – as well as wheeled Bath chairs and walking sticks, to enable infirm travellers to move around. Women seem to have constituted the majority of users taking advantage of these 'mobility aids': a magazine journalist wrote in 1847 (quoting from John Murray's *Handbook to Switzerland*) that the chaise meant that 'even the aged or invalid female is by no means debarred the pleasure of taking a part in difficult mountain expeditions'.

A woman in a chaise-à-porteurs, 1891, Switzerland

Mariana Fox Tuckett – who had walked and run through her native Cornwall as a young woman and whose sister, the mountaineer Lizzie Fox Tuckett, climbed extensively in the Tyrol in the 1860s and published books of humorous sketches of the women and men she encountered – was able to continue mountaineering into her sixties, by 'being carried on excursions in a *chaise-à-porteurs*' in Grindelwald.[20]

Another example of a woman whose mountaineering was enabled by mobility aids was a remarkable forty-three-year-old British woman called Martha 'Patty' Shaw (née Barkley), who, despite suffering permanent injuries from pregnancies and childbirths, made a four-year tour of Europe in the mid 1840s. She had recently lost her husband and mother and, since her final labour in 1839, Martha described how she had been 'almost wholly confined to my chair' with 'legs & feet still feel[ing] very dead & my hips disjointed' and had an additional diagnosis of asthma. She was determined to mountaineer nonetheless, and on 9 December 1845 she said goodbye to her neighbours, paid off her bills, bundled her six young children (ranging from six to nineteen years old) out of their London house and set off with them for the continent. Over the following year, she took them climbing in the Rigi massif in central Switzerland; the Brünig

Pass, between the Bernese Oberland and central Switzerland; the St Gotthard Pass, between northern and southern Switzerland; the Aare valley around Guttannen, in the Bernese Oberland; and Mount Vesuvius in Italy.

While Martha's children walked and ran beside her, her diaries draw attention to the geometry of motion that was specific to travelling in a *chaise-à-porteurs*: how the descent of the St Gotthard Pass involved 'long dreadful zigzags' and, 'when you come to the turn', the chaise's wide turning-circle meant that the porters had to momentarily overshoot the path, before slowly switching back, and 'it appears as if you were going into space'. Once, when 'rounding a point of rock', she was suspended over thin air, and the porters stopped to point out the river below. 'It was about 200 feet below me, the precipice perpendicular & my chair partly over it. I scarcely had breath to look down & yet it was so lovely I c[oul]d not resist a look.'[21] Martha's accounts show exploration in a very different way from the conventional non-disabled person's viewpoint which dominates mountaineering literature.*

Innovations such as these, as well as package tourism generally, encouraged growing numbers of women into the outdoors from the

* The shift in perspective that Martha's diaries bring about in the reader are similar to the dramatic change in outlook experienced by the British garden designer Humphry Repton, who was involved in a serious carriage accident in 1811, resulting in injuries that meant he used a wheeled Bath chair for the rest of his life. In his wheelchair, Repton realised that the landscape looked and felt very different to how he had previously experienced it. The gravel pathways he had previously favoured in his designs now brought a 'shaking and rattling [that] soon became intolerable to an invalid', and so in his future garden plans he started substituting gravel with 'glades of fine mown turf' meandering 'among shrubs, sometimes under trees', which, in Repton's own words, 'may be enjoyed by the cripple, with as much, and perhaps more, satisfaction from his wheeling-chair' than by a pedestrian. He also introduced radically elevated flower beds, and a wide pergola, both easily accessible to a user of an early 'wheeling-chair'. (Repton, 'Fragment 29: Concerning the Luxuries of a Garden', in *Fragments on the Theory and Practice of Landscape Gardening* (London, 1816). See also George McKay, *Radical Gardening* (London, 2013).)

1860s onwards. They helped young women like Yorkshirewoman Jemima Morrell – who bought 'tickets to Switzerland and back' with Thomas Cook in June and July 1863 – to decide that many of the purported 'dangers of Alpine travel' were actually 'imaginary'. Among the burgeoning ranks of female mountaineers, the number of women who were happy to travel freely, without male chaperones, alone or with female friends or relatives, also seems to have increased. In the 1850s, Jane Freshfield had described how '"unprotected females" evidently created some surprise', but in the 1870s and 1880s, Emily Hornby – who had an energetic quarter-century mountaineering career, from her early forties to her mid sixties – mostly travelled only with other women, through the Alps and the Carpathians: with an American friend, Hilda; with various other female friends, all designated in her books by initials (Mrs O, F and L, H and P); and with sisters and female cousins.[22]

In the early 1870s, Amelia Edwards trekked through the Dolomites with her friend Lucy. (Edwards always preferred female company: she lived with her companion Ellen Drew Braysher, and was affectionately berated by the landscape painter Marianne North, who told her: 'What love letters you do write, what a pity you waste them on a woman!') Frances Havergal – an enthusiast for Switzerland, who also wrote English hymns and poems – reflected in 1881 on 'what a combination of keen enjoyment and benefit to health [is] to be found in a pedestrians [sic] tour by unprotected females'. Back in the 1850s, a (male) mountain guide had predicted that women would soon 'go everywhere', and by the time Lizzie entered the mountains in the early 1880s, his prophecy was coming true.[23]

I want to know about the joys that these women found in the natural landscape and the outdoors. I want to discover if 'mountaineering' – rambling, running, riding and climbing – carried some of the same meanings for these foremothers as they do for me, today. So I immerse myself in their memoirs, letters, diaries and articles, and it quickly becomes evident that the pleasures these women took from interacting with the natural world were manifold – and arguably more complex than the search for respite from city-living that dominates histories of men's outdoor leisure.

Some women were searching for 'once-in-a-lifetime' escapes from the limited vistas of their usual routine; forms of extreme experience unlike anything they had ever encountered before. In 1775, one anonymous female traveller – possibly Elizabeth Cust, wife of the Welsh politician and antiquarian Philip Yorke – went up Snowdon, Wales's highest mountain, and described it as 'the most glorious day I ever spent'.

Women looked to outdoor activities for ways to find greater physical and emotional freedom than the restrictive world of corsets and stuffy withdrawing rooms permitted. In Jane Austen's 1813 novel *Pride and Prejudice*, Elizabeth Bennet derives great personal pleasure – but also attracts social censure – for being 'in the habit of running' and looking 'almost wild' as she rambles 'three miles, or four miles, or five miles, or whatever it is, above her ankles in dirt, and alone, quite alone!'[24]

Many women enjoyed consciously rebelling against codes that otherwise ruled their lives, on the basis of both their gender and class. Frances Havergal loved 'the delicious freedom and sense of leisure' that came from 'having no one to consult, or to keep waiting, or to fidget about us' as she and her female friend 'stormed' mountains with 'our alpenstocks and scrambled and leaped and laughed and raced as if we were not girls again but *downright boys!*' Back in the 1740s, the British poet, polymath and literary 'bluestocking' Elizabeth Carter had rejoiced when a rugged hike turned her and her friend into 'deplorable ragged figures . . . vagrants'. She was doubly thrilled to overhear 'some civil swains . . . signifying to one another, with a note of admiration, that *I am Parson Carter's daughter*'. She revelled in her sense of daring at transgressing the expectations that weighed upon her, as a woman, and the child of a curate.[25]

Many historians use the idea of 'separate spheres' to describe a gradual segregation of men and women's spaces which arguably accelerated around the turn of the nineteenth century, as the world of work transferred from domestic to public settings, and thus debarred some women – whose proper domain was considered to be the home – from economic power. Mountaineering offered a way for women to resist such segregation and the first woman to summit Mont Blanc experienced how it could directly confer financial authority. In 1809, a 'neat-looking peasant woman' called Maria Paradis reportedly came up with the idea of the ascent to drum up publicity for the tea stall she ran at the foot of the mountain. Guides subsequently directed tourists to Paradis's business, and she regaled them with stories of her climb while serving refreshments.[26]

Hiking and mountaineering repeatedly helped women to access a world of employment and status that was otherwise often out of reach. The 'sapphist' landowner Anne Lister mountaineered across Europe in the 1820s and 1830s, becoming one of the first people to climb a 'recognisable Alpine peak' (Mont Perdu), and only the second person – and the first amateur climber – to ascend Vignemale, in the French Pyrenees, in 1838. Lister's sporting activities complemented other ways in which she staked her claim to a public role, as a landowner with shares in canals, railways, mines and quarries.[27] Later in the century, Lizzie Le Blond would explicitly refer to her own climbing as 'the work', and the mountaineer Frederica Plunket – an Irish aristocrat and botanical illustrator (whose sister Katherine lived to be Ireland's oldest person, at 111 years and 327 days) – would reflect in the 1870s that, because middle- and upper-class women were often excluded from formal employment, they were also not considered in need of proper leisure time – 'as we have none of the hard work . . . we should have none of the play'. Mountaineering gave Plunket a taste of both: how much more beautiful a 'period of absolute rest' felt when it had been 'earned' by proper 'exertion and excitement'.[28] This was the taste of a rhythm of life, oscillating between work and play and rest, that was more typically enjoyed by men.

Mountains were also sources of intellectual power for female ramblers and climbers. In the early nineteenth century, girls' formal education was very different from boys', being primarily designed to create good wives and mothers. If working-class girls were taught at all, it was in small domestic or church schools in which they learned the basics of reading, writing and arithmetic and practical skills such as needlework. Middle- and upper-class girls were educated by governesses to be 'decorative, modest, marriageable beings', and Lizzie herself bemoaned her poor education, which had left her 'uninformed' as a young adult, and with a 'useless' 'smattering' of 'conversational French' – and this was despite the fact that, as a student, she had been hungry for knowledge and 'keenly interested in everything around me'.[29]

Scientific enquiry had prompted some of the first expeditions into the mountains – as opportunities for measuring altitude, air pressure or glaciers, or collecting samples of rocks or flowers – and women often relished the possibilities that mountaineering presented for ad hoc tutoring.[30] Many described how panoramic views from summits helped them to learn geography. At the top of the Sasso Bianco in the Italian Dolomites, Amelia Edwards 'set to work with maps and field-glasses, to identify all that is visible of the panorama', and Jane Freshfield repeatedly used wide-ranging views as the starting point for broader research, 'enabling us to correct our topography'. Traditionally, vistas from hilltops had been depicted by eighteenth-century landscape poets as symbols of the social and intellectual power of male landowners, and rambles to wide-ranging viewpoints gave women a taste of the same kind of authority. In 1807, the poet Charlotte Smith's *Beachy Head* was published posthumously, a long poem in which the view from the 'projecting head-land' on Britain's south coast gave her a comprehensive understanding of commerce, empire and war. Frederica Plunket, among others, acknowledged the practical and intellectual challenges of the outdoor world. She found that devising a route up a mountain was a form of problem-solving, and noted that 'to overcome a difficulty is . . . gratifying'.[31]

The educational and social benefits that countless women discovered in the mountains occasionally catalysed into public recognition. In 1786, as part of a Grand Tour around Europe, a party of four young women (sisters Jane and Mary Parminter, their cousin Elizabeth Parminter, and a friend, Miss Colville) climbed the mountain of Buet in the Mont Blanc chain. They – and Frenchwoman Marie

Desailloud, who had made one of the earliest recorded female ascents of a mountain anywhere in the world, when she reached the same summit the previous year – were memorialised when Buet was subsequently termed 'the Ladies' peak', 'Mont Blanc for the Ladies' and 'Parminter Peak'.[32]

But this fame was not permanent. The memory of the Parminters has not survived into the present day. The icons of early outdoor sport whom we remember now are almost all men.

Such accounts of mountaineering show me that the character of nineteenth-century outdoor culture for women was, indeed, complicated. In many respects, this world was far more welcoming and accommodating to women than I had ever realised, especially in the way that practical innovations that catered for the specific characteristics of female lives and bodies were on offer. But I also realise that, despite the fact that they explored the mountains in large numbers, women did not always find a halcyon feminist utopia there. The opportunities (for physical strength and comfort, for intellectual engagement, for social power and fame) that were available to middle- and upper-class women in outdoor resorts were generally agreed to be greater than back home, but those resorts were still mixed-sex arenas of a patriarchy, with all that that entailed. Female travellers experienced both overt and more routine forms of sexism in the hills.[33]

As the Parminters' descent into obscurity shows, men dominated public representations of outdoor leisure in the nineteenth century. Today, we instantly recall many of these male icons: the young man standing above the clouds in Caspar David Friedrich's 1818 painting *Wanderer Above the Sea of Fog*; the sensitive nature-loving young men of Goethe's *Werther* and Rousseau's *Emile*; the reclusive, peripatetic figures of William Wordsworth's poetry; Henry David Thoreau's experiment with living at Walden Pond in the 1840s; and Ralph Waldo Emerson's 'Philosophers' Camp' for ten academics – all male – in the Adirondacks. But the names of women like Eliza Cole, Jane Freshfield, Maria Paradis, Amelia Edwards, Frederica Plunket – and Lizzie Le Blond – are far less familiar.

Male discomfort with women's presence characterised the outdoor leisure movement from the beginning. This was partly because many men used the outdoors to experiment with their identities as men. Some were drawn to outdoor adventure to counteract what could be seen as the sedentary, 'effeminate' nature of city life, in which middle- and upper-class men rarely worked with their hands, and which many men also felt was indivisible from the feminised space of the home. As Charles Dickens put it, in outdoor leisure, a man could '[prove] to himself that he is neither effete nor effeminate'.[34]

Others used the outdoors to try out more unconventional ideas about manhood: to rediscover 'natural' authentic emotions that were being stifled in a mechanised society, or to take on domestic jobs usually assigned to women, such as cooking and cleaning in their camps. The importance of the outdoors as a crucible in which different ideas about masculinity could be forged drove many men to explicitly exclude women. In Japan, men banned women from sacred mountain sites until 1868, under formal limitations known as 'Nyonin Kinsei' (No Women Admitted) and 'Nyonin Kekkai' (Barrier to Women). (Sections of Mount Ōmine are still today closed to women.) Men's exclusion of women was bolstered by philosophical ideas. When in 1757 the young British intellectual Edmund Burke published his theories about the pleasures of natural landscapes, he portrayed men as instinctive observers and explorers who gained profound benefits from the outdoors. But for Burke, women were not active travellers, adventurers or athletes in their own right. 'It is impossible to discern any idea of use' in women's bodies, he declared, and the beauty of a 'well-turned leg' is completely irrelevant to whether it might be 'well fitted . . . for running'.[35] In his eyes, women were only beautiful objects; motionless things to be *looked at* by men.

Right from the off, men directly deterred women from the outdoors using harassment, intimidation and belittlement – and violence. In May 1809, a Lancashire governess called Ellen – or rather Nelly – Weeton wanted 'to traverse Wales on foot', entirely alone, but she was dissuaded by 'the many insults a female is liable to'. She wondered if she could 'dress in the plainest garments I had, that I might attract less notice' and was frustrated that, 'If I was but a man, now! I could soon do it.'

Because of her fear of assault, Nelly Weeton put aside her dream and instead took a position as governess for the Pedder family, at Ambleside in the Lake District. It was awful and traumatic. Mr Pedder was violent and abusive to the women of the household: 'He seems to think that by lording it over two or three women, he increases his own consequence; and the more we submit, the worse he grows,' she wrote. In February 1810, the ten-year-old girl for whom Nelly was responsible died from burn injuries after standing too close to an open fire. Nelly stayed on as housekeeper, companion and tutor to Mrs Pedder, the girl's mother. Walking alone in the Lakes, for whole days, was Nelly's only respite, in snatched moments away from her domestic hell. 'I admire this country exceedingly,' she wrote, 'and if my time were my own, would ramble the country over; would traverse the vales, glide over the surface of the lakes, and run up the hills like a mountain sheep – here, I could live a life of seclusion, and scarce heave a sigh for society.'

Later, rambling continued to offer Nelly a fleeting escape throughout an emotionally and physically abusive marriage, in which she was in 'extreme want and houseless at one time; [with] imprisonments and bruises at another; my life daily in danger'. In June 1825, aged forty-eight, Nelly finally realised a part of her early dream to hike through Wales, and took a carriage to Pont Aberglaslyn, from where she began her ascent of Snowdon. But the experience was marred by men's refusal to leave women alone outdoors. 'I saw a gentleman descending with his guide,' she wrote, and 'they espied me'. Scared and traumatised, she tried to hide but nevertheless 'the guide . . . called out'. She pretended to be '*quite* deaf', but the men didn't take the hint, and 'continued shouting and I was forced to hear'. It became evident that the guide assumed that, as a mere woman, she must be wanting his services, and Nelly walked past the pair 'as fast as I could, hanging down my head; the guide again giving me some directions'.[36] The encounter ruined her experience of the ascent.

As the numbers of women outdoors grew over the decades, misogynist hostility seems to have intensified. In the 1880s, a backlash against the general popularity of the outdoor leisure industry started to materialise, and one of its principal targets was women. In February 1881, the mountaineer Willy Coolidge complained that 'Zermatt and Chamonix, the Oberland and the Engadine are worked to death' in 'what our French neighbours would call *"la vulgarisation des montagnes"*'. Some men grumbled that the increasing numbers of female travellers was the nadir of this vulgarisation.[37]

In 1865, Charles Dickens stratified Switzerland into three 'different altitudes': the lowest 'valleys and lakes' comprised 'the Switzerland of ladies', he wrote, above which there was a 'second region', accessed by 'prudent lads and lasses . . . on foot or horseback', while the 'third and uppermost Switzerland' was reserved for men: members of the 'Alpine Club . . . scientific men and human donkeys'. But within a few years, as the number of talented and ambitious female mountaineers escalated, this spatial segregation of the sexes came under threat, and both Leslie Stephen – author, mountaineer and future father of Virginia Woolf – and climber Albert Mummery grimly plotted a 'decline' of mountaineering, in which peaks that had once been relished as 'inaccessible' were 'doomed to pass through' three further stages, as more and more tourists took up climbing. The men predicted that such routes would become known, first, as 'a good hard climb, but nothing out of the way', then 'a perfectly straightforward bit of work', and finally, the worst, 'an easy day for a lady'.[38] Women's refusal to know their place was perceived as an intrusion into men's worlds.

By the 1870s and 1880s, the achievements of world-leading female mountaineers were ruthlessly realising Leslie Stephen's prophecy. Lucy Walker was born in British North America (now Canada), moved to Liverpool as a child, and in 1858, in her early twenties, she was advised by doctors to start climbing to ease her early-onset rheumatoid arthritis. Over the course of a long mountaineering career, Walker made nearly a hundred expeditions, including a first overall ascent of the Balmhorn, and first female ascents of mountains including the

Eiger, Lyskamm and Aiguille Verte. She was a role model for Marguerite 'Meta' Brevoort, whose family had emigrated from Holland to run a large farm on a site that is now Union Square in New York. Brevoort was the carer for her sister's 'delicate' son, Willy Coolidge, who would later complain about the 'vulgarisation' of mountain resorts – and in 1865, when she was forty and Coolidge fifteen, she took him for a summer holiday in the Alps. During that trip, she climbed to the summit of Mont Blanc, where she drank champagne, sang the Marseillaise and danced a quadrille with her three team mates. Over the next eleven years, Brevoort would make twelve overall first ascents and fourteen first female ascents, and the Pointe Marguerite on the Grandes Jorasses would be named after her.

Elite superstars like Walker and Brevoort, and the abundance of less skilled but nevertheless enthusiastic female mountaineers, were so unapologetically unavoidable by the 1880s that some men began a concerted attempt to contain women's numbers and protect the all-male exclusivity of the mountains.

From the beginning of the decade, some male mountaineering writers pointedly stopped writing about women as individuals in their reports, and instead portrayed them as an undifferentiated mass – 'the ladies'. Early men's mountaineering literature had once described remarkable female mountaineers by name, including Walker and Brevoort, and also other climbers and hikers including Sophia Romilly (who made the first female ascent of St Théodule in 1840), Isabella Straton and Emmeline Lewis Lloyd (who ascended Monte Viso together in 1870), Jane Margaret Leman (who went up Le Brévent in 1871), Constance Gordon Cumming (who climbed in Yosemite Valley in the 1870s, and wrote *Granite Crags*) and Elizabeth Mazuchelli (who explored the 'Indian Alps' in 1876). But from around 1880 onwards, male writers increasingly anonymised female climbers. The women who made the third overall ascent (and first female ascent) of the Feuerstein, in the Stubai Alps in the Tyrol, on 5 August 1884, were reported as simply 'two English ladies'; peremptory phrasing which became commonplace in men's reports throughout the next two decades.[39]

Women's individuality became hidden behind stereotypes as men sorted them into groups, such as the hysterics who were 'striv[ing] to outdo nature, and make everything dreadful, admirable, or wonderful'. Such rhetoric dehumanised women and put them back in their place – and so too did Edward Whymper's decision in *Scrambles Amongst the Alps* to include a photograph of Lucy Walker, not as an individual, but in a group shot in which, as the mountaineering writer Marjorie Milsom later pointed out, Walker was 'standing well in the background . . . with twenty more or less famous' male climbers in the foreground.[40]

The mass-market outdoor leisure industry that emerged after the 1860s was characterised by far greater organisation and codification, and this, in turn, provided formal opportunities to both marginalise and push women out of mountaineering.

In 1857, Charles Edward Mathews – along with his brother, a male cousin and two male friends – established the world's first mountaineering society: the Alpine Club, in London. Hundreds of other local and national rambling, climbing and mountaineering clubs followed across Europe, North America and Australasia: the Alpine Club of Williamstown, Massachusetts, was founded in 1863 and the German and Austrian Alpine Club in 1869; and a flurry of societies including the Appalachian Mountain Club, the Club Alpin Française, the Bright Alpine Club in Australia and the Wallaby Club for bushwalking were established in the 1870s, 1880s and 1890s. These early societies were forums through which members could share advice, tips, information, history and scientific information; distribute reports of members' ascents; and train and talk about the mountains during long off-season periods when climbers were confined to home. They also provided opportunities to socialise: the London Alpine Club's premises fulfilled many of the functions of a gentleman's club, offering smoking evenings, lectures and dinners. Such clubs took over the publishing industry for mountaineering literature, producing journals and yearbooks, including the Alpine Club's *Alpine Journal*. These publications forged a written tradition of outdoor sport – but it was one in which men's achievements were paramount, and vastly more visible and respected than women's.

Outdoor clubs could bring like-minded people together, but they also had the power to keep people out – women being a particular target. As outdoor leisure became a mass pursuit after the 1860s, clubs and their members became preoccupied with differentiating 'real' mountaineers from, in Willy Coolidge's words, 'the never ceasing stream of Cook's tourists'. To 'mountaineer' had been coined as a verb in 1802 by the poet Samuel Taylor Coleridge, but it wasn't until this later period that the Irish physicist and climber John Tyndall used *mountaineer* as a noun and identity for the first time, in 1860, as 'a person who engages in or is skilled at mountain climbing'. Outdoor clubs demarcated the identity of a 'proper mountaineer' by setting criteria for membership, and Charles H. Sholes, president of the Mazamas club in Portland, Oregon, was clear that the club's 'greatest strength' was its 'sifting process'. Some clubs firmly placed women in the out-group, as *improper* mountaineers. Britain's Alpine Club, the Scottish Mountaineering Club, the Japanese Alpine Club and the Explorers' Club of New York all barred women from membership.[41]

A single early exception was made by the otherwise male-only British Alpine Club for Lady Florence Dixie (1855–1905), whose brother Lord Francis Douglas had died in an accident descending the Matterhorn in 1865, and who was allowed to attend an Alpine Club meeting in February 1881. In 1881, Dixie had recently returned from an 'outlandish . . . escape' to Patagonia, in which she was the only woman in an all-male shooting party, and in her resulting book, *Across Patagonia*, she described the 'egotistical pleasure' of being 'as far removed from [other people] as possible'. *Across Patagonia* sparked a remarkable career, in which Dixie corrected some of Charles Darwin's work on Patagonian fauna, wrote books for children and adults on women's rights (including the feminist fantasy *Gloriana, or the Revolution of 1900*, in which she predicted that Britain would have a female prime minister by 1999), was employed as a war correspondent in South Africa, supported women's suffrage, helped to establish women's football in Britain and was an enthusiastic blood sportswomen until a volte-face in 1890s saw her become vice-president of the London Vegetarian Association. Her outdoor adventures were, in her words, attempts to flee the 'shallow artificiality of modern existence'.[42]

The Alpine Club may have been a bastion of all-male sociability, but it is important to note that, between the 1860s and 1890s, such male-only mountaineering clubs were in the minority. Most *did* allow female members. Ernest Caron, president of the Club Alpin Française (CAF) in 1889, emphasised that '*Nos rangs sont ouverts à tous ceux et toutes celles qui aiment les montagnes*' ('Our ranks are open to all those men and women who love the mountains'). However, historian Cécile Ottogalli-Mazzacavallo warns against romanticising any of these clubs as havens of egalitarianism and points out that women's apparent inclusion could be superficial. Out of the CAF's 430 members in 1875, only four were women and, even though the CAF specifically encouraged female members to join in the 1880s, this encouragement was conditional: women were expected to enjoy leisurely walks in the foothills rather than competing with men for first ascents, and their presence was tolerated because it could make the mountains feel 'homely' for men, and they were expected to raise hearty and brave mountaineering sons.[43] Nevertheless, it was important to female travellers that they were – even nominally – welcomed into clubs like the CAF and Swiss Alpine Club and, in the accounts of female mountaineers such as Emily Hornby, Frederica Plunket, Amelia Edwards – and Lizzie – the world of 1880s mountaineering comes across as generally female-friendly. In this overall context, the few male-only clubs seem to be only a minor undercurrent of sexism.

There was, however, increasing hostility ahead. Women's participation in the outdoors was on the rise in the final decades of the nineteenth century and, with it, male discomfort. Some of those more inclusive clubs would soon change their policies and imperil women's inclusion, respect and visibility in outdoor sport and leisure.

I want to find out if men's resistance to sharing 'their' outdoor spaces purely targeted women, or if it was directed at other demographic groups too. I begin by investigating the constitution of the early outdoor clubs. Like the majority, the British Alpine Club's membership in the late Victorian period predominantly comprised professional middle-class men – lawyers, civil servants, doctors – with around 12 per cent from the landed classes, none from the working classes, and all its members were white.[44]

Alpinists frequently spoke about walking, running and climbing in terms of aesthetic, philosophical or athletic benefits, but rarely about more mundane incentives, like earning money or manual work. However, those pursuits, and even the word *mountaineer*, had all originated in labour. A *mountaineer* had once referred to a 'hillbilly', 'backwoodsman' or 'trapper': someone who worked, but not necessarily played, in the wilderness. Historically, long-distance running was a job too: the task of running footmen, who were employed by the European nobility to swiftly scout out routes for carriages and clear a way through crowds, and of couriers running long distances with messages for rulers and military leaders. Rambling was a daily reality for commercial trade, travelling salespeople, itinerants and beggars, the homeless and unemployed, farmers, nomadic tribes, indigenous communities, cattle drovers, gamekeepers and marching armies. In Australia, New Zealand and North America, 'wilderness camping' had been necessity, not leisure, for the earliest explorers and settlers, land selectors and squatters, navvies building railroads, surveyors, gold prospectors and bushrangers.[45] But despite these labouring-class origins, by the turn of the twentieth century many of those who rambled, ran and mountaineered for leisure were conflicted about whether people who did so *for work* were truly 'one of them'.

Outdoor leisure enthusiasts frequently romanticised the 'humble' origins of their activities, and some even pursued them with the explicit hope of going back in time, or down in class – 'beginning again' and finding a more 'authentic' way of being. But, in practice, there was reluctance among middle- and upper-class travellers to fully include the working classes in their outdoor world. The poet William Wordsworth felt that urban labourers did not possess the requisite 'vivid perception' or 'comprehensive education' to appreciate 'picturesque and romantic scenery' – and he campaigned against a railway that would allow Manchester workers to easily access the Lake District. The second woman to climb Mont Blanc, a French aristocrat called Henriette d'Angeville, deliberately distinguished herself from her predecessor Maria Paradis by insisting that the 'peculiar pleasure and happiness' of mountaineering lay, not in the vulgar financial gain that had reportedly motivated Paradis, but in admiration of 'the grandeur of natural landscapes'. Guides posed a conundrum because they were clearly workers, yet upper-class tourists had no choice but to climb with them and depend on their greater expertise. To negotiate this difficulty, many Alpine Club members presented mountain guides as individuals who fell outside the class system, or were their equals ('princes', 'gentlemen') in the mountains but 'peasants' in the valleys.[46]

Such ambivalence about the labouring classes means that the stories and achievements of those who mountaineered, rambled, ran and camped for work have rarely been recorded, preserved or celebrated alongside other representations of outdoor leisure. And working-class women's stories have suffered a double hit of historical amnesia, as such women were frequently deemed 'improper mountaineers' on grounds of both class and sex. But these working-class women's stories deserve attention, as they reveal how the range of meanings that people find in the outdoors is far greater than the narrow set of associations linked to the elite white men who have traditionally dominated the history of mountaineering.

In a 1739 poem called *The Woman's Labour*, West Sussex washerwoman Mary Collier emphasised that working-class women's experiences of the world outdoors were very different from men's. She described how she walked long distances carrying harvested crops and while 'charing' (begging, or looking for cleaning or household work) and how, unlike male labourers, she had to haul her children around while she worked. While men enjoyed pleasant ambles home at the end of each day's labour, she could not take a leisurely 'rest at ev'ry Stile' – as that was the time when she was expected to turn to 'Toil and Labour' in the home. (As I'll discover later on, similar experiences still constrain women's ability to participate in sport today.) Women who walked and ran in roles such as couriers and postal workers described how their outdoor activities were shaped by being vulnerable to assaults and abuse from men. In 1848, Mrs Dovey – whom a journalist calculated walked around ninety-six miles a week, and clocked up nearly 80,000 miles in her working life – was robbed while carrying parcels in Gloucestershire.[47]

Women who engaged in very early professional or competitive sporting events to earn an income also had different experiences of the outdoors from their male counterparts. Organised running had a history of coercion and humiliation, especially for women. In medieval Italy, prostitutes were made to race, sometimes alongside donkeys, as part of a series of 'insult races' to entertain soldiers and officials. This persisted into seventeenth-century Italy, Germany and Switzerland, where prostitutes were pelted with water, rotten fruit and stones by spectators as they ran in forced events. In eighteenth-century Britain, 'foot races' were a staple of fairs and fêtes in rural villages and country and city taverns, and were popular at agricultural fairs, wakes and landowners' coming-of-age feasts. Female foot races were known as 'smock-races', because the women and girls competed for payment in the form of smocks (a type of undergarment) or similar. Participation was largely voluntary, although often driven by poverty. However, the women's races were not taken as seriously as the men's and the competitors were ridiculed and sexualised. Organisers frequently stipulated that female runners had to be young, virgins and 'handsome in person', and that they run barefoot in 'petticoats', 'drawers only' or sometimes 'stark naked'.[48]

In nineteenth-century Britain and America, these events evolved into timed foot races known as 'female pedestrian' competitions, in which women speed-walked extraordinarily long distances on measured pieces of track – often in pub gardens in the early days – for money from bets or prizes. (On 8 April 1878, Ada Anderson became the 'Lady Champion Walker of the World' for covering over 1,500 miles in 1,000 consecutive hours – just under forty-two days – taking no more than around ninety minutes' rest at any one time.) Women's participation in these events was often coerced, by their families or their own financial desperation, and many *pedestriennes* were threatened with violence and other forms of abuse from male spectators. To mention but a few examples: in September and October 1864, Emma Sharp walked 1,000 miles in 1,000 hours at Quarry Gap, outside Bradford, and had to carry pistols to prevent male onlookers chloroforming her to throw the event. In 1874, in Staffordshire, a young girl called Rebecca Richards was attempting to walk 1,000 miles in 1,000 hours when she was sexually assaulted by a farmer. And in 1881, fifteen-year-old pedestrian Lucy Richards was assaulted by the landlord of the pub in whose grounds she was walking.[49]

These women were all impressive athletes, but the structures in which they ran were – at least partially – designed to humiliate them before men, and the pecuniary basis for their sport meant that many middle-class and elite men, including the members of the Alpine Club, did not consider them kindred spirits.

Women whose lives were shaped by additional intersecting axes of oppression – including race and ethnicity, as well as class and sex – fell even further outside the elite white male mould of outdoor leisure, and their stories have therefore suffered even greater marginalisation.

In the 1850s in North Carolina, American abolitionist, suffragist and former slave Harriet Tubman led – on foot, in carriages, by sea and by rail – around seventy enslaved men, women and children to freedom through a route known as the 'underground railroad', which traversed swamps, woods, hills and rivers. It is only very recently that Tubman's sophisticated knowledge of the outdoors has been recognised, and that she has been hailed as an 'unsung naturalist'.[50]

Sarah Mapps Douglass was born into one of the earliest elite free Black families in Philadelphia, and she rambled to collect rocks and minerals for a geological cabinet that she used in the 1830s to teach girls and young women about the natural sciences, and to gather botanical specimens for drawings. Douglass's walking, and its outcomes in the education of young Black women, showed how the natural world could be a source of authority for otherwise disenfranchised women. (Similarly, abolitionist and former slave Sojourner Truth found power in nature in the 1840s when she travelled long distances on foot as an itinerant preacher in camp meetings. On one occasion, a 'party of wild young men' abused her as she spoke – but she resisted the intimidation by climbing 'to the top of a small rise of ground' where she 'commenced to sing', and the group of men left.) But although natural landscapes had the potential to be sources of social, intellectual and physical power, Douglass was a Black woman pitted against the white masculine character of the scientific world, and her audience was limited to private (and semi-private) spaces – such as informal schooling in the church, garden and parlour – and she is almost unknown today.[51]

In their writings, women often devised a language and style that represented the natural world and outdoor leisure in very different ways to the tropes of white, elite men's literature. In her nature poetry collection *Forest Leaves*, dating from the late 1840s, Frances Ellen Watkins Harper – a little-known Black American abolitionist, suffragist, teacher and writer – specifically warned against the well-worn trope of romanticising the natural world because, she pointed out, it was also the location for slavery. None of Harper's personal papers (beyond a few letters and speeches) have been preserved, and *Forest Leaves* was considered 'lost' for 150 years.[52] But rediscovering depictions of the outdoors in lost voices like Harper's is particularly crucial in the present moment, when climate crisis requires us to make plans for the future of natural environments. In doing so, we need to take into account the full range of meanings and experiences that different demographic groups find in the outdoors, in order to ensure that our projects meet the needs of land users beyond white men.

The factors that led to the fading of women such as Sarah Mapps Douglass, Frances Watkins Harper, Mary Collier and Maria Paradis from mainstream narratives are comparable to the more rigid gate-keeping of outdoor leisure and its history that took place in the later nineteenth century. Women's achievements were recorded less frequently and publicised less widely than men's, in part because they lacked the same forums for circulation: male-dominated clubs, societies and institutions, with their dedicated journals and publications. The works of BAME and working-class women, whose social status differed from archetypal male mountaineers in more ways than sex, have suffered an extra level of historical amnesia.

It is therefore important not to be fooled by how the *his*tory of outdoor sport has been hitherto presented. Despite persisting claims that 'few' women walked, ran, hiked or climbed, a wealth of evidence attests that the hills were alive with the sound of women. It is worth paying attention to the voices of these women, because they show the pleasures and pitfalls, the meanings and values, of the natural world and the capabilities of the human body, in far greater and more astonishing variety than we are used to hearing.

I spend months immersed, poring over women's memoirs and travelogues (many of them privately published or in manuscript); diary entries and letters; stacks of railway timetables and guidebooks; brochures for hotels and sanatoria; novels and newspaper reports about holidaymakers in nineteenth-century Switzerland; old volumes of the *Alpine Journal* and histories of tourism, rambling, outdoor clubs and nature-writing. They all show me that Lizzie Le Blond was no outlier in the hills. By the 1880s, tourism, sports and leisure industries were consciously making efforts to accommodate the specific needs of women. The fact that women were – even superficially – welcomed into European mountaineering societies shows that there was a certain acceptance among men of their female companions. In the final decades of the nineteenth century, women in their numbers were flocking to 'the rooftops of the world' – wild open spaces, peaks, mountains and moors – where they found a nourishing way of life to repair the harms of the lives they'd left behind.

Frederica Plunket was optimistic that 'the mountains have room for all'.[53] But as the years passed and the numbers of women outdoors continued to swell, the more uncomfortable men would become. Mountains and mountaineering would form particularly heated battlegrounds in women's fights for greater freedom outdoors, partly because of their recent history as places where men fortified, and experimented with, their masculinity. Although many members of the mass-market outdoor tourist industry were enthusiastic and encouraging towards female consumers in the 1880s, that world's increasingly organised, codified character – its clubs, societies, results, records, journals and competitions – would give other men a way of keeping out certain people who did not share their own (white, male, middle-class or elite) social status. As women's rights outdoors made progress, a concerted physical and cultural backlash was starting to form.

Historians often have an impulse to assign neat and definitive personalities to particular phases: 'the age of revolution', 'the age of wonder', and so on. But this oversimplifies what occurs on the ground, and how it feels to those who live through periods of complex and sometimes opposing political dynamics. In periods of social change, processes of progress, backlash and regression are often at play at the same time. Just as a split-second snapshot of a runner cannot ascertain her overall direction or speed, at any single point in history it is impossible to say whether that moment is moving towards progress or backlash. We are always living on the pivotal points of potential fulcra. In the 1880s, female mountaineers were largely buoyant and optimistic about their freedoms outdoors, and were forging ahead despite the swirls, eddies and undercurrents trying to hold them back. If those women identified evidence of pushback, they may well have assumed that it would soon die out.

Over time, however, the pull of the undertow would become stronger and harder for women to swim against.

4.

Why can't you just run faster?

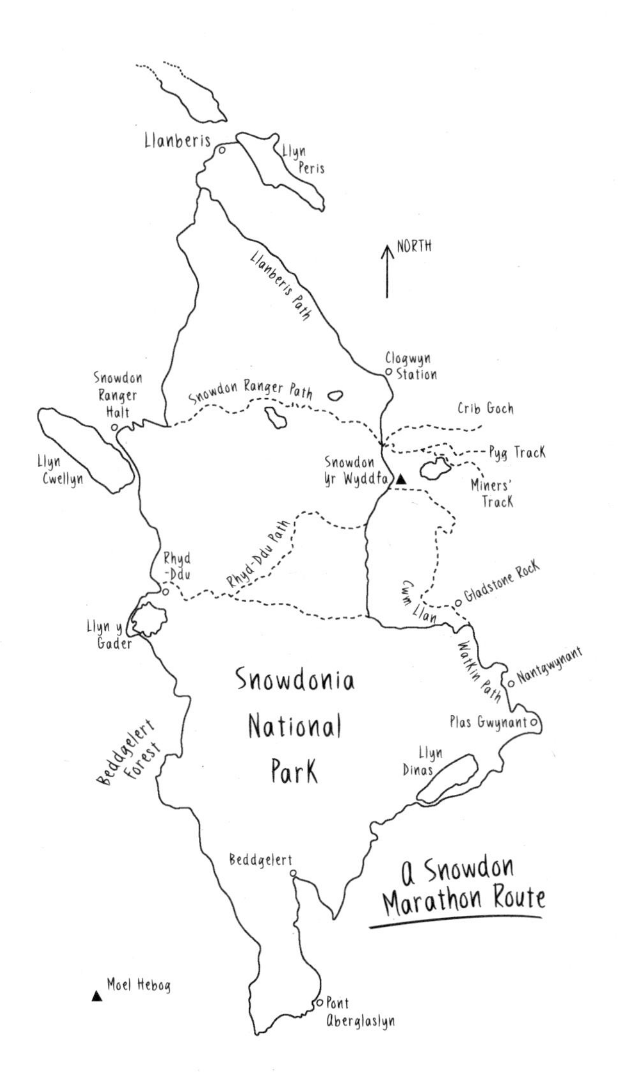

My stepfather's funeral takes place towards the end of August. A fortnight later I pack a wheeled suitcase so heavy with books that I can barely lift it into the taxi, and head for the station. I take the train to a village in north Wales, where I have been granted a writing residency. It was meant to begin two weeks earlier, but in the days after Willy's death I wrote to the director of research, Louisa – an email that was half-formal, half-deranged ('I've lost five family members in the space of five months . . .') – asking for the date to be put back.

I'm looking forward to pursuing more research into Lizzie during the residency and I'm excited about doing some running too. I hope to get to the mountains of Snowdonia, which will be a good training ground for the West Highland Way race, which I'm still aiming towards in June next year.

On the train, I've reserved a seat in the quiet carriage and, as it pulls out of the station, I fold down the micro-table on the back of the seat in front and get out my laptop. A man – plump, besuited, in his mid twenties – walks along the aisle and leans against the chair next to mine, talking rapidly and noisily into a microphone attached to his mobile, which he presses against his mouth. I look up at him and say, 'I'm sorry, but this is the quiet coach. Please could you talk somewhere else?'

He juts his chin away from the cable and whispers loudly to me, while the person on the other end continues speaking: 'I really need somewhere quiet to take this phone call and it's too noisy out in the foyer.' Then he returns to his conversation at full volume.

He's come to the quiet carriage to talk because it's so quiet.

I crossly ram small, pink plugs into my ear. I started wearing them at night a year or so ago, to muffle Pete's snoring, but in the last month I have worn them for much of the daytime too; at first, while trying to work, and then while walking around the house, to mask Pete's podcasts, my children's singing, their sneezes, laughter, all the sounds of life.

My train journeys have been regularly punctuated by conflicts in 'quiet coaches'. On a train to Oxford once, I requested that a group of four men take their conversation to a different carriage (their reply was: 'Oh no, that rule only applies to those electronic thingies. *We're* talking about Seneca'). On other quiet carriage journeys, I have asked: a group of drunk men to stop swearing in front of my children; a man doing a presentation to an online meeting of over a hundred or so people to take it somewhere else; and a young man watching porn on his iPad to turn the sound off.

I received the following responses:

'Fucking bitch.'

'Yes, *madam*' [petulant].

'Why don't *you* go somewhere else?'

At other times, I have been met with silence and blank stares, followed by a purgative shake of the head and a return to their conversation. As I remember them, all these encounters feature men. I don't know if that is because male passengers are more likely to transgress the quiet zone rules, or maybe it is because I find it scary to approach men in this way and therefore remember the confrontations. When I have to ask them to be quiet, I put on my reading glasses first, like some sort of chainmail visor.

Today it is too noisy to concentrate on writing, so I pass the time by using the train's Wi-Fi to find out if there are gendered differences in those who perpetrate, and those who are affected by, 'noise annoyance'. I click on a study whose authors estimate that highly noise-sensitive individuals comprise around 12 per cent of the population. These people are more likely to grow annoyed because of noise; to be woken up by noise; to respond to noise with negative emotions of greater strength; to have problems habituating to regular noise; to report general feelings of inadequacy, depression and anxiety; and to suffer from diagnosed psychological disorders. Highly noise-sensitive people are also more likely to be female.[1]

When men's and women's exposure to unwanted noise is equal, it is women who more frequently report health complaints (including muscle pains, stomach and intestinal problems and nervous symptoms), sleeping problems, higher anxiety, and an elevated use of prescription drugs. Noise places the body under stress and, if the person is already stressed from other causes, then the physiological and emotional impact is much greater. The way that many women describe 'noise annoyance' is as an intrusion into personal space. It feels physical, like claustrophobia, and a breach of consent. One woman, who spoke to communications experts Steve Love and Joanne Kewley in 2005, explained how she felt 'coerced into eavesdropping' by other people's mobile phone conversations.[2]

I recognise all this: as grief chugs away in the background, unexpected noise is a call on my attention that can push me from 'just coping' back to shutdown; back to being a spinning beachball.

Women are not less frequent users of mobile phones than men, but women appear to be 'more attentive to the potentially disruptive impact of cell phone use on the social environment' and are 'more irritated by social etiquette violations'. This is probably partly because women are more invested in using phones to maintain family relationships and because women tend to be more observant of written and unwritten rules of behaviour. A 2012 study found that 'females complained . . . significantly more [than men] about reachability' via mobile phones and, in numerous surveys, more women than men think that making and receiving mobile phone calls in public is harmful. A study of university students' attitudes across Sweden, the USA, Italy, Japan and Korea found that significantly more men than women considered it acceptable to speak on mobile phones when eating dinner with their family, when sitting with friends in cafés and when paying at cash registers. Men also felt that mobile phone use was 'more appropriate' during intimacy than women.[3]

Perhaps unsurprisingly, then, considering that we are more affronted by mobile phone use, women deploy a wider range of strategies to protect ourselves from unwelcome noise: working from home, erecting screens around desks in open-plan offices, wearing noise-cancelling headphones and earplugs . . . and approaching perpetrators to ask them to quieten. But these strategies often cause further anxiety on top of the stress stemming from noise: the risk of clashes with male strangers or colleagues, and the breach of expectations that women should be 'reachable' and acquiescent.[4]

The desire that many female interviewees express is simply 'to be left alone' in public, in silence. That is all I want too.

Over a century ago, in 1890, US lawyers Samuel D. Warren and Louis Brandeis wrote an essay for the *Harvard Law Review* on 'The Right to Privacy', in which they argued that the 'general right of the individual to be let alone' is 'a part of the more general right to the immunity of the person – the right to one's personality' and intrinsic to 'the right to enjoy life'.[5] In Britain and America, civil (tort) laws of nuisance protect individuals from 'offensive noises' as part of their defence of this 'right to ordinary enjoyment' of space.

This all makes me think back to Nelly Weeton, trying to climb Snowdon unmolested and in peace. It occurs to me that women's 'right to be left alone' in public is much more fragile than men's. This fragility affects *everything* that women do outdoors: sport and leisure, yes; but also work, education, shopping and – as I am currently experiencing – travelling. Early outdoor leisure enthusiasts had fantasised that their hobbies might provide respite from modern life, but the separation between work and play, mundanity and holiday, could never be definitive and impermeable. There are crucial spillages between the worlds, and sexism is one of them: men's intimidation and belittling of women occurs on the streets of daily urban life *and* in sporting clubs and group hikes. Women's 'right to be left alone' and 'right to enjoy life' is endangered everywhere.

I have definitely become more sensitive to noise since Willy died, but now I question whether my heightened awareness is a disorder, purely symptomatic of personal trauma and loss, or whether I am responding to some spike in hostility to women outdoors today.

I start to think about Lizzie Le Blond and her contemporaries and wonder how their era of competing currents – one driving towards greater acceptance of women outdoors, and the other pulling in the opposite direction – compares to ours today. I wonder if the same tension between progress and reaction is visible in the present moment too. On the one hand, I have started noticing more episodes of intimidation – catcalls, abuse, naked anger – visited by men upon women in public spaces. But in the realm of outdoor sports, women seem to be riding high on a tide of support. The trail-running magazine I have in my bag celebrates 'a line of incredible performances and high-profile outright wins by female endurance athletes in recent years'.[6] So what is going on? Unprecedented improvement and/or a mounting backlash? And how does this relate to women's rights and freedoms elsewhere, in public spaces. Are they expanding or contracting?

The train pulls into a small station, and I drag my suitcase up the road to the library, where a kind man carries it up two flights of stairs and shows me to an attic room with a small desk overlooking a graveyard. On the desk, there are leaflets explaining the building's history, the writing residency programme, opening hours for the reading room and canteen and three home-printed pages outlining local walking routes. I unpack, piling books and folders onto the desk, and I arrange my running kit in the tall, narrow wardrobe. The library is currently hosting a book festival – and there are people and their noise everywhere, in the corridors, garden, canteen and common room, in temporary tents outside the front and back entrances and in the car park beside the cemetery.

I spread out an Ordnance Survey map over the double bed and trace onto it one of the walking routes suggested by the pamphlets on my desk: a 7km circular course through a wood that is privately owned but, the author assures me, is open to library residents bearing permits. I put on shorts and a T-shirt, stuff the map into my running pack, queue to exit the building and, once onto the gravel drive, I break into a jog. The route leads me down a hill to a car park, where a footpath leads onto my favourite sort of track: soft, peaty earth through a cool, shaded forest. There are breaks in the trees with views out over to nearby hills and enough undulation to make my heart work hard on the inclines and then flood my system with the joy of release on the descents.

On my return to the library, I shower and go downstairs for dinner. It is 7.40 p.m. and I am sure that one of the leaflets said that the canteen serves dinner until 7.45 p.m., but a metal screen has been pulled down and the dining room is full of people chatting, eating the tail end of sponge puddings and custard, and trifles in glasses.

Louisa sees me standing in the doorway, rises from her chair and walks over. 'Oh no, have you missed dinner?' she asks. 'Wait, I'll go and see if they can put something together for you,' and she disappears through a doorway beside the metal screen, popping her head out to ask: 'Do you eat chicken?'

I nod, and she emerges a few minutes later with a plate on which a piece of meat, tomato sauce, couscous, salad and vegetables are arranged in neat quadrants. She puts it into my hands and says, 'Come and sit with us. I'll introduce you to the others.'

At the table, I meet a famous novelist, a less-famous novelist, and a nature-writer whose book I have coincidentally just finished reading. They are talking animatedly about a mutual friend's childhood memoir that is about to be published and the less-famous novelist turns to me: 'Where are you from, Rachel?'

It's one of my least favourite questions, and I find it strange how much it comes up in conversation. I start to answer – 'Well, it's hard to say. I moved around a lot as a kid' – but, in doing so, I realise how long it has been since I have had a sustained conversation with anybody other than my husband. My voice squeaks, as if my mouth is pursed against the lip of a balloon. I start explaining that, because of my parents' jobs and divorces and remarriages, I was born in the Midlands; lived in Paris for a year or so; went back to the Midlands, but a different part; moved to York; then to Cambridge; then Oxford, London, Wales, Cambridge again, London again and now back to York.

The nature-writer and famous novelist have started talking about something else. Although the less-famous novelist has his head turned towards me, he is listening to them. 'I've lost my thread,' he says. 'Sorry, Rachel, what were you saying?'

For as long as I can remember, I have found conversation difficult. I miss an organic sense of rhythm that others seem to possess. When I was younger, I could not control the tempo of my own speech. One morning, aged six or seven, I started telling my teacher about a book I was reading and, not knowing when to pause for breath, I simply didn't, but ploughed on, faster and faster, cramming more and more words into the rising pitch of my failing voice until I became dizzy and fainted.

I still cannot manage the mechanics of a genuine multiway conversation, and don't know when to interject. I often feel like my young daughters, who stand at my knee intoning 'Mum mum mum mum mum mumumumumumum', while Pete and I talk above them. I think that perhaps it is one effect of the split consciousness that the philosopher Iris Marion Young described, in which women perceive themselves as subject and object at the same time. A portion of my attention is always listening out for how I sound as I speak, and it becomes as distracting as talking on a malfunctioning phone line, when you can hear your own voice repeated back to you with a split-second delay. Just as Young described women's difficulties in realising our desires through our bodies, I also find it hard to use spoken language to convey what I want to say. My voice can feel like an impediment, rather than an instrument.

I had expected the residency to offer quiet and solitude; I had not expected it to be so *sociable*. I walk through clusters of people queuing for authors' talks; chatting over scones and jam in the garden; planning lunchtime visits to the nearby organic farm shop; coming and going from yoga classes. One morning I sign my name on the reading room's register with a scratchy biro that is running out of ink. When I come to sign out in the evening, I cannot find my earlier signature and, after minutes of searching, I realise another reader has unwittingly written their name over the top of mine. It reminds me of a story told by Rennie Sparks, one half of a band called the Handsome Family, at a gig that Pete and I attended a few years ago. She introduced a song by describing how she had been sitting in a departure lounge, waiting for a flight, when 'a middle-aged businessman,

McDonald's bag in one hand, rolling-bag handle in the other – walked up to [her] and, without pause, turned and sat down on her lap'.[7] He had thought she was an empty chair.

I, too, feel hollow and invisible. Like a ghost.

Towards the end of the book festival, I give a talk and, as soon as it is over, I decide to escape for the rest of the weekend.

After some googling, I find a trail race that is being held further into Wales, in the Snowdonia National Park, a few hours away by public transport. There are varying lengths: a 'short' run of around eleven miles, a 'middle' of fourteen miles, a 'long' of twenty-seven miles (basically a marathon) and an 'ultra' of forty miles. I am tempted by the ultra and it would be good training for the West Highland Way in nine months' time, but the route entails ascending Snowdon (in Welsh, Yr Wyddfa) twice, and it allows only eleven hours. I have run forty miles well within that time before, but trail races often underestimate distance and two ascents of Wales's highest mountain is a serious challenge: in my current slow, sad state, I am not sure I will make the cut-offs. So I enrol for the shorter, marathon event; reserve a room for two nights in an Airbnb; book a train ticket to Bangor and find a bus that will take me to Llanberis, at Snowdon's base. When I arrive, the owners of the Airbnb explain that the kitchen is out of bounds, but I can keep a bottle of milk and a small orange juice in their fridge, if I wish.

The following morning at nine, the race starts with a foghorn in Parc Padarn on the outskirts of Llanberis. Runners immediately start to climb up the Llanberis Path, the longest and most gradual and therefore busiest route to Snowdon's summit. The weather is extraordinary for early autumn – 25 degrees; skies denuded of cloud – and the wide, clearly demarcated path is packed with hikers, families with small children and charity walkers. Up we all go, up and up, over 900 metres up (measured vertically), from the start. The mountain railway occasionally overtakes. I march forward, trekking poles in front. *Tap plod tap plod*. It takes ninety-seven minutes to travel the five-ish miles from the start to the top, and, although a race marshal directs me onto a path skirting beneath the official summit, I duck up to the cairn and trig point at the top and take a happy, salty selfie. Sometimes the pleasures of running are just very simple and, right now, I feel great: no longer ghostly but full in body. 'God, I love running,' I think. 'I'm so lucky to be able to do this.'

I'm far from the only woman to be so in love with running and, in many ways, I know that women everywhere are benefitting from exercising in an era of unprecedented support for female sport. Some surveys show that, for the first time in history, there are more female recreational runners in the world than men: in the USA and Iceland, women comprise 58 per cent and 59 per cent of all runners. This is part of a mind-blowing global increase in numbers of sportswomen since the 1970s: compared to just 14.6 per cent in 1972, 48.7 per cent of participants at the most recent summer Olympics were female. And the lines on the graphs are still rising: numbers of female marathon runners seem to be swelling faster than their male counterparts, especially among women over the age of fifty, who are also healthily represented at ultra-marathons.[8] Likewise, the amount of time and money that women are spending on running is going up, and other aspects of outdoor sport are also becoming more equitable. Although men are still the majority among older generations of hikers, women take a marginal lead in younger cohorts and, because of this lead, in 2015 women accounted for 42 per cent of all recreational walkers in the USA. The same trends are visible in climbing. Women's membership of the British Mountaineering Council rose from 16 per cent in 2002 to almost 27 per cent in 2014 and is continuing to accelerate.[9] In lots of ways, the contemporary picture of women's outdoor sport is incredibly rosy.

Escalating numbers of girls and women playing sport means that, today, some truly remarkable, record-breaking female athletes have emerged. In my own world of ultra running, there are prime examples. Between 2005 and 2013, British trail-runner Lizzy Hawker won the *c.* 106-mile Ultra Trail du Mont Blanc (UTMB) five times, as well as the 100km world championships in 2006, and in 2011 she set the women's world record for the longest distance covered in twenty-four hours (153.5 miles). In 2021, US ultra-runner Courtney Dauwalter beat Hawker's UTMB performances to set a new female course record of 22 hours 30 mins 54 secs. Sharon Gayter, Mimi Anderson and Carla Molinaro have all broken and set new fastest female times to run the 830-mile vertical span of Britain, from John O'Groats in Scotland to Land's End in Cornwall, and the current women's record of 12 days, 30 mins 40 secs is Molinaro's. In April 2022, British runner Kate Jayden established a new female world record for completing the most marathons in consecutive days (106 marathons in 106 days, including 60 with a fractured knee). On 19 February 2022, at the Jackpot US championships in Nevada, American ultra-runner Camille Herron broke her own previous world record for running a hundred miles, whittling it down to 12 hours 41 mins 11 secs (maintaining a pace of around 7.37 minutes per mile, which, on a very good day, I can keep up for around two miles).[10]

Herron won that particular race overall, besting the fastest male participant, and this has become a recent theme in women's ultra running: women often outdo the men. Lizzie Hawker still holds the fastest time (63 hours 8 mins) out of men or women for running 199 miles between Everest Base Camp and Kathmandu, which she achieved in 2013. In 2016, Nicky Spinks set the record for running a *double* circuit of the famous fell-running challenge, the Bob Graham Round – a course of sixty-six miles over forty-two fells in the Lake District, which Spinks ran twice, in 45 hours 30 minutes – breaking the previous best time set by a male runner in 1979. In 2019, Jasmin Paris became the first woman to win outright at the notorious 268-mile Spine Race, smashing previous female and male course records over the length of the Pennine Way – and while expressing breast-milk at checkpoints.[11]

In press interviews after her Spine triumph, Paris was asked whether endurance sports epitomise an apparent trend throughout the twentieth century: the shrinking of the gap between male and female performance times. Do endurance sports draw on particular female physiological aptitudes and can women therefore expect to consistently prevail over men? Some sports scientists argue that women's endurance victories are partly down to the fact that female bodies have higher percentages of body fat, so women have greater reserves to fuel them for longer. Others point out that, while men have more 'fast twitch' muscle fibres that power explosive activities like sprinting, women benefit from 'slow twitch' fibres, which are weaker but may be more resistant to fatigue, and that men generate more body heat during exercise and are sometimes prone to overheating, whereas women stay cooler.[12]

Researchers speculate whether women's apparent endurance advantage is sociological as well as physiological. Paris herself reflected on whether recent wakeful nights with her baby had prepared her for running the Spine in 83 hours 12 mins 23 seconds on next-to-no sleep. A number of sports scientists have suggested that women might have higher pain thresholds than men, perhaps because of experiences of menstruation, pregnancy and childbirth. It has also been observed that women tend to be more cautious in race strategy and pacing, which is useful in endurance events that prioritise self-knowledge, self-care and the eking out of resources. Researchers note that female runners typically begin races at more sustainable speeds than men and finish stronger, whereas men have a tendency to begin too fast and later reluctantly slow down and even burn out. Runner, race company director and writer Keri Wallace spoke to me about how, anecdotally, she thinks that male ultra-runners often seem readier than women to adopt 'risky' strategies – entering races that are far outside their 'comfort zones' and trying to 'wing' challenges for which they haven't adequately trained; whereas women tend to be more 'conservative', and likely to select feasible events and train appropriately. This pattern seems to be confirmed in runner Mitch LeBlanc's analysis of the Leadville Trail 100 Race in 2011, in which the most likely group to finish were women aged 40 to 49 (59 per cent finishing rate), while the least likely were men aged 20 to 29 (32 per cent finished).[13]

The extraordinary rise of women's formal participation in sport since the 1970s has not just been fuelled by individual aptitudes but by societal changes, and some of the chief drivers are legislative protections such as 'Title IX', which was passed in 1972 in the United States. Title IX and a similar British act of 1975 both prohibited public discrimination on the grounds of sex, and Title IX specifically reshaped schools and education programmes to ensure greater equality in provision of athletics facilities, coaching and scholarship opportunities. An assessment of Title IX's impact discovered that female participation in college sports rose by 450 per cent between 1977 and 2006, and that, at high school level, the number of girls taking part became nine times greater over the same period. Sports sociologist Cheryl Cooky calculates that, today, one in three school-age girls play sport, compared to just one in twenty-seven in the 1970s, and she partly attributes this to the rise in scholarships for female sport.[14]

There are further institutional efforts to improve the visibility and respect granted to female athletes. Media representation of female sport has traditionally been very poor: only around 3–4 per cent of all sports coverage is dedicated to women, dropping to 2 per cent on television. But in March 2019, in the UK, the *Telegraph* newspaper launched its *Women's Sport* supplement, 'with a commitment to deliver unprecedented coverage of women's sport, across all platforms'. In 2020, 47 per cent of the BBC's coverage of the Tokyo Olympic Games featured female athletes, and in the following year, the BBC showed more women's singles matches than men's in its footage from Wimbledon. There is a similar drive in the USA: in 2021, Olympic athletes Alex Morgan, Chloe Kim, Simone Manuel and Sue Bird set up sports media platform Togethxr to address the gender imbalance. If these trends continue, then broadcasters predict that large sporting events will bring in unprecedented numbers of female viewers across traditional media and YouTube channels and Instagram, and industry specialists predict that the 'value of women's sport could treble by 2030'.[15]

As both cause and consequence of increasing numbers of female runners, race directors are getting better at accommodating women in organised events. In 2018, runner and researcher Lizzie Rosewell conducted a survey to query 'why don't more women take part in ultra running?' and she discovered that women report being deterred by constraints including lack of free time to train, low self-confidence, feeling intimidated, insufficient childcare, poor navigational skills, feeling unsafe, anxiety about injury, and lack of disposable income.[16]

The running industry is tackling some of these obstacles head-on. Race director and marketer Bev Logan agrees that 'for many women, entering a race can be really intimidating', and many female would-be participants describe being put off by branding images solely featuring athletic men. So Logan set up a female sportswear company (Badass Mother Runners), a running group for mothers and a women-only race – the Badass Epic 10K – to 'create an event that's more empowering, where all abilities, ages and body shapes are welcome'. As Logan suggests, studies of female outdoor pursuits have found that many women value female-only events because they instil greater confidence and opportunities for leadership and feel less competitive, and safer and friendlier, than mixed-sex activities. Race directors are encouraging female participants in further ways: the Loon Mountain Race in New Hampshire boosted the proportion of women entrants to 54 per cent by offering discounts for first-time female competitors, ensuring equal representation of women in marketing imagery, offering equal prizes for the fastest men and women and giving female finishers race T-shirts designed for women's bodies – a vanishing rarity, in my experience. Some races went one better than equal prizes: the Antelope Island 50K, Barr Trail Mountain Race, Legendary Races' Cloud City Multi-Stage race and the Ouray 100-Mile Endurance Race all offer women *larger* prizes than men, to compensate for the gender pay gap.[17]

Event directors are also increasingly attending to women's physiological and social needs. A few race companies – including Punk Panther and Hardmoors in the UK and Rainshadow Running in the US – provide free period and incontinence products at toilets en route, and the provision of on-site childcare was a priority for the organisers of the inaugural Salomon WMN women-only trail half-marathon in Lake Sonoma, California, and Trivium Racing in North Carolina.[18] Big Bear Events, in the British Midlands, is coordinating a race to fit in with the hours of a nearby holiday childcare scheme.

Over recent years, a major bone of contention for female runners

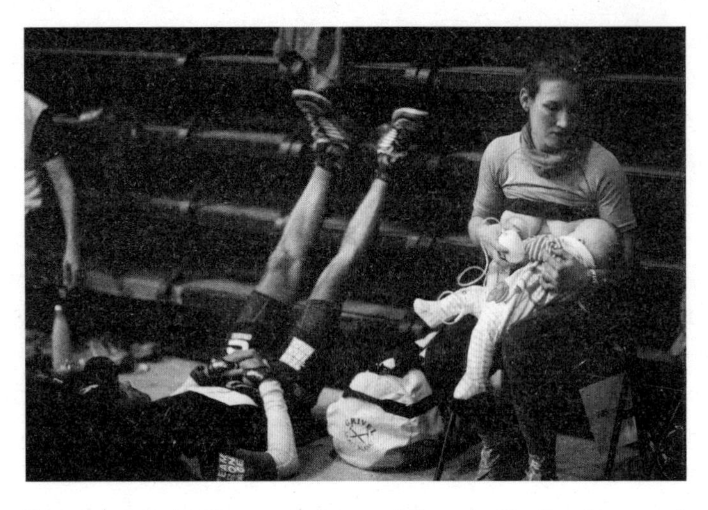

Ultra-runner Sophie Power, simultaneously breastfeeding her three-month-old baby and expressing milk at a checkpoint during 2018's Ultra Trail du Mont Blanc, a c. *106-mile mountain race*

has been organisers' attitudes to 'pregnancy deferrals', but these are finally improving and the Ultra Trail du Mont Blanc is the most famous example. The UTMB is oversubscribed each year, and runners earn places by amassing points or 'stones' at numerous qualifying races around the world in the two years prior to the race, and then enter a ballot. Competitors who secure hard-won entry tickets and subsequently cannot take part due to injury are allowed to defer their prized places to the following year – but the same courtesy has not been granted to female competitors who become pregnant or give birth in the weeks or months immediately prior to the race. In 2018, a photograph of British athlete Sophie Power breastfeeding her three-month-old son at a checkpoint at the UTMB, while simultaneously expressing milk into a pump, went viral. Power was hailed as a 'powerful and positive' icon of running motherhood, but she also drew attention to the lack of 'equal opportunity' in the differences between the UTMB's treatment of injured athletes and its attitude towards pregnant or postpartum competitors. She had lost a UTMB place four years earlier, when she was pregnant with her first child, and, as an elite athlete, she didn't want to lose another chance to race and to waste her accumulated qualifying points again. But, as Power admitted, she didn't really 'want to be on that UTMB start line 3 months postpartum', running *c.* 106 miles while having to express milk during the race, ensuring she was taking on enough extra calories for lactation and meeting her husband at checkpoints to breastfeed her baby son – and all on the back of a lighter recent training load, sleep deprivation and a looser pelvis from pregnancy hormones. Power would much rather have run the UTMB the following year, when she was in better condition, but that option wasn't open to her – so after she successfully completed the race in 2018, she campaigned for changes to the rules.[19] That same year, the Western States 100-Mile Endurance Run announced it would permit pregnancy deferrals, and in 2019 the Golden Gate Dirty 30 decided to offer full refunds to pregnant and postpartum women who were unable to race. The UTMB finally changed its policy in 2021.

Trends in kit, clothing and technology are following the same heartening direction, towards greater recognition and accommodation of women's distinct needs. Sales of women's sportswear started rising steadily from the 1960s: in 1972, for instance, female sports apparel sold in roughly equal quantities to dresses, but a decade later women were buying over twice the amount of leggings and running shorts as frocks. By 2013, sales of sportswear linked to women's colleges were seeing three-figure growth. We are currently living through a surge in availability of female running clothing, in which, fashion researcher Sam Dhanapala explains, 'women have become a key opportunity for growth and gaining market share, with not only products but also campaigns and sub-brands created for this market'. Women's sportswear is no longer simply categorised into footwear and clothing but is specialised into type of sport and level of technology and performance.[20]

Contemporary designers increasingly recognise that items previously marketed and sold as 'unisex' or 'gender-neutral' actually need different constructions for male and female users. For example, producers of camping mats and sleeping bags now acknowledge that women's typically shorter height and lower body temperature require smaller mats, and sleeping bags fitted to wider hips and narrower shoulders than men, with more insulation distributed around the core. Makers of 'unisex' hydration packs for running and hiking usually position flasks of water on the chest area, which can be uncomfortable on women's breasts over long periods, so designers are now experimenting with situating soft flasks below the breasts, with extra-long straws to extend up over the breasts towards the mouth. In the past, clothing manufacturers typically created male items first, which then underwent a 'pinking and shrinking' process to produce women's garments. However, designers such as Helen Stuart, apparel product and design manager at British company inov-8, do the opposite – they start with the female form and then adapt it for men. And the same recognition of female physiological needs is taking place in sports technology too: in April 2019, Garmin announced that its tracking app would give users the ability to log menstrual symptoms. Much of this work is underpinned by recent better inclusion of women in sports science research, and the development of training programmes designed around women's hormonal variations – such as New Zealand physiologist Stacy Sims's recommendations for training throughout the menstrual cycle and menopause, and the development of protocols for women returning to exercise after childbirth by British campaign group Pelvic Roar. Sims has a passionate vision of 'a world of healthy women who understand their bodies [and] know how to work with their unique physiology'.[21]

These are happy thoughts to have in mind as I stand at the top of Snowdon.

It seems to me that, if women had been driven out of sport in the early twentieth century, mercifully that exclusion does not seem to have been permanent. And in many ways, women's progress in sport since the 1970s has mirrored improvements elsewhere: over the same period, women's numbers in the workplace, education and political life have all rocketed too. Formal protections of female sport have been joined with defences of women's wider presence in the public sphere, in legislation (such as the US's Pregnancy Discrimination Act of 1978 and the UK's Equality Act 2010), and in campaigns for parity, empowerment and emancipation that seek to confer upon women the status of full and equal citizens.

I wonder if this is how it felt to Lizzie Le Blond's contemporaries: that they were entering a world in which the welcome that women received in sport offered hope for a female-friendly future more generally.

But I also know that that late nineteenth-century world was tainted by an undercurrent of misogynist hostility.

As I start to make my way down from the mountain's summit, it occurs to me that maybe I need to ask whether the same undertow is also detectable today. Are women's experiences in contemporary sport all as uplifting as the tale of Jasmin Paris, besting all male rivals, and the apparent 450 per cent rise of female participation in US college sport? Or are things actually more complicated – as they were in the late nineteenth century? Alongside the inspiring stories of 'badass women smashing it', is there now, too, a backlash simmering among men?

After the summit of Snowdon, the route divides. Runners on the shorter distances head back towards Llanberis, while those on the marathon and ultra routes descend along Snowdon's south ridge. As I start coming down, I keep an eye on the time. I have already taken nearly 1 hour 45 minutes to get this far, and the cut-off to reach the valley settlement of Nantgwynant is 2 hours 30 minutes. According to the race description, it's around five kilometres away, but with a very steep 1,000-metre loss of altitude, almost down to sea level. If I'm going to make it, the timing is going to be tight.

The narrow path weaves along the ridge and then begins to drop more severely and indiscernibly among fangs of rock. I'm not good at these types of descent. I get scared of catching my toes on a slab and tipping forward and I find the necessary concentration exhausting. Nevertheless, I run on, following advice I've read in running magazines; keeping my knees slightly bent and supple, my thighs' quadriceps muscles strong, heels lifted to allow my forefeet to lightly find their way and I constantly scan the route ahead, identifying tiny spaces of grass between the rocks to place rapid, short steps. It is as precarious as sprinting in stilettos down a wet, cobbled path.

On the way down, I overtake a woman and man. She is crying and he is shouting: 'Why can't you just run faster?'

I stop and ask her, 'Are you okay?'

'It's my first trail race,' she sobs. 'I hate it. I feel like I'm going to fall on my face.' She gestures towards the man, who is now standing ten metres below us, hands on hips, foot tapping against a rock, looking out towards the surrounding mountains. 'He's worried we're going to miss the cut-off. And it's my fault. I'm holding him up.'

'Why don't you go on?' I shout down to him. 'We'll walk down together and see you at the checkpoint.' Without a word or wave, he scampers on and is out of sight within a few seconds.

'He grew up in the Pyrenees,' she explains. 'This sort of terrain is nothing to him. But I've only ever done one road marathon. He said this would be good for me. But I hate it. I'm so slow.'

'I'm trying not to worry about the cut-off,' I reply. 'The race director told us that no one had ever been timed out at the first checkpoint in the whole history of this race, and in my experience, marshals tend to be pretty forgiving, as long as you look like you're going to finish the whole distance within the overall deadline. And there are lots of runners behind us. I think we'll be okay.'

About twenty minutes and 700 metres of altitude later, we join a broad path, clearly outlined by flagstones, which snakes gently downhill alongside a wide river for the remaining 300 metres or so of descent. This, according to the map, is the Watkin Path – one of six main routes up and down the mountain – named after the British MP and railway entrepreneur Sir Edward Watkin who, in his youth, campaigned for public parks for urban workers and later decided against building a railway to Snowdon's summit in favour of opening a footpath instead, in 1892. His was the first officially designated 'public footpath' in the world. Snowdon has a rich history of ascents by female climbers, around 200 of whom wrote accounts of their tours between 1700 and 1900, and I will later be pleased to learn that the very first walkers to take Watkin's trail all the way to the mountain's summit were women. Even after their male companions dropped out because of poor weather, Watkin's stepdaughter Emmeline and her friend Mary Drew, the daughter of Prime Minister William Gladstone, successfully completed their ascent. I feel an odd kinship with Emmeline and Mary, as if their ghosts are walking beside me.[22]

Here I leave my companion, after making sure she is happier, and I career down the Watkin Path until I spill out onto a small road that leads down to the checkpoint. It is two kilometres further than the race description had indicated and my watch tells me that I am seventeen minutes past the cut-off. There is a small group of runners, all women, huddled around the checkpoint's tent and none are wearing their race numbers.

As I slow and stop, I shout, 'Are we being timed out?'

The marshal nods. 'I need you to give me your race number and timing chip.'

As I do so, four runners, standing a little to the side of the tent, wave me over. One woman – with muscular legs encased in hot-pink compression socks, and whose accent, somewhere between south-eastern Australian and Geordie, disorients me – says, 'I'm pissed off by this. We're going to run anyway. Do you want to join us?'

The marshal overhears and interrupts. 'You can run, but we can't be responsible for your safety. And you won't be able to take any water or food from the checkpoints.'

We run anyway. Jen, in the hot-pink socks, introduces herself. She is indeed from the northeast of England, has lived in Sydney for a decade and is back in Britain visiting family. It is her twelfth marathon and she has come all the way from Newcastle-upon-Tyne, a drive of around four hours. As we run, we talk about being timed out.

I try to be cool with it. 'I mean, I *am* rubbish with technical descents,' I say. 'I always knew that going up and down Snowdon in two and a half hours was going to be a hard ask. And I guess checkpoints have to have a cut-off at some point.' I don't want to sound like a poor loser.

'Well, I think it's ridiculous,' says Jen. 'Last year, the cut-off at the first checkpoint was three and a half hours. This year they're giving us an hour less. An hour less! To run up and down Snowdon! And even though we've been timed out, we're all going to make it to the finish before the final cut-off. We're not running so slowly that we're unsafe. What's the point in having this macho deadline before the very first checkpoint?'

She is right, of course. And an hour or so later, a different marshal takes pity on us and reinstates us in the race, and we do make it around the route – all twenty-seven miles, all 2,000 metres of vertical ascent – before the event closes. At the finish, we are given medals and bottles of beer.

I take lots of photographs throughout the day. Usually, I'd text them to my stepdad, but instead I post them on Facebook, full of nonchalance and bravado: 'I was a bit out of condition, but it was so lovely to be out all day in the sun and I met some top trail-running women 💪♀⛰❤'

But really, it has been a strange race. It is so stressful to run with the constant awareness of cut-offs close at your heels. And I think back to the group of us who were timed out at the first checkpoint: we were all women. When I look at the race results when they're published later in the week, they mostly confirm it: of the men who started the race, only 6 per cent were timed out at checkpoint 1, whereas 15 per cent of the female starters were taken off the course there (not including those of us who were told to stop but persevered anyway). I remember that, earlier in the year, something similar had happened at the London Marathon – but on a much larger scale. 2019 was the first year that London had introduced a pacer to help runners achieve a time of 7 hours 30 minutes, and it was designed to open the race to slower participants: previously, there had been no pacers for finishing times over six hours. But competitors in the 7.5-hour group, and slightly faster ones too, were horrified when race officials started packing up well before the event was over. Sweeper cars yelled abuse at pacer Elizabeth Ayres and her fellow runners ('If you weren't so fat, you wouldn't be so slow'); crews started spraying hazardous cleaning fluids at the participants' feet (leaving at least one with chemical burns); checkpoints closed, and there was no water left on a scorchingly hot day. When the runners got to the end, the timing mats had been removed and there were none of the finish-line videos, photos, T-shirts or medals that runners cherish – and the thought of which often keeps us going during long, gruelling races. And, because women are, on average, slower than men, this maltreatment was levelled at a group of runners that was nearly two-thirds female.[23]

It strikes me that recent exultations that 'women [are] better ultra-endurance athletes' and are 'outperforming men at the extremes of endurance' are largely tales of a few outlying athletes. Such claims do not change the overall picture in which male and female physiological capabilities are very different, and in which the average woman is slower than the average man. Tables of results and records show that, at all levels, from amateur to elite, and at all distances and on all terrains, from 100 metres to 100 miles and more, male runners are typically faster than female runners of equivalent fitness. Compilations of world-record times display a remarkably consistent pattern: the fastest female runners in the world are generally between 10 and 15 per cent slower than the fastest men. This sex difference is actually one of the slightest in sporting performance: the gap between men and women is 16 per cent in track cycling, 18 per cent in jumping events, over 20 per cent in activities involving the upper body, such as weight-lifting, javelin and tennis serves, and it leaps to around 50 per cent in comparisons of the fastest basketball pitches.[24]

Men's sporting advantage is mostly down to physiological attributes, including their higher aerobic capacity, lower body fat, greater haemoglobin and muscle mass, larger heart and lungs and a larger proportion of fast-twitch muscles than women. Women may have certain aptitudes that come to the fore in endurance sport, but the salience of those characteristics is more debatable than I had first realised. For example, women's higher ratio of body fat, which some commentators hold responsible for extraordinary female performances in ultra-marathons, would only really be useful in long-distance races in which competitors are not allowed to eat – and, to my knowledge, such races don't exist. When individual female athletes triumph outright, including over men, it may be simply because there were no equivalently talented male runners on those specific start lines, rather than because the performance gap between men and women is closing in general. (Trail- and ultra-marathons tend to be rather niche affairs, with wildly varying casts of competitors, many drawn from local regions, unlike events such as the World Athletics Championships at which the highest level of runners in the world consistently race against one another.) The truth remains that, despite extraordinary performances by individual women, female runners are still significantly slower than men overall.

Because of this, women require specific accommodations in organised sport to protect our presence and visibility – such as a separate female category in which to compete. Without a female class in sport, women would fall so far down the results' lists that we would be almost invisible: as of 2019, around 10,000 men have sprinted the 100 metres faster than the current Olympic female champion. So, from the birth of organised sport in the late nineteenth century, men and women competitors have been routinely sex-segregated. But there are persisting ways in which female physiology is still not being adequately accommodated in events. Cut-offs are not usually differentiated by sex, and so, as I find on Snowdon, women need to work between 10 per cent and 25 per cent harder than men of equivalent fitness to beat such deadlines. As a consequence, women are more likely to be timed out in the middle of races, and to be deterred from even signing up for events that boast 'brutal' cut-offs: the eighty-two-mile 'Oner' ultra-marathon along Britain's Jurassic coastline only allows twenty-four hours to cover the distance (thirty-six hours would be closer to the norm for a race with this distance and ascent), and in 2017 women numbered only 4.5 per cent of participants.[25] Although the formal organisation of running has become more women-friendly in recent years, there is clearly still work to be done to encourage our participation.

*

I want to better understand the nature of the contemporary world of outdoor leisure. I want to more clearly ascertain whether sport and leisure offer a paradise of equality and hope for women, or whether they are still bogged down by sexism, deliberate or unintentional. When I get back to the library residency from Snowdonia, I spend the remainder of my time identifying and reading research papers and statistical tables. I realise that most existing studies focus on single aspects of women's inclusion in outdoor sport, but I want to read a fuller survey, a more holistic picture of the constraints that women face in outdoor sport and leisure throughout our lifetimes, and the ways we negotiate those interacting barriers. With scholars Kerri Andrews and Joanna Taylor, I draft an application to fund a research network that will bring together people working in different roles across the outdoor leisure industry – academics, conservation charities, athletes, women's trail-running companies, clothing designers, writers and artists, physiologists and sports scientists – with whom we can piece together this picture. The application is successful and the 'Women in the Hills' (WITH) network is born. Over the next few years, we will work with the sports sociologist Kerry Griffiths to produce that holistic report on the contemporary state of 'women's participation in outdoor sport and physical activity in rural areas'.

Kerry Griffith's work confirms my sense that the picture of increasing female participation in sport is not as entirely rosy as it may seem. In running, numbers of female road-runners have indeed exploded, but women are still a definite minority in other fields, such as off-road running: in 2018, only 23 per cent of competitors in trail races were female. Women are not, of course, a homogenous group, and some demographics take part far more than others: female city-dwellers report more opportunities for organised sport than rural women, and teenage girls from higher socio-economic groups receive significantly more assistance (such as lifts to matches, supply of clothing and equipment, and emotional support) than girls from lower socio-economic groups.[26]

Just as women in general are not homogenous, nor are sportspeople. The Outdoor Industries Association divides them into eight 'types': explorers; challengers; enthusiasts for fitness in nature; tribe members; adventurers; learners; freestylers; and thrill-seekers. Out of all of these categories, women only predominate in *one*: 'explorers' – people who spend time relaxing in natural scenery with friends and family, and prefer lower energy, 'softer' activities (such as camping and walking) to 'harder', riskier pursuits. All the other groups are male-dominated. 'Thrill-seekers' (who mountaineer, mountain-bike, ski and snowboard, canoe and kayak, sail, surf and base jump) comprise 80 per cent men.[27] As a rule, the longer the endurance activity, the smaller the proportion of female participants and, across the board, higher status roles – such as mountain leaders, instructors and coaches – tend to be occupied by men, even in women's teams and groups.

This slow rise of female participation in many areas of sport and leisure is mirrored by an equally slow rise – and, in some areas, stasis – in female representation. Even though market analysts are buoyant about the *future* of women's sports media coverage, the *current* picture remains rather gloomy: the proportion of all broadcast time that is given in the US to female sport, around 5 per cent, has not changed significantly for thirty years, and coverage of women's stories has been found to have lower technical quality and production values than men's. Although many competitions have equalised prize money for men and women, sponsorship deals are much less transparent: Julie German, co-founder of the Athletes' Coalition, cannot name a single big-industry sponsor who has agreed to a gender audit. Gina Lucrezi, founder of the online trail-running community Trail Sisters, surveyed thirty-three male and thirty-four female sponsored athletes, and found that men enjoy more cash and non-cash sponsorship deals, which offer a wider variety of stipends for longer periods and represent higher incomes: 71 per cent of women made less than $10,000 per year, whereas 71 per cent of men made over $10,000 per year.[28]

Sports publishing has made some recent efforts towards diversity – including memoirs by mountaineers with disabilities, such as Karen Darke's *If You Fall . . . It's a New Beginning*, and BAME runners, such as Alison Désir's *Running While Black*. However, in general, sports books remain dominated by white, non-disabled men. The semiotics of the representation of athletes also shows marked gender differences: a 2017 study of Instagram advertisements for leading sportswear companies found that in 33.4 per cent of images featuring women, 'more emphasis is placed on the physical appearance and attractiveness of the athlete rather than her athletic performance'.[29]

Similarly, although inclusion of women in sports science has marginally improved, researchers still overwhelmingly focus on male subjects. A 2019 survey found that over 70 per cent of studies concentrate entirely on men, whereas only 6 per cent are dedicated solely to women and, in that same year, in the first five issues of the *International Journal of Sports Physiology and Performance*, only 19 per cent of articles featured women at all. This represents an increase from 2013 – when a review found that only 3 per cent of sports science research from the last two years exclusively studied female athletes – but it is a very marginal one, and the discrepancy is even visible in research that specifically analyses hormonal variations in training. Despite the fact that female bodies undergo greater hormonal variations than male, women were excluded from at least one such study on the basis that 'female hormones were too complicated'. Even though training programmes are changing, such schedules still mostly ignore the characteristics of female physiology, meaning that, as Stacy Sims puts it, women 'most likely end up overtrained, slow, and have extra body fat' by following programmes that purport to be unisex but are actually designed for men. Women are deterred from returning to running, or taking it up in the first place, because of poor treatment of pelvic floor disorders following childbirth or in older age, and the lack of evidence-based advice about exercise from gynaecologists and physiotherapists. Peri- and menopausal women also tell me that there's an unmet need for 'more honest discussions about the issues we face' – including incontinence, fatigue and greater susceptibility to injury – 'and more importantly, solutions . . . [that] normalise some of the issues' and provide customised training advice for exercising during menopause.[30]

Clothing, equipment and technology may all be areas in which provision for women has significantly expanded, but 'activewear' remains 65 per cent male-dominated. Although the female market is perceived as a growth opportunity, much of that growth is still latent. It is also notable that the greatest rise has taken place in women's 'athleisurewear': comfortable daywear in a sporty style, but not necessarily truly functional outdoor clothing. And even though brands might target female consumers, they don't necessarily uphold equality in their corporate practices: footwear and clothing company Under Armour allowed male employees to put visits to strip clubs on expenses and Nike has recently been criticised for a 'boys' club atmosphere' and mistreating female athletes by reducing, or even ending, sponsorship payments on pregnancy.[31] (After a *New York Times* report in 2019, Nike changed this sponsorship policy.) There are still some glaring gaps in the female outdoor sportswear market, such as clothing that allows women to urinate discretely on the trail.

Technology also contains similar omissions: women's smart watches typically have fewer capabilities than men's, most significantly in terms of battery power and mapping. People of colour find that wrist heart-rate monitors take inaccurate readings from darker skin. Leonie Tanczer and Julia Słupska, researchers in emerging technologies, also point out how 'the tech sector has so far ignored' the ways in which smart technology, such as sports watches' location-trackers, can be used in intimate partner violence (IPV). Rose Stokes described to the *Independent* newspaper how an abusive ex-partner used the fitness-tracking platform Strava to follow her movements, and consequently sports tech 'went from being something I did to measure my progress to something that made me feel I couldn't ever be private or live online in any meaningful way without him finding me'. Until recently, Strava, by default, publicly displayed maps of users' runs, allowing random followers to easily locate those users' start and end points – that is, their homes. It also enabled the 'fly-by' function, via which (male) users can access information about (female) passers-by they might encounter en route, including their full names, photographs and maps of their walks or runs. One appalled Strava user labelled the platform 'a stalker's playground' and Tanczer is frustrated that tech companies have 'failed to implement technical responses to the daily privacy and security trade-offs that IPV victims/survivors must make'.[32]

For the most part, these examples demonstrate the painfully slow nature of progress in women's experiences of outdoor sport. Nevertheless, they are still pointing to the existence of improvement. But there are some areas which have seen reverses, retreats and declines. Although female participation in sport has increased since the 1970s, women's representation in leadership roles, in both mixed-sex and women-only sport, has *decreased*. There has been a tendency for women's clubs to combine with men's and, in such mergers, men have typically retained the lead coaching roles. In 1971, 90 per cent of head coaches in college women's sports in the USA were female, but by 2017 this had dropped to 43 per cent. Even in all-female sport, over half of coaching and management positions are held by men.[33]

The WITH report finds that women's readiness to participate in sport is also undermined by societal factors, such as gendered gaps in available leisure time and disposable income, childcare costs, and a generalised awareness of being observed and judged (for being unfeminine; for being bad mothers; for being incompetent at sport; for their appearance; and so on). Many of these gaps are widening. In 2018, the UK's Office of National Statistics released figures showing that men are enjoying more leisure time than they were fifteen years ago, while women are having less. In both the UK and USA, childcare costs have risen significantly in the same period: between 2008 and 2017, for the care of one-year-olds it rose by 48 per cent. Women today have less time and money for outdoor pursuits than in the early 2000s.[34]

In some of the more informal, less easily regulated arenas, such as sports culture and the sporting goods industry, there have also been reverses. In 2019, retail analyst Cara Salpini reported how Russ Kahn, the senior vice-president of Puma North America, admitted that the company had forgotten about 'athletics and the sport market, and . . . our female consumer', and had wrongly prioritised luxury over functionality in womenswear; as a consequence, the proportion of women buyers of Puma's collections went from 50 per cent to 30 per cent.[35]

Evidence for a mounting backlash against women outdoors is perhaps most heartbreakingly visible in abusive and aggressive behaviours from men. My eldest daughter, aged nine, recently returned from attending a football match with her girls' club, where teenage boys in the row above them threw sweets and crisps into her hair and possibly even urinated in her drink when she left it on her seat to go to the toilet. A recent survey of 2,000 fans finds that reports of harassment of female spectators at football matches has seen a sharp increase, from 8 per cent to 20 per cent in the space of seven years.[36] And at the most extreme end of the spectrum of male harassment of women outdoors – in fatal attacks – there is also a horrifying rise taking place. Between 2016 and 2022, more women were murdered (all by men) while they were out running than had been murdered, while running, in the previous twenty-eight years.

On the one hand, women now have better kit, protected competitive categories, more equal prizes, and we are attracting more sponsorship in sporting competitions. But on the other, we are losing leadership and coaching roles to men, we have less money and time to spend on leisure compared to our male counterparts – and this gap is widening further – and, while we are participating in sports in greater numbers, our safety outdoors has never been so much under threat. All this has so many knock-on consequences for women's progress and continued participation in sport. As I will explore in a later chapter, women's and girls' perception of our heightened physical vulnerability to abuse and threat from men is the greatest deterrent to our willingness to run, walk, bike, swim, explore and climb outdoors.

So are we living in a period of progress or backlash? It is not always easy to distinguish the two. In cross-country running, there is an ongoing global debate about the long-standing convention that female competitors race on a shorter course than men: 8K to the men's 12K in the National Championships. The British campaign group RunEqual sees the discrepancy as a sexist message that the women's race 'isn't as important, you aren't as capable and you aren't being welcomed on equal terms'.[37] But the issue is not straightforward and a number of elite female runners (including British long-time marathon world-record holder Paula Radcliffe and Olympians Mara Yamauchi and Laura Muir: staunch feminists all) feel that shorter distances might be preferable for women for a number of reasons – such as encouraging enrolments by attracting both middle- and long-distance female runners, and potentially better suiting female physiological capabilities. So, would equalisation of cross-country distances represent progress or regression? Is the status quo a remnant of sexist sporting history, or does it exemplify how the sporting world is making efforts to welcome women's biological aptitudes and desire for participation?

Similarly, there is a heated debate about the inclusion of trans athletes in organised sport, particularly around whether trans women should be allowed to compete in the female class. Trans women athletes often retain physiological benefits of male puberty – in what degree and for how long is currently under investigation by numerous sporting bodies and sports science researchers across the world, including exercise physiologist Tommy Lundberg, and Leonardo Azevedo Mobilia Alvares's team of endocrinologists at São Paulo University. Some organisations' and competitions' policies allow trans women to compete in female categories or teams, usually after a period of time on testosterone-suppressive medication and tests to confirm low testosterone levels in the body. Critics of such policies perceive the inclusion of trans women in female categories as an erosion of women's necessary protections in sport, which drive female athletes out of visibility and, in sports such as boxing and rugby, also threaten women's safety. However, other commentators interpret such guidelines as part of a trajectory towards greater diversity in sport, and they welcome the inclusion of trans athletes in the female category at a time when the gaps between male and female athletes' performances are often perceived to be diminishing. So, is the inclusion of trans women athletes in the female class a marker of progress or backlash? Is it an expression of how far the sports industry has come, in terms of accommodation of diversity; or is it an indication that the protections awarded to women are fragile and that our acceptance in organised sport has peaked, and is in retreat?[38]

It is difficult to straightforwardly identify whether particular changes like these represent progress or backlash. It is even harder to conclude whether the 1880s and the present day are periods of overall advancement in women's rights or phases of retreat. In many ways, the contemporary world appears as buoyant for athletic women as the 1880s must have seemed to Lizzie. In both eras, there have been significant efforts to facilitate female sport, examples of progress that mirror broader gains in women's rights in those periods. But, looked at in a different way, darker streaks are visible in both eras. In Lizzie's time, men were starting to mutter and organise against the prevalence of sporting women in 'their' spaces. And today, men are increasingly reluctant to share sports leadership roles and are more likely to harass, intimidate and even murder women outdoors.

It was impossible for Lizzie and her contemporaries to know how seriously to take the niggling underswell of sexism in the 1880s, and it is similarly hard to prophesy the future now. Will we continue to enjoy the steady, ongoing expansion of women's freedoms and will the sexist backlash fizzle out – and will female participation, visibility and authority in sport swell even further?

Or will men's hostility towards women's sport – and women's freedoms elsewhere – intensify? And will women be driven out?

5.

In the mountains, there you feel free

How severe does sexism need to be, to deter women from taking part in outdoor sport? From the research I've done so far, I've discovered that Lizzie Le Blond seems to have found something similarly important in mountaineering as I have in trail running. For both of us that importance is related to our femaleness, the way that we are treated in the world as women and the emancipation that outdoor sport can offer.

Back home in Yorkshire, I look at the next period of Lizzie's life. I want to understand how she built on the initial joy and liberation that she found in the mountains. But I also want to track the nature of the male backlash against women in the great outdoors, and how Lizzie fared in the face of it.

By the late 1890s, Lizzie was arguably the most famous female climber in the world. But this success was hard fought for, against a rising tide of misogyny: in each and every ascent, she had to negotiate constraints that threatened to bring her, and her entire generation of sportswomen, crashing down to earth.

After separating from her husband Fred in the summer of 1882, Lizzie returned to Chamonix, where she stayed in the Hôtel d'Angleterre, the oldest tourist hotel in the valley. That season, she realised the hopes of the previous year and made it to the summit of Mont Blanc – not once, but twice: from the Italian side as well as the French. She also made a few smaller scrambles, including the popular Aiguille du Belvédère, overlooking Chamonix; the Aiguille du Tacul, with its view down to the enormous valley glacier of the Mer de Glace; the Col du Géant; the Aiguille du Tour; and the Grandes Jorasses. By the end of the summer, 'I felt I might consider myself a climber,' Lizzie congratulated herself.[1]

In the early autumn, mountain resorts closed for the season and most travellers left the high life to return home or headed to warm beaches along the Riviera or north Africa. In September, Lizzie too left Chamonix, but she went in a different direction. She crossed the Alps, skirting south of the Italian lakes of Maggiore, Lugano and Como, and then travelled north to the spa resort of Bormio. However, 'the weather was as bad as it possibly could be', so she kept moving, crossing the Stelvio Pass – 'the highest pass in Europe crossed by a carriage-road' – and descended the other side, towards Trafoi and Meran, 'hoping for better things in Tyrol'. She found yet more snow, 'which often reached to her waist'. Then Italy was hit by flooding on a biblical scale: fifteen consecutive days of rain caused rivers across the north to overflow, resulting in what one journalist called 'the shipwreck of a whole population'. Lizzie gave up, and after spending 'six weeks of damp on the borders of the lake of Geneva', she returned to Chamonix in the depths of winter.[2]

The most popular season for mountaineering was mid July to mid September: snow levels were at their lowest and travellers could ramble, run and climb with ease. But long-term invalids often remained through the winter at sanatoria and hotels in Davos, Montreux and St Moritz, and by the 1880s proprietors had devised myriad ways to entertain winter guests. The grand Kulm Hotel installed electric lighting, heating and ventilation, rinks for curling and skating, indoor and outdoor tennis courts, and tobogganing and bobsleigh runs. (Skiing was not initially included in this array of leisure activities. It wasn't until 1896 that early pioneers – most famously, the author of the Sherlock Holmes stories, Arthur Conan Doyle – imported it into the Alps from Norway, and skiing still remained a largely 'alien sport' in Switzerland until later in the 1900s.)[3]

Despite the fiendishly cold air, the sun could be so strong in the Alpine resorts that parasols were necessary, and winter visitors continued to enjoy picnics, rambles and sleigh rides. It would be in these elite snow-covered playgrounds that, within a few years, Lizzie would begin photographing the women who skated, tobogganed, hiked and climbed alongside her, in what constituted the birth of winter sports.

Nevertheless, most guests drew the line at winter mountaineering. December and January brought vastly reduced hours of daylight, unpredictable weather, and depths of snow and ice that could turn 'the path to which the summer tourist is accustomed' into 'a nasty place', admitted Lizzie. *The Times* described how 'winter mountaineering' involved 'a great amount of gratuitous hardship and labour':

> The days are short, the side roads are gone out of repair, and accommodation in the villages is almost as precarious as the weather. You cannot ride or drive, as in the summer, to the point where the eventual climbing is to begin; and the mountain châlets or cabins which offer shelter for the night are, of course, abandoned and generally choked with snow. There are no ready means of making a fire; cookery must be carried out under extreme difficulties; while, in the daytime, with falls in the temperature, all fluids except cognac are apt to congeal, and everything solid, except biscuits, is hardened beyond the eating point. Above all, as might be imagined, the snow is too often in indifferent condition.[4]

Mountains contained crevasses, deep cracks in the ice hidden beneath bridges of snow which might collapse without warning.

A detail from Lizzie's photograph of a female mountaineer peering into a crevasse on the Forno Glacier, in the Bregaglia mountain range in Switzerland

There were walls of snow and ice which could only be climbed using axes to cut hundreds of steps. The afternoon sun melted the ice just enough to release cascades of enormous rocks onto climbers below. Thousands of tons of snow might be disturbed into avalanches and mountain summits were frequently adorned with cornices, overhanging snow shaped by the wind into cresting waves, with nothing but thin air beneath. Winter mountaineers had to learn to read the quality of snow and discern whether the ground beneath was solid or a fatal void; dig out huts from underneath drifts; edge cautiously with lanterns through darkness, blizzards and fog; accurately navigate routes across terrains of undifferentiated white, in which footprints were rapidly obliterated by falling snow; and glissade, sliding down snow-covered slopes by leaning on slanting alpenstocks that controlled the speed and direction of the descent.[5]

Despite – or because of – these dangers, Lizzie soon found that winter slopes also brought a 'flavour of excitement which was very enjoyable', and which set her apart from the usual run of tourists. Between 1 November 1882 and 3 March 1883, Lizzie made what even the male-dominated pages of the *Alpine Journal* admiringly called an 'unparalleled series of winter ascents executed by a lady', which, their correspondent predicted, 'will form one of the most brilliant chapters in the history of winter mountaineering'.[6]

She was led in them by her long-standing guide, Edouard Cupelin, who, instead of attempting a series of one-off ascents, linked mountains together into tours for Lizzie. That winter, Lizzie, Edouard and his brother Auguste first crossed what she thought was 'the one remaining untrodden col in the chain of Mont Blanc', ascending the Aiguille du Tacul by a new route. A month later, Lizzie made an astoundingly fast ascent of the Aiguille du Midi, during which Edouard had to stand above some smooth rocks on which Lizzie could find no footholds or handholds and pull her up 'like a fisherman landing an unwieldy salmon', she recalled laughingly. The season's adventures were capped off with a daring attempt at the first ever winter ascent of Monte Rosa at the beginning of March 1883 – the 'coldest month in the year in the mountains' – which had to be abandoned at the final stage, when a 'hurricane' whipped up, the temperature plummeted and Lizzie's nose turned white from frostbite. Although that particular ascent failed, it gave her plenty of material for stories of her exploits, and she started writing for the public about her new life in the mountains.[7]

Just over a fortnight after the Monte Rosa attempt, newspapers back in Britain announced that Lizzie's first book, *The High Alps in Winter*, was close to completion. But when it was published that June, the *Alpine Journal*'s (male) reviewer declared himself 'grievously disappointed'. It was clearly 'the book of a lady', he said, and 'probably the flimsiest and most trivial that has ever been offered to the alpine public'. In particular, he was affronted by Lizzie's realisation of Leslie Stephen's prophecy: that a peak which had been designated 'absolutely inaccessible' by mountaineer Albert Mummery three years earlier, had apparently been so effortless for Lizzie, as to merely form 'the fourth day in one of Mrs Burnaby's ideal high-level routes'. The once-revered route, against which men tested their macho mettle, had become *an easy day for a lady.*[8]

Lizzie's winter climbs gave her a taste of fame not, as she'd previously found, because of her marriage to Fred Burnaby, or as a society wife, but for her own accomplishments. Lizzie was experiencing a new social role, in which – despite the fact she was a woman of the upper classes – she was expected to take responsibility for managing her own fitness and safety, and in which 'all the party share the pleasures and the dangers'. She was also witnessing a new form of masculinity, very different to that she had previously encountered. Her guide Edouard was the same height as her husband Fred – 6 feet 4 – but much less intimidating. He did not take himself particularly seriously: when she idly compared the stone walls of their mountain chalet to a slab they'd been climbing, he set off up the wall 'like a monkey', and when she dared him to do so with 'the tea-things in your hands, and break nothing', he accepted the challenge and made the ascent with a teapot in one hand and a full cream jug and cup in the other, and landed on his feet without spilling a drop, while she sat, laughing, on the ground. She would describe mountain guides as 'unique as a class', with Edouard combining 'the qualities of an excellent cook, a lady's maid, a courier, and a first-rate carpenter, with those of a pleasant companion'.[9]

Lizzie was not the only woman to find that outdoor sport offered the opportunity to experiment with interactions between the sexes. Relationships between mountaineers and guides could be extremely physically intimate: Lizzie would later write about standing on a guide's shoulders to clamber up onto a ledge, as well as holding their hands, being caught in their arms when she slipped, having a rope tied around her waist, being wedged upright against a guide and turning in 'a flank movement', and having to bivvy on a tiny ledge, pressed against her guide's body, rolling over together at the same time. Women changed, slept and urinated near their guides and Lizzie thought a good relationship was characterised by a physical sixth sense by which her guide would 'know where I required a helping hand and where I could move alone'.[10]

Women were often more relaxed around their guides' bodies than around prospective (or actual) husbands and, unsurprisingly, this ease sometimes developed into romantic relationships. Isabella Straton, who climbed Monte Viso and the Aiguille du Moine with her friend Emmeline Lewis Lloyd in the early 1870s, married her guide Jean Charlet, and later they named the Pointe de la Persévérance after 'the perseverance that they had shown before they had dared to confess their affection for one another'. A Yorkshirewoman called Margaret Sophia Green married her Norwegian mountain guide, Knut Kvikne, in 1890. The outdoors was also the setting in which women experimented romantically with male companions who would otherwise have been out of bounds in their conventional lives. In 1872, Isabella Bird, who was suffering from a spinal complaint, headaches and insomnia, was instructed by her doctor to take up open-air pursuits and, after visiting Australia and Hawaii, she made her way to the Colorado Rockies, where she rode 800 miles on horseback (not side-saddle), met an outlaw called Jim Nugent, with whom she later entered into a romantic relationship, and wrote *A Lady's Life in the Rocky Mountains*. The mountaineer Lily Bristow, who made the first ascent of the Aiguille des Grands Charmoz in the Mont Blanc massif in 1892, shared tents with men and climbed with Albert Mummery, until his wife Mary forbade him. Bristow's relationship with Mummery was close enough that, after he died in 1895, she gave up her own mountaineering.[11]

Lizzie's relationship with Edouard does not seem to have been sexual, but they did become lifelong friends, and he was a passionate supporter of her early mountaineering career. In June 1883, Edouard suggested an expedition that, if it were successful, would be a first female ascent: of the higher of the two summits of the Dent du Géant, a mountain whose sharp pinnacle thrusts up into the air like a Giant's Tooth, with two distinct prongs, one loftier than the other and separated by what she knew to be an 'extremely awkward notch'. Lizzie understood that reaching the upper peak was a feat that had previously been thought impossible 'without artificial aid, as by fixing nails and ropes to the rocks'. After two false starts, thwarted by bad weather, on 13 July 1883 Lizzie and Edouard – accompanied by Auguste Cupelin and two porters (Michel Savoiz and Auguste Tairraz) – set off in the evening and walked through the night, reaching the foot of the prominent section of the mountain by lunchtime the following day. During climbing expeditions, Lizzie tended to dine on 'tinned soup, potted meat, champagne and marsala' and, like her forerunner Lucy Walker, sponge cake too. Champagne was often drunk at summits to celebrate noteworthy ascents, but it wasn't just a luxury: in sub-zero temperatures, Lizzie described how flasks of tea, 'chicken, soup . . . everything, except for the cognac', became 'frozen hard as a stone', even when insulated in 'tin gourds . . . enclosed in flannel bags, stuffed with cotton wool'.[12] The lower freezing temperatures of alcohol sometimes made it the only option for taking in fluids and calories.

After lunch, Lizzie, Edouard and Auguste began climbing up the Dent du Géant, roped together by a ninety-foot length which allowed each climber to negotiate the large distances separating the mountain's hand- and footholds. Later, Lizzie described how, from this point, 'the rock appears to rise in a sheer and unbroken wall', followed by a gully with 'an unpleasant amount of ice in it'. She made her way up to find yet more sheer slabs, 'the most difficult of the whole climb, as there really is hardly room for one or two nails in the side of one's boot, in the tiny ledges, and each step must be a long one'. To reach the pinnacle, the tooth itself, she then had to climb over a large rock that shifted perilously with her weight and ascend 'some perpendicular gullies' down which dangled fixed ropes. Lizzie pulled 'the whole weight of the body' up a rope with her arms alone ('very fatiguing'), and then momentarily recovered on a shoulder of rock, before making her way from the lower to the higher peak. The two prongs were joined by 'a ridge which falls away sheerly to a depth of many thousand feet on either side', which she accessed by getting past 'a hump of rock', hugging it, and 'gradually worming' her way around. This was 'extremely uncomfortable', she said, but not 'really dangerous or even very difficult', as Edouard was standing above her on the ridge, with 'a firm footing (what Cupelin would describe as *"solide comme un boeuf!"*) and could easily check a slip' by anchoring the rope between them with his bodyweight. Finally, all that was required was to climb the few remaining metres above the ridge and she was standing on the summit: 'a flat slab of rock perhaps six feet wide and as many long', from which the lower portion of the mountain was strangely concealed, 'as the rock falls away in vertical and, in some parts, in overhanging walls on all sides'. It felt, she said, 'as if our platform floated in mid-air, amongst the spires and domes of the great mountains'.[13]

The descent wasn't straightforward. Lizzie described how 'gusts of wind made frantic dashes at us and seemed as if they would tear us from our insecure positions'. By the time the party got back to the hotel, late in the afternoon of 14 July, she had been on her feet (and hands) for over twenty-one hours. Her team had been seen by another climber, a lawyer called James Walker Hartley, who was climbing the same peak, although he hadn't ascended to the highest summit. In his report for the *Alpine Journal*, Hartley described 'the first ascent by an English lady' of the Dent du Géant, but he did not refer to Lizzie by name. Rightly proud of her feat, Lizzie wrote up a long, detailed account, which would later make its way into her second book, *High Life and Towers of Silence*, which she would publish in 1886. She bought a photograph of the Dent du Géant by her friend, the mountaineer and photographer William Donkin; an image which was so faithful in capturing 'the horrors of the peak' that, when it was hung in her sitting room a couple of years later, she recounted how 'an invalid friend of mine . . . had such a severe nervous attack . . . that a doctor had to be called up during the night'.[14] Combined with Lizzie's previous accomplishments in winter mountaineering, the Dent du Géant climb cemented her reputation as one of the most adept climbers in the world, male or female.

Although Lizzie and her peers were enjoying newfound freedoms in the mountains, there was a sense that this liberation was fragile, partial and conditional – and always under threat. Like some female athletes today, many were aware that much remained to be done in the name of equality.

Despite being relatively accepting of women's involvement, the world of outdoor leisure was still unfairly weighted towards men. Female travellers often discovered that hotels, inns and mountain huts were designed for men. They felt vulnerable in hotel rooms that lacked locks and found that male residents often commandeered so-called 'shared' spaces with the 'sounds of men's voices and fumes of tobacco', making it clear to women that 'it will not do to intrude yourself upon these men'. On one occasion, Frederica Plunket was allotted a bedroom which was accessible only via the men's billiards room and so she had to relocate to a different hotel. On another, she was forced to eat dinner in the corridor because the dining hall was so suffocated with men's cigar-smoke that it was like 'a distant view of Manchester'. Mountain huts – basic refuges on the slopes – almost always contained 'but one room' and women were faced with the prospect of getting changed in front of, and sleeping alongside, strange men. As a result, women were often deterred from using the huts at all and had to relinquish the dream of multi-day, long-distance excursions that depended on safe accommodation en route. Female mountaineers often felt restricted to short trips that began and ended at their hotels. Even during Lizzie's overnight tours, she found it 'infinitely preferable' to 'bivouac under a great rock' than to spend 'a night in a hut'.[15]

Another key battleground was outdoor clothing. Female climbers frequently had to negotiate the desire for physical comfort and freedom versus the desire not to flout convention and attract unwanted attention. In the second half of the nineteenth century, a typical female 'mountaineering suit' tended to include some or all of the following, depending on the fashion of the particular year: warm woollen underclothing; a small or elastic corset; a blouse, often with a tie; a short woollen jacket; a waterproof cape; a thick 'plaid' (to use as a shawl or blanket); a hat (often a boater); strong boots (like 'gentlemen's shooting-boots' with 'Lund's glacier nails' driven into the soles, and no heels); one or more facial veils or masks, to preserve a pale complexion and defend against sunburn; snow goggles; a waterproof bag with a cross-body strap, or knapsack; and an alpenstock, the walking stick that Lizzie found had further uses as a tin-opener, a defensive weapon against animals and 'a means for rapidly passing through a crowd at a railway station'. What women wore to

A self-portrait of Lizzie, wrapped in veils to protect her skin from the sun

cover their legs was particularly contested, but the most socially acceptable option was a long skirt, which reached all the way down to the heels and was teamed with a petticoat and bustle and, until the late 1870s, a crinoline – a stiff underskirt that gave it greater volume and made the waist appear smaller. Sometimes women wore riding skirts made of light waterproof cloth: expertly tailored items, often with long, asymmetric hems which could be shortened with buttons or hooks and which could be 'slipped on and off in a moment'.[16]

Voluminous skirts had certain advantages. They gave the legs a wide range of motion; the folds of fabric contained enormous pockets that were big enough to accommodate small tents; they could function as blankets when sleeping out overnight; and they probably allowed women to urinate discreetly behind a screen. Emily Hornby found that her petticoat was brilliant as a sledge. But long skirts also caused serious problems. They were extremely heavy and bulky, trailed in snow and puddles and became wet and even heavier – especially when rain cascaded onto them from waterproof capes worn on the top half. They snagged on branches and sometimes brought rocks raining down on unsuspecting hikers below, and they

Lizzie and her friend, the tennis champion Lottie Dod, wading through deep snow in long skirts

could get frozen to icy surfaces. The wind turned them into parachutes, and they caught on saddles when riding. When they were wet, skirts lost their insulating qualities and instead of doubling as blankets at night, they made women freeze. They tended to get torn and, because women's clothing was mostly too bulky and heavy to carry spares, female climbers often found themselves 'darning the last rent in one's mountain suit' while the men were relaxing and drinking wine around the campfire. When Plunket got to her hotel after a rainy expedition, she realised she had the unenviable choice of either eating dinner in the communal dining room in sodden clothing or taking 'off our dripping garments and having none with which to replace them, to go supperless to bed'. She tried to dry her skirt in front of the fire in her room, but the wet muddy material smelled so bad that she compared the 'vapoury atmosphere [to] that which geologists attribute to our earth during one of the great pre-Adamite periods'.[17]

Women devised workarounds. Some made adaptations to their skirts: Eliza Cole recommended stitching 'small rings . . . inside the seams of the dress, and a cord passed through them, the ends of which should be knotted together in such a way that the whole dress may be drawn up at a moment's notice to the requisite height', like a Roman blind. But, on trying Cole's suggestion, mountaineer Meta Brevoort found that, when 'descending snow slopes the snow enters between the rings and stuffs up the hem and makes me heavy and wet'. Many women found a compromise between comfort and social acceptability by wearing their skirts over 'knickerbockers'. Mountaineering writer Marjorie Milsom described how, once female climbers were 'out of sight of the last chalet, the skirt was removed and carried in the guide's or porter's knapsack', or placed under a rock or by a cairn, so that the women could climb on unhindered. But this method was not foolproof: on one expedition, Lizzie returned to the rock under which she'd placed her skirt to find that it had been swept away by an avalanche. She had to send her guide down to her hotel to collect a new one. (He returned with 'her best evening gown', which she wore for the rest of the descent.[18])

Some women eschewed the skirt altogether. Henriette d'Angeville, the second woman to summit Mont Blanc, was inspired by the French female novelist and mountaineer George Sand's penchant for masculine clothing, and wore 'a climbing costume of checkered material, complete with wide trousers, long coat, huge feathered beret and a long black boa'. From 1851, the American women's rights activist Amelia Bloomer popularised 'bloomers', baggy Turkish trousers gathered at the ankles, with the hope that 'the costume of women should be suited to her wants and necessities. It should conduce at once to her health, comfort, and usefulness.' Thirty years later, Lady Florence Harberton founded the Rational Dress Society on similar principles, which protested against 'any fashion in dress that either deforms the figure, impedes the movements of the body, or in any way tends to injure the health', and 'the wearing of tightly fitting corsets; of high-heeled shoes; of heavily weighted skirts, as rendering healthy exercise almost impossible; and of all tie down cloaks or other garments impeding on the movements of the arms. It protests against crinolines or crinolettes of any kind as ugly and deforming.'[19] The society showed how 'freedom of movement' applied to the body as well as travel, and that women were sorely disadvantaged in both.

Inspired by these arguments, a few nineteenth-century female mountaineers adopted tighter trousers: 'puttees' (leggings made of strips of material wrapped tightly around the lower legs) or breeches, often with a short skirt on top. In 1895, Annie Smith Peck experimented with knickerbockers tucked into tall boots, paired with a hip-length tunic.[20]

Neither the Rational Dress Society nor Amelia Bloomer discounted the importance of 'grace and beauty', of 'personal adornment' and of conforming to 'ordinary dress'. Women mountaineers had to conduct their own personal 'risk assessments', weighing up comfort versus their tolerance for criticism. Lizzie could be scathing about women who came to different resolutions than her own, and she was often defensive about whether her femininity had been compromised by her participation in 'manly' activities like mountaineering. She ridiculed a party of ladies – whom she noticed whispering about her in the hotel dining room, and who eventually plucked up the courage to ask if climbing was responsible for the blisters and burns on her face – for prioritising their vanity and fashion over function. At other times, Lizzie could be fiercely critical of women who did the opposite and sacrificed their femininity to their sport. Similarly, the Egyptologist and explorer Amelia Edwards ridiculed a German woman who had travelled across Europe and Palestine alone: Edwards referred to her as 'it', and mocked her battered clothing, indeterminate age, 'man's' voice and 'tanned and travel-stained' face.[21]

It is notable that almost all adventurous women shared an acute self-consciousness, a perpetual awareness of being watched and judged, and that they frequently expressed anxieties about being condemned for – in the words of Lizzie's great-aunt – 'scandalising' society. Repeatedly, they wrote about the same split consciousness – the same sense of seeing themselves as simultaneous subjects and objects – that philosopher Iris Marion Young described as characteristic of women in sport, and which I myself undoubtedly experience. Lizzie wrote extensively about her painful sensitivity to the different audiences that watched her as she climbed: the telescopes trained on her from hotel windows far below; the 'critical pairs of eyes watching my awkward movements' from a nearby group of mountaineers; the 'people below' who fired a cannon when they saw her reaching the summit of the Aiguille du Midi, and whom she later tried to evade; the way in which her party must appear 'like flies on a church spire, as they creep slowly up the steep slabs'. Later, she would wistfully tell the Yorkshire Ramblers' Club that mountaineering 'brought out the best that was in people' only when it was 'carried on beyond the gaze of onlookers'. In the finest moments, when she managed to escape critical eyes, she felt that she was able to climb 'like a child, ardently, engrossingly, thinking not at all of on-lookers, and indeed unaware that such even existed'.[22] But that privacy and invisibility – that right to be left alone – was hard for women to find in the hills.

Women's worries about being watched and criticised were not hypothetical. They were on the receiving end of a wide range of criticisms, from a large number of men in the outdoors. Expeditions were usually accompanied by teams of guides and porters, who were almost always male. Their protection was considered to be especially important to women: Frederica Plunket felt that as women generally 'have neither the muscular strength, the activity, nor the training required' to be fully confident in the mountains and needed to be more cautious of their safety than men, they were more dependent than men upon guides' 'strong arm[s]'. But women commonly reported how guides reacted in patronising, hostile and theatrically aghast ways to the very concept of female mountaineers: Eliza Cole concluded that they were 'much disposed to magnify all dangers, especially when they have to conduct a lady'. She recounted how, on numerous outings with her husband and a team of male guides and porters – including trips to the Aletsch Glacier on the Jungfrau, the Belvedere Glacier on Monte Rosa and the northern ridge of the Valle di Bors – she was sent back to the hotel prematurely when the guides 'solemnly assured us that "Madame" could not go higher', leaving the men to climb alone. Such behaviour would dog women's experiences through the decades. In the late 1880s, Emily Hornby described how 'it aggravates me beyond endurance' when her guide, Peter Anderegg, insisted on holding her 'hand firmly, standing just in front so that I could not see where to put my foot next'. (She was relieved when Anderegg later broke his hand in an accident and was unable to undermine her ability to walk independently.)[23]

Other men – climbing companions, onlookers, writers and doctors – could be equally dispiriting. Some men worried that women were so physiologically feeble that the endurance, strength and flexibility required by mountaineering were far beyond them. Cole described how she had 'been told, by more than one person . . . that it was *impossible* for a lady to cross' the Monte Moro Pass between Switzerland and Italy. The Yorkshire physician Thomas Clifford Allbutt – who later became regius professor of physic at the University of Cambridge and president of the British Medical Association (and may have been the model for Dr Lydgate in George Eliot's *Middlemarch*) – warned in the mid 1870s: 'I have seen many women broken down in health for a year or years by a few days' mountaineering in the company of active men.' Allbutt compared women's physiological abilities to those of children, but warned that, unlike children, women would never outgrow their frailty.[24] In particular, physicians worried that vigorous pursuits would endanger women's reproductive capabilities, and that mountain sports like tobogganing – in which women lay face down – were particularly threatening to the health of their breasts.

Frederica Plunket described how one effect of men's doom-mongering was that women felt so 'beset with such dangers and difficulties' that their outdoor experiences were always marred by disproportionate fear. Eliza Cole openly worried 'lest my strength and courage should prove unequal' and she described her 'fear of over-fatigue'. Sometimes this anxiety and self-doubt led women to abandon long-planned and long-desired excursions: Plunket gave up on her hope of going up Piz Morteratsch after a guide pronounced it 'not fit for ladies'. Cole also spoke of how she was forced to halt various rambles in the face of men's naysaying, 'with much reluctance' and 'full of regret'. Some women rejected the idea of outdoor sports altogether, feeling that 'to attempt such performances would be absolute madness, risking other lives as well as their own'.[25]

Women were scared not just of criticism and ridicule, but of physical assaults too. Hornby gave up an ascent of a mountain in the Carpathians because 'I did not want to be robbed and murdered'. Female climbers, including Lizzie, were horrified by tales of attacks on women in the mountains, such as that memorialised on a plaque in the Stelvio Pass, where suspected serial killer Henri Perreau (posing as Count Henri de Tourville) murdered his wife, Madeleine Miller, on their honeymoon in July 1876, for an inheritance. (Although there were clear signs that Madeleine's body had been dragged over the edge of the pass, and despite the fact that Perreau's previous wealthy wife and mother-in-law had both died in suspicious circumstances, the coroner ruled Madeleine's death a suicide.)[26]

Despite their fears, women writers tried to encourage themselves, and other would-be female mountaineers, to go outdoors nevertheless. 'It requires neither very great strength nor a very dauntless spirit to make the Tour I have described,' Cole told her readers, and she stressed how many women found pleasure and freedom – safely – in the mountains. She emphasised that there was often 'not a word of truth in [the] representations' of guides and other men. Jane Freshfield turned the tables on men's tendency to alarmism about the dangers facing women by gleefully describing how often *male* mountaineers endangered themselves through incompetence. In her anecdotes, her hapless husband variously sprained his knees, got lost, fell over, slipped under a horse, had to stop for several long rests, was reluctant to leave his breakfast and had to be chivvied by his more dynamic and competent wife. Frederica Plunket emphasised that the dangers of mountaineering were relatively 'slight' compared to more mundane activities, such as travelling on an 'express train on an English railway'.[27] She reassured women that the mountains could offer a profoundly beneficial and statistically safer alternative to their day-to-day lives. Lizzie and her companions were eloquent about the constraints they faced – obstacles that arose largely because of men's attitudes towards women – and showed ingenuity and determination in trying to overcome them.

But, as is the case today, the cost–benefit analyses that these women made every time they went outside, weighing up the risks and the pleasures involved in mountaineering, were constantly in a state of flux. In some months, years or decades, the pleasures vastly offset the threats and women took to the hills in greater number; in others, however, the reverse was true, and in those periods, women were more likely to stay at home. But for now, for Lizzie in the 1880s, the 'sense of intense enjoyment' she found in the mountains was worth fighting for – and it mostly outweighed the potential costs and dangers that her sport entailed for women.

By the close of the 1883 summer season, Lizzie had, in addition to the Dent du Géant, made ascents of the Matterhorn, the Adler Pass, the Weissthor (also known as the Fillarjoch), the Col Durand and the Trift Pass. As the winter drew in, she made her way to a region of Switzerland that was new to her: the Engadin, a valley running diagonally from the Maloja Pass (on the border with Italy) in the southwest, up through the settlements of Sils Maria, Silvaplana and St Moritz, to the region's capital, Samedan, in the northeast. There, at Samedan, the Engadin meets the Bernina valley and the two part, like a pair of compasses, the latter running southeast through the village of Pontresina to the Bernina Pass, on the border with Italy, and the town of Tirano.

Lizzie described how, during the summer months, the region could be 'crowded to over-flowing', but in winter she – like many other visitors – found that the Engadin could be just perfect, with a combination of 'warm, bright sun, with the cold, crisp air' that 'makes the flesh tingle'.[28] She took a room in St Moritz at the lavish Kulm Hotel, where a vast south-facing window looked out across the lake to the enormous mountains of Piz Rosatsch, Piz Surlej and Piz Corvatsch, whose rich green firs and silver scree seemed close enough to touch through the glass.

Lizzie immediately started plotting excursions but, soon after her arrival in St Moritz, her partnership with Edouard unexpectedly ended. In the summer of 1884, a massive boulder fell from the side of the Aiguille Verte, crushing his knee and mostly ending his career. Lizzie initially tried climbing with a number of new guides, but none had long-term potential. By the following summer, though, she had been introduced to a forty-four-year-old guide called Josef Imboden, from the village of St Niklaus, a few miles up the Matter valley, north of Zermatt. He had travelled widely in Europe and further afield, including in the Himalayas, and spoke six languages, including impeccable English. Josef soon became Lizzie's 'constant companion summer after summer' for the next fifteen years, with another guide, Martin Schocher, assisting her in winter. In their first season together, Lizzie and Josef climbed most of the major peaks and passes between Zermatt and Saas Fee: the Strahlhorn, Col Durand, the Dom, Bruneggjoch, the Biesjoch and the Stellijoch. They made a secret expedition up an unnamed mountain beside the Weisshorn, sleeping out overnight in 'a sheltered spot under an overhanging cliff, near the foot of the Abberg glacier', and became the first to summit 'the

Bieshorn (as we christened it)'.[29] Later, the Bieshorn's eastern peak would be named 'Pointe Burnaby' in Lizzie's honour.

In September, Lizzie took a room in the Hotel Belvédère, in Davos, in the neighbouring valley, around forty kilometres due north of the Engadin. There she met a man who could hardly have been more different from Fred Burnaby. John Frederic Main was a thirty-one-year-old professor of mechanics, described by a former lover (the incipient social reformer Beatrice Potter (later Webb)) as 'a clever, sensitive man, short in stature with a pleasant, open, sympathetic face'. In John, Beatrice had found 'a refined and sympathetic mind, deeply appreciative of nature'. His admiration of the mountain environment was scientific and mathematical as well as aesthetic: he was fascinated by processes of crystallisation and liquefaction and was planning a series of scientific observations of how ice behaved when put under tensional stress.[30]

In John Main, Lizzie probably also saw a male version of her own escape to the mountains from the harms of late nineteenth-century society. Their meeting would pave the way for Lizzie's growing interest, not just in the benefits that mountains might bring to her as an individual woman, but in the communities that resided in the Alps and in the wider social advantages of outdoor leisure. Lizzie's relationship with John arguably spurred her determination to document and record those communities and the transformational experiences that they brought to female travellers, in particular.

John Main had first visited Switzerland in the summer of 1882, just over two years before he and Lizzie met. Back then, he had been seriously ill, in the midst of a mental collapse precipitated by overwork and a family crisis. His childhood had been lonely, 'without games or companions' – first in Jamaica (where his father had died), and then in Portsmouth, where he, his mother and sister Catherine had shared a tall, thin house on the harbour with his maternal family, a collection of publicans, brewers and spirit merchants. He worked hard to leave this depressing background behind and, after distinguishing himself at university – at Cambridge and then London – he was appointed lecturer in mathematics and applied mechanics at University College, Bristol, and was soon promoted to professor. But the workload – involving the establishment of a new engineering department, outreach activities and helping with the debating society and football club – was exhausting. John described how 'four professors' at Bristol had collapsed 'owing to the severe strain put on them by excessive mental labour' and, before long, he too began to experience a crisis that Lizzie would identify as characteristic of 'overworked breadwinners whose nerves had broken down'. He perhaps reminded her of her father, Vin, whose nervous exhaustion had been precipitated by overwork on the family estate.[31]

John's professional stress happened at the same time as a complicated family emergency, which would later reignite to destroy his and Lizzie's relationship. John had grown up alongside a younger cousin, Clarissa, who – following her mother's death – was looked after by their unmarried aunt Sarah Ann in the same household as John and his family. Some time after John had left for university, Clarissa was sexually assaulted by her uncle and John dedicated himself to finding a new start for his beloved cousin. He approached his late father's brother, Thomas, who was living across the Atlantic, in a town north-west of New York City, and who was reputed to be one of the 'most eminent engineers and marine engine builders in the United States'. Thomas was a recent widower, caring for two sons, David (aged nineteen) and Tommy (aged four). John seems to have arranged that Thomas would give Sarah Ann and Clarissa a new life in the United States, in return for their provision of domestic services (and marriage between Thomas and Sarah Ann). The two women docked in New York City on 9 September 1880, but the new start quickly turned sour. As Clarissa would later tell a court, Thomas's nineteen-year-old son David raped her, offered to marry her and presumed he now 'had the right to do as he liked'. When Clarissa became pregnant, she reminded David of his promise and, when he refused to honour the agreement, she launched legal proceedings against him for 'seduction and breach of promise of marriage'. In retaliation, Thomas violently ejected Sarah Ann and Clarissa from the house, leaving them to fend for themselves. This shocking news reached John Main around May 1882, and, on top of his work-related exhaustion, it was too much to bear. He resigned from Bristol University and took an easier post – a demotion – at London's Normal School of Science (now Imperial College). But he found that intolerable too, and before long he had fled to Switzerland on long-term sick leave. John did not return to Britain, and it was in the Hotel Belvédère in Davos that, two years later, in September 1884, he met Lizzie.[32]

When she first encountered John, Lizzie was still officially married. But a few months after their introduction, in mid January 1885, a telegram arrived for her at Davos: Fred was dead, speared in the throat in Sudan while fighting in a British military initiative to neutralise supporters of the religious leader Muhammad Ahmad bin Abd Allah, the 'Mahdi'.

Lizzie was Fred's executor and, although she initially prevaricated and remained in Davos, she eventually had to return to London to attend to the probate administration and her son Harry, whom newspapers described as 'a pretty lisping little boy, hardly old enough to realise how it is his father does not come back to play with him as he was used to do'. Lizzie and Fred's separation, and her residence in the Alps, had previously been glossed over by reporters as necessitated by ill health. But now she found herself criticised for having 'only lived with her husband for just one year', for not being 'fond of domesticity' and for preferring 'adventurous pursuits inconsistent with home life'. Lizzie was hurt. She worried about reputational damage, but the reports were hard to dismiss: it was true that she was not 'fond of domesticity'. Indeed, she used her time in London to arrange for guardians to take over the care of her son so that she could return to the mountains. Lizzie's mother Alice agreed to continue helping with Harry's care. The second custodian chosen by Fred – a well-connected soldier friend by the name of Colonel Valentine Baker – was unable to take on the role, partly because his wife and daughter had recently died, and also because he had been convicted of sexually assaulting a young woman and had left the country.[33]

Instead, Lizzie found an alternative carer for her son in Fred's private secretary, an ambitious young man called James Percival Hughes. However, it was legally complicated to appoint a new guardian when the official one was still living, so the family found an unconventional solution. James and Lizzie's mother – Lady Alice Hawkins-Whitshed, twenty-four years older than James, and from a very different social background – married in secret. The marriage meant that James, as the husband of one of Harry's official guardians, could help look after Lizzie's son and also assist with managing the family's Irish estate – no doubt in return for healthy remuneration. Once the arrangement had been finalised, Lizzie returned to Switzerland, where she rekindled her relationship with John Main and married him at the British embassy in Berne on 17 March 1886.[34]

John was no mountaineer (Lizzie complained that he did not possess 'an enthusiasm corresponding to my own' for adventure), and she did not climb much in the year of their marriage, nor the following year. Instead, the new couple moved from Davos to St Moritz and threw themselves into its social whirl: the balls, theatricals, dances, comedies and bazaars held at the Kulm and nearby hotels. John gave public lectures on mathematics, astronomy and ice. Lizzie helped to set up an English-language newspaper for tourists, and a charity, which was designed to assist individuals who needed to escape the pressures of modern life, but lacked her own wealth. She called her charity the 'St Moritz Aid Fund', to which predominantly 'male applicants' whose 'nerves and general health have suffered from overwork' – like John and her father – could apply to pay for travel, accommodation and medical treatment in the Engadin.[35]

Lizzie was also nurturing a love for photography, which she put to the benefit of the St Moritz Aid Fund, selling prints to raise money. She had started experimenting with photographing landscapes a couple of years earlier, in Chamonix, and now she wanted to learn how to do it all, 'developing, printing, etc., of an exposure'. She set up 'a dark room tent in my bedroom' in her hotel and, every evening, she tinkered with developing solutions and chemical baths. She used the collodion process to expose coated glass plates to the light

A particularly exquisite example of one of Lizzie's many landscape photographs: of the view from Alp Grüm, in the Swiss canton of Graubünden

and bring out ghostly images from them onto paper coated with egg white and salt.[36]

Many men were less critical of the idea of women's photography than of women's mountaineering. Photography arguably depended on 'feminine' skills such as composition and fine precision in focusing lenses and mixing solutions, rather than 'manly' brute strength and endurance. Even the male-only Alpine Club in Britain began to cater for female visitors at its photographic exhibitions in the 1880s. (In December 1885, it introduced electric lighting to allow women to inspect the photographs closely, without risk of their feathered hats being ignited by naked candle flames.) But the idea of women combining photography with mountaineering was more clearly strenuous and therefore problematic. Writing about the mid nineteenth-century Californian landscape photographer Eliza Withington, art historian Katherine Manthorne comments that 'it was almost unheard of' for a woman 'to travel alone in remote areas, conveying heavy equipment and necessary chemicals, finding her subjects without pictorial precedents to guide her'. And although the Alpine Club was prepared to display Lizzie's prints at its exhibitions, it seems to have done so anonymously.[37]

As with her mountaineering, many of the pleasures that Lizzie found in photography were related to being a woman. Photography gave her a way of capturing the complexity of the shifting scenery around the Engadin and it vastly improved her topographical knowledge, filling in gaps in her otherwise poor education. It also seems to have helped Lizzie to rid herself of her self-consciousness, her discomfort at being watched, and allowed her to become an observer in her own right. And, like mountaineering, it was an opportunity to engage in the world of work.

Under her new married name – Mrs Main – Lizzie began writing articles for British and American magazines illustrated with her own photographs. She provided images for other mountaineering writers too, and joined the Royal Photographic Society in Britain, sending prints to art exhibitions around the country. She was conscious of the role that photography could play in recording and protecting particular communities, and she may well have encountered the work of the North American landscape photographers William H. Jackson and Mary Jacobson, who used photography to document places and cultures – such as Yellowstone National Park, and the Mission San José on the San Antonio River in Texas – as part of campaigns for preservation.[38] Before long, Lizzie would be using her photographic skills to capture the personalities that populated her new life in the Engadin. Did she sense that the lifestyle there, in which women were relatively free in the outdoors, was fragile and in need of protection, like the landscapes that Jackson and Jacobson were memorialising?

Lizzie's own personal situation turned out to be more vulnerable than she had realised. On 22 October 1887, when the winter season began again in St Moritz, the English-language newspaper announced that Lizzie and John were resident at the Kulm, accompanied by Harry, who was now seven. But in the first week of November, John abruptly left and, seven weeks later, he and his sister boarded the *Britannic* steamer in Liverpool and docked in New York City on Christmas Eve. The *St Moritz Post* euphemistically reported that John was 'acting on the urgent advice of his doctors'. However, Lizzie did not go after him. Following his departure, she stopped calling herself 'Mrs John Main' and destroyed all photographs of him. Consequently, very few records of John's life and no images of him have survived, and many years later, even in her autobiography (in which she devotes *seven* chapters to Fred), she would not refer to her second husband once – despite the fact that her fame was mostly consolidated during the period in which she used his surname.[39]

Why had John left? Perhaps he was jealous of Lizzie's success; perhaps he missed his family. Maybe the differences between his and Lizzie's backgrounds were too great and John became tired of what even Lizzie affectionately derided as the 'smart dresses and idle gossip' of the St Moritz elite. She may have taken some of this criticism on board: her first action after John's departure was to send away her maid, and from then on she would mostly travel alone. Lizzie seems to have been subdued for the rest of the winter, and when the Kulm put on its annual fancy-dress ball in January, she went dressed as an icicle.[40]

As the snows melted in the early summer, Lizzie was struck by the sight of avalanches resting 'still unmelted in many high-lying Alpine valleys', and the fallen 'mass of winter snow'.[41] Her second marriage, like her first, had quickly come crashing down to earth, and four and a half years after John's departure, in May 1892, Lizzie, at the age of thirty-one, became a widow for the second time.

On arrival in America, John and his sister Catherine joined his cousin Clarissa and aunt Sarah Ann. Clarissa's baby son had been born while John was in Switzerland, and she had won her case against the baby's father and been awarded $10,000 in damages. After John and Catherine docked in New York, the party of four travelled across the United States together for a new life in Denver, Colorado, which was enjoying a boom in silver-mining and offered tantalising opportunities for those 'in search of wealth and health'. John drew on wealthy contacts he'd made back in Bristol and used their investments to establish a bank. It was a success – original shareholders quickly made a 24 per cent profit – and John then moved onto a new scheme: buying land in Buffalo Creek Park, Golden, fifteen miles from the centre of Denver, on which to build and run 'hotels [and] sanitaria . . . of all kinds' – no doubt drawing on his personal experience of luxury hotels and health tourism in Switzerland. But around Christmas 1891, John exhibited 'symptoms of paralysis'. The following spring, he contracted scarlet fever and the paralysis was 'revived in a more malignant form'. He died on 10 May 1892, aged thirty-seven. John's will divided his estate between his sister and his estranged wife, but Lizzie refused her share.[42]

In the wake of John's departure and death, Lizzie discovered that, in St Moritz, 'in moments of need the undercurrent of kindness becomes visible, and the tenderest, most united family could not furnish a better example of how to treat one of its stricken members than does this winter colony'. After around six months following John's exit from the Engadin, she gradually felt able to throw herself into Engadin's social world once more, and it is around this time that she began to document the resort and its sporting women in earnest.[43]

St Moritz's community functioned a little like a salon, such as the famous Thursday parties that would be hosted in 1910s London by Lizzie's younger cousin Ottoline Morrell, which inspired 'an exciting feeling of liberty' and 'a new set of rules of behaviour'. Many of St Moritz's residents in the 1880s and 1890s were intellectuals and aesthetes: writers, artists, musicians, philosophers, playwrights, journalists and actors, and almost all of them were in flight from the social conventions of home and were searching for various kinds of emancipation. Throughout the 1880s, the German philosopher Friedrich Nietzsche holidayed in Sils Maria, seven miles outside St Moritz, and lunched every day at the Alpenrose Hotel on steak and macaroni, with an occasional glass of beer. He gathered around him 'a levée . . . of intelligent female company' – perhaps including Lizzie, and certainly involving her friend and future collaborator, the writer and translator Helen Zimmern. Among the Engadin's outdoor tourists, there was also an upper-class British clique known as 'The Souls' – an aristocratic cult of around three dozen friends who, between 1888 and 1895, had a reputation for intellectualism, esoteric conversation and (relatively) egalitarian relationships between men and women.

Other visitors came from the theatrical world: an industry that, in both America and Britain, was famous for allowing women to stand 'on a footing of absolute equality with a man', as the actor Kate Claxton put it in 1894. In St Moritz, everybody seemed to be in costume or disguise: women among the smart set of European nobility went out in public behind a screen of veils and Lizzie photographed Arthur Conan Doyle 'admirably got up as a Viking' as he stumbled out of a fancy-dress ball in the early hours of the morning.[44]

St Moritz's guests pursued unconventional sex lives, hoping to avoid notoriety. Those whose divorces, affairs and remarriages had caused scandal back home – such as the politician Hugo Charteris, Lord Elcho, who visited the resort with his mistress Hermione Fitzgerald, the Duchess of Leinster – found greater permissiveness, or simply indifference, for their behaviour. The explorer Richard Burton – who had published the Kama Sutra in English and formed a private society for the circulation of illegal books – holidayed at the Maloja Hotel in 1890 and dined and drank with Lizzie. Burton was accompanied that year by his friend, the explorer Henry Morton Stanley, who was travelling with his servant, a young man from Zanzibar called Saleh bin Osman. Historian Brian Murray has discovered that Saleh was a 'seasoned traveller' in his own right and, in his own account of his travels, Saleh mentions visiting Switzerland with Stanley – but he does not explicitly say whether he climbed and rambled there. If he did – which seems possible; likely even – was he the first Black mountaineer in the Alps?[45]

One of Lizzie's closest friends was the gay novelist and figure-skater Edward Frederick Benson (E. F. Benson), who later shared a villa with the pianist and classical scholar John Ellingham Brooks on the Italian island of Capri – which, like St Moritz, was famed for being 'a hedonistic dreamland, a place where the rules do not apply'. She also found a close friend in Countess Marie Larisch, who had been shunned from Austria after acting as a go-between for Crown Prince Rudolf and his mistress, her friend Baroness Mary Vetsera. The affair had ended in violent tragedy when, in 1889, Rudolf shot Mary dead and killed himself, and Marie Larisch had had to flee to

Munich, where she divorced her husband and married the baritone of the Munich Opera, Herr Otto Brucks. Marie and Otto holidayed annually in St Moritz. In his 1922 poem *The Waste Land*, T. S. Eliot would quote from a conversation with Marie about a childhood sled ride she had enjoyed at the estate of her cousin, the archduke, in which she discovered, 'In the mountains, there you feel free.'[46] That same sentiment was shared by most of St Moritz's guests.

Lizzie certainly found greater personal freedom in the Engadin than she had ever experienced in Ireland or England. She attended lunch parties in the woods, dinners, dances, lectures and fancy-dress balls, played parlour games and continued to help out on what she called 'the local English rag'. She may even have had casual sexual encounters: after John's death, there were rumours of a fling with the mountaineer Harold Ward Topham and she became very close to a young man called Edward Lisle Strutt, who had been introduced to mountaineering by his family's governess, Beatrice Tomasson (who would later make the first ascent of the south face of the Marmolada, long considered the hardest climb in the Alps).[47] But mostly Lizzie threw herself into sport, which was the most common way for women to find emancipation in the mountains.

In both summer and winter (when the snow and ice had to be scraped off the courts), Lizzie and her friends played and watched lawn tennis, and in August 1895 Lizzie made it to the women's singles final of the first Swiss Lawn Tennis Championship (where she lost to Countess Paulina von Pálffy, who, the previous year, had beaten the male player Károly Demény to win the singles trophy of Hungary's Lawn Tennis Championships outright). Lawn tennis had emerged in the early 1870s in the grounds of English country houses and was transported by tourists to the United States, where wealthy Staten Islanders and New Englanders began to trace out courts on their lawns. Across both continents, players' priorities were usually social rather than competitive and they mostly played in mixed doubles teams. In June 1884, the tennis magazine *Pastime* quoted an earlier journalist who had noted how both sexes enjoyed opportunities for physical proximity while playing, 'exhibiting their social charms . . . in flirtation for their partners'. Men appreciated being able to move in expressive, dance-like ways and women developed self-worth, vigour, health, accuracy and competitiveness. Like mountaineering, early lawn tennis was said to appeal to mavericks and misfits of an intellectual and artistic persuasion: particularly those wanting to try out different ways of being men and women, in non-standard models of relationships.[48]

In the warmer months, Lizzie sailed, rowed and punted on Lac Léman (Lake Geneva) or the Rhône river, and these sports were also more female-friendly than is perhaps commonly known today. There is evidence of (upper-class) women rowing as early as 1493, when a regatta of fifty women was organised to mark the Italian Renaissance princess Beatrice d'Este's visit to Venice. Working-class women – 'rowing madams' or *roddarmadammer* – were almost entirely responsible for ferrying travellers and residents between the islands of Stockholm's archipelago, from the fifteenth century right up until the early 1900s. By the 1880s and 1890s in Europe and North America, water sports including canoeing, rowing, swimming and yachting were acceptable, even encouraged, for elite women and military wives. During a women's yachting contest in Portsmouth in 1885, a journalist reported that the competitors' skills deserved 'the admiration of many yachtsmen and others, and the hope was expressed that this was the beginning of a series of races of the kind'.[49]

In July 1895, Lizzie taught her friend Jeanette Holland how to cycle, and they took turns photographing one another wobbling around a grassed arena in St Moritz, in full skirts and boater hats. In the 1890s, women were enjoying what *Cycling* magazine called a 'rabid disease commonly known as cyclomania'. Through parks in and around London and New York, groups of women organised picnic rides, cycling games and fancy-dress bike parades and, in Britain, there were rumours that some women even preferred bikes to horses when fox-hunting. Cyclist and writer Hannah Ross has charted how modern cycling was born in 1885 when the Starley & Sutton Company in Coventry launched the Rover 'safety' bicycle, whose original model was designed for men but was soon followed by a women's bicycle, with a lower step-through frame and a chain guard to accommodate skirts and petticoats. What Lizzie referred to as her 'safety machine' – so-called because of the smaller wheels that reduced the likelihood of falls and head injuries compared to the lofty heights of the original penny-farthing bicycle – was an extraordinary success, adopted rapidly across western Europe, Australia and North America, especially in the cities of Copenhagen, Amsterdam and Toronto. By 1896, over 1.2 million bicycles were being made each year in the United States, and roughly a third of their owners were female.[50]

Lizzie first learned to cycle in England in the early 1890s, and she took her new bike by train and boat from London to Chur in Switzerland, where she then cycled the ninety-odd kilometres over the Julier Pass down into St Moritz. Lizzie found that her bicycle granted unprecedented independence. She used it to cycle to the beginning of climbs, instead of having to arrange hire of horses, mules or carriages, or slog long distances on foot. Sometimes alone, or with friends, she undertook cycling tours across the continent, stretching out over a week or two into months, and crossing 'all the Engadine passes'.

In March 1896, Lizzie set off on a three-month cycle tour through Switzerland, Italy, France and England, mainly with two new friends from St Moritz: tennis star Lottie Dod, who won the Ladies' Singles Championship at Wimbledon five times (for the first time at the age of fifteen – she is still the youngest ladies' singles champion), and Lottie's brother Tony, who seems to have developed a crush on Lizzie. Cycling allowed Lizzie to be self-sufficient and roam for hundreds of miles, carrying her own food and clothing and powered entirely by her own body. It was an emancipation that held particular meaning for women. Hannah Ross describes how the bicycle gave women 'freedom, mobility, autonomy and fearlessness' – even more so as the cost of the vehicles dropped and they became accessible to a wider demographic. The bicycle literally broadened women's horizons, enabling them to access educational, professional and civic opportunities and pleasures that had previously been out of reach. Over the following decades, British suffragettes such as Alice Hawkins (no relation to Lizzie's mother) would rely on their bicycles for their work, promoting upcoming meetings of the Women's Social and Political Union, staging rallies at factory gates and distributing campaign literature. The American women's rights activist Susan B. Anthony credited the bicycle with having 'done more to emancipate women than anything else in the world'.[51]

In the colder months in St Moritz, Lizzie spent days on local lakes that had frozen over, picnicking with friends and 'ice-boating' on frozen water (sailing on craft fitted with runners). She played bandy, a game that she described as 'hockey on the ice', and curling, which must have reminded her of childhood winters at Kinnaird, when she had cheered on her grandfather Pippy on the frozen pond in Logierait Woods. And she learned to ice-skate, fuelled by a 'full share of cussedness' after a man dismissed her efforts, telling her 'however hard you work you will never be a skater!' Historian Mary Louise Adams explains that, during the 1880s and 1890s, the culture of ice-skating was changing away from being 'the almost exclusive pastime of aristocratic gentlemen', to becoming '*relatively* gender balanced'. This change was, in large part, precipitated by women, like Lizzie, who learned to skate

Women curling in Switzerland, c. 1896–7, likely photographed by Lizzie's friend Tony Dod. (This is perhaps the earliest known photograph of women curling in Switzerland)

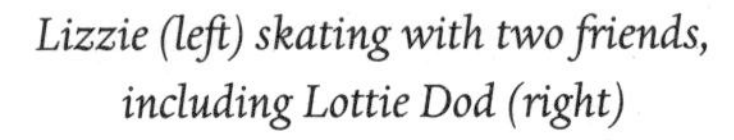

Lizzie (left) skating with two friends, including Lottie Dod (right)

A female rider zipping down the Cresta Run, with her skirts fastened down for greater speed and safety

in winter resorts, and by the visibility of elite female skaters such as virtuoso and future Olympic champion Madge Syers. One commentator thought that 'ladies not only skate as well as men, but . . . they are the better skaters . . . Their lack of physical muscularity, so far from being a disability, is a positive advantage, and serves to enhance the quality of their skating, making it more feathery and less compact than that of the male skater.'[52] A distinct school of skating emerged at St Moritz, and was codified by Lizzie's friends Cecil Watson, James Holland and Edward Benson, who established a Skating Club and introduced exams to judge skaters' skill. At first, the tests were sex-segregated, and even though Lizzie passed the ladies' one easily, initially she was not permitted to take the men's test, which was harder and more prestigious. But she pushed for change and the gate-keepers relented, and on 3 January 1893 Lizzie became the first woman to pass the men's exam.[53] After two more women passed the male test, the St Moritz Skating Club abolished such sex segregation.

The defining winter sport of St Moritz – tobogganing – was also a mixed-sex activity in the latter decades of the nineteenth century. In 1884, a committee headed by the Kulm's owner Caspar Badrutt commissioned a specialist toboggan run, and a British visitor, Major

Lizzie's photograph of the three fastest women in the Ladies Grand National skeleton race, on the Cresta Run in 1895: Frances Gibson, and Cissy and Esther Saunderson

William Henry Bulpett, oversaw the construction of a three-quarter-mile run with a 500-foot drop; a gradient of 1 in 8; and sharp turns with names like 'Scylla' and 'Charybdis', 'Battledore' and 'Shuttlecock', and high banks to allow riders to tip as they cornered, as in modern cycling velodromes.

Tobogganists zipped down the Cresta Run at speeds of around 120 kilometres per hour (75mph), head-first, lying on their stomachs, with thick leather pads on their knees and elbows and, on their feet, steel rakes – toe caps made of steel teeth – for guiding and braking the sleds or 'skeletons'. Nineteenth-century women were central to the tobogganing and bobsleighing worlds: it was mandatory for early bobsleigh teams to be mixed sex. Lizzie's friend Effie Bancroft was responsible for naming the Cresta's Battledore and Shuttlecock corners, and the latter referred to the vision of women travelling at high speed down the course, their skirts billowing. (Sometimes women strapped down their skirts, so as not to be slowed by the wind.)[54]

Lizzie deliberately recorded the names of these super-fast women, who included the American socialite Ava Willing, Frances Gibson (a talented hockey player too, who would work as the Dublin correspondent of *Christian Science Monitor*) and Barbara McLaren (who would be awarded an OBE for welfare work in Cairo during the Second World War). In February 1895, Lizzie photographed three winners of the ladies' competition of the 'Grand National' tobogganing competition. In the image, Frances Gibson and Cissy Saunderson stand upright, hugging their skeletons proudly, and Esther Saunderson lies sideways on hers, staring at the camera, her rakes protruding.*

Men mostly accepted and welcomed women's involvement in the sport. In 1894, Harry Gibson – the brother of Lizzie's friends Frances and Violet (who would later attempt to assassinate Mussolini) – published a guide to *Tobogganing on Crooked Runs* with a chapter by an anonymous 'Lady Tobogganer' entitled 'Tobogganing for Ladies', and at least six illustrations by Lizzie. The *Alpine Post* granted almost equal space to its coverage of women's sports, and photographs of female prize-winners were hung alongside images of their male counterparts on the Kulm's walls.[55]

From the late 1880s, more portable photographic equipment became available and Lizzie bought an 'admirable . . . very light and quickly ready' camera – a Shew's Xit – and later a 'No. 1 Folding Pocket Kodak', which used film rather than glass plates. Faster exposures allowed her to experiment with photographing human subjects rather than static landscapes, especially people moving quickly.[56] This was savvy: she found that fellow guests in St Moritz were willing to pay handsomely for photographs of themselves executing high-speed turns on their toboggans or elegant sashays on skates, and she put the money into her St Moritz Aid Fund. The new technology also allowed Lizzie to preserve a snapshot of the sporting world at this historical moment. Her photographs progressed from blurred images of skirts careering around snowy bends to sharp

* Esther and Cissy Saunderson's mother, the Irish aristocrat Lady Rachel Saunderson, loved tobogganing so much that she named another daughter 'Cresta'.

A photograph of Lizzie in winter, perhaps c. 1892 or 1893, after an attempt to ascend Piz Morteratsch in the Bernina mountain range, probably taken with her own camera

silhouettes of female forms tilting on skates, stretching for serves in tennis and floating serenely on sun-drenched lakes. She captured women congregating under snow-laden firs, picnicking on benches and hunched over curling stones and brooms, walking dogs on glaciers, balancing on bikes and slogging up the rocky slopes of mountains, alpenstocks resting on their shoulders as they paused for breath. Lizzie occasionally posed for photographs too, and in one particularly striking portrait on the side of Piz Morteratsch in winter she looks warily – even sullenly – at the camera, her face and hand the only flesh visible beneath layers of thick black wool, scarves swathed around her head, her legs mostly obscured by knapsacks and snow shoes. Her camera bag rests in the snow a little out of reach, and there is a rope running between Lizzie and the photographer, who seems to have snatched the camera and surprised its owner. She does not look particularly happy at this role-reversal.

The type of liberation that women found in St Moritz's sports partly reflected the town's identity as a holiday destination and expat community. Researchers have found that, in the words of Stephen Clift and Simon Forrest, holidays often 'offer a liminal environment away from the constraints of home, which reduce inhibitions and provide increased opportunities for sex'. The emancipation available in St Moritz, specifically, was also related to tourists' upper-class status: their wealth and privilege gave them the means to escape a breed of social elite that, back home, was becoming more and more obsessed with convention. The opportunities for rule-breaking that *fin-de-siècle* St Moritz offered to women were felt to rest on Switzerland's reputation as a country 'where everyone is as good as everyone else, and Jack very nearly as good as his master' (although its apparent egalitarianism didn't extend to Swiss women, who wouldn't get the vote until 1971). But it is clear that as the end of century drew near, women's accepted place in the outdoors, 'on top of the world' in St Moritz, was not unique to that specific location, and that something similar was being experienced by sporting women everywhere.[57]

Around the world, women were finding similar opportunities for physical and social emancipation in outdoor sport and leisure, on courts, pitches, mountains and trails. In the last two decades of the nineteenth century, women and girls across Europe and North America took part in calisthenics and gymnastics classes, learned cricket in single-sex public schools, began playing in football matches, formed university boat clubs and rowing programmes, founded a women's golf union, established female athletics competitions, signed baseball contracts and achieved extraordinary feats of endurance – such as Nelly Bly, who became the first woman to travel around the world alone. As the century drew to a close, commentators reflected that women's significant 'share in the outdoor sports and amusements of the day' was a bellwether for exactly the same type of 'freedom and energy' and 'growth' that women were displaying elsewhere in the public sphere, in 'the serious business of life'. Between 1885 and 1900, the figure of the 'New Woman' – young, middle class, single, financially independent, politically engaged, set on equality with men – was overwhelmingly imagined to be an athlete; her enthusiasm for sport was a natural accompaniment to her 'strong, skilled and competitive' personality in general.[58]

But things were about to change.

When T. S. Eliot wrote about Lizzie's friend Marie Larisch feeling free in the mountains, he was looking back on this moment as the high point before a decline. *The Waste Land*'s narrator subsequently leaves the mountains to go south, where he finds, not freedom, but dead trees, dry stone, red rock, fear and dust.

In 1900, Lizzie too departed St Moritz and the mountains – and she was not the only woman to do so. At hotels across the Alps, Lizzie left behind albums and catalogues of hundreds of photographs. By the time they were recovered and identified around a century later, the world they depicted – a snapshot of what one journalist called women's 'strong force' in outdoor sport – was no longer a familiar sight.[59]

Now it is strangely jarring to see these photographs of happy, healthy, vigorous late nineteenth-century women – muscular, sweaty, rosy-cheeked athletes – who demolished the stereotype of pale and wan Angels in the House, afraid to show an ankle. What happened, I wonder, to drive Lizzie and women like her from the mountains and to make us forget that they were ever there at all?

Perhaps the best place to start, to understand this exodus, is to ask: what happens today to make women feel uncomfortable and unwelcome outdoors, and even drive us out completely? And were the same factors in play in Lizzie's time?

PART TWO

Loss

6.

Lockdown

In the months following the Welsh writing residency, I spend very little time at home in Yorkshire. For most of the autumn–winter term at the end of 2019, I travel the four-hour train route between Newcastle, where I teach creative-writing students and attend meetings, and London, where I work on this book in the British Library and the Alpine Club.

When I first arrive in London, I stay in a flat half a mile from where we used to live. I had dreamed about the city for so long that I'd forgotten it existed outside my imagination. Perhaps for the first time, I notice the purple-orange haze of the capital's light pollution at night. I walk to the park at the end of our old road, where I used to take our children every day, and I half-expect to see us all there, my daughters digging in the sandpit, while I sit on a bench with a coffee, chatting to friends or perhaps to my stepfather, who is visiting for the day. But, of course, we are not there, and instead there are other children digging and other mothers talking. I feel like Patrick Swayze's character in the film *Ghost*; unseen and unheard in my own home.

The next day, I make my first visit to the Alpine Club. I have exchanged a few emails with the librarian, Nigel, and although I am neither a member nor an Alpine mountaineer, he is happy for me to look at the library's collections about Lizzie. The Alpine Club is in a five-storey townhouse on a small turning in Shoreditch. Even though it moved here in 1991, it feels like a Victorian relic amid the digital marketing agencies, art project spaces, retro speakeasies and Veggie Pret A Mangers. Nigel buzzes the door open for me and I climb to the first floor, entering the library via a lobby festooned with black-and-white portraits of the Alpine Club's presidents since its foundation in 1857: almost entirely men. I'd imagined Nigel to be a posh weather-worn mountaineer of post-retirement age, but he is younger than me and speaks gently with a Leeds accent. He feels like an exile, 'like the only Yorkshireman in London, sometimes', he says with a half-smile. The library is more utilitarian than I was expecting, with high metal bookcases, only one table and a window looking out onto air-conditioning units; but it is warm and I have the space to myself. As soon as I sit down, Nigel offers to make me tea, and I am suddenly overcome with an urge to cry. I have been travelling for so long that there has been no opportunity for these small human kindnesses. I return to the Alpine Club almost every week between October and December and it is the place I most look forward to being.

At the end of the year, I run a Hardmoors trail marathon, which is a few metres shy of thirty-one miles and follows a long loop around the top of the North York Moors, taking in the mini-Matterhorn peak of Roseberry Topping twice. Everyone is full of festive bonhomie, running in Santa hats; marshals dole out stollen and mince pies at the checkpoints. But it is the end of the week during which my estrangement from my mother becomes permanent and, right from the off, my legs feel heavy and stiff.

I am slow on rocky descents anyway, but on the way down from Roseberry I cannot lift my feet clear of the hill's ruts and protrusions, and I stumble again and again, while a steady stream of runners gambol past. After around ten miles, the path rises steeply back up onto the moors and takes us into the face of a freezing, damp December wind. I come to a halt, exhausted. I am being continually overtaken, and – cold, wet, tired, uncomfortable on my own legs, with twenty miles still to go – I feel a lump forming in my throat and know what's going to happen. As I reach the checkpoint, a cheerful woman notes down my race number and asks me how it's going.

'I can't do it!' I snivel. 'I just – I just don't want to be on my own right now.'

She unfolds a camping chair from her car and I sit down. I know I am going to pull out – to 'DNF' – the acronym for 'Did Not Finish' that appears on race results tables for runners who couldn't make the distance – and I am both hating the event and hating myself for being unable to complete it.

Then a familiar voice calls, 'Rachel?' I pull down my hood and turn to look. It is Jayne, one of my very first running friends, whom I met during my first marathon around Osmotherley, back in 2017. She gives me a hug and I burst into tears on her shoulder.

'Oh dear, you're having a bad run,' she says. 'Let's just walk for a bit.'

We leave the checkpoint and walk and chat, and then we jog and chat, and finally we run and chat. The remaining twenty miles pass somehow, and we finish the race together in 7 hours and 2 minutes. It is fifteen minutes slower than my time the previous year, but in a few weeks I will learn that it was just – by only one or two minutes – fast enough to place me 'third female' across a whole series of Hardmoors marathon races I have completed this year. An engraved trophy cup will arrive in the post from the race directors Jon and Shirley. It will be the first sporting accolade I have ever won in my life, and I will be ridiculously proud of it.

This race makes me think differently about the West Highland Way race, though. That event starts to feel too far, both in its actual length of ninety-five miles and in its distance from York. I am at home so rarely anyway. I cannot imagine spending multiple weekends alone, travelling up to the Scottish Highlands to recce sections of the route in winter darkness. Something in me, a faint thread whose existence I had been suppressing since my stepfather's death, which is pulling me back towards Pete and my children, starts to tug. I let the enrolment deadline for the race ballot come and go, and do not enter.

Christmas, my first with no extended family, is pared down, and on New Year's Eve I try my hardest to fall asleep before the midnight celebrations. The previous year, I had woken on New Year's Day with a faint hangover and a profound sense of foreboding. That black dread had lasted for a full week, far beyond the hangover, and it had felt like the contemplation of imminent, traumatic death. I still have no way of rationalising the sensation, which I have felt only once in my life before, at the beginning of 2014, and I feel embarrassed about admitting to it. I do not really believe in the supernatural, nor in premonitions, yet I have twice experienced what can only be described as a prophetic terror which, in both cases, has been borne out. I am terrified about feeling something similar tomorrow, so while Pete sits up watching New Year's Eve television with our eldest daughter, I lie in bed, pretending I'm asleep while messaging a friend who is worrying about the reports of a 'pneumonia of unknown etiology' that has broken out in a city called Wuhan in China.

'I think this might be the big one,' she types.

'The big what?'

'Pandemic,' she replies. 'It's spreading so fast. Look at the curve of infections. It's exponential.'

I do not reply and turn to face the wall.

And the following day, I feel nothing at all.

A few weeks later, at the end of January, I am sitting up in bed one weekend morning, skimming race calendars for 2020 on my laptop, and alternating the window with news reports of cases of 'the novel coronavirus' that are multiplying across Asia and further afield now: Australia, Canada, Germany, Japan and the USA are evacuating nationals from Wuhan, and several airlines have suspended flights to China. The World Health Organization declares the outbreak 'a Public Health Emergency of International Concern'.

I flick back to the race calendars. There is an event advertised for August along the eighty-two-mile length of the Dales Way, from Bowness-on-Windermere in the Lake District down to Ilkley in West Yorkshire, traversing almost the entire vertical span of the Yorkshire Dales National Park in one go. I could recce the route easily from York, and the idea of running through the Dales in soft summer light is so much more appealing than the rain and midges of the West Highland Way. I click on 'enter' and pay and feel better: I have a structure again, a plan for recovery from grief.

Soon after I enter to run the Dales Way Challenge, I am out on a short training run along the river near our house and notice that a hotel at the end of our road is cordoned off by ambulances and medical staff in hazmat suits. The local newspaper later quotes the leader of the city council confirming that two hotel residents, who have been taken to a hospital up in Newcastle, were 'the first two confirmed cases of coronavirus in the UK'. That weekend, another journalist reports that 'shoppers and tourists [are] packing York city centre – with hardly a face mask to be seen'. 'It seems to be business as normal,' he concludes.

Six weeks later, on 18 March, I am back in London, among the steel shelves of the Alpine Club library. I am drinking tea and leafing through G21, the library's classification of 'Newspaper cuttings relating to women's mountaineering 1908–75'. My phone buzzes with a notification from a national newspaper: 'UK schools to be closed indefinitely and exams cancelled'. I open the link and screenshot it. I want to preserve this moment, to halt time for a split-second while we teeter on the cusp of unknown change. I read the headline aloud to Nigel. He raises an eyebrow: 'The Alpine Club will never close. Even through a nuclear winter, we'd stay open.'

Still, I think it might be the last time I'm here for a while. I stop taking notes from G21, and start photographing – correspondence, mountaineering booklets, press cuttings, scrapbooks. I take 178 photographs. I feel like a crazed game-show contestant, sweeping stacks of pages from the library's shelves into my phone's memory, before the timer stops and the library shuts and I take my haul back to Yorkshire, for who knows how long.

Five days later, the prime minister addresses the nation: we must stay at home, all of us. As he speaks, my inbox fills with emails that empty out my diary. A five-day creative-writing course I had been organising is cancelled; so too a festival celebrating 'lost voices' in nature-writing. A trip I had planned to St Moritz, to go in search of the photograph albums that Lizzie left behind her, will not happen now. Races are called off, including a three-day running and camping event in the Lake District and, I notice, the West Highland Way ultra too. Neither my stepfather's memorial service, in Cambridge on his birthday, nor a conference organised to commemorate my father's work, can happen. But the Dales Way race still appears to be going ahead.

In this new coronavirus world, the newspapers report how 'that discomfort you're feeling is grief'. A man introduced as the 'foremost expert on grief' tells us that the 'loss of normalcy; the fear of economic toll; the loss of connection' during lockdown is coupled with 'anticipatory grief': 'that feeling we get about what the future holds when we're uncertain'.[1] I read it and feel at odds. This is perhaps the first time since losing my family that my grief has palpably diminished: suddenly everyone is estranged from their families; I am no longer unusual and I have no elderly parents to worry about losing. I have my husband Pete and three young healthy children, a demographic which seems mostly safe, and I am confident, for now, in my own body's resilience. I know how this goes, I think; this period of stripping away and hunkering down.

Then a friend's sister-in-law is hospitalised. Another friend's mother-in-law dies. Pete's childhood friend – a young woman with learning disabilities – dies suddenly and inexplicably and will later be found to have contracted Covid-19, the name that has been given to the disease. An old university friend, younger than me and a runner too, catches the virus and does not recover and will be bedbound for years to come. A self-employed friend worries about his business. A chronically ill colleague is told to shield and will not feel comfortable leaving the house for well over a year. A friend with health anxiety has a breakdown.

I realise that everyone is grieving, not just for the loss of normality, but for the loss of health and loved ones and livelihoods and ease while moving around public spaces. Almost everyone I know feels themselves to be at the centre of grief's concentric circles, alone at the top of the mountain, and so there is no one left further down for anyone to lean upon. How on earth will we all recover from this?

After a few days of lockdown, I am desperate to go outdoors. In England, guidelines allow us to leave the house for 'one form of exercise a day', and there are no official stipulations about distance or duration. I run alone in the evenings, after the children have gone to bed, and I watch how people behave now that there are fewer of us around and our proximity to one another is fraught with the danger of contagion. I watch how solitary walkers approaching one another veer apart as they get closer, as if magnetically repelled, and only return to the path when they're at a safe distance. I watch a runner fixing his eyes on a point two metres ahead and failing to give way to a pedestrian who, tutting, hops into the verge as he passes. A mother tries to shepherd her three children to one side of the path, to allow a cyclist to pass with plenty of space. Further along, a middle-aged man yanks his female partner's arm to pull her out of the way of the cyclist, who is coming up behind. Five or six walkers glance angrily from the side of the path at a young couple who sashay through, hand in hand, eyes locked, oblivious to the dance going on around them. A teenage girl treads slowly, headphones in ears, her eyes fixed downwards onto a mobile phone in her hand. Another runner swerves and slaloms around other walkers, and cheerfully cries out 'Thanking you!' to a man who steps back to let him pass and then nods his head in recognition.

I think too about the people who are not in the park. I live close to a block of sheltered accommodation for people with disabilities, but today there is nobody here in a wheelchair, and nobody elderly.

Politicians start using the phrase 'social distancing' to encourage us to put at least two metres, or six feet, between ourselves and other members of the public, to slow the virus's transmission. This edict has the effect of exaggerating the balletic manoeuvres we all make, every day in usual times, as we pass one another on foot, or on bikes, wheelchairs, skateboards, pushchairs, scooters and roller-skates. It enlarges the ducks and swerves, the giving-way and ploughing-through, which are part of the repertoire of moves we all make, often semi-consciously, on pavements and paths, to prevent collisions between ourselves and other passers-by. Now these shifts and dodges are magnified over a much larger range and are weighted with much greater consequence than usual.

Grief heightened my own personal sensitivity to ways in which I feel intimidated or out of place outdoors – and now lockdown is heightening *everyone's* sensitivity to the dynamics that shape our movements around public space. It feels like a momentous point in time, an abrupt end to freedoms I had taken for granted.

The term 'social distancing' was first used in relation to Covid-19 in the USA in mid January 2020 and became the official Center for Disease Control strategy by mid March. In the UK, the government first published a 'What is social distancing?' explainer the same month. But the phrase is much older. It was used in the nineteenth century to refer to the way that social class, and the degree of power that accompanies it, establishes physical distance between people.

Around 1830, Louis Antoine Fauvelet de Bourrienne wrote in his memoirs about seeing his old friend Napoleon Bonaparte enter a room after conquering Venice over three decades earlier: 'His position placed too great a social distance [*distance sociale*] between him and me not to make me feel the necessity of fashioning my demeanour accordingly.' Writer and artist Lily Scherlis describes how the phrase was often used in the United States to refer to the way in which 'practices of white supremacy' continued after the abolition of slavery, as white people tried to keep Black people out of 'their' spaces: 'In 1850, an abolitionist British Baptist church condemned US whites for "keeping your most injured brethren in Christ at so great a social distance."'[2]

In this context, 'social distancing' was the forerunner of a term coined by cultural anthropologist Edward T. Hall in the 1960s: *proxemics*. Hall defined proxemics as 'the inter-related observations and theories of humans' use of space as a specialized elaboration of culture'. That is, proxemics analyses how humans' movements around space are shaped by, and enforce, social differences such as power.[3] I think back to the male runner who pushed me off the path a few months after Willy died, and I wonder if proxemics are gendered: do men and women move differently around public space? How do the behavioural dynamics between men and women in public space affect women's ability to be free outdoors? This seems to be an important issue that makes women feel uncomfortable in public space, and I suspect that thinking carefully about similar factors might help me to understand both Lizzie's exit from the mountains and the deterrents to women's outdoor sport today.

In the 1970s, social psychology researchers built on Hall's ideas about proxemics by observing and measuring people as they made their way around city spaces. They did indeed find that men and women move in very different ways. Men were seen to walk faster and more powerfully, and to hold their course despite risk of collision. Women's routes, on the other hand, were more circuitous and more likely to be 'perturbed' – diverted or stopped – by approaching obstacles: either by people, by traffic or by static obstacles like signs or bollards. Across the world, male pedestrians expect that others will clear the way, and their expectations are usually met. In a 2001 study in Amman, the capital of Jordan, drivers were readier and faster to stop at pedestrian crossings for men rather than for women.[4] In the USA and UK, numerous studies from the 1970s to the present day show that women spend more time scanning pavements for other pedestrians and obstacles, and that women are more likely to attend to assumed rules of social movement (i.e. walking within lines drawn on pavements or roads).[5] Male pedestrians are more likely to engage in 'risk-taking behaviour' – walking out into traffic, crossing roads at pedestrian red lights and jay-walking – and male drivers are more likely to exhibit road rage and aggression to women (including female pedestrians) than the other way around. Researchers also find that there are differences in the amount of space granted to men and women on the streets. Passers-by (both male and female) are repeatedly seen to give male pedestrians wider berths than are granted to female pedestrians, possibly because men command more fear and respect. This is also the case at bus stops and at ATMs, where in Ankara, Turkey, in 1999, men waiting to use the cash machine encroached upon waiting women's personal space far more than they did to other men, or than women did to men or women.[6]

Women's personal space outdoors is 'crowded' more often and to a much greater extent than men's personal space: our right to be left alone is not respected to the same degree. In one social psychology study, different researchers sidled up beside individuals out walking, and measured the amount of time it took for the walkers to bolt. The quickest departure was by women when they were approached by unknown males, and they took off much faster than when men were approached by other men or women, or when women were approached by female strangers.[7]

More recent work has focused on how *groups* behave outdoors. Researchers find that groups of women take up much less space on the pavement than equivalent groupings of men. In an outdoor, large-scale version of 'manspreading', men tend to scatter more across pavements and parks – perhaps because they are less comfortable with intimate proximity, but perhaps also because men are more confident in taking up larger areas of public space. And groups of men are also less likely than female groups to be permeated by other pedestrians walking through them. This reflects men's power as a 'high status group', writes social psychologist Eric S. Knowles. Psychologist John R. Aiello further found that, when groups of women feel threatened, they expand the space taken up by their group on the pavement, confirming the idea that taking up space represents the shoring up of power. The lack of space typically granted to women outdoors underscores our status as a 'low status group'. 'Social power is the ability to move others, spatially or otherwise,' conclude the social psychologists James Dabbs Jr and Neil Stokes, and women have less of it than men.[8]

Running in lockdown, and watching the movements of my fellow pedestrians, illuminates these dynamics for me. I realise how women's experience of moving around the streets is one in which we are made to feel powerless and at risk on a daily basis.

On 28 May, the prime minister addresses us again, from the television screen. We will shortly go into 'Phase 2' of lockdown, and people from different households will be able to meet outdoors, in groups of no more than six. I invite three friends to our garden for evening wine, and right on cue the weather breaks and rain is forecast every day for the next two weeks. Nevertheless, small and not-so-small freedoms are opening up. The younger two of my three children are allowed back to school, and a few hours of writing each day becomes a possibility.

It feels like I have not written anything for months. But others clearly have. Colleagues at work begin a research newsletter, to document and share the 'research successes' that we are enjoying during lockdown. On 30 June, a publishing industry magazine reports that 'as authors have more time . . . their writing timeline is accelerating in lots of cases, helping speed up the publishing process'.

It also seems that lots of people are spending lockdown exercising. Usage of the exercise app MapMyRun doubles and of Strava, the running and cycling tracking service, trebles. Between March and June 2020, the 'Couch to 5K' app is downloaded 92 per cent more times than during those months the previous year. One of the largest online fitness stores sells 218 per cent more trainers, 243 per cent more running clothing and 268 per cent more running accessories than in the equivalent period in 2019. World Athletics president Seb Coe tells the Asian Athletics Federation that the world is seeing an 80 per cent increase in exercise, and he is buoyant about the future implications for sport.[9]

But women do not seem to be equally sharing this burst of activity. Sport England conducts a study showing that, contrary to the good-news stories, 42 per cent of women experience a *drop* in exercise levels during lockdown. Multiple newspapers start publishing reports showing that women's sport is being ' "left behind" during the pandemic': while boys' and men's training facilities remain open, clubs, programmes and competitions for women and girls close. In a retrospective analysis, the *Telegraph* online will find that 'women's sport has lost 664 more days than men's during the pandemic'. My own research network shows that, at all times during the pandemic, men were more likely than women to be active, and that, out of people whose activity levels fell during lockdown, it will take longer for women to return to exercise than men, especially women with children. This is partly because of women's greater caring responsibilities: for instance, 32 per cent women surveyed said they 'could not prioritise doing exercise during lockdown as they had too much to do for others'. But it is also because women proportionately engage more with *indoor* sport and exercise than men (such as running and cycling in gyms and at velodromes, in large part because of fear of male violence outdoors), and those indoor facilities closed during the pandemic. Women are also more likely to feel comfortable running outdoors only with friends or in club runs, and those possibilities, too, are temporarily ended during lockdown. Sports sociologist Ali Bowes publishes an article suggesting that the pandemic may have brought an end to the 'progress narrative' and 'upward trajectory' of contemporary women's participation in sport.[10] We may be at a turning point, at which the expansion of women's freedoms outdoors is peaking and going into retreat.

A similar gender gap applies to the explosion in writing and research. David Samuels, co-editor of the *Comparative Political Studies* journal, reports that submissions from male academics were up almost 50 per cent in April 2020, after a month of lockdown. But in the same period, Elizabeth Hannon, deputy editor of the *British Journal for the Philosophy of Science*, is astounded to find that there has been 'a negligible number of submissions to the journal from women in the last month. Never seen anything like it,' she says. Megan Frederickson, an ecologist at the University of Toronto, Canada, looks at the wider statistics for journal submissions across North America and finds that 'women's publishing rate has fallen relative to men's amid the pandemic'.[11] The effects will last: two years later, journal editors will feel embarrassed about the fact they are publishing issues without *any* contributions from women at all.

The 'second shift' was coined by sociologist Arlie Russell Hochschild in 1989 to describe the domestic labour that working women fit around their paid work. Uniquely capable of childbearing and breastfeeding, women have historically undertaken the bulk of caring, cooking, cleaning and coordinating households. As the workplace began to open up to women during the latter half of the twentieth century, we took on more professional roles on top of our labour in the home – but men did not take on a proportionate amount of domestic responsibility to equalise the situation. A report by the Pew Research Center found that, in the USA in 2011, men were spending six hours more per week on domestic labour than they had done in 1965, but women were still spending eight hours per week more than men (eighteen hours per week in total) on chores. And in 2016, researchers from the University of Oxford found that the narrowing of the gender housework gap has slowed in recent years; since the 1990s in fact. As journalist and writer Oliver Burkeman puts it: 'Men, it seems, conceded that they should be doing more than before – but then, having half-heartedly vacuumed the living room and passed a dampened cloth over the dining table, concluded that it was time for a nice sit-down.' In the UK in 2016, the Office of National Statistics reported that women still did almost 60 per cent more unpaid work than men, and even in relatively gender-egalitarian Sweden, women spend around forty minutes more than men each day on domestic tasks.[12]

All of this erodes the time available to women for leisure – and everything that goes with it, such as relaxation, re-energisation, the development of a wider variety of interests and strengths, and respite from all forms of labour. 'Just as there is a wage gap between men and women in the workplace,' Hochschild wrote, 'there is a "leisure gap" between them at home.' In the UK in 2018, men enjoyed five hours more leisure time per week than women, and that gap is growing. Women's ability to enjoy leisure (or, for that matter, anything) in uninterrupted peace is further undermined by what French graphic artist 'Emma' calls the 'mental load': the constant 'to-do' list of bill-paying, playdate-organising, present-buying, school-cake-sale-baking, children's-dentist-appointment-making, pet-flea-treatment-applying, form-filling, packed-lunch-making and so on, which ticks over constantly in the background of our attention, like some malevolent malware taking up our bandwidth.[13]

Women's ability to move freely and comfortably outdoors is eroded not just by displays of male power that eat into our space on the pavement, but by this persisting idea of 'separate spheres' which sees the indoor world of the home as women's natural domain, and the outdoors – with its opportunities both for leisure and for work, and everything they entail – as the realm of men. When women's time and energy are exploited by men's refusal to take on their share of domestic responsibility, our time to ramble, run and climb is eaten away. When women's disposable income is whittled away by the gender pay gap and by our greater likelihood of footing the bill for children's and household items, we have less to spend on our own outdoor projects. When women are denied equal visibility in sporting competitions, awarded inferior prize money and sponsorship, and excluded from networking opportunities at sports clubs, it has knock-on effects on women's power and status in public life. This reinforces my growing understanding that sport is not distinct from other activities in the public sphere, but that women's ability to participate in sport directly relates to how well we are treated in the world in general.

As summer dawns during 2020's first lockdown, I leave the house on 2 June for a run at five to eight in the evening, and jog my usual route, along the main road that runs outside our house, to a turning down towards the River Ouse. As I veer around the corner, a van drives past and beeps. I turn and a man leans out of the passenger window and yells: 'Nice legs!' I raise my middle finger and he shouts again – 'Fucking bitch!' – and falls back into his seat, laughing.

The global children's charity Plan International UK conducts a study around this time and finds that 'sexual harassment, including men indecently exposing themselves, has become worse during the lockdown'. Women runners report finding that 'lockdown . . . makes running alone more scary' because, with fewer people out on the streets, men seem to be less inhibited in their harassment. One woman tells me how, during 'lockdown when everyone really stayed in, my sister was running round a secluded bit of a large park and a man literally pulled a balaclava on to follow her'. Another describes being 'harassed by workmen who stopped their car at a traffic light who said they'd like to give me "boner virus" '. A third explains how 'I lost my love of running after being forced off the road so many times by men in white vans purposefully driving at me and pulling away at the last second. The roads were so empty. This happened 4 times before I packed [it] in.'[14]

Abuse has always been the backdrop to my running. Over the last five years, I've been surrounded by men on mopeds chanting 'Cunt! Cunt! Cunt!'; I've had cigarette smoke deliberately blown into my face, been spat at, tripped up, lunged at, my path blocked and been on the receiving end of catcalls, honks and heckles ('You look like a paedophile in those leggings!'; 'Can't you run faster than that?'; and the tedious old chestnut, 'Give us a smile, luv!'). I have been followed at least five times while running (and more times besides). One man jogged beside me, trying to coerce me into conversation, for almost a mile, and only fell back when I picked up speed. Another was more sinister. Dressed in black non-running clothes, he was walking when I passed him. He then pulled up his hood and broke into a fast, silent, unsmiling run behind me, and was set to catch me up as I approached a dark park. I evaded him only by ducking into a stranger's driveway and pretending to knock at the door. Another time, a male pedestrian I had overtaken subsequently ran to catch me up and stayed within an arm's distance for the next ten minutes, until I reached a group of strangers and stopped to pretend to talk to them. Yet another time, I was running along a cycle path as it was getting dark and a male runner overtook me, and then, a hundred or so metres ahead, paused to let me go by. This pattern repeated four or five times, as he overtook, paused, caught up, overtook, paused, caught up – until I confronted him: 'What on earth are you doing?' 'It's fun to chase you,' he grinned back.

A survey conducted by *Runner's World* in the United States in 2017 found that 43 per cent of women runners say they've been harassed while running, rising to 58 per cent for the under-30s. This compares to only 4 per cent of male runners. In Spain, a survey of 2,500 women showed that 28 per cent of female runners had been verbally or physically abused while running, and 90 per cent said they felt insecure running alone.[15] And, when I ask on social media for women runners to share 'their experiences of harassment while running', the response I receive is staggering. I do not have many followers on Twitter, but my request is retweeted and nearly a thousand people reply within the first twenty-four hours: they are almost all women, with their own personal experiences of facing verbal abuse, obscene gestures, men flashing and masturbating at them, throwing objects, blocking their way, following them, touching, grabbing, groping and raping them. It is a picture which is overwhelming in its ubiquitous nature: a vast and horrifying mosaic of relentless attempts to drive women out of the outdoors.

The harassment faced by women runners, specifically, is a microcosm of the abuse that is experienced by all women outdoors. The term 'street harassment' was coined in 1981 by anthropologist Micaela di Leonardo to refer to this phenomenon: 'when one or more strange men accost one or more women . . . in a public place which is not the women's worksite. Through looks, words, or gestures, the man asserts his right to intrude on the women's attention, defining her as a sexual object, and forcing her to interact with him.' Street harassment is so prevalent that, for many people, it has become normalised and therefore seems easy to overlook. One US judge called it 'generally accepted behaviour [which is] too frequent for a justice system to handle' and he refused to prosecute cases of street harassment on that basis. It didn't even have a distinct legal or cultural label in print, and therefore no means of formally identifying and challenging it, until di Leonardo coined her terminology (based on language used in the 1970s' rape crisis movement) in *Aegis Magazine on Ending Violence against Women* in the US in the 1980s. And still, today, prosecution of street harassment often depends upon a legal benchmark known as the 'reasonable man' standard, or colloquially in Britain, 'the man on the Clapham omnibus'.[16]

Shockingly, this point of reference assesses the harms caused by men's behaviour by wondering whether a 'reasonable man' would find it offensive. The problem is that harassment is rarely levelled at men, reasonable or not – but at women. As legal scholar Cynthia Grant Bowman explains, 'although the reasonable man may not be placed in apprehension of receiving a battery by a stranger yelling, "Hey, cunt", the response of a reasonable woman may differ, because of her constant awareness of the violent consequences of male hostility to women and her realistic fears of rape'.[17] Despite their veneer of objectivity, rules and laws are still often biased towards men's experiences of the world, not women's – even when it comes to crimes perpetrated against women, on the basis of misogyny.

A 2014 study by social scientist Heather R. Hlavka found that 'objectification, sexual harassment, and abuse appear to be part of the fabric of young women's lives'. Girls described being 'harassed and assaulted at parties, in school, on the playground, on buses, and in cars' to the extent that they had come to see 'unwelcome touching and grabbing as normal, commonplace behaviors'. But boys and men do not expect their morning walks or runs to be disfigured by sexual violence and, although street harassment is frequent for women, that does not mean that it is innocuous. Excluding non-verbal forms of intimidation (honking; whistling; inarticulate noises), 65 per cent of women in the USA report having been harassed in public, rising to over 99 per cent when such noises are included. A 2021 study by UN Women UK found that '86 per cent of women aged 18–24 have been sexually harassed' in public.[18] A 2000 study in Egypt has the figure at 83 per cent, and in 2009 a survey in Sana'a, Yemen, found that 90 per cent of women had experienced street harassment. Of 811 women who spoke to Holly Kearl, founder of the USA's Stop Street Harassment campaign, 75 per cent reported having been followed by a stranger (and more than 27 per cent having been followed more than six times); 62 per cent having had their path blocked at least once by a man; nearly 57 per cent having been touched or grabbed in a sexual way by a stranger; more than 37 per cent having experienced a stranger masturbating at them, or in front of them, in public; and 27 per cent having been assaulted at least once by a stranger in public space. Some demographics are subjected to street harassment more often and/or in different ways than others. In US surveys, 'persons of color were more likely than white people to say they experienced street harassment sometimes, often, or daily', and in the San Francisco Bay area, 68 per cent of women of colour experienced sexually suggestive speech 'every day' or 'often' compared to 55 per cent of white women. LGBT people, especially lesbians, are particularly targeted, reporting a higher frequency of daily street harassment than heterosexuals. Men are less likely than women to be targeted by male harassers, and the most common form of harassment for men is homophobic slurs.[19]

All women and girls are potential victims of street harassment, but this is a problem that is caused almost entirely by men. Researchers conclude that 'men are overwhelmingly the harassers of both women and men'. In the aforementioned Egyptian study, 62 per cent of surveyed men admitted perpetrating harassment. Lone men are the most common perpetrators of street harassment against both women and men, followed by groups of men (then lone women, mixed sex groups, and, least common of all, groups of two or more women). Historically, street harassment has been associated with 'men who work on the streets . . . as delivery men, construction workers, or gardeners, etc. . . . or unemployed men', but recent research finds that 'age, education, and income show little relation to harassing behavior (although younger men tended to be more aggressive, and older men tended to lower their voices)'. The only characteristic that reliably determines propensity to perpetrate street harassment is maleness. When asked, 'Why do you do this?' some of the replies from men who have harassed women include, it 'alleviated boredom', and it was 'fun'. Some described how it established camaraderie with, or earned kudos from, other men. Many denied that it caused harm and protested that it was intended as a 'compliment', but 15 per cent of male respondents plainly stated that they intended to anger, humiliate or intimidate their victims.[20] Street harassment is a problem visited on women by men and, consciously or not, it claims the outdoors as a male domain and drives women back indoors.

What many women fear is that the men who follow us while we're running, who hurl insults, who wolf-whistle or beep at us, will rape and kill us. These do not feel like completely different crimes from noises and verbal intimidation. Many women experience street harassment as a spectrum of male violence which ranges from the first unsolicited intrusion into our right to be left alone, all the way up to femicide. Many of us have experienced how men's harassment can escalate. An initial catcall is followed by a cry of 'Fucking bitch! Think you're too good to reply to me?!' which leads to a man shadowing, grabbing or groping us. I think that men often *intend* their behaviour towards women to evoke the full range of this spectrum: much 'minor' harassment is designed to hint at much worse, to deliberately scare women. A man on a Reddit thread with the title 'Frightening girls' describes regularly following teenage girls on the street, especially at night, and enjoying watching how they run 'like a newborn fawn, turning around every so often, trying to see if I am still following'. (It is 'kind of a good feeling', he elaborates: 'you are no longer some random insignificant face in the crowd'.)[21]

Such men know full well that women anticipate this behaviour escalating into violence – that's the whole point – but they're also protected by the seemingly innocuous nature of the intimidation in its own right. Women are gaslit: we're told that it was 'only' a catcall; that 'we can't take a joke'; that our reactions are unreasonable; that our fears are irrational; that we've imagined the man following us, or the man rubbing his groin against us on a packed train. But we know we're not imagining it and we also know about the cases that prove that 'minor' harassment can escalate into rape and murder.

In the summer of 2016, over a horrifying nine days, three women runners in the United States were murdered. Alexandra 'Ally' Brueger was a thirty-two-year-old nurse who worked long hours at a hospital in Michigan to fund her dream of becoming a writer. She was killed in broad daylight during her daily ten-mile run, on Saturday 30 July. Karina Vetrano, aged thirty, was also an aspiring writer, who worked as a speech pathologist with children with autism, and described herself as a 'thrill seeker' and 'day dreamer'. Around 5 p.m. on Tuesday 2 August she was running in Spring Creek Park in Queen's, New York City, when she was attacked and killed by a man. On 7 August, Vanessa Marcotte was killed during a run in Princeton, Massachusetts, at around 2 p.m. She was twenty-seven years old, and worked at Google, where she was known 'for her ubiquitous smile, passion for volunteer work, and love of Boston sports'.

The murders of Brueger, Vetrano and Marcotte reflect a marked acceleration of violence against female runners. As I've already discovered, more women were murdered by men, while running outdoors, in the six years between 2016 and 2022 (at the time of writing), than in the twenty-eight years before. They include Mollie Tibbetts (studying child psychology at the University of Iowa), Wendy Martinez (a passionate advocate for women's rights, who worked for a tech company and had got engaged six days before her murder), Laura Luelmo (a twenty-six-year-old teacher, artist and caricaturist, whose last tweet was an illustration she'd made to celebrate International Women's Day), Carolina Cano (who taught Spanish at her local church's Sunday School, to which she was running), Suzanne Eaton (professor of molecular biology and a talented pianist with a black belt in taekwondo, who was out for a run during a conference in Greece), Sarmistha Sen (a clinical research manager specialising in cancer, and a trained singer of Indian classical music), Sydney Sutherland (a registered nurse in Newport, Arkansas, nicknamed 'Sassy'), Ashling Murphy (a twenty-three-year-old primary school teacher in Tullamore, Ireland) and Eliza Fletcher (a kindergarten teacher and mother in Memphis, Tennessee).[22]

Even street harassment that doesn't kill women harms us in a variety of ways. It reminds us that we are being watched all the time, and that our presence outdoors is considered to turn us into public property. It thwarts the prospect of ever entering into relaxed conversation with male strangers, as men might do. Random, gratifying encounters with unknown men are a trope of male travel literature and nature-writing, but women have much more complex, negative reactions to such interactions. The possibility of male violence withholds these chances from us. Street harassment also interrupts our solitary thoughts, daydreams and emotions: commands to 'give us a smile' take us out of our own mental and emotional worlds and instruct us to perform in someone else's instead. Shilpa Phadke, Sameera Khan and Shilpa Ranade describe how, in Mumbai, loitering on the streets and in parks gives men the freedom to chat and laugh, sharing knowledge, 'exchanging corporate notes or planning protest meetings', 'reflecting on world politics and dissecting the rising sensex [stock exchange]', all while having fun. But women cannot loiter outdoors safely without being considered men's property, and so we are deprived of these social, intellectual and professional opportunities.[23]

Different axes of oppression – race, age, sexuality, dis/ability – intersect in street harassment. Women of colour often experience street harassment as misogynoir – intersecting misogyny and racism. Feminist author bell hooks describes how men's harassment of Black women conveys 'the assumption that all Black women, regardless of their class, are prostitutes and available as sex objects'. Legal scholar Deirdre Davis points out how street harassment is a traumatic reminder of the 'institutional memory of slavery' and the implied contract that 'the slave owner had free sexual access to the slave woman'. For trans women and trans men, abuse can come from intersecting misogyny and transphobia, and for lesbian women, street harassment can inflict misogyny and homophobia. One lesbian woman described how 'it's hard enough coming out to your family and to yourself . . . Becoming conscious of who you are', and that 'to have someone on the street try to convince you against it' is a denial of the right to be left alone and 'the right to personality'.[24]

Street harassment deprives its victims of a fundamental civil and socio-economic right: the right to freedom, comfort and safety in public space, and therefore in public life. This is often the explicit intention. Feminist activist Pam McAllister defines 'the first function of public harassment' as 'clearly stak[ing] out public space as male space'. In ancient Greece, the *agora* was a public gathering place in which the city's commercial, political, social, judicial and religious activities occurred. Denial of Greek citizenship to slaves, women and foreigners was carried out via the prohibiting of access to the *agora*'s political activities. Street harassment today does something similar. Sociologist Jarrah O'Neill describes how it overtly constrains women's political participation. In the 2011 Occupy Wall Street protests in Zuccotti Park, New York City, a Tumblr blog was set up called *Hot Chicks of Occupy Wall Street* ('the sexy side of protesting corruption'), and the sexual objectification of female protesters was amplified by physical assaults: 'Zuccotti Park became the venue of several alleged rapes and incidents of sexual assault, eventually forcing the protesters to create a tent for women to spend the night in safely.'[25] On that occasion, harassment and violence were used to deter women from effective political action; one example of how the spectrum of male violence against women outdoors denies women the rights and freedoms of full citizenship.

Women resist these attempts to be driven out of public spaces in a multitude of ways. We try to ignore or play down the harassment, or possibly even persuade ourselves of its 'just being friendly' nature. We wear headphones to establish a protective barrier around ourselves, though not at night, when we need to be especially alert. We like sunglasses and, during the pandemic, face masks, for the same reason: to ward off attention and hide in plain sight. We fix our gaze on our mobile phone screens to avoid eye contact; or pretend to be making calls. We tell harassers to 'back off' and push gropers away. We draw attention to the harassment and ask for help, or look for online advice. We wedge keys between our fingers, carry rape alarms, pre-dial 999 into our phones and ask friends to call the police if we don't text to confirm we've arrived home safely. We constantly assess our surroundings, giving a wide berth to unlit parking bays or scrubland, clocking the locations of security guards and taking the long way round to avoid crossing parks or walking down dark alleys.[26] Women in the United States seek recommendations online for brands of mace, knives and lightweight guns to carry while running. We weigh up whether to listen to music when we run, or whether it's too dangerous, and we sometimes get a dog to chaperone us. We tell loved ones of our intended routes, enable our mobiles or watches to act as tracking devices, set up silent FaceTime calls to operate in the background throughout our runs and debate whether to run alone, whether to run at night or whether to run at all. Women organise against street harassment. We establish campaigns (such as the US Stop Street Harassment and Hollaback! campaigns), collect stories, commission surveys, fight for more security cameras, argue for better training for law enforcement and transport workers and request 'community safety audits', in which local governments record usage of public space and assess risks to women's safety. We generate awareness campaigns, educational materials, website resources and toolkits (such as the *Know Your Rights* manual published by Stop Street Harassment) for victims of intimidation in public, and for bystanders. Individually and collectively, women innovate, adapt, improvise, and work very hard to manage street harassment, even though it is not of our making. Men do not have to do all this.

But however hard we try to contain the harms of street harassment, it still feels like a heartbreaking loss to not be able to move around outdoors safely, comfortably and freely. As activist and researcher Fiona Vera-Gray points out, the 'safety work' that women are expected to do means that 'we learn that keeping ourselves safe *from* violence is more important than feeling safe *to* express and expand ourselves freely in the world'. Sadness, resignation and grief – for experiences we may never have, but deserve and crave all the same – infuse the fantasies that women entertain, in answer to the hypothetical question: 'What would you do if, just for one night, a curfew was imposed upon men?' Me personally, I'd run alone in a forest in the dark. After an evening out, I'd go straight to bed, without waiting up to receive text messages from female friends confirming they'd arrived home safely. I wouldn't walk home with a precautionary makeshift weapon of keys wedged between my fingers, as I've done since, aged fourteen, we girls were taken aside at school and solemnly warned of the need to protect ourselves against rape – as if rape were an inevitable natural force, like black ice, and not the result of men's decisions. (The boys were not subjected to cautionary sessions advising them not to rape women.) Other women describe similarly mundane fantasies: wearing headphones or heels while out at night, travelling home alone from gigs, booking Airbnbs in cheap, potentially insalubrious locations.[27]

But, most often, women's dreams are variations of simply being able to 'walk alone at night, anywhere I want, and not be afraid'. In 1951, Sylvia Plath wrote in her journal of her profound desire to 'sleep in an open field, to travel west, to walk freely at night', and how 'being born a woman is my awful tragedy', which meant that such modest requests were out of bounds. Very little seems to have changed in the seventy or so years since Plath wrote this in her diary. The simplicity of women's daydreams highlights the severity of the constraints under which we live all the time, and grief is the reaction that many of us experience to the choking of our freedoms. In 1978, the feminist writer Andrea Dworkin described how she was no longer feeling anger in response to the fact that 'every woman walking alone is hunted, harassed, time after time harmed by psychic or physical violence'. Increasingly grief and hopelessness had become her prevailing emotions.[28]

Because of the spectrum of men's violence against women outdoors, women feel constantly 'at risk' and we engage in continual risk assessments and cost–benefit analyses every time we leave the house. Sometimes, though, it simply seems safer to stay indoors. Holly Kearl found that 24 per cent of women who had experienced street harassment stopped going to the locations in which it occurred; 5 per cent of women gave up a specific activity, such as running, explicitly because of street harassment; and 4 per cent of women made a big life decision entirely due to street harassment, such as changing job or moving home, to avoid a particularly threatening environment. Kearl cites a study showing that, in New and Old Delhi, 95 per cent of the 630 women surveyed said their mobility was restricted because of male harassment. Women are four times as likely as men to develop agoraphobia and, among sufferers, women are more impaired by symptoms than men – just as we are disproportionately affected by unwanted noise outdoors. Agoraphobia is, literally, fear of the *agora*, the public space that enables participation in public life, and some men seem to make special effort to make such communal environments as unpleasant for women as possible. In an MA thesis, Suzie Siegel described how agoraphobia can be seen as women's 'resistance to a hostile world': 'To be safe, most women restrict their public participation. When agoraphobic women stay home or rely on a companion, they are only doing what other women do, but to a greater extent.' In India, where both street harassment and cultural injunctions on women to remain in the home can be extremely high, researchers of one study found that it is 'very difficult to diagnose' and study agoraphobia 'in Indian women' because of the difficulty in distinguishing it 'from the culturally expected avoidance of public situations' that defines women's lives.[29] Every woman is forced to be agoraphobic, to a greater or lesser extent. Every woman lives under a degree of lockdown all the time.

We are living through an era in which the murder rates of female runners suggest that hostility to women outdoors has recently intensified. One result of that escalation is, as some commentators fear, that the increasing participation of women in sport may have been brought to an abrupt end; that our period of progress might have ended and shifted into reverse.

In history and society there are patterns, times when men's aggression and intolerance of women outdoors intensifies. This happens on a large scale, affecting whole generations of women across the world, and there is evidence that something like this is happening right now. I start to wonder if this takes place on a smaller scale too, in the lives of individual women; whether, just as there are historical periods in which men more violently drive women out of the outdoors, there are also times in the life cycles of each and every woman in which men are more prone to exerting such control. Do men target us more in childhood, adolescence, adulthood, menopause or old age? I hope that these combined investigations – into both the large- and small-scale dynamics of men's violence against women and girls outdoors – will help explain the circumstances in which so many women of Lizzie's generation were shepherded back inside.

7.

Separation anxiety

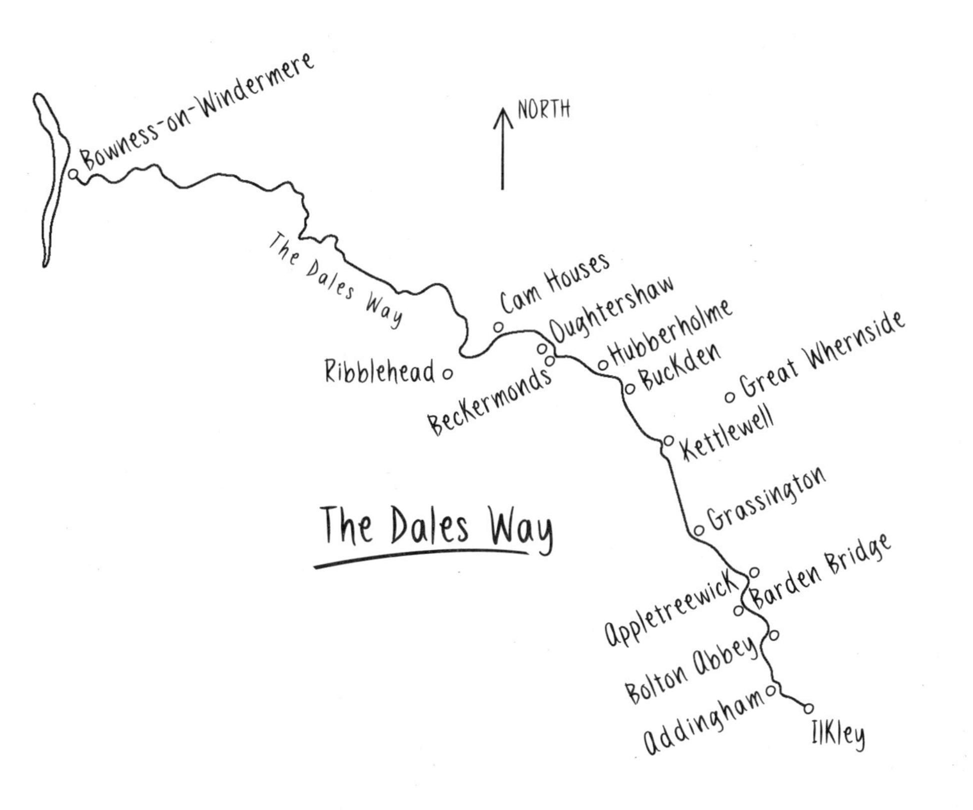

At the beginning of June 2020 – nearly three months after lockdown is first announced, and eleven months after the death of my stepdad – I decide to run the second half of the Dales Way course. If the race goes ahead in August, I will probably be running this section overnight, and a recce might help me avoid taking a wrong turn. The route I have in mind is around forty miles and I could do it in a day, but I would prefer to take it slowly and prolong my time outdoors. Pete and I have been taking it in turns to look after the children while they're off school during the pandemic, and he agrees to swap our shifts so that I have two consecutive days in which I can run.

Staying in a hotel feels out of the question, though. No one yet knows how Covid-19 is transmitted, and whether air or surfaces are more dangerous. When I tread across cattle grids while running, I balance on tiptoes to avoid touching gates. The idea of sleeping in a hotel – with every pore squashed against someone else's sheets and pillows, my fingers touching used keypads in lifts, my lips pressed against alien tea cups and inhaling air expelled from strangers' lungs – seems impossible. Sleeping outside, camping, feels like the only thing to do.

But I do not know how to camp. I email the Alpine Club's librarian, Nigel, who is incredulous that I have never camped before. He sends me a list of recommendations and I order a lightweight tent, a tiny inflatable mattress and pillow, a cloud-like sleeping bag I cannot believe will keep me warm, a towel that folds to the size of my palm, an eye mask, and a stove whose various elements fit neatly into a small plastic bowl. I already own a head torch and I set this out with a flat-lay of snacks and dehydrated powder meals, water flasks, incontinence pads, maps and a compass, first-aid kit, spork, a series of base layers (tights, long johns, thermal tops), waterproofs, underwear, a tiny tube of toothpaste, one of my children's mini-toothbrushes and my down jacket. All of this will just – *just* – compress into the 25-litre capacity of my largest running pack.

I have a dry run and attempt pitching the tent in our garden. I am generally good at DIY and flatpacks but I cannot fathom these instructions. I have no idea what is meant by a fly sheet, ground sheet or liner, and the tent's manual tells me that it goes up 'just like a standard tunnel tent', but I don't know what that means. I have to watch three YouTube videos before I manage to set it up. The instructions say it should take seven minutes: it takes me two hours. Ditto with the stove. When it first lights, I cannot see its pale blue flame, expecting it to be orange instead, and so I assume it is not lit and place a plastic bowl on it, which melts within seconds, clogging the element and plugging the gas. When I am lying in the tent in the garden that night, the expensive mattress deflates and I try to find a comfortable position on the cold, uneven ground. Since childhood, I've rarely tried out totally new activities. I am out of practice at being a clueless novice. But I remind myself that no one is watching and that *nobody cares if I'm rubbish at camping*, and I feel a small but palpable sense of release and expansion and even excitement.

On 14 July, I cycle to the station to take an early train from York to Leeds, where I will need to change onto another, along the famous Settle–Carlisle railway line, as far as Ribblehead. I miss the first train to Leeds. It comes into the platform unannounced, and sits invisibly behind a stationary train, before departing just as invisibly. I catch the following train, which leaves me only three minutes to make my connection and, if I miss that, there is a three-hour wait for the next train to Ribblehead, which would make it hard to recce the whole section in daylight. Just as I'm about to bound down the stairs to the platform at Leeds, a member of staff in a high-vis jacket stops me and points to a sign indicating that, because of the one-way system to enforce social distancing, the stairs are for ascent only. I must take the lift. I jog on the spot, waiting for the lift to trundle up from the platform, until the guard blows the whistle on the platform below and the station worker relents and lets me sprint down the empty steps. I leap onto the train just as the doors are closing and drop into a seat, panting through my face mask. There is only one other person on the carriage. The trains are following their usual commuter schedule, even though they are largely empty of people.

The other passenger and I both get off the train at Ribblehead, to a view of the famous mid nineteenth-century viaduct nestling against the flank of Whernside, one of Yorkshire's three highest peaks. The Dales Way footpath was conceived in 1968 as a riverside route: 'England's first major lower-level long-distance trail,' a guidebook tells me. It was designed to run south-to-north, covering the eighty-odd miles between Ilkley and Bowness-on-Windermere, and taking walkers from the urban settlements of West Yorkshire across the vertical span of one National Park – the Yorkshire Dales – and into a second – the Lake District. The trail made the most of the new 'rights to roam' that were granted after updates to the 1949 Access to Countryside Act in Britain, allowing hikers to wander more freely along riverside land as well as moors and mountains.[1] The Dales Way ultra-marathon will follow the footpath's original route in reverse, from north to south, beginning in Bowness and ending in Ilkley; so, over the next two days, I plan to recce the second half of the course and run from Ribblehead down to the finish line.

I career down the side lane leading from the station onto the main road, where I swiftly slow to a walk as it rises up across Blea Moor. After one and a half miles, the road tacks left and I veer right, onto a stretch of path that is incorporated into both the Dales Way and the Pennine Way (Britain's first long-distance footpath). The trail takes me towards the top of a hill called Cam Fell, which marks roughly the halfway point of the whole Dales Way route and lies on the main watershed of northern England. The northernmost half of the course – which I will not see until race day, unless I can fit in another recce first – follows paths beside the rivers Kent, Lune, Rawthey and Dee, which all flow west towards the Irish Sea. Its southern half, which I will be running today and tomorrow, clings to the River Wharfe, which feeds the Ouse and finally dispenses east, into the

North Sea. I am beginning my adventure at the middle of things – along the spine of the country, halfway through the Dales Way – on a hill between rivers flowing in opposite directions.

A little way before the highest point of Cam Fell, there is a junction, and the Dales Way turns off the Pennine Way onto an indistinct path, more like a sheep-trod, through tussocky, marshy ground. It leads me to Cam Houses, a tiny, semi-ruined hamlet of two conjoined buildings overgrown with waist-high nettles, which sting my bare calves as I wade through to find the gate. An old blue pick-up truck is parked outside one of the buildings. There are no other signs of humans in the overgrown plots or behind the black, cobwebbed windows, a few panes of which are broken, but some items of laundry have been hung out to dry – a brown shirt, yellow socks, a pair of boxer shorts – and I suddenly feel astonishingly alone. Cam Houses sits above one end of an enormous cauldron scooped out of the landscape, in which small plantations conceal the nearest settlements. Ribblehead station is now six kilometres behind me, and the nearest house at Swarthghyll is another two ahead. I take out my phone. It has no reception. I hold onto it tightly anyway, like a talisman.

Clambering over the rusted gate at Cam Houses as fast as I can, I head quickly out onto increasingly boggy ground. Firmer footing finally emerges: a flat path takes me past Swarthghyll, Nethergill and, after a mile or so, into the hamlet of Oughtershaw – where there are people in their gardens, drinking tea, and mowing, and a woman is walking her dogs down the road. I smile, say hi as I run past and feel slightly high as the adrenaline retreats. Then I swoop down the road which cascades steeply into the next hamlet, at the source of the River Wharfe. I am now in Langstrothdale, whose Germanic names I rehearse out loud as I jog: *Beckermonds. Yockenthwaite. Langstroth. Hubberholme. Cray*. I am momentarily struck by a memory of Hubberholme said in my stepdad's Leeds accent: *Ubberurm*. We went there together one day in my twenties, for lunch at the pub and a walk along Cray Gill, and that year, for Christmas, he bought me a woodcut of the church, whose pews each bear a small carved mouse, the insignia of the Arts and Crafts furniture-maker Robert 'Mouseman' Thompson.

I am strangely nervous as I approach Hubberholme. I think there is a small, irrational part of me that half-expects Willy to still be there, sat outside the pub with a pint and a bird book, or walking around the graveyard, inspecting the inscriptions, or striding beside the river, Australian bush hat on head, wooden hiking stick in hand, with his slightly uneven gait. We talk about places 'making an impression' on us, but what if we, too, make an impression on them – leaving behind some residue or surplus of ourselves in places that provoke strong emotions? There is a bar in Oxford I used to visit with a man I loved when I was younger and, for years afterwards when I walked past and glanced through its large high windows, I looked out for us both, at the back, perched on stools against the bar, and was ready to wave if I caught my eye. I wonder if this is what ghosts are.

But there is nobody sat outside the pub at Hubberholme, which is closed and shuttered up, so I run past and stop for lunch at the next village, Buckden, instead. An hour later I amble down the road to pick up the Dales Way again, at the riverside.

As I turn onto the path, there is a wooden fingerpost, pointing towards 'Kettlewell, 4 miles'.[2] And then I am struck by another recollection: one for which I have not steeled myself. I have been here before, in teenagehood, and standing by the fingerpost now, I am taken back there. It is a time in my life when my world out of doors is shrinking and I am in danger of losing many things. The recollections might help me answer one of my questions, which is whether there are times in women's lives in which we are particularly vulnerable to losing our freedom outdoors.

It's a Saturday in August 1995, and Willy and my mother drop me off in Hawes, Wensleydale, in the northernmost third of the Yorkshire Dales National Park – about thirteen miles due north of that fingerpost at Buckden. Over the next few hours, nine of my schoolfriends arrive – fifteen-year-old girls and boys spilling out of family cars or trekking from the train station. After producing a folder of maps, itineraries and accommodation lists to reassure our parents, we have been allowed a week without adult supervision to hike across the Dales.

The summer of 1995 is the hottest and driest on record. My best friend Josie arrives wearing a thin, self-designed T-shirt using words from an REM song, 'I Don't Sleep, I Dream'. She and I go to gigs at least twice a week, scouring the listings at the back of *NME* and *Melody Maker*; queuing in HMV to buy tickets from behind the counter; standing in line outside venues on the off-chance that a whispered rumour of a band's 'secret gig' might be true. Blur and Oasis have just released their singles 'Country House' and 'Roll with It', but I don't particularly like either band; too blokey for me. I much prefer listening to Pulp, and their fey, cavorting frontman Jarvis Cocker, or the gentle-seeming lead singer of REM, Michael Stipe. I go to sleep most nights listening to 'Find the River', the final track on my cassette of their album *Automatic for the People*. In that song, Stipe's elderly poet-narrator senses himself to be at the very end of things. His energy is emptying out, like a river into the ocean, and he wishes to hand on the joy-filled stories of his life on this miraculous planet, swimming amid its herbs and flowers and storms and moons, to the hard-driving city-dwelling dynamos of the new generation. I imagine myself in this latter role, kneeling at the poet's knee, being assured that all of this beauty is ready for me – if I choose.

The boys on our hostelling trip, however, are very invested in the battle of the bands between Blur and Oasis. My friend Henrik has crammed into his backpack a full hi-fi – amplifier, CD deck and two speakers – so we can all listen to 'Roll with It' in our dormitories at night. And we sing it loudly as we walk thirteen miles on the first day, from Hawes to the neighbouring village of Aysgarth; the boys hurrying us along to get to the hostel in time to listen to the radio chart show to hear who is at number 1. That evening Blur wins the battle and our disappointed friends try to get drunk on non-alcoholic cans of shandy from the vending machine in the hostel's communal dining area.

Two days later, after a day paddling at the top of Aysgarth Falls, we head out to hike the seventeen miles from Aysgarth down to Kettlewell, via Buckden. We set off at nine in the morning, leaving Josie determinedly asleep in her bunk.

Everything Josie does – from washing her hair and making cups of coffee, to painting, drumming and late-night conversations about philosophy and politics – she does with methodical, unhurried absorption. She contemplates ideas like a photographer carefully holding negatives up to the light. I don't think I've ever been listened to with such concentration, before or since. And so she is not just an extraordinary interlocutor, but also my stepdad's favourite of all my friends. I frequently arrive home from my evening waitressing job to find them – in age, over thirty years apart – sat across the table from one another, sharing a pint and discussing Keynesian economics or trade unionism in China.

In contrast, I find myself increasingly unable to enjoy each present moment. I am rarely able to talk without being distracted by anxieties about how I look and sound as I speak. I draw up 'to-do' lists and complicated schedules, coloured in with felt pen, which allot brief windows of time to each task. I set myself goals – to fit into size 8 hipsters, to get an A in A-level maths, to work my way through all the exercises in Charles-Louis Hanon's book *The Virtuoso Pianist* – and I sketch out a timetable to attain these objectives. I hate wasting or running out of time, and worry that, if each hour is not spent in 'doing' or achieving, there will be little to justify my continued existence. I am never late.

One side effect of Josie's immersion in the present is that she is often very late. In those years before mobile phones, I once waited for her outside a second-hand clothing sale, in the city centre, for three hours past our agreed meeting time.

And now, in the Dales, our ways of keeping time clash.

I am cross with Josie for failing to rise early, and I refuse to wait. Instead, I issue strict instructions to her sleeping form to check out by 11 a.m., and the rest of us set off on the long hike to Kettlewell. As we drop down into Buckden, after some five or six hours of walking, I worry out loud about her. I am frustrated that she could not fit in with our timetable. I am concerned about her, alone in the hills, getting lost as night draws in. And I resent the thought that I might need to go back and look for her.

And then our friend Dom says, 'Isn't that Josie down there?'

We peer down to see her tall, slim shape loping along the path below. She left Aysgarth two hours after us, but she has taken a more direct route and has ended up ahead. We catch up with her and laugh. I have been fearful and angry for nothing. Josie is fine; everything is fine, and we are all back on the same schedule, no longer out of time. We picnic briefly at that fingerpost in Buckden, which points us along the remaining four miles towards Kettlewell.

That evening, the genial, bearded hostel manager prophesies that Josie will have four children by the age of twenty-eight. Now I think he was probably patronising her, implying that her distinctiveness was 'just a phase', but she took him seriously and was adamant she would have none – and we agreed that we would all return to Kettlewell to prove him wrong in thirteen years' time, in 2008.

Looking at my diaries now, I can see that, between that holiday in 1995 and late 1997, something changed. The gigs disappear and are replaced by exam revision schedules. I start a Saturday job at a glass-blowing factory, where two men in their forties talk to my breasts about how to dip a rod into molten glass and spin it into a bowl and suggest I wear a shorter skirt to mitigate the heat of the furnaces.

In the summer of 1996, our group of friends go away again – to the Edinburgh Fringe Festival and then for a week hiking up the West Highland Way. We are made up of roughly equal numbers of boys and girls but, during that trip, we mostly go our separate ways, partitioned by sex. One evening at the Fringe, we girls go to a stand-up comedy show by a fifty-year-old comedian from our favourite TV series. When he asks Josie why she isn't laughing, she replies, simply, 'Because it's not funny', and he calls her a 'fucking bitch', and she walks out. In Edinburgh nightclubs, we are orbited by much older men, who attempt to kiss us on the backs of our necks as we dance, and propel each of us out of our circle, one at a time, pushing us up against a wall, where we dodge their lunging faces and hold bottles of Smirnoff Ice up to UV light. Sometimes, the men try again, and then we lean forward and shout, 'No, thank you', above the music, and then, sometimes, they yell back, 'Fucking bitch', and I understand how swiftly what looks like flattery can reveal itself as hatred.

My diary for the following year is almost empty. I go to college, and work at a bookshop in the evenings and at weekends. In the months after October 1997, I make plans to go to classes, concerts and sleepovers with friends, and then cross them all out. My territory shrinks to the mile between my bedroom, where I obsessively scrutinise myself in the mirror, and the municipal library, where I spend every day revising, instead of going to classes.

My handwriting gets smaller. I go to the chemists by the library early each morning and weigh myself on the electronic scales and paste each printed slip into my diary. I lose over a third of my body weight. I buy the size 8 hipsters and they are much too big, and I realise that the clothes on shop mannequins have to be pinned to fit, and I feel cheated. From January 1998, my life is so thin that I stop writing in my diary altogether. I do not bother to buy one for the following year.

A photograph from that year captures something of my teenage losses – the anorexia; the contraction of my interests; the shrinking of the territories I once roamed. I am eighteen and dressed entirely in black. I sit, partially hidden on both sides by friends, and I am hunching forward to hide my non-existent stomach. My hair is cropped into an angular bob, and I am smiling cautiously, not enough to risk squeezing my cheeks into pockets of fat.

It is radically different from a photograph of myself in 1994 or 1995, before things changed. In that earlier shot, I am wearing a long, sleeveless vest top over a turquoise tie-dyed dress and black tights, and a purple scarf wound around my neck, into which my long, unevenly parted hair falls. Below the photo's edge, I know I am wearing floral Doc Martens. I am holding something – a book or a purse? – offering or receiving a gift. I stand upright, smiling broadly, about to burst into laughter in the middle of a story or joke with the person behind the camera – who is probably Josie. I take up the whole frame. Perhaps it is my birthday.

In the 1990s, the feminist psychologist Carol Gilligan and educationalist Lyn Mikel Brown conducted interviews with girls aged between eight and fourteen years old, at the single-sex private Laurel School in Shaker Heights, Ohio. Aware of existing studies showing that 'girls at this time have been observed to lose their vitality, their resilience, their immunity to depression, their sense of themselves and their character' and that 'girls approaching adolescence are often victims of incest and other forms of sexual abuse', Brown and Gilligan wanted to see if and how such losses and traumas were audible in girls' own voices.[3]

They began by interviewing pre-adolescent girls, aged eight and nine. The researchers found that they were admirably willing to speak out to friends about hurt feelings, as well as emotions such as love and loyalty. These young girls had the capacity to be openly angry, as well as listening to others and learning from them. They also expressed a clear desire to talk and to be heard. A nine-year-old called Judy described knowing (in the researchers' words) 'her world through the evidence of her senses', and she was willing to trust and publicly defend this 'experience of being in a body that feels and knows feelings'. Brown and Gilligan concluded that the girls' relationships seemed genuine.[4] Times spent with friends, parents and teachers were opportunities to speak freely, to listen, to find a way forward through conflict without fear of anger – either their own or others'. Young girls frequently reported that they could *be themselves* while around family members and friends.

Over the next five years, Brown and Gilligan observed major changes. The same girls, now aged thirteen and fourteen, increasingly repeated 'I don't know' when asked questions. They spoke with their hands over their mouths and lowered their voices. They sounded tired and emotionally drained when speaking about friendships. One girl, thirteen-year-old Neeti, appeared detached from her life. Older girls described feeling pressure to put aside their own desires, priorities, feelings and experiences to obey teachers' and parents' injunctions to 'always be nice' and 'be kind'. Many were aware of the concept of a 'perfect girl' and expressed the need to become perfect themselves. They increasingly saw themselves – their lives, achievements, bodies – through the gaze of others. The split consciousness that philosopher Iris Marion Young described was taking up residence.[5]

To live up to what Brown and Gilligan call 'the tyranny of nice and kind', the adolescent girls became more willing to deny their own experiences and to agree with others' conflicting versions of reality: 'asked if she has ever been in a situation where what she knows to be true from experience is different from what others are saying and doing, thirteen-year-old Anna replied, "All the time . . . that's my life" '. Fearing that, if they passionately asserted their own discordant feelings and beliefs then they'd be socially ostracised, girls like Anna felt pressured to renounce the genuine relationships that characterised their childhood for false and unsatisfying ones, 'in which she silences herself because she is afraid of what will happen, and also how she will feel, if she expresses what she really thinks'.[6]

Such self-silencing required the girls to dissociate themselves from their own feelings and their bodies. Some described developing a double life, outwardly behaving in acceptable ways but inwardly harbouring anger and resentment. Others drove their feelings so far underground that they considered those feelings, when they inevitably emerged, to be alien, irrational and terrifying – not part of themselves at all. A third group resisted this pressure to deny their own reality in what Brown and Gilligan recognised as an 'act of relational heroism . . . a political struggle', but these girls knew their outspokenness made them unpopular outsiders.[7]

'Girls, we thought, were undergoing a kind of psychological footbinding,' Brown and Gilligan concluded. The girls feared adults' disapproval if they failed to be nice and kind. Many had directly experienced violence from authority figures, such as fathers, and their fears of being met with anger were not groundless. Some girls described witnessing adult women, often their mothers, silencing their own feelings in relationships, and of encountering media images of love that did not seem loving. Almost all the girls were terrified of being rejected from social groups, especially by boys. And they expressed acute awareness that, whereas acceptable adult masculinity is often defined by self-sufficiency, femininity entails the opposite: being skilled at being social. To conform to these standards, more than one teenage girl expressed a readiness to stay in relationships that were hurting them. The researchers realised they were witnessing a 'giving up of voice' by adolescent girls, an abandonment of self, for the sake of becoming a good woman and having relationships'.[8] They, and other psychologists, had seen the same behaviour later down the line, in adult women with abusive intimate partners.

In a 1926 essay called 'Inhibition, Symptom, and Fear', Sigmund Freud described how separation from the mother is the single most formative moment of loss that we all undergo. It is, for him, the moment when we begin to come to terms with our own fundamental separateness and solitude in the world, and the irreversible 'absence of the loved (and longed for) person'. Freud depicted this moment of separation taking place during infancy, when the baby is weaned from the mother's breast, and his ideas about this decisive moment of loss and separation have become foundationally important to the way we think about childhood development in the West. But some women-focused psychologists suggest that Freud's schema applies mainly to boys, who are indoctrinated into an adult masculinity defined by solitude and independence. Psychologist Dana Crowley Jack suggests that, for girls and women, the foundational moment of loss is not the same as for boys. Girls do not separate from their mothers in early infancy, but quite the reverse: they are expected to remain in close relationships with others – including and going beyond the mother – into and throughout adulthood.[9] But, within those relationships, girls lose themselves. Boys lose the mother, girls lose themselves. As Gilligan and Brown realised, girls are required to stifle their own voices, priorities and self-belief in order to become acceptable adult women who successfully maintain relationships with other people, even if those relationships are profoundly harmful to them – and this foundational loss for girls does not take place in infancy (as it does for boys) but in adolescence.

As I found during my own teenagehood, girls' loss of self is played out in the shrinking of our freedom of movement – a loss of comfort and safety outdoors which damages our experiences of being in public spaces and of living comfortably in our own bodies. Brown and Gilligan note that one of their interviewees, eight-year-old Noura, frequently 'wanted her parents out of the house so she and her friends could make as much noise as they wanted'. But five years later, 'she seems to have lost the capacity to imagine, let alone to create, this kind of space for herself and her friends'.[10]

Intensification of girls' discomfort in public space during teenagehood has been observed by sociologists, sports scientists, urban planners and leisure researchers. As health policy researcher Kelly Hallman succinctly puts it, 'with puberty, girls' worlds shrink, while boys' expand'. In a study in the KwaZulu-Natal province of South Africa, published in 2015, children were asked to map local spaces with which they were familiar. Aged eleven, girls mapped territories of similar areas to boys, but by the age of fourteen, girls' maps were only one-third the area of their male classmates' maps and two-fifths the size of the maps that they themselves had drawn three years earlier.[11] The spaces in which they felt safe had shrunk dramatically, especially in comparison to their male counterparts.

Studies from the 1970s up to the present day have produced similar findings. During adolescence, boys typically range further than girls. In towns and cities all over the world, teenage girls are observed to spend less time in public spaces and stay closer to their homes than boys. In Los Angeles, scholar of urban planning Anastasia Loukaitou-Sideris and her team of researchers find that adolescent boys prefer to spend their recreation time in parks and on the streets, whereas girls tend to remain within their own gardens or backyards. This sets a pattern into adulthood, in which men visit green spaces and parks more often, in greater numbers, and spend a longer time there than women and girls. Social scientist Margaret O'Brien discovered that, in UK cities, these gendered differences often intersect with ethnicity: Black and minority ethnic girls appear 'to be more restricted in their use of urban space' – more than both white girls and white and BAME boys. For example, in Tower Hamlets in east London, only 37 per cent of 'older Asian [Bengali] girls' were 'allowed to play out unaccompanied in contrast to 92 percent of Asian boys from the same neighbourhood'.[12]

The disparity between adolescent boys' and girls' freedom of movement is especially pronounced in the developing world. Martha Brady, a researcher and leader of health and development programmes for PATH (a global team working towards health equity), emphasises that, 'in many settings, adolescence is a time when the world expands for boys and contracts for girls, and gender disparities in opportunity and expectations become particularly pronounced'. She draws on surveys of adolescents by the international non-profit NGO the Population Council, in India, Mali, Pakistan and Vietnam, which all show that 'boys have greater freedom of movement, go to more places with greater frequency, and usually do not need to be accompanied in public'. In Brady's two particular areas of focus – rural upper Egypt and the slums of Nairobi, Kenya – she finds that 'girls' lives become increasingly restricted to the domestic sphere' during adolescence, and 'the kinds of public spaces that are considered okay for women are those that reinforce domestic roles as homemakers and mothers: markets, health clinics, tailors'. Girls and women are 'often completely excluded from spaces that men can visit freely: town halls, parks, sports stadiums'.[13]

Girls' loss of freedom outdoors in adolescence is mirrored in the drop-off of their participation in sport. In 2008, health researcher Anna Timperio found that eight-year-old girls and boys did roughly similar amounts of moderate-to-vigorous physical activity, but by the age of thirteen to fifteen, boys were doing around ninety minutes more exercise per week than girls. Across the world, studies show that far fewer girls than boys meet the World Health Organization's guidelines of sixty minutes of physical activity every day – only 10 per cent of girls achieve the recommendation – and that girls drop out of sports clubs and organised activities during adolescence at much higher rates than boys. A recent report by the UK charity Women in Sport has found that '64 per cent of girls will have quit sports by the age of finishing puberty (16–17)', and '80 per cent of girls feel they do not belong in sport'. Girls from lower socio-economic and BAME backgrounds are even less likely to be active than their white female, or male peers from higher socio-economic environments. This sets a trend for life, as physical activity in adolescence correlates to activity levels in adulthood: Women in Sport find that physically inactive children are more likely to be inactive adults.[14]

In many ways, the contraction of girls' movements around public space in teenagehood mirrors the historical narrative that I am discovering. Girls do not begin life with a childhood period in which they are completely confined indoors, and then forge their path into outdoor space in a linear, progressive fashion, developing ever greater confidence and freedom to roam as they get older. Similarly, women did not spend the latter years of the nineteenth century purely as Angels in the House, emerging into the sporting world bit by bit over the second half of the twentieth century, and achieving increasingly greater representation as the years passed. In both the large-scale shifts of history and the smaller-scale sequences of individual lives, the story of women in sport – and the visibility and respect accorded to us – is not one of consistent, if slow, advancement. Instead, both of these narratives trace the loss of earlier freedoms.

Around the turn of the twentieth century, women seem to have lost some of the emancipation that they previously found in sport. And in teenagehood, girls experience a dramatic curtailment of the comparative liberty of childhood. Women en masse only came back into widespread visibility in sport from the 1970s onwards and, likewise, if individual women are ever able to recover from the loss of ease in our own strong, sweaty, energetic bodies during adolescence, it can take decades. (I suspect that many women are, like me, only ready to re-enter the world of outdoor sport in our thirties, forties, or later.) As psychologists like Dana Jack describe, socialisation as a woman entails periods of profound dispossession and mourning.

According to many studies, the most influential factor that deters adolescent girls (and adult women too) from feeling free and safe in public space, and exercising within it, is the presence of boys and men. This discovery initially surprises and shocks me. When I first started my research for this book, I had expected that more technical obstacles – such as kit designed for male bodies, which is ill-fitting, uncomfortable and unflattering on women – would be the key dampeners on young women's enthusiasm for outdoor sport.

Perhaps I had hoped that the problem would be easier to fix.

But multiple investigations show that, as fifteen-year-old Australian female interviewees put it, girls would 'use [public] spaces more if boys weren't around', and that they purposely avoid 'active spaces that girls perceive to be dominated by boys'. Observations of park users in North Carolina, Texas and California find that the larger the number of recreational facilities in parks, and the larger the particular park 'zone' (i.e. an individual area, such as a basketball court or skate park), the more likely it is to be populated by adolescent boys; and this means that it is *less* likely that teenage girls are present and active. Far fewer girls than boys use basketball courts and other 'organized sport settings'; girls instead gravitate to swings and slides, because playgrounds are the only areas of parks to be dominated by adult women (often carers and their children), rather than boys and men.[15] Instead of formally structured zones, girls often voice a desire for informal spaces in which they can sit with friends, and be concealed enough to feel protected from harassment and ridicule, but not so hidden as to be vulnerable to assault.

The widespread closure of public toilets around the world has disproportionately affected women's ability to feel free in shared spaces, and men's presence in close proximity to sanitary facilities is an especial deterrent: in 2018, UNESCO shone a light on how the lack of sex-segregated toilet provision is a major obstacle for girls attending schools in low- and middle-income countries, and in Bangladesh, 41 per cent of teenage schoolgirls report missing at least three days of school per month because of a lack of women-only sanitary provision. During a 2018 heatwave in India, women and girls living in slums avoided eating and drinking because they 'face lewd remarks, harassment, and stares from local boys when they go out in the open to defecate'. In the UK, a consultation in Wales in 2019 found that, in secondary schools which mainly offer mixed-sex or 'gender-neutral' toilets, girls are more prone to missing school during their periods, more likely to avoid drinking water and that they tend to shun the toilets in general – because of fears of sexual assault, of being ridiculed and, for Muslim girls, of having to adjust hijabs in front of males. In the UK and USA, restrictions on women's liberty in the nineteenth century, caused by lack of free, safe, female public toilets has been called the 'urinary leash', as it kept women close to their homes and restricted their freedom outdoors – and it very much still exists across the world.[16]

Two principal reasons emerge from existing research for adolescent girls' reluctance to share public space with boys. The first is the same type of self-consciousness described by nineteenth-century mountaineers and Iris Marion Young. All the Western Australian girls interviewed by leisure researcher Kandy James – from the most to the least confident – said they felt conscious of the critical gaze of others, particularly boys and men, and that they would use school basketball courts and public swimming pools more if boys were not present. Girls describe being acutely conscious of their physical appearance and athletic competence, and attribute this to past experiences of being intimidated and embarrassed by boys through taunts aimed at their weight or sporting abilities. Girls also report being on the receiving end of harassment for being too good at sports, and therefore appearing like 'unfeminine tomboys'. Many had been ridiculed by PE teachers, who unfavourably compared girls to male students and, in 2013, girls in Edinburgh described being made to feel unwelcome in their local sports centre because of belittling behaviour from male members of staff.[17]

The second reason for girls' avoidance of public spaces containing boys and men is fear of violence and assault. Of girls aged thirteen to fourteen in Stockholm, 60 per cent of those surveyed report feeling scared in their own neighbourhoods, compared to 40 per cent of boys. In LA, far more girls than boys say that they find parks unsafe; and in Australia, girls rank parks as the least safe public space, followed by streets, then public transport. This is disturbing: parks are explicitly designed to encourage congregating and exercise, but something is clearly going wrong when over 50 per cent of the population consider them the *least* conducive place for those activities. In South Africa in 2015, not a single group of girls identified any public space as more than 'somewhat safe', and they ranked over 58 per cent of spaces – many of which, like schools, parks and even private homes, were designated as 'extremely safe' by boys – as 'unsafe' or 'very unsafe'. Some of these fears are to do with the built environment: more girls than boys worry about poor maintenance of public places like parks, and about being injured outdoors. But overwhelmingly, girls' fears centre on violence and sexual crime from boys and men. In LA, Loukaitou-Sideris and her colleagues find that the higher the density of crime within half a mile of home, the lower the physical activity rates of girls (but not boys). In interviews, girls express fear of 'undesirable users' of parks, including 'people doing drugs' and 'gangs', and in Stockholm, teenage girls identify the most prominent threat as originating from 'lone rapists – mainly threatening girls – or gangs of adolescent boys (threatening boys with violence and girls mainly with (sexual) harassment)'.[18]

Girls' fears are not imagined or hypothetical. They are often based on traumatic experiences. In 2013, adolescence was the period of highest risk for being on the receiving end of intentional injury across the world. In South Africa in 2008, the leading cause of death (36 per cent) among teenagers was male violence, and more than 40 per cent of adolescents had been victims of crime, with many more having witnessed crimes against their peers. In interviews, Swedish girls describe their own experiences of being harassed and assaulted by men in public spaces after dark, including being stalked or witnessing it happen to other women. Adolescence is when girls start being systematically subjected to street harassment. In studies in 2010 and 2014, Holly Kearl found that 22 per cent of girls had been harassed by the time they were twelve years old, leaping to 66 per cent by the age of fifteen and 87 per cent by age nineteen. Out of 168 girls in

Chicago aged between ten and nineteen, 86 per cent said they'd been catcalled, 36 per cent said men harassed them daily and 60 per cent said they felt unsafe walking in their own neighbourhood. In 2018, the British charity Plan UK found that, although street harassment of girls started at a young age, adolescence was the period when it became particularly pronounced, and that many women felt it was so inevitable as to be an expected 'part of growing up' – and it meant that girls were unable to feel safe 'in the classroom . . . or on the streets'.[19]

Girls find a number of ways to negotiate the new constraints that they experience during adolescence. Some describe trying to defy stereotypes of victimhood and behave confidently in public, such as pretending to speak on their mobile phones. Or they do the opposite and attempt to make themselves inconspicuous: in public swimming pools, girls evade boys' gaze by hiding, often covering themselves in towels until the last moment. They swim in T-shirts or conceal themselves among friends. Many report deliberately avoiding boisterous forms of behaviour – not jumping in, messing around or too obviously *having fun* – in order to avoid drawing attention to themselves. In parks, girls describe eschewing visible physical activity, preferring to walk slowly, sit or lie down, and they gravitate towards areas with grass, trees and natural screens. One girl, Beth, was quoted as saying she tries 'not to look too much out of place' in public space, as if it isn't really her space at all.[20]

Often, though, girls feel that it is simpler to avoid the outdoors altogether. Many female teenage interviewees tell researchers they prefer never to visit parks or basketball courts. Kandy James finds that, in the face of boy's and men's domination of public spaces such as streets and parks, adolescent girls frequently retreat to their bedrooms where, in the words of a girl called Leonie, 'I know that people won't be following me and looking at everything I do and watching me.' Another girl refers to her bedroom as 'the only place in the world' where she feels safe. But at home girls have less possibility for vigorous activity than outside the house. Although a few girls report trying to exercise in their bedrooms, the majority say they engage in 'relaxation activities' – but they also sometimes use those spaces to self-harm, or starve themselves, or to criticise their own appearance and compare themselves unfavourably to (social) media images.[21] And spending large amounts of time alone in a bedroom does not prepare young women for full participation in the world later on. We should not underestimate the magnitude of this loss, when girls are deprived of the ability to feel safe, comfortable and free outdoors.

In this light, I start to wonder if 'loss' is the wrong term for the damage that is done to teenage girls. This is no accident. We do not mislay our freedoms, like losing an earring in a nightclub. Instead, they are taken from us, by boys and men. Perhaps a better word for the traumas that girls face in adolescence is not 'loss', but *dispossession* or even *theft*.

I was unusual, and relatively lucky, I think, in that my own traumas took place so late in adolescence, between the ages of sixteen and eighteen. I am grateful that I had those earlier years of teenagehood, in which I glimpsed an adulthood characterised by hot summers of relative freedom and pleasure, before the fear and self-loathing truly set in.

My late teens were a reckoning. Until then, school reports had talked about my 'promise', but exams marked the gateway to an uncosseted world beyond and it seemed like a time when potential could no longer remain latent. I felt like I could not let anything slip. So I tried to perfect everything: my exam results, my appetites and weight, my stomach and thighs, my geometric bob haircut, my clothing – and my friendships.

Until my late teens, Josie had been my closest friend. We would spend hours after school lying side by side on her top bunk, or on the mattress on my bedroom floor, staring up at the tie-dyed mandala poster stuck to the ceiling. She rolled and smoked spliffs from cannabis she grew herself and talked about books she was reading – Fritjof Capra's *Tao of Physics*, Erich Fromm's *The Art of Loving*, Ian Stewart's *Does God Play Dice?* – and she gave elegantly filleted summaries that I would draw upon for decades to come, in my attempts to ape erudition. I admired and envied her hugely. It seemed like we were standing at the doorway to adulthood and Josie had gone through first, showing it to be a place of dangerous and tantalising ideas and pleasures. And although the paintings she produced had become much angrier – images of violent sexual encounters, knives, blood – it was only much later that I realised I'd been blind to how difficult things had often been for Josie, in the way that it is for many girls who don't entirely conform to the mould of 'perfect teenage girl'.

After reading Brown and Gilligan's book, I start to wonder if the changes that occurred in my friendship with Josie were the result of our different ways of negotiating the dispossessions that are inflicted on teenage girls as we all tried to negotiate entry into adult womanhood. I was desperate to be loved: there was not a single part of me I would not have jettisoned in order to be loved, or even merely deemed acceptable. I had no guiding values beyond that. But Josie did have stronger principles, a more robust selfhood. Our paths diverged. I started to draw dark kohl rings around my eyes and wear tight black polo necks and pencil skirts; she continued living in baggy jeans and cords, checked flannel shirts and Doc Martens or cowboy boots. I became more interested in *Vogue*'s reports on London Fashion Week than her philosophy. She still went to gigs every other night, but now I refused to go with her. When it came to organising a group summer holiday in 1998, I insisted that we did not invite her.

Years later, Josie told me how abandoned she had felt. I too had felt deserted by her: for her refusal to compromise her tastes and beliefs to the extent that I did, in the name of 'femininity'. Now I am angry with myself for the choices that I made. But I am also furious with the world, for offering us both such dreadful options as adolescent girls: to lose either our selves or our homes in that world, and possibly even both.

As we got older, and the traumas of teenage girlhood receded a little, Josie and I did become closer again, though we never regained the cherished intimacy of those early years. In 2013, she was asked to contribute to an exhibition, 'Advice to my Teenage Self'. 'Don't take anything too seriously,' she wrote in the catalogue. 'It's all complete nonsense. Just enjoy the days, and the people you're with.'

Josie's rage seemed to resolve into a quieter form of sadness. I too relaxed, put on weight, started running. When my first child was born, Josie painted an image of Pete and me – cocooned against the world, sheltering our daughter like a human canopy – which I hung in our entrance hallway. After our second and third children, twins, were born in the late spring of 2014, Josie came to visit us in London, and I snapped a photograph of her, bent over one of the babies in a similar protective position. I had deliberately given Josie's middle name to that daughter, and I planned on framing the photograph of the two of them together.

Josie had seemed tired that afternoon. Her skin had a faint yellow tinge. She said she had been working hard all summer, drawing caricatures outdoors, and had spent too much time in the sun. But, she said, her health 'hadn't been great'. She'd been having stomach pains since January, and often 'felt sluggish'. Her GP thought these might be symptoms of depression, and he had put her on a waiting list for cognitive behavioural therapy.

A month later, at the end of September, my new family of five came home from a hastily arranged holiday. There was a voicemail on our house answerphone, from a mutual childhood friend. Josie had been admitted to hospital: it seemed that she had stopped being able to keep food down. Doctors were worried she was bulimic, but after a week in which Josie was repeatedly encouraged to 'let herself digest' and still vomited everything she was fed, the hospital agreed to give her a scan. It showed that she had cancer of the duodenum, the first part of the small intestine: a very rare, aggressive cancer, which had spread to her lungs, her heart, her lymphatic system and her liver. She was allowed home in time to celebrate her thirty-fifth birthday. 'I've been sent home to die,' she told me. And she was right. She died less than two weeks later.

For this, Josie's final birthday, I put together a photo album – old snaps of us at secondary school, on a French exchange trip, and from that 1995 hiking holiday in the Yorkshire Dales. Beside a photograph of us picnicking beside the fingerpost at Buckden, I wrote a note: 'When the old man at the Kettlewell hostel made his prediction, I assumed we'd all lose touch. But I love that we didn't – and that it wasn't necessary after all to have a grand reunion in Kettlewell in 2008, to check whether you'd had four children or not! I love you just as much as I always have.'

But it was useless to pretend that nothing had changed. The different types of dispossession we'd undergone during female teenagehood had permanently driven us apart. I had discarded my self-belief in order to fit in with the world; Josie had preserved more of herself intact but found it hard to feel at home in the world because of it.

As I run out of Buckden and back onto the Dales Way, my attention returns to my feet hitting the path. As I pass that fingerpost, pointing me forward to Kettlewell, I wish I could go back to when I was last here, in 1995. I wish I could return to the point when things were starting to go wrong – for myself, and for Josie, and for our friendship – and try to put a stop to it, to do things differently. But I can't and, at this moment in time, I have no choice but to run on, following the fields and flagstones down into Kettlewell, where the hostel door is locked and bears a sign, 'Closed for Covid'. So I keep on running, down to the small town of Grassington, and then along the river to Appletreewick, where I'm going to camp for the night.

The campsite is a large field beside the River Wharfe. I set up my pitch close to the riverbank. In a barn, I shower and put on fresh clothes that I've stuffed into my running pack. My tent is minuscule in comparison to the family teepees and camper vans that share the field. It is barely longer and wider than my own body, and the lightweight fly sheet feels as defenceless as sunburned skin. I walk to the pub in Appletreewick (the landlord pronounced it *App'trick* when I phoned earlier to reserve a table for dinner). I have run around twenty-seven miles today and I am ravenous.

But the pub is shut. There is a sign, pinned to the door: 'Owing to breakdown, kitchen closed.' I remember having run past another pub, just over a mile earlier, in the village of Burnsall. I am no longer wearing a sports bra or incontinence pads and my legs are tired, but I need to eat, so I jog messily back along the river and find an empty table in the pub garden. I order chicken pie and mashed potato and drink a pint of lager shandy. I speak to Pete and my girls on FaceTime, before walking slowly back to the campsite in the late evening light, and I slot myself into my tent, where the rushing of the River Wharfe – which has acquired significant volume and pace in the miles between its source at Beckermonds and here – keeps me awake for hours.

In the morning, I open the tent's zipper to air that is thickly saturated, as if the river has exploded overnight. Fine droplets stud the fly sheet and the neighbouring hill is now hidden behind gluey mist. Inside the tent, I put on yesterday's running clothes and work damp leggings up over my thighs and bum like I'm attempting a Worm (my children's current favourite dance move) on my back. The campsite's coffee hut is open. I consume an Americano and two croissants and the vapour seems to lift a little. I shake off the water and roll up the tent and pack it tightly back into my pack, alongside the sleeping bag and mattress, which had, again, deflated in the night. I clamber through the hedge bordering the campsite and onto the footpath. I am back on the Dales Way.

This morning, I am stiff. As I start to run, muscles at the tops of my legs tug on other muscles, deep inside my buttocks. My skin is rough and red where the pack repeatedly hits my lower back and my shoulders ache where the straps pull. Each step on the firm path sends jolts up my spine, and it is just as well that today's run is much shorter than yesterday's: just twelve or thirteen miles. When, after around forty minutes, I reach Barden Bridge and enter the Bolton Abbey estate, where the path gives way to waterlogged grass, it is with relief.

After nearly an hour of dodging day-trippers and toddlers on reins, I jog out of the other side of Bolton Abbey and into the village of Addingham, and then, a few miles later, approach Ilkley and the end of the Dales Way. I realise that, if I get a move on, there is a train which will take me home in time to see my children before their bedtime, so I slalom between masked shoppers, swerve into the station and throw myself onto the train just before the doors close.

On a nearby seat, there is a young woman wearing a cropped T-shirt, emblazoned with the slogan 'You Are Not Your Body'.

Is it any wonder, I think, that women – especially young women – want to believe that message? For millennia, male philosophers and theologians have defined themselves in opposition to female flesh, which has been associated with apparently undesirable qualities such as irrationality, chaos and instinct – as opposed to the so-called masculine and attractive traits of reason, intellect and self-control. Men routinely disparage female bodies, and they turn them into commodities, trading them in marriage markets, buying and pimping them, enslaving them, and using them as passive receptacles for their desires. Women's value is conflated with our bodies, our ability to be fucked and to be controlled and to reproduce. 'Women are somehow [seen as] *more* biological, *more* corporeal, and *more* natural than men,' writes Australian feminist philosopher Elizabeth Grosz. We are thought to be 'closer to nature' – and it is not always meant as a compliment. As the third-century philosopher Porphyry put it, if women want to amount to anything, we should 'flee from every effeminate element of the soul as if [we] are clothed in a male body'.[22]

Nor are women's bodies housed well in the world. We are harassed on the streets and driven out of the built environment by design decisions that do not take account of our physiology or our lives. Feminist writer Caroline Criado Perez's 2019 book, *Invisible Women*, is a tapestry of the ways in which the human world is biased around 'default male' forms, often with catastrophic results for women. Our heart attacks go undiagnosed because of medical research that is entirely conducted on male bodies. We die at greater rates than men in car crashes because manufacturers use male-proportioned crash-test dummies. We cannot comfortably hold iPhones, open jar lids or play the piano as easily as men, because these are designed for men's hands.[23] And our bodies are subjected to men's violence and abuse, which is often suffered first and most intensely by girls in adolescence.

When the mistreatment and marginalisation of women's bodies is so endemic and traumatising, is it any wonder that so many girls attempt to seize control over our vulnerable flesh through disorders such as anorexia and self-harm? We are taught to set our conscious selves against our bodies, as if those bodies are some sort of enemy to loathe, tame, imprison, torture or even eradicate. Is it any wonder that, like the girl on the train, so many of us are tempted to protest that our value does not lie in our bodies, but in minds that we fantasise are completely and impossibly detached from their shells – like brains in jars?

It is an appalling bereavement for women and girls to lose the sense of our bodies and minds working together, towards what the ancient Greeks called our *eudaimonia*, our flourishing. We lose all the miraculous possibilities that are in store when we care for our own bodies and their capacity to ignite myriad sensations – of joy, pleasure, strength, confidence, freedom, self-knowledge, adventurousness and daring – and when we do so for ourselves alone, not for men.

The hope of forging a world in which all female bodies are better accommodated can feel impossible. Running during lockdown and on the Dales Way has made me reflect and read, and I have learned about the dynamics that shape women's and girls' psychological responses to the outdoors and its threats. Now I better understand some of the forces that make women reluctant to participate in vigorous exercise outside and I realise the enormity of the impact of male aggression. I have also seen how men's intimidation towards women outdoors can intensify and wane depending on the cultural mores of certain historical periods, and that it is visited most violently on women at certain stages of their lives – most notably, in adolescence.

As a result, women's rates of participation in outdoor sport (and public life) do not show consistent linear progress, either across the centuries or throughout individual lives. Instead, women's involvement in sport and leisure often follows patterns of advancement and reversal. In our attempts to move freely outdoors, many women experience backlashes that drive us indoors – and this occurs both to individual women and to whole generations. During the Covid lockdowns, the West seemed to witness one such decline in women's participation in sport, and, globally, an arguable intensification in hostility to women outdoors. We appear to be at a turning point at which our period of progress in women's rights in sport and beyond might have ended and shifted into reverse.

From the research I've already conducted, I suspect that the turn of the twentieth century – when prolific, ground-breaking female athletes such as Lizzie Le Blond left outdoor sport forever – was a comparable moment in time to the present day. Partly to better understand our contemporary era, I now want to find out what happened at the *fin de siècle* to make the outdoors seem particularly hostile to women. I want to discover how that hostility was visited by men onto women, and – perhaps hardest of all – I want to see if it's possible to discover some of the reasons *why* men seek to appropriate outdoor space for themselves and exclude women.

Only then will it be possible to turn to the women who fought – and continue to fight – for that seemingly impossible hope: of making a better home in the world for our bodies and our selves.

8.

Frozen out

The immediate trigger for Lizzie's departure from the mountains was death.

Of all her friendships in St Moritz, her most meaningful were with her guides, and especially with Josef Imboden. In 1887, Josef had first brought along his eldest son, Roman, on an expedition with Lizzie up the 11,213-foot (3,418-metre) Piz Kesch, the highest peak in the Albula Alps. Roman was then around seventeen years old, and Lizzie noticed that his climbing '"form" had already attained to a point which few amateurs could beat'. Roman soon became a guide in his own right and, over around a decade, he accompanied his father and Lizzie, and frequently guided her excursions on his own. In September 1895, she stood with both father and son at the summit of the Lyskamm and, once they had descended safely, she photographed Roman, seated in a wicker chair in a three-piece suit, coupled with mountaineering boots, smoking a pipe.[1] He was one of the most important people in her life.

Almost exactly a year later, Lizzie was in the Hotel Zermatt, writing in the salon, while Roman accompanied a climber up the Lyskamm. Out of the window, she noticed that the 'snow was atrocious and the weather grew worse and worse', but she wasn't worried – until two guests arrived, lamenting 'a horrible smash on the Lyskamm!' Lizzie ran outside to try to see what was going on up the mountain and found a silent crowd in the street. The hotel office confirmed that the accident had affected Roman's party, but it wasn't until another mountaineering team returned, sadly shaking their heads, that his death was confirmed. Lizzie was said to be inconsolable.[2]

She had lived through personal bereavements before and found comfort in the mountains. After Roman died, she saw how Josef was changed by grief, 'never . . . the same man again'. He asked her to help him raise funds for the wife and children of another guide killed in the same accident, and together they also erected a tombstone for Roman. In the longer term, Lizzie described how 'neither Imboden nor I cared to face the sad associations of the Alps', and she began to detach herself from her life there, sending away the Bernese mountain dog, Pluto, that she had kept as a pet for years. Then she left Switzerland herself, first for some tours of Spain, and then for an expedition in a new place to climb: Norway.[3]

Norway was a country in which women's outdoor sport had long flourished. The Yorkshire mountaineer William Cecil Slingsby had climbed there in the 1870s with his sister Edith (who wrote about her first female ascent of the Glittertinden mountain in the *Norwegian Tourist Association's Yearbook*) and in the 1880s with his wife Alizon (who made the first English climber's ascent of Lodals Kaupe). Slingsby greatly admired Norwegian women mountaineers such as Nikka Vonen and Therese Bertheau and, when Lizzie was planning her expedition there, he enthusiastically encouraged her. During her first summer in Norway, in 1897, Lizzie noticed the blithe ease with which groups of young women enjoyed 'long walking tours in the mountain district of their country, unescorted by any mere males': even though it is 'very likely they will hardly meet a single soul during the whole of their walk . . . they don't care at all. They feel perfectly safe – and well they may in that country!' Between autumn and spring, she flitted around Britain, Spain and Switzerland until she could go to Norway again in the summer. This time, she and Josef headed for the Arctic circle, to make the most of hiking and climbing in twenty-four hours of daylight.[4]

For seven weeks in 1898, Lizzie camped beside the Lyngenfjord, in a tent made more comfortable by her favourite Union flag pillow. By the end of the expedition, she and Josef had 'made 19 ascents, and of these 15 were first ascents'; and she had taken around 200 photographs, which she would exhibit at the Royal Photographic Society's gallery in the autumn. She returned to Norway for the third time the following year, 1899, and camped beside a derelict barn at

Holmebukta, south of Tromsø, using her Norwegian summers and Spanish winters to write two new books.[5]

Lizzie's writing in these years focused on loss and grief and was marked by a sense of unease. In January 1903, she published *True Tales of Mountain Adventure*, in which she collected almost every single memory of the mountains' capacity to exert 'appalling vengeance' on 'ignorant' climbers. She recounted story after story of fatal accidents, such as the avalanche on Mont Blanc in August 1820, which killed a scientist and three guides and deposited their bodies in a glacier, down which their remains inched over the next forty years until, in the early 1860s, pieces of bone and bags and clothing and equipment were disgorged piecemeal and perfectly preserved at the glacier's lower end. She dwelled upon her own near-misses too, including the time she had taken off her skirt and placed it under a 'heap of stones' so that she could climb more freely, and then watched it being swept away 'by the violence of the wind', like watching a ghostly double being blown off the mountain. It 'brought very strongly home to me . . . the escape we had had ourselves', she reflected.

Reviewers noticed Lizzie's newly macabre tone. In her earlier books, she had actively encouraged readers to head to the hills, but one reviewer thought that now 'her purpose was to frighten the would-be mountaineer and dissuade him or her from ever risking life and limb in Alpine climbing'.[6] The accounts articulated Lizzie's increasing discomfort in the mountains.

Lizzie was not the only prominent woman to turn away from the mountains at the close of the century. By the end of the first decade of the twentieth century, most of the earlier generations of female adventurers – women such as Meta Brevoort, Amelia Edwards, Margaret Sophia Green Kvikne, Jane Freshfield and Isabella Bird – had died. Many other remarkable women mountaineers stopped climbing around this time, including Lucy Walker, Isabella Straton, Mary Mummery, Margaret Jackson, Emily Hornby and the Pigeon sisters (Anna and Ellen, famous for making a particularly pioneering and hair-raising nine-hour descent of the 'formidable' Sesia-Joch Pass near Zermatt in 1869, after their guide got lost and the women had had to take control).

Some of those who persevered with mountaineering turned their attentions to much less well-trodden areas, well away from established tourist resorts. From 1897, Jane Inglis Clark focused on rock-climbing in Britain; in 1902, Gertrude Bell was the first to systematically explore the Engelhörner group of mountains in the Bernese Oberland in western Switzerland; and Käthe Bröske started climbing in the Slovak Alps. In 1902, Frances Emily Weston and her husband moved to Japan and mountaineered there, and she became the first non-Japanese woman to climb Togakushi, Tamkatsuma, Yari and Oku-Hodaka mountains. (Today, her achievements are marked by a memorial and an annual 'Mrs Weston' festival at Togakushi: a counterpart to the 'Weston Festival' that is held on the first Sunday in June each year to mark her husband's contribution to mountaineering in Japan.)[7] Gertrude Benham started climbing in Canada, and then Kenya, making a first ascent of Kilimanjaro in 1909.

The general trend, however, was a fading of the attention and respect that had been previously bestowed on women in the mountains.

On 5 September 1897, two climbers called Sarah Katharine 'Katy' Richardson and Mary Paillon reluctantly joined this group of women departing outdoor sport and made what would be their last ascent of any large mountain: Mont Pelvoux, a peak of nearly 4,000 metres in the Massif des Ecrins. By this time, both women – who lived as well as climbed together – were mountaineering celebrities: two of the most famous climbers in Europe. Katy, in particular, was renowned for having completed 116 of the Alps' *grandes courses* – the long, beautiful and challenging routes that had become embedded as classics in the mountaineering canon – including six overall first ascents and fourteen first female ascents.

On 5 September, Mary and Katy were making their way down from Mont Pelvoux's summit, when Mary, whose eyesight was failing, did not see a step hacked into the hard snow and placed all her weight in mid-air, lurching off the mountain. Katy braced herself and held tight to the rope, arresting Mary's fall. Neither were hurt but Mary was shaken and knew then that her time in the high mountains had come to an end. 'The state of my eyes no longer allowed me to rub shoulders with danger,' she wrote sadly. Katy knew what a profound loss this represented, and how much it would 'aggravate [Mary's] pain' to see her partner continuing to climb without her. So, with what Mary called 'exquisite sensitivity', Katy gave up serious mountaineering too. It seemed grimly fitting that, on that last ascent, she lost a much-loved engraved gold ring, her fingers having shrunk in the unseasonably icy weather.[8]

Mary and Katy's departure from mountaineering was prompted by personal circumstances, but what happened next points towards a wider marginalisation of such pioneering women.

After her retirement, Mary began recording, celebrating and memorialising the history of women's mountaineering, dictating her writings to an amanuensis as her eyesight deteriorated further. Articles about female climbers (*grimpeuses*) had been included in the yearbook of the French Alpine Club (the Club Alpin Français, CAF) since its first issue in 1874, in which female novelist and CAF member George Sand had contributed her memories of the Auvergne. Until 1903, women's writing was included regularly in the yearbook, and the publication of the Lyon section – of which Mary and Katy were members – contained a particularly high percentage of pieces by women, including by Mary, who wrote a series of articles about *les femmes alpinistes*. But in the years that directly followed Mary and Katy's retirement, female climbers faded from such visibility. Between 1906 and 1919, the CAF's *Annuaire* included only six articles by women, and female mountaineers were increasingly represented as being under the tutelage of men.

When Katy died in 1927, her obituary ended on a melancholy note: 'Except for short records in Alpine periodicals, no accounts of [Katy's] achievements were ever written.'[9] When Mary died nearly twenty years later, in 1946, there was no obituary for her at all – anywhere – unlike her father, brother and nephew, who had all been publicly commemorated for much lesser achievements.

As with Lizzie's departure from Switzerland, Katy and Mary's exit from mountaineering took place against the backdrop of a broader cultural shift in which outdoor sport was becoming less accepting of women. It was a discernible change that caused other women in sport to react similarly, by giving up their pursuits altogether. In a different, more female-friendly era, perhaps they might have persevered. Personal obstacles often seem more insurmountable when they are encountered in cultures that are obstructive in other ways too.

One of the features around the time of Katy and Mary's retirement from mountaineering was the disappearance of female role models from sporting literature. Over the second half of the nineteenth century, sport was formalised by structures such as competitions, clubs, societies, rules and institutions. From the 1850s onwards, an array of activities – including rowing, cricket and football – were more rigorously codified in contexts such as school sports lessons, university teams and sporting clubs. This transformed the nature of many sports and the way in which athletic activities were publicised. During this time, accounts of sporting achievements were increasingly produced under the aegis of formal institutions, rather than by the unattached individual writers who had been chiefly responsible for producing mountaineering books in the first half of the century. The *Alpine Journal* was an early example of such an affiliated publication. By the early twentieth century, yearbooks, results tables and lists of record holders – produced by universities, colleges and societies, and circulated more widely in newspapers – became the chief means of disseminating sporting endeavours. And because women were debarred from many of these institutions, their achievements were increasingly less visible than men's.

The definition of sport, in general, changed as it became formalised. For most of history, the word *sport* has meant a leisure activity undertaken for pleasure and 'merriment', often in a spirit of irreverent playfulness and humour, and with emphasis on *fun*. But in 1863, in a Victorian social science journal, one writer clearly distinguished recreations, pastimes and diversions (which were 'fun') from 'sport', which the writer described as being quite different: something organised and intentional, with an element of duress, in which participants '*set* ourselves to take part'. By 1884, a writer in *Longman's Magazine* was defining 'athletic sport' as activities governed by 'ruling bodies'. Participants still often found *sport* fun, but it was no longer necessary to do so: *sport* was *sport* because it was associated with rules, regulations, facilities and competitions, whether it was enjoyable or not. This still applies today. The question 'What's the difference between *sport, recreation* and *exercise*?' is frequently asked on English-language learning forums. One respondent explained that *sport* is 'always a competitive activity', whereas *exercise* is 'physical activity done to maintain one's physical condition' and *recreation* is 'laid back' and 'enjoyment based'. On Twitter, someone tells me that 'if it's not timed or producing finishing times it isn't sport'.[10]

The trend to codify, clubify and regulate sports over the second half of the nineteenth century directly involved the greater exclusion of women. For example, in the seventeenth and early eighteenth centuries, cricket had been what historian Rob Light described as a 'localised and informal game . . . not far removed from its folk origins', usually played on pieces of common land, in a laid-back, somewhat improvisatory manner. Women had enthusiastically participated in the early days of cricket: the first recorded women's cricket match was in July 1745, and overarm bowling was said to have been introduced to avoid the tendency for female bowlers' arms to become stuck in their skirts when bowling underarm. But as cricket was reformed, codified and clubified, women were made less welcome. Participation was increasingly structured by national and international championships and by the annual publication of *Wisden Cricketers' Almanack* from 1864, a reference book containing lists of awards, records, statistics about the game, rules and laws and winners – including, from 1889, lists of the 'five cricketers of the year'. No women were included in that list until 2009, 120 years after the accolade began, and the Marylebone Cricket Club – which owns Lord's Cricket Ground and is considered the 'guardian of the Laws of the game' – did not allow female members until 1998.[11]

Sport's new structured, disciplined identity was perceived as a way to take specifically boys and men in hand, in public schools and universities. Organised sport was a mechanism of social control, explicitly designed to prepare male students for future leadership roles in industry, politics and empire. The British soldier, explorer and colonial administrator Frederick Lugard claimed that public schools and universities – and, by implication, their systems of physical education – 'produced an English gentleman with an almost passionate conception of fair play, of protection of the weak, and of "playing the game". They have taught him personal initiative and resource, and how to command and to obey.' Historian Anthony Kirk-Greene summarises Lugard's argument: 'The best type of colonial administration would be found among those with a recognised record of above-average athletic success at school and university.'

As Lugard indicated, the relationship between sport and public life was not just symbolic. On pitches, tracks and courts, in clubhouses and changing areas, at competitions and regattas, and in sporting speeches, ceremonies, parties and dinners, boys and men nurtured the qualities and social networks they would draw upon professionally. In France, rowing regattas were opportunities for local industrialists and political leaders to give public speeches in '*l'intérêt national*'. Sport still has an overtly public significance today: the *Washington Post* describes how 'politics and golf have long been intertwined' and 'lobbyists have used it to cozy up to members of Congress'.[12]

Organised sport was a key conduit through which young men entered this public world, and sport's new codes and institutions gave men a way to gate-keep access to those activities. Men clamped down on women's presence, partly by introducing new sports with especially masculine identities from which women were excluded from the very beginning – such as American football, which originated around 1892 but which women were not permitted to play until over three decades later. And, as the example of cricket shows, the 'codification mania' also took pursuits in which women had once actively participated and remade them as male-only.

The activities that Lizzie and her peers had once loved in St Moritz were cases in point. Changes in those sports exemplified how attitudes towards female involvement shifted, as men reorganised sport around their own prerogatives and pushed women to the sidelines. In 1907, ladies' doubles tennis, which had been introduced at Wimbledon in 1899 as a mark of esteem for women's tennis, was removed from the championship. Tennis historian Robert Lake sees this as a key moment in a 'widespread backlash' against women's tennis, in which men increasingly worried that women's participation was making the sport 'unmanly' (and, vice versa, making 'women unwomanly'). Similarly, when Lizzie's friend Lottie Dod took up golf in the 1890s, it was a sport that was widely considered well suited to women. At the same time, however, there was mounting resistance from men like Lord Moncreiff (also known as Lord Wellwood) and amateur golfer Horace Hutchinson, who declared that 'constitutionally and physically women are unfitted for golf' and scorned the idea of a 'Ladies' Golf Union'. This anti-female feeling swelled, leading to the most prestigious golf clubs of the early twentieth century being male-only. Joyce Wethered, who was Ladies British Open Champion four times between 1922 and 1929, recalled having to wait outside in the cold 'for my male partners to emerge from the locker-room', and in 1946 the Royal Liverpool Golf Club denied entry to the wife of champion Sir Henry Cotton, declaring 'no woman ever has entered the clubhouse and, praise God, no woman ever will'. Today, golf clubs are still some of the last bastions of all-male sociability: the Royal and Ancient Golf Club of St Andrews, in Scotland, only admitted women as members as late as 2014.[13]

Cycling – which had geographically and politically emancipated women in the 1880s and 1890s – saw a similar retrenchment of female opportunities from the turn of the twentieth century onwards. In 1894, the League of American Wheelmen (LAW) took the decision to ban African-American men, immigrant men and all women from membership, despite the fact that women were already members of many regional chapters. The following year, the Massachusetts Bicycle Club reversed an earlier policy to include women and decided instead to uphold 'the old male club camaraderie'. In Britain in 1896, the Manchester Wheelers put to the vote a proposal to admit female members: it not only got voted down, it led to a permanent clause explicitly barring women from membership. In July 1895, a Black female cyclist – Katherine 'Kittie' Knox, a twenty-one-year-old seamstress from Boston who was already an LAW member before the new declaration – found herself, as a woman of colour, in contravention of two of the LAW's new rules. Cycling historian Hannah Ross describes how Knox protested by attending a meet in Asbury Park, New Jersey, and presenting her membership card. The *San Francisco Call* reported that Kittie's card was refused. The LAW's name wouldn't be changed until 1994, when it became the gender-neutral 'League of American Bicyclists'. Its 'colour ban' would not be revoked officially until 1999. And men found further ways to deter women from cycling. In 1895, the board of trustees at a school in Long Island, New York, worked with a local justice of the peace to ban female teachers from cycling and criminalise it as an 'improper practice' which 'had a tendency to create immorality' in women. In the early days of two colleges at the University of Oxford, Lady Margaret Hall and Somerville, 'neither cricket, hockey, nor bicycling were permitted to women students'.[14]

Even Lizzie's much-loved mixed-sex winter sports underwent the same reversals regarding female inclusion in the early decades of the new century. The official rules of bobsleighing, drawn up in the 1890s, had made mixed-sex teams mandatory, but in 1923 the Fédération Internationale de Bobsleigh et de Tobogganing did the opposite and banned women from international competition. Other national governing bodies followed suit and, by the end of the 1930s, women were entirely excluded from the sport's official face. (Today, female bobsleighers still compete in the Olympics in smaller teams than men, a symptom of the history of women's exclusion.) In 1929, the managing committee of the Cresta Run – where Lizzie had once photographed prize-winning female tobogganists whizzing down the course – banned women from the facility under the guise of concerns about the health of women's breasts. The ban effectively lasted until the winter of 2018/19, when the club voted to finally permit women to again use the Cresta on the same terms as men.

At first, ice-skating looked as if it was following the same trend. In the years after Lizzie successfully campaigned for female figure-skaters to be able to take the St Moritz Skating Club's advanced (previously male-only) test, a backlash gathered momentum which reversed the progress in women's rights. Numerous competitions in the early twentieth century restricted women from participating in the same number of events as men, or for the title of world champion. At the first Winter Olympic Games in 1924, no dressing room was provided for female figure-skaters, who instead squatted in the male Canadian speed-skating team's space. However, there was then an unexpected about-turn in this trajectory. Largely thanks to the influence of the popular Norwegian skater Sonja Henie, figure-skating became considered 'more and more of a woman's sport' after the 1920s, as one observer put it in 1941. However, this did not buck the trend of men refusing to share sporting spaces with women: women's presence continued to be thought of as compromising sport's ability to 'bolster manliness'. As figure-skating became more female-dominated, male involvement was increasingly considered effete and men kept women at arm's length, not by banning them, but by making their own exit from the sport. Today, as health studies scholar Mary Louise Adams reports, figure-skating is still considered a 'girly' or even 'sissy' pursuit, and male skaters – a minority – are often perceived as 'more feminine than other men'.[15]

As I have discovered, mountaineering had been historically more female-friendly than most other sports during the nineteenth century. The pursuit was initially populated by eccentrics and rebels who tended to sympathise with women wanting to escape their domestic prisons, and it was also much harder to stop women accessing open countryside than it was to bar them from clubhouses. Nevertheless, around the turn of the twentieth century, a more exclusionary attitude to women's participation in mountaineering swept across outdoor clubs and societies. Norway had a vibrant early history of women's rambling and climbing, but when the Norwegian Peak Club was established in 1908, it was male-only and women were banned from using its mountain hut in Skagadalen. In 1898 in

Britain, Charles Edward Mathews, who had helped to found the Alpine Club forty years earlier, set up the Climbers' Club mainly for rock-climbing in north Wales. As with his first club, it also excluded women from membership. On 24 January 1934, at the first annual general meeting of the Preston Mountaineering Club, its male founders 'resolved that ladies be barred from becoming members'. The first mountaineering club in Asia, the Japanese Alpine Club, was established as male-only in 1905. In January 1889, 'all interested parties' – men and women – were invited to discuss setting up a Scottish mountaineering club, but the founder member, William W. Naismith, considered climbing as 'one of the most manly . . . forms of exercise', and when the club was established it was male-only. Even more hurtfully, the Swiss Alpine Club – which had welcomed female members since 1863 and symbolised the progressive nature of Swiss mountain resorts for many women, including Lizzie Le Blond – took the decision in 1907, after a protracted, divisive debate, to kick women out. Women's exclusion from the SAC effectively lasted until 1980.[16]

Sexism had co-existed alongside support for women's sporting rights throughout the whole period in which Lizzie was climbing. But in the early twentieth century, that sexism intensified, and the balance between progress and backlash in relation to women's rights shifted so that the latter became more dominant. This occurred in almost every sporting discipline. In 1921, England's Football Association (FA) banned women from using FA grounds and female footballers were left to play on streets, 'in local parks and even dog-tracks'. In 1931, women were barred from professional baseball in the USA. In 1926, both the Home Secretary and the mayor of Hackney intervened to prevent a 'disgraceful' exhibition boxing match between two women. The Blackheath Ladies' Hockey Club closed on the outbreak of the First World War, and was lost until 1982, only two years after the first inclusion of women's hockey in the Olympics. Women's rowing was excluded from the earliest Olympics and, unlike their male counterparts, female rowers at Cambridge were long denied a 'Blue', the award recognising the commitment and skill required to compete at university level. When female teams played rugby between the 1880s and 1920s, the women faced riots, public outcries, cancellation of matches, suppression of publicity and formal bans that, in Samoa, lasted until the 1960s.[17]

The women who were predominantly affected by these turnarounds in female inclusion in sport were mostly white, middle- and upper-class and able-bodied – but they were certainly not the only victims. The men who reorganised sport in the latter half of the nineteenth century also excluded participants on the basis of further intersecting factors, which went beyond sex and gender and included social class, disability, race and ethnicity, and sexuality. The Royal Cinque Ports clubhouse in Deal, Kent, barred male golfers who were 'professionals' rather than gentlemen amateurs, and who were therefore apparently pursuing the sport for filthy lucre. The earliest Olympic Games were inaccessible to athletes with disabilities, and, at the turn of the century, deaf athletes were hindered by attempts to suppress sign language (leading to the establishment of the 'International Silent Games' in 1924, at which visual signals were permitted). In the 1870s and 1880s, Black men had been prominent in professional baseball but, as the game became more established and lucrative, those players were formally driven out, and Black baseball player Weldy Walker protested that the exclusion was 'a disgrace to the present age . . . and casts derision at the laws of the voice of the people – that say all men are created equal'.

The cultural punishments for homosexual sportspeople were so stringent that, as sociologist Eric Anderson points out, studying the history of gay sport has been very hard, verging on impossible, because very few could come out of the closet to male heterosexual teams. 'In the absence of a formal ban against gay athletes,' Anderson writes, straight men deterred their participation by 'creating a culture of silence surrounding gay athleticism' and 'by persistently using homophobic discourse to discredit homosexuality in general'. Straight men's appropriation of sport in the late nineteenth century to bolster heterosexual masculinity led to fears that gay athletes would undermine this project by rendering sport effete – and many also worried, along these same lines, that female involvement would both feminise sport and 'de-feminise' women. This anxiety particularly affected lesbian women. From around the turn of the twentieth century, horror at 'amazonian' female athletes – lesbian or straight – led to critics arguing that 'strenuous athletic pursuits endangered women and threatened the stability of society'; and that sport damaged women's ability to menstruate and reproduce, unleashed uncontrollable female sexual desire, eroded feminine respectability and eventually created 'failed heterosexuals' who embraced the 'homosexual menace'.[18] By the 1930s, lesbian athletes were being vilified as 'bogey women' whose 'mannishness' realised all of these anxieties.

Amid this broad commandeering of outdoor physical pursuits for white, non-disabled, heterosexual, middle- or upper-class men, the eviction of women from organised sport was a particularly pronounced and widespread trend. Each example of backlash against female participation in sport represented a profound loss for the individual women involved. And the cumulative impact – in which women all around the world were erased from the sports pages of publications, refused equal events in competitions, thrown out of clubs, and told they were morally and physically unsuited to vigorous physical activity – must have been devastating. Inevitably, many women must have given up sport entirely or didn't think it was ever for them in the first place and resigned themselves to lives lived mostly indoors.

Sport is never '*just* sport'. The ability to participate and be powerful in sport is directly linked to the ability to participate and be powerful in public life.

This is why male public schools were so keen on their pupils taking part in organised sport, and it is why men were so intent on excluding women. At the turn of the twentieth century, men protested against women's burgeoning influence in the public sphere by explicitly targeting their ability to play sport. When members of Cambridge University campaigned against women taking full degrees in 1897, it was not a replica of a female student, don or scientist that

Protesters against women being awarded full degrees at Cambridge University in 1897, hanging and mutilating an effigy of a female cyclist

they mutilated and hanged from the external walls of the Cambridge University Press bookshop, but an effigy of a female athlete: a cyclist, in fact – one of the most potent visualisations of how women could be liberated and empowered through sport. A *Tribune* journalist directly compared the refusal of 'the older English Universities' to grant degrees to women to the existence of 'sex disability' in sport, and specifically to the constraints that were newly imposed on female mountaineers.[19]

Male backlash against women's intertwined strengths in sport and the public arena was perpetrated in different ways. Sometimes men exacted their disapproval of women's sport at the same time as they imposed other constrictions on women's rights. At the University of Oxford, bans on women's participation in cricket, hockey and cycling were enforced along with fixed quotas on female students, which kept women's numbers far below men's. Both strictures worked together to limit women's freedom and power. At other times, women's sport was low-hanging fruit: it was an arena in which men could still control and constrain female athletes when they couldn't restrict women's power elsewhere. The FA's ban on female footballers is an example. The ban was issued relatively soon after two women's teams – Dick, Kerr Ladies and St Helens Ladies – played a particularly successful match in Liverpool in December 1920, at which the enormous numbers of spectators and the money raised for charity showed up the comparatively mediocre achievements of contemporary male footballers. Men could not stop women working for Dick, Kerr – an engineering company, where female workers had produced weapons to support the war effort, played football in their spare time, and gained status and camaraderie – but men could, and did, cut those women down to size by taking away their sporting facilities, spectators and press coverage.

As this suggests, the conjoined backlash from men against women's prominence in sport and public life was, in large part, a reaction against recent significant advances in women's rights. Over the second half of the nineteenth century, women's standing in the public sphere followed a trajectory close to that of female participation in sport. Female pioneers successfully fought for greater power, autonomy and rights, in law, the workplace, community leadership roles, education, business and politics. In Britain in the 1870s and 1880s, the Married Women's Property Acts, the Matrimonial Causes Acts and acts pertaining to the custody of children increased the rights of women within their marriages, and permitted wives to own property, retain their own income, engage in business and manage their own capital. Qualification of Women Acts meant that certain women could be elected to council positions and then, later, as MPs. Women were first allowed to serve on mixed juries in Britain in 1919 as part of the Sex Disqualification (Removal) Act, which also enabled women to join professions and professional bodies and to receive university degrees, and the Representation of the People Act in Britain in 1918 gave women (aged over thirty, and who owned sufficient property) the right to vote for the first time in Great Britain and Ireland. Similar legislation was passed across North America, and women's presence became more visible elsewhere in public too. By the end of the nineteenth century, in Europe and in North America, women were entering the workforce in swelling numbers as telephone operators, typists and cashiers, and also in professional roles, as doctors, journalists and lawyers. But just as women's success in sport was undercut by male backlash, so too were women's gains in public life destabilised by men's imposition of limits onto women's freedom outside the house and their ability to move around public space.

Such constraints on free movement were felt by women in many, if not most, outdoor spaces in the second half of the nineteenth century. Public transport is one example. When railways were first built across Britain and North America, they were hailed by many as a prospective 'engine of liberation' for women, which would enable them to travel more widely, cheaply and independently than before. But in Britain, the male-biased design of passenger trains put paid to that feminist emancipatory potential. Carriages were constructed to prioritise gentlemen's desire for privacy: they were divided into sealed compartments, none of which were visible from the next, with no connecting corridors, and each compartment was only accessible through external doors leading out of the train to the platform, which were usually locked between stations. There were often no alarm cords or means of communication with the guard's van. For women, this design could be terrifying, imprisoning them in closed boxes with male strangers and with no means of escape.

In June 1875, a twenty-one-year-old woman called Rebecca Kate Dickinson was sexually assaulted in one such carriage in broad daylight in Surrey. Many women had been attacked by men on the railways before – in July 1864, a newspaper described the 'insults and annoyance' that were directed at lone female travellers as a 'frequent' occurrence – but Dickinson's wealth and prestigious family connections, and her assailant's identity, meant that the case garnered an almost unprecedented amount of attention. Dickinson was assaulted by Colonel Valentine Baker, who was a close friend of Lizzie Le Blond's first husband, Fred Burnaby, and was travelling to London to dine with the commander-in-chief of the British Army, the Duke of Cambridge. Dickinson managed to evade Baker by getting out of the compartment door and balancing precariously on the footboard as the train sped through tunnels at 45mph, until the guard and driver wondered why so many passengers were staring out of the window and brought the train to an emergency stop. After a high-profile court case, Baker was found guilty of indecent assault, imprisoned and fined. He was thrown out of the army, after which he left the country.[20]

The Dickinson case prompted an outpouring of similar stories from women – a precursor to #MeToo – and a fierce debate about how to keep women safer outdoors. In key ways, that commentary anticipated present-day discussions about male violence against women in public space. Baker's identity as an 'officer and gentleman' sent a shockwave through the nation, much like the discovery that the attacker and murderer of thirty-three-year-old Sarah Everard in London in March 2021 was a serving police officer. Both cases highlighted the extent of women's vulnerability; that it is not just untrustworthy male members of the general public whom we have to fear, but also the very men – among the ranks of the police and army – who are supposed to be protecting us and upholding the law. Journalists argued too about whose responsibility it was to preserve women's safety outdoors: guards and drivers, carriage designers, the police – or women themselves? One idea that was mooted to preserve women's security was all-female carriages and women-only rooms in stations. But, although characters such as Margaret Hale in Elizabeth Gaskell's novel *North and South* were 'thankful to be able to turn into the ladies' waiting-room', sex segregation also had its critics.[21] There was very little to prevent men entering ladies-only coaches and rooms, so that many women felt that such spaces were really limiting the freedom of female victims, rather than curtailing the liberty of male perpetrators of violence.

Like trains, restaurants were another nineteenth-century public space in which men formally constrained women's movements. Restaurants first appeared in the United States in the 1830s, and in Britain shortly after and, like railway carriages, they were designed with men's preferences primarily in mind: many featured private supper rooms with adjoining bedrooms in which men hosted prostitutes. Initially proprietors strictly limited almost all other female presence, arguing that 'respectable' ladies should not share spaces with 'disreputable women'. In the US between the 1830s and 1860s, Black women were completely banned from restaurants and white women were only permitted in sex-segregated dining rooms – 'Ladies' ordinaries' or 'ladies' parlours' – which generally had separate entrances and were frequently hidden away on top floors. Like ladies' carriages on trains, these spaces limited women's liberty without impacting on men's freedom of movement: in establishments such as the United States Hotel in Boston, men walked around without restriction, including into the women's dining rooms, where they could take meals if they wished. In 1907, Harriet Stanton Blatch (suffragist and daughter of women's rights activist Elizabeth Cady Stanton) angrily noted that 'men, no matter what their characters may be, are admitted anywhere', whereas waiters and maître d's rigorously assessed female patrons' 'respectability' before granting them entry, and then confined them to small ladies-only rooms in the attic – where they were still harassed by male diners. (Blatch also pointed out that it was not the prostitutes from whom women were supposedly being protected who posed most 'annoyance' to women; it was men.) Something similar took place in American saloons, which sprang up in frontier towns from the 1820s to cater to soldiers, fur-traders and trappers. Saloons were important civic buildings, doubling as banks, post offices and employment agencies, and they were likewise male domains, where men met with prostitutes, and from which other women were sometimes formally excluded by laws and ordinances.[22]

After the 1860s, restaurant proprietors started doing away with ladies' parlours and regulated women's presence in different ways. In the 1860s and 1870s, the managers of Delmonico's on 14th Street (one of New York's oldest restaurants) did not allow women to enter its café space at all, and permitted all-female groups of diners in the restaurant at lunchtime only in private rooms; at dinner, women were tolerated solely in the company of men. By the end of the nineteenth century, most high-end restaurants and hotels in the United States did not permit women who were 'unescorted' by male chaperones to dine in the main dining rooms after around 7 p.m. When

Blatch and the Appalachian educationalist Hettie Wright Graham tried to eat dinner in the outdoor roof-garden restaurant of New York's Hoffman House in 1907, a waiter directed them to the indoor 'Ladies' Room'. After refusing and requesting a table in the main space, they were asked to leave. Blatch and Graham took the hotel to court and their case highlighted how women's right to move freely around public space was an urgent political issue – but they did not win.[23]

Restrictions on women's movements were not just a feature of new types of public space, such as restaurants and trains, which had not existed prior to the nineteenth century. Constraints on female presence were also introduced into older spaces, where women had once been tolerated or even welcomed. In the seventeenth and eighteenth centuries, women's drinking in British taverns and inns had been frowned upon, but not formally proscribed. But from the 1820s right up until the 1970s, female drinkers in Britain were generally allowed only in separate drinking rooms, called 'ladies' snugs'. In 1941, a male patron refused to call a mixed-sex drinking establishment a 'pub', because 'pub' was short for 'public house' and, he reasoned, women did not belong in a 'pub' in the same way that they did not belong in 'public'. (In the same interview, he linked his complaint about female pub-goers to women's presence in sport and grumbled that one problem with female patrons was that they arrived 'fresh from a tennis court or with their bicycles'.)[24]

Women's access to educational spaces also changed in the nineteenth century. In many ways, this was a story of progress: in the second half of the century, nations around the world passed statutes allowing some women (sometimes including women of colour) to attend state and private schools offering equivalent education to boys, receive college awards, serve as school governors and on school boards, enrol in mixed- and single-sex universities, study 'manly' subjects such as dentistry and medicine, take degrees and even become professors. But what was given with one hand was diluted or taken away by another. As Caroline Criado Perez shows, men's aggression towards female involvement in public life often intensifies as that participation swells, rather than fizzling out. Across academic culture, there was a passionate commitment from men to contain or diminish women's burgeoning presence. In the 1860s and 1870s, the universities of Cambridge and Oxford formally decided to allow women to study in all-female colleges – but both institutions introduced quotas that radically restricted the number of women students (to 500 – around one-tenth of the student body – at Cambridge, where limitation on female enrolment remained until 1987), and although women were allowed to study and even teach, Cambridge refused to award them degrees until 1948.

In some academic subjects, women found their credibility diminishing, rather than increasing, over time. At the end of the nineteenth century, women were actively encouraged to join the British Astronomical Association, and Dava Sobel's *The Glass Universe* shows how female astronomers were widely employed at the Harvard College Observatory in the same period. A few decades later, however, there was a change of heart in the culture of astronomy and Harvard's president, Abbott Lawrence Lowell, decreed that women such as astronomer Celia Payne-Gaposchkin should *not* be granted teaching appointments and J. J. Thomson, director of Cambridge's Cavendish Laboratory, expressed the view that women 'simply did not have the intellectual capacity to be world-class physicists'.[25]

Similarly, in the eighteenth and early nineteenth centuries, botany had been a discipline in which women were particularly active: historian Emanuel D. Rudolph has named 1,454 female botanists in the USA and Canada in this period. One was Jane Colden, who lived on a 3,000-acre farm on the Hudson in the 1750s and 1760s and systematically described around 140 wild plants per year, including a hitherto unidentified plant with the local name Gold Thread, which she named *Fibraurea* – and she corresponded with other leading botanists, male and female, about her discoveries. But in 1828, John Lindley was appointed the first professor of botany at University College, London, and he announced his intention to 'redeem one of the most interesting departments of Natural History from the obloquy which has become attached to it' – by which he meant botany's historical association with women. To 'redeem' his subject for men, Lindley downgraded women's role to 'unscientific readers' who only needed to glean enough knowledge to teach their 'little people'. Consequently, even though botany had been 'traditionally considered a relatively acceptable scientific pursuit for women', the reformulation of botany's identity in the nineteenth century as a manly subject means that female botanists' work has not been adequately recognised: a survey at Kew Gardens has found that, of all the new plant species named between 1753 and 2013, fewer than 3 per cent of their names were published by female authors.[26] The type of nonprofessional engagement pursued by women like Jane Colden was no longer taken seriously, and Colden is almost entirely forgotten today.

Women's education was also affected by the introduction and (re)design of public libraries, and the rules that managed women's presence there. From the early 1700s, circulating libraries had been popular among both men and women, charging a relatively cheap yearly subscription to lend books. Enlightenment moralists fretted about the effect on women of unregulated access to books, but these spaces were important in promoting the work of female writers and encouraging women's reading. Free public libraries were established in Britain and the US after the 1850s, to widen access to books even further, especially to working-class men – but, as they did so, the spaces offered to women became more strictly limited (on the rationale that the presence of working-class men endangered the reputation and safety of respectable ladies).

Some men openly depicted women as a threat to male dominion over spaces of learning. The creator of a cartoon from the 1890s – 'Chaos in the Lending Library' – embodied 'Chaos' as a woman, invading men's territory, climbing the bookcase's ladder (like a female mountaineer) and raining tomes on the male readers beneath. In 1855, Charles Folsom, librarian at the Boston Athenaeum, thought that 'a considerable portion of a general library should be to [a decent woman] a sealed book' and, the following year, the authors of the first American manual of library arrangement recommended the construction of 'a smaller reading room which may be used exclusively by females', separated from the main (men's) space. Historian Abigail A. Van Slyck found that, between 1884 and 1897, at least a third of the US libraries listed in the *Library Journal* directed female readers to use 'ladies' reading rooms'. These were often placed next to children's libraries and, instead of the gravitas of large tables, hefty chairs and portraits of public personages which adorned the main reading rooms, ladies' spaces were more often decorated with rocking chairs, fireplaces, flimsy coffee tables, and paintings of flowers, and contained magazines rather than books – more like domestic parlours rather than prestigious portions of the public sphere.[27]

Men also deterred women from leaving the home and venturing outdoors in much cruder ways. Reports of men harassing women on the street increased in the late nineteenth century to the extent that it was talked about as a distinct phenomenon, perhaps for the first time. US actor, writer and suffragist Elizabeth Robins described 'learn[ing] . . . to be afraid in broad daylight' after numerous encounters in the 1880s with 'the darker moods of men', including being 'helped over a dangerous crossing by two gentlemen' who 'said things that frightened me'. The same threat that excluded women from restaurants and saloons – that women might be mistaken for prostitutes and have men's sexual advances forced upon them – was also used to deter women from city streets. Historian Judith Walkowitz describes how late nineteenth-century conduct books and magazines 'frequently admonished their female readers not to window-shop or in any other way exhibit "lounging behavior" on the street' and insisted that it was generally a woman's fault if a man spoke to her. British suffragist and cyclist Helena Swanwick recalled that, when she was a young woman in London in the 1880s, she had been warned by her mother that: 'I would be taken for a "bad woman" if [I] went about Piccadilly or Oxford Street unaccompanied' and, in the 1890s, she was on the receiving end of jeering and catcalls while cycling in public.[28]

A perverse contract was at play here. Men claimed communal spaces as their own by treating women in them as if they were sexually available; and men then claimed that any women entering those spaces were doing so in full knowledge of the male sexual advances they would receive – and so must be acquiescent. Some men openly alluded to this contract. Zoologist Sir Edwin Ray Lankester, founder of the Marine Biological Association in 1884 and director of the Natural History Museum in London, recommended that if women 'really do wish to be left alone', they should '*avoid the haunts of men*'. By 'the haunts of men', he really meant everywhere outdoors, including nominally shared public spaces such as urban thoroughfares: it would be 'comic' or illogical for a woman to 'object to being spoken to in the street', he observed. Lankester practised what he preached. In October 1894, he was arrested for loitering (presumably with intent to harass, or to buy sex) in Piccadilly Circus at midnight.[29]

For women of colour in the nineteenth century, the limits imposed on free movement in public space were intensified by racial segregation. Civil rights conferred after the abolition of slavery in the US were effectively stalled by the 'Jim Crow laws' – a series of state statutes and Supreme Court decisions from the 1870s which permitted the exclusion of people of colour from 'Whites Only' spaces, including restaurants, transport, prisons, schools and in the armed forces. In American restaurants, people of colour were allowed to order food only to take away and were barred from dining spaces. Across the public sphere, women of colour faced a double form of exclusion, not just from areas claimed by white men, but from Black men's spaces (such as male-only Black youth groups) and often from white women's spaces too. Writer and activist bell hooks describes how white women's early twentieth-century campaigns to enter the work arena were often explicitly hostile to Black women workers, who were 'seen as a threat to white female security; [as they] represented more competition'. Black women and Jewish women were excluded from many white-women-only clubs – such as the General Federation of Women's Clubs – that were established to confer wider access to the worlds of education, work and politics. And there were other intersections too, through which many women found their freedom outdoors restricted in multiple ways. From 1867 in the US, women with certain disabilities were constrained by the so-called 'Ugly Laws', introduced in cities including San Francisco, New

Orleans, Portland, Chicago and Pennsylvania as part of an anti-vagrancy push to 'cleanse' public spaces of anyone who was 'diseased, maimed, mutilated or in any way deformed so as to be an unsightly or disgusting object'.[30]

As these examples show, the limitations that were imposed on women's participation in sport around the turn of the twentieth century were not unique. They were part and parcel of a raft of restrictions introduced over the second half of the nineteenth century, which constrained women's ability to move around freely outdoors, and which were imposed in reaction to the burgeoning success and authority of women in the public domain. In many cases, these new curbs on female freedom did not underline pre-existing customs. Instead, they represented a cultural shift which fundamentally altered – and diminished – women's freedoms to participate in social, political, intellectual and physical activity. In taverns and inns, libraries, academic disciplines such as astronomy and botany, and even as pedestrians on the streets, many women found themselves less welcome in supposedly communal spaces than they had been before. For many such women, these new limits on their free movement around towns and cities must have felt like a drastic reduction of earlier liberties. That sense of bereavement was perhaps similar to the grief that many women experienced when they married and lost the ability to behave like single, autonomous agents. In May 1860, Nellie Wetherbee, a young married woman in San Francisco, described how previously, when she had been single, she'd enjoyed 'festival-going'. But now, she wrote sadly in her diary, she was 'an old married woman' and so 'everyday' consisted of 'the same thing': she mostly 'staid in', indoors in her home, with an occasional walk to the park with her husband, if he agreed to act as her chaperone.[31]

If a woman is made to feel disobedient, unwelcome and unsafe every time she walks alone or with female friends on the street or in a park, eats in a restaurant, drinks in a pub, reads in a library, enrols in school, college or university, attends a meeting or protest, travels on public transport, enters a workplace, voting station, council offices or parliament, goes for a run or attempts a round of golf, then she faces significant obstacles to her ability to live a life outside the home. Despite the significant legislative advances that women made in the second half of the nineteenth century, many found their ambitions hamstrung by the myriad constraints that men devised to limit female presence outdoors. When men couldn't overturn women's formal legislative gains, they turned instead to the arena of culture to restrict women's freedoms.

These two currents pulled in opposite directions: one towards women's progress in the public arena, and the other towards women's return to domestic enslavement. And those currents co-existed in the same historical period. This underscores what I have already discovered: that backlash and progress do not always neatly alternate, one era tidily following the other. Instead, backlash and progress can occur in the same place, at the same time, and this is what was happening around the turn of the twentieth century. On the one hand, women's rights campaigns had achieved unprecedented successes, and numerous commentators saw the impressive achievements of women in sport as a natural parallel. But, at the same time, women in both sport and public life were also facing an intensification of the sexism that had always been an undercurrent in their daily lives. In the face of women's accomplishments, men were fighting back by claiming the outdoors as their exclusive domain – and, increasingly, the men were winning.

But *why*? Why were men so reluctant to share these spaces and activities with women? And are there similarities with what is happening today?

In 1883, Emile Zola published *Au Bonheur des Dames* (translated as *The Ladies' Delight* or *The Ladies' Paradise*), a novel set in a Parisian department store of the same name. The male proprietor of the shop, Octave Mouret, was, in Zola's words, 'at war' with femininity. He deliberately designed the store's layout to control female customers' behaviour – 'to hold [women] at his mercy', and, as literary critic Vaheed Ramazani observes, his 'sole passion' was to 'conquer woman', manipulating female customers and employees 'with mechanical regularity, an entire nation of women passing through the force and logic of the churning gears'. Au Bonheur des Dames was a 'machine for devouring women', in a country 'afflicted' by a debilitating new 'malady' – 'uncontrolled femininity'.[32]

Ramazani suggests that one motive for Mouret's attempts to control women's freedom of movement in his shop lay in France's defeat in the Franco-Prussian War (1870–71). In Zola's account, France subsequently became enfeebled, 'womanish', 'impotent' and 'sterile', suffering from an illness that resembled 'female nervous weakness'. To recover from such woeful degeneration of national strength, a 'virile healing' was necessary, in which women's influence must be suppressed and manliness revivified.

In Britain and the Empire, there were similar concerns about degenerating male strength. Valentine Baker's assault of Rebecca Kate Dickinson undermined the assumption that the British officer class embodied a morally upright form of masculinity of which the nation could be proud. Such worries deepened in the wake of the Boer War (1899–1902). As had happened in France in the Franco-Prussian War, British troops were overconfident and underprepared, and the Boers' guerrilla tactics prolonged the war much longer than possibly anyone had expected. The war drew attention to the poor physical condition of British men: a Committee on Physical Deterioration set up after the war found that 'close to 60 per cent' of all applicants to the British military had been rejected as physically unfit to serve. As imperial rulers, Britons had entertained a sense of racial pre-eminence, but the report highlighted how the national physique was far from superior: children of the working poor were malnourished from birth and they matured into underfed adults, suffering from rickets and other poverty-related diseases. Sport historians John Nauright and Timothy Chandler point out that the committee's conclusion – that Britain was a nation of deteriorating men – seemed to be borne out in sport in the following years when, during a series of rugby tours in 1905, 1908 and 1912, teams from New Zealand, South Africa and Australia 'beat nearly all the [British] teams they played and displayed vigorous and innovative styles of play previously unseen in Britain'.[33]

In the United States and Britain, anxieties about the impending 'end of men' were also reactions to economic and political changes in the second half of the nineteenth century. In 1886, Henry James's novel *The Bostonians* voiced fears that 'the whole generation is womanized; the masculine tone is passing out of the world; it's a feminine, nervous, hysterical, chattering age'.[34] In the States, many white middle-class and elite men linked such unease about 'degenerating manliness' to a perception that their domination of citizenship had been eroded by the fourteenth and fifteenth amendments in 1868 and 1870. These granted citizenship rights and equal protection under the law to formerly enslaved men and women. Male ascendancy over the public sphere was also felt to be eroded in the US from the 1830s, and Britain from the 1870s, by the legislative landslides that expanded women's rights within their marriages and in political and professional life. To many men, increasing numbers of female university students, doctors, lawyers and office workers represented an erosion of their command over the workplace. Some men derided the feminisation of offices – the unwelcome arrival of plants, rugs and lampshades – and held women responsible for their own perceived decline in status, autonomy, income and manliness.

Disquiet about the quality of 'male stock' was fuelled by nineteenth-century scientific theories of 'degeneration'. Psychiatrist Bénédict Augustin Morel and criminologist Cesare Lombroso claimed that criminality could be passed down from generation to generation, and in his 1880 book *Degeneration: A Chapter in Darwinism*, Ray Lankester – who would become the street-harassing director of the Natural History Museum – worried that humans were not evolving towards improvement, but that 'we are as likely to degenerate as to progress' over time. Psychoanalyst Sigmund Freud's ideas suggested that grown men were stymied by perverted desires stemming from traumatic childhood memories, and medical journals increasingly blamed men, rather than female prostitutes, for the transmission of syphilis. Physician and social critic Max Nordau's book – which, like Lankester's, was also called *Degeneration* – held men's 'effeminacy' responsible for deterioration in societies' artistic achievements. In the light of Nordau's theories, Oscar Wilde – whose sentencing for homosexual acts took place two months after the publication of Nordau's book in Britain – seemed to many like an example of an artist who could 'exert a disturbing and corrupting influence on the views of a whole generation'.[35]

In the face of this widespread paranoia about the degeneration of (white, heterosexual, able-bodied) male power, men invested sport with a particularly urgent importance. Many sporting and outdoor projects were explicitly aimed at boosting male strength in the public realm. In 1903, Robert Baden-Powell returned to Britain from the Boer War and composed *Scouting for Boys*, which used outdoor exercises, games and camps to 'take [boys] in hand in a practical way', and rescue them from weakness, smoking and 'girlitis'. Similar projects occurred on the European continent. Historian of science Vanessa Heggie charts how Frederick Ludwig Jahn formulated a system of exercise in Germany called *Turnen*, based on classical Greek exercises, to 'rebuild degenerate national bodies'. In early nineteenth-century Sweden, Per Henrik Ling felt that a light had been shone on Swedish men's physical decline by the loss of the northern territories during the Finnish War of 1809. He subsequently developed a form of gymnastics to improve Sweden's military capabilities and founded the Royal Central Institute of Gymnastics – from which women were excluded. And in 1844, the YMCA was imported into the United States from Britain, where it had a muscular Christian ideology that sought to provide young men, specifically, with opportunities for sport that would enable them to counter 'the degeneration of the white Protestant Anglo-Saxon race'.[36]

Key to sport's capacity to boost male strength was the exclusion of femininity and effeminacy from its spaces. The Olympic Games are one of the most famous examples of the way in which men used sport to boost manliness and eject women.

When the Franco-Prussian War broke out in 1870, Pierre de Frédy, Baron de Coubertin, was seven years old. Invading troops marched through his family's summer home at the Château de Mirville in Normandy, packing his croquet box with explosives. When he was twelve years old, a major excavation of Olympia took place and there was a fervour across Europe for the rituals of classical sport. These 'planted seeds of hope' in his mind and gave him an idea for a way in which France might be saved from its ignominy. As an adult, de Coubertin drew on the model of the ancient Olympic Games – as well as displays of Greek athleticism in English public schools – and he proposed that a similar competition in the modern era might repair the male fragility that had led to France's defeat: 'Whoever learns not to shrink from a football scrimmage will not retreat from the mouth of a Prussian cannon,' he wrote.[37]

The exclusion of women was a founding principle of the modern Olympic Games. De Coubertin emphasised that the Games were based on the concept of 'solemn and periodic exaltations of male athleticism.' Later, he stated that the very 'Philosophic Foundations' of the Olympics were that women's 'role should be above all to crown the [male] victors, as was the case in the ancient tournaments': women should be handkerchief-fluttering spectators. As late as the 1970s, Olympic officials were justifying their exclusion of women from any running events longer than 1,500 metres on the basis that 'women are too weak and fragile' and that their 'reproductive organs would get damaged'.[38] A women's marathon event wouldn't be introduced until 1984, and this was because of men who, like de Coubertin, believed that women's sports were 'against the laws of nature'.

In the early 1980s, anthropologist Peggy Reeves Sanday explored the circumstances in which men dominate public space and exclude women. For Sanday, the emergence of 'separate spheres' between men and women was not a specifically nineteenth-century phenomenon. Instead, she argued that the exclusion of women from the outdoors and from public life was characteristic of certain types of society at particular times. She linked these patterns to communities in which masculine roles involving violence are highly valued – such as those that depend on hunting big game or fighting off invasion. Sanday pointed out that, at times of stress, when the society feels itself to be internally poorly resourced and/or vulnerable to external attack, male violence becomes more prized. Men respond by making 'the whole of public life . . . synonymous with the male collective': they exclude and control women's presence outside the home, and visit violence upon them, becoming more 'rape prone'. There is 'a causal relationship' between 'depleting resources, cultural disruption . . . and the oppression of women', she concludes.[39]

I am not entirely convinced by Sanday's argument. It seems to me that men do not just oppress women when they're feeling under attack, but when they're feeling powerful too. And I'm not sure that men's violence against women is just a scapegoat for different anxieties: often pure hatred of women is enough of a motivating factor for violent men, in and of itself. Nevertheless, Sanday's blueprint fits the cultural disruptions of the nineteenth century. Driven by a sense of their own 'depleting resources', men devised projects to shore up masculinity against the menace of 'degeneration'. Those projects tried to boost male power by appropriating public spaces (including sporting facilities) for these aims and keeping out the supposedly weakening influence of women.

There are marked similarities between the turn of the twentieth century and our present times. In *More Than a Woman*, feminist writer Caitlin Moran describes talking with a man who expresses many of the same anxieties as his late nineteenth-century counterparts. He articulates his painful awareness that, over the last fifty years, women have made enormous progress in citizenship rights, public roles and professional life, while men have arguably lost power and status over the same period.[40] And women have done all this while also shouldering principal responsibility for their families and homes. A scan through the online chatboards of Mumsnet paints a picture of thousands of households across the world in which these dynamics are visible. Women skilfully juggle high-powered jobs, complex family arrangements, large networks of friends, hobbies and voluntary commitments, and engage in contemporary political debate, while their husbands retreat into childishness: refusing to take on equal responsibility for domestic life, not engaging with decisions about children or schooling, sulking when their needs don't always come first, envying and hating their impressive wives and withdrawing into escapist worlds of gaming, pornography, obsessions, addictions and extra-marital affairs.

Sanday suggested that men's misogyny intensifies in periods when there are panics about invasion, war and depleting national resources, and this is also visible today. Men's perceived loss of influence has been exacerbated by de-industrialisation, and by recent fears about climate crisis, immigration, Brexit and Putin's Russia. That men project their own sense of weakness and redundancy onto hatred for women is overtly visible on online forums occupied by incels and men who buy sex from prostitutes. And, just as they did in the early twentieth century, many men today react by trying to boost their manliness by commandeering public space. They do so via intensified street harassment and violence, intimidation of girls and women in sport, and workplace harassment, and by reversing feminist legislation such as *Roe v Wade*.

But Sanday was optimistic that this scenario is not set in stone in perpetuity. 'Change the cultural plot,' she wrote, 'and sex roles are conceived differently. Change sex roles and the plot will change.' We could hope that the social stressors of climate crisis, war and economic collapse might reduce in the future, and that, as a consequence, men will be impelled to oppress women with less force. Or, we could tackle the belief that male violence is necessary for ensuring countries' safety and security – and one way of doing so is for women to have more power.[41]

As men appropriated the outdoors – the public sphere and the sporting world – around the turn of the twentieth century, female athletes became key campaigners. Sport became a contested political space in which women vehemently resisted their wider marginalisation in public life. One example of female rebellion can be found in the first modern Olympic Games, in 1896. Women were banned from the marathon race, but a working-class Greek woman called Stamáta Revíthi insisted on running nonetheless, despite having been refused permission by the IOC. An anonymous artist imagined Revíthi in the aftermath of her defiant run. In the resulting painting, she bears muscular legs half-hidden by a hitched-up calf-length skirt.

Her sore feet have been removed from leather shoes and allowed to splay against the ground. Behind her, an audience of men and boys – priests, villagers, spectators, IOC officials, athletes – stare on with a mixture of curiosity, horror and condemnation. But her determined face turns up to the heavens. She is in her own world; a better world for women.[42]

Now, I more fully understand some of the methods how, and some of the reasons why, men try to drive women out of the outdoors. And so, next, I want to discover the ways in which women like Revíthi resisted. How did women fight against their ostracisation from mainstream sport at the turn of the twentieth century? How did they successfully take up their places again under the limelight, decades later? And might these earlier women's accounts suggest ways in which we can deal with men's hostility outdoors today?

I hope that those examples might also aid me, as an individual. I hope that these defiant women's stories might help me to feel more at home outdoors, in a world that has seemed crueller since losing my family.

PART THREE

Recovery

9.

Risk management

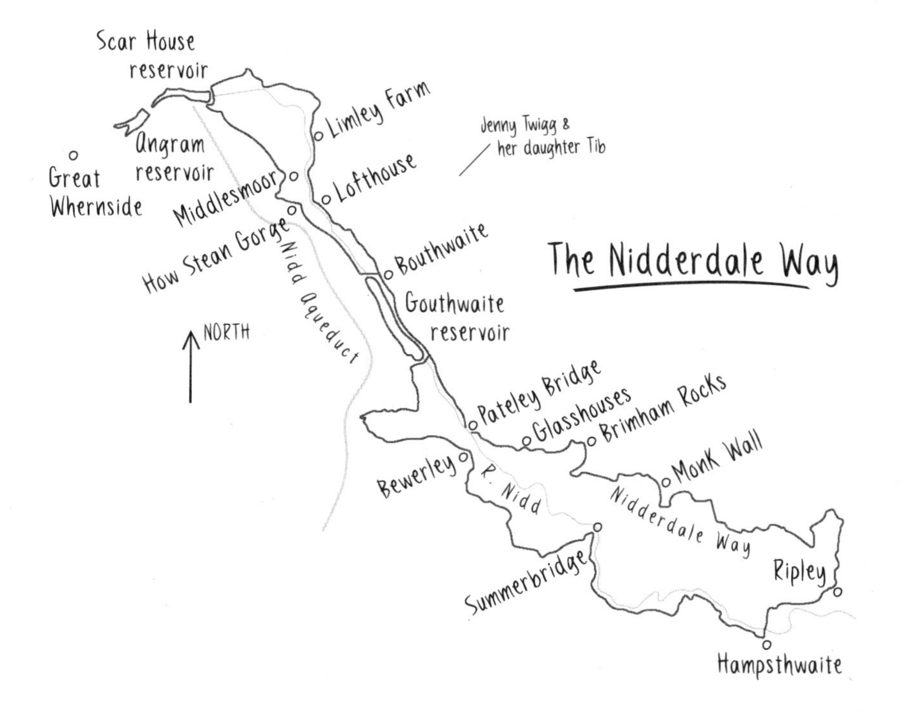

After my Dales Way recce in June 2020, I develop an injury at the top of my right foot. When I flex the big toe it creaks and the tendon moves like a splintering slat of wood. A physiotherapist says I have tenosynovitis, an inflammation of the sheath that usually lubricates motion of the extensor tendon to allow the toes to lift, splay and clutch. He is unsure what has caused it. Perhaps my shoes are too big and my toes have been forced to grip, too hard, too often, on descents. Perhaps my shoes are too tight across the top and the laces have irritated the tendon. Perhaps I have simply been running too much. He massages my foot, gives me a list of twice-daily exercises and suggests I have a short break from running.

This is not the first time I've been injured or ill and have had to stop running, and I'm sure it won't be the last. In a later, grimmer winter lockdown during early 2021, I will be rushing through domestic chores – at the same time as answering my three small children's questions about online phonics and maths home-schooling worksheets, while also half-participating in an online work meeting, and writing this book. Realising we are low on fresh milk, I take advantage of a moment when a colleague is speaking to run to the freezer. On my way back, I let a container of six pints of frozen milk slip through my fingers and fall squarely onto my left foot, smashing the phalange of the big toe and a smaller metatarsal, and confining me to the house for nearly six weeks.

These periods in which I cannot run make me confront anxieties that are usually suppressed by running. In particular, when I cannot run, I worry all the time about illness: about twinges in my sinuses, aches in my calf muscles, faint raspiness at the back of my throat, a stretched feeling across my sternum, audible clicks, pins and needles in my thumb, a previously undetected bump under my jaw or a liver spot on my hand. I latch onto the smallest pinprick of unexpected sensation and worry away at it, like a splinter that grows ever more painful with the rubbing. My symptoms never seem to be those of minor maladies, but of potentially terminal illness: cancer, a brain haemorrhage, deep-vein thrombosis, sepsis.

A pandemic is a bad time for those of us who are anxious about our health. We are now explicitly being encouraged to monitor ourselves for symptoms – coughing, loss of smell and taste, fatigue. Before Covid, these symptoms were considered mostly harmless, but now they portend a potentially fatal condition. In normal times, statistics show that women suffer more from anxiety disorders than men and, during the pandemic, researchers find that depression, fretfulness and expressions of trauma are rising significantly in women, who are '1.6 times as likely to report high anxiety' as men. An online study conducted by psychiatrist Bao-Liang Zhong and his team in 2020 reveals that in China, 'although women were better informed about the disease than men during the Covid-19 pandemic and complied more with advice, such as wearing masks and avoiding public spaces, they also reported not knowing whether the pandemic could be brought under control'.[1] And much of this rising unease in women is expressed in health anxiety.

Women's disproportionate propensity to health anxiety has a number of overlapping causes. As women globally are more likely to be carers, we are more likely to be in close proximity to sick and dying people – which is shown to fuel fears about our own health. Women have a higher life expectancy than men, meaning we are more likely to live with age-associated health conditions, and to live through more bereavements and illnesses, and severe health anxiety does seem to be 'more prevalent in older than younger adults'. Women are also statistically more vulnerable to traumatic physical events, such as sexual assault and difficult pregnancies and births, and so we frequently feel our bodies to be under attack and out of our control. And women are less likely to find adequate reassurance from doctors. Historically, female anatomy has been seen as a defective version of male anatomy: sixteenth-century physicians taught that the vagina and cervix were merely inverted forms of 'the penis of the male' and may be 'perfected' by being 'driven outside the body'. Things aren't a whole lot better now: around the world, women were not routinely included in clinical trials until the 1990s; 80 per cent of pain medication is tested only on men; and, as I have already found out, female bodies are shockingly underrepresented in sports science. Women's bodies are, to many doctors, like the unknown *dark continent* to which Freud compared women's sexual psychology. And so there are often few medical professionals whom anxious women trust to reassure us. A friend tells me how her own 'health anxiety [is] caused by being failed by doctors so many times'.[2]

In many ways, I worry about my health in the same way that I worry about going for a run alone at night. In both scenarios, I feel at risk from uncertain threats. I do not feel able to fully trust authorities like doctors or the police to keep me safe. I think that, for women, health anxiety and agoraphobia can both be internalisations of sensing that we are perpetually at risk in the world, with no safety nets.

Depression and melancholia are sometimes understood as forms of mourning or deprivation. They often relate to people, objects, experiences, relationships or states that we may not consciously recognise ourselves as having lost – perhaps we never possessed them in the first place – but they remain essential to human flourishing nonetheless. Women are statistically more prone to anxiety and depression than men. So does this suggest that women are more likely to be living with grief? Are women disproportionately depressed because we are being deprived of inalienable human needs, such as freedom, personal security and safety?

To minimise these feelings of loss and anxiety, I adopt certain safety behaviours as I make my way through the world. I buy gadgets to monitor my heart-rate, blood pressure, pulse oxygen levels and temperature; just as I carry a rape alarm, don't run on unlit paths and set my running watch so that Pete can track my movements. But sometimes the risks seem too great and the solution to both the risk of infection and the risk of assault is to stay at home.

Yet running outside is what most decreases my anxiety. It acts as proof of my health and, when I'm covering long distances, I can tell myself that my 'symptoms' are merely unsurprising side effects of very hard physical work.

I've come to think that risk – how we assess being at risk in the world and how we manage that risk – is a very complicated issue for women. Women are certainly at risk from illness and from male violence outdoors, but I think that we may feel that risk to be greater than its numerical probability. Women live in more fear than men do, partly because of the greater material risks that threaten us and because of men's infliction of constant reminders of their capacity to hurt us. I think we also experience higher levels of distress because of the way fear and risk are treated in society. Women's panic is not met with reassurance, but often the opposite. And both actual and exaggerated threats have the same effect: of keeping women out of full participation in the world, hindering us through anxiety disorders and a perpetual hum of fear.

During this enforced hiatus from running, it strikes me that the issue of how women manage risk is crucial to the question of how women resist attempts to drive us out of the outdoors. As I have found, from the female mountaineers of the nineteenth century to women outdoors today, every single time we step outside we make complex cost–benefit analyses; weighing up anticipated pleasures of adventure versus fears of being met with disapproval, ridicule, abuse and violence. At times of greater male tolerance towards women's presence outdoors, the likelihood and severity of those fears reduces and the cost–benefit analysis tips in favour of us going outside – and I suspect that the numbers of women in sport and public life rise. But at times of greater constriction of women's rights, the penalties for penetrating male-dominated outdoor spaces grow, and women are more likely to prioritise their safety over their freedom and stay indoors – and women's visibility in sport and public life decreases.

So I want to find out more about how women assess and negotiate the risks we face outdoors. What evidence do we draw upon and what techniques do we deploy to stay safe? I wonder if our assessments are always accurate, or if we are sometimes deterred from outdoor sport by a combination of real risks and over-inflated ones.

How did Lizzie and her contemporaries deal with risk in order to defend the embattled presence of women outdoors? And what threats did the women who came later, from the 1970s onwards, get the better of in order to successfully stake a claim for women's prominence in sport and public life?

Over the next few weeks, the tendon in my foot gradually stops creaking, and I feel more optimistic about running the Dales Way Challenge. But then the race is cancelled. It's inevitable, really: it's a point-to-point and starts and ends in different locations, requiring runners to be bused up to the start. It is hard to see how the risk of infection could have been contained on a minibus or coach. For similar reasons, a district council and various owners of buildings intended as checkpoints also withdraw their consent for the race to be held on their land.

It's not entirely all over, however. The race directors, an unflappable couple called Ryk and Bev who head up the Punk Panther Endurance Events company, poll runners for suggestions of alternative routes. I suggest the Nidderdale Way. It is a long-distance trail which extends over a fifty-four-mile loop, shaped somewhat like a tilted hourglass. I have hiked and run on sections of the Nidderdale Way many times, but I have never before covered it all in one go. As its name suggests, the long-distance path traverses Nidderdale, a valley surrounding the River Nidd and once called *Netherdale*, probably because of its southerly position in relation to the other thirty or so divisions of the Yorkshire Dales. The circuit can be started anywhere, but hikers and runners often set off from a sixteenth-century castle in the village of Ripley, at the base of the slanted hourglass. The route then covers around fourteen miles, travelling anticlockwise up to the small market town of Pateley Bridge at the hourglass's neck. The Nidderdale Way then departs on a twenty-six-mile loop north, out of the town and onto wilder, less-habited fells that bank onto the remote reservoirs of Upper Nidderdale – Scar House and Angram – before returning to the neck of the hourglass, near Pateley Bridge. And then it sets off on the roughly fourteen-mile semi-circle back down south to Ripley.

It is a good course for an event, yo-yoing from lively settlements to seemingly empty moorland, incorporating over 7,000 feet of ascent. And, as it starts and ends in the same place, runners can travel to and from the race independently, and avoid the risk of infection on communal transport. Although the official Nidderdale Way is fifty-three miles long, the race will end up covering around fifty-eight miles (nearly a hundred kilometres) once deviations to and from checkpoints are included. Other entrants like my suggestion, and Ryk negotiates access to a field on the outskirts of Ripley in which we can park and, if necessary, camp. The new Nidderdale Way Race will be significantly shorter than the Dales Way Challenge, but it will still be the longest distance I have ever run.

I also have personal reasons for suggesting the Nidderdale Way. Soon after the furthest point on the route away from Ripley, just as the path doubles back from the northernmost end of the hourglass, there is a small village called Middlesmoor. Like an Italian hill-town or citadel, Middlesmoor clings to the top of a long, high ridge that extends eastwards from the summit of Great Whernside, a hill lying on the boundary of the Yorkshire Dales National Park. Middlesmoor is where expanses of unbroken moorland disgorge pocked tracks that finally solidify into a proper road, which runs south to nearby towns. It is where the wilderness of Upper Nidderdale appears to meet with civilisation, and it is also where I first met my stepfather, many decades ago. It is where I first discovered how hiking and running outdoors could make me feel freer and stronger in the world, and its place in my life has been so important that at times I have told friends that Middlesmoor is the place where I feel most at home.

In the months since Willy's death, I have visited his grave only once, and that was not entirely intentional. The funeral of a friend's mother was held in the same burial ground, outside Cambridge, and I thought I should 'pop over to see him'. But his ghost was not there and, over the last year, I have been fruitlessly searching for it. My runs have sometimes felt like desperate pilgrimages across Willy's old stomping grounds. During the summer of 2020, on a quick visit to his widow Jackie, I even set up my tent in the garden of their house, beside the driveway on which he died, with some unspoken hope of being haunted overnight. But he did not come. If he's anywhere, though, he'll be in Middlesmoor.

Back in August last year, I had decided to structure my journey through grief by running. I wanted to believe there could be a schedule for mourning: a year's worth of training sessions that, if I made myself complete each and every one, would bring me steadily back from bereavement to belonging. I had first selected the West Highland Way as my finish line and then, when that no longer felt right, I turned instead to the Dales Way. And now that race has been cancelled. But even though the Nidderdale Way is shorter and less of a physical challenge than the Dales Way, I wonder if it may have been the most fitting goal all along.

I try to reserve a campsite in Ripley for the night before the race, but the owners are not taking bookings from travellers with tents (and therefore without their own toilet and shower facilities), so I get up early and drive over from York. Ryk and Bev have allocated entrants their own start times – two minutes apart to avoid any congregating and contagion. Mine is 7 a.m. I go through the usual pre-race preparations, which are simpler now that we cannot hang around at the start. I change from driving shoes to running shoes, use the portaloo, collect my tracker and fasten it to my pack, open the route I've downloaded to my running watch and set it to 'navigate', use the portaloo again and then, on getting the okay from Ryk and Bev, I wave back to them and start jogging out of the car park and along the road to a turning onto the Nidderdale Way. I press 'start' on my watch as I run.

The first few miles of the trail pass through farmland. I had been worrying about herds of aggressive cows, but they are all far off, at the other end of the fields. I catch up with a man running ahead, and we jog side by side and chat for a while. I am wearing shoes I bought only five days earlier, panicking that my favourite trainers, which have a padded tongue, might aggravate the recently recovered tendon in my foot. Just in case the new shoes don't work out, I have put the old ones in my drop bag, along with snacks and drinks, spare socks and incontinence pads, which will all be taken to a checkpoint at the halfway mark. It was a gamble to wear the new shoes, with so little experience of how they perform over different terrain and, seven miles in, I realise they are already rubbing against the arch of my left foot. I stop and unsuccessfully try to fix a plaster to a foot that is slippery with sweat and puddle-water. So I dry my arch with one of the squares of kitchen roll I carry for my nose and prise open a box of cushioned gel pads. Once upon a time, I bought them to wear with stilettos for partying, but now they are a staple of my running first-aid kit.

Nearly eight miles from the start, I take a turning north along a shaded track, which is named on the map in antique script as the 'Monk Wall'. Within a mile, the path starts to ascend onto moorland. The mist parts for a second and I realise where I am: the outskirts of Brimham Rocks, an elevated outcrop of millstone grit formations overlooking much of Lower Nidderdale. The rocks' exposed location has subjected them to 325 million years of water and wind erosion, which has carved them into improbable shapes: the Druid's Idol, like a giant bear sat on a tiny bowler hat, a Porpoise Head and Monkey Face. Some rocks seem placed by design, like furniture in a room – reflected in names such as the 'Writing Desk', 'Pulpit', 'Parlour' and 'Coffin'. Eighteenth-century antiquarians thought that they were the work of the Druids, but by the beginning of the nineteenth century, people were coming around to the idea that 'the extraordinary position of these rocks is . . . owing to some violent convulsion of nature'. For novelist Maria Edgeworth in 1801, 'Brimham Craggs' were proof that, however much we might wish the world was made of foreseeable 'reasonings', 'facts' and certainties, we are really shaped by an unpredictable 'variety of accidental circumstances'.[3]

I had visited Brimham Rocks six months earlier, with two friends, both called Chloe. On previous family day trips here, I had been jealous of the blithe way my children scampered up and through the boulders. In contrast, I'd stood stock still, shaking with fear that they might fall from the tops and break their necks. So I'd phoned an outdoor adventure company, based at How Stean Gorge outside Middlesmoor, and booked a day's rock-climbing tuition at Brimham Rocks in February, a month before the first lockdown. Chloe, Chloe and I had arranged that our husbands would do the school-run, and we had driven out to Nidderdale on a cold misty morning that the weather forecast promised would dissolve into sunshine. Our instructor, Connor, met us in the car park and walked us out to a slab of rock he called 'the U-Tube' – because two-thirds of the way up there is a tunnel or alcove indented by a horseshoe-shaped pock. At the top of the slab, Connor set up a pulley around the base of a large rock above it, and two ends of the rope dropped down to where we stood. He explained that one end would be securely attached to a climber's harness, and the other would be held by a person standing on the ground, in a belay device which pulled in slack rope as the climber moved up the rock, to arrest any fall. This was 'top-roped climbing', Connor said: the safest kind. The three of us took it in turns to belay one another and make our way slowly up the slab.

When it was my turn to climb, I was surprised by how quickly the ground came to seem a long way away. When running and walking, I fear falling *down*. But in my harness, I was aware of the possibility of falling in multiple dimensions: down to the ground, yes, but also of slamming my nose forward or missing a foothold and skating sideways against the rock face. I had thought of climbing as a simple range of motion – up and down – but the reality disrupted my ideas about the laws of physics. In the same way that I can barely believe that my books at home are kept aloft by the six small screws that fix the shelves' brackets to the wall, it seemed equally ludicrous that a few tiny points of contact between the tips of my fingers and toes and the rock were supposed to support my whole body weight. And yet, they did.

The exhilaration of identifying a potential fingerhold, and realising it was just within reach and my strength was just sufficient to propel my body towards it, reminded me of yoga. The first time I successfully managed a 'crow pose', I had thought it impossible that my legs would ever lift off the floor. But then I realised that, if I shifted my torso and centre of gravity fractionally forward, and resisted my chin's tendency to tuck inwards, then my arms could become a fulcrum on the ground and my toes could lift towards my bum, and I could fly. Climbing felt similar: not gravity-defying, exactly, but chipping away at my ideas of my body's limitations.

I also found it very scary. After climbing the U-Tube, we abseiled down a much larger crag called the 'Notice Board Wall'. One of the reasons I hate driving a car is because the responsibility for a hunk of metal hurtling at speeds exceeding 100kph seems too great for one inexpert individual. It felt similarly absurd that I was being placed in control of my own descent off this rock. I checked my watch afterwards and, although the abseil was not physically strenuous, my heart-rate had shot up to nearly 140 beats per minute – my usual measurement during a comfortable run. Whatever this adrenal sensation was – fear, excitement, stress, what psychiatrists might call 'arousal' – it did not feel particularly pleasurable.

Later that week, back in the Alpine Club library in London – one of my last trips before lockdown was imposed – I had told Nigel about my introduction to climbing and how terrifying I had found it. He had paused for a few seconds and then said: 'I dunno, climbing *is* scary; you *should* find it scary. There are dangers involved and fear helps you take them seriously. You don't want the fear to overwhelm you, though.'

The way that Nigel described fear was not as a disorder – irrational or debilitating – but as something necessary and useful, which communicates to climbers that they are potentially at risk and helps them to devise a plan of action. I think that the conventional view is that women are less able to take such a constructive view of fear: that we try to steer clear of it and are 'naturally' more risk-averse than men.[4] But female climbers voluntarily put themselves at risk and immerse themselves in scary situations. My experience at Brimham made me want to learn more about how adventurous women experience and deal with danger and threat. Learning to take risks and to manage fear is essential for women who insist on their right to freedom outdoors, even – *especially* – in the face of pronounced hostility. I would do anything to not be ruled by fear.

Women are commonly thought of as more risk-averse than men. This has been observed across a wide variety of activities, from drug and alcohol consumption and crime, to sports, gambling, driving and sexual behaviour. Researchers Sylvia Maxfield and Mary Shapiro find that, in the workplace, women are more risk-averse in areas such as health and safety, and that women place greater emphasis on protecting workers from injury and are more likely to wear personal protective equipment (PPE). The report from my 'Women in the Hills' network finds that outdoor activities that are considered especially 'risky' – such as base jumping, skydiving and snowboarding – tend to be male-dominated, often dramatically so. Some researchers suggest a hormonal origin to this gendered difference, in women's lower levels of testosterone. Others suggest social explanations. A skydiver called Nadia spoke to sociologist Riley Olstead about how she felt that women's risk aversion is partly linked to the issue of *responsibility*. Nadia's family constantly reminded her of her duty to them to curtail her skydiving and she described how her dad 'worries that I am really going to get hurt or killed . . . [He said] it's like I am holding them hostage and purposely making them upset'. Her brother, she said, got 'a lot of [positive] attention' from them for his skydiving, 'but I have to hide it'.[5]

Gendered beliefs about women's responsibility to their families also shape societal attitudes to the risk-taking of female climbers who have children. In 2010, sports sociologists Amanda West and Linda Allin found that 'men reported being less likely than women to restrict their climbing practices' because of a sense of familial duty. Climbing mothers spoke about feeling especially guilty for taking risks. That men and women face different expectations about risk management was obvious after the death of mountaineer Alison Hargreaves on K2 in 1995. News of Hargreaves's death 'provoked moral outrage' in the British press, as 'not only reckless, but selfish' behaviour for a mother. Political commentator Polly Toynbee compared Hargreaves's climbing to 'a taste for crack' and criticised her for having 'behaved like a man'. A few days before Hargreaves's disappearance, two other British mountaineers – Paul Nunn and Geoff Tier – died on Haramosh II, a mountain close to K2, and, the following year, Rob Hall died on Everest. Nunn and Tier both had children and Hall's wife was pregnant – but, as fathers, they received no such criticism for irresponsible risk-taking. Climber Alison Osius described the 'especially painful' effects of Hargreaves's public vilification on other 'women climbers, many of whom had been trying to sort out their own conflicting obligations to self and family'.[6]

So there is evidence that, perhaps for physiological reasons and certainly for societal ones, women are indeed more risk-averse than men. But it seems to me that this commonplace idea is complicated by ways in which the public sphere, the outdoors and risk itself are (mis)represented. The reality of the risks that face women can be skewed in order to deter and marginalise us from purportedly dangerous activities.

Research shows that the degree to which women are risk-averse, and the ways in which women *do* readily take risks, are not accurately reported. The majority of women in business who spoke to Maxfield and Shapiro reported willingly pursuing major change initiatives and new programmes, new jobs and significant business development opportunities. But they described how these are not always recognised as 'business risks', which is an area of study typically focused on the male-dominated area of financial investment and gambling. 'Ability to demonstrate risk-taking' is often a key element of promotion criteria, and the narrow assumption that men are natural risk-takers – and women are not – can be used to exclude women from the upper strata of the industry. The same is true in climbing. There is still a tenacious sexist belief that, as US writer Clyde Lawrence expressed way back in 1909, 'women are not natural climbers' because of a seemingly greater tendency to risk aversion.[7] Such claims serve to ring-fence climbing, like the financial sector, as inherently 'risky businesses' that are therefore unsuited to supposedly risk-averse women and are 'naturally' men's domains.

But when the risks involved in activities like climbing or business are presented in a different light, they can seem more fitted to conventional ideas of women's aptitudes. Many of West and Allin's interviewees spoke about climbing as an activity that draws on skills in risk *management* rather than risk-*taking*. And the careful management of risk is something in which women are thought to excel: in the financial sector, some psychologists have concluded that 'women are [particularly] well-suited to risk *management*'. This suggestion – that climbing is about calm and calculated risk management, rather than maverick risk-taking – is echoed in sociologists Tommy Langseth and Øyvind Salvesen's conversations with Norwegian climbers, who describe how 'credibility' within the climbing community depends on knowing one's abilities and tackling 'forms of risk that can be managed', rather than recklessly exposing oneself to risks outside one's control or capability. When we think about climbing (and other pursuits) in this way, then – even if we subscribe to the belief that women are more reluctant than men to take wild risks – it is no longer possible to conclude that women are intrinsically unsuited to those activities. In fact, because of our aptitude for risk management, women can actually feel *more* at home in outdoor sports than in many public spaces we enter during our day-to-day lives, in which the threats we face are often harder to define, manage and control. My friend Maria, a rock climber and fell runner, describes how some people might 'see running on your own in the dark on a mountain as risky', but she insists that, 'for me, it feels safer than running in a city because [out on the hillside] the risks can be managed (carry appropriate gear, have the right skills etc.). When the danger comes from other people [in a city],' she continues, 'you can't manage that in any meaningful way.'[8]

Anthropologist Mary Douglas wrote about different types of risk in exactly these terms. She theorised that there are some situations in which knowledge about relevant threats 'is certain', and that these can be managed via 'technical' solutions – such as choosing handholds, footholds and protection in climbing, or carrying GPS trackers, waterproof kit, and a map and compass for fell running. But she also thought there are very different situations in which 'knowledge is uncertain' (it is impossible to calculate the risks), and then solutions are harder to find and the scenario feels much more dangerous.[9] In Douglas's schema, negotiating male violence and abuse outdoors in our day-to-day lives can be a much trickier form of risk management for women than the physical dangers presented by sport.

Words like *risk*, *probability*, *assessment* and *calculation* suggest objectivity: the possibility of precisely computing our vulnerability and devising solutions. But often the risks we perceive are obscure and undefined, and they can be misrepresented to deter women from certain activities. I realise that there are multiple factors at play when women negotiate risk: we have to assess and deal with statistically likely threats, but we also have to be wise to the ways that specific risks and the general idea of risk can all be manipulated against our interests.

The Nidderdale Way does not stay in Brimham Rocks for long. I follow the path as it descends rapidly into a darkly wooded valley bordering a small beck and then rises up again on the other side. I run along increasingly well-paved tracks overlooking the lower-lying settlements of Glasshouses and Smelthouses – reminders of Nidderdale's lead-mining past – until I am careering down the steeply sloping high street of the small market town of Pateley Bridge. A marshal standing by a pick-up truck in the car park at the bottom of the hill waves me over and tells me to help myself to water and cereal bars from crates at the back. I dash to the public toilets to change my pad and return to the van. This is the centre of the route's hourglass shape and I am just under a quarter of the way through the race. The event splits here: runners who prefer a shorter, roughly marathon-length distance will cross the bridge to the neighbouring settlement of Bewerley and go back to Ripley without covering the top loop. Everyone on the ultra-marathon course will keep heading north, up to Scar House reservoir and Middlesmoor. From this point on, I am on familiar territory, on paths I've trodden since childhood. When the marshal asks me how it's going, I reply that I'm feeling strong; although, when a fellow runner diverts onto the shorter course my gaze follows his path with more interest – is it jealousy or longing? – than usual.

The trail out of Pateley Bridge runs north for four miles, alongside a reservoir called Gouthwaite, up to the next checkpoint at a tiny hamlet called Bouthwaite. (There was, in fact, once a third: Outhwaite – Old Norse and Germanic variations on a *thwaite*, meaning a meadow or clearing in the wood that used to blanket the dale.) After that, the Nidderdale Way crisscrosses the narrow road up to the village of Lofthouse, under the gaze of two standing stones, marked on the OS map as 'Jenny Twigg and her daughter Tib'. Outside the pub, two couples shelter under the colonnade, sipping pints of beer and staring out onto the misty garden, a black dog barking around their feet. There are no other runners in sight, neither ahead nor behind me, and I think that this might be my last glimpse of humans for a while. I know from many past visits here that, after Lofthouse, the route will leave the road to strike out into the wild, uninhabited reaches of Nidderdale, onto the sides of a long valley which arches like a sickle before being bookended at the hill of Great Whernside.

For a few miles, I run alone along a path which clings to the River Nidd, travelling upstream towards its source, and then cuts through Limley Farm. At a distance, the farm's fences appear to be woven of dark willow or hazel, but as I get closer I realise they're heavy with the corpses of dead moles – a tradition by which mole-catchers show landowners their work, and charge them for it. At Limley, the way turns sharply east and up through bracken. Cranking my forearms against my thighs, I lever myself up a hundred metres of brisk ascent, towards the top of the ridge, where I stand for a moment, letting my heart-rate slow, wiping the sweat from my cheeks and chewing on a blackcurrant energy jelly as I turn around and look down onto pillowy fog in the valley's base. Then I start moving again, following the track along the ridge that traces the dale's edge, dipping in and out of the mist for the next three miles. As I jog forward, the black crenellated dam at Scar House reservoir comes gradually into view, silhouetted against white cloud, like a barricade at the end of the universe.

I begin the gentle descent towards the reservoir, and the surrounding hills emerge one by one from the vapour: Dead Man's Hill, Little Whernside, Great Whernside, Riggs Moor, Kay Head and Rain Stang. I run across Scar House dam and into the car park at the other side, which roughly marks the halfway point for the race and is where a marshal in a camper van has our drop bags. My new shoes have stopped rubbing, but they have less cushioning than I'd like and my arches are aching, so I try on the spare pair I'd put in the drop bag. But even without standing I can feel the tongue constricting my troublesome tendon, so I take them off again and sit shoeless on the floor and open a freezer bag of malt loaf and butter. It is unexpectedly disgusting, yeasty and stale. I try something else: a chocolate-filled cake in the shape of a teddy bear, stolen from my children's snack box. It tastes the same: of musty feet. I realise that the smell from my old trainers has infected everything in my drop bag. I want to cry but there is nothing to be done, so I get up, put my original shoes back on, take a packet of crisps and a bottle of energy drink from the marshal and leave the checkpoint to start trudging up the steep, high-sided track from the reservoir towards the top of Rain Stang. After a cairn near the summit, the track tilts and begins a gradual rocky descent over three kilometres into Middlesmoor, where the path begins to smooth and widen into a tarmac road which curves sharply around the village pub.

Here I take a cobbled side-turning, a few metres from the race route. I run to a small, plain, empty, eighteenth-century farm labourer's cottage, which faces the church. I stand momentarily in the doorway and then move a little way down the path to the entrance to the churchyard, where I have a view down the whole upper dale, right through to Pateley Bridge. Willy's extended family own this cottage, and in 1980 he first brought two friends from work here – my mother and father, with me, their six-month-old baby, along in a sling. A decade later, after my parents had divorced and Willy's own relationship had ended, he invited us again; this time, just my mother, my younger sister and me. The weekend began with my mother and Willy kissing politely on each cheek, and ended with them wrapped around one another on a picnic blanket overlooking the reservoirs.

I was not a light-hearted child. My parents' world appeared to be one of angry indecipherable words in French and my father's bitterly repeated motto: 'Your mother is always right.' I do not know if I was unusually sickly, but many of my early childhood memories are of illness: of my mother pressing thermometer strips against my hot forehead; of spending days in bed in dark rooms with drawn curtains, tormented by swollen cheeks and the glassy pain of urinary tract infections and raw, sore throats that repeatedly left me mute. Illness seemed to be something of terrifying, life-changing significance – but I also sensed that, in my family, it was something of which I had no right to complain. Nevertheless, I worried, all the time and silently – that I was dying of a brain tumour; that my legs were being eaten by necrotising fasciitis; that I was somehow, miraculously, pregnant, despite not yet being pubescent.

I felt 'at risk' from disease and I tried to mitigate other apparent dangers in the world too. I tried to be sparkling enough company for my father to not want to drink. I tried to be 'a good girl' for my mother, sitting still and not running around. I was an only child until the age of six, and I often played in the hollow heart of a large shrub on the pavement outside the house, where I'd pretend I was camping, cocooned in a sleeping bag, my body warm and dry and strong against the cold air. I'd sleep in bed at night beneath an open window, listening to rain hitting the tarmac road and imagining a breeze drifting across my body laid out on the grass.

But against these fantasies of safety, real-life outdoor environments seemed terrifying to me – with their bone-imperilling climbing frames, slides with vertiginous stepladders, and large dogs that jumped up and barked. Such places might bring injury, or physical disturbances like a raised heart-rate or a film of sweat, which were portents of illness. So I said that I hated sport, and when I was eight and my school participated in a county competition in which each pupil accrued points for physical activity, I came last.

I do not have a brother, so I have no sense of whether things would have been different if I had been a boy. But studies show that many girls grow up with a similar sense of panic about playing outdoors. Pre-pubescent girls are arguably less restricted than their teenage counterparts, who report their younger worlds 'shrinking' upon adolescence – but female childhood is not a golden age of liberty. From infancy, there is a marked gendered difference in the permission given by adults to children to play freely and to take risks, in which boys are granted significantly more latitude. Parents even demonstrate different attitudes towards male and female foetuses in the womb, and are more likely to perceive boys as kicking vigorously and girls as moving in a subdued fashion, even when their movements are actually similar. Teenagehood is worse than infancy, in terms of the intensification of these dynamics, but neither before nor afterwards is there a belle époque of freedom for women and girls.

In the 1990s and 2000s, Canadian psychologist Barbara Morrongiello and her colleague Kerri Hogg studied parents' attitudes to their children's risk-taking in playgrounds. They discovered that 'parents made more statements encouraging risk-taking for sons than for daughters and more cautions highlighting . . . vulnerability [to injury] to daughters than to sons'. Moreover, they found that 'parents spontaneously provided more physical support to daughters than to sons during risky play activities, and they made more explicit demands of sons than of daughters to perform these activities without parental assistance'.[10]

In 2007, psychologists Lisa Kindleberger Hagan and Janet Kuebli looked at two variables: the sex of the children *and* the sex of the parents. Complicating Morrongiello and Hogg's conclusions, they found that mothers did not treat sons and daughters particularly differently – but what was notable was that *fathers* 'monitored their daughters . . . to a much greater degree than did fathers of sons'. A recent study of 'gender role attitudes and parenting practices' by psychologist Jordan Montgomery and her co-researchers also found that, while both parents discussed 'fostering the independence of their sons', it was 'fathers [who] frequently remarked on the increased risks for daughters and relatedly their need for additional monitoring and guidance'. One of the dads interviewed by Montgomery's team expressed the belief that 'boys is boys' – that boys and men are naturally predisposed to take risks – and he recognised that boys' risk-taking sometimes jeopardises girls' safety. But he concluded that it was therefore *his daughter* – not her male peers – who needed to be constrained to avoid these threats, and that this became even more urgent upon adolescence. Another father voiced the same opinion: 'When [girls] get in the . . . age of thirteen and fourteen, you gotta tighten down on 'em then. Can't let 'em run the streets.'[11] From infancy onwards, girls' freedoms are curtailed by male authority figures, and these restrictions are justified by adults because of potential threats from men and boys. Violent or inappropriate male behaviour is not regulated and subdued in the same way.

Gendered differences in parents' feelings about their children's risk-taking do not always reflect statistical evidence about who is most at risk. Paradoxically, parents are observed to report less concern and demonstrate fewer monitoring behaviours towards children who have a history of moving around recklessly and injuring themselves more often than others. And the former can be the result of the latter, rather than vice versa. A child's tendency to injury appears to subsequently inoculate parents to concern, whereas they become more cautious when a child remains safe and unharmed. I think I understand this apparent contradiction. One of my daughters hurls herself around playgrounds with reckless abandon and – even though she's been stung by nettles and wasps countless times, fallen off skateboards and bikes, twisted ankles dropping from monkey bars, skinned her knees, bruised her shins, bumped her head and even broken her leg – her motion exudes such self-confidence that I worry about and monitor her far less than I do her twin sister, who treads cautiously and is injured far less frequently, but on whom I find myself training an anxious eye. In general, this paradoxical pattern of parental behaviour is gendered, and parents, especially fathers, worry about and constrain girls' behaviour more often and more strictly than boys', even though, for example in the US, boys aged over two years old are two to four times more at risk of injury in playgrounds than girls.[12]

Illogical gendered beliefs about risk persist into adulthood too. Across the world, women and girls are much more at risk of violence and abuse from known men inside the home than from attacks by strangers outdoors. But when rapists or murderers are 'on the loose', messaging from police forces frequently instructs women to stay at home – instead of imposing a curfew on men. This is despite the fact that women are, in general, more at risk from male violence indoors than outside. Sometimes the outdoors can be portrayed as far riskier than it really is, as a deliberate strategy to deter women from leaving the home. The feminist writer Victoria Smith describes how her parents represented the world outside as a source of peril in order to minimise the abuse she faced within the family, and to keep her indoors where she was more easily controlled: she was brought up to believe that 'we shouldn't talk about bad things happening at home [because] every danger, every disease, is outside, with the others'.[13] This shows how gendered attitudes to risk outdoors do not necessarily reflect reality or statistical calculations of risk, but can be based on societal beliefs that men's freedom takes precedence over women's. Such parental behaviour tells children that boys' liberty to take risks and behave dangerously is more important than girls' freedom of movement, and that girls' outdoor play should be constrained to give boys more latitude – even the latitude to behave in violent or anti-social ways towards them.

I think about my attitude to my daughters' outdoor play. It strikes me that, although a parent's close monitoring of a child can appear to be motivated by care, concern and love, perhaps sometimes standing back and allowing a child to take risks might be the more generous gesture. I realise that I am particularly intolerant of my children playing in risky ways when I'm feeling hurried, stressed or distracted:

when I feel like I don't have the time to wipe up blood, get out my first-aid kit, or make that trip to A&E. Then I tell them sharply to 'Stop doing that!' or 'Oh, for goodness' sake, hold my hand!' It makes me wonder if granting children the freedom to graze knees or break legs sends a message that it's okay for them to get hurt, because the world will stop to look after them. Whereas, when we ask children to be 'nice' and 'kind' and 'good', to sit quietly and not get dirty, we're telling them that the world will not necessarily stop for them, nor care for them, and so they had better fit in with other people's plans. I wonder if, by granting boys more liberty than girls to take risks, we're reassuring boys that their desires and education come first, and that we're warning girls that theirs do not.

When I arrived in Middlesmoor, aged ten, I was scared of everything. I had never before met anyone like my stepfather, who seemed so unafraid and uncomplicated. My own father's interests had lain entirely in cities and in men who were, like him, heavy-hearted, difficult and private: Louis-Ferdinand Céline, André Malraux and Leonard Cohen. After Dad's death, when I came to box up his books, it struck me that there was an almost complete absence of publications about sport or the countryside or leisure – or by or about women, for that matter. But Willy's cottage at Middlesmoor had books about wild flowers, birds of the British Isles and autobiographies by Yorkshire shepherdesses. Dad's jumper had smelled of pub carpets and cigarettes, but Willy just smelled of soap, and he did not ever seem to be ill.

My stepdad had been raised on a diet of *Swallows and Amazons*, *Just William* and the humorous series of books about Nigel Molesworth, a schoolboy at the fictional school St Custard's. He saw no reason not to pass on these 1950s childhood loves to my sister and me. When we all moved in together, he brought with him a wooden coffee table with a small rodent running up its leg and instead of 'Dad', 'Stepdad' or 'Willy', he suggested that his new stepdaughters should call him 'Mr Mousetrousers'. I was not used to adults being silly. From what I could glean from overheard conversations, Willy's job seemed to be extremely serious – concerned with wages and unfairness and politicians – but he read me stories about characters called Violet Elizabeth Bott and Basil Fotherington-Thomas, from which he often had to break off, incapacitated by mirth.

We visited Middlesmoor often, where Willy shook out an Ordnance Survey Explorer map over the kitchen table and encouraged me to imagine myself as a tiny speck, crawling over the paper landscape. He explained that the more tightly the orange contour lines were bunched, the heavier I'd feel as I made my way up them. He taught me about northings and eastings and showed me how to line up a compass and navigate a path; and he told me the difference between a 'public right of way' and a 'permissive footpath', and how to behave around cows in a field. He showed me how to stack and light a fire outdoors; how to build a dam in a stream and knock it down again; and which side of a winding country road to walk upon. He encouraged my mother to buy me an outdoor coat. He pointed out constellations in the night sky and birds in the daytime (confidently declaring that many of them were 'LBBs' and later admitting, when I couldn't find that species in the guidebook, that the acronym stood for 'Little Brown Birds' and was his late mother's invention).

I was frequently scared outdoors – of tripping face-first down rocky paths or of my feet slipping out from under me on stones half-submerged beneath streams – but Willy waited patiently, offering his hiking stick or a hand for stability, until I could continue trotting after him. Once, during a family holiday on the Isle of Skye when I was a teenager, I got stuck in the middle of a solo hike across the 'Bad Step' near Loch Coruisk, and was hours late in getting back to our cottage. As I finally emerged onto the road in Elgol, where we were staying, he ran towards me in relief, one arm outstretched high above his head and waving, shouting: 'Oh, love! You're safe!' He had been looking out for hours, and I realised that, in him, I had a safety net for when things went wrong.

During this childhood training, I learned to trust the evidence of senses, to locate myself according to what the 'natural navigator' Tristan Gooley calls the 'observation and deduction' of 'natural clues including the sun, the moon, the stars, the land, the sea, the weather, the plants, and the animals'.[14] I had previously been used to mistrusting my body but, largely thanks to my stepdad and this outdoor education, I gradually came to think that perhaps my body could be depended on after all. When Willy and my mother divorced in my early twenties, I initially worried that the 'step' between us – our relationship, which was no longer formalised by law – would dissolve. But, even after his remarriage to Jackie, he continued to give me a home to which I could, and did, return, many times. He showed me that the closest bonds are not always the result of bloodlines and inherited traits, but that it is possible to forge our own alternative families; communities who are brought together, not by genetics, but by mutual qualities, values and choices – and voluntary love.

I suddenly and desperately want to be with someone who knew him, to reassure me I had not dreamed it all. Willy had been good friends with a couple in Middlesmoor, Anthony and Valentina, who live a few doors down from the churchyard where I am now standing, and impulsively I knock on their door, not expecting them to be in. But they answer and now I do not know what to say. They do not recognise me as the grown-up version of the child and teenager and young woman who used to come here every vacation with my stepdad. 'I'm Willy's stepdaughter,' I explain, and we talk for a few minutes, but none of us mention the fact that Willy is dead. I feel completely out of place, talking to these polite, bemused people when I am thirty tired, sweaty miles into a nearly sixty-mile race and so sad; like turning up drunk to a gathering of sober people and talking much too loudly. They invite me inside for a cup of tea, but I tell them that I have to be getting on, and I say goodbye with a promise of bringing my daughters up to see them soon, and run on.

The second half of the race is hard. My feet ache and I am so very tired. Revisiting Middlesmoor has made me wish intensely for things I cannot change or cannot have right now. A happier childhood. A family home. A cold pint of lager with friends in a pub garden on a sunny evening. A not-dead father and stepdad and uncle and cousin and best friend and cat. A cup of hot sweet tea. A world in which I'm able to run at night without fear. The end of coronavirus and lock-down. A slice of chocolate cake. The finish line.

The kilometres tick down agonisingly slowly and it starts raining. I finally get to the next checkpoint, which is back at the neck of the route's hourglass shape and marks roughly the three-quarter point of the race. But there are still around fifteen miles left to go. A camping chair is set up beside the checkpoint, and I sit down heavily and tell the marshals I am thinking of pulling out. 'My head's just not in it,' I say. And, 'I have tendonitis in my foot, and I'm not sure it's a good idea to keep going.' And, 'I've been doing high mileage this summer and I think my reserves are depleted.' The marshals look on silently and hand me a cup of tea.

Why should I keep going? I only want running to be a joy in my life, never a punishment, and currently it does not feel good. The thought of stopping – DNFing – feels fraught, though. I'd be risking self-reproach, and a loss of confidence; the worry that maybe I'm not up to these distances after all. But a decision to continue running when it is causing me pain is also complicated.

Sitting in my camping chair, debating whether to continue or not, I realise that the idea of *making myself run when I don't really want to* taps into unhealthy associations that running has held for me in the past. And later it will strike me that this is another aspect of the complexity of risk for women. For many women – and some men too – sport is not always uncomplicatedly beneficial, but it can be used to exert control over a body that otherwise feels wayward and terrifying. For me, at one time in my life, running was a way of keeping a lid on certain dangers; namely the risk that, without it, I would be fat, lazy, undisciplined and unremarkable – and unloveable. Now I know these are dreadful reasons to run. But I also think they are not uncommon, and that assessing risk can be difficult for women because many of the things we are encouraged to fear are really not worth our energy.

As this suggests, I have a history with running in which it has not always been a positive force in my life. Like the adolescent girls who spoke to Lyn Mikel Brown and Carol Gilligan for their research in the 1990s, during late teenagehood I too lost the ability to trust the evidence of my senses and to stand up for my 'experience of being in a body that feels and knows feelings'.[15] For a long time in my twenties, I had no strong beliefs; nothing I internally felt to be true or right to defend. I founded all my judgements of value on external touchstones. All I cared about was that I was judged by others as likeable, pretty, 'nice and kind' – and thin. I sought proof in numerical benchmarks. On the face of it, I had recovered from the anorexia of my adolescence, and my weight was healthy and my diet adequate, but I still weighed myself every day, recording the number along with my body fat percentage in a notebook. I listed the foods I consumed and their calorific value on a piece of paper stuck to the fridge. I kept numerous spreadsheets enumerating every item of income and expenditure, the articles and books I made myself read per day, the volume of words I had got onto paper, the time I had spent in the gym. My therapist was shocked by the fact I did not own a sofa or comfortable chair – but I could not imagine wasting my time in just sitting. The idea of *winging it* seemed impossible. I was not convinced that anything lay within the scaffolding of numbers I had built around myself.

In my early twenties, I was working on a dissertation on surveys and maps in the early nineteenth century. I read that, in the eighteenth century, optimists like the natural philosopher Joseph Priestley had believed in a form of providence that is always moving towards greater 'virtue and happiness'. They believed that risks either paid off or they didn't, but either way those gambles and their outcomes contributed new knowledge about God's system, and all results were part of general progress in the direction of 'the improvement and happiness of each'. But by the early nineteenth century, in the wake of bloody revolutions and failures of political hope around Europe, such buoyancy was harder to sustain. Without the safety net of a providence that reassured people that everything was tending to the good, risk-taking became more loaded and momentous. People turned to statistics, surveys and numerical calculations of probability as new safety nets, to safely manage risk and fend off calamity. By

1838, quantifying habits were so embedded in everyday mental processes that mathematician Augustus De Morgan concluded: 'Probability is the feeling of the mind.'[16]

I recognised that deep psychological craving for a numerical safety net, and I found one in running. In April 2004, when I had just turned twenty-four, my friend Sally, who worked in a sports marketing agency, got me a job on an energy drink stall at the London Marathon Exhibition. Visitors walked around the venue clutching 'pacebands' to wear on race day: simple paper bracelets listing the times at which runners should pass each mile marker in order to meet their overall target time. One stall showed off a brand new sports watch – the Garmin Forerunner – which superseded the paceband by using GPS for the first time to accurately measure distance, time and pace, as well as calculations of energy expenditure. Everybody at the exhibition seemed to be engaged in mental arithmetic.

Running offered a perfect way to prove my value in a number. I had never run before but a man at the exhibition told me that completing a marathon in 3 hours 45 minutes was 'good for my age' and I felt that, if I could do that, then I would have numerical evidence that *I* was therefore 'good'. I bought a running magazine with a 'sub-3:45 marathon training programme', and started running on the treadmill at the gym, fixated by red numbers tracking my increasing distance and calorie outlay. My goal was rapid metamorphosis: to become faster, fitter, thinner, cleverer, funnier, prettier, nicer, better. I knew there was historical precedent for the idea that moral reassurance might be found in running. I remembered reading as an undergraduate the British priest William Law's 1729 book, *A Serious Call to a Devout and Holy Life*, in which he too alighted on running as an ideal method for women to impose 'order and regularity' onto our lives and bodies. Law used training regimes and dieting as metaphors for the spiritual self-regulation required to make a woman's mind and 'body fitter', in order 'to run a *race* for her life'. Success, for Law, meant that his morally robust female runner 'will never have her eyes swell with fatness, or pant under a heavy load of flesh'.[17] I was terrified of such 'fatness' and all it meant to me.

But running did not offer instant transformation. It was only much later that I learned first-hand that running is a slow, gradual process of building muscular strength, lung capacity, a sturdy heart, self-confidence, self-knowledge and experience. A non-runner cannot be transformed into a fast marathon racer in the space of a few months, as I had hoped. Just three weeks after taking up road running, I inevitably developed an injury: Achilles tendonitis. Even when that healed, I continued to refuse to stretch or weight-train, not seeing the point of exercise that didn't burn hundreds – preferably thousands – of calories. So my alignment got worse, my knees knocked inwards and I endured constant pain along my iliotibial band, the fibrous stabilising band that runs from knee to hip. I was also continually disappointed in myself: my performance never lived up to my arbitrary goals. I never achieved that sub-3:45 marathon time and its numerical proof that I was a good runner and therefore a good person. So, eventually, I gave up running altogether.

When I came back to running in my mid thirties, in late 2015, I had resolved to do things differently. I liked the fact that trail running is less competitive than road, track or treadmill running, and that Personal Best times are largely meaningless, because there is little point in comparing times over routes that vary wildly in elevation and 'technicality' (a term relating to the trickiness of ground cover: flat tarmac is not technical, but a steep slither down boulders and scree qualifies as a 'technical descent'). I started to pay attention to how my runs felt inside, rather than how they might be judged by others. And I experimented with different ways of making running feel good: sometimes keeping my heart-rate low and giving myself permission to walk, sometimes sprinting fast and strong but slowing before the point of nausea. I stopped listening to music and enjoyed the sounds around me, and I packed picnics so I could sit and enjoy the views. I chose races as excuses for nights away in beautiful locations and I gave myself rewards: spaghetti bolognese and a glass of red wine the evening before an event and, afterwards, a soak in a bath with a cold lager and a cwtch on the sofa with Pete and Netflix. I signed up for a beginner's yoga course to stretch out my tight muscles. When, in the first class, the instructor suggested we begin by 'moving in a way that feels good', I literally did not know what she meant. I watched my classmates writhing on all fours, tilting hips, twisting spines, arching and dipping, and I copied them, and gradually discovered the small movements that pulled pleasantly at my outer pelvis or unfurled the muscles between my shoulder blades.

In this later running life, I was no longer hoping it would transform me into someone entirely different, as I had done in my twenties. Instead, in my mid thirties, I wanted to gently nurture and expand who I already was. This opened the door to a glorious new existence outdoors. It was wildly different to the past, when I had spent so long trying to manage the risks that girls are taught to fear – that we might not be thin, pretty, fast, clever, self-disciplined, hardworking, 'nice and kind' or perfect enough. I had been blinded by these aspirations to such an extent that I had forgotten to question whether it is even desirable to care about such 'dangers'. I had lost sight of the importance of my own freedom, comfort and wellbeing in my body and in the world – the foundation and starting point of all human action. Some of this shift in perspective came on the back of a lot of personal change. I had been through therapy, fallen in love with Pete, published a successful book, become a mother, and started to believe that perhaps I was not such a dreadful person after all. And some of it was simply a factor of age: putting some temporal distance between myself and adolescence; reaching greater self-confidence; refusing to suffer fools and foolish ideas. It is a perspective that many women report discovering as they approach menopause.

As I sit here, debating whether to continue and finish the Nidderdale Way, I draw upon what I have learned. I tell myself that I'm allowed to *walk* the rest of the way, and to enjoy the late summer twilight: the sounds of livestock being fed, the flashes of white as rabbits charge into their burrows. I tell myself that it doesn't matter if I am slow and end up placed way down the results tables. And the pep talk is enough. I get out of the chair, thank the marshals for their tea and, after walking along the road for a mile or two, I reach a descent, down which my sore legs are able to move fractionally faster. After a couple of hours of this pattern – plodding the flats, jogging the downhills, stumbling up slopes – I finally enter the shady wooded path that marks the approach to Ripley. A male silhouette emerges in the dark a hundred or so metres away, running towards me. The muscles all around my torso, from beside my armpits down to my buttocks, clench as he passes. The strange runner waves and says, 'Congratulations! Nearly done!' Nevertheless, I do not relax until he is out of sight and I am under the streetlights on the village high street.

The car park is a little way out of Ripley, so it is not quite all over yet. But a few minutes later I am running along the main road and a woman with a head torch greets me and guides me into the turning, and I trot into an open tent where Ryk is sitting behind a table. I put on the face mask I've been carrying in my pack, sink into a camping chair, press 'stop' on my watch, detach my tracker and hand it over. 'That was so hard,' I say.

I have been running for 14 hours 22 minutes and have covered over ninety-three kilometres. All I want to do now is to lie flat and still for a very long time, but I have to drive back to York. It is late and pitch black and I find it hard to make sense of the car lights that stretch and flicker in the rain; but I make it home in one piece, and Pete is on the sofa, and I tell him that I missed him and that I need a cuddle.

While I am recovering over the next few days, I think about the past year. Immediately after Willy's death, I was completely unmoored and became acutely sensitive to further ways in which I felt myself to be dispossessed in the world. I even started to doubt my ability to run.

At first, I thought these were purely symptoms of grief. But, as I've been reading and running and writing over the past months, I have come to think that perhaps what I was feeling was not a disorder, but a clearer view of the mourning that many women experience for the losses we suffer in relation to our freedom outdoors. I have learned how the bereavements that shape women's relationships with outside space are multiple and vast. Some are shortfalls which point to women's unequal treatment in relation to men and are 'technical' in character. These include the relative dearth of sporting clothing, kit and technology that are designed for women's bodies and lives; races and events whose rules and regulations prioritise male competitors; sponsorship deals that favour men; and male-centred sports science research that leaves female athletes following training plans that do not account for our physiology or cycles. Female wanderers negotiate public spaces – including streets, parks, municipal sporting facilities, train carriages, hotels and mountain huts – that don't recognise women's concerns about safety and we contend with poor public toilet provision that keeps us close to home.

Some of the other ways in which women lose out outdoors are in the realm of representation. In literature and theory, male philosophers represent men as active explorers of the natural world, and women as naturally passive objects. Male bodies are idealised in literature and the visual arts as honed and self-controlled, whereas female physicality is denigrated as chaotic and animalistic. Sport and 'the great outdoors' have long been conceptualised as training grounds for male domination of nations and empires, and adventurous women are therefore perceived as 'manly' aberrations of femininity, who undermine these important male projects. Skill in outdoor sport is represented as dependent on risk-taking, and women are portrayed as risk-averse and thus inherently disinclined to activities such as climbing. Girls in books, advertisements and TV series are shown to be quiet and static, whereas boys romp boisterously. Records, histories, manuals, guides, memoirs and media coverage of sport and outdoor leisure frequently concentrate on men's achievements, assume their consumers are male and, when women feature at all, it is often anonymously or as stereotypes. Women's own accounts of sporting endeavour lack opportunities for wide dissemination and are repeatedly missed out of review pages and anthologies. The history of women's participation in sport is misrepresented and forgotten, to the extent that many early female athletic role models – such as Lizzie and her friends – have been entirely lost to women today.

I have learned that many of the losses that women suffer outdoors are wide-ranging, long-standing and social and structural in nature.

Women find it harder than men to access outdoor leisure because of changes in work that led to the solidification of 'separate spheres' and assigned public space to men and domestic space to women. Relative to men, women have enjoyed significantly less authority in relation to land, property, their families, the workplace, education and even our own bodies, which means that we experience the outdoors very differently to men, and with a sense of disempowerment. Today, there are marked gender gaps in income and free time which deter women from participating in sport and leisure, and we are further hindered by disproportionate responsibility for childcare and the 'second shift' of domestic duty. We contend with social pressures around beauty and physical appearance which celebrate thinness, weakness, paleness and fragility in women, and we are painfully conscious of how sweating in sport contradicts these ideals of femininity. We rarely escape the perception of being judged and criticised outdoors. Women's right to freedom outside is also obstructed by failures in the social infrastructure that is necessary to uphold that right: by police officers, lawyers and law-makers who do not adequately tackle intimidation and violence against us, and by a patriarchal medical system which fails to support women's participation in sport through menstruation, pregnancy and menopause, and frequently dismisses our physiological concerns.

Often women are put off from outdoor sport by particular, identifiable men, as well as by more amorphous patriarchal structures. Men are more likely to occupy leadership roles, even in mixed-sex and female-specific sporting groups, and such men – including PE teachers, guides, personal trainers and coaches – are often experienced to be patronising and pessimistic about women's abilities. They sometimes wield power over female athletes via sexual abuse. On the streets, men take greater risks than women do. This endangers men's own safety (in the case of male pedestrians who walk in front of cars) and it also threatens women's lives (in the case of reckless male drivers with female passengers). At football matches, recent studies show that there is a rise in male fans jeering and hurling abuse at women, and at political protests, women face male sexual violence. Men deploy formal mechanisms to deter women from sport, concocting bans on female presence on mountains and football pitches and in club-houses and competitions. And men are not afraid to use violence and intimidation to claim the outdoors as an exclusively male domain. In towns and cities, men commandeer public space by bashing into female pedestrians, crowding us at ATMs and crossings, expanding their groups to take up entire pavements and perpetrating 'noise annoyance'. On the streets and trails, men catcall, abuse, follow, grope, assault and even murder women as we walk to and from work, amble through parks, stroll to the shops and go for runs.

When I began my search for women who fought for freedom outdoors, I naively assumed that those women would have mainly been tackling technical irritations, such as poor clothing design. But I have realised that my hope of quick-fix solutions to relatively simple problems is in vain. The fight for women's freedom outdoors cannot be accomplished purely by designing better running packs (although that would be nice). Nor can it be achieved by changing *ourselves*, as individual women; by enrolling in self-defence classes, wedging keys between our fingers, leaning in in boardrooms or 'putting on our big girl pants' and trying to overcome fear. The problems we face in moving freely around outdoor space largely do not reside within ourselves, but are exerted through the behaviour of the world's men. Upholding women's right to freedom outdoors is a long-term, global, societal endeavour, and it needs to tackle both the material threats we face outdoors as well as ideological beliefs, including pervasive expectations about masculinity and femininity which are inculcated from infancy upwards.

As I rest and recover from the Nidderdale Way, I spend lots of time with my daughters. I don't want my girls to be as scared in the world as I was, both as a female child and as an adult woman. I want them to have the confidence and freedom outdoors that I partially gained from my stepdad and then later reinforced in trail running. And I want them to have all this much earlier than I found it.

I need to work out how to make that happen. What interventions and projects can protect women's freedom outdoors, and where can I find examples? Lizzie always spoke of mountaineering as emancipating her from 'shackles' that otherwise threatened to imprison women. How did she fight for women's liberty when she stopped mountaineering in a period of heightened backlash against women's rights? How did she, and her contemporaries, resist men's attempts to drive them out of sport and public life?

And what is being done now, to repel the risks women face outdoors? and what can we all do, as individuals and collectively?

10.

Resistance training

In June 1900, Lizzie left the mountains and headed for Britain to marry her third husband, a man she had recently met in St Moritz.

Aubrey Le Blond had arrived with a friend at the Kulm Hotel a few days into the new year. He was nearly a decade younger than Lizzie and small, like her, with an athletic build, and light eyes – rather like those of the late Roman Imboden. Aubrey had played tennis for Pembroke College, Cambridge, from where he'd graduated with a third in modern languages, and he had been travelling around Europe for the last three years. Lizzie was back in St Moritz to see in the new century and, the week after Aubrey's arrival, there was a fancy-dress ball at which both she and Aubrey made half-hearted efforts: respectively attiring themselves as a 'Member of the Cyclists' Touring Club' and in 'Evening dress, period 1900'. Aubrey, nonetheless, had a flair for theatricals and possessed a rich singing voice. When Lizzie organised fundraising concerts for the Boer War effort and for her St Moritz Aid Fund, he agreed to perform.

By the end of January, the *Alpine Post* reported that Aubrey had 'already established himself as a favorite with a Kulm audience', and the same could be said of Lizzie's attitude towards him. But the promising new relationship was soon jeopardised when Aubrey's family's business got into trouble, and he had to return to Britain to help his parents. Lizzie soon followed him back and, on 12 June, two weeks before her fortieth birthday, they were married in what newspapers reported to be a 'very quiet' wedding at St Mary Abbot's parish church, Kensington.[1]

To all intents and purposes, Lizzie had left mountaineering forever. In the years immediately after her marriage, she made only a few small climbs around Zermatt, including the Wellenkuppe, in 1903. Her health began to deteriorate. She suffered repeated bouts of phlebitis: a venous inflammation that caused her to experience intense pain, throbbing, burning sensations and fever, leaving her laid up for months at a time. Lizzie plotted a new career using the stories and contacts she had collected during two decades of outdoor sports. She became a professional public speaker and mountaineering journalist, donating her income to charities, including the Society for the Prevention of Cruelty to Children and the St Moritz Aid Fund.

In these years, there were few role models of athletes who successfully monetised sport via books and lecture tours. As a woman, Lizzie was largely excluded from high-profile audiences at grand male-dominated bastions, such as the Royal Geographical Society, so she instead fostered connections at national and regional newspapers and at mixed-sex societies such as the Croydon Camera Club. Her articles were popular enough to form the backbone of two books, including *Adventures on the Roof of the World*, which was published in March 1904 and acclaimed as 'difficult to praise too highly'.[2]

By 1903, Lizzie was designated as 'probably the most widely known' female climber in the English-speaking world: 'a voluminous writer as well as an indefatigable mountaineer'. In 1904, the *Gentlewoman* included her in a 'Roll of Honour for Women', a feature spotlighting 'women who have achieved distinction in work for the public good'.[3] The first sportswoman to professionalise her pursuits to this extent, Lizzie was an inspiration for other women, including Fanny Bullock Workman, an American travel writer and mountaineer. Fanny travelled through Europe, north Africa and Asia with her husband, cycling thousands of miles, and she was one of the first Western travellers to climb in the high-altitude ranges of the Himalayas and Karakoram, where she set the women's altitude record at Pinnacle Peak. She also pursued a career in public speaking, and in November 1904 she became the first American woman to lecture at the Sorbonne, in Paris. It was Lizzie who had shown Fanny that such a career could be possible for an adventurous woman.

In the summer of 1907, a 'fearless and ardent mountaineer' called Adeline Edwards resolved to set up 'a women's Alpine Club . . . thus doing for women what the Alpine Club has striven to do for men'. Adeline had approached the Lyceum Club, recently founded (in 1904) by the disabled artist and writer Constance Smedley as one of a number of new clubs to help elite women meet in the capital in comfort and safety. One reporter described how, as the women moved into the Lyceum Club – the first women's club to 'invade' the territory of male clubland – men could be seen 'from the windows of the eleven other clubs on Piccadilly . . . with shocked faces . . . First Dover Street, now Piccadilly, what would the women conquer next?'[4]

The Lyceum's executive committee liked Adeline's idea for a women's Alpine club, and suggested she write a short proposal and present it to the club. Constance's father, who was a financial backer of the Lyceum, read Adeline's suggestion and wrote to Lizzie, inviting her to be president of his daughter's mooted 'Alpine Section'. At the time, Lizzie was at her family estate at Killincarrick, writing a biography of her great-great-great-grandmother, Countess Charlotte Sophie Von Aldenburg Bentinck (who, like Lizzie, had also been accused of abandoning her family 'and all that should be dearest to you in the world, to retire with your delicate health'). Lizzie, already a member of the Lyceum Club and active in 'the Italian and Swedish circles, and on the Council of the Photographer's Section', dropped everything to accept the invitation, travelling across the sea from Dublin to Wales, and then by train to London. A few days after Adeline's presentation on 12 August, Lizzie gave an interview to the *Telegraph* about the new 'Ladies' Alpine Club', in which she angrily described how 'many men are not enthusiastic about women climbers at all; and, perhaps, would rather be without us'. This meant, she continued, that 'women have had no place at which to meet and discuss mountaineering'.[5] She explained how the new all-female club would resist men's sidelining of women in the sport.

Together Lizzie and Adeline thrashed out the details. In particular, they noted how male mountaineers usually segregated their clubs by nation, region or state; but Adeline and Lizzie wanted the Lyceum Alpine Club to be for women everywhere, with 'members drawn from all parts of the world' so that 'their membership might form a bond of union among all countries for every lover of mountains'. They also emphasised the need for 'an extensive and authoritative library' of publications by women mountaineers, to share practical female-oriented information about 'the formation of climbing parties, the provision of guides, means of travelling, and general accommodation' – and to raise awareness about the existence of a distinct and impressive tradition of female mountaineering, which had hitherto gone mostly unrecorded. Lizzie further stressed the importance of a club room, 'some place where [women] can meet each other to discuss the sport they so much enjoy', and an opportunity 'to promote that spirit of comradeship'.[6]

On 16 December 1907, the Lyceum Alpine Club held its inaugural dinner. Over sixty guests attended, including Fanny Bullock Workman and her husband; Lucy Walker, arguably the first really famous female climber, who was now seventy-one and living in Liverpool; a 'great authority on volcanoes' called Dr Tempest Anderson; and Lizzie's publisher, Thomas Fisher Unwin, a keen mountaineer married to the suffragist and campaigner Jane Cobden, whom Lizzie had first met in St Moritz. As a courtesy, Lizzie invited members of the men's Alpine Club, but they were busy and sent their apologies. The women ate a nine-course meal of French haute cuisine, and Lizzie – her small frame dressed in a long, pale, lace gown with a voluminous, floor-length shawl, with hair pinned back tightly or perhaps even cropped – made a rousing speech, celebrating 'the energy and initiative of Miss Edwards' and 'the movement she has initiated'. Fanny expressed her hopes that the club would encourage members to tell stories like her own, of being 'a woman [and] a pioneer', so that 'others may be induced also' to go to the mountains, 'as women geologists, or women surveyors, and so on'.[7]

After the dinner, Adeline invited all interested women to form a committee. Lizzie became president, Adeline vice-president and an indefatigable woman called Edith Emily Mudd – who had 'climbed all the principal peaks in Switzerland', walked over 2,500 kilometres from Uganda to Sudan and would become one of the first female almoners in England, working for St George's Hospital in

London – was made treasurer. As honorary secretary, they elected Alice Carthew, a Hellenist, translator, watercolourist, collector of antiquities, Brazilian ceramics, and prints by Albrecht Dürer and William Blake, who would go on to become a politician and council member. Six further women joined as founding members: from France, the retired mountaineering couple Katy Richardson and Mary Paillon, and another female climber called Eugénie Vail; Fanny Bullock Workman; Lucy Walker; and the travel writer and linguist Susette Taylor, who had studied modern languages at Lady Margaret Hall in Oxford, spoke German, Italian, Greek and Spanish fluently and had travelled in Tibet, where her sister Annie lived alone, dressed in Tibetan costume, and was said to be 'the only Englishwoman who can claim to have lived continuously in the Forbidden Land'. Before 1 December 1909, another seventeen women enrolled in the Lyceum Alpine Club, including Lily Bristow (possibly the model for Lily Briscoe in Virginia Woolf's *To The Lighthouse*), Violet Roy-Batty (née Paget), Ada Hatfield (née Tippetts), Ada Cossey, Countess Ida Felicia Lewenhaupt (née Gosling), Maria Howard Fox, Louise Nettleton (née Dyer, who went on to become a world champion archer in her sixties and seventies), cousins Emily and Lucy Western, and Ina Brodigan (who would later champion the rights of women workers).[8]

Many of these early members shared certain characteristics at the time of the Lyceum Alpine Club's foundation. They were mainly in their forties and based in London or the south of England. Some were married but most were single, and a few cohabited with other women: Alice Carthew would later live and travel with a Greek stockbroker's daughter called Loucia 'Lucy' Agelasto. They were all white and, despite some exceptions, the majority described themselves as having 'independent means' stemming from ancestors with significant wealth. Many had nurtured an early love for mountaineering within adventurous families who travelled extensively. But they were a very different group of women from the light-hearted, fashionable 'smart set' of St Moritz, who had 'failed to see the fun of . . . Women's Rights', as even Lizzie herself may have admitted. As she would discover soon after the birth of the Lyceum Alpine Club, most of its members were seriously committed to social and political work, and they thought of their mountaineering in alignment with those projects. Many volunteered for charitable associations, educational establishments and political movements across a spectrum of affiliations, and with an emphasis on women's rights. By 1 December 1909, the 'Lady Alpinists' numbered twenty-seven women and, over the next decade or so, their commitment to defending women's freedoms in the mountains would become particularly relevant to wider campaigns for female participation in the public sphere in the face of increasing male hostility.[9]

In October 1909, the new club separated from the Lyceum Club and established itself as an independent 'Ladies' Alpine Club'. The Great Central Hotel in Marylebone offered 'the sole use of a separate room – in which to keep photographs of interest & literature . . . & in which our own Members may gather', and by the time of the third annual dinner, on 6 December 1909, the women were ensconced within their new surroundings. They decorated the club room's walls with members' Alpine photographs and drawings, alongside portraits of Queen Margherita of Italy (who accepted an invitation to be honorary president of the new club), and of Lizzie, Mary Paillon, Lucy Walker, Fanny Bullock Workman and a distinguished climber called Margaret Jackson (who had recently died and who, over her career, had made 140 major climbs, including overall first ascents of the Weissmies, the Dom and the Dent Blanche, and first winter ascents of the Gross Lauteraarhorn, the Klein and Gross Viescherhorn, the Jungfrau and the Wengern Alp, all in the 1880s).[10]

Members donated furniture and other essentials: an antique bookcase, a cupboard, clock, wastepaper basket and noticeboard. Alice Carthew obtained the pièce de resistance: a 'lantern' (like a projector) and table, and a screen on which images could be shown during public talks. Maria Howard Fox – who came from a well-known outdoorsy family, and was related to Quaker mountaineering siblings Francis, Mariana and Elizabeth Fox Tuckett – drew a menu card featuring the Jungfrau mountain anthropomorphised into a *jung frau*, a young

'To the Spirit of the Jungfrau': A drawing of a female mountain and mountaineer on the menu of the Ladies' Alpine Club's annual dinner in 1910, by member Maria Howard Fox

woman sharing a toast with a female climber. The women designed a bookplate to be stuck into the library's collection, and a logo of interlocking white letters – 'L,' 'A' and 'C' – on a grey background, encircled by a dark green rim studded with silver, which was engraved onto a brooch (with a 'design of the Weisshorn [in] blue, grey and white enamel, on the reverse'). The women had held a couple of lectures at the Lyceum Club the previous year, but now they could do so far more frequently, and they organised talks by speakers including Fanny and Lizzie, and hosted 'At Homes' – convivial get-togethers in the club room, with tea, once a month in the afternoon.[11]

The Ladies' Alpine Club members sought to push back against the increasing marginalisation of female climbing from male-dominated mainstream mountaineering literature, and to make women's achievements more visible. In 1909, Adeline encouraged the idea 'that members should be invited to send in reports of their season's work . . . in order that a record may be kept, and annually brought up to date'. But this wasn't a straightforward decision. In its favour, the women knew, first-hand, the importance of role models and foremothers. But they also understood how 'codification mania' had meant that, in historian Carol Osborne's words, success in organised sport had become 'synonymous with the recording of results'. Some members of the Ladies' Alpine Club worried that encouraging the dissemination of mountaineering achievements could impel women to climb primarily in order to be the first, or the fastest, or for fame. The explorer Amelia Edwards had described how 'those words "*prima ascenzione*" are Cabalistic', and Lizzie was scathing about those who only wanted to 'ascend peaks in order to boast of their achievements'. She thought that such behaviour was the hallmark of 'Mountain Midgets' who made the Alps their 'running-ground' in order to boast to girls about 'cutting records' – and was more characteristic of male than female climbers.[12] And so the Ladies' Alpine Club found a compromise and began publishing small annual *Reports*, which were less ostentatious and less competitive than the men's *Alpine Journal*, but still did important work in preserving the tradition of women's outdoor sport.

The women also defended the value of their distinct, female-specific experiences of kit and clothing. Between 2 and 7 May 1910, the Ladies' Alpine Club organised a public 'Exhibition of Mountaineering Equipment' and 'Women's Alpine Kit', led by member Louise Nettleton. The exhibition showed that women did not climb like honorary men, but had their own characteristics and needs. All outdoor kit – both male and female – had to balance 'the minimum of weight and the maximum of protection', but the exhibition showed how it was hard to design along these lines for women, whose typical clothing was heavier and could not be significantly minimised without social censure. Manufacturers demonstrated that they were trying to create women's lightweight kit that was functional, fashionable and respectable, in waterproof silk 'mackintoshes, which . . . could be carried in a pocket or handbag', 'waterproof silk hats, trimmed with brilliant-hued plumage, which could be rolled up and slipped in the pocket without fear of injury' and tents that could similarly be tightly packed and weighed 'only 1¼ lb, and can be stowed in a pocket'. There was a nod to the popularity of photography among mountaineering women, and James Sinclair, who owned a photographic shop on Whitehall, advertised ultralight photographic equipment and 'snow spectacles' suitable for women's smaller facial dimensions. Burberry sent in 'an assortment of their well-known rough weather garments', and Jaeger displayed 'woollen wraps'.[13]

Women climbers still struggled with full-length skirts, and the exhibition displayed a number of work-arounds, in varieties 'that can be shortened for climbing, and dropped to normal length on returning to the flat'. The firm of Thomas and Son, on London's Brook Street, hired a model to demonstrate their new women's 'climbing costume, consisting of a Norfolk coat with skirt made to button down the front, which by an ingenious arrangement could be converted when necessary into a cape, with knickerbockers of the same material'. A different company manufactured a variation on this theme, an article they called 'the aviation' which could be 'converted into wide loose trousers at a moment's notice'. One manufacturer encouraged women to eschew the long skirt altogether, in favour of a cropped version 'made of rough Irish or Scotch tweed' which should 'reach not more than just over the knee' and could be worn over 'puttees' or with 'a plain pair of knickerbockers, well pouched at the knees so as to give plenty of movement'.[14] But although such shorter garments were lighter (especially when wet) and less hazardous than their ankle-length equivalents, they did not offer the same capacious pockets, and many female climbers would stick with their long skirts. It would not be until the late 1920s and 1930s that the combination of improvements in rucksack design, female participation in manual labour during the First World War, and Coco Chanel's designs would make trousers more attractive for women.

The Ladies' Alpine Club exhibition insisted that, despite the exclusion of women from mainstream sport, 'woman as a climber means business' (in the words of a journalist who reported on the event). But, beneath the bravado, a pronounced shift had occurred. This affected how women thought of their relationship with the world of male mountaineering. In the 1880s and 1890s, Lizzie and her friends had mostly participated in sport in mixed-sex settings but, around a quarter-century later, there was much greater emphasis on single-sex spaces. This was arguably one result of men's commandeering of public space around the turn of the century: women were forced to respond to heightened misogyny outdoors by creating all-female refuges offering safety and opportunities for women to recuperate their strength.

Ladies-only clubs and societies were sometimes the only ways for certain women to hold authority in a public sphere that was characterised by hostile masculinity. The Ladies' Alpine Club was among a number of all-female institutions established at this time, which included the Pinnacle Club, a woman's rock-climbing club founded in 1921 by Emily 'Pat' Kelly, and the British Federation of University Women, which was founded by Constance Smedley's sister Ida (who had studied at the women's college, Newnham, in Cambridge). In the same era, a phenomenon known as 'manless climbing' or *cordées féminines* became popular: all-female mountaineering teams, in which women took on the roles of guides and porters as well as climbers. (Lizzie's friend Edward Lisle Strutt would claim that Lizzie herself had been 'the first lady to make "manless" ascents', following her ascent of Piz Palü in 1892, accompanied only by another woman, Lady Evelyn McDonnell, with no male guides or assistants.) The same trend towards single-sex clubs, activities and spaces can be seen in the present moment. Contemporary feminist debates involve impassioned defences of the value of all-female spaces, such as single sex rape and domestic violence refuges, prisons and public toilets. I think that, among other things, this articulates a perception that public space in general has become more dangerous for women: that, at this present moment, there is heightened danger in our close proximity to men and that all-female spaces are necessary for women to be able to function in public.[15]

Some women were wary of sex segregation and all-female spaces, though. When ladies-only train carriages were mooted as a remedy to male violence on public transport, a journalist stressed that many among 'the band of women suffrage agitators' were critical of the idea: perhaps 'the attempted separation of the sexes [was] a ruse ingeniously devised for the purpose of indicating female inferiority'. Women's societies tended to be less well resourced than male equivalents: the Ladies' Alpine Club operated out of a small single room, in comparison to the men's expensive quarters which, since 1895, had been located on Savile Row in London's Mayfair. And, as I've already encountered, women like Harriet Stanton Blatch criticised spaces like all-female carriages and waiting rooms for constraining the freedom of women, rather than that of male perpetrators of harassment and violence. Some commentators thought that solutions to men's aggression lay not in women-only spaces, but elsewhere, in much more far-reaching forms of change. A correspondent in the *Liverpool Daily Post* mused in 1875 that, in order to make women freer and safer, perhaps 'it is not only railway travelling, but the whole structure of social habits that will have to be changed'.[16]

Again, similar discussions reverberate today. In a radio programme about the history of violence against women in public spaces, Mandu Reid, leader of the British Women's Equality Party, emphasised that, instead of sticking-plaster solutions such as ladies-only carriages, 'what we need to see is a political response that acknowledges' that 'male violence against women and girls is a deeply entrenched problem'.[17] There is something shocking and depressing about the fact that such conversations about how to protect women's safety and freedoms in public space have changed so little. Men in 2022 are deploying almost exactly the same tactics to constrain and intimidate women outdoors as they did 150 years earlier – and they are still being allowed to get away with it.

The members of the Ladies' Alpine Club considered it entirely apposite that, as mountaineers, they should be hotly engaged in debates of this nature. They knew how closely outdoor leisure was bound up with modern politics and economics.

Rambling had always been a political activity. In Britain, nineteenth-century urbanisation had evolved at the same time as an acceleration in the Enclosure Acts, through which over six million acres of common land were enclosed by private landowners. As numbers of outdoor leisure enthusiasts looking for respite from city life were rising, accessible open countryside was diminishing. Recreational walkers and mountaineers clashed with landowners who illegally closed footpaths across their estates, and societies and campaigns in the UK and US fought for the construction and preservation of trails and defended the 'absolute necessity' of 'walking unrestrainedly through the fine fields' as a 'counterbalance' to 'the dirt and smoke of a great town'. These campaigns intensified in the 1880s, when Scottish MP and lawyer James Bryce proposed an 'Access to Mountains Bill'. This sought to permanently protect people's right to access 'mountain land, moor or waste land' and to 'walk along the bed or bank of any river, stream, or lake'. His friend, the liberal MP Charles Trevelyan, held up European mountaineering as an exemplar of continental democracy that put Britain to shame: 'Who had ever been forbidden to wander over an Alp? . . . Who had ever been prosecuted for trespassing among Norwegian mountains?' Bryce's bill was voted down every year for two decades and, on 27 June 1930, the first mass trespass would take place on Ilkley Moor in Yorkshire, when two or three thousand ramblers would congregate to make their 'demand for access to mountains'. This was followed by a more famous protest on Kinder Scout in the Peak District in 1932. But it would not be until 1949 that the Access to the Countryside Act would finally pass into law.[18]

Such campaigns have conventionally been analysed in terms of class politics. Historian E. P. Thompson called enclosures 'a plain enough case of class robbery' in which landowners dispossessed the working classes of their 'birthright' to freely access, and graze animals upon, common land. The very idea of a *right to roam* was also gendered. As Simon Thompson describes in a brilliant PhD thesis on 'the origins of the mass outdoor movement', women played an active role in the politicised world of rambling, and a journalist noted that the Ilkley rally in 1930 'included many girls in shorts'.[19] Female ramblers and mountaineers knew that, as women, their right to roam around public space was undermined by multiple forms of discrimination. They campaigned, not just against greedy private landowners, but also against men who constrained their freedoms outdoors in other ways.

Female mountaineers had long been dynamically involved in

feminist political movements that were fighting for women's freedom and power in public space. Such women used climbing as both symbol and microcosm of the wider women's rights for which they were campaigning. There was direct overlap between the two worlds of early feminism and early mountaineering: many female political campaigners were also climbers. In the US, Quaker-turned-Methodist Anna Dickinson lectured and wrote on temperance, women's rights and the abolition of slavery, and was the first recorded white woman to ascend Gray's Peak, Lincoln Peak and Elbert Peak in Colorado's Rocky Mountains. Mary Taylor – who was photographed in 1875 taking five other women up Mont Blanc and was a lifelong friend of novelist Charlotte Brontë – wrote numerous articles on women's rights for *Victoria Magazine* in the 1860s, which she collected into a book called *The First Duty of Women*. Mountaineer Emily Hornby was a member of the Ladies' Grand Council of the Primrose League in the 1890s and helped to establish the Liverpool Women's Suffrage Society in 1893, and then served on its committee.

When the 'New Woman' ideal emerged in the late nineteenth century, and emphasised women's intellectual and physical independence, female mountaineers – including Gertrude Bell, Maud Meyer and the author and traveller Ménie Muriel Dowie – became icons of the mould. Multiple female members of a prominent Quaker family in northeast England, the Richardsons, were both enthusiastic outdoorswomen and campaigners for women's education in the nineteenth and early twentieth centuries: Elizabeth Spence Watson (née Richardson) was a mountaineer and member of the Women's Liberal Association. Her sister Anna Deborah Richardson helped to found the women's college, Girton, in Cambridge and also built a house called Heugh Folds, above Grasmere in the Lake District, where the sisters rambled and where their niece Teresa Merz held 'reading parties' for female friends from Cambridge's Newnham College. Teresa later turned Elizabeth's house in Gateshead into an educational settlement with an emphasis on lessons for women – including on public speaking – and she set up Hope House, a lodging house for women and girls in need. All these women's outdoor pursuits and their public work alike were guided by the conviction that, in Teresa's words, 'women are citizens of this country. Their health, happiness and convenience should be as important as that of any other section of society.'[20]

In the US, the connection between women's participation in sport and women's access to the public sphere was also made evident in campaigns for African-American women's rights. Historian Gwendolyn Captain describes how organisations such as the National Association of Colored Women's Clubs (NACWC) and the Young Women's Christian Association (YWCA) used sport to foster 'intellectual and moral growth', education about 'health, hygiene and physical efficiency' and the development of leadership skills. These institutions looked to Black athletes – including tennis players Lucy Diggs Slowe (who won the American Tennis Association's first tournament in 1917), Anita Gant (who won singles championships in 1925 and 1926, and doubles in 1929 and 1930) and hockey player, swimmer and track athlete Inez Patterson – as role models. In 1896, the NACWC adopted the motto 'Lifting as We Climb', which explicitly linked mountaineering to the wider struggle for emancipation; its emblem featured two girls helping one another up a steep slope.[21]

Mountaineering specifically, and women's sport in general, became important symbols of women's rights during campaigns for female suffrage in the UK and US. When demonstrating for women's political representation, suffragists stormed sporting facilities, including race courses, and in 1913 suffragette Emmeline Pankhurst pointed out how the male monopoly of 'golf links' encapsulated men's takeover of public space more generally. Many female suffragists were sportswomen. Hilda Webb, one of eight women arrested for throwing stones at government buildings in Dublin during protests by the Irish Women's Franchise League, had helped to establish women's hockey in Ireland in the 1890s. The openly lesbian mountaineer, tennis player, golfer, equestrian (and composer) Ethel Smyth put her musical career on pause to demonstrate with the Women's Social and Political Union. She wrote the suffragette anthem 'The March of the Women' and served two months in Holloway Prison for throwing stones at the home of colonial secretary Lewis Harcourt. Disabled suffrage activist May Billinghurst knew first-hand how important cycling was in female emancipation, especially for women with disabilities, and she took part in protest marches using a specially adapted tricycle. Florence Dixie was both a suffragist and president of the British Ladies' Football Club and a passionate hunter and explorer. Suffragist Sophia Duleep Singh played for East Molesey Ladies' Hockey Club: she felt hockey was more woman-friendly than golf, which had become male-dominated, and she declared the outdoors to be 'the birthright of every happy, healthy girl, be she princess or peasant'. In this, she was using rhetoric directly associated with the 'right to roam' movement in order to refer to women's rights.[22]

Out of all sports, mountaineering was especially relevant to suffragists' fight for representation; in part because outdoor leisure activities such as hiking were already widely accepted to be fundamentally political pastimes in the context of 'right to roam' campaigns. In a 1908 short story called 'The Suffragette', author Frank Savile made sure that the fictional women's rights activist was a 'lady mountaineer'. Marjorie Milsom thought that early twentieth-century female climbers brought to mind 'thoughts of window-breaking suffragettes . . . emancipation, in fact – another aspect of the new feminine attack on masculine sanctuaries'. Suffragist mountaineers directly embraced the political symbolism of their sport. In 1909, a group of women ascended Mount Rainier (in the Cascade mountain range of the Pacific Northwest) and placed a 'Votes for Women' pennant at its summit. One of the group's members, Cora Smith Eaton, was a founder of the Grand Forks Equal Suffrage Association and treasurer for the Washington Equal Suffrage Association, and when she subsequently climbed Glacier Peak in the same range, she wrote 'Votes for Women' after her name on the register. In 1911, the American mountaineer and suffragist Annie Smith Peck unfurled a yellow 'Votes for Women' banner on the 21,000-foot peak of Nevado Coropuna in Peru, and the following year, Fanny Bullock Workman was photographed holding up a newspaper with a 'Votes for Women' headline on the Siachen Glacier in the Himalayas.[23]

Fanny Bullock Workman proclaims 'Votes for Women' on Silver Throne Plateau in the Karakoram, 1912

Enough members of the female Alpine Club were ardent suffragists that, in 1909, the British *Votes for Women* newspaper suggested that its membership roster would make a good recruiting ground for militant campaigners. The club's most prominent mountaineer-suffragists were friends Eva McLaren and Frances Heron-Maxwell. Eva was known to be engaged in 'long and strenuous work for the enfranchisement of women': she served on the central committee of the National Society for Women's Suffrage, was a leading member of the Women's Liberal Federation, active in the Union of Practical Suffragists and the Liberal Women's Suffrage Union and, with Frances Heron-Maxwell, she co-founded the Forward Suffrage Union in 1908. Although a few upper-class women were wary of associating themselves with the militant suffragettes who smashed the windows of gentlemen's clubs, the majority of the Ladies' Alpine Club's members were sympathetic to the cause. Early member Violet Roy-Batty served on the ladies' council of the Conservative and Unionist Women's Franchise Association, which expressed the conviction that women should play a greater part in 'the government of the country'.[24]

Lizzie herself confessed that 'I am not a suffragette, because I lack the courage of my opinions' – but she promised that, privately, her views 'entirely coincide with those of that courageous sisterhood' and that she hoped that, if the suffragists 'make themselves sufficiently unpleasant during a sufficiently long time, they will get [the vote]'. All of the female climbers who comprised the Ladies' Alpine Club had experienced how mountaineering could radicalise women and offer a taste of freedoms that they subsequently wanted to be granted elsewhere. As Mary E. Crawford – a member of the Alpine Club of Canada, president of the Political Equality League in Winnipeg and campaigner for women's rights in the Province of Manitoba – explained in 1909, outdoor leisure helped a woman to 'know herself as never before – physically, mentally, emotionally', to 'gain confidence with every step' and to 'gaze out upon a new world'.[25]

Lizzie spent her middle age with the Ladies' Alpine Club, finding ways to claw back freedoms despite the marginalisation of women in sport and public life that had stolen many of the glorious liberties of her youth. Her final two decades were also seen out in this long-lasting era of male backlash. In those years, Lizzie came to see how her skills in mountaineering were relevant to political issues beyond female suffrage – such as international relations and women's role in global diplomacy.

When she had first left Ireland in her teens in the 1870s, Lizzie had worried that her education was slight and her conversational skills frivolous. But after a nearly twenty-year residence in Switzerland, she was able to speak multiple languages fluently and had met and socialised with some of the key politicians, journalists, news editors and diplomats of the period, during their own continental holidays. Lizzie would always uphold what she called the 'international ideal' that lay at the Ladies' Alpine Club's heart: the hope that patriotism and competitiveness might be supplanted by camaraderie across nations. But it was not an age in which women could easily act as official diplomats or foreign correspondents. There were female journalists, but they were frequently told that their sex 'physically debarred' them from certain commissions, and women wouldn't be formally appointed to international diplomatic positions in the UK or US until the late 1940s. But, as Helen McCarthy describes in her history of 'the rise of the female diplomat', women were tenacious and found alternative, unofficial routes to these professions.[26]

Lizzie used her mountaineering expertise in the theatre of international relations but, because she was a woman, her roles were often covert and undercover – mirroring the way in which women persevered in sport in this period, often without visibility or widespread respect.

After the outbreak of the First World War, Lizzie realised that, because of mountaineering, she had certain skills that might be transferable to the war effort. On the eve of war, she was in Flims, Switzerland, visiting her son Harry, who was now in his mid thirties and 'whose health', she claimed, 'obliges him to live out of England'. After a hairy series of train journeys across the continent, Lizzie managed to get back to the UK where she quickly applied her experience in public speaking to give 'enthusiastic [army] recruiting speeches' at local meetings and wrote a pamphlet to encourage young men to enlist. After Italy joined the Allies, her leaflet would be 'translated into Italian, and distributed in large quantities in Italy'.

Lizzie wanted to help the war effort in more hands-on ways too. Now fifty-four, she was too old to volunteer with the Red Cross in Britain, but she had heard that unskilled help might be welcome in France. The decades she had devoted to outdoor sport meant that she was adept at logistics, bodily care, problem-solving and she possessed extraordinary endurance. (Her desire to leave Britain may also have been prompted by distress after she – or her chauffeur – accidentally killed an elderly man, a chimney sweep, who had suddenly stepped in front of her car in Tunbridge Wells in April 1914.) That autumn, she travelled to a hotel in Dieppe and was welcomed at 'a large, improvised military hospital in the Collège', where she signed up as an orderly. She described how her 'job was to make myself generally useful: that is to say, I made beds, washed patients, helped them with their meals, gave medicines, took temperatures, sterilized instruments and did so many other trifling jobs'.[27]

Over the winter, Lizzie returned to Britain, and offered herself as a volunteer in London. At first, she did clerical work at the British Red Cross Society's London enquiry office for wounded and missing soldiers, and then she became attached to the British Ambulance Committee, through her cousin Dartchie, now the 6th Duke of Portland, who was its president. The vice-president, a wealthy Dorset landowner and car enthusiast called Bradby Peyman, spoke of the need for 'a motor kitchen for the Englishmen attached to the Ambulance Corps in the Vosges', in the mountainous border region between France, Germany and Switzerland. Lizzie had resigned as the Ladies' Alpine Club's president back in June 1912, but she knew that she and the society still had the specific expertise, resources and connections to help the campaign and assist the Chasseurs Alpins – the elite infantry of the French Army, which operated in the mountains and included many Alpine guides known personally to her mountaineering friends. In March 1915, Lizzie rallied the club's membership and immediately raised over £150 (around £10,000 to £12,000 today) in donations, with over a quarter coming from a fundraising lecture she gave in May. The money directly funded the motor kitchen, which was duly made and sent to the mountain soldiers.[28]

Lizzie wanted to do more. When representatives of the French Red Cross and 'Pro Italia Committee' got in touch with lists of items required by the French and Italian Alpine troops – socks, climbing boots, belts, helmets, mufflers, scarves and layer upon layer of woollen garments ('for the cold is often intense and climatic conditions terrible') – Lizzie and fellow club member Beatrice McAndrew appealed for donations to mountaineers everywhere in Britain, and Beatrice turned the women's club room at the Great Central Hotel into a storage depot, where she sorted, parcelled and sent thousands of items to Contessa Greppi and the Vicomtesse de la Panouse in Italy and France. Surplus clothing was posted to Mary Paillon and Katy Richardson in France, who coordinated a separate scheme to collect garments for 20,000 refugees.[29]

In August 1915, Lizzie returned to front-line work. She went back to Dieppe, where she worked as part of a 'pleasant little group of

English' volunteers, including fellow club member Mabel Capper, at 'Hôpital 37', one of the British base hospitals at which casualties were treated before being evacuated to longer-term care. Lizzie stayed for over a year this time: through the Battle of the Somme and the torpedoing of the SS *Sussex*, in which she was shocked to find a friend, the suffragist and journalist Vera Collum, among the seriously injured casualties. Lizzie would be awarded a Victory Medal for her work in France. When she travelled back to Britain by early December 1916, it was to find that the Ladies' Alpine Club room at the Great Central Hotel was gone, requisitioned by the War Office as 'a Hospital for Convalescent Officers'.[30] And the club room was not the only loss that Lizzie suffered on her return.

In a rare candid moment in her autobiography, Lizzie confessed that her hasty departure from France in the winter of 1916 had been prompted by 'family reasons'. While she was overseas, her husband Aubrey had moved to Gloucestershire and bought a farm called the Ploddy House. There he grew potatoes, donated produce to the local hospital and kept pedigree pigs, naming his herd 'Greystones', after the town that, with Delgany, bordered Lizzie's Irish estate.[31] Lizzie came back to help him establish himself as a farmer, but their lives were growing apart. Over the next fifteen or so years, she was rarely with Aubrey or, indeed, in Britain at all.

After returning from France, Lizzie used her fundraising experience in her role as head of the British Ambulance Committee's Appeal Department and was then sent by the War Office to lecture to troops in France during the winter of 1918/19 – one of the severest on record (she had to sleep in bed at night hugging her glass projector slides to stop them shattering from the cold). In January 1920, she went alone to north Africa, to meet the French colonial administrator Hubert Lyautey, who had been Resident-General in Morocco since 1912, and later that year she set up a charity for the restoration of Reims Cathedral, which had been heavily bombed in 1914. She fought the 1921 Football Association ban on women's football in England to organise a fundraising match between Hey's Ladies (a women's team based at Hey's Brewery in Bradford) and a visiting French female team, the

Olympique de Paris. She made numerous trips during this time to the US, ostensibly to see her son, Harry – who had moved to California and renamed himself 'Arthur' – but also to meet with 'many prominent men and women in America – journalists, bankers, business men, and millionaires', in order to gauge public opinion about the USA's postwar relationship with Germany. In January 1926, Lizzie established an 'Anglo-French Luncheon Club', which she hoped would do 'admirable work in keeping together English people who love France and in entertaining distinguished Frenchmen who visit London'. In March 1933, she was delighted to be made a chevalier de la Légion d'honneur, France's highest order of merit, for her commitment to her 'international ideal'.[32]

Lizzie coordinated these projects from one, and then two, flats in London: 87 Victoria Street, close to Victoria station, and 134 Whitehall Court, an iconic block on the north side of the Thames, near Charing Cross station, which resembled an enormous French chateau and housed famous residents including George Bernard Shaw, as well as societies such as the Farmers' Club and the Authors' Club and, until 1919, SIS (Britain's Secret Intelligence Service, now MI6). While Lizzie was in the capital and abroad, Aubrey at first remained in Gloucestershire and then took a series of houses in Suffolk and Sussex. He was not living alone. In 1921, he employed a young Gloucestershire woman called Edith (or, as she preferred, 'Edythe') Hayward, sometimes known as Jane, to help him look after his pigs and organise a large agricultural show. When Aubrey moved to Suffolk, Jane came too and they lived together for the rest of their lives. Occasionally Lizzie resided with Aubrey and Jane, and sometimes they went out in public as a threesome: they all attended a Ladies' Alpine Club dinner together and, in the winter of 1924/25, they travelled to the States. But most of the time, Aubrey and Jane were a couple, taking long retreats *à deux* in Algiers, Genoa and the Canary Islands, while Lizzie lived apart and on her own.[33]

In what would be her final few years, in the early 1930s, Lizzie moved into new quarters in London, at St Ermin's Court, a hotel with apartments. It was perhaps fitting that Lizzie – who had rarely anchored herself to a permanent home during her lifetime and who had lived at the Kulm in St Moritz for nearly twenty years – should see out her last days in a hotel, surrounded by fellow travellers. St Ermin's was meaningful in other ways too. In 1926, the Secret Intelligence Service had taken up premises at 54 Broadway, just around the corner, and St Ermin's subsequently became an unofficial meeting place for its officers, known as the 'house of spies'.[34] In the communal dining, reading and smoking rooms, Lizzie, in her seventies, sat surrounded by intelligence agents and their contacts.

I wonder to myself: could Lizzie Le Blond have been a spy? Historian Christopher Andrew has described how the British intelligence community originated in professional travellers, including surveyors, soldiers and imperial officials, adventurers, explorers, scientists, photographers – and mountaineers. Women's travels were often underestimated and dismissed as trivial holidays, but many of Lizzie's adventures – such as her honeymoon in Algeria, when she may have hoped to monitor the French railway – were information-gathering missions. In fact, she had been employed as a foreign correspondent on some of her own trips. In 1901 and 1905, she reported for the *Daily Express* from northern Norway about Russian attempts to annex the Lofoten Islands and Lyngenfjord as ports. In 1912 and 1913, she and Aubrey visited the Yangtze valley in China during unrest following the Wuchang Uprising (the rebellion of the southern provinces against the Qing court), and there she interviewed railway engineers about the vulnerability of British trade in the region, as well as speaking to personal contacts of one of the new presidential candidates and writing up reports for the *Daily Mail*. She travelled further afield, too, to other places of urgent political significance: Spain during the US–Philippines War; Russia and Germany in the year before the outbreak of the First World War; and America during the Depression, where she wrote in the *Daily Mail* that she'd found 'a keen desire for an alliance between France, Great Britain and the USA'. During the First World War, Lizzie had established lines of communication between London, northern France and the Vosges front via the Ladies' Alpine Club's distribution of kit to soldiers.[35]

According to historian Tammy M. Proctor, there was a drive to recruit female intelligence agents specifically, because women were considered less likely to attract suspicion. Even back in the 1870s, Lizzie and Fred's friends, Henry and Alice Colvile, had pointed out that female travellers were rarely suspected of 'serious designs'. Though it is not possible to ascertain whether Lizzie was *formally* employed as an intelligence officer, her mountaineering expeditions did indeed offer ideal cover for spying missions. In general, Lizzie's international projects encapsulated the type of political influence she possessed throughout her life: in a period in which women could not officially act as diplomats, politicians or journalists, Lizzie's wider political impact had to be stealthy. She found a way of negotiating the male-dominated public sphere by carving out a distinct, but limited, niche for herself and other women; often covertly, rather than enjoying full public recognition for her achievements.

Lizzie died, aged seventy-four, on 27 July 1934, at 'Mangalore', an Arts and Crafts house in the Welsh countryside near Llandrindod Wells. She had been staying with Aubrey's sister Evelyn and her doctor husband, who were caring for her after a traumatic operation on a cancerous tumour in her rectum. She died the same day as the colonial administrator Hubert Lyautey, whom she had met in person fourteen years earlier, and whose letters she had later translated for publication in English. But, unlike Lyautey, whose demise was front-page headline news, Lizzie's death was met with a few small notices, tucked away in the corners of newspapers' inner pages. She was buried in Brompton Cemetery in Kensington, London, in a plot with her mother Alice, who had died in 1908; her mother-in-law Mary; and Aubrey's younger brother Royston, who had died of appendicitis in 1915. The group burial glossed over the complexities of Lizzie's family life but, six months after her death, Lizzie's husband Aubrey married his long-time partner in adultery, Jane Hayward. Jane's surviving family tell me that she subsequently dispersed Lizzie's private papers and photographs, which have ended up at car boot sales and auctions, in rubbish dumps, and in private and public collections around the world, from Kansas to Switzerland to Dunkeld.[36]

Despite being a celebrity in her lifetime, today Lizzie has no full-length biography. Would Lizzie have expected to have disappeared from public memory? Perhaps. She chose to end her autobiography with an account of a total eclipse of the sun and, like many of her depictions of natural phenomena in her writing, it can be read as a mirror of her own life. On 29 June 1927, three days after her sixty-seventh birthday, Lizzie had taken a chartered train to Southport, north of Liverpool, to watch the solar eclipse from the beach. As the moon passed over the sun, and the light grew 'dimmer and dimmer', Lizzie recalled how 'my glasses nearly dropped from my hands in sheer amazement'. For a matter of seconds, 'the corona stood out far more vividly than I had expected, and crimson flames flickered along the edge of the black circle, startlingly bright'.[37] It had only lasted a moment, but it was against the darkness that the sun had burned most brightly.

The subdued quiet that met Lizzie's death reflected women's marginalisation from the public gaze elsewhere over the next few decades, including in sport.

In the 1920s, many mountaineers switched their focus from the familiarity of the Alps towards the Himalayas, which were represented as an opportunity for men to 'climb for the nation' in a region whose significance was compared to a 'Third Pole'. In the run-up to British-led Himalayan expeditions, men wrote in to the Mount Everest Committee, offering their services and describing their prior experience as soldiers, sportsmen, hikers, climbers, linguists, cooks and porters. A few women wrote in too, including a remarkable Frenchwoman called Marie Marvingt. She had been the first woman to finish the Tour de France, one of the first women to fly alone across the Channel and she was a record-breaking swimmer, figure-skater, bobsleigher and mountaineer. During the First World War, Marvingt had designed an 'ambulance plane', worked as a nurse and war correspondent and served on the front line disguised as a man, before using her skiing talents to evacuate injured soldiers from the Italian front. She was well qualified for a Himalayan attempt, but

Francis Younghusband, president of the Royal Geographical Society and chair of the Mount Everest Committee, read her letter aloud to its members – sarcastically reporting that she 'was evidently a great "sportsman" '; Marvingt's proposal was met with guffaws of laughter and rejected. When Anne Bernard, another Frenchwoman, also volunteered, she received the reply that 'it would be quite impossible for the Mount Everest Committee to contemplate the appointment of a lady'.[38]

Despite the proven competence of female mountaineers for high-altitude climbing – such as in Fanny Bullock Workman's expeditions in the Himalayas and Karakoram – men fiercely guarded their expeditions as 'the natural domain of the gentleman amateur'. This remained a defining feature for decades. Women were entirely excluded from the American Everest team of 1963, and in 1969 the American climber and scientist Arlene Blum was rejected from a mountaineering expedition in Afghanistan on the basis that a woman's presence was 'unpleasant' in the midst of 'the easy masculine companionship which is so vital a part of the joy of an expedition'. (In 1970, Blum was permitted to take part in a high-altitude expedition, as far as base camp, on the basis that she could 'assist in the cooking'.) In 1961, Irene Miller, an American mountaineer and physicist at IBM, accompanied her husband on Edmund Hillary and Griffith Pugh's Himalayan Scientific and Mountaineering Expedition, which was designed to experiment with acclimatising climbers to altitude. Miller later spoke to Blum about the experience and told her that Hillary had not wanted women in his expedition, so she and other wives were hurried dangerously fast by their husbands to 19,000 feet and down again, to get an illicit glimpse of base camp, and so they consequently suffered altitude-related problems. In his subsequent book, Hillary used this as evidence that 'women could not adapt well to high altitude'.[39]

Public attention focused on these prestigious all-male high-altitude trips – but women continued organising their own expeditions in the same years, even though they often went unnoticed or uncelebrated. Japanese mountaineer Junko Tabei described how hard it was for women to put together an overseas expedition. Whereas men could draw upon members of local clubs, women could not do similarly because even mixed-sex clubs usually contained only two or three (often inexperienced) female members, not enough to form an expedition team. In the 1930s, the German mountaineer Hettie Dyhrenfurth participated in two Himalayan ventures: the 1930 and 1934 International Himalaya Expeditions (IHE) to Kangchenjunga and the Gasherbrum mountains in the Karakoram. She published a memoir of the first trip, *Memsahb im Himalaja*, and, on the second, she climbed Sia Kangri, breaking the women's altitude record. But in her writings, she represented herself as an assistant and companion to her husband, rather than as an accomplished climber in her own right.

In the 1950s, there were a number of all-female Himalayan expeditions. In 1955, Monica Jackson led the first party of women, many from the Ladies' Scottish Climbing Club, to reconnoitre the Jugal Himal. Their project was met with widespread anxiety – that the women would be assaulted; that they would be unable to lead a team – and historian Carol Osborne describes how 'these climbers were placed under pressure from the outset to get things "right" in a way that never impinged upon male climbers. If they "slipped up", there would be plenty of people who would say "These women should never have been allowed out in the mountains on their own".'[40]

Such pressure reached fever pitch in the 1959 international Expédition Féminine au Nepal to climb Cho Oyu: the first attempt by a women's team to climb an 8,000-metre peak. It ended in tragedy when an avalanche killed four climbers, including leader Claude Kogan and renowned climber Claudine van der Stratten. Despite the women's protests, male journalist Stephen Harper tagged along on the expedition and in 1965 he published a bestselling account entitled *Lady Killer Peak* (reissued in 2007 with the only marginally less sensationalising title *A Fatal Obsession*). Harper used the tragic event to demonstrate how the female mountaineers' 'strange inexplicable urge to battle against rock and ice and thin air until the highest places of the earth lie conquered beneath their tiny, feminine feet' was a form of unnatural 'rebellion against man's natural assumption of command'. For Harper, the avalanche was a reassertion of the natural patriarchal order; a reminder of the 'verdict that even the toughest and most courageous of women are still "the weaker sex" in the White Hell of a blizzard and avalanche torn mountain'.[41] Harper wasn't a climber, didn't ascend the mountain himself and only heard about the women's deaths from second-hand reports while lodging in the town of Namche Bazaar – but the cover of *Lady Killer Peak*'s first edition shows a man bravely leading the women's mountaineering expedition up the treacherous, icy face of Cho Oyu, while the women cower further down the rope, and the book sells itself as 'the story of one man, twelve women and a killer mountain' when, in reality, the man was not part of the story at all.

Similar examples of women being pushed to the sidelines occurred across the rest of the sporting world. In running, men whittled the marathon world record down from 2:55:18 in 1908 to 2:15:16 in 1960. But, in the same period, women were mostly excluded from organised events greater than three miles in distance and their achievements garnered much less coverage. On 29 May 1954, less than a month after Roger Bannister became the first person to run a mile in under four minutes, a twenty-one-year-old analytical chemist called Diane Leather became the first woman to run the same distance in less than five minutes. This was a commensurate achievement, considering the physiological performance gap between men and women and taking into account the fact that, unlike Bannister, Leather ran without pacers. Bannister's run received front-page coverage but Leather's achievement wasn't mentioned in Britain's largest newspapers and it was never classed as a world record because the International Association of Athletics Federations (IAAF) would not recognise the mile as an allowable distance for women until 1967.

Historian of female athletics Katie Holmes points out that Leather's run took place in the same year as a landmark in sporting sexism. In 1954, Adolphe Abrahams published *Woman: Man's Equal?* Abrahams was medical officer to the British Olympics athletics teams and is now widely regarded as the founder of sports science. He chaired a National Fitness Council committee on the 'Desirability of Athletics for Women and Girls' and his report admitted that he had failed to 'obtain adverse criticism on violent exercise for women and girls'. Nevertheless, he concluded that sport threatened women's 'capacity to bear the burdens of womanhood' – these 'burdens' included women's 'femininity and charm' and abilities in 'motherhood, home-making and nursing' – and that female athletics disciplines were less interesting and impressive than their male counterpart.[42] Women were seen as disappointing men, not competitors with our own distinct physiology, history and achievements.

Female athletes who wanted to participate in organised sport often had to do so outside official races. In 1955, sixteen-year-old Kathleen Connochie completed the Ben Nevis fell-race but, because women were banned from the event, she set off one minute before the men's start. Women continued running on their own, but often without events for which to train or in the knowledge that permission to race was fragile. The Lake District Mountain Trial held ladies' races in 1953 and 1954, but then these disappeared and would not be organised again until the late 1960s. And women's participation in sport was especially vulnerable at certain times in the life cycle: in particular, women were expected to stop running upon marriage. Florence Scott remembered working at the Withnell Fold paper mill in Lancashire in the 1930s and taking part in 'the Inter-Mill Sports'. She was delighted when her name 'was called to run in several races, the highlight being the girls' relay race which we proudly won', but she also described how, 'when any female working at the mill got married she had to leave as [her employers] were great believers in the old adage "a woman's place is in the home" '.[43]

During the two world wars, it became nearly impossible to coordinate formal sporting societies and competitions, especially international ones. The Olympic Games did not take place between 1936 and 1948, and activities organised by climbing clubs ground to a halt. But in the interwar period, informal and independent exercise flourished among both women and men, especially walking, which rose to the level of a craze in Britain by the early 1930s. Historian Simon Thompson emphasises that rambling in the 1920s and 1930s was very much a youth movement, especially for young women, whose economic independence and social mobility increased in the interwar years. By 1931, women represented 42 per cent of the clerical workforce, and the average age of marriage had slightly risen to the mid twenties, so there emerged the idea of female youth, after adolescence and before marriage, as 'a life stage marked by a degree of personal independence and commercial consumption'. Women used this brief window of freedom to go hiking. The first edition of *Ruc-Sac* magazine, in July 1931 – which had a circulation of 50,000 – ran a front cover entirely populated by women, and it contained a regular column, 'Jill on the Jaunt', which offered recommendations for female-specific kit and techniques 'to lighten the woman hiker's load'.[44]

This rise of young female pedestrians met with much disapproval. Men who had been walking for recreation since well before the First World War, and called themselves 'ramblers', criticised the new 'hikers' – an American import into the English language, they said – for their supposedly poor taste, vulgar bright jumpers, reported tendency to drop litter and apparent insistence on music in the countryside (from ukeleles, mouth organs, and gramophones playing American jazz records). Especial criticism was levelled at female hikers, who were pejoratively referred to as 'open-air girls', 'carefree girls', 'fat girls in shorts', young women who were 'hatless, raucous, yellow-jerseyed, slung with concertinas' and 'ladies [who] have cast convention to the winds and returned to nature'. Women's hiking was represented by such men as a 'tide of invasion' in which 'ramblerette[s]' 'staked their claim' to a formerly male world. Older male ramblers complained that it was impossible to distinguish male and female hikers, as the seemingly androgynous women appeared to have relinquished femininity, and everyone was 'dressed in shorts and bright coloured shirts without distinction as to sex'. They were revolted by the social intermixing of men and women, with one rambler complaining that hiking is 'only a modern form of "petting party" '. These mostly older, middle-class men tried to limit the threatening presence of young women in the countryside. The Cooperative Holidays Association placed a quota on the number of female members and the Manchester Ramblers' Federation set up a system of (entirely male) 'warden-guides' to teach hikers how to behave – which was especially aimed at young, working-class, female hikers. Elizabeth Coxhead, an enthusiastic walker, later remembered how 'the established . . . clubs froze the ill-connected female beginner with a glance'.[45]

Something similar happened in mountaineering. The interwar and postwar years saw a large increase in independent climbers who were unaffiliated to clubs. Echoing the earlier backlash to the 'vulgarisation' of the Alps in the 1880s, British mountaineer Geoffrey Winthrop Young condemned the new climbers as an 'influx of unordered and untutored scramblers . . . flooding in rapidly increasing numbers over our crags'. Young had first-hand experience of remarkable women climbers: his wife Eleanor 'Len' Slingsby was the daughter of Norwegian mountaineering pioneer William Cecil Slingsby and a champion of female climbing in her own right (she co-founded and was first president of the all-female Pinnacle Club).[46] But Young was still disapproving of the swelling presence of less elite adventurers in the hills – and many men's censure especially targeted women.

After the British Mountaineering Council was inaugurated in 1946, it tried to regulate novice climbers' behaviour with an instructional pamphlet that stressed 'the value of mountain adventure and of the discipline of climbing in developing . . . the character of adolescent boys'. Historian Carol Osborne emphasises how profoundly damaging this ongoing insistence on the manliness of climbing was 'to women's status within the activity' and in 'continuing to shape perceptions of who would or would not climb'.[47] Even when women tried to evade organised sport – in the form of male-dominated clubs, societies and competitions – and to strike out independently, men still attempted to limit women's freedom of movement.

Throughout the mid twentieth century, women's access to sport remained fundamentally shaped by institutions – and this meant that, in male-biased organisations, female athletes suffered. In universities across the UK and US, women's sport was often under-resourced and poorly rewarded in comparison to men's. At Cambridge, female rowers were denied a Blue until the 1940s, and then were disqualified again in 1948. Men's hostility to female athletes could be violent: when a women's boat competed in their first inter-collegiate race (known as 'bumps') at Cambridge in 1962, a male crew deliberately rammed the boat off the river. Two years later, the president of the men's boat club proposed an outright ban on female participation. Women in the Cambridge University Women's Boat Club wouldn't have their own boathouse, nor even access to the men's, until 2012 – 2012! – when they raised enough money to fund a women's extension to the men's facilities. Until then, female rowers stored their boats on a grass embankment at Ely – seventeen miles outside Cambridge – and got changed in bike sheds. And whereas the men's rent, kit and training were mostly paid for by external sponsorship, the women had to cover it themselves, at a rate of around £2,000 each per year.

Institutions did not just curtail women's access to sport, but their visibility and fame too. Lucy Diggs Slowe – who won the American Tennis Championship in 1917, the year before the US Lawn Tennis Association banned Black athletes – saw sport as one component of her wider campaigns for women's rights. She was passionate about the part that educational institutions could play in furthering Black women's 'professional achievement and personal fulfilment', and, in 1922, she was selected as the first 'Dean of Women' at Howard University, a historically Black research university in Washington DC. But the university's president, Mordecai Wyatt Johnson, was reportedly 'venomous' in his attempts to quash her leadership. *The New York Times* described how he denied her a pay rise, cut her department's budget, ousted her from committees and even tried to eject her from the house she shared with her intimate partner, playwright Mary Burrill. When Slowe was dying, Johnson gave her a ridiculous and spiteful ultimatum – to return to campus within twenty-four hours or forfeit her role as dean – and after her death, he belittled her achievements to the extent that Burrill had to write to her colleagues to defend her reputation. Partly because of such institutionalised misogyny and racism, Slowe's significant achievements have largely been forgotten and she has become one of what *The New York Times* termed 'the overlooked': 'remarkable people whose deaths . . . went unreported' at the time, and whose lives have subsequently become invisible.[48]

Yet this poor respect granted to women's sport did not last forever.

Over the space of three years in the 1970s, tennis star Billie Jean King won the 'Battle of the Sexes' match against male player Bobby Riggs, as well as founding the Women's Sports Foundation, persuading the US Open to offer equal prize money for men and women and becoming the first female athlete to earn over US$100,000 from sport.

How on earth was this possible – just a few years after Arlene Blum was excluded from Himalayan mountaineering expeditions and women were barred from running further than a mile in IAAF events? How did this extraordinary change come about?

As I near the end of my project, I want to understand what happened in the 1970s.

How did women finally succeed in their long-running fights against exclusion and marginalisation in sport?

Did this only happen in the sporting world – or did something similar take place in the public sphere too?

And is this mainly a story of sweeping structural shifts, or are there personal lessons to be gleaned?

It is around a year since my stepfather's death, and I am desperate for tales of recovery. I need ideas about how to feel more at home in the world. Are there lessons that I can learn from the stories of the sportswomen of the 1970s and beyond: the women who finally found greater freedom outdoors?

11.

Recovery run

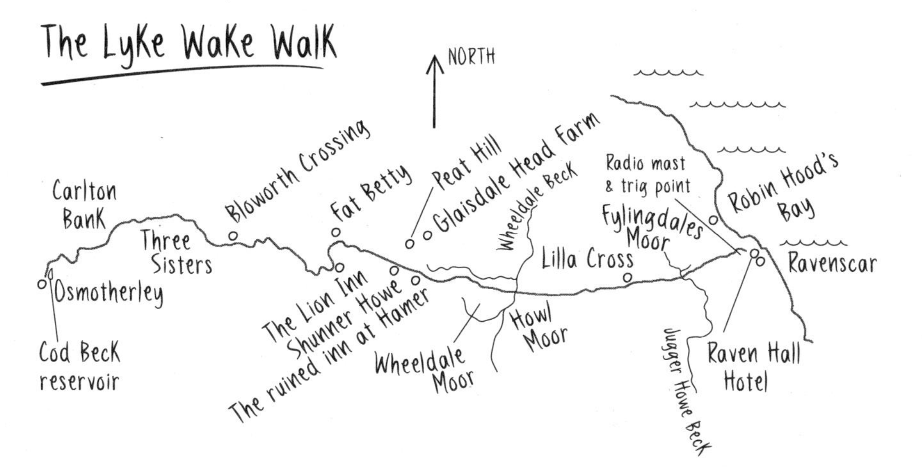

On 1 August 2020, it is the first anniversary of Willy's death. I had hoped that this would be the end of my training schedule; that I would have run my way out of mourning by now. A year ago, I thought of grief as a sudden, temporary injury and running as physio: a regime that would help me to come back fitter, faster, stronger, better. I assumed that, if I worked hard, then the universe or karma would send me my just rewards, perhaps even a period of happiness. But life doesn't work like that, I have realised.

Friends tell me that I 'must be due some good luck', but death is often random. Being good or hard done by is no protection against further loss. And anyway, I don't think that the last year has made me a better or more deserving person. I don't believe that 'what doesn't kill us makes us stronger'. These days, I am brittle, distracted, reproachful, quick to anger and my intolerance for noise has got worse, not better. I wear earplugs day and night. Grief still chugs away in the background, hampering my ability to engage with the present.

Sometimes it all seems very straightforward. People die. Their bodies just stop working. I simply miss all the people and places that have gone, and life is, and always will be, worse for these losses.

But, on other days, it feels far from straightforward. I think I now understand that bereavement is not a discrete event, but a long process of coming to terms with loss, exploring its significance and learning to live with (and around) it as best we can. When Josie died, I told a friend that it felt as if a thread had been yanked out of a tapestry and the whole structure had become loose and unstable, in danger of permanently unravelling. Over the following years, I came to think of mourning and recovery as processes of repair: identifying where that thread had been woven, visibly or invisibly, and seeing how scenes and images from the past depended upon it. I realised that no replacement thread could be inserted in the old one's place, but the tapestry could be embroidered with new stories and images, which strengthened the structure and kept it intact.

In a 1940 essay, the psychoanalyst Melanie Klein referred to mourning in similar terms: as a process of managing our 'internalised objects', our hoard of memories and ideas about lost people and what they meant to us. It involves bringing our inner world (which can be slow to catch onto the dreadful actuality of loss) into closer proximity to the reality of life and death. And the process is assisted by placing 'greater trust in actual people and things, and help received from the external world'.[1] Mourners cannot return to life as it was before bereavement; but, with support, they can grow stronger over time and move forward.

Now I know that grief is not a quick process, but a lifelong change and, over the last month or so, I've felt so tired from the hard labour of mourning. I have started to wish that running could be less onerous; not a regime of improvement but more like retreat or respite. In the running world, there is the concept of a 'recovery run': a slow, relaxed jog taken soon after a long, tough outing. Physiotherapists are uncertain whether recovery runs actually assist physical repair, but they do seem to loosen the muscles, bring some pleasure and offer the reassurance that, even after extreme exhaustion, it is possible to find a second wind. I need this reminder that, even when I'm shattered and there's no end in sight, there is still the possibility of renewal.

I do not want to be at home on the first anniversary of Willy's death, distressed and irritable in front of the children and Pete – so I plan a weekend away, for myself alone. I decide to run the Lyke Wake Walk as a recovery run. At forty miles, it is much longer than typical recovery runs – which are usually just a few miles – but it feels like a satisfying distance: substantial but not punishing, spanning a day of summer light, but no more. And I am excited by the notion of covering the entire width of the North York Moors in one go.

The Lyke Wake Walk has been on my mind since my decision, just under a year ago, to 'run my way through' grief – but now I no longer expect running to do the work of grieving for me and, instead, it will be reprieve. I suppose there is something grimly fitting in marking the anniversary of a death by following a route with such morbid connotations. And I have also been listening to, and reading about, Benjamin Britten's setting of the words of the 'Lyke Wake Dirge' in his *Serenade for Tenor, Horn and Strings*. Written in 1942, shortly after Britten had returned to the UK from the States, to find a land of wartime blackouts, military mobilisation and a tribunal for conscientious objectors like himself, the music is suffused with a sense of displacement and homelessness – which sums up much of my temperament over the last year.[2]

On Friday 31 July, I cycle to the station at 4.30 in the afternoon. The streets and roads are the busiest I've seen them since lockdown lifted. It is a warm day and there are clusters of drunk men congregating around cars with music blaring, and by the banks of the river and on the station platform. Although I tense as I pass, nobody speaks to or looks at me. I catch the train to Northallerton and then a bus to Osmotherley and, after a sustaining dinner in a pub garden, I walk up the hill towards the youth hostel – the same one I stayed in the night before my first marathon, all those years ago. The communal kitchen is closed to prevent Covid transmission, so I try to keep a bottle of milk cold by standing it in a basin of water. I sleep naked. All my belongings will have to come with me tomorrow, so I have tried to pack light. I brush my teeth with a toothbrush I have cut to a stump.

At five the next morning, the alarm on my phone sounds and I get dressed, taping up my back behind my sports bra so that its clasp does not rub my skin raw. I walk just over a mile from the hostel, through woods where a small group is wild camping and a man is standing outside his tent, stretching, yawning and then looking straight at me. I amble along the length of Cod Beck reservoir, which is astonishingly blue in the early morning sun, like an Alpine thermal spring. In my running pack, I have a copy of *Lyke Wake Walk*, a guide to its history, folklore and route, by its creator Bill Cowley, and, in the last fortnight, I have also been to the British Library's reading room at Boston Spa, Yorkshire, to read Cowley's articles in the *Dalesman* magazine about how he first came up with the idea.

In those pieces, Cowley described how, one evening in the summer of 1955, he climbed up from his farm at Glaisdale Head onto the ridge that runs along the top of the moor and walked up to the highest point: the cairn at Peat Hill. In the clear evening light, the view was magnificent. He could see over neighbouring Great Fryup Dale and Little Fryup Dale, north to the moors that hunker over the settlements of Danby and Lealholm, and east as far as the great blue arc of the sea. Then he turned to the south and gazed out over Howl and Wheeldale Moors, the ruined inn at Hamer and the burial mounds and standing stones of 'the Bronze Age Round-Barrow People or Urn Folk'. Here, Cowley wrote:

> the brown moors undulated endlessly, dotted with tumuli, and, as always at such a time, I began to imagine them peopled with ghosts of a remote past, little men with stone axes or flint arrows, coming to the edge of the moor and looking down into valleys thick with frost, or full of marshes and lakes. What rites and ceremonies had marked the burial which had taken place so long ago on the point where now I stood?[3]

He started to imagine a walking route through this ghost world: a footpath traversing the entire panorama, the whole width of the North York Moors, which would cling mostly to the tops and kick 'up a cloud of pollen from the purple heather at every step for forty miles'. By September, Cowley decided to hike his creation, which he had named 'after the traditional Cleveland Lyke-Wake Dirge': the poem whose comparison of purgatory to the crossing of a 'whinny moor' had, a year ago, seemed such an apt metaphor for my own attempt to run through grief. He even resolved to form 'a new Club, the qualification for which shall be the completion of this Scarth Wood to Ravenscar walk, and [to] call it the Lyke-Wake Club'.[4]

The walk originated in death, but Cowley's attitude was light-hearted. Despite his Yorkshire understatedness, he had a flair for the dramatic and joked that he had felt like a corpse, a *lyke*, himself, after hiking his own trail. He and the Lyke Wake Club developed an arcane liturgy surrounding the walk. Any man who managed a successful 'crossing' in under twenty-four hours would be a 'dirger', an equivalent woman was a 'witch' and Cowley himself was the 'Chief Dirger'. Ramblers who registered their crossings with the club (and paid a shilling) were sent black-edged condolence cards and, over time, more macabre merchandise was produced too: pins, scarves, ties, cufflinks, all decorated with black coffins. The club's gatherings were referred to as 'wakes', and members aspired to notch up seven crossings (one in winter, and one a solo unsupported hike) to earn the qualification of 'Doctor of Dolefulness'. The route was subtly redrawn so that, instead of beginning at the trig point above Scarth Wood Moor – which now rears up to my left – walkers set off instead from a new carved stone, which prefigures the standing stones that punctuate the rest of the route and is closer to the car park at the northern end of Cod Beck reservoir. Along the walk, enthusiasts erected waymarkers daubed with black coffins or the letters 'LWW'. A misconception arose, and was widely repeated, that the Lyke Wake Walk traced the course of an old coffin path leading from the moors to the sea.

Word spread fast after the *Dalesman* published Cowley's articles. The first walkers came from local organisations such as York Technical College and Stockton-on-Tees scouts, and then the BBC made a programme about it in October 1961, and hikers and runners arrived from around the country (and indeed the world), with numbers sharply rising in the 1970s.

In 1978, between 20,000 and 30,000 pedestrians attempted the crossing in the space of that year (only 6 per cent of whom were women). Many would-be dirgers were accompanied by loud support crews who revved engines in small settlements, and ramblers woke locals at night with loud voices and bright torches and were accused of dropping cigarette butts and starting fires on the moorland. Under their perpetual footfall, paths expanded from the size of sheep-trods to conduits said to be 'wide enough for two tanks to cross side by side'. In 1982, the North York Moors National Park Committee commissioned a report, which pointed out the harm that was being caused and called for 'a substantial reduction in use'.[5] So Britain's national mapping agency, the Ordnance Survey, took the Lyke Wake Walk off its maps and the numbers of pedestrians dropped nearly straight away. It became a ghost walk in more ways than one: the ghost *of a* walk, as well as a hike through the ghosts that haunted the burial mounds. Now that the route is no longer marked by the OS – nor, in some places, clearly visible on the ground either – I have had to resurrect it from dotted traces on maps, boundary stones, rumours, advice on Facebook forums and route descriptions in out-of-print books.

At around 6.40 a.m., I find the Lyke Wake Walk stone near the car park at Cod Beck reservoir. It glows pink in the early morning sunshine and I photograph it on my phone. Then I press 'start' on my watch and jog along the road to the cattle grid. From here, the route turns into the woods and I'm immediately overtaken by the smell of human excrement. I look around, and see a man, a few metres from the path, squatting by a tree, and he smiles and waves as I pass. For the next fourteen kilometres, the Lyke Wake Walk mostly follows the same paths that I ran during my first ever marathon around Osmotherley back in 2017: trails that are designated on the map in thick green lines, studded with diamonds and labelled as the 'Cleveland Way'. I emerge from the woods into Scugdale, climb up onto Carlton Bank and, when I dip down into Lordstones campsite a few miles later, although it is only just gone 8 a.m., it is already so hot that I have to use the outside tap to refill my water bottles.

From now on, I head straight for the hills; up and down, over the Three Sisters, nodding and smiling at a man and his young son who are photographing the view towards the city of Middlesbrough. At the Osmotherley marathon nearly three years ago, the route doubled back after traversing these three hills, but today I don't turn around and instead keep going east, towards the sea. The water will be my benchmark throughout the day, revealing itself from time to time in glimpses, reminding me that I am on the right track, that I am getting closer, but that I cannot stop just yet.

The path crosses a road and then takes me up again, onto another heathery ridge and the highest point of the North York Moors. This moor is called Urra, from the Old Norse *haugr*, 'the dirty hill', and it is a misnomer: although the heather appears brown for much of the year, today it is in flower and is the purple of laundry detergent. (I will later be pleased to discover that the Latin name for heather, *Calluna*, means 'to sweep clean'.) I jog past a burial mound and a standing stone carved with an unamused face, which marks both the way ahead and the boundary line between two adjacent civil parishes. I am running along the western cliff edge of the moors and green plains lie far beneath to my left. Ahead of me, those lowlands cleave into the moors like an arrowhead, taking a slice out of the hills. In wet and windy weather, it can be bleak here, with gusts accelerating through the inland cove and dumping sheets of rain onto the sides. Today, though, it is still and, in the heat, the uppermost layers of heather quaver and flex against the blue sky.

At the tip of the arrowhead, I reach a crossroads: Bloworth Crossing. To my left, the Cleveland Way jack-knifes north to continue tracing the border of the moors, while the Lyke Wake Walk continues ahead, advancing east into the heart of the heather and gorse on a wide, yellow, serpentine path I have often seen in the distance, but never before run upon. This is an old railway line, which was built in the late 1850s to reach ironstone mines in Rosedale – requiring empty wagons to be hauled up the 1-in-5 incline onto the moors – and which closed almost a century ago. After the Three Sisters' sharp undulations and the trip hazards of Urra Moor's heather, this path is a pleasure to run upon: relatively flat and broad, with a view to my right down into the neon bracken of Farndale.

I jog past a group of four teenage girls, hiking with daypacks, and stop to ask if they're doing the Lyke Wake Walk too. *They are*, they smile, and they set off far earlier than me, at daybreak, and hope to finish before it gets too dark. We wish each other good luck and I run on. In a few miles' time, a building comes into view further along the railway line: the Lion Inn, on the main road on Blakey Ridge, one of only four or five roads that form vertical conduits across the moors, bridging the gentle Yorkshire Wolds' market towns of the south with Teesside's industrial cities further north. Not counting Lordstones campsite, the Lion is one of only two habited buildings that populate the entire Lyke Wake Walk – the other is the hostel at Wheeldale Beck, eleven miles ahead – and, although I am not yet at the halfway point of today's run, the pub feels like a landmark: the end of the largely familiar sections of the route, and the beginning of unknown, wilder paths. I've taken it slowly so far and don't feel too tired, but I could do with using the toilet and I am also very hot. Sweat has evaporated to leave small dry salt plains across my cheeks and forehead; and I cannot wait to buy a pint of iced Fanta and a packet of salty crisps, and to rest for a while.

Unfortunately, it is only 11.30 a.m. and the pub won't open for another half-an-hour. As I run around the Bronze Age barrow by the outer wall – burial mounds are *everywhere* on this route – and clock the pub's closed doors, another runner, clad entirely in black, overtakes me and sprints towards the car park. A woman is leaning against a car, and she has laid out a selection of food inside its open boot. Unsmiling, the runner nods at her and picks up a pot of instant porridge, which he wolfs, and then hands his flasks over for her to refill with water. Once she has returned them, he sprints off, shouting 'See you at Hamer'. She looks familiar with the scenario, and bored.

I find the pub's outside tap, soak my headband and put it back on, letting the cold water splash down my hot back. Even the toilets are still locked, so there is no reason to hang around, and instead I do a quick wee in a nearby clump of heather, squatting low and relatively hidden. I had anticipated a rest so, even though I did not get my Fanta, I permit myself to walk for much of the next mile. It takes me along the side of the busy road, beside speeding motorbikes and camper vans, until I reach a dumpy white stone, topped with a round face, and surrounded by a group of walkers taking photographs.

'This is Fat Betty,' one tells me; 'the only female stone cross on the moors.'

I smile at Betty in some sort of imagined sisterhood, and take a selfie with her, and then continue on my way. Here Cowley tells me to plot a path between a line of white boundary stones, and I locate the first stone and follow it into knee-high gorse to the second, before realising that I am only a few metres from a road, from which a group of young hikers are looking at me curiously. Embarrassed, I clamber out of the undergrowth and run along the tarmac until there really is no option but to head onto the moor. The path here is narrow and the earth is peat bog, and every time I place my weight upon it, I am unsure if my feet will spring back or be sucked down. On one occasion, the peat clutches my ankle, like a small child playing a prank, and I fall flat on my face. Even today, when it is scorching and there has been no rain for a week or two, much of the ground is still sloppy, and I dread to imagine what it is like to cross this moor in winter.

After around an hour, I reach the round barrow of Shunner Howe, which Cowley's guide tells me means 'look-out hill'. Because of the conditions under-foot, I certainly feel like I have climbed a hill to get here from Fat Betty, but, when I look at the map, I realise I have actually come down in altitude; like the confounding M. C. Escher prints I loved as a child, in which staircases impossibly ascend and descend at the same time. There is a view of the sea, far in the distance, and I also look for a sight of the ruined inn at Hamer, which should be a few hundred metres ahead of me. When Cowley was making his first crossing in October 1955, the sun had set by this point and, as he dropped down from Shunner Howe in the darkness, he saw lights at the ruined inn, where friends had set up a tent for him, and he 'gave a great shout and rushed on down'. He 'had covered twenty-one miles in seven hours, and had earned a rest', he wrote.[6] I love the idea of a ruined inn coming to life at night, and it reminds me of a book I sometimes read to my younger children, in which ghost-skeleton animals party in the dark while everyone sleeps. But as I peer down the path in front of me, I can see nothing at all, not even a ruin, and the inn appears to have returned to the heather.

The inn was only around two miles from both Cowley's farm at Glaisdale Head and Peat Hill, where he had first conjured up the Lyke Wake Walk. As he was resting here, I wonder, was he tempted by the idea of giving up on his crossing and returning home to sleep? After all, there was no need to leave Glaisdale to find the supernatural. His neighbourhood had a rich folklore, and the mythology that grew up around the Lyke Wake Walk was comparable to local mutterings about magical beings like 'the Glaisdale Hob'. When I looked into some of these stories in my research in the weeks before this run, I learned that many of Glaisdale's (and neighbouring Danbydale's) superstitions revolved around witches. The hill opposite Cowley's farm was known as Witch Hill, and the next settlement, Mountain Ash Farm, was named after 'witch wood', and the belief that mountain ash or rowan that had been cut from a previously unvisited tree with a household knife on St Helen's Day could be laid around the house (or carried in pockets) to deter witches from entering.[7]

On another sweltering, cloudless day earlier in the summer, on my way home from buying new shoes at my favourite running shop in nearby Stokesley, I detoured to Glaisdale Rigg and parked in a layby three-quarters of a mile above Cowley's farm. I had heard that there was a collection of sandstone boulders hidden in a plantation near the rigg, and on a specialist bouldering blog I found a list of the climbs' tantalising names: Maleficium, Trial by Ordeal, Cunning Folk, Supernatural, White Witch, Dark Witch, Witch Way Down. The author said that one slab bore a very old carving of a witch, and I wondered if Cowley himself had been responsible. I followed a path – unmarked on the map, but distinct on the ground – through the heather to the top of the boulders, which were dispersed down the hillside. The blog noted that the sun only falls on them in the late afternoon and, indeed, even though the outside temperature was scorching, among the boulders it was cool and damp, like a cathedral. I found a small rock on which to perch and, shivering, took from my bag a long-sleeved top and packet of crisps. I turned and behind me loomed a large slab in deep shadow, whose top half was riven by a vertical crack, like a lightning bolt. Towards the bottom of the crag, there was a carved outline of a horned animal head, underneath an unmistakeable 'W': the witch!

In local stories of the supernatural, Glaisdale residents were less interested in stereotypically occult activities – such as making potions, casting spells or summoning evil spirits – than in witches' freedom of movement. The desire to run outdoors alone was especially considered to mark a woman out as a witch. It reminds me of the story of Atalanta in Greek mythology, in which Atalanta's talent for running, her insistence upon selecting her own suitor (a man who could beat her in a footrace) and her passionate sexual desire for him marked her out as a figure of exceptional, potentially rebellious strength. Awe and disgust similarly characterised stories that local moors historians recorded about female runners – supposedly witches – from the seventeenth to the twentieth centuries – many of which featured the same woman called 'Nanny' or 'Nan'. John Atkinson, vicar of Danby from 1847 to 1900, recounted a tale of how Nanny, who liked to walk and run alone in the heather, was driven out of the undergrowth by a group of 'young fellows of the farming persuasion', who chased and 'chivvied' her up the hill, and down 'along the slope from the moor-end towards the hamlet called Ainthorpe' at 'headlong speed'. One evening, a young man called Thomas Prudom decided to annoy this nineteenth-century female trail-runner, and he sat on the track leading down to her cottage 'with his legs a little apart, to form a barrier'. As Nanny ran down the slope towards him, she apparently became invisible and he 'felt something rush full force between his legs', whooshing him down the path and hurling 'him over on one side like a sucked orange'.[8]

Around the same time, probably the same local woman – here referred to as 'Au'd Nan Hardwick . . . witch though she was' – applied for, and was refused, parish relief by the overseer of the poor, who happened to be young Thomas Prudom's father. Walking out of the village of Castleton one day, at the top of Danbydale, Prudom senior had an awkward encounter with Nan on a bridge that was 'just wide enough to let one person pass at a time'. The nineteenth-century antiquarian William Henderson described how 'no feeling of courtesy prompted [Prudom] to stand back till Auld Nan had crossed, so he marched sturdily on to the middle of the bridge'. But 'there her power fell upon him, and he stood like a statue, unable to move hand or foot, till she was pleased to set him free – which was not at once'. This makes me think back to what I'd learned, months ago, about the gendered dynamics of pedestrians' motion. Nan was a woman who fought back against men's attempts to dominate the streets, and she was labelled a 'witch' for it. And if confidence in taking up space – through a passion for running, or refusal to give way to imperious men on narrow footpaths – was thought to mark out women as witches, then local methods of constraining those women's power focused on suppressing their freedom of movement. A couple of old Glaisdale houses still bear 'witch posts', wooden posts close to the entrances or hearths of houses, carved with the cross of St Andrew, to prevent witches from entering.[9]

Before my Lyke Wake Walk run, I tried to find the real Nan Hardwick. 'Nan' was a common term of endearment for Ann or 'Mine Ann', and, in Danby's parish registers for the 1790s – when Thomas Prudom (junior) was in young adulthood, and his father in his sixties – I located an 'Ann Hardwick' who lived in the dale. Ann's husband had died in 1778. By the 1790s, when she was in her fifties or sixties, her children had probably all left home and she seemed to be living alone in a small cottage outside Ainthorpe. I was childishly excited to discover that Nan Hardwick's surname before her marriage had been the same as mine, Hewitt, and I tried to find a direct line of descent from her to me. It was in vain, but nevertheless I was pleased by the idea that a trail-running witch might be my foremother.

As I descend from Shunner Howe, I realise that the invisibility of the ruined inn is not a trick of the light, but that the building no longer exists. Disappointed, I cross a small, empty road and stand at the border between Rosedale and Wheeldale Moors. On the map, it looks as if the way ahead should be a pleasant, lightly sloping, runnable descent, but appearances are deceptive. In reality the path is indistinct amid heather that, here, is not purple but brown and dull, obstructed with roots. When the trail emerges more clearly in a few miles, my tired legs cannot lift my feet above the rocks that stud the path and, over and over again, I stumble and trip, hurtling forward like a clumsy superhero trying to take off. Cowley thought that 'the wild stretch of Wheeldale Moor' was the 'worst part' of the whole Lyke Wake Walk. In the time it has taken me to descend from Shunner Howe, the glaring sunshine has become blanketed in cloud, and it is starting to rain.

Over this last year, I have been living among ghosts, but it occurs to me that, by my side, there have been witches too: women who, like Nan Hardwick, insisted on their freedom of movement outdoors.

I am reaching the final stages of researching and writing this book, and I have recently turned my attention to Nan's twentieth-century descendants: a whole movement of women who defended their right to roam outdoors.

In the 1960s and 1970s, sport and public space became widely recognised as political battlegrounds again – just as they had been at the turn of the twentieth century. Black women took on what Elise Johnson McDougald, campaigner and first African-American female headteacher, called the 'double task' of challenging racial and sexual discrimination outdoors. In 1955 in the US, Jo Ann Robinson and the Women's Political Council organised a boycott of buses in Montgomery, Alabama, to protest the ongoing legal segregation of Black passengers on public transport – four days after Rosa Parks was arrested – and, five years later, Ella Baker formed the Student Non-Violent Coordinating Committee to arrange sit-ins and freedom rides to resist Jim Crow laws. Disability rights campaigners urged that designers of the built environment should 'allow us to participate fully in society' and they staged sit-ins on Madison Avenue, in New York City, and demonstrations in Washington DC.

Like first-wave campaigners for women's rights, second-wave feminists insisted that it was urgent that freedom and safety in public space should be restored to women. Debates about free speech, pornography, the sexual revolution and male violence were part of what historian Claire Bond Potter calls 'a contest over physical and cultural space'. The grief and hopelessness that Andrea Dworkin had felt in response to male violence outdoors found both expression and remedy in 'a revolutionary movement' in which women walked together freely. Feminists marched on Times Square, the geographical centre of the pornography industry. 'Take Back the Night' demonstrations across the world countered male violence on the streets and rebelled against police forces' advice for women to keep ourselves safe by staying at home. The National Organization for Women drew up a list of political goals that included open access to public space and set up a dedicated task force. In February 1969, it organised 'Public Accommodations Week', which featured sit-ins and drink-ins at male-only establishments such as the Oak Room at the Plaza Hotel in New York.[10]

Campaigners in this era drew a clear link between women's marginalisation in public life and women's impoverished access to sport. Membership of private clubs and facilities was still frequently male-only, and such exclusivity had knock-on effects on the public sphere. The 'world's most exclusive golf club', the Augusta National in Georgia, was whites-only until 1990 and male-only until 2012, and it was (and still is) a prime site for networking among (white male) ultra-wealthy politicians and CEOs. Feminist protesters targeted the gate-keeping mechanisms of sport: its exclusionary rules and regulations, private spaces and competitions. Some feminist activists turned to sport in this era as a direct extension of their political principles: the feminism came first, and participation in sport naturally followed. Historian Andrew D. Linden interviewed female players of American football who were part of the 1970s feminist movement. Julie Sherwood, a working-class lesbian who played for the Columbus Pacesetters, told Linden how sport (and especially sport with hyper-masculine associations, like American football) 'was kind of seen as the feminist thing to do': it offered her 'the first place that I ever was where your weight wasn't something to be ashamed of' and a space where lesbian women could find acceptance. For other women, it was vice versa: sport came first, and then opened gateways to a feminist political consciousness. Olivia Flores, who grew up in a conservative working-class household and played for the Toledo Troopers in the 1970s, described to Linden how, unlike Sherwood, she did not enter sport thinking 'we're feminist and we're out here going to prove that women can play football', but that her political convictions emerged because of her sporting career.[11]

Second-wave campaigners fought for legislative change as a crucial way to rebut ways in which women were formally excluded from sporting spaces. In Britain, the 1975 Sex Discrimination Act and 1976 Race Relations Act achieved something similar to the earlier Civil Rights Act of 1964 in the US, which criminalised discrimination based on race, colour, religion, sex and nationality, and was followed up in 1972 with Title IX legislation (which ensured that 'no person in the United States shall, based on sex, be excluded from participation in' state education). Title IX led to a significant increase in female participation in school and college athletics and, in 1973, this was extended to athletes with disabilities, when section 504 of the 1973 Rehabilitation Act stated that no 'individual with a disability in the United States' shall 'be excluded from the participation in . . . any program or activity receiving federal financial assistance', and placed an onus on institutions and employers to 'take reasonable steps to accommodate disability'.[12] Women targeted further regulatory mechanisms in the 1970s, such as licensing arrangements in boxing. In 1978, boxers Marian 'Tyger' Trimiar, Jackie Tonawanda and Cathy 'Cat' Davis won a lawsuit in New York to become licensed fighters, after years of having to compete illegally. But legislative obstacles were not always toppled quickly. In 1992, Gail Grandchamp finally succeeded in an eight-year case of sex discrimination to be licensed as an amateur boxer in New England, by which point she was no longer young enough to qualify as an amateur and had to compete as a professional instead. A bill introduced in 1947 to outlaw female professional boxing matches in Mexico was used as late as 1998 to ban a fight with Laura Serrano (but it was overturned the following year). Women's boxing was only included in the Olympics for the first time in 2012.

Female competitive runners were particularly active in targeting their sports' exclusionary regulations, and the Boston Marathon was a fraught battleground in the late 1960s and 1970s. The Boston race had been established in 1897 and, although nothing in the USA's Amateur Athletics Union (AAU) rule book explicitly banned women from entering, the event had been inspired by the Olympics and its alignment of sport with male strength. The AAU's omission of women from its regulations was not implicitly permissive, but because 'the authors of this rule book . . . couldn't even conceive of women's participation'. In 1966, Roberta 'Bobbi' Gibb applied and was refused permission to run the Boston Marathon, but she ran nevertheless, without a number and disguised in a hoody, and finished in 3 hours 21 minutes and 40 seconds. The following year, German-American student Kathrine Switzer was encouraged by Gibb's proof that 'a woman can run a marathon', but she wanted to do so legitimately and visibly, so she entered the Boston marathon and was approved – but on the basis of her initials alone, 'K. V. Switzer'. On the start line, Switzer described how she felt 'very welcome . . . special and proud of myself' among the other runners, but then, after a few miles, she 'heard the scraping noise of leather shoes coming up fast behind me'. 'When a runner hears that kind of noise, it's usually danger,' Switzer explained, and she turned around to see:

> the most vicious face I'd ever seen. A big man, a huge man, with bared teeth was set to pounce, and before I could react he grabbed my shoulder and flung me back screaming, 'Get the hell out of my race and give me those numbers!' Then he swiped down my front, trying to rip off my bib number, just as I leapt backward from him. He missed the numbers but I was so surprised and frightened that I slightly wet my pants, and turned to run . . . I was dazed and confused. I'd never been up close to physical violence; the power was terrifying and I was shocked at how helpless I, a strong woman, felt against it . . . I wished I was not there.[13]

Race director Jock Semple attempts to prevent Kathrine Switzer from running the Boston Marathon, 1967

Race manager Jock Semple's attack was not (just) a cold, calculating adherence to sexist rules; it replicated the same violent aggression that women experience in street harassment and assault. Semple's behaviour was captured by press photographers and viewed around the world, but it did not persuade the race organisers to permit women to run – even though Switzer had successfully completed the marathon, in around 4 hours 20 minutes. In fact, in the wake of Switzer's feat, the AAU filled in the gap in its rule book and formally banned women from competing in races alongside men.

Nevertheless, many male-only races did relax their restrictions and open their gates to women. For example, the Isle of Wight Marathon in the UK had been all-male since 1957, and only allowed a one-off female runner in 1964, when Dale Greig achieved a record-breaking time of 3 hours 27 minutes 25 seconds, becoming the first woman in the world to be recorded as running a marathon in sub-3:30. In 1976 the race became permanently mixed-sex. In the long stretch between 1928 and 1960, female athletes had not been permitted to run further than 200 metres at the Olympics, but in 1972 the women's 1,500 metres was added, and then, in 1984, a female marathon. Despite women's prowess in long-distance pedestrianism in the nineteenth century, when competitive racewalking became an Olympic event in 1908, women were barred from participating – and that ban lasted until 1992, when women were finally allowed to compete (but were only permitted to cover half the distance of male athletes). Nevertheless, female racewalkers found other forums to practice their sport, and in 1977 the Bristol 100 allowed women's participation for the first time: Ann Sayer became the first female 'Centurion', covering one hundred miles in under twenty-four hours.[14]

Some aspects of this revolution in women's sport were driven by all-female initiatives. In 1978, the International Women's Running Circuit, headed by Switzer and sponsored by the beauty company Avon, was created to promote elite female athletes' competitive running. But, in this period of change, opinions of women-only spaces and events were shifting. For decades, men's domination of public space had felt so insurmountable that all-female societies had been necessary to provide women with opportunities for respite, recovery and resistance. But, from the 1970s, as male authority started to feel less intractable, there was a swing towards campaigning for women's full participation in mixed-sex space. In order to ensure fairness and safety, the female category was still physiologically necessary in most competitive sporting events, as were all-female teams – but women also pushed for equal inclusion alongside men in umbrella organisations and competitions. In 1976, the Ladies' Alpine Club was subsumed within the Alpine Club. In 1971, the Football Association in England rescinded its fifty-year ban on women playing football on affiliated pitches, and – although it took almost another twenty years – in 1993 the FA agreed to include female members in their organisation, and the Women's Football Association disbanded. In 1998, the Women's Cricket Association merged with the England and Wales Cricket Board.

Female cricketers later reported that there had been both benefits and drawbacks to the union with previously all-male institutions. Their sport enjoyed greater financial investment as a result of the merger – but many women also felt that they had lost influence over the club's organisation, which remained male-dominated in number and still prioritised men's interests.[15] This was a theme of many of the mergers. Sportswomen frequently felt they had been allowed entry into clubs as 'honorary men', but that male members were not willing to change their practices for women. Some competitions that had once admitted only men now allowed women to compete, but often on an unequal basis to their male counterparts in terms of permitted distances and events, prize money, sponsorship or media coverage: outside Grand Slam tennis tournaments, the top 100 women still earn only 80p for every £1 won by the top 100 men today. Men's commitment to mixed-sex sport could feel superficial and tokenistic. When the FA ran a Women's Cup for the first time in 1994, many female members were not happy, feeling that the men 'just rode roughshod all over us': failing to consult women and demonstrating lack of commitment to female grassroots football. Sheila Edmunds, founder of the women's football team the Doncaster Belles, interpreted the merger not as a demonstration of inclusivity, but as an attempt by the men 'to control us, to keep us in our place', by keeping the women closer.[16] It often seemed that female sport was seen by men as an extension or supplement to the main business of male sport, and this perception was literalised when the National Football Museum placed women's football history in an extension to the permanent gallery in 2018.

As it was in the early twentieth century, from the 1970s mountaineering again became a potent symbol of women's broader freedoms of movement and authority in the public sphere. When three female Everest summiteers – Junko Tabei, Pan Duo and Wanda Rutkiewicz – were interviewed in 1979 and were asked, 'Why Everest?' Rutkiewicz replied, 'For women's liberation.' Seven years earlier, Rutkiewicz had been descending from Noshaq, in Afghanistan, when she had met Arlene Blum ascending and greeted her with the injunction: 'We must climb to 8,000 meters together, all women.' Before Blum could put an expedition into place, other women climbers achieved that goal, but Blum had been repeatedly rejected and patronised by male Himalayan expeditions and the idea of making a visible feminist mountaineering statement still appealed to her. So she organised the first all-woman expedition to be approved by the American Alpine

Club: an ascent in August 1978 to the summit of Annapurna I, in Nepal. Blum described how their challenge was 'even greater than the mountain. We had to believe in ourselves enough to make the attempt in spite of social convention and two hundred years of climbing history in which women were usually relegated to the sidelines.' The women gave their expedition a feminist slogan – 'A Woman's Place is on Top' – and sold T-shirts, gave interviews and invited film-makers, in order to try to mitigate Blum's weary prediction that the press would disparage the climbers.* (They did anyway: one article was headlined, 'What Will Their Husbands Think?') The first summit team reached the top on 15 October 1978, but two members of their party, Alison Chadwyck-Onyszkiewicz and Vera Watson, tragically died in a second summit attempt. Nevertheless, *The New York Times* called the expedition 'an inspiration to women', which showed that all-female mountaineering had 'come of age', and Blum hoped that it had given participants the necessary experience to organise their own expeditions in future.[17]

As Blum hinted, the liberation that mountaineering offers women is not just symbolic, but practical and literal. Mountaineering plays a significant role in tourist industries around the world and, from the 1990s, there has been increasing awareness of its potential to confer economic and social power onto women. Until the 1970s, Nepalese women had mostly been involved in expeditions as porters and kitchen helpers, but not in higher-status roles as guides or high-altitude assistants. In the early 1990s, the Nepalese ministry of tourism tackled this inequality by encouraging expeditions designed to bring the first Nepalese woman to the summit of Everest. When Pasang Lhamu Sherpa reached the summit on 22 April 1993, but died on the descent, there was both national celebration and mourning, with a public funeral ceremony, commemorative postage stamp, and a highway and a strain of wheat named after her. The Pasang Lhamu

* In the same year, Blum's geophysicist friend Tanya Atwater led a pioneering oceanographic expedition to the middle of the Atlantic, for which she made T-shirts emblazoned with 'A Woman's Place is on the Bottom'.

Mountaineering Foundation was established in Kathmandu, aiming to 'uplift deprived and marginalized Women and children from Mountainous and Hilly region[s] in the country' via education, training and provision of health, legal and social security facilities. Pasang Lhamu had 'proved that Nepalese women are as brave and strong as their men', and 'as competent as men' in education, and therefore as deserving of resources.[18]

Similar links between female mountaineering and women's economic and social enfranchisement were made in Pakistan. In 2007, the Alpine Club of Pakistan and the American Alpine Club formed the Pakistani Women's Climbing Camp, a course designed to expose a hundred women to 'the world of climbing', with an eye to 'careers not previously available to them in a growing tourism industry' and to challenge the fact that – at that point – no Pakistani woman had made significant ascents in the country's mountains. The camp was (perhaps indefinitely) delayed because of military conflict, but from 2011 Samina Baig was hailed as 'Pakistan's female role model' when she climbed a hitherto unascended peak in Pakistan – now named after her, as Samina Peak. In 2013, Baig became the first Pakistani woman to climb Everest and then all Seven Summits (the highest mountains on each continent) by 2014. She hoped that her achievements would 'motivate more women to participate in climbing, as this will give a message of confidence to females everywhere', and that mountaineering and trekking might open up economic opportunities for women, especially in her home region of Gilgit Baltistan.[19]

In 2015, Marina LeGree set up the 'Ascend: Leadership Through Athletics' programme in Afghanistan. The project selected twenty women for participation in a two-year programme in which five components of mountaineering were explored in ways that were directly transferable to roles in the public sphere, including 'leadership, service, [and] psycho-social well-being'. Two members of Ascend, Hanifa Yousoufi and Freshta Ibrahimi, described to the British Mountaineering Council how 'really unusual' it is 'for Afghan women to do sport', and how exciting they found it to see 'strong women' moving freely outdoors. The women of Ascend faced significant obstacles in their mountaineering: on one expedition, Afghan police 'didn't want the little ladies to go climbing', to which Freshta responded, 'you can shoot us, but we are going to go', and strange men made intimidating sexual gestures and abusive remarks. Male family members were disapproving, and the women climbed in the mountains in the constant knowledge that the Taliban were nearby.

But Hanifa described the profound benefits she derived from the programme: increased confidence, sociability and experience of travelling without family members. She learned management skills and took on leadership roles including programme assistant at Ascend and climbing tutor, and she assumed responsibility for looking after climbing gear. She and Freshta even hoped to become the first guides in Afghanistan to hold formal climbing qualifications, after doing a single-pitch instructor course. Marina, Freshta and Hanifa ultimately wanted to establish an outdoor industry in Afghanistan, in which women would play a central role. 'Mountaineering is the hook. It symbolises to everybody what women are capable of,' wrote Marina.

However, since the Taliban regained power in Afghanistan in 2021, Ascend has had to refocus on simply keeping its members safe. Instead of working with women to 'strengthen communities; create change' in their country, Ascend is instead helping them to leave.[20] This is a horrific reminder that the history of women's liberation is not a linear march towards progress, but a series of waves, in which the constrictions that men place on women's lives tighten and loosen at different points in time, and women grieve profoundly when temporary freedoms are stolen again.

I reach the road on the eastern edge of Wheeldale Moor and pick my way slowly down a steep bank to Wheeldale Beck, at its base. I have completed just under three-quarters of my Lyke Wake Walk crossing and have come to the end of the uninhabited section. It is good timing: I have drained my flasks dry, but I have a filter bottle in my bag and I sit for a while, drinking freezing water out of the clear, fast-running stream and chewing on a flapjack. There are stepping stones across the beck and I wonder if this means I have reached the 'Brig o' Dread' of the Lyke Wake Dirge.

It doesn't feel very dreadful. The sun is shining again, and the grass is lush and cool and damp after the rain, and it is wonderful to lie back against the hill and let my legs thrum now that the weight has been taken off them. The hostel on the other side of the beck is officially closed, but there is a woman with a wheelbarrow in its garden, and I wave cheerily and she waves back. It is so nice to be back in the land of the living. And there are only ten or so miles to go until I am at the sea.

I think about the serious risks that women like Hanifa and Freshta have to take, just to do something as simple as going for a hike. For women, breaking the rules or breaching conventions always involves conducting an assessment: weighing our desires against the likely punishments we will incur for attempting to realise them. Change is only brought about by taking risks, but sometimes these risks are simply too great – as they are, currently, for many women in Afghanistan to contemplate running or climbing again. And as I've learned while writing this book, the calculation of risk is not as straightforward as it might seem.

I get up from the riverbank and start walking up the hill on the other side. As I walk, I think about how we – as individual women, and as societies – might better manage the risks that women face outdoors in order to fight for our freedom. It strikes me that a two-pronged strategy is required, which involves managing the material threats to women's wellbeing as well as tackling the representation of risk itself.

My reading over the last year has shown me that the most powerful barriers to women's enjoyment of outdoor sport and leisure – both in the nineteenth century and today – are the risks posed by violence. A wealth of research shows that perpetrators of violence are overwhelmingly male, and that these men tend to subscribe to certain beliefs and expectations – including the notions that women must be submissive to male family members; that men have the right to discipline women; that women cannot deny sex to male partners; that women's value is derived from their relationship to men; and that family honour is more important than women's safety. Campaigners against male violence – such as White Ribbon, UN Women, Women's Aid, and End Violence Against Women – have devised interventions to help erode these beliefs, which include collaborating with role models in public messaging, running workshops with parents and employers, producing research, reports and toolkits, and working with young people and schools. In the US, the Stop Street Harassment and Hollaback! campaigns provide educational programmes and resources and bystander intervention training to encourage men to confront other men who perpetrate misogynistic abuse in public.

The justice system is also important – not just as punishment and deterrent, but because it reinforces the unacceptability of threats to women's freedom and safety. It can be a moral guide, setting out what members of a society collectively agree is right and wrong. In 1993, legal scholar Cynthia Grant Bowman pointed out that 'existing legal concepts, fashioned primarily by male judges and legislators in light of the experiences encountered by men, fail to provide effective remedies for the peculiarly female-directed experience of street harassment'. And the situation has only moved on a little during the last few decades. In the UK, street harassment is currently prosecuted by the 1986 Public Order Act, but some campaigners complain that it is not understood as a crime that has misogyny at its heart: instead, it is compared to the gender-neutral idea of 'affray'. The US legal system also prosecutes street harassment, not as a distinct phenomenon that aims to keep women out of public life, but by dividing it into assault and battery, following and stalking, and with 'hate crime' added as an 'aggravating circumstance'. UK activists and charities, such as Plan International and a cross-party group of MPs, are instead urging the recognition of street harassment as a distinct 'form of gender-based violence' that is fundamentally perpetrated for misogynistic aims.[21]

It is also important to look at the effectiveness of the police's enforcement of the current law. British MP Stella Creasy points out that, although street harassment already exists as a crime in the

British legal system, the police's failure to recognise, record and prioritise it is an equally pressing issue, and that using legislation around 'hate crimes' and 'aggravating offences' to tackle street harassment might impel the police to take it more seriously. However, Creasy is dismayed by the stasis of the contemporary situation and the failure to include misogyny in hate-crime legislation. The severity of the problems involved in policing street harassment was indicated when Sue Fish, leader of Nottinghamshire Police's trial of new methods to tackle the crime, resigned after the experiment, describing how the force were 'institutionally misogynistic in terms of their approach' to sexual harassment and assault. Such endemic sexism can intersect with racism and homophobia, and it not only creates a toxic environment for female officers but deters women from reporting sexual violence. In public messaging, the police still frequently place the onus on women, to keep ourselves safe, rather than on male perpetrators of public sexual harassment; and female victims often describe feeling intimidated and uncomfortable when being interviewed. When Sarah Everard was abducted from a residential street in London in March 2021, and then raped and murdered by a serving police officer – and became the sixteenth woman to be killed by a serving or former police officer in the UK since 2009 – her death prompted an outcry which voiced a widespread suspicion that *women have no safety net*; that, not only can we not depend on the police or justice system to protect us, but that they may even contribute to the ways in which our freedom and safety are jeopardised. Because of the extent of institutional misogyny within the police, campaigners are divided as to whether reforms need to be targeted at challenging such sexism, because the police remain the key way to deter street harassment, or whether the police are a lost cause and alternative remedies need to be sought. The American campaign group Stop Street Harassment feels unable to recommend 'over-policing' of men's public abuse of women, because 'over-arresting in low-income neighbourhoods and among communities of color is a problem in the United States' and the police are not always 'safe places to turn to for help'. The report concludes that 'law enforcement agencies need more training on respect, empathy, and cross-cultural understanding'.[22] For women to be freer outdoors, it is necessary to tackle the beliefs that drive men to intimidate and restrict women, and also the judicial mechanisms which demonstrate a society's commitment to women's rights. Clearly, we are not there yet.

Some feminist campaigners emphasise that 'women aren't raped by bad street lighting', highlighting a tendency for governments to misdirect attention onto quick, temporary sticking-plaster solutions rather than the necessary profound societal change. But, despite such reasonable concerns, nevertheless certain aspects of the built environment can make it easier for men to perpetrate crimes against women outdoors. Planners, developers and campaigners are working on ideas to redesign public space with an eye to reducing the risks that women face. Stop Street Harassment advises that local governments should track reports of men's public abuse of women to identify hotspots, peak times and the ways in which specially vulnerable demographics are affected. Technology, such as the app My Safetipin, allows individuals to draw on informally submitted reports to assess the safety of walking or running in particular areas. In the UK, certain local authorities (such as Plymouth City Council) subject plans for new public spaces to 'gender audits', to identify spatial characteristics which might deter women's presence (such as the closure of public toilets) or put us at risk from male violence (such as poor lighting, narrow passageways and spaces hidden from public view), and to suggest remedies.

Campaign groups highlight the need to consult female users in the design of public spaces. Through conversations with female teenagers, the British charity Make Space for Girls has discovered that girls' tastes in park design differ significantly from boys', confirming the conclusions of some existing research. Whereas adolescent males gravitate towards dedicated zones, such as basketball courts or outdoor gyms, girls often prefer open-ended spaces in which a variety of activities can take place – such as artificial hollows or dips in the ground, in which girls can lounge, roll, cartwheel, chat and read, with a sense of enclosure and privacy, but not so concealed as to make girls anxious about being harassed, robbed or assaulted. Some planners are trialling female-friendly designs. Anna Livia Cullinan tells me that she has a long-standing interest in how 'everything from sports bra design to crime prevention through environmental design' shapes women's experience of public space, and in 2018 she conducted research with girls in Yangon in Myanmar about interventions to improve their experiences outdoors. Together they designed Mya Malar Park, described as 'one of Asia's first parks to be designed by teenage girls . . . who were tired of social pressure to stay indoors and needed safe places to gather in their own neighborhoods'.[23] The park contains lighting, trees, sitting areas, with a permanent team of caretakers, and Cullinan's observations show that girls are using the park more frequently and for longer periods than in male-biased equivalents. Such assessments need to become common practice, and women and girls should be involved in decision-making about the design of public space at the highest levels – otherwise the built environment will continue to primarily reflect the preferences of men and, at best, deter female usage and, at worst, make it easier for predatory men to commit violence against women.

As I've learned, improving women's experiences outdoors does not just involve tackling the risks that we face, but also tackling the ways in which risk is (mis)represented. This is not solely down to the individual but requires societal change. Participants in certain high-status activities, including financial investments and climbing, often propagate tenuous beliefs about women's risk aversion that can diminish women's standing. From birth, girls receive messages about their vulnerability that far exceed their probability of being physically hurt and are raised to fear the consequences of freedom outdoors, while boys are socialised from infancy into a more confident, entitled attitude to their right to occupy public space. Such cultural mores can later become one underpinning of the behaviour of male adults who grow up to harass, abuse, assault and murder women outdoors.

But these discourses and beliefs are not set in stone, and it is possible to promote different visions of male and female aptitudes. As campaign groups such as 'Let Clothes Be Clothes' and 'Let Toys Be Toys' urge, advertising, children's books, films and TV programmes, clothing and kit, and educational resources need to show more girls engaged in adventurous, strong, brave, exploratory physical play. And tackling the misrepresentation of gender and risk also needs to include men's attitudes. It is women who are most often stereotyped as hysterical paranoiacs, but men's perception of risk is often illogical too. During the Covid-19 pandemic, men have been less likely to wear masks and follow lockdown rules and worry about becoming infected, despite the fact that male patients have much higher odds of intensive care treatment and death than women. Male pedestrians take more risks than women, and they die from road traffic collisions at much higher rates than female pedestrians: in 2002, 70 per cent of pedestrian fatalities were men. As I've learned, male runners adopt riskier strategies than women, setting overambitious time goals and adopting 'risky' fast starts and, as in these other examples, men's risk-taking frequently doesn't pay off: men seem to be more prone to 'hitting the wall' than female runners.[24] Women are encouraged to feel more 'at risk' than statistics justify, and this constrains our freedoms. Men are encouraged to feel more invincible and *less* 'at risk' than statistics justify, and this injures and kills them.

Men's unhealthy attitude to risk not only threatens their own wellbeing: it directly impacts on women's safety too. Men are more likely to take risks with health and safety at work, and in doing so they endanger all their colleagues, male and female. In India, women are disproportionately affected by HIV/AIDS, and epidemiologist Sunil Solomon finds that they are not usually endangered by 'their own risks, but by those of their partners, generally their [male] spouses' – who have unprotected sex or inject drugs, and then pass on HIV to their wives. A study in Ghana between 1998 and 2005 found that men were overwhelmingly more likely to drive (and drive badly) than women, and were responsible for 99 per cent of road traffic accidents, in which – as Jeff Turner, a specialist in transport and poverty reduction in developing countries, explains – passengers and pedestrians (mostly female) suffered from men's 'higher levels of risk taking and risky behaviour (alcohol and drug use, for example)' while behind the wheel.

In an article about the causes of women's supposedly 'stick-in-the-mud' risk-averse nature, novelist Lucy Ellmann asks (light-heartedly), 'Why can't women be more like men, and enjoy failing?' But, as a society, we also need to encourage boys and men to be more like women, and to be *more cautious* about failing. This is for the sake of themselves, and for everyone else who is caught up in men's cavalier attitudes to risk.

As one man says to me on Twitter, boys and men need to be 'given more leeway to be afraid'.[25] And if men had more latitude to be openly scared, and therefore more cautious and mindful of others' safety, then women might be able to be less afraid, and more free.

I trudge up the aptly named Howl Moor towards another burial mount, Simon Howe. From here, the path broadens and becomes clearer of rocks, and I'm able to scamper down the other side of the hill and over the railway line, and then cross the main road and enter Fylingdales Moor. There is a distinctive US surveillance station here, which stands in the Yorkshire heather like a book of matches propped open on a beermat. I see a wide 4x4 track across the bog, but I have been told by other runners that this is MOD property and that, if I walk upon it, then admonitory soldiers will appear from nowhere in jeeps. So I try to follow the route indicated by my watch's GPX file, and it leads me through deep cold troughs of water hidden beneath the long grass until, after around a kilometre, the barely visible trail I am pursuing comes back towards the forbidden comfort of the wide 4x4 track. I merge with it and ascend to Lilla Cross, another burial-mound marker. A rainbow appears in the distance, against the dark rain cloud that is now receding far into the distance, and I get a flapjack out of my running pack.

While I'm eating, I think a bit about my own attitude to risk and how it's changed over the last year.

The research I've done has, perhaps unexpectedly, countered some of my fear of male violence in public space. I've realised that the probability of being murdered for women is still extremely small: at the time of writing, 1 in 35,336 women aged 18–44. Even though levels of male violence towards female runners are rising, they are still lower than rates of violence experienced by women moving through public space in other contexts: 43 per cent of women running report harassment, compared to 65–99 per cent (depending on the study) of women outdoors in general. So, statistically, running seems to make women *less* vulnerable than activities such as walking, and the aspects of running that can feel most dangerous, such as running alone at night, are not necessarily so: very few of the men who have killed female runners since 2015 have done so in the dark. Many of those murdered women did everything we are supposed to do – they set their watches as trackers, told people where they were going, ran in broad daylight – and men still killed them. In a strange way, this makes me feel absolved of the anticipatory guilt I harbour for repeatedly putting myself 'at risk' by running at night: it seems there is little I could do to keep myself safe anyway.

However vulnerable I may feel when I'm alone on a dark moor, worrying about a male silhouette emerging on the path, I also know that my actual danger is probably marginal compared to the statistical threat that men pose to women in the home. Strangers on hilltops are less dangerous to women than known men, such as intimate partners and family members, and 'lethal violence experienced by women and girls in the private sphere appears to be a more intractable problem than killings of women and girls outside the home', as the UN Office on Drugs and Crime reported in 2020. I also try to remind myself that studies suggest that the majority of men are not violent, and the fact that I often don't believe this may be more symptomatic of my own history of trauma than a reflection of statistical reality. On that basis, I have – occasionally – experimented with answering back when men yell abuse at me outdoors. Holly Kearl finds that one of street harassment's pernicious 'psychological harms' is how it disempowers women, and the female subjects of her research tell her that when they respond to abusive men outdoors – angrily or calmly – it counters that sense of impotence.[26]

I am also attempting to manage other dangers that can damage the pleasures I gain from running.

I know I am susceptible to certain social pressures that are put on women, which make me liable to turn sport into an internal competition and try to be faster, fitter and thinner. But I do not want to be running away from myself, as I am, any more – not like I did in my twenties. So now I am endeavouring to 'run to feel', as it is sometimes called by running coaches; to move more often without looking at my watch. I am trying not to worry whether my training is 'productive' or if my VO2 max is increasing. I have found it surprisingly hard to do this, but nevertheless, I am persevering: exploring what it feels like to simply run – day in, day out – without a long-term trajectory in mind, and without the objective of improving all the time. I tell myself that I'm okay as I am, and that I am out for a run *because it feels good*: nothing more, nothing less. After all, every evening before bed, I enjoy the ritual of warming up a cleanser on my palms before smoothing it over my face, sensing the cream melt against my skin, then dipping a flannel into a basin of steaming water and wiping the cleanser away to leave new pink flesh that, for a few seconds, reminds me of my children's bodies when they were babies, hot from a bath. I do this every night, and I love it and it is good for me, this minor act of renewal – but there is no suggestion that I should have a long-term strategy of getting better at washing my face. Could running not be something similar in my life – simply pleasure in the present moment – perhaps not all the time, but at least sometimes? Over the next decade, as I approach menopause and the age at which women's physiology makes it harder to get faster, I suspect I will be having these conversations with myself more often.

There are a few outdoor events – such as the annual Terry Fox Run, held around the world to raise money for cancer research – in which participation replaces competition as the guiding principle. The idea reminds me of the character of outdoor pursuits before the codification mania of the nineteenth century. It recalls an era when sport was chiefly about fun, rather than rules and competitions and record-breaking and the aspiration of endless improvement. When I was working in the Alpine Club archives, I came across clippings from national newspapers in the 1920s, which reported on women's outdoor excursions in the mountains, not because they broke any records – but because the participants' joy was infectious.[27] Competitions unquestionably have a place in sport: they are ways of conferring status, recognition and reward on talented sportspeople, including women, and of exploring the furthest limits of human athletic capabilities. But there are more stories in sport than simply those of the fastest and strongest. I wonder how it would feel, today, to open a newspaper's sports supplement and to read about the adventures, experiences and pleasures of amateurs outdoors – and to see a wider range of bodies in motion than we are used to viewing.

Nevertheless – despite my worries about the quantification involved in running, and the obsessions it can foster – I always run with my sports watch on my wrist. This is because it records every run I do, and I don't want to forget, and I don't want anyone else to forget, that we women were here, all the time, in the outdoors.

Perhaps it seems silly to doubt that the vast numbers of women out running in the world today might be lost to memory in the future. But I suspect that Lizzie and her friends never imagined that they would be forgotten. They surely would have been horrified to learn that, one day, scholars would confidently proclaim that 'women's historic role [in sport] was that of handkerchief-fluttering spectators' and that 'few women' were mountaineering in the nineteenth century. We can never know, in each present moment, whether the near future will tend towards progress or backlash, and today women's freedoms feel so very fragile. I do not trust future historians to be on our side. Instead, I hope that data of the type my sports watch collects will insist beyond possible refutation on the fact of our presence outdoors.

*

The sugar from the flapjack hits, and I suddenly feel amazing: a proper second wind. There is a long clear downhill slope off Fylingdales Moor to Jugger Howe Beck, a descent which lasts for almost three miles and, as I always do when I feel this good and happy, I stretch my arms to the sides and pretend I am a plane. From the beck there is another sharp pull up to the road, and I slow down to a walk and cross it. From here, I can see the radio mast close to where the Lyke Wake Walk ends: it is a straight one-mile (or so) line from where I'm currently standing, and it is all uphill, but I run the whole way without stopping and then sit heavily on the ground against the trig point that stands beside the mast. I hug it and take a selfie.

Is this the end, though? I thought there was supposed to be an official Lyke Wake Walk marker stone and, as I try to locate it and get out Cowley's guidebook for assistance, I read that, in the early days, the finish was about another mile away, at the bar of the Raven Hall Hotel.

It seems wrong not to take the route right up to the seafront and cross the moors in their entirety, and I am staying at the hotel anyway. So I do not press 'stop' on my watch just yet, but lean heavily on the trig point to raise myself to my feet. I slowly accelerate enough to tip walking into jogging, through a field of sheep who seem unusually interested in the contents of my running pack and cluster around me, nudging my back. The gate on the other side of the field takes me out onto a street of squat white houses and, at its end, I turn a corner onto a broader road leading straight to the gateposts of the hotel. I speed up as I run through an avenue of trees, as if on a victory lap, smiling and waving at an imaginary crowd of cheering spectators, and finally, while a panorama of the sea opens out to my left, I touch the hotel's wall and stop my watch. I've run the entire horizontal span of the North York Moors in 10 hours and 55 minutes and, according to Lyke Wake Walk mythology, now I'm a witch.

I take my trainers off at the hotel's door and check in at reception. Before I climb upstairs to my room, I go to the bar and order a pint of lager.

The young woman behind the bar looks down at my peat-splattered legs, and asks, 'Have you walked here?'

'I've run!' I reply triumphantly. 'From Osmotherley! The whole width of the moors!'

The bar must get a lot of Lyke Wake Walkers, but she doesn't seem to have heard of it. She does a double-take, and asks, 'But how far is that?'

'Forty miles.'

'Wow,' she says, sincerely. 'That's incredible. I wish I could do that.'

'You can,' I say. 'I only started running a few years ago. It's just a matter of building up distance, slowly. And it's so worth it: I've had the best day.'

'Wow,' she says again, thoughtfully, and hands me my pint.

I take my lager up to my bedroom, which is on the northwestern side of the hotel, and has spectacular views across Robin Hood's Bay. I run myself a bath, and when it is full, I balance my cold glass on the side, and lower myself into the hot water. Flakes of peat float free from my skin, and I let my legs rise up too, and hover just below the surface. I lie completely still in the warmth – head tipped back and ears plugged by water; torso suspended and floating – and although my shins tingle where they have been scratched by heather, and my muscles are well used, nothing hurts, and it is so lovely I could cry.

A year ago, this ease was all I wanted. I was wrong in thinking that running could do my grieving for me, but running has helped me, nonetheless. It doesn't stop me from missing all the loved people I have lost, but it teaches me how to move around the world more assertively, to prioritise my own needs and to look after myself. When it feels like I've lost everything, running reminds me that I still have my body and all the stories and sensations it holds. That is not nothing; not at all.

I always knew that my project would be a dual one: to both run and write my way through grief. And now I think that the writing has been just as important as the running; that they have worked together in a way I hadn't necessarily expected. Amid so much of my own personal loss, I have sometimes felt unable to bear the disappearance of the women in these pages from our collective memory. And women fade from the historical record *all the time*. Every time a woman married, her own name was replaced with her husband's and she became, for example, a Mrs Frederick Burnaby or a Mrs John Main or a Mrs Aubrey Le Blond; a shadow behind a man, ghostly in her own lifetime and one further step out of reach for the researcher who, decades later, is trying to find her. I have tried to bring some of these women out of the shadows again; among other reasons, in order to mitigate my own sense of mourning for foremothers, my own homelessness.

Grief made me acutely sensitive to the multiple ways in which women are alienated from outdoor space and our own bodies, and to the far-reaching consequences of those dispossessions. Running has helped restore me to my own body and to an outdoor world in which it can best flourish – and writing this book about the restorative potential of running has made me think about what it means to tell stories about bodies, and about women's bodies in particular.

Towards the end of my research, a woman called Jacquelyn, the archivist at a museum in Kansas where many of Lizzie's photographs ended up after her death, emails me an image of Lizzie and Aubrey on their honeymoon, and I open it on my phone and zoom in. Aubrey is seated on a folding chair outside a Norwegian hut, hunched forward with a towel around his shoulders, and Lizzie is leaning over him from behind. She pinches a snippet of his hair between the thumb and forefinger of her left hand, and with her right, she starts to cut from below with an enormous pair of scissors. As she bends forward, her tie, which is tucked into her skirt, sags forward, and her shirt starts to crease and pull against the high waistband. The material on her left shoulder gathers and strains as her arm raises. Her feet are placed flat on the ground, but she is leaning forward and therefore having to shift her weight into her backside and heels to stop herself tipping face-first onto Aubrey. Her face is focused and intent, and the pose probably lasted no more than a second or two, as she made a quick snip and righted herself again. But nevertheless, the photograph is so detailed that, for a second, I can feel the shirt tugging, the shoulders constricting, the weight in my heels, the stretch along my calf muscles, the metal against my thumb, the hair in my fingers. It is as if she has possessed me.

Lizzie knew the power of photographs to preserve bodily experiences.

But my sense of an actual physical encounter with Lizzie in this photograph is, of course, an illusion. Neither photographs nor books can resurrect a person physically. Photographs and stories of actual people are all translations from one mode – the world of breathing, sweating, moving bodies – to another – static black and white words or images; mere outlines. Something necessarily gets lost in that translation. When I miss my stepdad and Josie, and all the other people I've lost, it is their full-bodied physical presence in the world that I long for the most. I miss the way that Josie dunked dry bread in tap water and threw her head back in open-mouthed laughter. I miss the way that my stepfather lifted his hat in greeting; guffawed until his voice ran out; hugged me so tightly to his chest that I could not breathe; and ran towards me down the road, one hand outstretched high above his head, waving in relief. I crave the things that *cannot* be resurrected. The relics that *can* be preserved after a person has died – their letters, emails, text messages, the books my stepdad published, the drawings that Josie made – are poor consolation.

Grief is not rational. In this book, I had so desperately wanted to translate my memories of my stepdad and Josie into physical form. I had hoped that this book might revive them, and give me something material to hold onto – to hug – again. But, in writing it, I have had to come to terms with the fact that it is an impossible task to preserve bodies in the form of text. The earliest photographs of humans were thought by viewers to be ghostly, uncanny, insubstantial things. Stories are the same.

Nevertheless, there is still something extremely valuable in the attempt to translate living bodies into stories. I have not managed to repair the loss of people I love; but writing this book has helped to mitigate further mourning: the grief I felt for the apparent absence of women in the outdoors, and my deep-seated fear that this absence meant that I did not belong there either. Unearthing the stories of the physical achievements of Lizzie and her generation of tenacious women has helped to mend two different, but related, forms of bereavement: some of my discomfort and dispossession in an outdoor world that is unremittingly hostile to women, and some of my alienation from my own body. I cannot resurrect Lizzie in person; but discovering her story has gone some way in returning me to myself.

In our society, it is ingrained to value reason over instinct, culture over nature, mind over body – and men over women. But we need celebratory stories about bodies as well as about minds, and it is especially important to preserve stories of women's bodies. Female bodies are not accommodated well in our world, and that failure lasts after death. What women's bodies have achieved, and the impact they have made on the world, has not been well preserved.

With that loss, we've all been impoverished. In losing the rich history of women's sport, we've lost half the wealth of experiences and meanings associated with the outdoors, and we have been left with only a fragmentary set of ideas and tales: about *his* city, *his* mountain, *his* moor, *his* river, *his* park, *his* football pitch, *his* street. This is bad for women today who need to feel at home in the outdoors, and it is bad for our understanding of sport and the natural world, which is radically diminished when it omits the experiences of over half the population.

I still want to know more, so much more, about the women who have run, walked and climbed outdoors. I want to discover more about those women's bodies and their capacities and their joys, and to see the vast possibilities of what might be 'in our nature' to achieve. I want to immerse myself even more deeply in women's representations of the outdoors, and to see the myriad guises in which 'her nature' appears, and what women of diverse eras and places found there, and how women's perceptions differ from 'his' stories of the natural world.

And seeing as we cannot raise those women's living bodies, then stories and photographs will have to do. I think and hope that such stories might help women today to live more fully and freely, both in the outdoors and in our own bodies.

The next morning, I leave the hotel and amble along the Cinder Path up the coastline to Robin Hood's Bay, where I catch a bus and train back to York. I let myself in through the front door, and my three girls run into the corridor, with Pete standing behind them. My eldest daughter takes my hand and shouts: 'We've made something for you, Mummy.' They pull me into the kitchen and on the table there is an enormous papier-mâché hill, painted in various shades of green, with dark brown moorland on its top and a blue river running around it. On the summit is a wire figure, and she is running, and she is making her way down the mountain.

Afterword

In January 2022, my husband, Pete Newbon, took his own life.

In Her Nature is not about his death – and, in the days and months after he died, I realised that in these pages I might have been in danger of portraying my earlier experiences of grief in 2019–20 as something universal. If so, that was wrong. Now I know that losing parents is very different to mourning a spouse. And bereavement through suicide is different from enduring the death of loved ones from natural causes. Someone, I can't remember who, described the emotional effects of suicide as a 'grief dial turned up to eleven', and there have certainly been times when I have felt strangely nostalgic for the lesser agony of the way I felt after my father and stepfather died.

Nevertheless, I am finding some similarities between these periods of mourning. After Pete died, I could not get out of bed again; this time, for nearly six months. I could not begin to run until July 2022 and, as I write this in late autumn 2022, the world outside my house still seems terrifying and confusing. But, despite the fear, spending time outdoors, on my own two feet, once more feels essential to the process of learning to live around catastrophic loss. I have found that the only way to endure such sadness is to take life an hour – or even a few minutes – at a time, and that is something I have learned from long-distance running: to simply eat and drink enough to propel myself to the next bend in the path, and then to take it from there. And when it feels like everything is broken, running also reminds me that I still have my own body and all the pleasures and stories of which it is capable, and that it is worth caring for it and building up my strength once more.

And I have my girls, my three extraordinary daughters: Molly, Martha and Esme.

In 2019, grief following my dad's and stepdad's deaths magnified many of the losses that women endure in the world, which I started to sense on a deeply personal level. Now, after Pete's death, I feel redoubled grief for those losses and dispossessions; and I am not just sad for myself, but for my daughters too and for everything they have been and will be bereaved of, as they mature into women. And so now it seems even more urgent than it did a year or so ago, when I was writing early drafts of this book, for women and girls living in such an inimical world to be able to find solace, security and freedom *somewhere* – perhaps on the moors and mountains, and in the act of running, where I get a degree of comfort; or perhaps in other spaces and activities. But my worry and fury, that girls might continue to be deprived of safety and ease in the world, when their need is so great, is now so much stronger too.

Acknowledgements

The production of *In Her Nature* has taken place through more changes than anything I've written before – including both creative shifts and events that blew my life apart – and one consequence is that there are an unusually large number of people and institutions to thank for helping me to get this book into print.

My wonderful agent, Tracy Bohan at the Wylie Agency, has championed the idea of this book from the very start. My brilliant editor at Chatto & Windus, Poppy Hampson, trusted and encouraged me when it became clear that the book I was writing was very different to the text I'd originally proposed. She patiently helped me to turn the manuscript from a compendium of research nuggets into an actual coherent book, and was infinitely flexible and reassuring throughout the horrors of 2022. I was devastated when Poppy left Chatto in August 2022, and I am so grateful to my new editor, Rose Tomaszewska, for taking on the book with such genuine dedication, efficiency and tact. I also want to thank everyone else at Chatto (and elsewhere) who has worked so hard on bringing *In Her Nature* out into the world: Anna Redman Aylward, Asia Choudhry, Polly Dorner, Eoin Dunne, Nicola Evans, Clara Farmer, Oli Grant, Graeme Hall, Rosanna Hildyard, Kate Johnson, Victoria Murray-Browne, Stephen Parker, Priya Roy, Kit Shepherd and Sinead Ussher.

I was delighted and honoured to receive a British Library Eccles Writer's Award in 2019, which supported my work on *In Her Nature* in multiple ways. It was a huge vote of confidence from the judges, at an important time in the book's gestation. The staff of the Eccles Centre and the British Library in general (both in London and Boston Spa) were invaluable in helping me to develop a sense of the global nature of the patterns I describe in the book, and to learn about the extraordinary North American women who broke barriers outdoors.

The award's funds allowed me to conduct essential research at the British Library, and in the Alpine Club too, and I am particularly grateful to Nigel Buckley, the Alpine Club's indefatigable librarian during 2019–20, for making it into such a rewarding experience. I also owe a lot to the Gladstone's Library Political Writing Residency, which gave me the opportunity to fully immerse myself, without distractions, in Lizzie's life and writings at a crucial early stage in my research. In particular, I want to say thank you to Louisa Yates and Peter Francis for being so accommodating.

My profound gratitude is due to further archivists and organisations from whose expertise I benefitted enormously. In alphabetical order of institution, these include: James Webster at the Bristol Naturalists' Society; Ruth Brown at the Chapter House Museum Archive, Dunkeld; Dora Lardelli, Diana Pedretti and Gian-Nicola Bass at the Cultural Archive of the Upper Engadin in Samedan, Switzerland; Andreas Augustin at Famous Hotels; the staff of the General Register Office of England and Wales; Natasha Rangno at the Hotel Belvédère, Davos; Ronda Frazier at the Jefferson County Archives, USA; Alison Gillies at Kinnaird House, Dunkeld; Evelyne Lüthi-Graf, archivist of the Kulm Hotel and Badrutt's Palace Hotel in St Moritz; Katja Schneider at the Kulm; Jacquelyn Borgeson and Conrad Froelich at the Martin and Osa Johnson Safari Museum; the National Archives (of England and Wales) as a whole and, in particular, Stephanie Markins; Elizabeth McEvoy at the National Archives, Ireland; Maggi Gonsalves at the New York State Archives (and Joshua Newton for liaising with Maggi and even paying for the digitisation of the documents I needed); Susan Norwebb at the Nottinghamshire Archives; Yvonne Marse at the Orange County Clerk's Office; Julie Carrington at the Royal Geographical Society; Stephen Bartley at the St Moritz Tobogganing Club; Karen Anderson at the University of Bristol's Special Collections department; Elizabeth Ennion-Smith at the University of Cambridge, Pembroke College library and archives; Frank Bowles at the University of Cambridge, University Library, Department of Archives and Modern Manuscripts; and Jayne Amat at Manuscripts and Special Collections in the University of Nottingham's Libraries.

In Her Nature follows my search for foremothers in the great outdoors, and that search was only made possible by my foremothers in the research world: the extraordinary writers whose rigorous, trail-blazing labour opened my eyes to a historical landscape of women's sport that I had never known existed until I read their work. In particular, I am hugely grateful to Madie Armstrong, who was incredibly generous in sharing her own ground-breaking research into Lizzie's life and writings, which I really hope she'll be able to publish before long; Eliza Cox and Joan Robins, who researched the provenance of Lizzie's aunt Renira Pollard's notebooks and traced them back to the presence of Lizzie's family at Kinnaird House; Liz O'Donnell, for telling me about Anna Deborah Richardson and Teresa Merz; and the staff of the Cultural Archive of the Upper Engadin, and the Martin and Osa John Safari Museum, for so painstakingly digitising Lizzie's photos and making them available to the world. In putting together a broad picture of late nineteenth-century women's sport and its relationship to women's rights, I leant on the work of many historians, particularly Mary Louise Adams, Gwendolyn Captain, Martina Gugglberger, Sheila Hanlon, Kathleen E. McCrone, Carol Anne Osborne, Cécile Ottogalli-Mazzacavallo, Clare Roche, Britt Rusert, Mary P. Ryan, Karen J. Stockham, Patricia A. Vertinsky, Kathryn Walchester, Judith R. Walkowitz and Cicely Williams. My eyes were opened to the reality of women's experiences in contemporary public space, and the psychological effects of 'outdoor misogyny', by researchers and activists including Cynthia Grant Bowman, Anna Livia Cullinan, Deirdre Davis, Micaela di Leonardo, Dana Crowley Jack, Kandy James, Holly Kearl, Anastasia Loukaitou-Sideris, Caroline Criado Perez, Shilpa Phadke, Sameera Khan and Shilpa Ranade, Fiona Vera-Gray, and Susannah Walker of the charity Make Space for Girls. The scholarship of Lyn Mikel Brown and Carol Gilligan, and Iris Marion Young, had a particularly formative influence on me. I am extremely grateful to female athletes including Keri Wallace, Maria Dixon and Sophie Power for talking to me about their experiences of running and mountaineering as women; and to Arlene Blum, Kathrine Switzer and Marina LeGree for writing publicly about their achievements and campaigns. Thanks are also due to my former colleagues at Women in the Hills, Kerri Andrews and Joanna Taylor, and to sports sociologist Kerry Griffiths at the Sheffield Hallam Sports Industry Research Group, for working so hard to identify, quantify, analyse and tackle numerous constraints negotiated by women in the outdoors today; and to UKRI, the AHRC, and the Universities of Newcastle, Manchester and Edge Hill for supporting this research. I'm particularly grateful to Jo Robinson at Newcastle for a great deal of support over 2021–3, and to Laura Elliott, Louise Jones and David Hill for support as the book went to press. And none of my work would have been possible without the extraordinary earlier generations of women in the hills, who broke cultural and sporting barriers, and made sure that their achievements were recorded for posterity. In particular, I loved reading the writings of Isabella Bird Bishop, Eliza Cole, Amelia Edwards, Jane Freshfield, Emily Hornby, Margaret Jackson, Mary Paillon, Anna Pigeon and Ellen Abbot, Frederica Plunket, Martha Shaw, Mariana Starke, Elizabeth Fox Tuckett, Fanny Bullock Workman – and, of course, Lizzie Le Blond. I am profoundly indebted to every person listed in these acknowledgements, and many more besides, and I take full and sole responsibility for any errors or differences of opinion that may occur in these pages. If, in these acknowledgements, I have inadvertently missed anyone who needed thanking, I apologise and extend my gratitude.

I am also grateful to some men(!): Tom Alban, for encouraging my work on the history of street harassment in two BBC radio programmes; Ben Griffin for describing nineteenth-century inheritance laws; Mike Heffernan for talking to me about the trans-Saharan railway and early British intelligence communities; Brian Murray for sharing his research into Saleh Bin Osman; John Spencer, for outlining the current laws regarding street harassment; Tim Walsh, who was so generous in telling me about his great-great-uncle Aubrey Le Blond; and historians Sasha Abramsky, Silas Chamberlin, Ronald W. Clark, Bill Garner, Peter H. Hansen, John Hawkins and Simon Robert Thompson for their respective research into the history of outdoor leisure and the role of women such as Lizzie in that history.

For their kind permission to include the images on these pages, I am very grateful to Alamy and the Antiqua Print Gallery; the Alpine Club;

Alexis Berg and Sophie Power; the Bettman Archive; the Cultural Archive of the Upper Engadin in Samedan; the Dod family, especially Bill Dod; Getty Images; the Hulton Archive; the Library of Congress; the Martin and Osa Johnson Safari Museum; and the St Moritz Tobogganing Club. Huge thanks to designer Bill Donohoe for the maps that accompany chapters 1, 4, 7, 9 and 11, and to Stephen Parker for the front cover, with Alex Green's illustrations, and to Diana Patient for the author shots. Appreciation is due to Faber, for permission to reproduce text by T.S. Eliot from *The Waste Land* and Sylvia Plath from *The Journals of Sylvia Plath*; and to Harvard University Press for allowing me to cite Lyn Mikel Brown and Carol Gilligan's *Meeting at the Crossroads*. For their generous agreement to having my descriptions of them, and their words and their actions, included in this book, I am grateful to Anthony and Valentine Bamber, Nigel Buckley, Connor Cannings, Ryk and Bev Downes, Victoria Dutchman-Smith, Sophie Gosling, Kate Jackson, Dominic Lash, E. Parry, Henrik Salje, Harriet Shields, Chloe Smee, Chloe Wigston Smith, Jon and Shirley Steele, Keri Wallace, Jayne Wetherley, Sally Wyatt, and everyone who took the time to respond to my queries and conversations on social media. Thank you to Eddie Arthur for going on a fact-checking mission along the Dales Way for me. And I owe profound gratitude to the family of my much-loved and intensely missed friend Josie – her parents Joanna and Jean-Jacques Camus, and her brothers Bernie and Dom Camus – for their permission to write about her.

As I say in the final chapter of this book, its production has not just come from reading and writing, but also from my own running and hiking. So I want to thank everyone who has made running into such a joyous and meaningful experience for me, especially Hardmoors race directors Jon and Shirley Steele; Punk Panther race directors Ryk and Bev Downes, and Mark Limon; my running friends Harriet, Jayne and Kate; Claire and Jon Pitchford; my sports masseur Karen Leaf; the adventure company at How Stean Gorge; and Alan Middlebrook and Kim Cavill, who are both brilliant athletes, trainers and friends. In my depictions of some running events, I have implicitly altered the calendar order for narrative purposes: for example, the Nidderdale Way race actually took place after my Lyke Wake run in August 2020.

I also want to show my appreciation for those who directly helped the writing of the book by reading and responding to very early drafts: the audience of a talk I gave at GladFest in 2019, about my initial ideas for the book; Rosie Blau, who gave brilliant editorial advice on my long-read article on women's running for *1843* magazine; Sarah Ditum, Daisy Hay and Caroline Criado Perez, whose comments and suggestions were enormously insightful; and Stella Creasy and Mary Curtin, who generously fact-checked sections of the text. Responsibility for any remaining errors in these pages is entirely mine.

Getting this book from its first full draft (which was ready in autumn 2021) to a complete manuscript suitable for publication in late 2022 was not easy. I am grateful to everyone who supported me to get the book ready for production over the unimaginably hard months following my husband's sudden and traumatic death in January 2022 – and especially the friends who stuck around after the funeral was over: in particular, Chris Cotton, Penni Grodzicka, Daisy Hay, Nathan Martin, Juliet Oosthuysen, Isla Rowland, Jackie Scott, Chloe Wigston Smith, Andrew Spencer, and Joe and Laura Wilson. I especially need to thank Caroline Criado Perez for her love, friendship and care: I honestly don't know how I'd have got through these last months without her. Some people won't consider themselves as having directly assisted the book, but I know that I couldn't have finished *In Her Nature* without their help with practical matters relating to finances, legal situations, my house, my children and my mental state. So I need to say a heartfelt thank you to Marion Bates, Ruth Brady, Chris and Angela Brooks, Greg Callus, Bethany Fennell, Francesca Floris, Shelli Gordon, Ruth Hendry, Paul Inman, Gary Lyons, Antony Smith, Raymond Shaw and Brian Swales; as well as everyone who set up and contributed to fundraisers; Helen Lewis; and my children's lovely godparents.

This book would not exist without the influence of my wonderful late stepfather, Willy Brown. And its entire raison-d'être is the love, hope, wonder, admiration, anger and determination I feel on behalf of my three extraordinary and brave daughters, Molly, Martha and Esme, who are my whole world.

List of illustrations

6 Elizabeth Le Blond (aka Mrs Main), 'Double Run on the St Moritz Cresta', Cultural Archive of the Upper Engadin in Samedan. Reproduced with the kind permission of the Kulturarchiv Oberengadin.

7 Attributed to Tony Dod, Women Playing Bandy in 1890s Switzerland, Dod Family Album, reproduced with the kind permission of the Dod family (especially Bill Dod) and the St Moritz Tobogganing Club.

46 Certificat d'Ascension aux Grands-Mulets, Elizabeth Burnaby, 25 July 1881, Ladies' Alpine Club Archives, Alpine Club, London, G21. Reproduced with the kind permission of the Alpine Club.

72 F. and G. Charnaux, 'Ladies and Guides on the Mer de Glace, Mont Blanc', c. 1886. Reproduced with the kind permission of the Alpine Club.

76 'The Chaise-à-Porteurs, 1891, Switzerland', in Samuel Manning, *Swiss Pictures*, London, 1891. Reproduced with the kind permission of Antiqua Print Gallery and Alamy.

112 Alexis Berg, Sophie Power during the 2018 UTMB. Reproduced with the kind permission of Alexis Berg (and Sophie Power).

133 Elizabeth Le Blond (aka Mrs Main), 'On the Forno Glacier', Cultural Archive of the Upper Engadin in Samedan. Reproduced with the kind permission of the Kulturarchiv Oberengadin.

140 Elizabeth Le Blond (aka Mrs Main), 'Self-Portrait: Summer', Cultural Archive of the Upper Engadin in Samedan. Reproduced with the kind permission of the Kulturarchiv Oberengadin.

141 Tony Dod, 'The Snow was Very Deep in Places', c. 1895–6, Dod Family Album, reproduced with the kind permission of the Dod family (especially Bill Dod) and the St Moritz Tobogganing Club.

153 Elizabeth Le Blond (aka Mrs Main), 'From Alp Grüm', Cultural Archive of the Upper Engadin in Samedan. Reproduced with the kind permission of the Kulturarchiv Oberengadin.

161 Attributed to Tony Dod, Women Curling in Switzerland, c. 1896–7, Dod Family Album, reproduced with the kind permission of the Dod family (especially Bill Dod) and the St Moritz Tobogganing Club.

162 **t/l** Tony Dod, 'Mrs Main, Mrs Rutherford, L[ottie] D[od]', c. 1896, Dod Family Album, reproduced with the kind permission of the Dod family (especially Bill Dod) and the St Moritz Tobogganing Club; **t/r** 'Tobogganing', c. 1895, reproduced with the kind permission of the Hulton Archive and Getty Images.

163 Elizabeth Le Blond (aka Mrs Main), 'Hon. Frances Gibson, Cissy Saunderson, Esther Saunderson. The First Three in the Ladies Grand National, 1895, St Moritz', Martin and Osa Johnson Safari Museum Archives, Chanute, Kansas, EMLB SB4 4.197. Reproduced with the kind permission of the Martin and Osa Johnson Safari Museum Archives.

165 Elizabeth Le Blond (aka Mrs Main), 'Mrs. Main after a Winter Attempt on Piz Morteratsch', Cultural Archive of the Upper Engadin in Samedan. Reproduced with the kind permission of the Kulturarchiv Oberengadin.

245 'Women at Cambridge', 1897, reproduced with the kind permission of the Hulton Archive and Getty Images.

311 Maria Howard Fox, 'To the Spirit of the Jungfrau', from the First Report of the Ladies' Alpine Club, 1913, Ladies' Alpine Club Archives, Alpine Club, London, G10. Reproduced with the kind permission of the Alpine Club.

320 Fanny Bullock Workman and William Hunter Workman, 'On Silver Throne Plateau at Nearly 21,000 Feet', from *Two Summers in the Ice-Wilds of Eastern Karakoram*, New York, 1917, facing p. 128. Reproduced with the kind permission of the Library of Congress.

355 'First Women in Boston Marathon', 1967, reproduced with the kind permission of the Bettmann Archive and Getty Images.

Bibliography

Archives

LADIES' ALPINE CLUB ARCHIVES, ALPINE CLUB, LONDON

G1: Ladies' Alpine Club Visitors' Book (1910 onwards); G2: Ladies' Alpine Club Minute Book (1909–29); G3: Ladies' Alpine Club Minute Book (1947–70); G4: Ladies' Alpine Club Minute Book (1970 onwards); G5: Ladies' Alpine Club Minute Book (1929–47); G6: Records re. merger of Ladies' Alpine Club with Alpine Club in 1970s; G7: List of members (1924–7); G8: List of graduating members (1924–9); G9: List of guides; G10: Press cuttings, lecture cards, badge designs, menus, etc. (1907–13); G11: Scrapbook (1914–24); G12: List of names, dates and climbs; members' climbing records; G13: List of graduating members (1925–30); G14: List of members; G15: Application forms with list of climbs; G16: Application forms with lists of climbs; G17: List of members who have retired or died (1920–75); G18: Lyceum Club papers and correspondence around move from Lyceum Club to Great Hotel, Marylebone; G19: Papers re. merger of Ladies' Alpine Club with Alpine Club in 1970s; G20: Mountaineering pamphlets with women mountaineers; G21: Newspaper cuttings relating to women's mountaineering (1908–75); G22: Ladies' Alpine Club motor kitchen (1915); G23: Artwork (1910–25); G24: Old prints of Zermatt region; G25: Members' records (1910–75); G26: Booklets produced during time of Ladies' Alpine Club; G27: Article in the *Nursing Times* by Peter Steele, 'Women in High Places'; G28: Recording of *Woman's Hour* programme on Women and Climbing; G29: Pinnacle Club dinner menu (1976); G30: Typewritten list of members; G31: Correspondence between Alpine Club librarian Margaret Ecclestone and Kevin Higgins about a life of Lizzie Le Blond; G32: Material re. Frances Emily Weston festival in Japan (1872–1937)

See also Johanna Merz (ed.), *Index to the Ladies' Alpine Club Year-Books, 1910–1975* (London, 2000)

ANCESTRY.COM AND THE CHURCH OF JESUS CHRIST OF LATTER-DAY SAINTS

1880 US Census, Rockland County, Orangetown, population schedule, Orangetown, pp. 7–296, schedule 1, p. 2, supervisor's district 4, enumeration district (ED) 54, dwelling 20, family 20, Thomas Main: NARA microfilm publication T9, roll 924

BADRUTT'S PALACE HOTEL, ST MORITZ, SWITZERLAND

See Kulm Hotel, St Moritz, Switzerland

BRITISH LIBRARY, LONDON

Martha Shaw, Diary (1839–42), Mss Eur F 197/2; Martha Shaw, Diary (1845–6), Mss Eur F 197/3; Martha Shaw's diaries were transcribed by Madeleine Symes in 2018, and are available online at: https://sites.google.com/site/fenwickoflambton/jane-hornby-barkley/martha-shaws-journals

Letter from Elizabeth Le Blond, Add. MS. 89076/2/1: Miscellaneous letters received by Ernest Gardner

Letters from Elizabeth Le Blond, Add. MS. 89076/2/4: Miscellaneous letters received by Delphis Gardner

COLORADO STATE ARCHIVES, DENVER

John Frederic Main probate, Denver 1892, archive loc 52179, case 2890, ID 2825510

DUNKELD COMMUNITY ARCHIVE, SCOTLAND

Notebooks of Renira Pollard née Whitshed, written 1864–9 at Kinnard, 2001.0409. Box 62

Folder of research made by Eileen Cox and Joan Robins, which accompanies the Notebooks of Renira Pollard née Whitshed, Robins 003

GENERAL RECORD OFFICE OF ENGLAND AND WALES, SOUTHPORT

Marriage certificate of Frederick Gustavus Burnaby and Elizabeth Alice Frances Hawkins-Whitshed, 1879, 2nd Quarter, District Kensington, Vol. 1a, p. 164

Death certificate of Elizabeth Frances Alice Le Blond, Year 1934, Quarter: Sep., District: Radnor W, Vol. 11b, p. 135

JEFFERSON COUNTY ARCHIVES, GOLDEN, COLORADO

Incorporation Records for Buffalo Creek Park Land and Improvement Company, Jefferson County Clerk and Recorder Incorporation Records, 1862–1969, Series #168, box 2, folder 44

KULM HOTEL, ST MORITZ, SWITZERLAND

I am very grateful to Evelyne Lüthi-Graf, archivist of the Kulm and Badrutt's Palace Hotels, and Katja Schneider at the Kulm, for showing me their uncatalogued copies of Lizzie's photo albums, which functioned as catalogues of prints that she was selling for the St Moritz Aid Fund

LIDDELL HART CENTRE FOR MILITARY ARCHIVES, KING'S COLLEGE LONDON

Spears 6/1/4: Letters written from Elizabeth Le Blond to Spears following publication of first edition of *Liaison 1914*, 3 Mar. 1931

LINCOLNSHIRE ARCHIVES, LINCOLN

Letters to/from Elizabeth Le Blond, 1924–9, Goulding Papers 3/D/20

MARTIN AND OSA JOHNSON SAFARI MUSEUM ARCHIVES, CHANUTE, KANSAS

Elizabeth Le Blond Album 1: 'My Home in the Alps' (1886–1890), EMLB SB1; Album 2: 'My Camera's First Swiss Tour' (1890–1893), EMLB SB2; Album 3: 'Guide to the Old Gardens of Italy' (1894–1906), EMLB SB3; Album 4: 'Winter in the High Alps: Pictures of Snow Sports' (1894–5), EMLB SB 4; Album 5: 'High Life and Towers of Silence' (1896), EMLB SB5; Album 6: 'Mountaineering from a Woman's Point of View' (1895–6), EMLB SB6; Album 7: 'A Holiday in the Wilds of Arctic Norway' (1901–2), EMLB SB7; Album 8: 'Day In, Day Out' (1901–1903), EMLB SB8 – all of which have been digitised and catalogued at: https://safarimuseum.wixsite.com/lizzieleblond

THE MORGAN LIBRARY AND MUSEUM, NEW YORK

Letter from Marjorie Bowen to Elizabeth Le Blond, 30 Dec. 1923, Unbound Ray Bowen MA 13420.13; Letter from Marjorie Bowen to Elizabeth Le Blond, 2 May 1924, Unbound Ray Bowen MA 13420.16

Bibliography

NATIONAL ARCHIVES OF IRELAND, DUBLIN

Grants of probate and wills, Elizabeth Le Blond, died 27 Jul. 1934, CS/HC/PO/4/88/4515

THE NATIONAL ARCHIVES, LONDON

Admiralty: Officers' Service Records, ADM 196/37/1406, Whitshed, James H., Rank: Lieutenant: Officers' Service Records, ADM 196/70/174, Whitshed, James Hawkins, Rank: Commander; Admiralty

'Cabinet Photograph of Col and Mrs Burnaby', 26 Jan. 1885: COPY 1/371/60

1861 England, Wales and Scotland Census, RG09/644 folio 85 page 5; 1881 England, Wales and Scotland Census, RG11/51 folio 44 page 13

Incorporation Records for Denver Investment and Banking Corporation Ltd, BT 34/781/34247

Merz, Teresa, 'Lodging Houses', NRO 2281/15

Medal Card of Le Blond, Aubrey, WO 372/23/23867

1939 Register, RG101/0307D/013/33

'UK and Ireland, Incoming Passenger Lists, 1878–1960', Board of Trade: Commercial and Statistical Department and successors: Inwards Passenger Lists; Class: BT 26/748/8; Piece: 748 (Lizzie's return from the USA on 16 Mar. 1923)

'UK and Ireland, Incoming Passenger Lists, 1878–1960', Board of Trade: Commercial and Statistical Department and successors: Inwards Passenger Lists; Class: BT 26; Piece: 852; Item: 1 (Aubrey and Jane's voyage to Algiers, 28 Oct. 1926)

NATIONAL ARCHIVES, WASHINGTON

'Passenger and Crew Lists of Vessels Arriving at New York, 1897–1957', Microfilm Publication T715, 8892 rolls. NAI: 300346. Records of the Immigration and Naturalization Service, Year: 1924; Arrival: New York, New York, USA; Microfilm Serial: T715, 1897–1957; Line: 7; Page Number: 14

NATIONAL LIBRARY OF WALES, ABERYSTWYTH

Anon., 'A Tour through North Wales, 1775', MS 9279–9280A, ff. 19–21. This has been transcribed, and potentially attributed to Elizabeth Cust, by Michael David Freeman in *Early Tourists in Wales: 18th and 19th Century Tourists' Comments about Wales*: https://sublimewales.wordpress.com/attractions/snowdon/list-of-all-transcriptions/snowdon-descriptions-of-ascents-by-women/

NATIONAL RECORDS OF SCOTLAND, EDINBURGH

Death certificate: Elizabeth Sophia Bentinck, 1858, Statutory Registers: Deaths, 373/2

Sir St Vincent Keene Hawkins-Whitshed probate, 7 Nov. 1870, Edinburgh, SC/70/6/7

NEW JERSEY STATE ARCHIVES, TRENTON

Main v Main, 24 A. 1024 (Ch. Div. 1892), 18 Aug. 1892, Court of Chancery of New Jersey; *Main v Main*, 50 N.J. Eq. 712 (Ch. Div. 1892), 22 Nov. 1892, Court of Chancery of New Jersey

NEW YORK STATE ARCHIVES, ALBANY

Dale v Main, 101 N.Y. 654 (1886), Vol. 144, Series J2002–82A, New York State Court of Appeals Cases and Briefs, New York State Archives

NOTTINGHAMSHIRE ARCHIVES, NOTTINGHAM

Glass negative of painting of Lady Hawkins Whitshed (née Sophie Henriette Bentinck, 1765–1852) and her son James, by James Northcote, DD/P/6/19/18/8

PEMBROKE COLLEGE ARCHIVES, UNIVERSITY OF CAMBRIDGE

'Tennis Team, 1894', GBR/1058/COL/9/1/15/1/1894

PRINCIPAL PROBATE REGISTRY (DUBLIN PROBATE OFFICE), IRELAND

Sir St Vincent Keene Hawkins-Whitshed probate, Dublin; 19 Nov. 1870; Irish double probate sealed at Principal Registry, Jan. 1871

PRINCIPAL PROBATE REGISTRY OF ENGLAND AND WALES, LONDON

Frederick Gustavus Burnaby probate, proved 13 Apr. 1885, died 17 Jan. 1885, Principal Registry

ROYAL GEOGRAPHICAL SOCIETY, LONDON

MEC archives, Madam M. Marvingt, 13 Jun. 1919, EE Box 5, File 2, Item 35

Letter from M. Anne Bernard, to Sir Francis Younghusband, 19 Mar. 1926, EE Box 26, 'Other Correspondence – B'

ROYAL INSTITUTION, LONDON

Invitation from Elizabeth Le Blond to William Henry Bragg to join Anglo-French Luncheon Club, W. H. Bragg/11A/66; Reply: W. H. Bragg/11A/39

ST MORITZ TOBOGGANING CLUB, SWITZERLAND

Elizabeth Le Blond, photograph albums

Lottie and Tony Dod's album of photographs from Norwegian excursion, 1897 (on loan from the Dod family)

UNIVERSITY OF BRISTOL ARCHIVES, BRISTOL

Photograph of Katherine Furse racing on a bobsleigh, Additional Papers of the Symonds Family, *c.*1859–1963, DM375/1/folio 15v/4

Photograph of Madge Vaughan and Harold Freeman at the start of a toboggan race, Additional Papers of the Symonds Family, *c.*1859–1963, DM375/1/folio 7/9

UNIVERSITY OF NOTTINGHAM MANUSCRIPTS AND SPECIAL COLLECTIONS, NOTTINGHAM

Marriage settlement of Capt. James Hawkins Whitshed, RN, and Sophia Henrietta Bentinck, 23 Apr. 1793, University of Nottingham, Manuscripts and Special Collections, PI F4/5/3

Letters in French from Charlotte Sophie, Countess Bentinck, Emsbuttel, to her granddaughter Sophia Hawkins Whitshed [née Bentinck], 1790–99, Pw F 10081–10343

WELLCOME LIBRARY ARCHIVES, LONDON

'Queen Alexandra Sanatorium Fund', SA/NPT/D

WEST SUSSEX RECORD OFFICE, CHICHESTER

Letter from Elizabeth Le Blond to Leopold J. Maxse, 1929, MAXSE/480/f.221

Published Texts

AAA Foundation for Traffic Safety, *2019 Traffic Safety Culture Index* (Jun. 2020); https://aaafoundation.org/wp-content/uploads/2020/06/2019-Traffic-Safety-Culture-Index.pdf

'Abraham Le Blond', *The New Baxter Society*; https://newbaxtersociety.org/leblond.aspx

Abrahams, Adolphe, *Woman: Man's Equal?* (London, 1954)

Abrams, Cleone, '"We Wear Our Boots Just Like the Men": Women's Roles in Pacific Northwest Mountains and Society, 1890–1939', honours thesis (University of Washington, 2019)

Abramsky, Sasha, *Little Wonder: The Extraordinary Story of Lottie Dod, the World's First Female Sports Superstar* (Edinburgh, 2021)

'Access to Mountains Bill', *Hansard*, vol. 188, HC Deb (15 May 1908), c1440

Adams, Mary Louise, 'From Mixed-Sex Sport to Sport for Girls: The Feminization of Figure-Skating', *Sport in History* (2010), 30:2, 218–41

——— *Artistic Impressions: Figure Skating, Masculinity, and the Limits of Sport* (Toronto, 2011)

Adams, Trevor, *The A La Ronde Story: Its People* (2011); https://www.devonmuseums.net/includes/documents/BOOK%20%20-%20The%20people%20ver2%20COMPRESSED.doc

Agerholm, Harriet, '"Single-Sex Toilets Needed to Overcome Girls' Barriers to Education," Says Unesco', *Independent* (8 Mar. 2018); https://www.independent.co.uk/news/world/single-sex-toilets-unesco-un-international-womens-day-period-a8244776.html

Aiello, J. R., 'Human Spatial Behavior', in D. Stokols and I. Altman (eds.), *Handbook of Environmental Psychology* (New York, 1987), pp. 1359–504

Akenson, Donald Harman, *Discovering the End of Time: Irish Evangelicals in the Age of Daniel O'Connell* (Montreal and London, 2016)

Al-Gabalawy, R., C. S. Mackenzie, M. A. Thibodeau, G. J. G. Asmundson and J. Sareen, 'Health Anxiety Disorders in Older Adults: Conceptualizing Complex Conditions in Late Life', *Clinical Psychology Review* (2013), 33:8, 1096–105

All-Party Parliamentary Group for UN Women, *Prevalence and Reporting of Sexual Harassment in UK Public Spaces* (London, Mar. 2021), https://www.unwomenuk.org/site/wp-content/uploads/2021/03/APPG-UN-Women-Sexual-Harassment-Report_Updated.pdf

Alexander, Michael, *The True Blue: The Life and Adventures of Colonel Fred Burnaby, 1842–85* (London, 1957)

Allbutt, T. Clifford, 'On the Health and Training of Mountaineers', *Alpine Journal* (Aug. 1876–May 1878), 8, 30–40

'Alpine Climbing for Consumptives', *Lancashire Evening Post* (9 Jun. 1899), 3

Altintas, Evrim, and Oriel Sullivan, 'Fifty Years of Change Updated: Cross-National Gender Convergence in Housework', *Demographic Research* (2016), 35, 455–70

'American Guides to Teach Climbing to Pakistani Women this Summer', *Climbing* (16 May 2007); https://www.climbing.com/news/karakoram-tower-first-ascent-paragliding/

Anand, Anita, *Sophia: Princess, Suffragette, Revolutionary* (London, 2015)

Andersen, Jens Jakob, 'Marathon Statistics 2019 Worldwide', *RunRepeat* (6 Aug. 2021); https://runrepeat.com/research-marathon-performance-across-nations

———'Research: Women Are Better Runners than Men', *RunRepeat* (21 Sep. 2021); https://runrepeat.com/research-women-are-better-runners-than-men

Anderson, Ben, 'A Liberal Countryside? The Manchester Ramblers' Federation and the "Social Readjustment" of Urban Citizens, 1929–1936', *Urban History* (2011), 38:1, 84–102

Anderson, Dorothy, 'Baker, Valentine [*called* Baker Pasha] (1827–1887)', *Oxford Dictionary of National Biography* (Oxford, Sep. 2004; online edn, Sep. 2015)

Anderson, Eric, 'Openly Gay Athletes: Contesting Hegemonic Masculinity in a Homophobic Environment', *Gender and Society* (2002), 16:6, 860–77

Anderson, Mimi, *Beyond Impossible: From Reluctant Runner to Guinness World Record Breaker* (Chichester, 2017)

Andrew, Christopher, *Secret Service: The Making of the British Intelligence Service* (London, 1985)

Angell, Shirley, *Pinnacle Club: A History of Women Climbing* (Glasgow, 1988)

Anker, Daniel, Ursula Bauer, Markus Britschgi and Cordula Seger (eds.), *Elizabeth Main (1861–1934): Alpinist, Photographer, Writer* (Lucerne, 2003)

'The Army', *The Army and Navy Gazette* (31 Jan. 1885), 6

Ashwell, Samuel, *A Practical Treatise on the Diseases Peculiar to Women* (London, 1845)

Askwith, Richard, *Feet in the Clouds: A Tale of Fell-Running and Obsession* (London, 2004)

Asmundson, G. J., J. S. Abramowitz, A. A. Richter and M. Whedon, 'Health Anxiety: Current Perspectives and Future Directions', *Current Psychiatry Reports* (2010), 12:4, 306–12

Atkinson, Revd J. C., *Forty Years in a Moorland Parish: Reminiscences and Researches in Danby in Cleveland* (London, 1891)

Atrey, Shreya, 'Lifting as We Climb: Recognising Intersectional Gender Violence in Law', *Oñati Socio-Legal Series* (2015), 5:6, 1512–35

Austen, Jane, *Pride and Prejudice*, edited by Donald Gray (1813; New York and London, 2001)

Baden-Powell, Robert, *Scouting for Boys: A Handbook for Instruction in Good Citizenship*, edited by Elleke Boehmer (Oxford, 2004; first published 1908)

Baedeker, Karl, *Switzerland, and the Adjacent Portions of Italy, Savoy and the Tyrol. Handbook for Travellers*, 2nd edn (Coblenz, 1864), 10th edn (Leipzig, 1883), 13th edn (Leipzig, 1889), 16th edn (Leipzig, 1895)

Bailey, Jane, Asher Flynn and Nicola Henry (eds.), *The Emerald International Handbook of Technology-Facilitated Violence and Abuse* (Bradford, 2021)

Baker, W., and J. A. Mangan (eds.), *Sport in Africa: Essays in Social History* (New York, 1987)

Ballard, Jamie, 'Most Women Say They Regularly Take Steps to Avoid Being Sexually Assaulted', *YouGov America* (28 Mar. 2019); https://today.yougov.com/topics/lifestyle/articles-reports/2019/03/28/women-safety-sexual-assault-awareness

Band, George, *Summit: 150 Years of the Alpine Club* (London, 2006)

Baran, Perver K., William R. Smith, Robin C. Moore, Myron F. Floyd, Jason N. Bocarro, Nilda G. Cosco and Thomas M. Danniger, 'Park Use among Youth and Adults: Examination of Individual, Social, and Urban Form Factors', *Environment and Behavior* (2014), 46:6, 768–800

Baron, Naomi S., and Elise M. Campbell, 'Gender and Mobile Phones in Cross-National Context', *Language Sciences* (2012), 34:1, 13–27

Barrell, John, *The Idea of Landscape and the Sense of Place, 1730–1840: An Approach to the Poetry of John Clare* (Cambridge, 1972)

Barrow, Robin J., 'Rape on the Railway: Women, Safety, and Moral Panic in Victorian Newspapers', *Journal of Victorian Culture* (2015), 20:3, 341–56

Bartlett, John, John Harrington and Paul Hodgson, *Blackheath Hockey Club, 1861–2011: A Subjective History of Blackheath Hockey Club* (2011); https://s3-eu-west-1.amazonaws.com/files.pitchero.com%2Fclubs%2F23752%2FBHCSubjective History1961-2011.pdf

Barton, Susan, *Healthy Living in the Alps: The Origins of Winter Tourism in Switzerland, 1860–1914* (Manchester, 2008)

Bateman, Anthony, and Jeffrey Hill (eds.), *The Cambridge Companion to Cricket* (Cambridge, 2011)

Bauer, Carol, and Lawrence Ritt (eds.), *Free and Ennobled: Source Readings in the Development of Victorian Feminism* (Oxford and New York, 1979)

Baynton, Douglas C., *Forbidden Signs: American Culture and the Campaign against Sign Language* (Chicago and London, 1996)

Beecher, Donald, 'Concerning Sex Changes: The Cultural Significance of a Renaissance Medical Polemic', *The Sixteenth-Century Journal* (2005), 36:4, 991–1016

Bekker, Marrie H. J., 'Agoraphobia and Gender: A Review', *Clinical Psychology Review* (1996), 16:2, 129–46

Bell, Morag, and Cheryl McEwan, 'The Admission of Women Fellows to the Royal Geographical Society, 1892–1914', *Geographical Journal* (1996), 162:3, 295–312

Berinato, Scott, 'That Discomfort You're Feeling Is Grief', *Harvard Business Review* (23 Mar. 2020); https://hbr.org/2020/03/that-discomfort-youre-feeling-is-grief

Berry, David, *A People's History of Tennis* (London, 2020)

Bertrand, Gilles, 'When Travel Is for the Purpose of Inventing a New Space: The French Public Works Inspectors Posted to Italy in the Napoleonic Era', translated by Joan Johnson, *Annales Historique de la Révolution Française* (2016), 385:3, 133–52

Biasillo, Roberta, and Marco Armiero, 'The Transformative Potential of a Disaster: A Contextual Analysis of the 1882 Flood in Verona, Italy', *Journal of Historical Geography* (2019), 66, 69–80

Bindel, Julie, 'Why Are London Police Telling Women to Stay at Home?', *Spectator* (10 Mar. 2021); https://www.spectator.co.uk/article/why-are-london-police-telling-women-to-stay-at-home/

——— *Feminism for Women: The Real Route to Liberation* (London, 2021)

Bin Osman, Saleh, 'The Story of My Life', *St. Nicholas: An Illustrated Magazine for Young Folks* (Aug. 1891), 18, 795–8

Birch, Herbert George, and Joan Dye Gussow, *Disadvantaged Children: Health, Nutrition and School Failure* (New York, 1970)

Bird Bishop, Isabella, *A Lady's Life in the Rocky Mountains* (London, 1879)

——— *Unbeaten Tracks in Japan* (London, 1880)

——— *The Golden Chersonese and the Way Thither* (1883; Cambridge, 2010)

——— *Among the Tibetans* (1894; London, 2019)

——— *Korea and Her Neighbours : A Narrative of Travel, with an Account of the Recent Vicissitudes and Present Position of the Country* (London, 1898)

———*The Yangtze Valley and Beyond : An Account of Journeys in China, Chiefly in the Province of Sze Chuan and Among the Man-Tze of the Somo Territory* (London, 1899)

Birkett, Bill, and Bill Peascod, *Women Climbing: 200 Years of Achievement* (London, 1989)

Birley, Derek, *Sport and the Making of Britain* (Manchester, 1993)

'Birnam', *Dundee Advertiser* (16 Mar. 1871), 4

Birnie, Lionel, and Ellis Bacon (eds.), *The Cycling Anthology*, Vol. 1 (London, 2014)

Blond, Stéphane J. L., 'The Trudaine Atlas: Government Road-Mapping in Eighteenth-Century France', *Imago Mundi: The International Journal for the History of Cartography* (2013), 65:1, 64–79

Bloomer, Amelia, *The Life and Writings of Amelia Bloomer* (Boston, 1895)

Blum, Arlene, *Annapurna: A Woman's Place* (1980; Berkeley, 2015)

Blunden, John, and Nigel Curry (eds.), *A People's Charter?: Forty Years of the National Parks and Access to the Countryside Act 1949* (London, 1989)

Boase, Tessa, *Mrs Pankhurst's Purple Feather: Fashion, Fury and Feminism – Women's Fight for Change* (London, 2018)

Boehmer, Elleke, 'At Once A-Sexual and Anal: Baden-Powell and the Boy Scouts', in George Rousseau (ed.), *Children and Sexuality: From the Greeks to the Great War* (Basingstoke, 2007), pp. 299–311

Booth, Alison, 'Gender, Risk and Competition', *Vox EU* (14 Sep. 2009); https://voxeu.org/article/gender-risk-and-competition-experimental-evidence-environmental-influences

Bordewich, Fergus M., *Bound for Canaan: The Underground Railroad and the War for the Soul of America* (New York, 2005)

Bosen, Ralph, 'Violence against Women Occurs Mostly at Home', *DW* (25 Nov. 2018); https://www.dw.com/en/violence-against-women-occurs-mostly-at-home/a-46439823

Botta, Renée A., and Lynne Fitzgerald, 'Gendered Experiences in the Backcountry', *Journal of Outdoor Recreation, Education and Leadership* (2020), 12:1, 27–40

Bowes, Ali, Lucy Lomax and Jessica Piasecki, 'A Losing Battle? Women's Sport Pre- and Post-COVID-19', *European Sport Management Quarterly* (2021), 21:3, 443–61

Bowman, Cynthia Grant, 'Street Harassment and the Informal Ghettoization of Women', *Harvard Law Review* (1993), 106:3, 517–80

Brady, Martha, 'Creating Safe Spaces and Building Social Assets for Young Women in the Developing World: A New Role for Sports', *Women's Studies Quarterly* (2005), 33:1–2, 35–49

Briggs, Eva, 'My Adventures on the Appalachian Trail', *55 Plus: For Active Adults in Upstate New York* (15 Oct. 2016); http://www.cny55.com/features/my-adventures-on-the-appalachian-trail/

'Bristol University College', *Western Daily Press* (21 Nov. 1879), 6

Brown, Lyn Mikel, and Carol Gilligan, *Meeting at the Crossroads: Women's Psychology and Girls' Development* (New York, 1992)

Brown, Rebecca A., *Women on High: Pioneers of Mountaineering* (Boston, 2002)

Brunn, Stanley D. (ed.), *Engineering Earth: The Impacts of Mega-Engineering Projects*, 3 vols. (London and New York, 2011)

Buman, Matthew P., Britton W. Brewer, Allen E. Cornelius, Judy L. Van Raalte and Albert J. Petitpas, 'Hitting the Wall in the Marathon: Phenomenological Characteristics and Associations with Expectancy, Gender and Running History', *Psychology of Sport & Exercise* (2008), 9:2, 177–90

Burgdorf, Marcia Pearce, and Robert Burgdorf Jr, 'A History of Unequal Treatment: The Qualifications of Handicapped Persons as a Suspect Class under the Equal Protection Clause', *Santa Clara Law Review* (1975), 15:4, 855–910

Burke, Edmund, *A Philosophical Enquiry into the Origin of Our Ideas of the Sublime and Beautiful*, edited by Adam Phillips (1757; Oxford, 1990)

Burkeman, Oliver, 'Dirty Secret: Why Is There Still a Housework Gender Gap?', *Guardian* (17 Feb. 2018); https://www.theguardian.com/inequality/2018/feb/17/dirty-secret-why-housework-gender-gap

Burman, B., 'Racing Bodies: Dress and Pioneer Women Aviators and Racing Drivers', *Women's History Review* (2000), 9:2, 299–326

Burnaby, Elizabeth – for all Lizzie's publications, including those under her first married name, see 'Le Blond, Elizabeth'

Burnaby, Frederick, *On Horseback through Asia Minor* (London, 1877)

———*A Ride to Khiva: Travels and Adventures in Central Asia* (London, 1877)

———*A Ride Across the Channel, and Other Adventures in the Air* (London, 1882)

———*Our Radicals: A Tale of Love and Politics* (London, 1886)

Burrells, Anna, Steve Ellis, Deborah Parsons and Kathryn Simpson (eds.), *Woolfian Boundaries: Selected Papers from the Sixteenth Annual International Conference on Virginia Woolf* (Clemson, S.C., 2007)

Burton, Isabel, *The Life of Captain Sir Richard Burton*, 2 vols (London, 1893)

Busk, Rachel Harriette, *The Valleys of Tirol: Their Traditions and Customs and How to Visit Them* (London, 1874)

Butler, Ruth, and Sophia Bowlby, 'Bodies and Spaces: An Exploration of Disabled People's Experiences of Public Space', *Environment and Planning D: Society and Space* (1997), 15:4, 411–33

Cahn, Susan K., 'From the "Muscle Moll" to the "Butch" Ballplayer: Mannishness, Lesbianism, and Homophobia in US Women's Sport', *Feminist Studies* (1993), 19:2, 343–68

Caine, Barbara, *English Feminism, 1780–1980* (Oxford, 1997)

Cantrell, Mrs John Blackwell, *Melodies from the Mountains* (London, 1861)

Captain, Gwendolyn, 'Enter Ladies and Gentlemen of Color: Gender, Sport, and the Ideal of African American Manhood and Womanhood during the Late Nineteenth and Early Twentieth Centuries', *Journal of Sport History* (1991), 18:1, 81–102

'Captain R. C. Gore to Miss Rachel C. Saunderson', *Gentlewoman* (22 Jul. 1899), 43

Caron, Ernest, 'Chronique du Club', *Annuaire du Club Alpin Française* (1889)

Carpenter, Linda Jean, and R. Vivian Acosta, *Women in Intercollegiate Sport: A Longitudinal National Study, Twenty-Nine Year Update, 1977–2006* (West Brookfield, Mass., 2006)

Carson, Jennifer, 'Sexism and the Stars', *Science* (20 Mar. 2020), 367:6484, 1311

Carter, Elizabeth, and Montagu Pennington, *Memoirs of the Life of Mrs Elizabeth Carter*, 4th edn, 2 vols (London, 1825)

Carter, Neil, *Medicine, Sport and the Body: A Historical Perspective* (London, 2012)

Casey, Meghan M., Rochelle M. Eime, Warren R. Payne and Jack T. Harvey, 'Using a Socioecological Approach to Examine Participation in Sport and Physical Activity among Rural Adolescent Girls', *Qualitative Health Research* (2009), 19:7, 881–93

Catlow, Agnes and Maria, *Sketching Rambles; or, Nature in the Alps and Apennines* (London, 1861)

Cavendish-Bentinck, William Arthur, *Men, Women and Things: Memories of the Duke of Portland* (London, 1937)

CEQUIN (Centre for Equity and Inclusion), *Perception and Experience of Gendered Violations in Public Places in Delhi: Baseline Report*, (New Delhi, Nov. 2009); https://cequinindia.org/wp-content/uploads/2018/01/PerceptionandExperience.pdf

Chakelian, Anoosh, 'Are UK Police Forces Institutionally Misogynistic?', *New Statesman* (17 Mar. 2021); https://www.newstatesman.com/politics/uk-politics/2021/03/are-metropolitan-uk-police-cressida-dick-sarah-everard-institutionally-misogynist-vigil

Chamberlin, Silas, *On the Trail: A History of American Hiking* (New Haven and London, 2016)

Chamonix: Le Mauvais Pas (film footage from 1900); https://www.youtube.com/watch?v=UsVJKymRrPc

Chandler, Tertius, Gerald Fox and Lewis Mumford, *3000 Years of Urban Growth* (New York and London, 1974)

'The Charge against Colonel Valentine Baker', *Evening Mail* (25 Jun. 1875), 7

'Charge of Assaulting a Female Pedestrian', *Nottinghamshire Guardian* (24 Jun. 1881), 6

Chhabria, Pooja, 'Why Many Women in India Refuse Water during a Heatwave', *BBC News* (5 Jul. 2018); https://www.bbc.co.uk/news/world-asia-india-44613522

Choudhury, Nishat, 'Research Finds That 97% of Women in the UK Have Been Sexually Harassed', *Open Access Government* (11 Mar. 2021); https://www.openaccessgovernment.org/97-of-women-in-the-uk/105940/

Christopherson, Ingrid (ed.), *To Heaven's Heights: An Anthology of Skiing in Literature* (Greensboro, N.C., 2021)

Christofi, Elena, Yuliya Samboryk and Jonathan Bernabe, 'Men's Participation in Feminine Sports', presentation, John Jay College of Criminal Justice, City University of New York; https://www.jjay.cuny.edu/sites/default/files/content-groups/sasp/poster_gallery/poster13.pdf

Clark, Ronald W., *The Early Alpine Guides* (London, 1949)

———*The Victorian Mountaineers* (London, 1953)

———*An Eccentric in the Alps: The Story of the Rev. W. A. B. Coolidge, the Great Victorian Mountaineer* (London, 1959)

Cleghorn, Elinor, *Unwell Women: A Journey through Myth and Medicine in a Man-Made World* (London, 2021)

Clennett, Margaret, *Presumptuous Pinnacle Ladies: A Selection from the Early Journals of Britain's First Women's Rock Climbing Club* (Disley, 2009)

Clift, Stephen, and Simon Forrest, 'Gay Men and Tourism: Destinations and Holiday Motivations', *Tourism Management* (1999), 20:5, 615–25

'Climbing in the Arctic Circle', *English Lakes Visitor and Keswick Guardian*, (1 Oct. 1898), 6

Coffey, Maria, *Fragile Edge: Loss on Everest* (London, 2003)

Cole, Mrs Henry Warwick, *A Lady's Tour around Monte Rosa* (London, 1859)

Coleridge, Samuel Taylor, *The Notebooks of Samuel Taylor Coleridge*, edited by Kathleen Coburn, 5 vols (London, 1957)

Coletti, Jennifer T., Veronica Allan and Luc J. Martin, 'Reading Between the Lines: Gender Stereotypes in Children's Sport-Based Books', *Women in Sport and*

Physical Activity (2021), 29:1, 1–11; https://journals.humankinetics.com/view/journals/wspaj/29/1/article-p1.xml

Colley, Ann C., *Victorians in the Mountains: Sinking the Sublime* (Burlington, V.T., 2010)

Collier, Mary, *The Woman's Labour: An Epistle to Mr. Stephen Duck* (London, 1739)

Collins, Tracy J. R., 'Athletic Fashion, "Punch", and the Creation of the New Woman', *Victorian Periodicals Review* (2010), 43:3, 309–35

'Colonel Fred Burnaby at Home', *Leicester Chronicle* (22 Jul. 1882), 13

Colston, Marianne, *Journal of a Tour in France, Switzerland and Italy, during the Years 1819, 20 and 21* (Paris, 1822)

Colvile, Capt. Henry E., *A Ride in Petticoats and Slippers* (London, 1880)

Conefrey, Mick, *How to Climb Mt Blanc in a Skirt: A Handbook for the Lady Adventurer* (Richmond, 2011)

Connley, Courtney, 'The US Open Awards Men and Women Equal Prize Money – But Tennis Still Has a Pay Gap', *CNBC* (11 Sep. 2019); https://www.cnbc.com/2019/09/11/despite-equal-grand-slam-tournement-prizes-tennis-still-has-a-pay-gap.html

Conolly, John, 'Description and Treatment of Puerperal Insanity', Lecture XIII: 'Clinical lectures on the principal forms of insanity, delivered in the Middlesex lunatic-asylum at Hanwell', *Lancet*, (28 Mar. 1846), 1:1178, 349–54

'Conservative and Unionist Suffrage Meeting', *The Queen*, (27 Feb. 1909), 360

Conway, William Martin, 'Alpine Notes: Review of the Alpine Club's Annual Picture Exhibition', *Alpine Journal* (Aug. 1886–May 1888), 13, 175–6

———'New Routes in 1886, and the Question of New Routes in General', *Alpine Journal* (Aug. 1886–May 1888), 13, 161–6

Cooky, Cheryl, LaToya D. Council, Maria A. Mears and Michael A. Messner, 'One and Done: The Long Eclipse of Women's Televised Sports, 1989–2019', *Communication & Sport* (2021), 9:3, 347–71

Coolidge, William Augustus Brevoort, 'Explorations amongst the Cottian Alps', *Alpine Journal* (Aug. 1880–May 1882), 10, 123

———'Alpine Notes', *Alpine Journal* (Aug. 1882–May 1884), 11, 242–3

———'New Expeditions: Stubaithal District', *Alpine Journal* (Aug. 1884–May 1886), 12, 124–5

[Coolidge, William Augustus Brevoort], 'Proceedings of the Alpine Club', *Alpine Journal* (Aug. 1880–May 1882), 10, 239

Copeland, J., *Roads and Their Traffic, 1750–1850* (Newton Abbot, 1968)

Corbett, Catra, *Reborn on the Run: My Journey from Addiction to Ultramarathons* (New York, 2018)

Costa, Marco, 'Interpersonal Differences in Group Walking', *Journal of Nonverbal Behavior* (2010), 34:1, 15–26

'County Wicklow Church Defence', *Wicklow News-Letter and County Advertiser* (4 Jul. 1868), 1

Cowley, Bill, 'A Cleveland Farmer's Diary, from Goulton Grange and Glaisdale Head Farms', *Dalesman* (Aug. 1955), 17:5, 245–7

———'A Cleveland Farmer's Diary', *Dalesman* (Nov. 1955), 17:8, 408–10

———*Lyke Wake Walk and the Lyke Wake Way* (Clapham, 1988)

Craig, Malcolm, *Shackles of Convention: Women Mountaineers before 1914* (Ammanford, 2013)

Crawford, Mary, 'Mountain Climbing for Women', *Canadian Alpine Journal* (1909), 2, 86–91

Cregan-Reid, Vybarr, *Footnotes: How Running Makes Us Human* (London, 2016)

Criado Perez, Caroline, *Invisible Women: Exposing Data Bias in a World Designed for Men* (London, 2019)

Cripps, Suzy (ed.), *The Joy of Walking* (London, 2020)

Cuk, Ivan, Pantelis Theodoros Nikolaidis and Beat Knechtle, 'Sex Differences in Pacing during Half-Marathon and Marathon Race', *Research in Sports Medicine* (2020), 28:1, 111–20

Cullen, Lynsey T., 'The First Lady Almoner: The Appointment, Position, and Findings of Miss Mary Stewart at the Royal Free Hospital, 1895–99', *Journal of the History of Medicine and Allied Sciences* (2013), 68:4, 551–82

Cumming, Constance Frederica Gordon, *From the Hebrides to the Himalayas: A Sketch of Eighteen Months' Wanderings in Western Isles and Eastern Highlands* (London, 1876)

———*In the Himalayas and on the Indian Plains* (London, 1884)

———*Memories* (London, 1904)

Cunningham, C. D., 'The Decline of Chamonix as a Mountaineering Centre', *Alpine Journal* (Aug. 1882–May 1884), 11, 459–71

Cunningham, C. D., and W. de W. Abney, *The Pioneers of the Alps* (London, 1887)

Cunningham, John, 'Interview: On the Foundation and Character of the Creag Dhus', *Mountain* (1971), 14, 24–9

Curl, Jordyn, and Elizabeth Cobb, 'Biographical Sketch of Mary P. Burrill', *Alexander Street* (2018); https://search.alexanderstreet.com/view/work/bibliographic_entity%7Cbibliographic_details%7C3957480

Curry, Jane Kathleen, *Nineteenth-Century American Women Theatre Managers* (Westport, Conn., 1994)

'Cuttings from Society Papers', *Lichfield Mercury* (26 Aug. 1881), 8

Daamen, Winnie, and Serge Hoogendoorn, 'Controlled Experiments to Derive Walking Behaviour', *European Journal of Transport and Infrastructure Research* (2003), 3:1, 39–59

Dabbs, James M., 'Sex, Setting, and Reactions to Crowding on Sidewalks', *Proceedings of the Annual Convention of the American Psychological Association* (1972), 7:1, 205–6

Dabbs, James M., and Neil A. Stokes, 'Beauty Is Power: The Use of Space on the Sidewalk', *Sociometry* (1975), 38:4, 551–7

Dangar, D. F. O., and T. S. Blakeney, 'The Rise of Modern Mountaineering and the Formation of the Alpine Club, 1854–1865', *Alpine Journal* (1957), 62, 17

D'Angeville, Henriette, *My Ascent of Mont Blanc*, translated by Jennifer Barnes (London, 1992)

Darke, Karen, *If You Fall . . . It's a New Beginning* (Winchester, 2006)

Dart, Jon, and Stephen Wagg (eds.), *Sport, Protest and Globalisation: Stopping Play* (London, 2016)

Davenport, Romola J., 'Mortality, Migration and Epidemiological Change in English Cities, 1600–1870', *International Journal of Paleopathology* (2021), 34, 37–49

Davenport-Hines, Richard, 'Browning, Oscar (1837–1923)', *Oxford Dictionary of National Biography* (Sep. 2004; online edn, Jan. 2008)

Davidoff, Leonore, and Catherine Hall, *Family Fortunes: Men and Women of the English Middle Class, 1780–1850* (London, 1987)

Davies, Pete, 'Football: Tough Test for the Team England Forgot', *Independent* (6 Oct. 1994); https://www.independent.co.uk/sport/football-tough-test-for-the-team-england-forgot-as-england-s-women-prepare-for-their-biggest-ever-fixture-and-the-game-continues-to-flourish-at-club-level-the-fa-s-commitment-to-the-grassroots-is-being-questioned-pete-1441525.html

Davis, Deirdre, 'The Harm That Has No Name: Street Harassment, Embodiment, and African American Women', *UCLA Women's Law Journal* (1994), 4:2, 133–78

'Day to Day in Liverpool', *Liverpool Mercury* (23 May 1894), 6

De Coubertin, Pierre, 'Causerie du Samedi', *Sports Athlétiques* (13. Feb. 1892), 3

———'Forty Years of Olympism, 1894–1934', pp. 742–6 in Pierre de Coubertin, *Pierre de Coubertin, 1863–1937: Olympism – Selected Writings*, edited by Norbert Müller (Lausanne, 2000)

———'Les Femmes aux Jeux Olympiques', *Revue Olympique* (Jul. 1912), 79, 109–11, in translation as 'The Women at the Olympic Games' in *Pierre de Coubertin*, Pierre de Coubertin, pp. 711–13

———'The Philosophic Foundation of Modern Olympism', in Pierre de Coubertin, *Pierre de Coubertin*, pp. 580–83.

'The Death Has Occurred . . . of Captain Royston Le Blond', *South Eastern Gazette* (1 Jun. 1915), 7

Della Croce, Marco, 'Stamáta Revíthi: Melpomene o la Maratona Negata', *Storie di Sport* (2019); http://www.storiedisport.it/?p=10430

Dent, Clinton Thomas, *Above the Snow Line: Mountaineering Sketches between 1870 and 1880* (London, 1885)

DePauw, Karen P., 'The (In)Visibility of DisAbility: Cultural Contexts and "Sporting Bodies"', *Quest* (1997), 49:4, 416–30

Désir, Alison Mariella, *Running While Black: Finding Freedom in a Sport That Wasn't Built for Us* (London, 2022)

Deville, Nancy, 'Needles, Not Knives, to Treat Sports Injuries and Degeneration', *The Three Tomatoes: The Insider's Guide for Women Who Aren't Kids* (15 Sep. 2015); https://www.thethreetomatoes.com/needles-not-knives-to-treat-sports-injuries-and-degeneration

Dhanapala, Sam, 'An Overview of the Sportswear Market', in Steven George Hayes and Praburaj Venkatraman (eds.), *Materials and Technology for Sportswear and Performance Apparel* (Boca Raton, Fla., 2016), pp. 1–22

Di Blasio, Sonja, Louena Shtrepi, Giuseppina Emma Puglisi and Arianna Astolfi, 'A Cross-Sectional Survey on the Impact of Irrelevant Speech Noise on Annoyance, Mental Health and Well-Being, Performance and Occupants' Behavior in Shared and Open-Plan Offices', *International Journal of Environmental Research and Public Health* (2019), 16:2, 280

Di Leonardo, Micaela, 'Political Economy of Street Harassment', *Aegis* (1981), 51–7

'Diana', 'Sports and Sportswomen', *Gentlewoman* (2 Aug. 1890), 20

Dickens, Charles, 'Hardihood and Foolhardihood', *All the Year Round* (19 Aug. 1865), 14, 85–7

———'Foreign Climbs', *All the Year Round* (2 Sep. 1865), 14, 135–7

Diethe, Carol, *Nietzsche's Women: Beyond the Whip* (Berlin and New York, 1996)

Digby, A., 'Women's Biological Straitjacket', in Susan Mendus and Jane Rendall (eds.), *Sexuality and Subordination: Interdisciplinary Studies of Gender in the Nineteenth Century* (London, 1989), pp. 192–220

Dixie, Florence, *Across Patagonia* (London, 1880)

Djordjevic, Milos, '20+ Mind-Blowing Sportswear Industry Statistics: How the Pandemic Affected the Numbers', *Fashion Discounts* (18 Mar. 2022); https://fashiondiscounts.uk/sportswear-industry-statistics/

'D.M.N', 'Book Review: *Lady Margaret Hall*', *Vote* (2 May 1924), 6

Dockrill, Michael L., *British Establishment Perspectives on France, 1936–40* (Basingstoke, 1999)

Dollman, James and Nicole R. Lewis, 'The Impact of Socioeconomic Position on Sport Participation among South Australian Youth', *Journal of Science and Medicine in Sport* (May 2010), 13:3, 318–22

Doughan, David, and Peter Gordon, *Women, Clubs and Associations in Britain* (Oxford, 2006)

Douglas, Mary, and Aaron Wildavsky, *Risk and Culture: An Essay on the Selection of Technological and Environmental Dangers* (Berkeley, 1983)

Dowie, Ménie 'Mary' Muriel, *A Girl in the Karpathians* (London, 1891)

Dronsart, Marie, *Les Grandes Voyageuses* (Paris, 1894)

Du Mont, Janice, Maryam Woldeyohannes, Sheila Macdonald, Daisy Kosa and Linda Turner, 'A Comparison of Intimate Partner and Other Sexual Assault Survivors' Use of Different Types of Specialized Hospital-Based Violence Services', *BMC Women's Health* (2017), 17, 59

Duis, Perry R., and Cathlyn Schallhorn, 'Chicago', *Encyclopedia Britannica* (online edn, 17 Dec. 2021); https://www.britannica.com/place/Chicago

Duncan, Isabelle, *Skirting the Boundary: A History of Women's Cricket* (London, 2013)

Dunning, Eric, and Dominic Malcolm (eds.), *Sport: Critical Concepts in Sociology, Volume III: Sport and Power Relations* (London, 2003)

Dworkin, Andrea, 'Pornography and Grief', speech given in San Francisco in 1978, in *Letters from a War Zone* (Atlanta, 1993), pp. 19–26

Dyhouse, Carol, 'Troubled Identities: Gender and Status in the History of the Mixed College in English Universities since 1945', *Women's History Review* (2003), 12:2, 169–94

———*Girls Growing up in Late Victorian and Edwardian England* (London, 2012)

Dyos, Harold James, and Derek Howard Aldcroft, *British Transport: An Economic Survey from the Seventeenth Century to the Twentieth* (Harmondsworth, 1974)

'Early Winter on the Continent', *Aberdeen Press and Journal* (22 Oct. 1879), 6

Edgeworth, Maria, *Belinda*, edited by Kathryn J. Kirkpatrick (1801; Oxford, 1994)

'Editor's Table', *The Knickerbocker; or, New York Monthly Magazine* (Dec. 1850), 36, 571

'Editor's Trip: Co. Wicklow, Killincarrick', *Irish Farmer's Gazette and Journal of Practical Horticulture* (31 Jan. 1863), 10

Edwards, Amelia B., *Untrodden Peaks and Unfrequented Valleys: A Midsummer Ramble in the Dolomites* (London, 1873)

Edwards, Emory, *Modern American Marine Engines, Boilers and Screw Propellers* (Philadelphia, 1881)

Eliot, T. S., *The Waste Land and Other Poems* (1940; London, 1972)

'Elizabeth Hawkins-Whitshed', *Wikipedia*; https://en.wikipedia.org/wiki/Elizabeth_Hawkins-Whitshed

Ellenberger, Nancy W., 'The Souls and London "Society" at the End of the Nineteenth Century', *Victorian Studies* (1982), 25:2, 133–60

Ellmann, Lucy, 'Why Can't Women Be More Like Men, and Enjoy Failing?', *Independent* (12 Jan. 1997); https://www.independent.co.uk/voices/why-can-t-women-be-more-like-men-and-enjoy-failing-1282832.html

Elrick, Gail, 'Obituary of Ann Sayer', *LDWA* (17 Apr. 2020); https://ldwa.org.uk/news/news_story.php?news_id=587

'Emma', *The Mental Load: A Feminist Comic* (New York, 2018)

Emsley, Clive, Tim Hitchcock and Robert Shoemaker, 'London History: A Population History of London', *Old Bailey Proceedings Online*, version 7.0: www.oldbaileyonline.org

Engel, Claire-Elaine, 'Early Lady Climbers', *Alpine Journal* (1943), 54, 51–9

'English Ramblers', *The Daily News*, Perth, Western Australia (16 Jun. 1931), 1

Epstein, David, *The Sports Gene: Talent, Practice and the Truth about Success* (London, 2014)

Ernie-Steighner, Jennifer A., 'Beyond the Summit: Traversing the Historical Landscape of Annie S. Peck's and Fanny Bullock Workman's High-Altitude Ascents, 1890–1915', MA thesis (Miami University, 2009)

Esson, Dylan Jim, 'Selling the Alpine Frontier: The Development of Winter Resorts, Sports, and Tourism in Europe and America, 1865–1941', PhD thesis (University of California, Berkeley, 2011)

'Fancy Dress Ball', *Alpine Post* (13 Jan. 1900)

'Fancy Dress Ball', *St Moritz Post and Davos News* (7 Jan. 1888) 164

'Farmer's Death on a Rick', *Gloucestershire Echo* (19 Sep. 1907), 3

Farr, Martin, and Xavier Guégan (eds.), *The British Abroad since the Eighteenth Century*, 2 vols (Basingstoke, 2013)

Farr, William, *Appendix to the Second Annual Report of the Registrar-General of Births, Deaths, and Marriages, in England, 1838–1839*, BPP 1840 XVII, p. 37

Fazackerley, Anna, 'Women's Research Plummets during Lockdown – But Articles from Men Increase', *Guardian* (12 May 2020); https://www.theguardian.com/education/2020/may/12/womens-research-plummets-during-lockdown-but-articles-from-men-increase

'A Female Pedestrian', *Morning Post* (30 Jun. 1874), 6

'The Female Pedestrian at Darlington', *Northern Echo* (15 Dec. 1876), 4

'A Female Pedestrian Carrier of Long Standing', *Hereford Times* (25 Nov. 1848), 5

Finch, Robert (ed.), *Norton Book of Nature-Writing* (New York and London, 2002)

Finison, Lorenz, *Boston's Cycling Craze, 1880–1900: A Story of Race, Sport, and Society* (Amherst, Mass., 2014)

'The First Lady Mountaineer', *Alpine Post* (1 Sep. 1897), 21:23, 303

Fletcher, Sheila, *Women First: The Female Tradition in English Physical Education* (London, 1984)

Foner, Eric, *Gateway to Freedom: The Hidden History of the Underground Railroad* (New York and London, 2015)

Ford, Joseph, *Some Reminiscences and Folk Lore of Danby Parish and District* (Whitby, 1953)

Forgays, Deborah Kirby, Ira Hyman and Jessie Schreiber, 'Texting Everywhere for Everything: Gender and Age Differences in Cell Phone Etiquette and Use', *Computers in Human Behavior* (2014), 31, 314–21

'Forthcoming Cattle Sales', *Gloucestershire Chronicle* (22 Apr. 1922), 6

Fox, Hubert (ed.), *Marion Fox: Quaker* (London, 1951)

Freedman, Paul, 'Women and Restaurants in the Nineteenth-Century United States', *Journal of Social History* (2014), 48:1, 1–19

Freeman, Michael David, *Early Tourists in Wales: 18th and 19th Century Tourists' Comments about* Wales; https://sublimewales.wordpress.com/attractions/snowdon/list-of-all-transcriptions/snowdon-descriptions-of-ascents-by-women/

'Fremdenliste von Davos', *Davoser Blätter* (13 Sep. 1884), 32, 3–4

[Freshfield, Douglas W.], 'Review of Walter White's *On Foot through Tyrol* and *Holidays in Tyrol*', *Alpine Journal* (Aug. 1876–May 1878), 8, 119

Freshfield, Jane, *Alpine Byways; or, Light Leaves Gathered in 1859 and 1860* (London, 1861) (published under 'A Lady')

———*A Summer Tour in the Grisons and Italian Valleys of the Bernina* (London, 1862) (published under Mrs Henry Freshfield)

Freud, Sigmund, *The Standard Edition of the Complete Psychological Works of Sigmund Freud,* Vol. XIX (1923–25), translated by James Strachey, in collaboration with Anna Freud, Alix Strachey and Alan Tyson (1961; London, 2001), especially 'The Ego and the Id' (1923), pp. 3–68

———*Beyond the Pleasure Principle and Other Writings*, translated by John Reddick, edited by Adam Phillips (London, 2003), especially 'Inhibition, Symptom, and Fear' (1926), pp. 151–240

Fried, Y., S. Melamed and H. A. Ben-David, 'The Joint Effects of Noise, Job Complexity, and Gender on Employee Sickness Absence: An Exploratory Study across 21 Organizations – The CORDIS Study', *Journal of Occupational and Organizational Psychology* (2002), 75:2, 131–44

Gaillard, Emile, *Une Ascension Romantique en 1838: Henriette d'Angeville au Mont Blanc* (Chambéry, 1947)

Gardien, Claude, translated by Katie Ives, 'Jean-Esteril Charlet and Mary Isabella Straton: A Fairy Tale', *Alpinist* (16 Jun. 2015), 50; http://www.alpinist.com/doc/ALP50/77-mountain-profile-the-aguille-du-drus-1871-1925

Garner, Bill, *Born in a Tent: How Camping Makes Us Australian* (Sydney, 2013)

Gaskell, Elizabeth, *North and South* (1855; London, 2008)

Gavin, Hector, *The Unhealthiness of London and the Necessity of Remedial Measures* (London, 1847)

'Gender and Road Traffic Injuries', *Gender and Health* (Geneva, Jan. 2002); https://apps.who.int/iris/bitstream/handle/10665/68887/a85576.pdf

'Gentlemen Only, Ladies Forbidden: A History', *Women's Golf Journal* (1 Aug. 2017); https://womensgolfjournal.com/golf/women-banned-golf/

George, Rose, *The Big Necessity: Adventures in the World of Human Waste* (London, 2008)

'G.H.P.', 'Young Women as Journalists', *Girls' Own Paper* (21 Mar. 1891), 395–6

Gibson, Harry, *Tobogganing on Crooked Runs* (London, 1894)

Gibson, Owen, 'R&A Golf Club Ends 260-Year Ban on Women Members', *Guardian* (18 Sep. 2014); https://www.theguardian.com/sport/2014/sep/18/royal-and-ancient-golf-club-women-ban

Gifford, Terry, 'Early Women Mountaineers Achieve Both Summits and Publication in Britain and America', in Teresa Gómez Reus and Terry Gifford (eds.), *Women in Transit through Literary Liminal Spaces* (Basingstoke, 2013), pp. 91–106

Gigerenzer, Gerd, Zeno Swijtink, Theodore Porter, Lorraine Daston, John Beatty and Lorenz Krüger, *The Empire of Chance: How Probability Changed Science and Everyday Life* (Cambridge, 1989)

Gilder, Lucy, and Jennifer Clarke, 'How Many Violent Attacks and Sexual Assaults on Women Are There?', *BBC News* (20 Mar. 2021); https://www.bbc.co.uk/news/explainers-56365412

'Gloucestershire Chamber of Agriculture', *Cheltenham Chronicle* (7 Jun. 1919), 5

'Gloucestershire Root, Fruit and Grain Society Annual Show: Potatoes', *Gloucestershire Chronicle* (10 Nov. 1917), 5

Glover, Tim, and Hugh Mellor, 'Obituary: Joyce Wethered', *Independent* (21 Nov. 1996); https://www.independent.co.uk/news/obituaries/obituary-joyce-wethered-1295292.html

Godwin, William, 'On Avarice and Profusion', in *The Enquirer: Reflections on Education, Manners and Literature, in a Series of Essays* (London, 1797)

Goffman, Erving, *Relations in Public: Microstudies of the Public Order* (New York, 1971)

Golson, Hodges L., and James M. Dabbs, 'Line-Following Tendencies among Pedestrians: A Sex Difference', *Personality and Social Psychology Bulletin* (1974), 1:1, 16–18

Goodwin, R. D., C. Faravelli, S. Rosi, E. Truglia, R. de Graaf, and H. U. Wittchen, 'The Epidemiology of Panic Disorder and Agoraphobia in Europe', *European Neuropsychopharmacology* (2005), 15:4, 435–43

Gooley, Tristan, *The Natural Navigator* (London, 2010)

———*The Walker's Guide to Outdoor Clues and Signs: Their Meaning and the Art of Making Predictions and Deductions* (London, 2014)

Goulstone, J., *Smock Racing* (Erith, 2005)

Grande, Julian, 'Swiss Alpine Club: Jubilee Celebrations in Lucerne', *Sheffield Daily Telegraph* (15 Sep. 1913), 6

Grant, Anne MacVicar, *Letters from the Mountains: Being the Real Correspondence of a Lady, between the Years 1778 and 1803* (London, 1806)

The Greater Manchester Coalition of Disabled People, *A Brief History of Disabled People's Self-Organisation* (Manchester, 2010)

Greaves, John Neville, 'The Last of the Railway Kings: The Life and Work of Sir Edward Watkin, 1819–1901', PhD thesis (Durham University, 2002; http://etheses.dur.ac.uk)

Green, Karen, 'Urban Innkeepers, Their Inns and Their Role in the Economic and Cultural Life of Leeds and York, 1720–1860', MA thesis (University of York, 2015)

Greenwood, Rosemary, 'A Grindelwald Centenary', *Alpine Journal* (1992–3), 97, 198–9

Gribble, Francis, 'Lady Mountaineers', *The Lady's Realm* (Oct. 1897), 2:12, 684–7

Griffin, Emma, *England's Revelry: A History of Popular Sports and Pastimes, 1660–1830* (Oxford, 2005)

Griffin, Susan, *Woman and Nature: The Roaring Inside Her* (Berkeley, 1978)

Griffiths, Kerry, 'Women in the Hills: A Literature Review on Women's Participation in Outdoor Sport and Physical Activity in Rural Areas', Sheffield Hallam Sports Industry Research Centre and Women in the Hills Research Network (Jan. 2022; unpublished at the time of going to press; will later be available via the Women in the Hills website and in future project outputs)

Gronim, Sara Sidstone, 'What Jane Knew: A Woman Botanist in the Eighteenth Century', *Journal of Women's History* (2007), 19:3, 33–59

Grosz, Elizabeth, *Volatile Bodies: Towards a Corporeal Feminism* (London, 1994)

Gugglberger, Martina, 'Climbing beyond the Summits: Social and Global Aspects of Women's Expeditions in the Himalayas', *International Journal of the History of Sport* (2015), 32:4, 597–613

Gupte, Manjushe, 'Gender, Feminist Consciousness, and the Environment: Exploring the "Natural" Connection', *Women and Politics* (2002), 24:1, 47–62

Hagan, Lisa Kindleberger, and Janet Kuebli, 'Mothers' and Fathers' Socialization of Preschoolers' Physical Risk Taking', *Journal of Applied Developmental Psychology* (2007), 28:1, 2–14

Hailu, Ruth, 'Fitbits and Other Wearables May Not Accurately Track Heart Rates in People of Color', *Stat* (24 Jul. 2019); https://www.statnews.com/2019/07/24/fitbit-accuracy-dark-skin/

Haley, Andrew P., *Turning the Tables: Restaurants and the Rise of the American Middle Class, 1880–1920* (Chapel Hill, N.C., 2011)

Hall, Edward T., *The Hidden Dimension* (1966; New York, 1969)

Hall, Harry, *The Pedestriennes: America's Forgotten Superstars* (Indianapolis, 2014)

Hall, Jenny, 'Women Mountaineers: A Study of Affect, Sensoria and Emotion', PhD thesis (York St John University, 2018)

Hall, M. Ann, *Feminism and Sporting Bodies: Essays on Theory and Practice* (Champaign and Leeds, 1996)

Hall, Mrs Marshall, 'Zermatt and the New Weissthor in 1849', *Alpine Journal* (Aug. 1878–May 1880), 9, 173

Hallman, Kelly K., Nora J. Kenworthy, Judith Diers, Nick Swan and Bashi Devnarain, 'The Shrinking World of Girls at Puberty: Violence and Gender-Divergent Access to the Public Sphere among Adolescents in South Africa', *Global Public Health* (2015), 10:3, 279–95

Hambleton, Brittany, 'British Runner Sets Guinness World Record for Most Consecutive Marathons', *Canadian Running* (13 Apr. 2022); https://runningmagazine.ca/the-scene/british-runner-sets-guinness-world-record-for-most-consecutive-marathons/

Hamed, Mohammed M., 'Analysis of Pedestrians' Behavior at Pedestrian Crossings', *Safety Science*, 38:1 (2001), 63–82

Hamilton, Michelle, 'Running While Female', *Runner's World* (8 Aug. 2017); https://www.runnersworld.com/training/a18848270/running-while-female/

Hamilton, Mrs, 'A Lady's Ascent of Mont Blanc', *Leader* (1854), 5, 845

'The Handsome Family', *The Trades Club* (8 Mar. 2018); https://thetradesclub.com/events/the-handsome-family

Hankinson, Alan, *Geoffrey Winthrop Young: Poet, Mountaineer, Educator* (London, 1995)

Hanlon, Sheila, 'Ladies Cycling Clubs: The Politics of Victorian Women's Bicycling Associations', *sheilahanlon.com* (15 Sep. 2015); http://www.sheilahanlon.com/?p=1889

Hansen, Peter H., 'Albert Smith, the Alpine Club, and the Invention of Mountaineering in Mid-Victorian Britain', *Journal of British Studies* (1995), 34:3, 300–24

———'Le Blond [*née* Hawkins-Witshed], Elizabeth Alice Frances (1860–1934)', *Oxford Dictionary of National Biography* (Oxford, Sep. 2004; online edn, Oct. 2006)

Harding, J. G. R., 'The Other Anne Lister', *Alpine Journal* (2019), 123, 234–40

Hargreaves, Jennifer, 'Playing Like Gentlemen While Behaving Like Ladies: Contradictory Features of the Formative Years of Women's Sport', *International Journal of the History of Sport* (1985), 2:1, 40–55

———'Taking Men on at Their Games', in Eric Dunning and Dominic Malcolm (eds.), *Sport: Critical Concepts in Sociology, Volume III: Sport and Power Relations* (London, 2003), pp. 147–56

Harper, Joanna, Emma O'Donnell, Behzad Sorouri Khorashad, Hilary McDermott and Gemma L. Witcomb 'How Does Hormone Transition in Transgender Women Change Body Composition, Muscle Strength and Haemoglobin? Systematic Review with a Focus on the Implications for Sport Participation', *British Journal of Sports Medicine* (2021), 55:15, 865–72

Harper, Stephen, *Lady Killer Peak* (London, 1965)

Harrant, Valérie, and Nicolas G. Vaillant, 'Are Women Less Risk Averse than Men? The Effect of Impending Death on Risk-Taking Behavior', *Evolution and Human Behavior* (2008), 29:6, 396–401

Hartley, James Walker, 'Aiguille du Géant', *Alpine Journal* (Aug. 1882–May 1884), 11, 302

Havergal, Frances, *Swiss Letters and Alpine Poems*, edited by J. M. Crane (London, 1881)

Hawker, Lizzy, *Runner: A Short Story about a Long Run* (London, 2015)

Hawkins, John, *Fred: The Collected Letters and Speeches of Colonel Frederick Gustavus Burnaby*, 2 vols. (Solihull, 2014)

Hayes, Nick, *The Book of Trespass: Crossing the Lines That Divide Us* (London, 2020)

Hayes, Steven George, and Praburaj Venkatraman (eds.), *Materials and Technology for Sportswear and Performance Apparel* (Boca Raton, Fla., 2016)

Healey, Edna, 'Coutts, Angela Georgina Burdett-, *suo jure* Baroness Burdett-Courts (1814–1906)', *Oxford Dictionary of National Biography* (Oxford, Sep. 2004; online edn, Jan. 2012)

Heffernan, Michael, 'The Limits of Utopia: Henri Duveyrier and the Exploration of the Sahara in the Nineteenth Century', *Geographical Journal* (1989), 155:3, 342–52

———'Shifting Sands: The Trans-Saharan Railway,' in Stanley D. Brunn (ed.), *Engineering Earth: The Impacts of Mega-Engineering Projects*, Vol. 1 (London and New York, 2011) pp. 617–26

Heggie, Vanessa, 'Long before the Paralympics There Was the Deaflympics', *Guardian* (5 Sep. 2012); https://www.theguardian.com/science/the-h-word/2012/sep/05/paralympics-deaflympics

———'Bodies, Sport and Science in the Nineteenth Century', *Past & Present* (2016), 231:1, 169–200

Helms, Karey, '"Do You Have to Pee?": A Design Space for Intimate and Somatic Data', *DIS '19: Proceedings of the 2019 ACM Designing Interactive Systems Conference* (New York, 2019), 1209–222

Henderson, Karla A., M. Deborah Bialeschki, Susan M. Shaw and Valeria J. Freysinger, *Both Gains and Gaps: Feminist Perspectives on Women's Leisure* (State College, Pa., 1996)

Henderson, L. F., and D. J. Lyons, 'Sexual Differences in Human Crowd Motion', *Nature* (1972), 240, 353–5

Henderson, William, *Notes on the Folk-Lore of the Northern Counties of England and the Borders* (London, 1879)

Heshka, Stanley, and Yona Nelson, 'Interpersonal Speaking Distance as a Function of Age, Sex and Relationship', *Sociometry* (1972), 35:4, 491–8

Hewitt, Rachel, *Map of a Nation: A Biography of the Ordnance Survey* (London, 2010)

———*A Revolution of Feeling: The Decade That Forged the Modern Mind* (London, 2017)

———*Repeating Patterns in the Street Harassment of Women*, BBC Radio 4 (25 Apr. 2021); https://www.bbc.co.uk/programmes/m000vk7s

Hewitt, Rachel, Jonathan Freedland and Tom Alban, *The Long View: Violence against Women in Public Spaces*, BBC Radio 4 (22 Jun. 2021); https://www.bbc.co.uk/programmes/m000x69z

'Hey's Ladies of Bradford, the Forgotten Football Champions of Yorkshire', *Yorkshire Coast History*; https://yorkshirecoasthistory.wordpress.com/home/heys-ladies-of-bradford-the-forgotten-football-champions-of-yorkshire/

Hickey, Georgina, 'Barred from the Barroom: Second Wave Feminists and Public Accommodations in US Cities', *Feminist Studies* (2008), 34:3, 308–408

'The High Alps in Winter', *The Times* (18 Jul. 1883), 5

'High Sheriffs for 1865', *Wexford People* (19 Nov. 1864), 4

Hill, Erin M., 'Noise Sensitivity and Diminished Health: The Role of Stress-Related Factors', PhD thesis (Auckland University of Technology, 2012); https://core.ac.uk/download/pdf/56363435.pdf

Hill, Howard, *Freedom to Roam: The Struggle for Access to Britain's Moors and Mountains* (Ashbourne, 1980)

Hilton, Emma N., and Tommy Lundberg, 'Transgender Women in the Female Category of Sport: Perspectives on Testosterone Suppression and Performance Advantage', *Sports Medicine* (2021), 51, 199–214

Hingston, James, *Guide for Excursionists from Melbourne: Dedicated to All in Search of Health, Recreation and Pleasure* (Melbourne, 1898)

Hirthler, George, 'Celebrating Pierre de Coubertin: The French Genius of Sport Who Founded the Modern Olympic Games' (2 Sep. 2019); https://www.

olympic.org/news/celebrating-pierre-de-coubertin-the-french-genius-of-sport-who-founded-the-modern-olympic-games

Hlavka, Heather R., 'Normalizing Sexual Violence: Young Women Account for Harassment and Abuse', *Gender & Society* (Jun. 2014), 28:3, 337–506

Hochschild, Arlie Russell, *The Second Shift* (1989; revised edition, London, 2012).

Holmes, Katie, 'Diane Leather and the 5 Minute Mile', *Run Young 50* (8 Mar. 2018); https://runyoung50.co.uk/diane-leather-and-the-5-minute-mile/

'Home and Domestic', *Illustrated Weekly News* (28 Sep. 1867), 2

hooks, bell, *Ain't I a Woman: Black Women and Feminism* (London, 1981)

Hornby, Emily, *A Tour in the Alps of Dauphiné and A Tour in the Carpathians* (Liverpool, 1906)

———*Mountaineering Records; Tour of the Alps of Dauphiné; A Tour in the Carpathians* (Liverpool, 1907)

Hornibrook, T., E. Brinkert, D. Parry, R. Seimens, D. Mitten and S. Priest, 'The Benefits and Motivations of All Women Outdoor Programs', *Journal of Experiential Education* (1997), 20:3, 152–8

'Horse Guards Ball in London', *Hermann Advertiser and Advertiser-Courier* (18 Aug. 1800), 8

Hübner, Stefan, 'Muscular Christianity and the Western Civilizing Mission', *Diplomatic History* (2015), 39:3, 532–56

Hunt, Arnold, 'Who Wants to Be a Millionaire? Angela Burdett-Coutts and the Man Who Wouldn't Go Away', *Untold Lives Blog*, British Library, 7 Feb. 2014; https://blogs.bl.uk/untoldlives/2014/02/who-wants-to-be-a-millionaire-angela-burdett-coutts-and-the-man-who-wouldnt-go-away.html

Hynes, Samuel Lynn, *The Edwardian Turn of Mind* (Princeton, N.J., 1968)

'Important Sale at Gloucester', *Gloucestershire Echo* (22 May 1922), 3

Inbar, Ohad, Gesche Joost, Fabian Hemmert, Talya Porat and Noam Tractinsky, 'Tactful Calling: Investigating Asymmetric Social Dilemmas in Mobile Communications', *Behavior and Information Technology* (2014), 33:12, 1317–32

'Infantine Female Pedestrian', *Salisbury and Winchester Journal* (21 Jul. 1823), 2

Ingala Smith, Karen, *Defending Women's Spaces* (London, 2022)

Ingle, Sean, 'Jasmin Paris Becomes First Woman to Win 268-Mile Montane Spine Race', *Guardian* (17 Jan. 2019); https://www.theguardian.com/sport/2019/jan/17/jasmin-paris-first-woman-win-gruelling-286-mile-montane-spice-race-ultrarunning

Irwin, M. R., M. Daniels, S. C. Risch, E. Bloom and H. Weiner, 'Plasma Cortisol and Natural Killer Cell Activity during Bereavement', *Biological Psychiatry* (1988), 24:2, 173–8

Isserman, Maurice, *Continental Divide: A History of American Mountaineering* (New York and London, 2016)

Jack, Dana Crowley, *Silencing the Self: Women and Depression* (Cambridge, Mass., 1991)

Jackson, Mrs E. P., 'A Winter Quartette', *Alpine Journal* (Aug. 1888–Nov. 1889), 14, 200–10

——— 'Winter Mountaineering in 1888', *Yorkshire Ramblers' Club Journal* (1903), 2, 97

Jackson, Monica, and Elizabeth Stark, *Tents in the Clouds: The First Women's Himalayan Expedition* (London, 1957)

Jahncke, Helena, Staffan Hygge, Niklas Halin, Anne Marie Green and Kenth Dimberg, 'Open-Plan Office Noise: Cognitive Performance and Restoration', *Journal of Environmental Psychology*, edited by Richard Lansdown, (2011), 31:4, 373–82

Jallat, Denis, and Sébastien Stumpp, 'French Sailing in the Late Nineteenth Century and the Debate about Parisian Centralism', *French History* (2015), 29:4, 550–70

James, Henry, *The Bostonians*, edited by Richard Lansdown (1886; London, 2000)

James, Jamie, *Pagan Light: Dreams of Freedom and Beauty in Capri* (London, 2020)

James, Kandy, '"You Can *Feel* Them Looking at You": The Experiences of Adolescent Girls at Swimming Pools', *Journal of Leisure Research* (2000), 32:2, 262–80

——— '"I Just Gotta Have My Own Space!": The Bedroom as a Leisure Site for Adolescent Girls', *Journal of Leisure Research* (2001), 33:1, 71–90

James, Tori, *Peak Performance: The First Welsh Woman to Climb Everest* (Cardiff, 2013)

Janssen, Megan, 'Trail Races Continue Making Strides toward Gender Equality', *Trailrunner* (22 Apr. 2019); https://www.trailrunnermag.com/races/buzz-updates-races/trail-races-continue-making-strides-toward-gender-equality/

Jarvis, Robin, *Romantic Writing and Pedestrian Travel* (Basingstoke, 1997)

Javed, Saman, '"Keep Your Whereabouts to Yourself!": Women Discuss Whether It Is Safe to Share Running Routes Online', *Independent* (16 Jun. 2021); https://www.independent.co.uk/life-style/women/run-social-media-women-strava-b1866880.html

'Jill on the Jaunt', *The Ruc-Sac: For Men and Women Lovers of the Open* (Jul. 1931), 1:1, 21–2

Johansson, Klara, Lucie Laflamme and Miriam Eliasson, 'Adolescents' Perceived Safety and Security in Public Space: A Swedish Focus Group Study with a Gender Perspective', *Young* (2012), 20:1, 69–88

John, Emma, 'Where Are All the Great Books about Women in Sport?', *Guardian* (28 Jul. 2017); https://www.theguardian.com/books/2017/jul/28/where-are-the-great-books-about-women-in-sport

Jones, Bethany Alice, Jon Arcelus, Walter Pierre Bouman and Emma Haycraft, 'Sport and Transgender People: A Systematic Review of the Literature Relating to Sport Participation and Competitive Sport Polices', *Sports Medicine* (2017), 47:4, 701–16

Jones, Jeffrey S., Barbara N. Wynn, Boyd Kroeze, Chris Dunnuck and Linda Rossman, 'Comparison of Sexual Assaults by Strangers versus Known Assailants in a Community-Based Population', *American Journal of Emergency Medicine* (2004), 22:6, 454–9

Jordan, Jennifer, *Savage Summit: The Life and Death of the First Women of K2* (New York, 2005)

Kaarlela-Tuomaala, A., R. Helenius, E. Keskinen and V. Hongisto, 'Effects of Acoustic Environment on Work in Private Office Rooms and Open-Plan Offices: Longitudinal Study during Relocation', *Ergonomics* (2009), 52:11, 1423–44

Kaya, Naz, and Feyzan Erkip, 'Invasion of Personal Space under the Condition of Short-Term Crowding: A Case Study on an Automatic Teller Machine,' *Journal of Environmental Psychology* (1999), 19:2, 183–9

Kearl, Holly, *Stop Street Harassment: Making Public Places Safe and Welcoming for Women* (Santa Barbara, 2010)

———*Unsafe and Harassed in Public Places: A National Street Harassment Report* (Reston, 2014)

Keyes, Allison, 'Harriet Tubman, an Unsung Naturalist, Used Owl Calls as a Signal on the Underground Railroad', *Audubon Magazine* (25 Feb. 2020); https://www.audubon.org/news/harriet-tubman-unsung-naturalist-used-owl-calls-signal-underground-railroad

Kimberley, Hannah, *A Woman's Place Is at the Top: A Biography of Annie Smith Peck, Queen of the Climbers* (New York, 2017)

Kimmerer, Robin Wall, *Braiding Sweetgrass: Indigenous Wisdom, Scientific Knowledge and the Teachings of Plants* (2013; London, 2020)

King, Revd S. W., *The Italian Valleys of the Pennine Alps: A Tour through all the Romantic and Less Frequented 'Vals' of Northern Piedmont* (London, 1858)

King, Sherilyne J., 'Crags and Crinolines', *Hypoxia: Women at Altitude*, Tenth Biennial Hypoxia Symposium, Lake Louise, Canada (18–22 Feb. 1997), 134–8

Kirby, Joanna, Kate A. Levin and Jo Inchley, 'Socio-Environmental Influences on Physical Activity among Young People: a Qualitative Study', *Health Education Research* (2013), 28:6, 954–69

Kirk-Greene, Anthony, 'Imperial Administration and Athletic Imperative: The Case of the District Officer in Africa', in W. Baker and J. A. Mangan (eds.), *Sport in Africa: Essays in Social History* (New York, 1987), pp. 81–113

Klein, Melanie, 'Mourning and Its Relation to Manic-Depressive States' (1940), in Melanie Klein, *Love, Guilt and Reparation, and Other Works, 1921–1945* (New York, 1975), pp. 344–69

———*Love, Guilt and Reparation, and Other Works, 1921–1945* (New York, 1975)

Knowles, E. S., 'Boundaries around Social Space: Dyadic Responses to an Invader', *Environment and Behavior* (1972), 4:4, 437–45

Knox, Alexander A., *The New Playground; or, Wanderings in Algeria* (London, 1881)

Kropp, Phoebe, 'Wilderness Wives and Dishwashing Husbands: Comfort and the Domestic Arts of Camping in America, 1880–1910', *Journal of Social History* (2009), 43:1, 5–30

LaBastille, Anne, *Woodswoman* (New York, 1976)

'A Ladies' Alpine Club', *Daily Telegraph and Courier* (17 Aug. 1907), 5

'Ladies' Letter', *Surrey Gazette* (5 Jun. 1900), 7

'Ladies' Reserved Railway Carriages', *Brechin Advertiser* (6 Jul. 1875), 4

'Lady Cyclist Effigy at the Cambridge University Protest, 1897', SheilaHanlon.com (16 Apr. 2011); http://www.sheilahanlon.com/?p=292

'A Lady Mountaineer in Norway', *Lake's Falmouth Packet and Cornwall Advertiser* (16 Sep. 1899), 2

'A Lady's London Letter', *Cheltenham Examiner* (4 Feb. 1885), 2

Lake, Robert J., 'Gender and Etiquette in British Lawn Tennis, 1870–1939: A Case Study of "Mixed Doubles"', *International Journal of the History of Sport* (2012), 29:5, 691–710

Lamb, Sharon, and Lyn Mikel Brown, *Packaging Girlhood: Rescuing Our Daughters from Marketers' Schemes* (New York, 2006)

'Land League Hunts', *Derry Journal* (9 Jan. 1882) 5

Landreth, Jenny, *Swell: A Waterbiography* (London, 2017)

Langelan, Martha, *Back Off! How to Confront and Stop Sexual Harassment and Harassers* (New York, 1993)

Langhamer, Claire., *Women's Leisure in England, 1920–1960* (Manchester, 2000)

Langseth, Tommy and Øyvind Salvesen, 'Rock Climbing, Risk and Recognition', *Frontiers in Psychology* (2018), 9, 1793

Lankester, Edwin Ray, *Degeneration: A Chapter in Darwinism* (London, 1880)

Larcom, Lucy, *A New England Girlhood, Outlined from Memory* (Boston, 1889)

Lascelles, Rowley, *Sketch of a Descriptive Journey through Switzerland* (Berne, 1796)

'The Latest Photography', *Lloyd's Weekly Newspaper* (25 Sep. 1898), 2

Law, William, *A Serious Call to a Devout and Holy Life* (London, 1729)

Lawrence, Clyde, 'The Chaperon', *Topeka Daily State Journal* (27 Jul. 1909), 4

Le Blond, Mrs Aubrey – for all Lizzie's publications, including those under her third married name, see 'Le Blond, Elizabeth'

Le Blond, Elizabeth, *The High Alps in Winter; or, Mountaineering in Search of Health* (London, 1883) (published under Elizabeth Burnaby)

———'Wetterhorn: Descent by the Renfen Glacier', *Alpine Journal* (Feb. 1890–Nov. 1891), 15, 369–70 (published under Mrs Main)

———*High Life and Towers of Silence* (London, 1886) (published under Elizabeth Main)

———'Over Mont Blanc from Courmayeur to Chamounix', *St Moritz Post* (7 Dec. 1886), 1–3

———'An Ascent of the Gross Glockner', *The Hour Glass* (Feb. 1887), chapter 2 (published under Mrs Main and Mrs Fred Burnaby)

———'Winter in the Engadine' (published under Mrs Main), *Graphic* (2 Mar. 1887), 6

———'The Engadine in Winter', *St James's Gazette* (24 Oct. 1889), 6 (published under Elizabeth Main)

———*Cities and Sights of Spain: A Handbook for Tourists* (1899; London, 1904) (published under Mrs Aubrey Le Blond (Mrs Main))

———*My Home in the Alps* (London, 1892) (published under Elizabeth Main)

———*Hints on Snow Photography* (London, 1894/5) (published under Mrs Main)

———'The Frozen Lakes of the Engadine', *Black and White Budget* (6 Dec. 1902), 331 (published under Mrs Aubrey Le Blond)

———*True Tales of Mountain Adventure* (London, 1903) (published under Mrs Aubrey Le Blond)

———'Alpine Winter Photography', *The Queen* (4 Feb. 1905), 53

———'The Coveted Lyngen Fjord', *The Queen* (5 Aug. 1905), 48

———*The Art of Garden Design in Italy* (London, 1906) (authored by Henry Inigo Triggs, 'with twenty-eight plates from photographs by Mrs Aubrey Le Blond')

———*Adventures on the Roof of the World* (London, 1907) (published under Mrs Aubrey Le Blond (Mrs Main))

———*The Story of an Alpine Winter* (London, 1907) (published under Mrs Aubrey Le Blond)

———*Mountaineering in the Land of the Midnight Sun* (London, 1908)

———*Charlotte Sophie Countess Bentinck: Her Life and Times, 1715–1800* (London, 1912) (published under Mrs Aubrey Le Blond)

———*The Old Gardens of Italy: How to Visit Them* (London, 1912) (published under Mrs Aubrey Le Blond)

———*The Autobiography of Charlotte Amélie, Princess of Aldenburg, née Princess de la Trémöille, 1652–1732*, translated and edited by Mrs Aubrey Le Blond (London, 1913)

———'Germany Will Never "Give" ', *Daily Mail* (19 Mar. 1923), 8 (published under E. Le Blond)

———'In Memoriam: Miss Katherine [sic] Richardson (1854–1927)', *Alpine Journal* (1928), 40, 160–2

———*Day In, Day Out* (London, 1928) (published under Mrs Aubrey Le Blond)

———*The Dunkelgraf Mystery*, authored by O. V. Maeckel 'with the collaboration of Mrs Aubrey Le Blond' (London, 1929)

———*Intimate Letters from Tonquin*, authored by Louis Hubert Gonzalve Lyautey, translated by Mrs Aubrey Le Blond (London, 1932)

LeBlanc, Mitch, 'Leadville 2011 Data Analysis', *mitchleblanc.com* (28 Jul. 2012); http://www.mitchleblanc.com/2012/07/leadville-2011-data-analysis/

Lee, Katharine, *In the Alsatian Mountains: A Narrative of a Tour in the Vosges* (London, 1883)

Lee, Maurice S., *Uncertain Chances: Science, Skepticism, and Belief in Nineteenth-Century American Literature* (New York, 2012)

Lennartz, Karl, 'Two women ran the marathon in 1896', *Citius, Altius, Fortius* (1994), 2:1, 19–20; https://library.olympics.com/Default/doc/SYRACUSE/2288307/two-women-ran-the-marathon-in-1896-by-karl-lennartz

Lerner, Gerda (ed.), *Black Women in White America: A Documentary History* (New York, 1972)

Lewis, Helen, *Difficult Women: A History of Feminism in 11 Fights* (London, 2020)

Lewis, Tiffany, 'The Mountaineering and Wilderness Rhetorics of Washington Woman Suffragists', *Rhetoric and Public Affairs* (2018), 21:2, 279–316

Lichtenstein, Grace, 'Himalayan Scaling Called an Inspiration to Women', *New York Times* (11 Nov. 1978), 8

Linden, Andrew D., 'American Football and the 1970s Women's Movement', *Sport in American History* (29 May 2014); https://ussporthistory.com/2014/05/29/american-football-and-the-1970s-womens-movement-3/

Lindon, Heather L., Lauren M. Gardiner, Abigail Brady and Maria S. Vorontsova, 'Fewer than Three Percent of Land Plant Species Named by Women: Author Gender over 260 Years', *Taxon* (2018), 64:2, 209–15

Ling, R., and P. Pedersen (eds.), *Mobile Communications: Renegotiation of the Social Sphere* (London, 2005)

Light, Rob, 'Cricket in the Eighteenth Century', in Anthony Bateman and Jeffrey Hill (eds.), *The Cambridge Companion to Cricket* (Cambridge, 2011), pp. 26–40

Lippincott, Sarah Jay, *Haps and Mishaps of a Tour in Europe* (London, 1854)

'The List of Killed and Wounded', *Portsmouth Evening News* (22 Jan. 1885), 3

'Local Government (England and Wales) Bill: Second Reading', *Hansard*, HC Deb (13 Apr. 1888), vol. 324, cc1210–86

Lombroso, Cesare, *Criminal Man*, edited and translated by Mary Gibson and Nicole Hahn Rafter (Durham, N.C., 2006)

'London Notes', *Daily Gazette for Middlesbrough* (24 Jan. 1885), 2

Loretta, Ashley, 'Trend Alert: More Women Are Running Races than Men, Brilliant!', *Gone Runners* (8 Jul. 2020); https://gonerunners.com/full-blog-posts/f/trend-alert-more-women-are-running-races-than-men-brilliant

Louie, Siri Winona, 'Gender in the Alpine Club of Canada, 1906–1940', MA thesis (University of Calgary, 1996)

Loukaitou-Sideris, Anastasia, and Athanasios Sideris, 'What Brings Children to the Park? Analysis and Measurement of the Variables Affecting Children's Use of Parks', *Journal of the American Planning Association* (2009), 76:1, 89–107

Love, Steve, and Joanne Kewley, 'Does Personality Affect Peoples' Attitudes towards Mobile Phone Use in Public Places?', in R Ling and P. Pedersen (eds.), *Mobile Communications: Renegotiation of the Social Sphere* (London, 2005), pp. 273–84

Lovesey, Peter, 'Women Behaving Madly'; http://www.vrwc.org.au/tim-archive/articles/wo-ada-anderson.pdf

Lovett, Lorcan, 'Yangon Puts "Girl Power" into Green Spaces', *Nikkei Asia* (28 Aug. 2019); https://asia.nikkei.com/Editor-s-Picks/Tea-Leaves/Yangon-puts-girl-power-into-green-spaces

Lucrezi, Gina, 'Women's versus Men's Pay in Trail and Ultrarunning', *I Run Far* (26 Apr. 2017); https://www.irunfar.com/womens-versus-mens-pay-in-trail-and-ultrarunning

Lugard, Frederick, *The Dual Mandate in British Tropical Africa* (London, 1922)

Lumpkin, Angela, 'The Contributions of Women to the History of Competitive Tennis in the United States (1874–1974)', PhD thesis (Ohio State University, 1974)

Lund, John W., 'Historical Impacts of Geothermal Resources on the People of North America', *Geo-Heat Center Quarterly Bulletin* (1995), 16:4, 7–14

Lyautey, Louis Hubert Gonzalve, *Intimate Letters from Tonquin*, translated by Mrs Aubrey Le Blond (London, 1932)

McAllister, Pam, 'Wolf Whistles and Warnings', *Heresies* (1978), 6, 37

McCarter, Christy, 'Overlooking Her Shot: Women's Sports Need an Assist as Coverage Remains the Same as 30 Years Ago', *Purdue University News* (24 Mar. 2021); https://www.purdue.edu/newsroom/releases/2021/Q1/overlooking-her-shot-womens-sports-need-an-assist-as-coverage-remains-the-same-as-30-years-ago.html

McCarthy, Helen, *Women of the World: The Rise of the Female Diplomat* (London, 2014)

McCarty, J. W., and C. B. Schedvin (eds.), *Australian Capital Cities: Historical Essays* (Sydney, 1978)

McCaskill, Steve, '"We've Got to Keep Pushing Forward": Why Greater Media Coverage of Women's Sport Will Provide the Platform for Equality', *Sports Pro Media* (31 Mar. 2022); https://www.sportspromedia.com/categories/broadcast-ott/media-rights/womens-sport-media-tv-equality-dazn-ata-football-togethxr/

McCrone, Kathleen E., *Playing the Game: Sport and the Physical Emancipation of English Women, 1870–1914* (London, 1988)

McDermott, L., 'Exploring Intersections of Physicality and Female-Only Canoeing Experiences', *Leisure Studies* (2004), 23:3, 283–301

McDonald, Bernadette, *Keeper of the Mountains: The Elizabeth Hawley Story* (Toronto, 2012)

McDougald, Elise Johnson, 'The Double Task: The Struggle of Negro Women for Sex and Race Emancipation', *Survey Graphic* (Mar. 1926), 6

McElwee, Molly, 'Outnumbered or Not, Sportswomen Are Leading the Way in Addressing Racism Worldwide', *Telegraph* (12 Jun. 2020); https://www.

telegraph.co.uk/womens-sport/2020/06/12/outnumbered-not-sportswomen-leading-way-addressing-racism-worldwide/

McElwee, Molly, Fiona Tomas, Tom Garry and Oliver Brown, 'Revealed: The True Scale of How Women's Sport Was Left Behind in Lockdown', *Telegraph* (23 Mar. 2021); https://www.telegraph.co.uk/sport/2021/03/23/revealed-true-scale-womens-sport-left-behind-lockdown/

MacLachlan, Jill Marie, 'Peak Performances: Cultural and Autobiographical Constructions of the Victorian Female Mountaineer', PhD thesis (Vancouver, 2004)

Mackay, Finn, *Radical Feminism: Feminist Activism in Movement* (Basingstoke, 2015)

McKay, George, *Radical Gardening: Politics, Idealism and Rebellion in the Garden* (London, 2013)

[Mackenzie, Georgina Muir and Adeline Paulina Irby], *Across the Carpathians* (London, 1862)

McKenzie, Precious, *The Right Sort of Woman: Victorian Travel Writers and the Fitness of an Empire* (Newcastle upon Tyne, 2012)

McKim, Richard, 'A Different Sort of Society', *Astronomy & Geophysics* (2016), 57:4, 4.14–17

McMahan, Ian, 'The Physiological Differences between Male and Female Runners', *Podium Runner* (8 Oct. 2015); https://www.podiumrunner.com/training/the-physiological-differences-between-male-and-female-runners/

[MacMorland, Elizabeth], *Davos-Platz: A New Alpine Resort for Sick and Sound in Summer and Winter* (London, 1878)

McNee, Alan, *The New Mountaineer in Late Victorian Britain: Materiality, Modernity and the Haptic Sublime* (Cham, Switzerland, 2017)

McNuff, Anna, *The Pants of Perspective: One Woman's 3,000 Kilometre Running Adventure through the Wilds of New Zealand* (published by the author, 2017)

'A Magic Lantern Exhibition', *Alpine Post* (12 Feb. 1898), 22, 176–7

Main, Elizabeth – for all Lizzie's publications, including those under her second married name, see 'Le Blond, Elizabeth'

Main, John Frederic, 'The Upper Engadine in Winter', *Fortnightly Review* (1885), 43, 168–76

———'Note on Some Experiments on the Viscosity of Ice', *Proceedings of the Royal Society of London* (1887), 42, 491–501

Maksimow, Peter, 'Tips for Women on the Trails: Introducing Helen Stuart', *American Trail Running Association* (15 May 2017); https://trailrunner.com/trail-news/tips-women-trails-introducing-helen-stuart/

Malcomson, A. P. W., *The Pursuit of the Heiress: Aristocratic Marriage in Ireland, 1740–1840* (revised edn, Belfast, 2006 ; first published 1982)

Manek, Nish, 'Olympics Marathon: Why Women Could Make for Better Endurance Athletes than Men', *Science Focus* (6 Sep. 2021); https://www.sciencefocus.com/the-human-body/women-endurance-sports/

Mann, R. K., *The Life, Adventures and Political Opinions of F. G. Burnaby* (London, 1882)

Manthorne, Katherine, *Women in the Dark: Female Photographers in the US, 1850–1900* (Atglen, Pa., 2020)

Marcus, David K., and Shelly E. Church, 'Are Dysfunctional Beliefs about Illness Unique to Hypochrondriasis?', *Journal of Psychosomatic Research* (2003), 54:6, 543–7

Marland, Hilary, *Dangerous Motherhood: Insanity and Childbirth in Victorian Britain* (Basingstoke, 2004)

'Marriages', *Galloway News and Kirkcudbright Advertiser* (2 Apr. 1886), 5

'Marriages in High Life', *Brighton Gazette* (30 Dec. 1858), 8

Mathews, Charles Edward, 'The Growth of Mountaineering', *Alpine Journal* (Aug. 1880–May 1882), 10, 251–63

Matthews, Peter, *House of Spies: St Ermin's Hotel, the London Base of British Espionage* (Stroud, 2016)

Maxfield, Sylvia, and Mary Shapiro, 'Gender and Risk: Women, Risk Taking and Risk Aversion', *Gender in Management: An International Journal* (2010), 25:7, 586–604

Mayfield, Ben, 'Access to the Countryside: The Tragedy of the House of Commons', *Legal Studies* (2017), 37:2, 343–62

Mazel, David (ed.), *Mountaineering Women: Stories by Early Climbers* (College Station, Tex., 1994)

Mazuchelli, Elizabeth Sarah, *The Indian Alps, and How We Crossed Them: Being a Narrative of Two Years' Residence in the Eastern Himalaya and Two Months' Tour into the Interior* (London, 1876) (published under 'A Lady Pioneer')

Mendus, Susan, and Jane Rendall (eds.), *Sexuality and Subordination: Interdisciplinary Studies of Gender in the Nineteenth Century* (London, 1989)

Menzies-Pike, Catriona, *The Long Run: A Memoir of Loss and Life in Motion* (New York, 2016)

Mertens, Lieze, Jelle Van Cauwenberg, Jenny Veitch, Benedicte Deforche and Delfien Van Dyck, 'Differences in Park Characteristic Preferences for Visitation and Physical Activity among Adolescents: A Latent Class Analysis', *PLOS One* (2019), 14:3, 1–16

Merz, Johanna (ed.), *Index to the Ladies' Alpine Club Year-Books, 1910–1975* (London, 2000)

Meschke, Jacob, 'Back-of-the-Pack London Marathoners Say They Were Shamed for Being "Fat" and "Slow"', *Runner's World* (7 May 2019); https://www.runnersworld.com/news/a27367110/london-marathon-slower-runners-bullied/

———'In Spain, a Young Woman's Killing Galvanizes Women to Assert Their Freedom to Run', *Runner's World* (22 Jul. 2019); https://www.runnersworld.com/women/a28368894/running-as-a-woman-in-spain/

'Metropolitan Notes', *Nottingham Evening Post* (23 Jan. 1885), 2

Metzler, Brian, 'Courtney Dauwalter Breaks UTMB Record to Win', *Trail Runner* (30 Aug. 2021); https://www.trailrunnermag.com/people/courtney-dauwalters-record-breaking-utmb/

Michael, T., U. Zetsche and J. Margraf, 'Epidemiology of Anxiety Disorders', *Psychiatry* (2007), 6:4, 136–42

Midorikawa, Emily, and Emma Claire Sweeney, *A Secret Sisterhood: The Hidden Friendships of Austen, Brontë, Eliot and Woolf* (London, 2017)

Milroy, Andy, 'In the Beginning: Native Americans', *UltraRunning Magazine* (15 Aug. 2013); https://ultrarunning.com/features/destinations/in-the-beginning-native-americans/

Milsom, Marjorie, 'The Ladies' Alpine Club', *Listener* (28 Nov. 1957), 881–2

Miragaya, Ana, 'Female Olympians in the Early Olympic Games (1900–12) through the Minutes of the IOC Sessions, Official Reports of Olympic Games, and Other Documents Found at the Olympic Museum: A Tribute', paper submitted to the Postgraduate Research Grant Program, Museum and Olympic Studies Centre, IOC, Switzerland (2005); http://www.sportsinbrazil.com.br/artigos/female_olympians.pdf

'Miscellaneous Dottings', *Shields Daily Gazette* (16 Feb. 1880), 5

Moffat, Gwen, *Space Below My Feet* (London, 1961)

Montaño, Alysia, and Lindsay Crouse, 'Nike Told Me to Dream Crazy, Until I Wanted a Baby', *New York Times* (12 May 2019); https://www.nytimes.com/2019/05/12/opinion/nike-maternity-leave.html

Montgomery, Ben, *Grandma Gatewood's Walk: The Inspiring Story of the Woman Who Saved the Appalachian Trail* (Chicago, 2014)

Montgomery, Janey Weinhold, *A Comparative Analysis of the Rhetoric of Two Negro Women Orators: Sojourner Truth and Frances E. Watkins Harper*, Fort Hays Studies Literature Series, 6 (Hays, Kans., 1968)

Montgomery, Jordan E., Casey L. Chaviano, Allison D. Rayburn and Lenore M. McWey, 'Parents At-Risk and Their Children: Intersections of Gender Role Attitudes and Parenting Practices', *Child & Family Social Work* (2017), 22:3, 1151–60

A Monthly Bulletin (Supplement): Adolescents in Public Houses (London, Aug. 1942), Warwick Digital Collections, 420/BS/4/41/1

Moon, Brenda, *More Usefully Employed: Amelia B. Edwards, Writer, Traveller, and Campaigner for Ancient Egypt* (London, 2006)

Moran, Caitlin, *More Than a Woman* (London, 2020)

Morin, Micheline, *Encordées* (Paris, 1936)

Morin, Nea E., *A Woman's Reach: Mountaineering Memoirs* (London, 1968)

Morrell, Jemima, *Miss Jemima's Swiss Journal: The First Conducted Tour of Switzerland* (London, 1963)

Morrissey, Joseph, 'Remaking Romantic Love in Maria Edgeworth's *Belinda*', *The European Legacy: Towards New Paradigms* (2021), 26:2, 170–87

Morrongiello, Barbara A., and Kerri Hogg, 'Mothers' Reactions to Children Misbehaving in Ways That Can Lead to Injury: Implications for Gender Differences in Children's Risk-Taking and Injuries', *Sex Roles* (2004), 50, 103–18

Mort, Helen, *No Map Could Show Them* (London, 2016)

Mort, Helen, Claire Carter, Heather Dawe and Camilla Barnard (eds.), *Waymaking: An Anthology of Women's Adventure Writing, Poetry and Art* (Sheffield, 2018)

Moss, Rachel, 'We Were Convinced We Weren't Runners. Lockdown Changed Everything', *Huffington Post* (3 Jun. 2020); https://www.huffingtonpost.co.uk/entry/it-makes-me-feel-strong-x-people-on-discovering-the-joy-of-running-during-lockdown_uk_5ed61763c5b65d90b0208883

'Motor Fatality', *Kent & Sussex Courier* (17 Apr. 1914), 2

Mount, Harry, 'How Conan Doyle Pioneered Skiing . . . in a Tweed Suit and 8ft-Long Wooden Skis', *Daily Mail* (30 Jan. 2012); https://www.dailymail.co.uk/news/article-2093609/How-Conan-Doyle-pioneered-Skiing--tweed-suit-8ft-long-wooden-skis.html

Mountjoy, Guido, 'The Comic Alpenstock', *The Daguerreotype: A Magazine of Foreign Literature and Science* (1847), 1, 562–7

Mu, Dennis Wenzhao, and Sharron J. Lennon, 'Objectification of Women in Sportswear Brands' Instagram Accounts', *International Textile and Apparel Association Annual Conference Proceedings* (2018), 75:1; https://www.iastatedigitalpress.com/itaa/article/id/1498/

Mujika, Iñigo, and Ritva S. Taipale, 'Sport Science on Women, Women in Sport Science', *International Journal of Sports Physiology and Performance* (2019), 14:8. 1013–14

Müller, Norbert (ed.), *Pierre de Coubertin, 1863–1937 – Olympism: Selected Writings* (Lausanne, 2000)

Mummery, Albert, *My Climbs in the Alps and the Caucasus* (London, 1895)

Mundy, Liza, *Code Girls: The Untold Story of the American Women Code Breakers of World War II* (New York, 2017)

Murakami, Haruki, *What I Talk about When I Talk about Running* (London, 2009)

Murphy, Mary, 'Bootlegging Mothers and Drinking Daughters: Gender and Prohibition in Butte, Montana', *American Quarterly* (1994), 46:2, 174–94

Murray, Brian, 'The Journeys of "Kalulu" and Saleh Bin Osman: African Travellers in the Archive of Exploration', *19th Century Studies Unit Guest Lecture Series* (Anglia Ruskin University, 22 Feb. 2021)

Musa, Ghazali, Anna Thompson-Carr and James Higham (eds.), *Mountaineering Tourism: Contemporary Geographies of Leisure, Tourism and Mobility* (London, 2015)

Nande, Anushree, 'World War, Mon Amour: A Brief History of Women's Football', *Football Paradise* (18 Oct. 2017); https://www.footballparadise.com/womens-football-part-1-origins-world-wars/

Nauright, John, and Timothy John Lindsay Chandler, *Making Men: Rugby and Masculine Identity* (London, 1996)

Ndee, H. S., 'Public Schools in Britain in the Nineteenth Century: The Emergence of Team Games and the Development of the Educational Ideology of Athleticism', *International Journal of the History of Sport* (2010), 27:5, 845–71

Neejer, Christine, 'The Bicycle Girls: American Wheelwomen and Everyday Activism in the Late Nineteenth Century', PhD thesis (Michigan State University, 2016)

'The New Conservative Agent', *Leamington Spa Courier* (11 Jan. 1907), 2

'News of the Day', *Liverpool Daily Post* (29 Jun. 1875), 5

Nivison, Mary Ellen, and Inger M. Endresen, 'An Analysis of Relationships among Environmental Noise, and the Consequences for Health and Sleep', *Journal of Behavioral Medicine* (1993), 16:3, 257–76

Nordau, Max, *Degeneration* (London, 1895)

'Notes on the Magazines', *The Queen* (13 Aug. 1904), 33

Nowell, Mrs W. G., 'A Mountain Suit for Women', *Appalachia* (1876–8), 1, 181–3

Nye, Robert, *Masculinity and Male Codes of Honor in Modern France* (New York, 1992)

'Obituary: John Frederic Main', *Minutes of the Proceedings of the Institution of Civil Engineers* (1892), 110, 394–6

O'Brien, Margaret, Deborah Jones, David Sloan and Michael Rustin, 'Children's Independent Spatial Mobility in the Urban Public Realm', *Childhood* (2000), 7:3, 257–77

O'Donnell, Elizabeth A., 'Doing Good Quietly: The Life and Work of Teresa Merz (1879–1958) of Newcastle upon Tyne', *Women's History: The Journal of the Women's History Network* (2017), 2:7, 4–12

Office for National Statistics (ONS), 'Women Shoulder the Responsibility of "Unpaid Work"' (10 Nov. 2016); https://www.ons.gov.uk/employmentandlabourmarket/peopleinwork/earningsandworkinghours/articles/womenshouldertheresponsibilityofunpaidwork/2016-11-10

——— 'Men Enjoy Five Hours More Leisure Time Per Week Than Women' (9 Jan. 2018); https://www.ons.gov.uk/peoplepopulationandcommunity/wellbeing/articles/menenjoyfivehoursmoreleisuretimeperweekthanwomen/2018-01-09

——— 'Coronavirus and Anxiety, Great Britain: 3 Apr. 2020 to 10 May 2020' (15 Jun. 2020); https://www.ons.gov.uk/peoplepopulationandcommunity/wellbeing/articles/coronavirusandanxietygreatbritain/3april2020to10may2020

——— 'The Nature of Violent Crime in England and Wales: Year Ending March 2020' (25 Feb. 2021); https://www.ons.gov.uk/peoplepopulationandcommunity/crimeandjustice/articles/thenatureofviolentcrimeinenglandandwales/yearendingmarch2020

'"An Officer and Gentleman" in a Railway Carriage', *Northern Echo* (21 Jun. 1875), 3

Olstead, Riley, 'Gender, Space and Fear: A Study of Women's Edgework', *Emotion, Space and Society* (2011), 4:2, 86–94

'On Ilkley Moor', *Yorkshire Post and Leeds Intelligencer* (12 Feb. 1934), 5

'On the Alps – without Tartarin', *St James's Gazette* (8 Mar. 1904), 19

O'Neill, Jarrah, 'Gender in Public Space: Policy Frameworks and the Failure to Prevent Street Harassment', BA thesis (Woodrow Wilson School of Public and International Affairs, Princeton University, 2013)

Onslow, Barbara, 'New World, New Woman, New Journalism: Elizabeth Banks, Transatlantic Stuntwoman in London', *Media History* (2001), 7:1, 7–15

Oppenheim, Janet, *'Shattered Nerves': Doctors, Patients, and Depression in Victorian England* (New York and Oxford, 1991)

Oppenheim, Maya, 'Almost Three-Quarters of Women Scared of Exercising Outside in Dark Amid Lockdown', *Independent* (22 Nov. 2020); https://www.independent.co.uk/news/uk/home-news/women-lockdown-exercising-dark-harassment-b1759283.html#comments

Ortner, Johanna, 'Lost No More: Recovering Frances Ellen Watkins Harper's *Forest Leaves*', *Commonplace: The Journal of Early American Life*, (summer 2015), 15:4; http://commonplace.online/article/lost-no-more-recovering-frances-ellen-watkins-harpers-forest-leaves/

Osborne, Carol Anne, 'Gender and the Organisation of British Climbing, *c.* 1857–1955', PhD thesis (University of Lancaster, 2004)

——— '"Deeds, Not Words": Emily Wilding Dickinson and the Epsom Derby 1913 Revisited', in Jon Dart and Stephen Wagg (eds.), *Sport, Protest and Globalisation: Stopping Play* (London, 2016), pp. 17–34

O'Sullivan, Suzanne, *It's All in Your Head: Stories from the Frontline of Psychosomatic Illness* (London, 2016)

Ottogalli, Cécile, 'Quand le Club Alpin Français Écrit au Féminin (1874–1919)', *Amnis* (2004), 1; https://journals.openedition.org/amnis/1080

Ottogalli-Mazzacavallo, Cécile, 'Femmes et Alpinisme au Club Alpin Français à l'Aube du xxe Siècle: au Recontre Atypique?', *STAPS* (December 2004), 66:4, 25–40

'Our London Letter', *Dundee Courier* (27 Jan. 1885), 5

Outdoor Industries Association, *Getting Active Outdoors: A Study of Demography, Motivation, Participation and Provision in Outdoor Sport and Recreation in England* (2015); https://www.theoia.co.uk/wp-content/uploads/2017/06/outdoors-participation-report-v2-lr-spreads.pdf

Özdin, Selçuk, and Şükriye Bayrak Özdin, 'Levels and Predictors of Anxiety, Depression and Health Anxiety during COVID-19 Pandemic in Turkish Society: The Importance of Gender', *International Journal of Social Psychiatry* (2020), 66:5, 504–11

Paillon, Mary, 'En Souvenir de Miss. K. Richardson (1854–1927)', *La Montagne* (1927), 23, 326–34

Park, J., 'Dress Reform and the Emancipation of Women in Victorian England: A Reappraisal', *International Journal of the History of Sport* (1989), 6:1, 16

Parker, Mike, 'Whatever Happened to the Lyke Wake Walk?', *Map Addict* (1 Aug. 2015); http://mapaddict.blogspot.com/2015/08/whatever-happened-to-lyke-wake-walk.html

Parlour, Tammy, and Women's Sport Trust, 'Visibility Uncovered: Review and Debate the Latest in Women's Sport Data' (26 Oct. 2021); https://www.womenssporttrust.com/visibility-uncovered-jan-sept-2021/

———'Visibility Uncovered: The Year in Review (2021)' (7 Feb. 2022); https://www.womenssporttrust.com/research-from-womens-sport-trust-reveals-2021-was-a-record-breaking-year-for-womens-sport/

Parry, Jonathan, 'Adrenaline Junkie', *London Review of Books* (21 Mar. 2019), 41:6; https://www.lrb.co.uk/the-paper/v41/n06/jonathan-parry/adrenaline-junkie

Parsons, Mike C., and Mary B. Roses, *Invisible on Everest: Innovation and the Gear Makers* (Philadelphia and London, 2003)

Pasang Lhamu Foundation, 'The History: Pasang Lhamu Sherpa', *Pasang Lhamu Foundation*; https://pasanglhamufoundation.org/index.php?option=com_content&view=article&id=4&Itemid=110

Pashigian, B. Peter, 'Demand Uncertainty and Sales: A Study of Fashion and Markdown Pricing', *American Economic Review* (1988), 78:5, 936–53

'Paul', 'This Must Be the Place: Killincarrick House', *Greystone's Guide* (28 Jun. 2018); https://www.greystonesguide.ie/this-must-be-the-place-killincarrick-house/

Paumgarten, Nick, 'Inside the Cultish Dreamworld of Augusta National', *New Yorker* (14 Jun. 2019); https://www.newyorker.com/magazine/2019/06/24/inside-the-cultish-dreamworld-of-augusta-national

Peckham, Hannah, Nina M. De Gruijter, Charles Raine, Anna Radziszewska, Coziana Ciurtin, Lucy R. Wedderburn, Elizabeth C. Rosser, Kate Webb and Claire T. Deakin, 'Male Sex Identified by Global COVID-19 Meta-Analysis as a Risk Factor for Death and ITU Admission', *Nature Communications* (9 Dec. 2020), 11, 6317

'Pedestrianism', *Leeds Intelligencer* (15 Oct. 1864), 7

'Pedigree Large Black Pigs', *Gloucester Citizen* (22 Oct. 1921), 6

Perkins, Kenneth J., 'So Near and Yet So Far: British Tourism in Algiers, 1860–1914', in Martin Farr and Xavier Guégan (eds.), *The British Abroad since the Eighteenth Century* (Basingstoke, 2013) Vol. 1, pp. 217–35

'Personal', *Alpine Post* (5 Mar. 1898), 22:19, 216

Pew Research Center, 'Modern Parenthood, Chapter 4: How Mothers and Fathers Spend Their Time' (14 Mar. 2013); https://www.pewresearch.org/social-trends/2013/03/14/chapter-4-how-mothers-and-fathers-spend-their-time/

Phadke, Shilpa, Sameera Khan and Shilpa Ranade, *Why Loiter? Women & Risk on Mumbai Streets* (New Delhi, 2011)

Phillips, Kristine, and Amy B. Wang, 'Authorities Say They Have Found the Killer of Google's Vanessa Marcotte', *Washington Post* (16 Apr. 2017); https://www.washingtonpost.com/news/morning-mix/wp/2017/04/16/police-say-they-believe-they-have-found-the-killer-of-googles-vanessa-marcotte/

'The Picture Exhibition', *Alpine Journal* (Aug. 1884–May 1886), 12, 462–4

Pigeon, Anna, and Ellen Abbot, 'The Passage of the Sesia-Joch from Zermatt to Alagna by English Ladies', *Alpine Journal* (May 1870–May 1872), 5, 367–72

———*Peaks and Passes* (published by the authors, 1885)

Pilley, Dorothy, 'Christmas Climbing for Ladies', *Daily Mail* (22 Dec. 1920), [page unknown]

———*Climbing Days* (London, 1935)

Plan International UK, *The State of Girls' Rights in the UK: Early Insights into the Impact of the Coronavirus Pandemic on Girls* (London, 2020); https://plan-uk.org/file/plan-uk-state-of-girls-rights-coronavirus-reportpdf/download?token=gddEAzlz

Plath, Sylvia, *The Unabridged Journals of Sylvia Plath, 1950–1962*, edited by Karen V. Kukil (New York, 2000)

Pleasance, Chris, Wills Robinson and Chris Summers, '"I Wonder What Would Happen if I Died?": Haunting Diary Entries of New York Jogger Who Was Sexually Assaulted and Strangled before Her body Was Found by Her Father', *Daily Mail* (4 Aug. 2016); https://www.dailymail.co.uk/news/article-3722861/I-wonder-happen-died-Haunting-diary-entries-New-York-jogger-sexually-assaulted-strangled-body-father.html

Plunket, Frederica, *Here and There among the Alps* (London, 1875)

Pollard, Tessa M., and Janelle M. Wagnild, 'Gender Differences in Walking (for Leisure, Transport and in Total) across Adult Life: A Systematic Review', *BMC Public Health* (2017), 17, 341

Pomfret, Gill, and Adele Doran, 'Gender and Mountaineering Tourism', in Ghazali Musa, Anna Thompson-Carr and James Higham (eds.), *Mountaineering Tourism: Contemporary Geographies of Leisure, Tourism and Mobility* (London, 2015), pp. 138–55

Porphyry, *To Marcella*, translated by Kathleen O'Brien Wicker (Atlanta, 1987)

Potter, Alex, 'An Interview with Camille Herron after Her 2022 100-Mile World Record', *I Run Far* (22 Feb. 2022); https://www.irunfar.com/the-master-an-interview-with-camille-herron-after-her-100-mile-world-record-at-the-2022-jackpot-ultrarunning-festival

Potter, Claire Bond, 'Taking Back Times Square: Feminist Repertoires and the Transformation of Urban Space in Late Second Wave Feminism', *Radical History Review* (2012), 113, 67–80

Powell, Kerry, *Women and Victorian Theatre* (Cambridge, 1997)

Prentice, Archibald, *Historical Sketches and Personal Recollections of Manchester* (London, 1851)

'The Primrose League', *Morning Post* (23 Nov. 1892), 2

Prince, Cathryn J., *Queen of the Mountaineers: The Trail-Blazing Life of Fanny Bullock Workman* (Chicago, 2019)

Proctor, Tammy M., *Female Intelligence: Women and Espionage in the First World War* (New York and London, 2003)

'The Property Market: The Ploddy House Estate', *Gloucester Journal* (27 May 1922), 12

Putney, Clifford, *Muscular Christianity: Manhood and Sports in Protestant America, 1880–1920* (Cambridge, Mass., 2001)

'The Queen's Drawing Room', *Evening Mail* (10 May 1878), 8

Radford, Peter F., 'Women's Foot-Races in the 18th and 19th Centuries: A Popular and Widespread Practice', *Canadian Journal of the History of Sport* (1994), 25:1, 50–61

Raeburn, Gordon David, 'The Long Reformation of the Dead in Scotland', PhD thesis (University of Durham, 2012; http://etheses.dur.ac.uk/6926/)

'A Railway Grievance', *Morning Post* (14 Jul. 1864), 3

Ramazani, Vaheed, 'Gender, War and the Department Store: Zola's "Au Bonheur des Dames"', *SubStance* (2007), 36:2, 126–46

'The Ramblerette', *Out-o'-Doors* (Nov. 1927), 111

Ranalli, Ralph, 'A New Mountain to Climb', *Harvard Kennedy School* (Winter 2022); https://www.hks.harvard.edu/faculty-research/policy-topics/poverty-inequality-opportunity/new-mountain-climb

Ranlett, John, '"Checking Nature's Desecration": Late-Victorian Environmental Organization', *Victorian Studies* (1983), 26:2, 197–222

Rappaport, Erika, *Shopping for Pleasure: Women in the Making of London's West End* (Princeton, N.J., and Oxford, 2000)

Reichel, Oswald J., 'Extracts from a Devonshire Lady's Notes of Travel in France in the Eighteenth Century', *Transactions of the Devonshire Association for the Advancement of Science, Literature and Art* (1902), 34, 265–75

Reid, James, 'On the Causes, Symptoms and Treatment of Puerperal Insanity', *Journal of Psychological Medicine and Mental Pathology* (1848), 1, 128–51

Reidy, Michael S., 'Mountaineering, Masculinity, and the Male Body in Mid-Victorian Britain', *Osiris* (2015), 30:1, 158–81

Reinke-Williams, Tim, 'Women, Ale and Company in Early Modern London', *Brewery History* (2010), 135, 88–106

Report of the Inter-Departmental Committee on Physical Deterioration (London, 1904)

Repton, Humphry, *Fragments on the Theory and Practice of Landscape Gardening* (London, 1816)

Reus, Teresa Gómez, and Terry Gifford (eds.), *Women in Transit through Literary Liminal Spaces* (Basingstoke, 2013)

'Review of *The High Alps in Winter; or, Mountaineering in Search of Health* (by Mrs Fred Burnaby)', *Alpine Journal* (Aug. 1882–May 1884), 11, 306–7

Richards, Dan, *Climbing Days* (London, 2016)

Richings, Emily, *In the Shadow of Etna* (London, 1890)

Robertson, Harry, 'The Business of Running: Trainer Sales and Fitness Apps Boom in Lockdown', *City A.M.* (5 Jun. 2020); https://www.cityam.com/how-running-took-off-during-the-uks-coronavirus-lockdown/

Robbins, David, 'Sport, Hegemony and the Middle Class: The Victorian Mountaineers', *Theory, Culture & Society* (1987), 4:4, 579–601

Robins, Elizabeth, *Both Sides of the Curtain* (London, 1940)

Robinson, Lilias Napier Rose, *A Short Account of Our Trip to the Sierra Nevada Mountains* (London, 1884)

Roche, Clare, 'Women Climbers, 1850–1900: A Challenge to Male Hegemony?', *Sport in History* (2013), 33:3, 236–59

———'The Ascent of Women: How Female Mountaineers Explored the Alps, 1850–1900', PhD thesis (Birkbeck, University of London, 2015)

Roche, David and Megan, 'Women Are Underrepresented in Exercise Science, and That Is a Problem', *Trail Runner* (9 Mar. 2021); https://www.trailrunnermag.com/training/trail-tips-training/women-are-underrepresented-in-exercise-science-and-that-is-a-problem/

Rogers, Charlotte, 'Value of Women's Sport Could Treble by 2030 as UK Viewership Hits 33 Million', *Marketing Week* (8 Feb. 2022); https://www.marketingweek.com/womens-sport-record-year/

'The Roll of Honour for Women', *Gentlewoman* (3 Sep. 1904), 21

Rom, Zoë, 'How Childcare Responsibilities Limit Women's Participation in Trail Running', *Trail Runner* (7 May 2020); https://www.trailrunnermag.com/people/culture-people/how-childcare-responsibilities-limit-womens-participation-in-trail-running/

Ronto, Paul and Vania Nokolova, *The State of Ultra-Running 2020: RunRepeat.com and the IAU* (21 Sep. 2021); https://runrepeat.com/state-of-ultra-running

Rooke, Hayman, 'Brimham Rocks in Yorkshire', *Sheffield Register* (13 Dec. 1788), 4

Rose, David, and Ed Douglas, *Regions of the Heart: The Triumph and Tragedy of Alison Hargreaves* (London, 1999)

Rosenbloom, Tova, 'Crossing at a Red Light: Behaviour of Individuals and Groups', *Transportation Research* (2009), 12:5, 389–94

Rosewell, Lizzie, 'Why Don't More Women Take Part in Ultrarunning?', *Lizzie Running* (25 Jul. 2018); https://lizzierunning.wordpress.com/2018/07/25/why-dont-more-women-take-part-in-ultrarunning/

Rosqvist, Leif, 'Stockholm Rowing Madams', *New Sweden Cultural Heritage Society*; https://www.newsweden.org/lib/doc/walkabout/Roddar-Madammerna.pdf

Ross, Hannah, *Revolutions: How Women Changed the World on Two Wheels* (London, 2021)

Rothman, Benny, *The Battle for Kinder Scout* (Altrincham, 2012)

Rousseau, George (ed.), *Children and Sexuality: From the Greeks to the Great War* (Basingstoke, 2007)

'Royal Irish Academy', *Saunders's Newsletter* (13 Jan. 1864), 1

Rudolph, Emanuel D., 'Women Who Studied Plants in the Pre-Twentieth Century United States and Canada', *Taxon* (1990), 39:2, 151–205

Rusert, Britt, '"Nor Wish to Live the Past Again": Unsettling Origins in Frances Ellen Watkins Harper's *Forest Leaves*', *Commonplace: The Journal of Early*

American Life (2016), 16:2; http://commonplace.online/article/nor-wish-to-live-the-past-again-unsettling-origins-in-frances-ellen-watkins-harpers-forest-leaves-2/

———*Fugitive Science: Empiricism and Freedom in Early African American Culture* (New York, 2017)

Ryan, Mary P., *Women in Public: Between Banners and Ballots, 1825–1880* (Baltimore and London, 1990)

'S', 'Sojourning with the Swiss', *Gloucester Journal* (10 and 17 Sep. 1881), 6

Sabbadini, Linda Laura, and Maria Giuseppina Muratore, *Violence and Abuses against Women Inside and Outside Family* (Rome, 2006); https://www.istat.it/it/files//2011/07/Full_text.pdf

'The Sahara', *The Times* (22 Jan. 1880), 7

Salpini, Cara, 'Game-Changers: Have Women Reshaped the Sports Market?', *Retail Dive* (3 Sep. 2019); https://www.retaildive.com/news/game-changers-have-women-reshaped-the-sportswear-market/561607/

Sand, George, 'Souvenir d'Auvergne', *Annuaire du Club Alpin Français* (1874), 1, 3–8

Sanday, Peggy Reeves, *Female Power and Male Dominance: On the Origins of Sexual Inequality* (Cambridge, 1981)

Sargent, Shirley, *Pioneers in Petticoats: Yosemite's Early Women, 1856–1900* (Palm Springs, 2011)

Saunders, Frances Stonor, *The Woman Who Shot Mussolini* (London, 2010)

Savile, F., 'The Suffragette', *Strand Magazine* (Jul. 1908), 36:211, 3–10

Schaverien, Anna, '"Because She's a Girl": Lockdown Exposes Gender Gap in UK Sports', *New York Times* (29 Nov. 2020); https://www.nytimes.com/2020/11/29/world/europe/uk-lockdown-sports-women.html

Scherlis, Lily, 'Distantiated Communities: A Social History of Social Distancing', *Cabinet* (30 Apr. 2020); https://www.cabinetmagazine.org/kiosk/scherlis_lily_30_april_2020.php

Scott, Florence, *Memories of Old Withnell Fold* (1988); http://www.boydharris.co.uk/sys1693.htm

Sellers, Kate, 'Real-Life Races to Book Now', *Women's Running* (29 Mar. 2021); https://www.womensrunning.co.uk/events/real-life-races-to-book-now/

'Serious Charge', *Morning Post* (19 Jun. 1875), 5

Seymour, Miranda, *Ottoline Morrell: Life on the Grand Scale* (London, 1992)

Shepherd, Nan, *The Living Mountain* (1977; Edinburgh, 2019)

Shoard, Marion, *This Land Is Our Land: The Struggle for Britain's Countryside* (1987; London, 1997)

Shoker, Sandish, 'Woman Completes 100 Marathons in 100 Days World Record', *BBC News* (12 Apr. 2022); https://www.bbc.co.uk/news/uk-england-derbyshire-61067808

Shteir, Ann B., 'Gender and "Modern" Botany in Victorian England', *Osiris* (1997), 12, 29–38

Siddique, Haroon, 'Childcare Costs in England Rise up to Seven Times Faster than Wages', *Guardian* (20 Oct. 2017); https://www.theguardian.com/money/2017/oct/20/childcare-costs-in-england-rise-up-to-seven-times-faster-than-wages

Siegel, Suzie, 'Safe at Home: Agoraphobia and the Discourse on Women's Place', MA thesis (University of South Florida, 2001)

Silk, Susan, and Barry Goldman, 'How Not to Say the Wrong Thing', *Los Angeles Times* (7 Apr. 2013); https://www.latimes.com/opinion/op-ed/la-xpm-2013-apr-07-la-oe-0407-silk-ring-theory-20130407-story.html

Simon, John, *Second Report of the Medical Officer of the Privy Council*, BPP 1860 XXIX, p. 201

Simri, Uriel, *Women at the Olympic Games*, Wingate Monograph Series 7 (Netanya, 1979)

'A Sister's Vow: How It Caused Trouble in Mr Main's Family', *Brooklyn Daily Eagle* (21 Jul. 1884), 1

Skidelsky, William, 'A People's History of Tennis by David Berry Review: A Game for Everyone?', *Guardian* (12 Jun. 2020); https://www.theguardian.com/books/2020/jun/12/a-peoples-history-of-tennis-by-david-berry-review-a-game-for-everyone

Slingsby, Edith, 'An English Lady in Jotunheimen', *Den Norske Turistförenings Årbog* (1875), 75, 102–18

Słupska, Julia, and Leonie Maria Tanczer, 'Threat Modeling Intimate Partner Violence: Tech Abuse as a Cybersecurity Challenge in the Internet of Things', in Jane Bailey, Asher Flynn and Nicola Henry (eds.), *The Emerald International Handbook of Technology-Facilitated Violence and Abuse* (Bradford, 2021), pp. 663–88

Small, Helen, 'Currie [*née* Lamb], Mary Montgomerie, Lady Currie [*pseud.* Violet Fane] (1843–1905)', *Oxford Dictionary of National Biography* (Oxford, Sep. 2004; online edn, May 2007)

Smil, Vaclav, *Growth: From Microorganisms to Megacities* (Cambridge, Mass., 2019)

Smith, Bill, *Forty Years of the FRA* (St Ives, 2010)

Smith, Charlotte, *The Poems of Charlotte Smith*, edited by Stuart Curran (New York and Oxford, 1993)

Smith, Janet Adam, *Mountain Holidays* (London, 1946)

———'Walker, Lucy (1836–1916)', *Oxford Dictionary of National Biography* (Oxford, Sep. 2004; online edn, May 2021)

Smith, Nicole L., 'The Problem of Excess Female Mortality: Tuberculosis in Western Massachusetts, 1850–1910', MA thesis (University of Massachusetts, 2008)

Smith, Victoria, 'On Correctly Curating the Past', *The OK Karen* newsletter (26 Feb. 2021); https://tinyletter.com/Glosswitch/letters/the-ok-karen-25-on-correctly-curating-the-past

'Smoking Concert at the Kulm', *Morning Post* (14 Jun. 1900)

Sobel, Dava, *The Glass Universe: How the Ladies of the Harvard Observatory Took the Measure of the Stars* (London, 2017)

'Society', *The Queen* (17 Aug. 1907), 37

'Society Gossip', *Bicester Herald* (13 Jan. 1888), 6

Solnit, Rebecca, *Wanderlust: A History of Walking* (London, 2001)

Solomon, Sunil S., Shruti H. Mehta, Amanda Latimore, Aylur K. Srikrishnan and David D. Celentano, 'The Impact of HIV and High-Risk Behaviours on the Wives of Married Men Who Have Sex with Men and Injection Drug Users: Implications for HIV Prevention', *Journal of the International AIDS Society* (2010), 13, S7–S7

Southgate, Jessica, and Lucy Russell, *Street Harassment: It's Not OK: Girls' Experiences and Views* (London 2018); https://plan-uk.org/file/plan-uk-street-harassment-report-summarypdf/download?token=K1HXe-Dv

Sparks, Elisa Kay, '"The Evening under Lamplight . . . with the Photograph Album": *To The Lighthouse* as Family Scrapbook', in Anna Burrells et al. (eds.), *Woolfian Boundaries: Selected Papers from the Sixteenth Annual International Conference on Virginia Woolf* (Clemson, S.C., 2007), pp. 164–71

Speakman, Colin, and Tony Grogan, *50 Years of the Dales Way* (Shipley, 2019)

Spielmann, Benjamin, 'Swiss Road History between State Consolidation and Private Interests: The Development of the Road Infrastructure in Switzerland between 1740 and 1850', paper delivered to the Conference of the International

Association for the History of Transport, Traffic and Mobility (Mexico City, 27–30 Oct. 2016); https://boris.unibe.ch/96063/

Spinks, Nicky, 'Nicky Spinks: My Double Bob Graham Round', *Inov-8*; https://www.inov-8.com/nicky-spinks-double-bob-graham-record

'Sport Will Benefit from People Taking up Running during Lockdown: Sebastian Coe', *Hindustan Times* (10 Aug. 2020); https://www.hindustantimes.com/other-sports/sport-will-benefit-from-people-taking-up-running-during-lockdown-sebastian-coe/story-FapBRQJlk77YpX3H84K6dP.html

SportScotland: Women's Sport and Fitness Foundation, *Barriers to Women and Girl's Participation in Sport and Physical Activity* (Edinburgh, 2008); https://www.funding4sport.co.uk/downloads/women_barriers_participation.pdf

Spyrka, Katie Campbell, 'Ultrarunner Sophie Power: Motherhood and Mountain Ultras', *Lessons in Badassery* (27 Oct. 2021); https://lessonsinbadassery.com/ultrarunner-sophie-power-motherhood-and-mountain-ultras/

Starcevic, V., A. Djordjevic, M. Latas and G. Bogojevic, 'Characteristics of Agoraphobia in Women and Men with Panic Disorder with Agoraphobia', *Depression and Anxiety* (1998), 8:1, 8–13

Starke, Mariana, *Travels on the Continent, for the Use of Travellers on the Continent*, 8th edn (London, 1833)

Starling, Mike, 'Women's Sport "Left Behind" during the Pandemic', *The Week* (11 Feb. 2021); https://www.theweek.co.uk/951951/womens-sport-left-behind-during-the-pandemic

'Statement and Editorial Note', *The Rational Dress Society's Gazette* (Jan. 1889), 4, 1

Statistiska centralbyrån (SCB), *Swedish Time Use Survey, 2010/11* (Örebro, 2012)

Staurowsky, E. J., N. Watanabe, J. Cooper, C. Cooky, N. Lough, A. Paule-Koba, J. Pharr, S. Williams, S. Cummings, K. Issokson-Silver and M. Snyder, *Chasing Equity: The Triumphs, Challenges, and Opportunities in Sports for Girls and Women: A Women's Sports Foundation Research Report* (January 2020); https://www.womenssportsfoundation.org/wp-content/uploads/2020/01/Chasing-Equity-Full-Report-Web.pdf

Stearn, Roger T., 'Burnaby, Frederick Gustavus (1842–1885)', *Oxford Dictionary of National Biography* (Oxford, Sep. 2004; online edn, May 2014)

Stein, Murray B., Ariel J. Lang, Charlene Laffaye, Leslie E. Satz, Rebecca J. Lenox and Timothy R. Dresselhaus, 'Relationship of Sexual Assault History to Somatic

Symptoms and Health Anxiety in Women', *General Hospital Psychiatry* (2004), 26:3, 178–83

Stephen, Leslie, *The Playground of Europe* (London, 1871)

Stephenson, Tom, *Forbidden Land: The Struggle for Access to Mountain and Moorland* (Manchester, 1989)

Stevens, E. H., 'Dr Paccard's Lost Narrative', *Alpine Journal* (1929), 41, 118–19

Stirling, Sarah, 'Climbing against Repression: The Afghan Women with High Mountain Dreams', *Summit Magazine* (7 Oct. 2019); https://www.thebmc.co.uk/climbing-against-repression-the-afghan-women-with-high-mountain-dreams

Stockham, Karen J., '"It Went down into the Very Form and Fabric of Myself": Women's Mountaineering Life-Writing, 1808–1960', PhD thesis (University of Exeter, 2012)

Stokes, Catherine, 'Global Recovery: Export Publishing Sales Post COVID', *Bookseller* webinar (1 Jul. 2020); https://www.youtube.com/watch?v=-MXIXoUkBFhM

Stokols, D., and I. Altman (eds.), *Handbook of Environmental Psychology* (New York, 1987)

'Strava Releases 2020 Year in Sport Data Report', *Strava* (16 Dec. 2020); https://blog.strava.com/press/yis2020/

Strutt, Edward Lisle, 'In Memoriam: James Walker Hartley (1852–1932)', *Alpine Journal* (1932), 44, 110–12

———'In Memoriam: Mrs Aubrey Le Blond (1861–1934)', *Alpine Journal* (1934), 46, 382–4

Sturgis, India, 'Meet the First Woman to Run the Boston Marathon (Illegally) 50 Years Ago – Now 70, She's about to Do It Again', *Telegraph* (17 Apr. 2017); https://www.telegraph.co.uk/health-fitness/body/meet-first-woman-run-boston-marathon-illegally-50-years-ago/

Summers, Martin, 'Manhood Rights in the Age of Jim Crow: Evaluating "End-of-Men" Claims in the Context of African-American History', *Boston University Law Review* (2013), 93:3, 745–67

Svrluga, Barry, 'U.S. Open: Golf Is a Bipartisan Game for Washington's Politicians', *Washington Post* (13 Jun. 2011); https://www.washingtonpost.com/sports/golf/us-open-golf-is-a-bipartisan-game-for-washingtons-politicians/2011/06/12/AG8qNZTH_story.html

Swale Pope, Rosie, *Just a Little Run around the World* (London, 2009)

Swanwick, Helena M., *I Have Been Young* (London, 1935)

Switzer, Kathrine, *Marathon Woman: Running the Race to Revolutionize Women's Sports* (New York, 2007)

Tabei, Junko and Helen Y. Rolfe, *Honouring High Places: The Mountain Life of Junko Tabei* translated by Yumiko Hirako and Rieko Holtved (Calgary, 2017)

Taylor, Simon, Matthew Whitfield and Susie Barson, *The English Public Library, 1850–1939*, Historic England Introductions to Heritage Assets (Jul. 2016); https://historicengland.org.uk/images-books/publications/iha-english-public-library-1850-1939/heag135-the-english-public-library-1850-1939-iha/

Taylor, Ula, 'The Historical Evolution of Black Feminist Theory and Praxis', *Journal of Black Studies* (1998), 29:2, 234–53

'Telegraph Women's Sport Celebrates Third Anniversary with "Close the Gap" Campaign', *Newsworks* (25 Mar. 2022); https://www.newsworks.org.uk/news-and-opinion/telegraph-womens-sport-celebrates-third-anniversary-with-close-the-gap-campaign/

Thompson, E. P., *The Making of the English Working Class* (Harmondsworth, 1991; 1st pub. 1963; revised paperback 1968; reprinted with a new preface 1980)

Thompson, Simon Robert, 'The Fashioning of a New World: Youth Culture and the Origins of the Mass Outdoor Movement in Interwar Britain', PhD thesis (King's College, London, 2018)

Thoreau, Henry David, *Walden; or, Life in the Woods* (1856; London, 2017)

———'Walking', *Atlantic Magazine* (Jun. 1862), 658

Timperio, Anna, Billie Giles-Corti, David Crawford, Nick Andrianopoulos, Kylie Ball, Jo Salmon and Clare Hume, 'Features of Public Open Spaces and Physical Activity among Children: Findings from the CLAN Study', *Preventive Medicine* (2008), 47:5, 514–18

Tindal, M., 'The Champion Lady Mountaineer', *Pearson's Magazine* (Jan.–Jun. 1899), 7, 354–64

Todd, Selina, 'Poverty and Aspiration: Young Women's Entry to Employment in Inter-War England', *Twentieth Century British History* (2004), 15:2, 119–42

Tomas, Fiona, 'Report Finds 61 Per Cent of Women Intend to Be More Active after Coronavirus Lockdown', *Telegraph* (16 Jul. 2020); https://www.telegraph.co.uk/womens-sport/2020/07/16/report-finds-61-per-cent-women-intend-active-coronavirus-lockdown/

'The Trans-Sahara Railway', *The Times* (29 Dec. 1879), 8

Trexler, Richard C., 'Correre la Terra: Collective Insults in the Late Middle Ages', *Mélanges de l'Ecole Française de Rome* (1984), 96:2, 845–902

Triggs, Henry Inigo, *The Art of Garden Design in Italy* (London, 1906) ('with twenty-eight plates from photographs by Mrs Aubrey Le Blond')

Trotter, Thomas, *A View of the Nervous Temperament; being a Practical Enquiry into the Increasing Prevalence, Prevention and Treatment of those Diseases Commonly Called Nervous* (London, 1807; reprinted Boston, 1808)

'True Tales of Mountain Adventure: Review', *Scotsman* (22 Jan. 1903), 2

Truth, Sojourner, *Narrative of Sojourner Truth*, narrated to Olive Gilbert, edited by Frances Titus (New York, 1875; first published 1850)

Tucker, Ross, 'Why Transgender Athletes Threaten Fairness in Women's Sport', *The Real Science of Sport Podcast*, (20 May 2021) 3:8; https://podcasts.apple.com/za/podcast/s3-e8-why-transgender-athletes-threaten-fairness-in/id1461719225?i=1000522515770

Tuckett, Elizabeth Fox, *How We Spent the Summer; or, a Voyage en Zigzag in Switzerland and Tyrol* (London, 1864)

Tuckett, Mariana Fox, *A Victorian "Teenager's" Diary; or, Mariana Fox Tuckett's Journal, December 1857–March 1859*, edited by Gerald Franklin (Frenchay, 2011); https://foxlinks.com/wp-content/uploads/2015/07/Mariana-Fox-Tuckett-Diary-1857-59.pdf

Tuke, John Batty, 'On the Statistics of Puerperal Insanity as Observed in the Royal Edinburgh Asylum, Morningside', *Edinburgh Medical Journal* (1864–5), 10, 1013–28

Tullis, Julie, *Clouds from Both Sides* (London, 1986)

'Tunbridge Wells War Notes', *Kent & Sussex Courier* (25 Sep. 1914), 5

Turban, Jack, 'Trans Girls Belong on Girls' Sports Teams', *Scientific American* (16 Mar. 2021); https://www.scientificamerican.com/article/trans-girls-belong-on-girls-sports-teams/

Turner, Jeff, and John Fletcher, 'TI-UP Enquiry: Gender and Road Safety', *TI-UP*, (May 2018); https://assets.publishing.service.gov.uk/media/57a08b8fed915d622c000d61/TI_UP_HD_May2008_Gender_and_Road_Safety.pdf

Turner, Thomas, 'The Production and Consumption of Lawn Tennis Shoes in Late-Victorian Britain', *Journal of British Studies* (Jul. 2016), 55, 474–500

Tynan, Katharine, *Twenty-Five Years: Reminiscences* (London, 1913)

Uings, Joy Margaret, 'Gardens and Gardening in a Fast-Changing Urban Environment: Manchester, 1750–1850', PhD thesis (Manchester Metropolitan University, 2013 https://pdfs.semanticscholar.org/7fd5/e29e3929321e498f2136c97904ce61777f96.pdf)

Underhill, Miriam, *Manless Alpine Climbing: The First Woman to Scale the Grépon, the Matterhorn and Other Famous Peaks without Masculine Support* (London, 1934)

——— *Give Me the Hills* (London, 1956)

Van Hecke, Linde, Benedicte Deforche, Delfien Van Dyck, Isle De Bourdeaudhuij, Jenny Veitch and Jelle Van Cauwenberg, 'Social and Physical Environmental Factors Influencing Adolescents' Physical Activity in Urban Public Open Spaces: A Qualitative Study Using Walk-Along Interviews', *PLOS One* (2016), 11:5, 1–24

Van Mead, Nick, 'Lizzy Hawker: "I Might Run around 180 miles in a Week" ', *Guardian* (28 Jun. 2013); https://www.theguardian.com/lifeandstyle/the-running-blog/2013/jun/28/lizzy-hawker-friday-flyer-interview

Van Slyck, Abigail A., 'The Lady and the Library Loafer: Gender and Public Space in Victorian America', *Winterthur Portfolio* (1996), 31:4, 221–42

Velija, Philippa, Aarti Ratna and Anne Flintoff, 'Exclusionary Power in Sports Organisations: The Merger between the Women's Cricket Association and the England and Wales Cricket Board', *International Review for the Sociology of Sport* (2012), 49:2, 211–26

Vera-Gray, Fiona, *The Right Amount of Panic: How Women Trade Freedom for Safety* (Bristol, 2018)

Verongos, Helen T., 'Overlooked No More: Lucy Diggs Slowe, Scholar Who Persisted against Racism and Sexism', *New York Times* (1 Oct. 2020); https://www.nytimes.com/2020/10/01/obituaries/lucy-diggs-slowe-overlooked.html

Vertinsky, Patricia A., *The Eternally Wounded Woman: Women, Doctors, and Exercise in the Late Nineteenth Century* (Urbana and Chicago, 1984)

Vibe, Anne-Mette, *Therese Bertheau: Tindestigerske og Lærerinde* (Oslo, 2012)

Viglione, Giuliana, 'Are Women Publishing Less during the Pandemic? Here's What the Data Say', *Nature* (2020), 581, 365–6; https://www.nature.com/articles/d41586-020-01294-9

'Visitor's List', *St Moritz Post* (22 Oct. 1887), 2:1, 9

——— (5 Nov. 1887), 2:3, 33–4

Von Cramm, Helga, *Sunbeams from the Alpine Heights* (Lahr, 1880)

Von Mallinckrodt, Rebekka, 'Attractive or Repugnant? Foot Races in Eighteenth-Century Germany and Britain', in John Zilcosky, and Marlo A. Burks (eds.), *The Allure of Sports in Western Culture* (Toronto, 2019), pp. 145–67

Wade, Becky, *Run the World: My 3,500 Mile Journey Through Running Cultures Around the Globe* (New York, 2016)

Walchester, Kathryn, '"My Petticoat Encumbrances": The Female Adventurer and the North', *Nordlit: Tidsskrift i Litteratur og Kultur* (2014), 32, 161–76

———'Alpine Guides, Gender, and British Climbers, 1859–1885: Swiss Guides and the Boundaries of Female Propriety in the British Periodical Press', *Victorian Periodicals Review* (2018), 51:3, 521–38

———'"A Fisherman Landing an Unwieldy Salmon": The Alpine Guide and Female Mountaineer', *Nineteenth-Century Contexts* (2018) 40:2, 1–16

Walker, Amanda, 'Why Are Women so Well-Suited to Risk Management?', *LinkedIn* (23 Feb. 2016); https://www.linkedin.com/pulse/why-women-so-well-suited-risk-management-amanda-walker/

Walkowitz, Judith R., 'Going Public: Shopping, Street Harassment, and Streetwalking in Late Victorian London', *Representations* (1998), 62, 1–30

Wallace, Keri, 'Follow a Strong Lead', *Trail Running* (Jun./Jul. 2019), 50, 40–3

Walmsley, D. Jim, and Gareth J. Lewis, 'The Pace of Pedestrian Flows in Cities', *Environment and Behavior* (1989), 21: 2, 123–50

Ward, Margaret, 'Gendering the Union: Imperial Feminism and the Ladies' Land League', *Women's History Review* (2001), 10:1, 71–92

Ware, J. Redding, *The Life and Times of Colonel Fred Burnaby* (London, 1885)

Ware, Susan, 'Climbing Mountains for the Right to Vote', *Lit Hub* (13 May 2019); https://lithub.com/climbing-mountains-for-the-right-to-vote/

———*Why They Marched: Untold Stories of the Women Who Fought for the Right to Vote* (Cambridge, Mass., 2019)

Warren, Samuel D., and Louis D. Brandeis, 'The Right to Privacy', *Harvard Law Review* (15 Dec. 1890), 4:5, 193–220

'Water Diviner, Alpinist, Lady Almoner . . .', *Worthing Gazette* (2 Apr. 1941), 5

Watkin, Absalom, *Absalom Watkin: Extracts from His Journal, 1814–1856,* edited by A.E. Watkin (London, 1920)

Webb, Beatrice, *The Diary of Beatrice Webb, Volume One: 1873–1892, 'Glitter Around and Darkness Within'*, edited by Norman and Jeanne MacKenzie (Cambridge, Mass., 1982)

'Wednesday, June 25, 1884', *Pastime* (25 Jun 1884), 410

Weeton, Ellen, *Miss Weeton: Journal of a Governess, 1807–1811*, edited by Edward Hall, 2 vols (Oxford, 1936)

Wesely, Jennifer K., and Emily Gaarder, 'The Gendered "Nature" of the Outdoors: Women Negotiating Fear of Violence', *Gender and Society* (2004), 18:5, 645–63

West, Amanda, and Linda Allin, 'Chancing Your Arm: the Meaning of Risk in Rock Climbing', *Sport in Society* (2010), 13:7–8, 1234–48

White, Eric Walter, *Benjamin Britten: His Life and Operas* (London, 1983)

Whymper, Edward, *The Ascent of the Matterhorn* (London, 1880)

——— 'Two Lady Climbers', *Girl's Own Paper* (15 Dec. 1885), 164–7

Wightwick, Abbie, 'Pupils Are Missing School because They Don't Like Mixed Sex Toilets and "Period Shaming" Is One of the Main Issues', *Wales Online* (15 Feb. 2019); https://www.walesonline.co.uk/news/education/pupils-missing-school-because-dont-15839558

Willet, Maxine, 'Beatrice Tomasson (1859–1947)', *Mountain Heritage* (6 Aug. 2006); https://web.archive.org/web/20140408212241/http://www.mountain-heritage.org/entity.php?ID=207

Williams, Cicely, *Women on the Rope: The Feminine Share in Mountain Adventure* (London, 1973)

——— 'The Feminine Share in Mountain Adventure, Pt 1', *Alpine Journal* (1976), 81, 90–100

Winnicott, D. W., *Playing and Reality* (1971; London, 2008)

Wirz, Tanja, *Gipfelstürmerinnen: Eine Geschlechtergeschichte des Alpinismus in der Schweiz, 1840–1940* (Baden, 2007)

Wohl, Anthony S., *Endangered Lives: Public Health in Victorian Britain* (London, 1983)

Wolfe-Robinson, Maya, and Vikram Dodd, 'Institutional Misogyny "Erodes Women's Trust in UK Police"', *Guardian* (16 Mar. 2021); https://www.theguardian.com/uk-news/2021/mar/16/institutional-misogyny-erodes-womens-trust-in-uk-police

'Women Footballers', *Pall Mall Gazette* (22 Mar. 1922), 11

Women in Sport, 'Reframing Sport for Teenage Girls: Building Strong Foundations for their Futures' (2019); https://www.womeninsport.org/wp-content/uploads/2019/04/Reframing-Sport-for-Teenage-Girls-small.pdf

——— 'Reframing Sport for Teenage Girls: Tackling Teenage Disengagement' (2022); https://www.womeninsport.org/wp-content/uploads/2022/03/Tackling-Teenage-Disengagement-March-2022.pdf

———'Transgender Inclusion in Women's Sport – July 2022'; https://womeninsport.org/statement/transgender-inclusion-in-womens-sport-july-2022/

'Women Mountaineers', *Field* (13 Jun. 1903), 27

'Women's Boxing Bouts Abandoned', *Hackney and Kingsland Gazette* (1 Feb. 1926)

'Wonders of Thibet: Lady Traveller's Curious Experiences', *St Andrew's Citizen* (20 Feb. 1904), 6

Wordsworth, William, *Kendal and Windermere Railway: Two Letters Re-Printed from the* Morning Post, *Revised, with Additions* (Kendal, [1845])

———*Wordsworth's Guide to the Lakes*, edited by Ernest de Sélincourt (first published as anonymous introduction to Joseph Wilkinson, *Select Views in Cumberland, Westmoreland, and Lancashire* (London, 1810). This edition – Oxford, 1877 – is based on the 5th edition, titled *A Guide Through the District of the Lakes in the North of England* (Kendal, 1835)

Workman, Fanny Bullock, *Algerian Memories: A Bicycle Tour over the Atlas to the Sahara* (London, 1895)

———*Sketches Awheel in Fin de Siècle Iberia* (London, 1897)

———*In the Ice World of Himálaya: Among the Peaks and Passes of Ladakh, Nubra, Suru, and Baltistan* (London, 1900)

———*Ice-Bound Heights of the Mustagh: An Account of Two Seasons of Pioneer Exploration and High Climbing in the Baltistan Himalaya* (London, 1908)

———*Two Summers in the Ice-Wilds of Eastern Karakoram: The Exploration of Nineteen Hundred Square Miles of Mountain and Glacier* (London, 1917)

Wrack, Suzanne, 'Survey Reveals Increase in Female Football Fans Being Harassed at Games', *Guardian* (9 Nov. 2021)'; https://www.theguardian.com/football/2021/nov/09/survey-reveals-increase-in-female-football-fans-being-harassed-at-games

Wraight, John, *The Swiss and the British* (Salisbury, 1987)

Wright, F. W., 'A Wonderful American City', *Derby Mercury* (2 Sep. 1891), 3

Wright, Thomas, *The Life of Colonel Fred Burnaby* (London, 1908)

'Yachting Ladies', *Penny Illustrated Paper* (12 Sep. 1885), 11

Young, Eleanor, and Geoffrey Winthrop (eds.), *In Praise of Mountains: An Anthology for Friends* (London, 1948)

Young, Iris Marion, 'Throwing Like a Girl: a Phenomenology of Feminine Body Comportment, Motility, and Spatiality', *Human Studies* (1980), 3:2, 137–56, reprinted in Iris Marion Young, *On Female Body Experience: 'Throwing Like a Girl' and Other Essays* (Oxford, 2005), pp. 27–45.

Young, Julian, *Friedrich Nietzsche: A Philosophical Biography* (Cambridge, 2010)

Young, Terence, *Heading Out: A History of American Camping* (Ithaca and London, 2017)

Yu, Christine, 'Where Are the Women in Sports Science Research?', *Outside* (8 Nov. 2018); https://www.outsideonline.com/2357391/where-are-women-sports-science-research

Zenic, Natasa, Rehda Taiar, Barbara Gilic, Mateo Blazevic, Dora Maric, Haris Pojskic and Damir Sekulic, 'Levels and Changes of Physical Activity in Adolescents during the Covid-19 Pandemic: Contextualising Urban vs. Rural Living Environment', *Applied Sciences* (2010), 10:11, 1–14;

Zhong, Bao-Liang, Wei Luo, Hai-Mei Li, Qian-Qian Zhang, Xiao-Ge Liu, Wen-Tian Li and Yi Li, 'Knowledge, Attitudes, and Practices towards COVID-19 among Chinese Residents during the Rapid Rise Period of the COVID-19 Outbreak: A Quick Online Cross-Sectional Survey', *International Journal of Biological Sciences* (2020), 16:10, 1745–52

Zhu, Motao, Songzhu Zhao, Jeffrey H. Coben and Gordon S. Smith, 'Why More Male Pedestrians Die in Vehicle–Pedestrian Collisions than Female Pedestrians: A Decompositional Analysis', *Injury Prevention* (2013), 19:4, 227–31

Zilcosky, John, and Marlo A. Burks (eds.), *The Allure of Sports in Western Culture* (Toronto, 2019)

Zsigmondy, Emile, *Les Dangers dans la Montagne* (Paris, 1886)

Notes

The following abbreviations are used in the Notes:

BPP	British Parliamentary Papers
DCA	Dunkeld Community Archive, Scotland
GRO	General Record Office of England and Wales
LAC	Ladies' Alpine Club archives, Alpine Club, London
MOJSM	Martin and Osa Johnson Safari Museum Archives
NA	The National Archives, London
NJSA	New Jersey State Archives
ODNB	*Oxford Dictionary of National Biography*

Introduction

1 Richard Askwith, *Feet in the Clouds*, London, 2004, p. 68.

2 Haruki Murakami, *What I Talk about When I Talk about Running*, London, 2009, p. 94; Vybarr Cregan-Reid, *Footnotes*, London, 2016, p. 205.

3 Emma John, 'Where Are All the Great Books about Women in Sport?', *Guardian*, 28 Jul. 2017, accessed 8 Jul. 2022. For further examples of male bias in sport and nature-writing anthologies, see Suzy Cripps (ed.), *The Joy of Walking*, London, 2020, which includes thirty-one extracts by male authors and thirteen by women; Ingrid Christopherson (ed.), *To Heaven's Heights*, Greensboro, N.C., 2021, whose extracts are almost entirely by male authors, except for introductions to various sections by the female editor; and Lionel Birnie and Ellis Bacon (eds.), *The Cycling Anthology*, Vol. 1, London, 2014, which includes no female contributors' writings. When the 'Landlines' research project at the University of Leeds endeavoured to discover 'the UK's favourite nature book', its members drew up a longlist on which 227 works by men, but only 51 by women, were included; and, on the shortlist, 8 works by men and 2 by women.

Robert Finch (ed.), *Norton Book of Nature-Writing*, New York and London, 2002, anthologised 96 men and 34 women, but of writers from the period prior to the early twentieth century, the ratio was much more disproportionate: 47 men to only 7 women. Nancy Deville, 'Needles, Not Knives . . .', *The Three Tomatoes*, 15 Sep. 2015, accessed 8 Jul. 2022.

4 Eva Briggs, 'My Adventures on the Appalachian Trail', *55 Plus*, 15 Oct. 2016, accessed 8 Jul. 2022; Precious McKenzie, *The Right Sort of Woman*, Newcastle upon Tyne, 2012, p. 108; Derek Birley, *Sport and the Making of Britain*, Manchester, 1993, p. 246.

5 Peter H. Hansen, 'Le Blond [*née* Hawkins-Whitshed], Elizabeth Alice Frances (1860–1934)', *ODNB*, and 'Elizabeth Hawkins-Whitshed', *Wikipedia*: (both accessed 8 Jul. 2022).

6 Pierre de Coubertin, 'Forty Years of Olympism, 1894–1934', pp. 742–6 in Pierre de Coubertin, *Pierre de Coubertin, 1863–1937: Olympism – Selected Writings*, edited by Norbert Müller (Lausanne, 2000); see also Uriel Simri, *Women at the Olympic Games*, Netanya, 1979, pp. 12–14.

7 Susan Silk and Barry Goldman, 'How Not to Say the Wrong Thing', *Los Angeles Times* online, 7 Apr. 2013, accessed 8 Jul. 2022.

Part One: Freedom

1: Running like a girl

1 Iris Marion Young, *On Female Body Experience*, Oxford 2005, pp. 38, 34.

2: The high life

1 Mariana Fox Tuckett, *A Victorian "Teenager's" Diary*, Frenchay, 2011, and online: entry 26 Sep. 1858, pp. 71–2, accessed 19 Feb. 2021. Although Tuckett did not measure the time it took her to finish the run, she did compare her pace to that of her family's carriage, and she was delighted that she and Helen 'got home first', 'feeling very proud of our achievement'.

2 Mrs Aubrey Le Blond, *Day In, Day Out*, London, 1928, p. 30.

3 Across her publications, Lizzie contradicts herself in the dating of many of her excursions, particularly her early ones, but the chronology offered here

is, I believe, the most likely. All the quotations in this paragraph derive from Le Blond, *Day In, Day Out*, p. 87, and Elizabeth Burnaby, *The High Alps in Winter*, London, 1883, p. 186.

4 Le Blond, *Day In, Day Out*, pp. 87–8. A description of the same excursions, conducted by a different mountaineer in the same season as Lizzie, can be found in a pair of articles by 'S', entitled 'Sojourning with the Swiss', *Gloucester Journal*, 10 and 17 Sep. 1881, 6. There is also a short silent film of mountaineers – mostly women – crossing Le Mauvais Pas in 1900, said to be the earliest existing footage of mountaineering: *Chamonix: Le Mauvais Pas*, 1900, accessed 12 Apr. 2021.

5 Le Blond, *Day In, Day Out*, pp. 88.

6 Le Blond, *Day In, Day Out*, pp. 88–9.

7 'Cuttings from Society Papers', *Lichfield Mercury*, 26 August 1881, 8.

8 'Alpine Climbing for Consumptives', *Lancashire Evening Post*, 9 Jun. 1899, 3; Mrs Aubrey Le Blond, *Adventures on the Roof of the World*, London, 1907, p. 173.

9 LAC G21: Elizabeth Le Blond, 'Certificat d'Ascension aux Grands-Mulets'.

10 'Marriages in High Life', *Brighton Gazette*, 30 Dec. 1858, 8; Le Blond, *Day In, Day Out*, p. 98.

11 University of Nottingham archives, Nottingham: 'Marriage settlement of Capt. James Hawkins Whitshed, RN and Sophia Henrietta Bentinck, 23 Apr. 1793', PI F4/5/3; Donald Harman Akenson, *Discovering the End of Time*, Montreal and London, 2016, pp. 138, 142.

12 See A. P. W. Malcomson, *The Pursuit of the Heiress*, Belfast, 2006; Le Blond, *Day In, Day Out*, p. 28.

13 Elizabeth is designated as 'Mimmy' by her daughter Renira in DCA, 'Notebooks of Renira Pollard née Whitshed, written 1864–9 at Kinnard', 2001.0409. Box 62; National Records of Scotland: 'Death certificate: Elizabeth Sophia Bentinck, 1858', Statutory Registers: Deaths, 373/2.

14 James Reid, 'On the Causes, Symptoms and Treatment of Puerperal Insanity', *Journal of Psychological Medicine and Mental Pathology*, 1848, 1, 134–5, cited in Hilary Marland, *Dangerous Motherhood*, Basingstoke, 2004, p. 38.

15 John Batty Tuke, 'On the Statistics of Puerperal Insanity . . .', *Edinburgh Medical Journal*, 1864–5, 10, 1015, cited in Marland, *Dangerous Motherhood*, p. 129.

16 Eliza's death certificate and information about her burial are included in the folder of research ('Robins 003') made by Eileen Cox and Joan Robins, which

accompanies DCA, 'Notebooks of Renira Pollard née Whitshed'. For information about mid nineteenth-century conventions surrounding the burial of those who took their own lives, see Gordon David Raeburn, 'The Long Reformation of the Dead in Scotland', PhD thesis, University of Durham, 2012, pp. 214–23. Later, a monument would be erected to Eliza in the churchyard of St Winifred's, Holbeck, Nottinghamshire, on the Cavendish-Bentincks' estates, inscribed 'To the memory of Elizabeth Sophia wife of Lieutenant General Arthur Cavendish Bentinck and eldest daughter of Sir St Vincent and the Hon. Lady Hawkins Whitshed. Died Jan 4th 1858 aged 22': https://historicengland.org.uk/images-books/photos/item/ioe01/01837/02 (accessed 6 May 2021).

17 John Conolly, 'Description and Treatment of Puerperal Insanity', *Lancet*, 1, (28 Mar. 1846), 1:1178, 349–54; Samuel Ashwell, *A Practical Treatise on the Diseases Peculiar to Women*, London, 1845, pp. 731–2: both cited in Marland, *Dangerous Motherhood*, pp. 160, 77 (see also pp. 8, 202); Robert Boyd, cited in Marland, *Dangerous*, p. 161.

18 Admiralty: Officer's Service Records: Whitshed, James Hawkins, Rank: Commander, National Archives, London, ADM/70/174; and Whitshed, James H., Rank: Lieutenant, ADM 196/37/1406; 'High Sheriffs for 1865', *Wexford People*, 19 Nov. 1864, 4 (similar announcements are made regarding Bentinck's presence as a high sheriff for Co. Wicklow for 1866 and 1867); 'County Wicklow Church Defence', *Wicklow News-Letter and County Advertiser*, 4 Jul. 1868, 11; 'Royal Irish Academy', *Saunders's Newsletter*, 13 Jan. 1864, 1; 'Editor's Trip: Co. Wicklow, Killincarrick', *Irish Farmer's Gazette and Journal of Practical Horticulture*, 31 Jan. 1863, 10.

19 William Arthur Cavendish-Bentinck, *Men, Women and Things: Memories of the Duke of Portland*, London, 1937, p. 6.

20 'Home and Domestic', *Illustrated Weekly News*, 28 Sep. 1867, 2; DCA, 'St Vincent Keene Hawkins-Whitshed, death certificate, 13 Sep. 1870, Edinburgh', in Robins 003.

21 'Birnam', *Dundee Advertiser*, 16 Mar. 1871, 4. Vin was his father's executor, but he was too unwell to execute his father's will, and his brother-in-law Arthur Cavendish-Bentinck had to take over; Sir St Vincent Keene Hawkins-Whitshed probate, 7 Nov. 1870; Irish double probate sealed Jan. 1871; both at Principal Registry, Dublin, Ireland.

22 John Hawkins, *Fred: The Collected Letters and Speeches of Colonel Frederick Gustavus Burnaby*, Solihull, 2014, II, p. 39.

23 Le Blond, *Day In, Day Out*, p. 23–4. Rosemary Raughter describes the early history of Killincarrick House in 'Paul', 'This Must Be the Place: Killincarrick House', *Greystone's Guide*, 28 Jun. 2018, accessed 13 Apr. 2021; Katharine Tynan, *Twenty-Five Years: Reminiscences*, London, 1913, pp. 212–13, 229; Helen Small, 'Currie [*née* Lamb], Mary Montgomerie, Lady Currie [*pseud.* Violet Fane] (1843–1905)', *ODNB*, accessed 19 Apr. 2021.

24 Le Blond, *Day In, Day Out*, p. 87.

25 Cavendish-Bentinck, *Men, Women and Things*, p. 2; 'The List of Killed and Wounded', *Portsmouth Evening News*, 22 Jan. 1885, 3; 'The Queen's Drawing Room', *Evening Mail*, 10 May 1878, 8; Thomas Wright, *The Life of Colonel Fred Burnaby*, London, 1908, pp. vii, 1, 34, 35, viii, x, 88, 102.

26 Hawkins, *Fred*, II, p. 39.

27 'Land League Hunts', *Derry Journal*, 9 Jan. 1882, 5.

28 I am very grateful to Madie Armstrong, who is working on a PhD thesis on the juxtaposition of the public/private persona in autobiography, biography and memoir in the life, writings and photography of Lizzie Le Blond, at De Montfort University, Leicester. Madie was kind enough to talk with me for several hours about Lizzie, and she made the excellent suggestion that Fred's late interest in marriage was motivated by the retirement of his anti-marriage colonel.

29 GRO: Marriage certificate of Frederick Gustavus Burnaby and Elizabeth Alice Frances Hawkins-Whitshed, 1879, 2nd Quarter, District Kensington, Vol.1a, p. 164; 'London Notes', *Daily Gazette for Middlesbrough*, 24 Jan. 1885, 2.

30 NA: 1881 England, Wales and Scotland Census, RG11/51 folio 44 p. 13; Hawkins, *Fred*, II, p. 40.

31 Le Blond, *Day In, Day Out*, pp. 28–9.

32 Kenneth J. Perkins, 'So Near and Yet So Far: British Tourism in Algiers, 1860–1914', in Martin Farr and Xavier Guégan (eds.), *The British Abroad since the Eighteenth Century*, Basingstoke, 2013, Vol. 1, pp. 219–20.

33 'Early Winter on the Continent', *Aberdeen Press and Journal*, 22 Oct. 1879, 6; Alexander A. Knox, *The New Playground; or, Wanderings in Algeria*, London, 1881, p. 8; Le Blond, *Day In, Day Out*, pp. 29–30.

34 Michael Heffernan, 'Shifting Sands: The Trans-Saharan Railway', in Stanley D. Brunn (ed.), *Engineering Earth*, London and New York, 2011, 1, p. 619; Michael Heffernan, 'The Limits of Utopia . . .', *Geographical Journal*, 1989, 155:3, 347; Roger T. Stearn, 'Burnaby, Frederick Gustavus (1842–85)', *ODNB*, accessed 13 Apr. 2021.

35 'The Trans-Sahara Railway', *The Times*, 29 Dec. 1879, 8; 'The Sahara', *The Times*, 22 Jan. 1880, 7; Capt. Henry E. Colvile, *A Ride in Petticoats and Slippers*, London, 1880, pp. 169, 232.

36 Wright, *Life of Colonel Fred Burnaby*, p. 163; 'Miscellaneous Dottings', *Shields Daily Gazette*, 16 Feb. 1880, 5; Colvile, *Petticoats and Slippers*, p. 301

37 Le Blond, *Day In, Day Out*, p. 30; 'Horse Guards Ball in London', *Hermann Advertiser and Advertiser-Courier*, 18 Aug. 1800, 8.

38 Wilfrid Scawen Blunt, diary entries, 3 and 30 Apr. 1884, cited in Hawkins, *Fred*, II, pp. 184–6; 'A Lady's London Letter', *Cheltenham Examiner*, 4 Feb. 1885, 2; Le Blond, *Day In, Day Out*, p. 28.

39 Mrs Aubrey Le Blond, *The Story of an Alpine Winter*, London, 1907, pp. 13, 21, 129.

40 Burnaby, *High Alps*, pp. 185–6.

41 Edna Healey, 'Coutts, Angela Georgina Burdett-, *suo jure* Baroness Burdett-Courts (1814–1906)', *ODNB*, accessed 15 Apr. 2021.

42 Healey, 'Coutts', *ODNB* ; Arnold Hunt, ''Who Wants to Be a Millionaire?', *Untold Lives Blog*, British Library, 7 Feb. 2014, accessed 15 Apr. 2021.

43 Barbara Caine, *English Feminism, 1780–1980*, Oxford, 1997, pp. 123–30; Margaret Ward, 'Gendering the Union: Imperial Feminism and the Ladies' Land League', *Women's History Review*, 2001, 10:1, 71–92.

44 Malcolm Craig, *Shackles of Convention: Women Mountaineers before 1914*, Ammanford, 2013, pp. 11–12.

45 Letter Fred Burnaby to his mother, 24 Aug. 1881, in Hawkins, *Fred*, II, p. 167; 'Colonel Fred Burnaby at Home', *Leicester Chronicle*, 22 Jul. 1882, 13.

46 Le Blond, *Day In, Day Out*, p. 90.

3: The mountains have room for all

1 Vaclav Smil, *Growth: From Microorganisms to Megacities*, Cambridge, Mass., 2019, p. 336; Perry R. Duis and Cathlyn Schallhorn, 'Chicago', *Encyclopedia Britannica*, 17 Dec. 2021, accessed 10 Jul. 2022; J. W. McCarty and C. B. Schedvin (eds.),

Australian Capital Cities: Historical Essays (Sydney, 1978), p. 21; Clive Emsley et al., 'London History: A Population History of London', *Old Bailey Proceedings Online*, accessed 10 Jul. 2022; Romola J. Davenport, 'Mortality, Migration and Epidemiological Change in English Cities, 1600–1870', *International Journal of Paleopathology*, 2021, 34, 37–8; Tertius Chandler, Gerald Fox and Lewis Mumford, *3000 Years of Urban Growth*, New York and London, 1974, pp. 373–7.

2 William Farr, *Appendix to the Second Annual Report of the Registrar-General of Births, Deaths, and Marriages, in England, 1838–1839*, BPP 1840 XVII, p. 37 (p. xi), and Hector Gavin, *The Unhealthiness of London and the Necessity of Remedial Measures*, London, 1847, both cited in Anthony S. Wohl, *Endangered Lives: Public Health in Victorian Britain*, London, 1983, pp. 1, 5.

3 Henry David Thoreau, 'Walking', *Atlantic Magazine*, Jun. 1862, 658; Silas Chamberlin, *On the Trail: A History of American Hiking*, New Haven and London, 2016, pp. 5–6; James Hingston, *Guide for Excursionists from Melbourne: Dedicated to All in Search of Health, Recreation and Pleasure*, Melbourne, 1868, cited in Bill Garner, *Born in a Tent: How Camping Makes Us Australian*, Sydney, 2013, p. 164.

4 Watkin, pp. 229, 76, cited in John Neville Greaves, 'The Last of the Railway Kings: The Life and Work of Sir Edward Watkin, 1819–1901', PhD thesis, Durham University, 2002, p. 27; *Report from the Select Committee on Public Walks*, BPP 1833 XV, p. 337, cited in Emma Griffin, *England's Revelry: A History of Popular Sports and Pastimes, 1660–1830*, Oxford, 2005, pp. 167–70; Joy Margaret Uings, 'Gardens and Gardening in a Fast-Changing Urban Environment: Manchester, 1750–1850', PhD thesis, Manchester Metropolitan University, 2013, p. 205; Lucy Larcom, *A New England Girlhood, Outlined from Memory*, Boston, 1889, p. 163, cited in Chamberlin, *On the Trail*, p. 19.

5 Robin Jarvis, *Romantic Writing and Pedestrian Travel*, Basingstoke, 1997, pp. 11–14; Rachel Hewitt, *Map of a Nation . . .*, London, 2010, p. 237; Samuel Taylor Coleridge, *Notebooks*, ed. Kathleen Coburn, London, 1957, Vol. I: *Text*, entry 1207.

6 Phoebe Kropp, 'Wilderness Wives and Dishwashing Husbands . . .', *Journal of Social History*, 2009, 43:1, 7–8; Garner, *Born in a Tent*, p. 53.

7 Charles Edward Mathews, 'The Growth of Mountaineering', *Alpine Journal*, Aug. 1880–May 1882, 252–4.

8 C. D. Cunningham, 'The Decline of Chamonix as a Mountaineering Centre', *Alpine Journal*, Aug. 1880–May 1882, 11, 467; Jemima Morrell, *Miss Jemima's Swiss Journal: The First Conducted Tour of Switzerland*, London, 1963, p. 4.

9 Amelia B. Edwards, *Untrodden Peaks and Unfrequented Valleys*, London, 1873, p. viii.

10 Dyos and Aldcroft, p. 35, cited in Jarvis, *Romantic Writing*, pp. 19–20; Stéphane J. L. Blond, 'The Trudaine Atlas: Government Road-Mapping in Eighteenth-Century France', *Imago Mundi: The International Journal for the History of Cartography* (2013), 65:1, 64–79; Giles Bertrand, trans. Joan Johnson, 'When Travel Is for the Purpose of Inventing a New Space . . .', *Annales Historique de la Révolution Française*, 2016, 385:3, 133–52; Benjamin Spielmann, 'Swiss Road History between State Consolidation . . .', International Association for the History of Transport, Traffic and Mobility, Mexico City conference, 27–30 Oct. 2016, accessed 15 May 2021; J. Copeland, *Roads and Their Traffic 1750–1850*, Newton Abbot, 1968, p. 85; Jarvis, *Romantic Writing*, p. 21.

11 Chamberlin, *On the Trail*, pp. 27, 1–2.

12 Jane Freshfield, *Alpine Byways; or, Fresh Leaves Gathered in 1859 and 1860*, London, 1861, pp. 40, 2; Mrs Henry Warwick Cole, *A Lady's Tour around Monte Rosa*, London, 1859, p. 9.

13 Karl Baedeker, *Switzerland, and the Adjacent Portions of Italy, Savoy and the Tyrol. Handbook for Travellers*, 10th edn, 1883, p. v (my emphasis), compared to Baedeker, 2nd edn, 1864, p. iii. Baedeker also replaced earlier references to 'the fair sex' with the more respectful 'ladies' in the 10th edition. Baedeker (1864), p. xviii ('The traveller who avails *himself* of all the public conveyances'), is edited to remove gendered pronouns in Baedeker, 16th edn, 1895, p. xvii ('the traveller prefers driving & riding to walking'). Similarly, Baedeker (1864), p. xxi ('The Pedestrian is unquestionably the most independent of all travellers; beyond all others is he able both physically and morally to enjoy a tour in Switzerland'), is edited in Baedeker (1895), p. xx, to read in a gender-neutral way ('In a mountainous country like Switzerland it is to pedestrians alone that many of the finest points are accessible, and even where driving or riding is practicable, walking is often more enjoyable').

14 Cunningham, 'The Decline of Chamonix', pp. 467, 461.

15 Cole, *A Lady's Tour*, pp. 261, 9; Freshfield, *Alpine Byways*, p. 64; Anne-Mette Vibe, *Therese Bertheau*, Oslo, 2012, p. 19; *Le Courrier des Alpes*, 1874, 93, cited in Cécile Ottogalli-Mazzacavallo, 'Femmes et Alpinisme au Club Alpin Français à l'Aube du xxe Siècle: au Recontre Atypique?', *STAPS*, 2004, 66:4, 31.

16 John W. Lund, 'Historical Impacts of Geothermal Resources on the People of North America', *Geo-Heat Center Quarterly Bulletin*, 1995, 16:4, 7; John Davy cited in Susan Barton, *Healthy Living in the Alps*, Manchester, 2008, p. 10.

17 See Barton, *Healthy Living in the Alps*, p. 21; Dylan Jim Esson, 'Selling the Alpine Frontier . . .', PhD thesis, University of California, Berkeley, 2011, p. 8; [Elizabeth MacMorland], *Davos-Platz*, London, 1878, p. i.

18 Herbert George Birch and Joan Dye Gussow, *Disadvantaged Children*, New York, Harcourt, 1970, p. 149; Wohl, *Endangered Lives*, pp. 12–13; John Simon, *Second Report of the Medical Officer of the Privy Council*, BPP 1860 XXIX, p. 201 (p. lxiv), cited in Wohl, *Endangered Lives*, p. 26.

19 Wohl, *Endangered Lives*, pp. 130–2; Nicole Smith, 'The Problem of Excess Female Mortality: Tuberculosis in Western Massachusetts, 1850–1910', pp. 17, 35, 43, MA thesis, University of Massachusetts, 2008, cited in Janet Oppenheim, *Shattered Nerves*, New York and Oxford, 1991, p. 193.

20 Guido Mountjoy, 'The Comic Alpenstock', *The Daguerreotype*, 1847, 1, 564; Rosemary Greenwood, 'A Grindelwald Centenary', *Alpine Journal*, 1992–3, 97, 198; Elizabeth Fox Tuckett, *How We Spent the Summer*, London, 1864.

21 British Library, Mss Eur F 197/2, Martha Shaw, Diary (1839–42), 9 Mar. 1839, 24 Aug. 1839, 10 Sep. 1839, 14 Jun. 1846, 1 Oct. 1846, 8 Aug. 1846.

22 Jemima Morrell, *Swiss Journal*, p. 4; Freshfield, *Alpine Byways*, p. 33; Emily Hornby, *Mountaineering Records*, Liverpool, 1907, pp. 3, 45, 48, 58.

23 Edwards, *Untrodden Peaks*, pp. 347–8; Frances Havergal, *Swiss Letters and Alpine Poems*, ed. J. M. Crane, London, 1881, p. 169; Cole, *A Lady's Tour*, p. 165.

24 National Library of Wales, MS9279–9280A, Anon., 'A Tour through North Wales, 1775'; Michael David Freeman, *Early Tourists in Wales: 18th and 19th Century Tourists' Comments about Wales*, accessed 17 May 2021; Jane Austen, *Pride and Prejudice*, ed. Donald Gray 1813, New York and London, 2001, pp. 195, 24–5.

25 Havergal, *Swiss Letters*, p. 169, cited in Clare Roche, 'Women Climbers, 1850–1900', *Sport in History*, 2013, 33:3, 243; Letter Elizabeth Carter to Catherine Talbot, 1746, cited in Elizabeth Carter and Montagu Pennington, *Memoirs of the Life of Mrs Elizabeth Carter*, London, 1825, I, pp. 134–5.

26 For perhaps the most influential exploration of the idea of 'separate spheres', see Leonore Davidoff and Catherine Hall, *Family Fortunes: Men and Women of the English Middle Class, 1780–1850*, London, 1987, pp. 32–3. Mrs Aubrey Le Blond, *True Tales of Mountain Adventure*, London, 1903, pp. 274–6, describes Paradis's ascent.

27 J. G. R. Harding, 'The Other Anne Lister', *Alpine Journal*, 2019, 123, 234–40. I am very grateful to Nigel Buckley, Alpine Club librarian, for pointing me in the direction of this article.
28 Elizabeth Main, *High Life and Towers of Silence*, London, 1886, p. 189; Frederica Plunket, *Here and There among the Alps*, London, 1875, pp. 181, 194, 195.
29 Le Blond, *Day In, Day Out*, p. 23.
30 Cited in Carol Dyhouse, *Girls Growing up in Late Victorian and Edwardian England*, London, 2012, p. 43; R. W. Clark, *An Eccentric in the Alps*, London, 1959, p. 30.
31 Edwards, *Untrodden Peaks*, p. 311; Freshfield, *Alpine Byways*, p. 164; John Barrell, *The Idea of Landscape and the Sense of Place, 1730–1840*, Cambridge, 1972, pp. 24–5; Charlotte Smith, *The Poems of Charlotte Smith*, ed. Stuart Curran, New York and Oxford, 1993, p. 217; Plunket, *Here and There*, p. 179.
32 Craig, *Shackles of Convention*, pp. 35–8; According to Trevor Adams (*The A La Ronde Story: Its People*, 2011), the Parminters' ascent was reported in the 1791 edition of Marc-Théodore Bourrit's *Nouvelle Description des Glaciers de Savoie*, and in *l'Esprit des Journaux François et Étrangers* in Nov 1786. Jane Parminter kept a travel diary which was destroyed in 1942 but had been partly transcribed: see Oswald J. Reichel, 'Extracts from a Devonshire Lady's Notes . . .', *Transactions of the Devonshire Association for the Advancement of Science* (1902), 34, 265–75.
33 Ann C. Colley, *Victorians in the Mountains*, Burlington, V.T., 2010, p. 5.
34 Charles Dickens, 'Hardihood and Foolhardihood', *All the Year Round*, 19 Aug. 1865, 14, 86 cited in Michael S. Reidy, 'Mountaineering, Masculinity, and the Male Body in Mid-Victorian Britain', *Osiris*, 2015, 30:1, 159.
35 Chamberlin, *On the Trail*, p. 37; Edmund Burke, *A Philosophical Enquiry*, ed. Adam Phillips, *1757*, Oxford, 1990 p. 97.
36 Ellen Weeton, *Miss Weeton: Journal of a Governess 1807–1811*, edited by Edward Hall, 2 vols, Oxford 1936–1939, II, pp. 168–9, 231–9, 258–9, 265, 140, 386–93. Michael David Freeman's website, *Early Tourists in Wales*, contains valuable transcriptions of early female mountaineers' accounts of ascending Welsh peaks, including Weeton's accounts. See https://sublimewales.wordpress.com/attractions/snowdon/list-of-all-transcriptions/snowdon-descriptions-of-ascents-by-women/.
37 W. A. B. Coolidge , 'Explorations amongst the Cottian Alps', *Alpine Journal* (Aug. 1880–May 1882), 10, 123; Cunningham, 'The Decline of Chamonix', 459–71.
38 Charles Dickens, 'Foreign Climbs', *All the Year Round*, 2 Sep. 1865, 14, 135–6; Leslie Stephen, *The Playground of Europe*, London, 1871, p. 304; Albert

Mummery, *My Climbs in the Alps and the Caucasus*, London, 1895, p. 120; see also Reidy, 'Mountaineering, Masculinity', 164.

39 W. A. B. Coolidge, 'New Expeditions: Stubaithal District', *Alpine Journal*, Aug. 1884–May 1886, 12, 124–5.

40 Douglas W. Freshfield, 'Review of Walter White's *On Foot through Tyrol* and *Holidays in Tyrol*', *Alpine Journal*, Aug. 1876–May 1878, 8, 119; LAC G21: Marjorie Milsom, 'The Ladies' Alpine Club', *Listener*, 28 Nov. 1957, 881–2.

41 Coolidge, 'Explorations amongst the Cottian Alps', 123; 'mountaineer, *n.* and *adj.*', *Oxford English Dictionary,* online edition, Oxford, Mar. 2022, accessed 11 Jul. 2022; Scholes, cited in Chamberlin, *On the Trail*, p. 62.

42 W. A. B. Coolidge, 'Proceedings of the Alpine Club', *Alpine Journal*, Aug. 1880–May 1882, 10, 239; Florence Dixie, *Across Patagonia*, London, 1880, p. 2.

43 Ernest Caron, 'Chronique du Club', *Annuaire du Club Alpin Française*, 1889, 16, 465–71 (466), cited in Ottogalli-Mazzacavallo, 'Femmes et alpinisme', 32.

44 David Robbins, 'Sport, Hegemony and the Middle Class', *Theory, Culture & Society*, 1987, 4:4, 593–4.

45 'Mountaineer, *n.* and *adj.*', *Oxford English Dictionary*; Rebekka von Mallinckrodt, 'Attractive or Repugnant? Foot Races in Eighteenth-Century Germany and Britain', in John Zilcosky and Marlo A. Burks (eds.), *The Allure of Sports in Western Culture*, Toronto, 2019, pp. 148–9; Andy Milroy, 'In the Beginning: Native Americans', *UltraRunning Magazine*, 15 Aug. 2013, accessed 11 Jul. 2022; Garner, *Born in a Tent*, pp. 27, 52.

46 Garner, *Born in a Tent*, p. 132; William Wordsworth, *Kendal and Windermere Railway: Two Letters Re-Printed from the Morning Post, Revised, with Additions*, Kendal, [1845], pp. 8, 16; Henriette d'Angeville, *My Ascent of Mont Blanc*, translated by Jennifer Barnes, London, 1992, pp. xx–xxi. D'Angeville's ascent, and its class politics, are discussed in Karen J. Stockham, 'Women's Mountaineering Life-Writing 1808–1960', PhD thesis, University of Exeter, 2012, pp. 58–61, and in 'The First Lady Mountaineer', *Alpine Post*, 1 September 1897, 21:23, 303. For a discussion of how the relationships between climbers and guides were shaped by social class, see Kathryn Walchester, 'Alpine Guides, Gender, and British Climbers, 1859–1885', *Victorian Periodicals Review*, 51:3, 523–4.

47 Mary Collier, *The Woman's Labour: An Epistle to Mr. Stephen Duck*, London, 1739, pp. 11, 12, 10, 15; 'A Female Pedestrian Carrier of Long Standing', *Hereford Times*, 25 Nov. 1848, 5.

48 Richard C. Trexler, 'Correre la Terra: Collective Insults in the Late Middle Ages', *Mélanges de l'Ecole Française de Rome*, 1984, 96:2, 866–8; Von Mallinckrodt, 'Attractive or Repugnant?', p. 149; Peter F. Radford, 'Women's Foot-Races in the 18th and 19th Centuries', *Canadian Journal of the History of Sport*, 1994, 25:1, 50–61; quotations from organisers of smock-races cited in J. Goulstone, *Smock Racing*, Erith, 2005, p. 25.

49 In July 1823, eight-year-old Emma Freeman was made to speed-walk thirty miles in under eight hours ('Infantine Female Pedestrian', *Salisbury and Winchester Journal*, 21 Jul. 1823, 2), and in December 1876, Jane Toner, a woman who was reported to be in her nineties, attempted to walk 300 miles but collapsed after 165.5 miles, 'exhausted by the soft nature of the ground' ('The Female Pedestrian at Darlington', *Northern Echo*, 15 Dec. 1876, 4). Ada Anderson collapsed with breathing difficulties after ninety-six miles, when attempting to walk 100 miles in 28 hours in Plymouth in January 1878 (Harry Hall, *The Pedestriennes*, Indianapolis, 2014, p. 49); Peter Lovesey, 'Women Behaving Madly', http://www.vrwc.org.au/tim-archive/articles/wo-ada-anderson.pdf, accessed 22 Nov. 2018; 'Pedestrianism', *Leeds Intelligencer*, 15 Oct. 1864, 7; 'A Female Pedestrian', *Morning Post*, 30 Jun. 1874, 6; 'Charge of Assaulting a Female Pedestrian', *Nottinghamshire Guardian*, 24 June 1881, 6.

50 Eric Foner, *Gateway to Freedom*, New York and London, 2015, pp. 190–215; Fergus M. Bordewich, *Bound for Canaan*, New York, 2005, pp. 344–72; Allison Keyes, 'Harriet Tubman, an Unsung Naturalist . . .', *Audubon Magazine*, 25 Feb. 2020, accessed 11 Jul. 2022.

51 Britt Rusert, *Fugitive Science: Empiricism and Freedom in Early African American Culture*, New York, 2017, pp. 181–218; Sojourner Truth, *Narrative of Sojourner Truth*, dictated to Olive Gilbert, edited by Francis Titus, New York, 1875, first published 1850, p. 116, cited in Janey Weinhold Montgomery, *A Comparative Analysis of the Rhetoric of Two Negro Women Orators*, Fort Hays Studies Literature Series, 6, Kansas, 1968, pp. 34–5.

52 Britt Rusert, '"Nor Wish to Live the Past Again" . . .', *Commonplace: The Journal of Early American Life* (2016), 16:2, accessed 5 Sep. 2021; Johanna Ortner, 'Lost No More: Recovering Frances Ellen Watkins Harper's *Forest Leaves*', *Commonplace: The Journal of Early American Life*, 15:4, Summer 2015; accessed 18 Oct. 2022.

53 Plunket, *Here and There*, pp. 11–12.

4: *Why can't you just run faster?*

1 Much research on men's and women's responses to unwanted noise has focused on open-plan offices. Background conversations and laughter – termed 'irrelevant speech noise', or ISN – are consistently found to be the biggest causes of annoyance in such environments. Again, it is women who report being most damaged by ISN, reporting a greater negative impact on 'motivation and cognitive performance, as well as on fatigue', than men. See Y. Fried, S. Melamed and H. A. Ben-David 'The Joint Effects of Noise, Job Complexity, and Gender on Employee Sickness Absence . . .', *Journal of Occupational and Organizational Psychology*, 2002, 75:2, 131–44; Helena Jahncke et al., 'Open-Plan Office Noise: Cognitive Performance and Restoration', *Journal of Environmental Psychology*, 2011, 31:4, 373–82.

2 Mary Ellen Nivison and Inger M. Endresen, 'An Analysis of Relationships among Environmental Noise, and the Consequences for Health and Sleep', *Journal of Behavioral Medicine*, 1993, 16:3, 257–76; M.R. Irwin, M. Daniels, S.C. Risch, E. Bloom and H. Weiner, 'Plasma Cortisol and Natural Killer Cell Activity during Bereavement', *Biological Psychiatry*, 1988, 24, 173–8, cited in Erin M. Hill, 'Noise Sensitivity and Diminished Health: The Role of Stress-Related Factors', PhD thesis, Auckland University of Technology, 2012, p. 58, accessed 9 Oct. 2020; Steve Love and Joanne Kewley, 'Does Personality Affect Peoples' Attitudes towards Mobile Phone Use in Public Places?', in R. Ling and P. Pedersen (eds.), *Mobile Communications: Renegotiation of the Social Sphere*, London, 2005, p. 274.

3 Deborah Kirby Forgays et al., 'Texting Everywhere for Everything . . .', *Computers in Human Behavior*, 2014, 31, 319; Naomi S. Baron and Elise M. Campbell, 'Gender and Mobile Phones in Cross-National Context', *Language Sciences*, 2012, 34, 13–27.

4 A. Kaarlela-Tuomaala et al., 'Effects of Acoustic Environment on Work in Private Office Rooms and Open-Plan Offices . . .', *Ergonomics*, 2009, 52:11, 1423–44; Sonja Di Blasio et al., 'A Cross-Sectional Survey on the Impact of Irrelevant Speech Noise on Annoyance . . .', *International Journal of Environmental Research and Public Health*, 2019, 16:2, 280; Ohad Inbar et al., 'Tactful Calling: Investigating Asymmetric Social Dilemmas in Mobile Communications', *Behavior and Information Technology*, 2014, 33:12, 1317–32.

5 Samuel D. Warren, and Louis D. Brandeis, 'The Right to Privacy', *Harvard Law Review*, 1890, 4:5, 207.

6 Keri Wallace, 'Follow a Strong Lead', *Trail Running*, Jun/Jul 2019, 50, 40–3.

7 'The Handsome Family', *The Trades Club*, 8 Mar 2018, accessed 11 Jul. 2022.

8 https://www.statista.com/statistics/531146/women-participants-in-olympic-summer-games/ (accessed 11 Jul. 2022); Jens Jakob Andersen, 'Marathon Statistics 2019 Worldwide', *RunRepeat*, 6 August 2021, accessed 11 Jul. 2022; Ashley Loretta, 'Trend Alert: More Women are Running Races Than Men, Brilliant!', *Gone Runners* 8 Jul. 2020. Running historian and blogger Katie Holmes points out that, while younger women predominate at short events like parkrun, older women also make up a much larger – and increasing – proportion of ultra-marathon participants ('Diane Leather and the 5 Minute Mile', *Run Young 50*, 8 Mar. 2008, accessed 11 Jul. 2022).

9 'Strava Releases 2020 Year in Sport Data Report', *Strava*, 16 Dec. 2020, accessed 11 Jul. 2022; Tessa M. Pollard and Janelle M. Wagnild, 'Gender Differences in Walking . . .', *BMC Public Health*, 2017, 17, 341, accessed 11 Jul. 2022; Renée A. Botta and Lynne Fitzgerald, 'Gendered Experiences in the Backcountry', *Journal of Outdoor Recreation, Education and Leadership*, 2020, 12:1, 27–40; Gill Pomfret and Adele Doran, 'Gender and Mountaineering Tourism', in Ghazali Musa et al. (eds.), *Mountaineering Tourism,* London, 2015, p. 141.

10 Nick Van Mead, 'Lizzy Hawker: "I Might Run around 180 Miles in a Week" ', *Guardian*, 28 Jun. 2013; Brian Metzler, 'Courtney Dauwalter Breaks UTMB Record to Win', *Trail Runner*, 30 Aug 2021; Sanish Shoker, 'Woman Completes 100 Marathons in 100 Days World Record', *BBC News*, 12 Apr. 2022; Brittany Hambleton, 'British Runner Sets Guinness World Record for Most Consecutive Marathons', *Canadian Running*, 13 Apr. 2022; Alex Potter, 'An Interview with Camille Herron after Her 2022 100-Mile World Record', *I Run Far*, 22 Feb. 2022 (all accessed 11 Jul. 2022).

11 Van Mead, 'Lizzy Hawker . . .'; Nicky Spinks: 'Nicky Spinks: My Double Bob Graham Round', *Inov-8*; Sean Ingle, 'Jasmin Paris Becomes First Woman to Win 268-Mile Montane Spine Race', *Guardian*, 17 Jan. 2019 (all accessed 11 Jul. 2022).

12 Nish Manek, 'Olympics Marathon . . .', *Science Focus*, 6 Sep. 2021; Ian McMahan, 'The Physiological Differences between Male and Female Runners', *Podium Runner*, 8 Oct. 2015 (both accessed 11 Jul. 2022).

13 Jens Jakob Andersen, 'Research: Women are Better Runners than Men', *Run-Repeat*, 21 Sep. 2021; Mitch LeBlanc, 'Leadville 2011 Data Analysis', *mitchleblanc.com*, 28 Jul. 2012, accessed 11 Jul. 2022.

14 Linda Jean Carpenter and R. Vivian Acosta, *Women in Intercollegiate Sport*, West Brookfield, Mass., 2006, p. i; Cheryl Cooky et al., 'One and Done . . .', *Communication & Sport*, 2021, 9:3, 347–71.

15 Christy McCarter, 'Overlooking Her Shot . . .', *Purdue University News*, 24 Mar. 2021; 'Telegraph Women's Sport Celebrates Third Anniversary . . .', *Newsworks*, 25 Mar. 2022; Tammy Parlour and Women's Sport Trust, 'Visibility Uncovered: Review and Debate . . .', 26 Oct. 2021; Steve McCaskill, ' "We've Got to Keep Pushing Forward" . . .', *Sports Pro Media*, 31 Mar. 2022; Tammy Parlour and Women's Sports Trust, 'Visibility Uncovered: The Year in Review (2021)', 2021', 7 Feb. 2022; Charlotte Rogers, 'Value of Women's Sport Could Treble by 2030 as UK Viewership Hits 33 Million', *Marketing Week*, 8 Feb. 2022 (all accessed 11 Jul. 2022).

16 Lizzie Rosewell, 'Why Don't More Women Take Part in Ultrarunning?', *Lizzie Running*, 25 Jul. 2018, accessed 11 Jul. 2022.

17 Kate Sellers, 'Real-Life Races to Book Now', *Women's Running*, 29 Mar. 2021; L. McDermott, 'Exploring Intersections of Physicality and Female-Only Canoeing Experiences', *Leisure Studies*, 2004, 23:3, 283–301; T. Hornibrook, E. Brinkert, D. Parry, R. Seimens, D. Mitten and S. Priest, 'The Benefits and Motivations of All Women Outdoor Programs', *Journal of Experiential Education* (1997), 20:3, 152–8, cited in Kerry Griffiths, 'Women in the Hills . . .', Sheffield Hallam Sports Industry Research Centre and WITH Research Network, Jan. 2022 (unpublished), p. 17; Megan Janssen, 'Trail Races Continue Making Strides toward Gender Equality', *Trailrunner*, 22 Apr 2019 (all online sources accessed 11 Jul. 2022).

18 Janssen, 'Trail Races . . .'; Zoë Rom, 'How Childcare Responsibilities Limit Women's Participation . . .', *Trail Runner*, 7 May 2020: (both accessed 11 Jul. 2022).

19 Katie Campbell Spyrka, 'Ultrarunner Sophie Power: Motherhood and Mountain Ultras', *Lessons in Badassery*, 27 Oct. 2021, accessed 18 Oct. 2022.

20 B. Peter Pashigian, 'Demand Uncertainty . . .', *American Economic Review*, 1988, 78:5, 936–53; Sam Dhanapala, 'An Overview of the Sportswear Market', in Steven George Hayes and Praburaj Venkatraman (eds.), *Materials and Technology for Sportswear and Performance Apparel*, Boca Raton, Fla., 2016, pp. 8.

21 https://www.seatosummit.co.uk/products/sleep/sleeping-mats/ultralight-si-wmn/; Peter Maksimow, 'Tips for Women on the Trails: Introducing Helen

Stuart', *American Trail Running Association*, 15 May 2017; https://www.garmin.com/en-US/newsroom/press-release/sports-fitness/2019-garmin-announces-menstrual-cycle-tracking-feature-for-garmin-connect/; https://www.drstacysims.com (all accessed 11 Jul. 2022).

22 'Climb up Snowdon', *Carnarvon and Denbigh Herald*, 16 Sep. 1892, cited by Freeman, *Early Tourists*, accessed 11 Sep. 2020.

23 http://www.maverick-race.com/results/2019/9/21/the-maverick-inov-8-x-amp-ultra-series-snowdonia-results; Jacob Meschke, 'Back-of-the-Pack London Marathoners . . .', *Runner's World*, 7 May 2019; 182 of the final 282 finishers at the 2019 London Marathon were registered in the female category: http://www.marathonguide.com/results/browse.cfm?RL=1&MIDD=16190428&Gen=B&Begin=42201&End=42300&Max=42485: (all accessed 18 Sep. 2020).

24 https://runhive.com/running/world-records (accessed 18 Sep. 2020); Emma N. Hilton and Tommy Lundberg, 'Transgender Women in the Female Category of Sport: Perspectives on Testosterone Suppression and Performance Advantage', *Sports Medicine*, 2021, 51, 201–3; David Epstein, *The Sports Gene*, London, 2014, pp. 56–74. Over 5km, the female record-holder is 12.4 per cent slower than the male record-holder; 11.4 per cent slower over 10km; 12.7 per cent slower over 10 miles; 11.2 per cent slower over a half-marathon; 10.2 per cent slower over a full marathon (26.2 miles); and 15.3 per cent slower over 50km.

25 Hilton and Lundberg, 'Transgender Women . . .', 204; Janssen, 'Trail Races . . .', accessed 11 Jul. 2022. The Dragon's Back Race was the first ultra-marathon to be won outright by a woman (Helene Whitaker, née Diamantides, in 1992), but it has very tough cut-offs and, in general, far fewer female than male participants: in 2021, 368 runners enrolled, of whom women constituted only 10 per cent, and of the 90 finishers who managed to stay within the deadlines, only 7 (7.8 per cent) were female.

26 Griffiths, 'Women in the Hills . . .', p. i; Paul Ronto and Vania Nokolova, *The State of Ultra-Running 2020: RunRepeat.com and the IAU*, https://runrepeat.com/state-of-ultra-running, accessed 11 July 2022; Natasa Zenic, Rehda Taiar, Barbara Gilic, Mateo Blazevic, Dora Maric, Haris Pojskic and Damir Sekulic, 'Levels and Changes of Physical Activity in Adolescents during the Covid-19 Pandemic: Contextualising Urban vs. Rural Living Environment', *Applied Sciences*, 2010, 10:11, 1–14; James Dollman and Nicole R. Lewis, 'The Impact of

Socioeconomic Position on Sport Participation among South Australian Youth', *Journal of Science and Medicine in Sport*, May 2010, 13:3, 318–22.

27 Griffiths, 'Women in the Hills . . .', p. 11; Outdoor Industries Association, *Getting Active Outdoors: A Study of Demography, Motivation, Participation and Provision in Outdoor Sport and Recreation in England*, 2015, accessed 11 July 2022.

28 McCarter, 'Overlooking her Shot . . .'; Gina Lucrezi, 'Women's versus Men's Pay in Trail and Ultrarunning', *I Run Far*, 26 Apr. 2017: (both accessed 11 Jul. 2022).

29 Jennifer T. Coletti et al., 'Reading Between the Lines: Gender Stereotypes in Children's Sport-Based Books', *Women in Sport and Physical Activity*, 2021, 29:1, 1–11; Dennis Wenzhao Mu and Sharron J. Lennon, 'Objectification of Women in Sportswear Brands' Instagram Accounts', *International Textile and Apparel Association Annual Conference Proceedings*, 2018, 75:1, https://www.iastatedigitalpress.com/itaa/article/id/1498/ (both accessed 11 Jul. 2022).

30 Iñigo Mujika and Ritva S. Taipale, 'Sport Science on Women, Women in Sport Science', *International Journal of Sports Physiology and Performance*, 2019, 14:8, 1013–14; David and Megan Roche, 'Women Are Underrepresented in Exercise Science, and That Is a Problem', *Trail Runner*, 9 Mar. 2021; McMahan, 'The Physiological Differences . . .'. I am very grateful to Sophie Gosling for talking to me, and giving me permission to quote her, about the ways in which menopause has shaped her experiences of running.

31 Milos Djordjevic, '20+ Mind-Blowing Sportswear Industry Statistics . . .', *Fashion Discounts*, 18 Mar. 2020; Cara Salpini, 'Game-Changers . . .', *Retail Dive*, 3 Sep. 2019; Alysia Montaño, and Lindsay Crouse, 'Nike Told Me to Dream Crazy, Until I Wanted a Baby', *New York Times*, 12 May 2019 (all accessed 11 Jul. 2022).

32 Ruth Hailu, 'Fitbits and Other Wearables . . .', *Stat*, 24 Jul. 2019; Julia Słupska and Leonie Maria Tanczer, 'Threat Modeling Intimate Partner Violence . . .', in Jane Bailey et al. (eds.), *The Emerald International Handbook of Technology-Facilitated Violence and Abuse*, Bradford, 2021, p. 666; Saman Javed, '"Keep Your Whereabouts to Yourself!" . . .', *Independent*, 16 Jun. 2021; https://twitter.com/MrAndrew/status/1305530276127428609; https://www.letsrun.com/forum/flat_read.php?thread=9250424> (all accessed 11 Jul. 2022).

33 E. J. Staurowsky et al., *Chasing Equity*, New York, 2020, p. 12.

34 Griffiths, 'Women in the Hills . . .', pp. 1–29; SportScotland: Women's Sport and Fitness Foundation, *Barriers to Women and Girl's Participation in Sport and*

Physical Activity, Edinburgh, 2008, pp. 1–2; Rosewell, 'Why Don't More Women Take Part . . .'; Women in Sport, 'Reframing Sport for Teenage Girls: Tackling Teenage Disengagement', 2022, pp. 10, 23; Office for National Statistics, 'Men Enjoy Five Times More Leisure Time . . .', 9. Jan. 2018; Haroon Siddique, 'Childcare Costs in England Rise up to Seven Times Faster than Wages', *Guardian*, 20 Oct 2017 (all online sources accessed 11 Jul. 2022).

35 Salpini, 'Game-Changers . . .', accessed 11 Jul. 2022.

36 Suzanne Wrack, 'Survey Reveals Increase in Female Football Fans Being Harassed at Games', *Guardian*, 9 Nov. 2021, accessed 11 Jul. 2022.

37 https://runequal.org/goals-and-principles/ (accessed 11 Jul. 2022).

38 Research into whether trans women athletes retain male physiological advantage post-transition, relative to their abilities prior to undergoing transition and relative to female athletes of equivalent fitness, is still in its infancy, and is a complex area of study. The nature of retained male advantage varies according to which sports and which physiological attributes are being studied (trans women might retain an advantage in athletics, but not perhaps in sports such as snooker or equestrianism), whether the subjects are elite athletes or untrained amateurs, the age at which trans subjects transitioned and whether they experienced the full course of male puberty, the nature of the transition and whether it included hormone therapy, and how many years of hormone treatment have been undergone. For an overview of some of the issues and research, see, for example, Joanna Harper, Emma O'Donnell, Behzad Sorouri Khorashad, Hilary McDermott and Gemma L. Witcomb, 'How Does Hormone Transition in Transgender Women Change Body Composition, Muscle Strength and Haemoglobin? Systematic Review with a Focus on the Implications for Sport Participation', *British Journal of Sports Medicine*, 2021, 55:15, 865–72; and Ross Tucker, 'Why Transgender Athletes Threaten Fairness in Women's Sport', *The Real Science of Sport Podcast*, 20 May 2021, 3:8. While Tucker (among others) is concerned about how the inclusion of trans women in the female category might jeopardise the visibility and protection (in terms of both safety and fairness) accorded to female sportspeople, greater weight is placed on the value of trans inclusion by commentators and researchers including Bethany Alice Jones, Jon Arcelus, Walter Pierre Bouman and Emma Haycraft, 'Sport and Transgender People: A Systematic Review of the Literature Relating to Sport Participation and Competitive Sport Polices', *Sports Medicine*, 2017, 47:4, 701–16 (702); and Jack Turban, 'Trans Girls Belong on Girls'

Sports Teams', *Scientific American*, 16 Mar. 2021. As the charity Women in Sport summarises, 'there is a genuine conflict between safety and fairness and trans inclusion in most women's sport' (Women in Sport, 'Transgender Inclusion in Women's Sport – July 2022'; all online sources accessed 13 Feb. 2023).

5: In the mountains, there you feel free

1 Burnaby, *High Alps*, preface; Le Blond, *Day In, Day Out*, pp. 90–1, in which Lizzie dates these climbs to summer 1881 (but contradicts herself in *High Alps*, which dates them to summer 1882). Clare Roche, 'The Ascent of Women . . .', PhD thesis, Birkbeck, University of London, p. 361.

2 Main, *High Life*, p. 59. My description of the 1882 floods in Italy is taken from 'Le Inondazioni', *La Perseveranza*, 21 Sept. 1882, 3, and Roberta Biasillo and Marco Armiero, 'The Transformative Potential of a Disaster: A Contextual Analysis of the 1882 Flood in Verona, Italy', *Journal of Historical Geography*, 2019, 66, 69–80 (72). Lizzie describes her return to Chamonix from Lake Geneva in Burnaby, *High Alps*, p. vii.

3 Baedeker, *Switzerland* . . ., 13th edn, 1889, included for the first time a section on winter resorts for 'invalids' (p. xvii) and noted how the price of a room at the Hôtel Kursaal-Maloja, in St Moritz, dropped from 10–15 francs per night to 8–12 francs in winter, in the hope of establishing itself 'as a winter-resort, especially by sufferers from nervous complaints' (pp. 384–5). For a brief account of Conan Doyle's role in importing skiing to Switzerland, see Harry Mount, 'How Conan Doyle Pioneered Skiing', *Daily Mail*, 30 Jan. 2012, accessed 12 Jul. 2022.

4 Burnaby, *High Alps*, p. 28; 'The High Alps in Winter', *The Times*, 18 Jul. 1883, 5.

5 Burnaby, *High Alps*, pp. 28–38, x.

6 Burnaby, *High Alps*, pp. 41, 21, 28–37, 52, 99, 162–4; Coolidge, 'Alpine Notes', 242–3.

7 Clinton Thomas Dent, *Above the Snow Line*, London, 1885, p. 93; Le Blond, *Day In, Day Out*, pp. 137–8.

8 'Review of *The High Alps in* Winter', 306–7.

9 Le Blond, *True Tales*, p. ix. The same sentiment is expressed by Dixie, *Across Patagonia*, pp. 171–2; Burnaby, *High Alps*, p. 78; Elizabeth Main, *My Home in the Alps*, London, 1892, p. 27.

10 Burnaby, *High Alps*, p. 6.

11 Claude Gardien, trans. Katie Ives, 'Jean-Esteril Charlet and Mary Isabella Straton: A Fairy Tale', *Alpinist*, 16 Jun. 2015, 50, accessed 12 Jul. 2022; Vibe, *Therese Bertheau*, p. 27; Carol Anne Osborne, 'Gender and the Organisation of British Climbing, *c.*1857–1955', PhD thesis, University of Lancaster, 2004, pp. 163, 166–9.

12 Main, *High Life*, pp. 62, 70–71; Roche, 'Women Climbers, 1850–1900', 247; Burnaby, *High Alps*, pp. 82–3, 178–9.

13 Main, *High Life*, pp. 135–8.

14 James Walker Hartley, 'Aiguille du Géant', *Alpine Journal*, Aug. 1882–May 1884, 11, 302; Edward Lisle Strutt, 'In Memoriam: James Walker Hartley . . .', *Alpine Journal*, 1932, 44, 110–12; Main, *High Life*, p. 140.

15 Plunket, *Here and There*, pp. 32, 110, 138; Main, *My Home in the Alps*, pp. 117–18; Le Blond, *True Tales*, p. 85.

16 LAC G10: Press cutting from Julian Grande, 'Woman out of Doors: Lady Alpinists from a Man's Point of View', *Daily Mail*, 6 May 1910; Le Blond, *True Tales*, p. 3. See also Mrs W. G. Nowell, 'A Mountain Suit for Women', *Appalachia*, 1876–8, 1, 181–3.

17 Hornby, *Mountaineering Records*, pp. 7, 12; Plunket, *Here and There*, pp. 19–20.

18 Cole, *A Lady's Tour*, p. 7; Brevoort, cited in Clark, *Eccentric in the Alps*, p. 39; LAC G21: Marjorie Milsom, 'The Ladies' Alpine Club', *The Listener*, 28 Nov. 1957, 881–2.

19 Rebecca A. Brown, *Women on High*, Boston, 2002, pp. 18–19; Cicely Williams, *Women on the Rope*, London, 1973, p. 21; Stockham, 'Women's Mountaineering Life-Writing', p. 61; Amelia Bloomer, *The Life and Writings of Amelia Bloomer*, Boston, 1895, p. 81; 'Statement and Editorial Note', *The Rational Dress Society's Gazette*, Jan. 1889, 4, 1.

20 Hannah Kimberley, *A Woman's Place Is at the Top*, New York, 2017, front cover image.

21 Main, *High Life*, pp. 24–5; Edwards, *Untrodden Peaks*, pp. 361–3.

22 Le Blond, *Day In, Day Out*, pp. 91–2.

23 Plunket, *Here and There*, p. 21; Cole, *A Lady's Tour*, pp. 12, 163, 274; Emily Hornby, *A Tour in the Alps of Dauphiné and A Tour in the Carpathians*, Liverpool, 1906, p. 27.

24 Cole, *A Lady's Tour*, p. 106; T. Clifford Allbutt, 'On the Health and Training of Mountaineers', *Alpine Journal*, Aug. 1876–May 1878, 8, 30–40.

25 Plunket, *Here and There*, pp. 2, 58; Cole, *A Lady's Tour*, pp. 131, 163, 274.

26 Hornby, *A Tour in the Alps*, p. 93; Le Blond, *Day In, Day Out*, p. 107.

27 Cole, *A Lady's Tour*, pp. 391–2, 158–9, 274; Freshfield, *Alpine Byways*, pp. 32, 55, 53, 78, 150; Plunket, *Here and There*, p. 3.

28 Main, *High Life*, pp. 169–70; John Frederic Main, 'The Upper Engadine in Winter', *Fortnightly Review*, 1885, 43, 169.

29 Ronald W. Clark, *The Early Alpine Guides*, London, 1949, pp. 86, 174; Le Blond, *Day In, Day Out*, p. 123; Le Blond, *True Tales*, p. 33; Main, *High Life*, pp. 102–3.

30 Beatrice Webb, 22 Jul. 1882, *The Diary of Beatrice Webb, Vol. One: 1873–1892*, ed. Norman and Jeanne MacKenzie, Cambridge, Mass., 1982, p. 53; Le Blond, 'Winter in the Engadine', *Graphic*, 2 Mar 1887, 6.

31 Webb, *Diary*, p. 53; NA: 1861 England, Wales and Scotland Census, RG09/644 folio 85 p. 5; 'Bristol University College', *Western Daily Press*, 21 Nov. 1879, 6; Le Blond, *Day In, Day Out*, p. 114.

32 Accounts of the circumstances surrounding Clarissa and Sarah Ann's move to the USA, and their experiences at the hands of Thomas and David Main, are given in trial transcript, *Dale v Main*, 101 N.Y. 654 (1886), Vol. 144, Series J2002-82A, New York State Court of Appeals Cases and Briefs, New York State Archives (NYSA), pp. 48, 3–9, and also in 'A Sister's Vow: How It Caused Trouble in Mr Main's Family', *Brooklyn Daily Eagle*, 21 Jul. 1884, 1. Thomas Main's career is described in Emory Edwards, *Modern American Marine Engines, Boilers and Screw Propellers*, Philadelphia, 1881, pp. 84–95. The residence of Thomas Main – and his sons David and Thomas – in 1880 in Orangetown, New York, is indicated in 1880 US Census, Rockland County, Orangetown, population schedule, Orangetown, p. 7–296, schedule 1, p. 2, supervisor's district 4, enumeration district (ED) 54, dwelling 20, family 20, Thomas Main: NARA microfilm publication T9, roll 924. Further details of Thomas and Sarah Ann's separation, and the case brought by Clarissa against David, are provided in *Main v Main*, 24 A. 1024 (Ch. Div. 1892), 18 Aug. 1892, Court of Chancery of New Jersey, New Jersey State Archives (NJSA), p. 1; and *Main v Main*, 50 N.J. Eq. 712 (Ch. Div. 1892), 22 Nov. 1892, Court of Chancery of New Jersey, NJSA, pp. 1–4. John Main's academic career and departure for Switzerland is given in 'Obituary: John Frederic Main', *Minutes of the Proceedings of the Institution of Civil Engineers*, 1892, 110, 394–6 (395). I am very grateful to Andreas Augustin for locating the visitors lists from the Sep. 1884 edition of the *Davoser Blätter*, which shows that Lizzie and John were staying in the

same hotel in Davos at the same time (see 'Fremdenliste von Davos', *Davoser Blätter*, 13 Sep. 1884, 32, 3–4).

33 The last will and testament of Fredrick Gustavus Burnaby, Principal Probate Registry of England and Wales, Frederick Gustavus Burnaby probate; 'Metropolitan Notes', *Nottingham Evening Post*, 23 Jan. 1885, 2; 'The Army', *The Army and Navy Gazette*, 31 Jan. 1885, 6. 'Our London Letter', *Dundee Courier*, 27 Jan. 1885, 5; Dorothy Anderson, 'Baker, Valentine [*called* Baker Pasha] (1827–1887)', *ODNB*, accessed 12 Jul. 2022.

34 In 1907, in an article about Hughes, the *Leamington Spa Courier* would report that 'after Burnaby's heroic death with his face to the foe at Abu Klea, his friend and secretary [James Percival Hughes] was then left trustee of his estates in Ireland, on behalf of the colonel's only son' ('The New Conservative Agent', *Leamington Spa Courier*, 11 Jan. 1907, 2). Lizzie and John's marriage is described in 'Marriages', *Galloway News and Kirkcudbright Advertiser*, 2 Apr. 1886, 5. Interestingly, the GRO has no record of a marriage certificate between Lizzie and John at the British embassy in Berne.

35 Elizabeth Le Blond, 'Over Mont Blanc from Courmayeur to Chamounix', *St Moritz Post*, 7 Dec. 1886, 2; Elizabeth Le Blond, 'The Engadine in Winter', *St James's Gazette*, 24 Oct. 1889, 6; 'Society Gossip', *Bicester Herald*, 6; Wellcome Library Archives, London: 'Queen Alexandra Sanatorium Fund', SA/NPT/D. The St Moritz Aid Fund would survive independently for another forty years after its establishment in 1888, and would later merge with the Queen Alexandra Sanatorium Fund, in Davos, and, twenty-six years later, with Britain's National Association for the Prevention of Consumption and Other Forms of Tuberculosis, which subsequently became the Chest and Heart Association, and then the Stroke Association, which survives today.

36 Le Blond, *Day In, Day Out*, p. 129.

37 'The Picture Exhibition', *Alpine Journal*, Aug. 1884–May 1886, 12, 462–4; Katherine Manthorne, *Women in the Dark: Female Photographers in the US, 1850–1900*, Atglen, Pa., 2020, p. 94; William Martin Conway, 'Alpine Notes: Review of the Alpine Club's Annual Picture Exhibition', *Alpine Journal*, Aug. 1886–May 1888, 13, 175–6. Conway's review refers to how it was 'an open secret that the very good platinotypes of views in the Engadine and the neighbourhoods of Saas and the Montenvers were done by Mrs. Main', suggesting that the photographs were not overtly attributed to her.

38 In *Mountaineering in the Land of the Midnight Sun*, London, 1908, p. 213, Le Blond describes how photographing panoramas means that she is 'sometimes more familiar' with topography than her guide; Examples of some of her earliest illustrated articles are Mrs Main, 'An Ascent of the Gross Glockner', for *The Hour Glass* (the issue was first advertised in *St James's Gazette*, 1 Feb. 1887, 16) and Mrs Main, 'Winter in the Engadine', *Graphic*, 2 Mar. 1887, 6. Le Blond's photographs accompanied William Martin Conway's 'New Routes in 1886, and the Question of new Routes in General', *Alpine Journal*, Aug. 1886–May 1888, 13, 161–6. The importance of photography in nineteenth-century preservation campaigns in the US is described by Manthorne in *Women in the Dark*, p. 98.

39 'Visitor's List', *St Moritz Post*, 22 Oct. 1887, 2:1, 9; 'Visitor's List', *St Moritz Post*, 5 Nov. 1887, 2:3, 33–4.

40 Le Blond, *Adventures*, p. 187; 'Fancy Dress Ball', *St Moritz Post and Davos News*, 7 Jan. 1888, 164.

41 Main, *My Home in the Alps*, p. 76.

42 Details about the case brought by Clarissa against David can be found in *Main v Main*, 24 A. 1024 NJSA; and *Main v Main*, 50 N.J. Eq. 712 (Ch. Div. 1892), NJSA. Denver's character in the 1890s is described in F.W. Wright, 'A Wonderful American City', *Derby Mercury*, 2 Sep. 1891, 3. Records of John Main's banking and investment projects can be found in Incorporation Records for Denver Investment and Banking Corporation Ltd, The National Archives, BT 34/781/34247. His scheme for building hotels and sanitaria in Golden is described in Incorporation Records for Buffalo Creek Park Land and Improvement Company, Jefferson County Clerk and Recorder Incorporation Records, 1862–1969, Series #168, box 2, folder 44, Jefferson County Archives, Golden, Colorado (I am very grateful to archivist Ronda Frazier for finding this document for me). John Main's death is described in 'Obituary: John Frederic Main', 396. His probate documents can be found under John Frederic Main probate, Denver 1892, archive loc 52179, case 2890, ID 2825510, Colorado State Archives, Denver.

43 Le Blond, *Adventures*, p. 187.

44 Miranda Seymour, *Ottoline Morrell*, 1992, p. 206; Nietzsche cited in Julian Young, *Friedrich Nietzsche*, Cambridge, 2010, p. 277 (fns. 29, 30); Carol Diethe, *Nietzsche's Women: Beyond the Whip*, Berlin and New York, 1996, p. 99; Nancy W. Ellenberger, 'The Souls and London "Society" at the End of the Nineteenth Century', *Victorian Studies*, 1982, 25:2, 147–8; Jane Kathleen Curry,

Nineteenth-Century American Women Theatre Managers, Westport, Conn., 1994, p. 1; Kerry Powell, *Women and Victorian Theatre*, Cambridge, 1997, p. xi; Le Blond, *Adventures*, p. 147; Le Blond, *Day In, Day Out*, p. 101.

45 Isabel Burton, *The Life of Captain Sir Richard Burton*, London, 1893, Vol. II, p. 403; Brian Murray, 'The Journeys of "Kalulu" and Saleh Bin Osman: African Travellers in the Archive of Exploration', *19th Century Studies Unit Guest Lecture Series*, Anglia Ruskin University, 22 Feb. 2021, p. 10; Saleh Bin Osman, 'The Story of My Life', *St. Nicholas: An Illustrated Magazine for Young Folks*, Aug. 1891, 18, 798.

46 Le Blond, *Day In, Day Out*, pp. 93–4; Richard Davenport-Hines, 'Browning, Oscar (1837–1923)', *ODNB*, accessed 30 Jun. 2021; Jamie James, *Pagan Light*, London, 2020, p. 5; T. S. Eliot, *The Waste Land and Other Poems*, 1940, London, 1972, p. 23.

47 Le Blond, *Day In, Day Out*, p. 96; Le Blond, *Adventures*, p. 63; Maxine Willet, 'Beatrice Tomasson (1859–1947)', *Mountain Heritage*, 6 Aug. 2006, accessed 10 Aug. 2021.

48 LAC G31: Correspondence from Kevin Higgins; Angela Lumpkin, 'The Contributions of Women to the History of Competitive Tennis in the United States (1874–1974)', PhD thesis, Ohio State University, 1974, pp. 15–16; Kathleen E. McCrone, *Playing the Game*, London, 1988, pp. 162–3; 'Wednesday, June 25, 1884', *Pastime*, 25 Jun. 1884, 410 (cited in Robert J. Lake, 'Gender and Etiquette in British Lawn Tennis 1870–1939 . . .', *International Journal of the History of Sport*, 2012, 29:5, 694, and also in Thomas Turner, 'The Production and Consumption of Lawn Tennis Shoes in Late-Victorian Britain', *Journal of British Studies*, Jul. 2016, 55, 474–500 (479)); William Skidelsky, 'Review of David Berry, *A People's History of Tennis – a Game for Everyone?*', *Guardian*, 12 Jun. 2020, accessed 15 Jul. 2022.

49 MOJSM: Elizabeth Le Blond, Photobook 4, 'My boat off St. Gingolph', EMLB SB4 4.199; Leif Rosqvist, 'Stockholm Rowing Madams', *New Sweden Cultural Heritage Society*, accessed 12 Jul. 2022; McKenzie, *The Right Sort of Woman*, p. 127; 'Yachting Ladies', *Penny Illustrated Paper*, 12 Sep. 1885, 11.

50 MOJSM: Le Blond, Photobook 4, EMLB SB4 4.216–19; Hannah Ross, *Revolutions: How Women Changed the World on Two Wheels*, London, 2021, pp. 25–7; Le Blond, *Day In, Day Out*, p. 103.

51 Lizzie's account of her cycling tour can be found in Le Blond, *Day In, Day Out*, p. 103. Sasha Abramsky's *Little Wonder: The Extraordinary Story of Lottie Dod, the World's First Female Sports Superstar*, Edinburgh, 2021, describes her

relationship with Lizzie – and its tensions. Ross's description of cycling's emancipatory feminist potential is in *Revolutions*, p. 1.

52 Le Blond, *Adventures*, pp. 23, 69; Le Blond, *Day In, Day Out*, p. 141; Mary Louise Adams, 'From Mixed-Sex Sport to Sport for Girls . . .', *Sport in History*, 2010, 30:2, 219; Le Blond, *Adventures*, p. 194; Sportswomen of the Day', 1907, source unknown, cited in Adams, 'From Mixed-Sex Sport to Sport for Girls . . .', 221.

53 Le Blond, *Day In, Day Out*, pp. 99–100, 141; Abramsky, *Little Wonder*, p. 79; *Alpine Post*, 19 Feb. 1898, 22:17, 188.

54 Le Blond, *Day In, Day Out*, p. 183; University of Bristol Archives, Additional Papers of the Symonds Family, *c.* 1859–1963, DM375/1/folio 15 verso/4, 'Photograph of Katherine Furse Racing on a Bob-Sleigh', 'Photograph of Madge Vaughan and Harold Freeman at the Start of a Toboggan Race'. I am very grateful to Stephen Bartley, archivist of the St Moritz Tobogganing Club, for providing me with the information about the provenance of the 'Shuttlecock' name.

55 'Captain R. C. Gore to Miss Rachel C. Saunderson', *Gentlewoman*, 22 Jul. 1899, 43; Frances Stonor Saunders, *The Woman who Shot Mussolini*, London, 2010, p. 42; Harry Gibson, *Tobogganing on Crooked Runs*, London, 1894, p. vii.

56 Elizabeth Le Blond, 'Alpine Winter Photography', *The Queen*, 4 Feb. 1905, 53.

57 Stephen Clift and Simon Forrest, 'Gay Men and Tourism: Destinations and Holiday Motivations', *Tourism Management* (1999), 20:5, 616; Julian Grande, 'Swiss Alpine Club: Jubilee Celebrations in Lucerne', *Sheffield Daily Telegraph*, 15 Sep. 1913, 6.

58 'Ladies' Letter', *Surrey Gazette*, 5 Jun. 1900, 7; Tracy J. R. Collins, 'Athletic Fashion, "Punch", and the Creation of the New Woman', *Victorian Periodicals Review*, 2010, 43:3, 313.

59 'Diana', 'Sports and Sportswomen', *Gentlewoman*, 2 Aug. 1890, 20.

Part Two: Loss

6: Lockdown

1 Scott Berinato, 'That Discomfort You're Feeling Is Grief', *Harvard Business Review*, 23 Mar. 2020, accessed 12 Jul. 2022.

2 Cited in Lily Scherlis, 'Distantiated Communities . . .', *Cabinet*, 30 Apr. 2020, accessed 12 Jul. 2022.

3 Edward T. Hall, *The Hidden Dimension*, 1966, New York, 1969, p. 101.

4 D. Jim Walmsley and Gareth J. Lewis, 'The Pace of Pedestrian Flows in Cities', *Environment and Behavior*, 1989, 21:2, 123–50; Marco Costa, 'Interpersonal Differences in Group Walking', *Journal of Nonverbal Behavior*, 2010, 34:1, 15–26; L. F. Henderson and D. J. Lyons, 'Sexual Differences in Human Crowd Motion', *Nature*, 1972, 240, 353–5; Mohammed M. Hamed, 'Analysis of Pedestrians' Behavior at Pedestrian Crossings', *Safety Science*, 38:1, 2001, 63–82.

5 Erving Goffman, *Relations in Public: Microstudies of the Public Order*, New York, 1971, p. 31; Hodges L. Golson and James M. Dabbs, 'Line-Following Tendencies among Pedestrians: A Sex Difference', *Personality and Social Psychology Bulletin* (1974), 1:1, 16–18, cited in Winnie Daamen and Serge Hoogendoorn, 'Controlled Experiments to Derive Walking Behaviour', *European Journal of Transport and Infrastructure Research*, 2003, 3:1, 42.

6 Motao Zhu, Songzhu Zhao, Jeffrey H. Coben and Gordon S. Smith, 'Why More Male Pedestrians Die in Vehicle–Pedestrian Collisions than Female Pedestrians . . .', *Injury Prevention*, 2013, 19:4, 227–31; Tova Rosenbloom, 'Crossing at a Red Light . . .', *Transportation Research*, 2009, 12:5, 389–94; James M. Dabbs and Neil A. Stokes, 'Beauty Is Power . . .', *Sociometry*, 1975, 38:4, 551–75; AAA Foundation for Traffic Safety, *2019 Traffic Safety Culture Index*, Jun. 2020, p. 28 (see also examples of male road rage towards female pedestrians, such as https://www.bbc.co.uk/news/uk-england-norfolk-62011504); Naz Kaya and Feyzan Erkip, 'Invasion of Personal Space under the Condition of Short-Term Crowding . . .', *Journal of Environmental Psychology*, 1999, 19:2, 187.

7 James M. Dabbs, 'Sex, Setting, and Reactions to Crowding on Sidewalks', *Proceedings of the Annual Convention of the American Psychological Association*, 1972, 7:1, 205–6.

8 E. S. Knowles, 'Boundaries around Social Space . . .', *Environment and Behavior*, 1972, 4:4, 437–45; J. R. Aiello, 'Human Spatial Behavior', in D. Stokols and I. Altman (eds.), *Handbook of Environmental Psychology*, New York, 1987, pp. 1359–504; Stanley Heshka and Yona Nelson, 'Interpersonal Speaking Distance as a Function of Age, Sex and Relationship', *Sociometry*, 1972, 35:4, 491–8; Costa, 'Interpersonal Differences . . .', 15–26; Dabbs and Stokes, 'Beauty is Power . . .', 557.

9 Catherine Stokes, 'Global Recovery . . .', *Bookseller* webinar, 1 Jul. 2020; Rachel Moss, 'We Were Convinced We Weren't Runners . . .', *Huffington Post*, 3 Jun.

2020; Harry Robertson, 'The Business of Running . . .', *City A.M.*, 5 Jun. 2020; 'Sport Will Benefit from People Taking up Running during Lockdown: Sebastian Coe', *Hindustan Times*, 10 Aug. 2020: (all accessed 12 Jul. 2022).

10 Anna Schaverien, '"Because She's a Girl" . . ., *New York Times*, 29 Nov. 2020; Mike Starling, 'Women's Sport "Left Behind" during the Pandemic', *Week*, 11 Feb. 2021; Molly McElwee et al., 'Revealed: The True Scale of How Women's Sport Was Left Behind in Lockdown', *Telegraph*, 23 Mar. 2021; Griffiths, 'Women in the Hills . . .', p. 5; Fiona Tomas et al., 'Report Finds 61 Per Cent of Women Intend to Be More Active after Coronavirus Lockdown', *Telegraph*, 16 Jul. 2020; Ali Bowes et al., 'A Losing Battle? Women's Sport Pre- and Post-COVID-19', *European Sport Management Quarterly*, 2021, 21:3, 443–61: (all accessed 12 Jul. 2022).

11 Anna Fazackerley, 'Women's Research Plummets during Lockdown . . .', *Guardian*, 12 May 2020; Viglioni Giuliana, 'Are Women Publishing Less during the Pandemic? . . .', *Nature*, 2020, 581, 365–6: (both accessed 24 Nov. 2020).

12 Arlie Russell Hochschild, *The Second Shift*, 1989, revised edn, London, 2012; Pew Research Center, 'Modern Parenthood, Chapter 4 . . .', 14 Mar. 2013; Evrim Altintas and Oriel Sullivan, 'Fifty Years of Change Updated . . .', *Demographic Research*, 2016, 35, 455–70; Oliver Burkeman, 'Dirty Secret . . .', *Guardian*, 17 Feb. 2018; Office for National Statistics, 'Women Shoulder the Responsibility of "Unpaid Work" ', 10 Nov. 2016; Statistiska centralbyrån, *Swedish Time Use Survey, 2010/11*, Örebro, 2012, p. 64 (all online sources accessed 24 Nov. 2020).

13 Hochschild, *The Second Shift*, p. 4, cited in Helen Lewis, *Difficult Women: A History of Feminism in 11 Fights*, London, 2020, p. 264. The data from 2018 is from Office for National Statistics (2018). The term 'mental load' was popularised in Emma, *The Mental Load: A Feminist Comic*, New York, 2018.

14 Plan International UK, *The State of Girls' Rights in the UK: Early Insights into the Impact of the Coronavirus Pandemic on Girls*, London, 2020, https://plan-uk.org/file/plan-uk-state-of-girls-rights-coronavirus-reportpdf/download?token=gddEAzlz, accessed 1 February 2023, cited in Maya Oppenheim, 'Almost Three-Quarters of Women Scared of Exercising Outside in Dark Amid Lockdown', *Independent*, 22 Nov. 2020; https://twitter.com/sjgeek/status/1328323764099092480?s=20; https://twitter.com/cattherunner/status/1328324246448254976?s=20; https://twitter.com/BacktothePhys/status/1329771755834126336?s=20 (all

accessed 12 Jul. 2022). I am very grateful to all the women who told me about their experiences of being harassed or assaulted while running.

15 Michelle Hamilton, 'Running While Female', *Runners World*, 8 Aug. 2017; Jacob Meschke, 'In Spain, a Young Woman's Killing Galvanizes Women . . .', *Runners World*, 22 Jul. 2019 (all accessed Jul. 2022).

16 Micaela di Leonardo, 'Political Economy of Street Harassment', *Aegis*, 1981, 51–2; US judge cited in Cynthia Grant Bowman, 'Street Harassment and the Informal Ghettoization of Women', *Harvard Law Review*, 1993, 106:3, 558.

17 Bowman, 'Street Harassment', 554.

18 Heather R. Hlavka, 'Normalizing Sexual Violence: Young Women Account for Harassment and Abuse', *Gender & Society*, Jun. 2014, 28:3, 337–506 (344), cited in Holly Kearl, *Unsafe and Harassed in Public Places . . .*, Reston, 2014, p. 12. The references to 65 per cent and 99 per cent of US women having experienced street harassment derive from Kearl, p. 6, and Jarrah O'Neill, 'Gender in Public Space . . .', BA thesis, Princeton University, 2 Apr. 2013, p. 16. The 2021 UN Women study refers to the All-Party Parliamentary Group for UN Women, *Prevalence and Reporting of Sexual Harassment in UK Public Spaces*, London, Mar. 2021, https://www.unwomenuk.org/site/wp-content/uploads/2021/03/APPG-UN-Women-Sexual-Harassment-Report_Updated.pdf, accessed 1 February 2023. The UN Women's study's finding that 'only 3% of 18–24 year-olds reported having not experienced any . . . harassment' was translated by Nishat Choudhury into the title claim of her article, 'Research Finds that 97% of Women in the UK have been Sexually Harassed', *Open Access Government*, 11 March 2021, https://www.openaccessgovernment.org/97-of-women-in-the-uk/105940/, accessed 1 February 2023.

19 Kearl, *Stop Street Harassment*, pp. 8–10, 11–15; Kearl, *Unsafe and Harassed*, pp. 18, 46, 6.

20 Kearl, *Unsafe and Harassed*, pp. 7, 22–23; Kearl, *Stop Street Harassment*, pp. 8–10, 54; Bowman, 'Street Harassment', 531, 543.

21 https://twitter.com/JosephineLehaff/status/1435521337829830665/photo/1.

22 Chris Pleasance, et al., '"I Wonder What Would Happen if I Died?" . . .', *Daily Mail*, 4 Aug. 2016; Kristine Phillips and Amy B. Wang, 'Authorities Say They Have Found the Killer of Google's Vanessa Marcotte', *Washington Post*, 16 Apr. 2017. Subsequent evidence showed Laura Luelmo was killed while walking

from the supermarket, not while running, but a Spanish resident described how her death 'brought to light our vulnerabilities as women, and as runners', Meschke, 'In Spain, a Young Woman's Killing . . .'.

23 Bowman, 'Street Harassment', 538, 540; Deirdre Davis, 'The Harm That Has No Name: Street Harassment . . .', *UCLA Women's Law Journal*, 1994, 4:2, 143; Shilpa Phadke, Sameera Khan and Shilpa Ranade, *Why Loiter? Women & Risk on Mumbai Streets*, New Delhi, 2011, pp. vii, xiii.

24 bell hooks, *Ain't I a Woman*, Boston, 1981, pp. 58–9, cited in Bowman, 'Street Harassment', 533; Davis, 'The Harm That Has No Name', 163, 167; Kearl, *Unsafe and Harassed*, p. 42.

25 Pam McAllister, 'Wolf Whistles and Warnings', *Heresies*, 1978, 6, 37, cited in Bowman, 'Street Harassment', 541–2; Phadke et al., *Why Loiter?*, p. 9; O'Neill, 'Gender in Public Space . . .', pp. 6–7.

26 Kearl, *Unsafe and Harassed*, pp. 20–21; Jamie Ballard, 'Most Women Say They Regularly Take Steps to Avoid Being Sexually Assaulted', *YouGov America*, 28 Mar. 2019 (accessed 12 Jul. 2022).

27 Fiona Vera-Gray, *The Right Amount of Panic: How Women Trade Freedom for Safety*, Bristol, 2018, p. 73.

28 Sylvia Plath, diary entry no. 93, 1951, *The Unabridged Journals . . .*, ed. Karen V. Kukil, New York, 2000; Andrea Dworkin, 'Pornography and Grief', *Letters from a War Zone*, Atlanta, 1993, pp. 24, 19.

29 Kearl's finding that 24 per cent of women avoided locations where they'd experienced harassment derives from Kearl, *Unsafe and Harassed*, pp. 20–21. The study of women in Delhi is CEQUIN (Centre for Equity and Inclusion), *Perception and Experience of Gendered Violations in Public Places in Delhi: Baseline Report*, New Delhi, Nov. 2009, https://cequinindia.org/wp-content/uploads/2018/01/PerceptionandExperience.pdf, accessed 1 Feb. 2023, p. 35 – it is among a number of international studies valuably cited in Kearl, *Stop Street Harassment*, pp. 8–10. Marrie H.J. Bekker, 'Agoraphobia and Gender: A Review', *Clinical Psychology Review*, 1996, 16:2, 129–46. Suzie Siegel, 'Safe at Home: Agoraphobia and the Discourse on Women's Place', MA thesis, University of South Florida, 8 Nov. 2001, pp. 3–4. The discussion about difficulties of diagnosing agoraphobia in Indian women derives from V. Starcevic et al., 'Characteristics of Agoraphobia in Women and Men with Panic Disorder with Agoraphobia', *Depression and Anxiety*, 1998, 8:1, 8–13 (8).

7: Separation anxiety

1 Colin Speakman and Tony Grogan, *50 Years of the Dales Way*, Shipley, 2019, pp. 14, 8–9.

2 I am grateful to Eddie Arthur for checking the inscription on the fingerpost when he was out running on the Dales Way.

3 Lyn Mikel Brown and Carol Gilligan, *Meeting at the Crossroads: Women's Psychology and Girls' Development*, New York, 1992, p. 2.

4 Brown and Gilligan, *Meeting at the Crossroads*, pp. 43, 45, 93, 125.

5 Brown and Gilligan, *Meeting at the Crossroads*, pp. 163, 217, 179, 198, 53, 58, 164.

6 Brown and Gilligan, *Meeting at the Crossroads*, pp. 165–6.

7 Brown and Gilligan, *Meeting at the Crossroads*, pp. 193, 112, 213, 183.

8 Brown and Gilligan, *Meeting at the Crossroads*, pp. 218, 96, 173, 160, 62, 2.

9 Sigmund Freud, 'Inhibition, Symptom, and Fear', 1926, in *Beyond the Pleasure Principle and Other Writings*, trans. John Reddick, ed. Adam Phillips, London, 2003, pp. 198, 205; D. W. Winnicott, *Playing and Reality*, 1971, London, 2008, p. 15; Melanie Klein, 'Mourning and Its Relation to Manic-Depressive States', 1940, in Melanie Klein, *Love, Guilt and Reparation, and Other Works, 1921–1945*, 1975, p. 346; Sigmund Freud, 'The Ego and the Id', 1923, *The Standard Edition of the Complete Psychological Works of Sigmund Freud*, Vol. XIX (1923–25), trans. James Strachey (in collaboration with Anna Freud, Alix Strachey and Alan Tyson), 1961, London, 2001, pp. 35, 31; Dana Crowley Jack, *Silencing the Self*, Cambridge, Mass., 1991, pp. 9–16.

10 Brown and Gilligan, *Meeting at the Crossroads*, p. 118.

11 Kelly K. Hallman, et al., 'The Shrinking World of Girls at Puberty . . .', *Global Public Health*, 2015, 10:3, 279.

12 Perver K. Baran et al., 'Park Use among Youth and Adults . . .', *Environment and Behavior*, 2014, 46:6, 787; Margaret O'Brien et al., 'Children's Independent Spatial Mobility . . .', *Childhood*, 2000, 7:3, 259–60; Anastasia Loukaitou-Sideris and Athanasios Sideris, 'What Brings Children to the Park? . . .', *Journal of the American Planning Association*, 2009, 76:1, 90, 94, 95; Baran et al., 'Park Use among Youth and Adults . . .', 784; O'Brien et al., 'Children's Independent Spatial Mobility . . .', 267–8.

13 Martha Brady, 'Creating Safe Spaces and Building Social Assets for Young Women in the Developing World . . .', *Women's Studies Quarterly*, 2005, 33:1–2, 39, 40, 48.

14 Anna Timperio et al., 'Features of Public Open Spaces . . .', *Preventive Medicine*, 2008, 47:5, 515; Joanna Kirby et al., 'Socio-Environmental Influences on Physical Activity among Young People . . .', *Health Education Research*, 2013, 28:6, 954–60; Kandy James, '"You Can *Feel* Them Looking at You" . . .', *Journal of Leisure Research*, 2000, 32:2, 262–80; Loukaitou-Sideris and Sideris, 'What Brings Children to the Park? . . .', 90; Meghan M. Casey et al., 'Using a Socioecological Approach to Examine Participation in Sport and Physical Activity among Rural Adolescent Girls', *Qualitative Health Research*, 2009, 19:7, 881; Women in Sport, 'Reframing Sport for Teenage Girls: Building Strong Foundations for their Futures', 2019, pp. 8, 10 and fn. 16, accessed 13 Jul. 2022.

15 Kandy James, '"I Just Gotta Have My Own Space!": The Bedroom as a Leisure Site for Adolescent Girls', *Journal of Leisure Research*, 2001, 33:1, 72, 87; Timperio et al., 'Features of Public Open Spaces . . .', 514–16.

16 Baran et al., 'Park Use among Youth and Adults . . .', 782, 783, 785; Loukaitou-Sideris and Sideris, 'What Brings Children to the Park? . . .', 94; Harriet Agerholm, '"Single-Sex Toilets Needed to Overcome Girls' Barriers to Education", Says Unesco', *Independent*, 8 Mar. 2018; Pooja Chhabria, 'Why Many Women in India Refuse Water during a Heatwave', *BBC News*, 5 Jul. 2018; Karey Helms, '"Do You Have to Pee?" . . .', *DIS '19: Proceedings of the 2019 ACM Designing Interactive Systems Conference*, New York, 2019, 1212; Abbie Wightwick, 'Pupils Are Missing School Because They Don't Like Mixed Sex Toilets and "Period Shaming" Is One of the Main Issues', *Wales Online*, 15 Feb. 2019 (all accessed 13 Jul. 2022). I am also very grateful to Susannah Walker, of the UK charity Make Space for Girls, for conversations on this topic.

17 James, '"You Can *Feel* Them Looking at You" . . .', 262–80; Casey et al., 'Using a Socioecological Approach', 885–6, 889; Kirby et al., 'Socio-Environmental Influences . . .', 963.

18 Klara Johansson et al., 'Adolescents' Perceived Safety . . .', *Young*, 2012, 20:1, 69–70; Loukaitou-Sideris and Sideris, 'What Brings Children to the Park? . . .', 90–2, 94–5; James, '"I Just Gotta Have My Own Space!" . . .', 84, 72; Hallman et al., 'Shrinking World . . .', 287–8; Linde Van Hecke et al., 'Social and Physical Environmental Factors Influencing Adolescents' Physical Activity in Urban Public Open Spaces . . .', *PLOS One*, 2016, 11:5, 19, 16; Lieze Mertens et al., 'Differences in Park Characteristic Preferences for Visitation and Physical

Activity among Adolescents . . .', *PLOS One*, 2019, 14:3, 16; Casey et al., 'Using a Socioecological Approach . . .', 889.

19 Hallman et al., 'Shrinking World . . .', 280; Johansson et al., 'Adolescents' Perceived Safety . . .', 70–8; Kearl, *Unsafe and Harassed*, pp. 12, 18, 56; Jessica Southgate and Lucy Russell, *Street Harassment: It's Not OK*, PLAN International UK, 2018, accessed 13 Jul. 2022.

20 Johansson et al., 'Adolescents' Perceived Safety . . .', 83; Mertens et al., 'Differences in Park Characteristic Preferences . . .', 1–16; Van Hecke et al., 'Social and Physical Environmental Factors . . .', 2; Timperio et al., 'Features of Public Open Spaces . . .', 514–17; James, ' "You Can *Feel* Them Looking at You" . . .', 271–4.

21 James, ' "I Just Gotta Have My Own Space!" . . .', 72, 77, 84.

22 Elizabeth Grosz, *Volatile Bodies*, London, 1994, p. 14; Manjushe Gupte, 'Gender, Feminist Consciousness, and the Environment . . .', *Women and Politics*, 2002, 24:1, 48–9; Porphyry, *To Marcella*, trans. Kathleen O'Brien Wicker, Atlanta, 1987, p. 75.

23 Caroline Criado Perez, *Invisible Women: Exposing Data Bias in a World Designed for Men*, London, 2019, pp. 215–18, 156–8.

8: Frozen out

1 Main, *My Home in the Alps*, p. 21; MOJSM: Elizabeth Le Blond, Photobook 4, EMLB SB4 4.250, 1895.

2 Le Blond, *True Tales*, pp. 34–5.

3 Le Blond, *True Tales*, pp. 36–7. Lizzie's description of sending her dog back to England is in 'Personal', *Alpine Post*, 5 Mar. 1898, 22:19, 216. (Photographs of Pluto exist, such as MOJSM, Photobook 4, EMLB SB 4 4.102.) Accounts of Lizzie's travels in Spain are given in numerous issues of the *Alpine Post*, including in the 'Personal' article above. Her first trip to Norway is detailed in the *Alpine Post* issue of 30 Oct. 1897, 21:1, 3.

4 Edith Slingsby, 'An English Lady in Jotunheimen', *Den Norske Turistförenings Årbog*, 1875, 75, 102–18. For details about William Cecil Slingsby's admiration for Norwegian female mountaineers, see Vibe, *Therese Bertheau*, p. 14. Lizzie describes her experiences in Norway in Le Blond, *Mountaineering*, pp. 272–3, 22, 75. I am very grateful to Stephen Bartley, archivist of the St Moritz Tobogganing Club, for showing me Lizzie's photograph albums, and the album of photographs taken by Lottie and Tony Dod, who accompanied Lizzie on her

first Norwegian excursion in 1897 (and I am grateful, too, to the Dod family, from whom this album is on loan).

5 'The Latest Photography', *Lloyd's Weekly Newspaper*, 25 Sep. 1898, 2. Descriptions of Lizzie's later Norwegian excursions featured in numerous contemporary newspapers, including 'Climbing in the Arctic Circle', *English Lakes Visitor and Keswick Guardian*, 1 Oct. 1898, 6, and 'A Lady Mountaineer in Norway', *Lake's Falmouth Packet and Cornwall Advertiser*, 16 Sep. 1899, 2. She published her accounts in *Mountaineering in the Land of the Midnight Sun*.

6 Le Blond, *True Tales*, pp. 251, 155, 43, 90–91; 'True Tales of Mountain Adventure: Review', *Scotsman*, 22 Jan. 1903, 2.

7 Anna Pigeon and Ellen Abbot, 'The Passage of the Sesia-Joch from Zermatt to Alagna by English Ladies', *Alpine Journal*, May 1870–May 1872, 5, 367–72 (for an account of the Pigeon sisters' descent, see also Le Blond, *True Tales*, pp. 153–61); LAC G32: Frances Emily Weston festival in Japan.

8 Mary Paillon, 'En Souvenir de Miss. K. Richardson (1854–1927), *La Montagne*, 1927, 330–1; Cicely Williams, 'The Feminine Share in Mountain Adventure, Pt 1', *Alpine Journal*, 1976, 96.

9 George Sand, 'Souvenir d'Auvergne', *Annuaire du Club Alpin Français*, 1874, 1, 3–8; Claire-Elaine Engel, 'Early Lady Climbers', *Alpine Journal*, 1943, 54, 56; Ottogalli, accessed 23 Feb. 2021; LAC, G18: Lyceum Club papers, list of Lyceum Alpine Club members, Jul. 1909; Elizabeth Le Blond, 'In Memoriam: Miss Katherine [sic] Richardson (1854–1927)', *Alpine Journal*, 1928, 40, 160–2.

10 'Sport, *n.1*', *Oxford English Dictionary*, online edition, Oxford, Jun. 2022; https://english.stackexchange.com/questions/274948/sport-vs-exercise; https://twitter.com/Woodywing/status/1360309902166654978 (all accessed 13 Jul. 2022).

11 Rob Light, 'Cricket in the Eighteenth Century', in Anthony Bateman and Jeffrey Hill (eds.), *The Cambridge Companion to Cricket*, Cambridge, 2011, p. 31; Isabelle Duncan, *Skirting the Boundary*, London, 2013, pp. 11–13; https://www.lords.org/mcc/the-club/about-the-mcc (accessed 25 Oct. 2022).

12 H. S. Ndee, 'Public Schools in Britain in the Nineteenth Century . . .', *International Journal of the History of Sport*, 2010, 27:5, 845–71; Frederick Lugard, *The Dual Mandate in British Tropical Africa*, London, 1922, cited in Anthony Kirk-Greene, 'Imperial Administration and Athletic Imperative: The Case of the District Officer in Africa', in W. Baker and J. A. Mangan (eds.), *Sport in Africa*, New York, 1987, p. 82, 85; Denis Jallat and Sébastien Stumpp, 'French Sailing in

the Late Nineteenth Century and the Debate about Parisian Centralism', *French History*, 2015, 29:4, 551; Barry Svrluga, 'U.S. Open: Golf Is a Bipartisan Game for Washington's Politicians', *Washington Post*, 13 Jun. 2011, accessed 8 Jul. 2021.

13 McCrone, *Playing the Game*, p. 162; Lake, 'Gender and Etiquette in British Lawn Tennis', 707 (fn. 50), 701–4; 'Gentlemen Only, Ladies Forbidden: A History', *Women's Golf Journal*, 1 Aug. 2017; Tim Glover and Hugh Mellor, 'Obituary: Joyce Wethered', *Independent*, 21 Nov. 1996; Owen Gibson, 'R&A Golf Club Ends 260-Year Ban on Women Members', *Guardian*, 18 Sep. 2014 (all accessed 13 Jul. 2022).

14 Ross, *Revolutions*, pp. 88, 90; Lorenz Finison, *Boston's Cycling Craze, 1880–1900*, Amherst, Mass., 2014, pp. 163–70; Sheila Hanlon, 'Ladies Cycling Clubs . . .', *sheilahanlon.com*, 15 Sep. 2015, accessed 13 Jul. 2022; Christine Neejer, 'The Bicycle Girls . . .', PhD thesis, Michigan State University, 2016, p. 114; 'D.M.N.', 'Book Review: *Lady Margaret Hall* ', *Vote*, 2 May 1924, 6.

15 The idea that figure-skating was 'more and more of a women's sport' is cited in Adams, 'From Mixed-Sex Sport to Sport for Girls . . .', 235–6, 241; Mary Louise Adams, *Artistic Impressions* . . ., Toronto, 2011, p. 22; Elena Christofi et al., 'Men's Participation in Feminine Sports', presentation, John Jay College of Criminal Justice, City University of New York, accessed 13 Jul. 2022.

16 Osborne, 'Gender and the Organisation of British Climbing . . .', pp. 378–9, 180. Male members of the Preston Mountaineering Club subsequently dithered about whether women could attend meets, social functions, or use the club's hut. For the history of women's inclusion and exclusion from the Swiss Alpine Club, see Tanja Wirz, *Gipfel stürmerinnen: Eine Geschlechtergeschichte des Alpinismus in der Schweiz, 1840–1940*, Baden, 2007.

17 Anushree Nande, 'World War, Mon Amour: A Brief History of Women's Football', *Football Paradise*, 18 Oct. 2017, accessed 13 Jul. 2022; 'Women's Boxing Bouts Abandoned', *Hackney and Kingsland Gazette*, 1 Feb. 1926; John Bartlett et al., *Blackheath Hockey Club, 1861–2011* . . ., 2011, p. 7.

18 https://members.royalcinqueports.com/light_hearted; Vanessa Heggie, 'Long before the Paralympics There Was the Deaflympics', *Guardian*, 5 Sep. 2012; Douglas C. Baynton, *Forbidden Signs*, Chicago and London, 1996, pp. 36–55; Gwendolyn Captain, 'Enter Ladies and Gentlemen of Color . . .', *Journal of Sport History*, 1991, 18:1, 90; Eric Anderson, 'Openly Gay Athletes . . .', *Gender and Society*, 2002, 16:6, 860; Susan K. Cahn, 'From the "Muscle Moll" to the

"Butch" Ballplayer" . . .', *Feminist Studies*, 1993, 19:2, 350 (all online sources accessed 13 Jul. 2022).

19 *Cambridge Daily News*, 21 May 1897, cited in Hanlon, 'Lady Cyclist Effigy at the Cambridge University Protest, 1897', SheilaHanlon.com, 16 Apr. 2011, http://www.sheilahanlon.com/?p=292, accessed 1 Feb. 2023; LAC G10: Press cutting from *Tribune*, 14 Aug. 1907.

20 'A Railway Grievance', *Morning Post*, 14 Jul. 1864, 3. Detailed news reports about the Dickinson case and trial – such as 'Serious Charge', *Morning Post*, 19 Jun. 1875, 5, and 'The Charge against Colonel Valentine Baker', *Evening Mail*, 25 Jun. 1875, 7 – were printed in a large number of newspapers throughout 1875. For a radio programme that I helped to make about the Baker–Dickinson assault and trial, see Rachel Hewitt, Jonathan Freedland and Tom Alban, *The Long View: Violence against Women in Public Spaces*, BBC Radio 4, 22 Jun. 2021.

21 ' "An Officer and Gentleman" in a Railway Carriage', *Northern Echo*, 21 Jun. 1875, 3; Robin J. Barrow, 'Rape on the Railway . . .', *Journal of Victorian Culture*, 2015, 20:3, 343; Elizabeth Gaskell, *North and South*, 1855, London, 2008, p. 328.

22 Paul Freedman, 'Women and Restaurants in the Nineteenth-Century United States', *Journal of Social History*, 2014, 48:1, 4, 7; Blatch, cited in Andrew P. Haley, *Turning the Tables*, Chapel Hill, N.C., 2011, p. 146; Mary Murphy, 'Bootlegging Mothers and Drinking Daughters . . .', *American Quarterly*, 1994, 46:2, 181. A 1907 ordinance in Montana prohibited women from entering saloons.

23 Freedman, 'Women and Restaurants . . .', 7; Blatch, cited in Haley, *Turning the Tables*, pp. 145–7. For a detailed survey of the ways in which public space was regulated by gender, see Mary P. Ryan, *Women in Public*, Baltimore and London, 1990, pp. 58–94.

24 Tim Reinke-Williams, 'Women, Ale and Company in Early Modern London', *Brewery History*, 2010, 135, 88; Karen Green, 'Urban Innkeepers, Their Inns and Their Role in the Economic and Cultural Life of Leeds and York, 1720–1860', MA thesis, University of York, 2015, p. 2; *A Monthly Bulletin (Supplement): Adolescents in Public Houses*, London, Aug. 1942, Warwick Digital Collections, 420/BS/4/41/1, p. 3.

25 Dava Sobel, *The Glass Universe: How the Ladies of the Harvard Observatory Took the Measure of the Stars*, London, 2017; Richard McKim, 'A Different Sort of Society', *Astronomy & Geophysics*, 2016, 57:4, 4.14–17; Jennifer Carson, Sexism and the Stars', *Science*, 20 Mar. 2020, 367:6484, 1311.

26 Carol Dyhouse, 'Troubled Identities . . .', *Women's History Review*, 2003, 12:2, 169–94; Ann B. Shteir, 'Gender and "Modern" Botany in Victorian England', *Osiris*, 1997, 12, 33–36, 40; Sara Sidstone Gronim, 'What Jane Knew . . .', *Journal of Women's History*, 2007, 19:3, 38; Emanuel D. Rudolph, 'Women Who Studied Plants in the Pre-Twentieth Century United States and Canada', *Taxon*, 1990, 39:2, 151–205; Heather L. Lindon et al., 'Fewer than Three Percent of Land Plant Species Named by Women: Author Gender over 260 Years', *Taxon*, 2018, 64:2, 209–15.

27 Abigail A. Van Slyck, 'The Lady and the Library Loafer . . .', *Winterthur Portfolio*, 1996, 31:4, 237; Simon Taylor et al., *The English Public Library, 1850–1939*, Historic England Introductions to Heritage Assets, Jul. 2016, pp. 6–7.

28 Elizabeth Robins, *Both Sides of the Curtain*, London, 1940, p. 167; Judith R. Walkowitz, 'Going Public . . .', *Representations*, 1998, 62, 1, 7; Helena M. Swanwick, *I Have Been Young*, London, 1935, p. 82.

29 Letter Sir Edwin Ray Lankester to Karl Pearson, 1887, Pearson Papers, University College, London, 10/47; cited in Walkowitz, 'Going Public . . .', 6, 28 (my emphasis).

30 Martin Summers, 'Manhood Rights in the Age of Jim Crow: Evaluating "End-of-Men" Claims in the Context of African-American History', *Boston University Law Review*, 2013, 93:3, 758–9; bell hooks, *Ain't I a Woman*, p. 132; cited in Marcia Pearce Burgdorf and Robert Burgdorf Jr, 'A History of Unequal Treatment . . .', *Santa Clara Law Review*, 1975, 15: 4, 863; Ruth Butler and Sophia Bowlby, 'Bodies and Spaces . . .', *Environment and Planning D: Society and Space*, 1997, 15:4, 420.

31 Nellie Wetherbee, 'Diary', Bancroft Library, 4 May 1860, cited in Ryan, *Women in Public*, p. 85.

32 Vaheed Ramazani, 'Gender, War and the Department Store . . .', *SubStance*, 2007, 36:2, 126–46.

33 Report of the Inter-Departmental Committee on Physical Deterioration, London, 1904, p. 142; Samuel Lynn Hynes, *The Edwardian Turn of Mind*, Princeton, N.J., 1968, p. 22; John Nauright and Timothy Chandler, *Making Men: Rugby and Masculine Identity*, ed. Richard Lansdown, 1886, London, 1996, p. 121.

34 Henry James, *The Bostonians*, ed. Richard Lansdown, 1886, London, 2000, p. 260.

35 Cesare Lombroso, *Criminal Man*, ed. and trans. Mary Gibson and Nicole Hahn Rafter, Durham, N.C., 2006, p. 53; Edwin Ray Lankester, *Degeneration: A*

Chapter in Darwinism, London, 1880, pp. 59–60; Max Nordau, *Degeneration*, London, 1895, p. viii. I am very grateful to Pete Newbon for sharing with me his own research into degeneration and the 'end-of-men'.

36 Robert Baden-Powell, *Scouting for Boys*, ed. Elleke Boehmer, Oxford, 2004, p. 299. The Girl Guides was formed in 1910 and associated with Robert's sister, Agnes Baden-Powell, but as editor Boehmer describes, Robert 'saw women as representing another realm of experience and sentiment entirely . . . boy-children represented Baden-Powell's primary focus' (*Scouting for Boys*, pp. 303–4); Vanessa Heggie, 'Bodies, Sport and Science in the Nineteenth Century', *Past & Present*, 2016, 231:1, 173; Clifford Putney, *Muscular Christianity: Manhood and Sports in Protestant America, 1880–1920*, Cambridge, Mass., 2001, cited in Stefan Hübner, 'Muscular Christianity and the Western Civilizing Mission', *Diplomatic History*, 2015, 39:3, 536.

37 George Hirthler, 'Celebrating Pierre de Coubertin . . .', 2. Sep. 2019, accessed 3 Mar. 2021; De Coubertin, 'Causerie du Samedi', *Sports Athlétiques*, 13. Feb. 1892, 3, cited in Robert Nye, *Masculinity and Male Codes of Honor in Modern France*, New York, 1992, p. 220.

38 Pierre de Coubertin, 'Les Femmes aux Jeux Olympiques', *Revue Olympique*, Jul. 1912, 79, 109–11 (111), which appears in translation as 'The Women at the Olympic Games' in Pierre de Coubertin, *Pierre de Coubertin*, pp. 711–13 (713). Pierre de Coubertin, 'The Philosophic Foundation of Modern Olympism', in Pierre de Coubertin, *Pierre de Coubertin*, pp. 580–83 (583). The idea that women are 'too weak and fragile' to run competitively is attributed to coach Arnie Briggs, in India Sturgis, 'Meet the First Woman to Run the Boston Marathon (Illegally) 50 Years Ago . . .', *Telegraph online*, 17 Apr. 2017, accessed 9 Oct. 2020.

39 Peggy Reeves Sanday, *Female Power and Male Dominance*, Cambridge, 1981, pp. 9, 153, 8.

40 Caitlin Moran, *More Than a Woman*, London, 2020, pp. 147–8.

41 Sanday, *Female Power and Male Dominance*, p. 12.

42 Karl Lennartz, 'Two Women Ran the Marathon in 1896', *Citius, Altius, Fortius* (1994), 2:1, 19–20; ; Ana Miragaya 'Female Olympians in the Early Olympic Games (1900–12)', Switzerland, 2005; Marco Della Croce, 'Stamáta Revíthi: Melpomene o la Maratona Negata', *Storie di Sport*, 2019, accessed 9 Oct. 2020.

Part Three: Recovery

9: Risk management

1 Suzanne O'Sullivan, *It's All In Your Head*, London, Vintage, 2016, p. 281; David K. Marcus and Shelly E. Church, 'Are Dysfunctional Beliefs about Illness Unique to Hypochrondriasis?', *Journal of Psychosomatic Research*, 2003, 54:6, 546; Selçuk Özdin and Şükriye Bayrak Özdin, 'Levels and Predictors of Anxiety, Depression and Health Anxiety during COVID-19 Pandemic in Turkish Society . . .', *International Journal of Social Psychiatry*, 2020, 66:5, 504–11; Office for National Statistics, 'Coronavirus and Anxiety . . .', 15 Jun. 2020, accessed 13 Jul. 2022; R. D. Goodwin et al., 'The Epidemiology of Panic Disorder and Agoraphobia in Europe', *European Neuropsychopharmacology*, 2005, 15:4, 435–43; T. Michael et al., 'Epidemiology of Anxiety Disorders', *Psychiatry*, 2007, 6:4, 136–42; Bao-Liang Zhong et al., 'Knowledge, Attitudes, and Practices Towards COVID-19 among Chinese Residents during the Rapid Rise Period of the COVID-19 Outbreak . . .', *International Journal of Biological Sciences*, 2020, 16:10, 1745–52.

2 G. J. Asmundson et al., 'Health Anxiety . . .', *Current Psychiatry Reports*, 2010, 12:4, 306–12; R. Al-Gabalawy et al., 'Health Anxiety Disorders in Older Adults . . .', *Clinical Psychology Review*, 2013, 33:8, 1096–105; Murray B. Stein et al., 'Relationship of Sexual Assault History to Somatic Symptoms and Health Anxiety in Women', *General Hospital Psychiatry*, 2004, 26:3, 178; Donald Beecher, 'Concerning Sex Changes . . .', *The Sixteenth-Century Journal*, 2005, 36:4, 991; Christine Yu, 'Where Are the Women in Sports Science Research?', *Outside*, 8 Nov. 2018, accessed 17 Feb. 2021. Thank you so much to E. Parry for her permission to quote her comment.

3 Hayman Rooke, 'Brimham Rocks in Yorkshire', *Sheffield Register*, 13 Dec. 1788, 4; Joseph Morrissey, 'Remaking Romantic Love in Maria Edgeworth's *Belinda*', *The European Legacy*, 2021, 26:2, 170–87; Maria Edgeworth, *Belinda*, ed. Kathryn J. Kirkpatrick, 1801, Oxford, 1994, pp. 249, 255.

4 Alison Booth, 'Gender, Risk and Competition', *Vox EU*, 14 Sep. 2009, accessed 14 Mar. 2021.

5 Valérie Harrant and Nicolas G. Vaillant, 'Are Women Less Risk Averse than Men? . . .', *Evolution and Human Behavior*, 2008, 29:6, 396–401; Sylvia Maxfield

and Mary Shapiro, 'Gender and Risk . . .', *Gender in Management: An International Journal*, 2010, 25:7, 586–604; 'Women in the Hills . . .', p. 8; Riley Olstead, 'Gender, Space and Fear . . .', *Emotion, Space and Society*, 2011, 4:2, 91.

6 Amanda West and Linda Allin, 'Chancing Your Arm . . .', *Sport in Society*, 2010, 13:7–8, 1234–48; David Rose and Ed Douglas, *Regions of the Heart*, London, 1999, pp. 273–5 (including citations from Polly Toynbee and Alison Osius).

7 Clyde Lawrence, 'The Chaperon', *Topeka Daily State Journal*, 27 Jul. 1909, 4.

8 West and Allin, 'Chancing Your Arm . . .', 13:7–8, 1234–48; Amanda Walker, 'Why Are Women so Well-Suited to Risk Management?', *LinkedIn*, 23 Feb. 2016, accessed 14 Jul. 2022 (my emphasis); Tommy Langseth and Øyvind Salvesen, 'Rock Climbing, Risk and Recognition', *Frontiers in Psychology*, 2018, 9, 1973; I am very grateful to Maria Dixon for talking to me about risk and fell running.

9 Mary Douglas and Aaron Wildavsky, *Risk and Culture: An Essay on the Selection of Technological and Environmental Dangers*, Berkeley, 1983, pp. 5–6.

10 Barbara A. Morrongiello and Kerri Hogg, 'Mothers' Reactions to Children Misbehaving in Ways That Can Lead to Injury . . .', *Sex Roles*, 2004, 50, 103–18.

11 Lisa Kindleberger Hagan and Janet Kuebli, 'Mothers' and Fathers' Socialization of Preschoolers' Physical Risk Taking', *Journal of Applied Developmental Psychology*, 2007, 28:1, 2–14; Jordan E. Montgomery et al., 'Parents At-Risk and Their Children: Intersections of Gender Role Attitudes and Parenting Practices', *Child & Family Social Work*, 2017, 22:3, 1151–60.

12 Morrongiello and Hogg, 'Mothers' Reactions', 103–18.

13 Jeffery S. Jones et al., 'Comparison of Sexual Assaults by Strangers versus Known Assailants in a Community-Based Population', *American Journal of Emergency Medicine*, 2004, 22:6, 454–9; Linda Laura Sabbadini and Maria Giuseppina Muratore, *Violence and Abuses against Women Inside and Outside Family*, Rome, 2006; Ralph Bosen, 'Violence against Women Occurs Mostly at Home', *DW*, 25 Nov. 2018. In a 2017 study in Canada, strangers were responsible for 17.9 per cent of sexual assaults on the studied cohort of women, versus 82.1 per cent by assailants known to the victim (Janice Du Mont et al., 'A Comparison of Intimate Partner and Other Sexual Assault Survivors' Use of Different Types of Specialized Hospital-Based Violence Services', *BMC Women's Health*, 2017, 17). ONS figures show that in England and Wales, from 2019 to 2020, 92 per cent of violent attacks on women were perpetrated by 'people the victim

knows' (Lucy Gilder and Jennifer Clarke, 'How Many Violent Attacks and Sexual Assaults on Women Are there?', *BBC News*, 20 Mar. 2021; Office for National Statistics, 'The Nature of Violent Crime in England and Wales . . .', 25 Feb. 2021). Julie Bindel, 'Why Are London Police Telling Women to Stay at Home?', *Spectator*, 10 Mar. 2021; Victoria Smith, 'On Correctly Curating the Past', *The OK Karen* newsletter, 26 Feb. 2021, accessed 24 Mar. 2021.

14 Tristan Gooley, *The Natural Navigator*, London, 2010, p. 5.

15 Brown and Gilligan, *Meeting at the Crossroads*, p. 125

16 William Godwin, 'On Avarice and Profusion', in *Enquirer*, London, 1797, p. 169. For a longer account of this transition from eighteenth-century optimism to nineteenth-century pessimism, see Rachel Hewitt, *A Revolution of Feeling*, London, 2017, pp. 414–38; Gerd Gigerenzer et al., *The Empire of Chance*, Cambridge, 1989, p. 38, cited in Maurice S. Lee, *Uncertain Chances*, Oxford, 2012, pp. 23–4. This tendency, to adopt mathematical risk assessments in everyday psychology, was satirised by a writer in New York's *Knickerbocker* magazine in Dec. 1850, who spoke about using 'the calculus of probabilities' to predict whether a block of cheese had been made from one particular pail of milk he'd drunk in 1848 ('Editor's Table', *The Knickerbocker; or, New York Monthly Magazine*, Dec. 1850, 36, 571).

17 William Law, *A Serious Call to a Devout and Holy Life*, London, 1729, pp. 3, 110–11.

10: Resistance training

1 Pembroke College archives: 'Tennis Team, 1894', GBR/1058/COL/9/1/15/1/1894; 'Abraham Le Blond', *The New Baxter Society*, https://newbaxtersociety.org/leblond.aspx, accessed 14 Jul. 2022; 'Fancy Dress Ball', *Alpine Post*, 13 Jan. 1900, 26:12, 124, and 27 Jan. 1900, 26:14, 150; 'Smoking Concert at the Kulm', *Morning Post*, 14 Jun. 1900.

2 LAC G12: List of members' climbs; 'A Magic Lantern Exhibition', *Alpine Post*, 12 Feb. 1898, 22:16, 176–7; Jonathan Parry, 'Adrenaline Junkie', *London Review of Books*, 21 Mar. 2019, 41:6, accessed 14 Jul. 2022; Morag Bell and Cheryl McEwan, 'The Admission of Women Fellows to the Royal Geographical Society, 1892–1914', *Geographical Journal*, 1996, 162:3, 297–8; 'On the Alps – without Tartarin', *St James's Gazette*, 8 Mar. 1904, 19.

3 'Women Mountaineers', *Field*, 13 Jun. 1903, 27; 'The Roll of Honour for Women', *Gentlewoman*, 3 Sep. 1904, 21.

4 LAC G10: Elizabeth Le Blond, Speech at inaugural dinner at the Lyceum Club, 16 Dec. 1907; Erika Rappaport, *Shopping for Pleasure*, Princeton, N.J., and Oxford, 2000, p. 110.

5 LAC G18: Adeline Edwards, 'Statement re Lyceum Alpine Club prepared for the information of the Executive Committee', Oct. 1908; G18: Letter J. Hambling to Miss Carthew, 19 Feb. 1909; G18: Lizzie Le Blond to Trustees of the Lyceum Club, 20 Apr. 1910; Le Blond, *Charlotte Sophie Countess Bentinck, 1715–1800*, London, 1912, p. 30; 'Society', *The Queen*, 17 Aug. 1907, 53; 'A Ladies' Alpine Club', *Daily Telegraph and Courier*, 17 Aug. 1907, 5.

6 LAC G18: Edwards, 'Statement re Lyceum Alpine Club . . .'; G10: Press cutting, *Morning Post*, 8 Dec. 1908, re Le Blond Lyceum Club speech; G10: Press cutting, *Tribune*, 14 Aug. 1907; G21: Press cutting, 'The Highest Society', *The Times*, 5 Aug. 1957; G10: Press cutting, *Ladies' Field*, 18 Dec. 1907.

7 LAC G10: Press cutting, *Ladies' Field*, 28 Dec. 1907. Coincidentally, Jane Cobden was the daughter of Richard Cobden, and had grown up in Durnford House, which was later leased to the family of Rebecca Kate Dickinson, the woman who brought to trial her assault by Valentine Baker on a British train. G10: Menu card for Lyceum Alpine Club, 16 Dec. 1907; G10: Fanny Bullock Workman, Speech at inaugural dinner at the Lyceum Club dinner, 16 Dec. 1907.

8 LAC G18: Edwards, 'Statement re Lyceum Alpine Club . . .'; 'Water Diviner, Alpinist, Lady Almoner . . .', *Worthing Gazette*, 2 Apr. 1941, 5; Lynsey Cullen, 'The First Lady Almoner . . .', *Journal of the History of Medicine and Allied Sciences*, 2013, 68:4, 551–82; 'Notes on the Magazines', *The Queen*, 13 Aug. 1904, 33; 'Wonders of Thibet . . .', *St Andrew's Citizen*, 20 Feb. 1904, 6; Elisa Kay Sparks, '"The Evening under Lamplight . . ."', in Anna Burrells et al. (eds.), *Woolfian Boundaries*, Clemson, S.C., 2007, p. 169.

9 Alice Carthew's cohabitation with Lucy Agelasto is given in NA, 1939: Register, RG101/0307D/013/33. An overview of the LAC's early members, their climbs, and their social character, can be pieced together from LAC G12: List of members' climbs, and G10: List of members' climbs in 1908. The comment about St Moritz tourists failing to see the fun of feminism is made in a review (possibly written by Lizzie; certainly edited and published by her) of a

'minstrel performance' which contained a 'lecture on Women's Rights', published in *Alpine Post*, 13 Feb. 1897, 20:16, 123.

10 LAC G18: Minutes from Lyceum Alpine Club meeting, 3 Oct. 1909; G18: Alice Carthew, 'Lyceum Alpine Club', 3 Mar. 1909; G2: Minute book 1909–11, entry for 22 Nov. 1909; G26: *First Report of the Ladies' Alpine Club*, 1913; Mrs E. P. Jackson, 'A Winter Quartette', *Alpine Journal*, Aug. 1888–Nov. 1889, 14, 200–10, and 'Winter Mountaineering in 1888', *Yorkshire Ramblers' Club Journal*, 1903, 2, 97; Roche, 'Women Climbers, 1850–1900', 248–9.

11 LAC G26: *First Report of the Ladies' Alpine Club*, 1913; G10: Logo and bookplate designs.

12 LAC G10: Report to be presented at the first annual meeting of the Lyceum Alpine Club, 27 Nov. 1908; Osborne, 'Gender and the Organisation of British Climbing . . .', p. 445; Edwards, *Untrodden Peaks*, pp. 208–9; Main, *My Home in the Alps*, pp. 127–31.

13 LAC G10: Press cuttings about women's Alpine kit exhibition in May 1910; G26: *First Report of the Ladies' Alpine Club*, 1913, pp. 26–7; G10: Press cutting, *The Times*, 3 May 1910; G10: Press cutting, *Morning Post*, 2 May 1910; G10: Press cutting, *Daily Graphic*, 4 May 1910; G10: Press cutting, *Daily Mirror*, 3 May 1910.

14 LAC G10: Press cutting, *Daily Telegraph*, 2 May 1910; G26: *First Report of the Ladies' Alpine Club*, 1913, pp. 26–7; G10: Press cutting, 'Mountaineering Costumes: Lady Alpinists Organise an Exhibition', *Daily Graphic*, 4 May 1910; G10: Press cutting, Julian Grande, 'Woman out of Doors: Lady Alpinists from a Man's Point of View', *Daily Mail*, Friday 6 May 1910.

15 LAC G10: Press cutting, *Daily Telegraph*, 2 May 1910; G10: Press cutting, 'Lady Mountaineer', *Morning Leader*, 3 May 1910; Edward Lisle Strutt, 'In Memoriam: Mrs Aubrey Le Blond . . .', *Alpine Journal*, 1934, 46, 382–4; see Miriam Underhill, *Manless Alpine Climbing*, London, 1934; Roche, 'The Ascent of Women', p. 221. See, for example, Julie Bindel, *Feminism for Women*, London, 2021, and Karen Ingala Smith, *Defending Women's Spaces*, London, 2022.

16 'Ladies' Reserved Railway Carriages', *Brechin Advertiser*, 6 Jul. 1875, 4; 'News of the Day', *Liverpool Daily Post*, 29 Jun. 1875, 5.

17 Hewitt, Freedland and Alban, *The Long View*, 22:00.

18 Archibald Prentice, *Historical Sketches and Personal Recollections of Manchester*, London, 1851, p. 289; Uings, 'Gardens and Gardening . . .', pp. 248–50; John

Ranlett, '"Checking Nature's Desecration" . . .', *Victorian Studies*, 1983, 26:2, 204; 'Local Government (England and Wales) Bill: Second Reading', *Hansard*, HC Deb (13 Apr. 1888), vol. 324, cc1210–86; 'Access to Mountains Bill', *Hansard*, vol. 188, HC Deb 15 May 1908, c1440; 'On Ilkley Moor', *Yorkshire Post and Leeds Intelligencer*, 12 Feb. 1934, 5.

19 E. P. Thompson, *The Making of the English Working Class*, Harmondsworth, 1991, p. 237; Simon Robert Thompson, 'The Fashioning of a New World . . .', PhD thesis, King's College, London, 2018, pp. 237, 52–7; Ben Mayfield, 'Access to the Countryside . . .', *Legal Studies*, 2017, 37:2, 343–62; 'English Ramblers', *Daily News*, Perth, 16 Jun. 1931, 1.

20 Emily Midorikawa and Emma Claire Sweeney, *A Secret Sisterhood*, London, 2017, pp. 77–140; 'The Primrose League', *Morning Post*, 23 Nov. 1892, 2; 'Day to Day in Liverpool', *Liverpool Mercury*, 23 May 1894, 6; Roche, 'The Ascent of Women', pp. 273–4; Elizabeth A. O'Donnell, 'Doing Good Quietly . . .', *Women's History: The Journal of the Women's History Network*, 2017, 2:7, 2–7; NA: Teresa Merz, 'Lodging Houses', NRO 2281/15. I am very grateful to Liz O'Donnell for talking to me about the Richardson sisters and Teresa Merz, 'Lodging Houses', NRO 2281/15. To hear O'Donnell speaking further about these remarkable women, see Rachel Hewitt, *Repeating Patterns in the Street Harassment of Women*, BBC Radio 4, 25 Apr. 2021.

21 Captain, 'Enter Ladies and Gentlemen of Color . . .', 101–2; Shreya Atrey, 'Lifting as We Climb . . .', *Oñati Socio-Legal Series*, 2015, 5:6, 1515.

22 Osborne, '"Deeds, Not Words": Emily Wilding Dickinson and the Epsom Derby 1913 Revisited', in Jon Dart and Stephen Wagg (eds.), *Sport, Protest and Globalisation*, London, 2016, p. 30; Osborne, 'Gender and the Organisation of British Climbing . . .', p. 140; Molly McElwee, 'Outnumbered or Not . . .', *Telegraph*, 12 Jun. 2020, accessed 14 Jul. 2022; Anita Anand, *Sophia: Princess, Suffragette, Revolutionary*, London, 2015, p. 132.

23 F. Savile, 'The Suffragette', *Strand Magazine*, Jul. 1908, 36:211, 3–10; LAC G21: Press cutting, Milsom. Accounts of the close relationship between mountaineering and women's suffrage campaigns are given in Rebecca A. Brown, *Women on High*, p. xii; Tiffany Lewis, 'The Mountaineering and Wilderness Rhetorics of Washington Women Suffragists', *Rhetoric and Public Affairs*, Summer 2018, 21:2, 297–316; Susan Ware, *Why They Marched: Untold Stories of the Women Who Fought for the Right to Vote*, Cambridge, Ma., 2019, pp. 18194;

Cleone Abrams, '"We Wear Our Boots Just Like the Men" . . .', honors thesis, University of Washington, 15 Mar. 2019, pp. 1–2; Susan Ware, 'Climbing Mountains . . .', *Lit Hub*, 13 May 2019, accessed 14 Jul. 2022.

24 The *Votes for Women* comment is preserved as a press cutting in LAC G10: 24 Dec. 1909. A brief account of Eva McLaren's work is contained in LAC G26: *Ladies' Alpine Club Annual Report*, 1922, pp. 25–7. Violet Roy-Batty's presence on the ladies' council is described in 'Conservative and Unionist Suffrage Meeting', *The Queen*, 27 Feb. 1909, 360.

25 Lizzie describes her lack of courage in Le Blond, *Mountaineering in the Land of the Midnight Sun*, London, 1908, pp. 268–9. Mary Crawford's description of the benefits of mountaineering for women is in Mary Crawford, 'Mountain Climbing for Women', *Canadian Alpine Journal*, 1909, 2, 86–91 (and is cited in Siri Winona Louie, 'Gender in the Alpine Club of Canada, 1906–1940', MA thesis, University of Calgary, 1996, p. 8). Not all the Ladies' Alpine Club members had the same views about women's rights. In the club's archives during these years, there is evidence of a conflict between one woman who preferred to use the female-specific term 'Chair*woman*' for the female chair of LAC meetings, and another person, who went through the meeting minutes and corrected this on multiple occasions to the default male term 'Chair*man*'. (See, for example, G2: Minute book 1909–11, entry for 19 June 2012, pp. 71–2).

26 'G.H.P.', 'Young Women as Journalists', *Girls' Own Paper*, 21 Mar. 1891, pp. 395–6; Barbara Onslow, 'New World, New Woman, New Journalism . . .', *Media History*, 2001, 7:1, 7–15; Helen McCarthy, *Women of the World*, London, 2014, pp. xi, 6.

27 Le Blond, *Day In, Day Out*, p. 178; 'Tunbridge Wells War Notes', *Kent & Sussex Courier*, 25 Sep. 1914, 5; LAC G26: *Ladies' Alpine Club Annual Report*, 1916, p. 15; Le Blond, *Day In, Day Out*, pp. 188–9; NA: 'Medal Card of Aubrey Le Blond', WO 372/23/23867, dates the beginning of Lizzie's war service as a nurse in the French Red Cross to Oct. 1914. 'Motor Fatality', *Kent & Sussex Courier*, 17 Apr. 1914, 2.

28 LAC G26: *Ladies' Alpine Club Annual Report*, 1916, p. 15; Le Blond, *Day In, Day Out*, p. 189; LAC G21: Advertisement for Lizzie Le Blond's lecture 'Mountaineering from a Woman's Point of View', delivered 12 May 1915.

29 LAC G26: *Ladies' Alpine Club Annual Report*, 1916, pp. 21–2; 'The Death Has Occurred . . . of Captain Royston Le Blond', *South Eastern Gazette*, 1 Jun. 1915,

7; LAC G11: Scrapbook 1914–24 (press cuttings from Jul. 1915–16, including *The Queen*, 6 Feb. 1916); G26: *Ladies' Alpine Club Annual Report*, 1917, pp. 14–15.

30 Le Blond, *Day In, Day Out*, pp. 191–3; LAC G26: *Ladies' Alpine Club Annual Report*, 1917, pp. 17–18.

31 Le Blond, *Day In, Day Out*, p. 193; 'Gloucestershire Root, Fruit and Grain Society Annual Show: Potatoes', *Gloucestershire Chronicle*, 10 Nov. 1917, 5; 'Gloucestershire Chamber of Agriculture', *Cheltenham Chronicle*, 7 Jun. 1919, 5; 'Important Sale at Gloucester', *Gloucestershire Echo*, 22 May 1922, 3; 'The Property Market: The Ploddy House Estate', *Gloucester Journal*, 27 May 1922, 12.

32 Le Blond, *Day In, Day Out*, pp. 194, 131–2; LAC G26: *Ladies' Alpine Club Annual Report*, 1917, 13; *Day In, Day Out*, pp. 216–17; 'Women Footballers', *Pall Mall Gazette*, 22 Mar. 1922, 11; Le Blond, *Day In, Day Out*, p. 204; 'Hey's Ladies of Bradford, the Forgotten Football Champions of Yorkshire', *Yorkshire Coast History* online; Michael L. Dockrill, *British Establishment Perspectives on France, 1936–40*, Basingstoke, 1999, pp. 23–4; Hansen, 'Le Blond', (online sources accessed 14 Jul. 2022).

33 From Dec. 1923, Lizzie received correspondence at both 134 Whitehall Court and 87 Victoria Street (Morgan Library, Letter Marjorie Bowen to Elizabeth Le Blond, 30 Dec. 1923 Unbound Ray Bowen MA 13420.13 and Letter Marjorie Bowen to Elizabeth Le Blond, 2 May 1924, Unbound Ray Bowen MA 13420.16). 'Pedigree Large Black Pigs', *Gloucester Citizen*, 22 Oct. 1921, 6, describes Aubrey's collaboration with Jane in organising an agricultural fair; 'Farmer's Death on a Rick', *Gloucestershire Echo*, 19 Sep. 1907, 3, provides more information about Jane's background. 'Forthcoming Cattle Sales', *Gloucestershire Chronicle*, 22 Apr. 1922, 6, describes Aubrey's intention to sell the Gloucestershire farm and move to Suffolk. Upland Hall, Bungay, was given by Lizzie as her address on the passenger list of the SS *Majestic*, when she travelled from New York to Southampton in March 1923, returning from her first visit to see Arthur in California, implying she lived with Aubrey and Jane at least some of the time (NA: 'UK and Ireland, Incoming Passenger Lists, 1878–1960', Board of Trade: Commercial and Statistical Department and successors: Inwards Passenger Lists; Class: BT 26/748/8; Piece: 748, 16 Mar. 1923). Lizzie listed Aubrey and Jane as guests at the Ladies' Alpine Club on 18 Nov. 1925 (LAC G1: Visitors' book). Lizzie, Aubrey and Jane's arrival in New York is documented in National Archives, Washington, 'Passenger and Crew Lists of Vessels

Arriving at New York, New York, 1897–1957', Microfilm Publication T715, 8892 rolls. NAI: 300346. Records of the Immigration and Naturalization Service, Year: 1924; Arrival: New York, New York, USA; Microfilm Serial: T715, 1897–1957; Line: 7; Page Number: 14. Jane and Aubrey's trip to Algiers is documented in NA: 'UK and Ireland, Incoming Passenger Lists, 1878–1960, Board of Trade: Commercial and Statistical Department and successors: Inwards Passenger Lists.; Class: BT26; Piece: 852; Item: 1', 28 Oct. 1926.

34 GRO: Death certificate of Elizabeth Frances Alice Le Blond Year 1934, Quarter: Sep., District: Radnor W, Vol. 11b, p. 135; Peter Matthews, *House of Spies: St Ermin's Hotel, the London Base of British Espionage*, Stroud, 2016, pp. 59, 88.

35 Christopher Andrew, *Secret Service*, London, 1985, pp. 25–6; Elizabeth Le Blond, 'The Coveted Lyngen Fjord', *The Queen*, 5 Aug. 1905, 48. In this, she refers to having written for the *Daily Express* on 21 Sep. 1901 about Russian attempts to buy the Lofoten Islands to supply an ice-free port. Le Blond, *Day In, Day Out*, pp. 157–61; E. Le Blond, 'Germany Will Never "Give"', *Daily Mail*, 19 Mar. 1923, 8; Tammy M. Proctor, *Female Intelligence*, New York and London, 2003, p. 2.

36 GRO: Death certificate of Elizabeth Frances Alice Le Blond. I am grateful to Tim Walsh, Aubrey's great-grand-nephew, for generously sharing a lot of information with me about Aubrey, Jane and 'Mangalore'.

37 Le Blond, *Day In, Day Out*, p. 250.

38 Osborne, 'Gender and the Organisation of British Climbing . . .', pp. 344, 319; Royal Geographical Society, MEC archives, Madame M. Marvingt, 13 Jun. 1919, EE Box 5, File 2, Item 35 and Letter from M. Anne Bernard, both cited in Osborne, 'Gender and the Organisation of British Climbing . . .', pp. 352–4.

39 Osborne, 'Gender and the Organisation of British Climbing . . .', p. 364; Arlene Blum, *Annapurna*, 1980, Berkeley, 2015, pp. xvii, 60.

40 Junko Tabei and Helen Y. Rolfe, *Honouring High Places*, Calgary, 2017, p. 72; Martina Gugglberger, 'Climbing beyond the Summits', *International Journal of the History of Sport*, 2015, 32:4, 598–9; Osborne, 'Gender and the Organisation of British Climbing . . .', pp. 426–7.

41 Stephen Harper, *Lady Killer Peak*, London, 1965, p. 5.

42 Adolphe Abrahams, cited in Holmes, 'Diane Leather and the 5 Minute Mile'. See also Neil Carter, *Medicine, Sport and the Body: A Historical Perspective*, London, 2012, pp. 161–3.

43 Bill Smith, *Forty Years of the FRA*, St Ives, 2010, pp. 8–12; Florence Scott, *Memories of Old Withnell Fold*, 1988, accessed 14 Jul. 2022.

44 Claire Langhamer, *Women's Leisure in England, 1920–1960*, Manchester, 2000, pp. 76–83; Thompson, 'The Fashioning of a New World . . .', p. 52; Selina Todd, 'Poverty and Aspiration', *Twentieth Century British History*, 2004, 15:2, 119–42; 'Jill on the Jaunt', *The Ruc-Sac*, Jul. 1931, 1:1, 21–2.

45 Cited in Thompson, 'The Fashioning of a New World . . .', pp. 15–17, 53–5, 63; 'The Ramblerette', *Out-o'-Doors*, Nov. 1927, 111; Ben Anderson, 'A Liberal Countryside? . . .', *Urban History*, 2011, 38:1, 84–102.

46 Alan Hankinson, *Geoffrey Winthrop Young*, London, 1995, pp. 59–60, 222, plates between pp. 244–5.

47 Osborne, 'Gender and the Organisation of British Climbing . . .', pp. 397–99.

48 Jordyn Curl and Elizabeth Cobb, 'Biographical Sketch of Mary P. Burrill', *Alexander Street*, 2018; Helen T. Verongos, 'Overlooked No More . . .', *New York Times*, 1 Oct. 2020: (both accessed 14 Jul. 2022).

11: Recovery run

1 Klein, 'Mourning . . .', p. 359.

2 Eric Walter White, *Benjamin Britten*, London, 1983, p. 46.

3 Bill Cowley, 'A Cleveland Farmer's Diary, from Goulton Grange and Glaisdale Head Farms', *Dalesman*, Aug. 1955, 17:5, 245–7; Bill Cowley, *Lyke Wake Walk and the Lyke Wake Way*, Clapham, 1988, p. 16.

4 Cowley, 'A Cleveland Farmer's Diary, from Goulton Grange'; Bill Cowley, 'A Cleveland Farmer's Diary', *Dalesman*, Nov. 1955, 17:8, 408–10.

5 Cowley, *Lyke Wake Walk*, p. 11; Mike Parker, 'Whatever Happened to the Lyke Wake Walk?', *Map Addict*, 1 Aug. 2015, accessed 14 Jul. 2022.

6 Cowley, *Lyke Wake Walk*, p. 12.

7 Joseph Ford, *Some Reminiscences and Folk Lore of Danby Parish and District*, Whitby, 1953, pp. 97–100.

8 Revd J. C. Atkinson, *Forty Years in a Moorland Parish*, London, 1891, pp. 85–7.

9 William Henderson, *Notes on the Folk-Lore of the Northern Counties of England and the Borders*, London, 1879, p. 212; Atkinson, *Forty Years*, pp. 63, 111; Ford, *Some Reminiscences and Folk Lore*, pp. 95–6.

10 Ula Taylor, 'The Historical Evolution of Black Feminist Theory and Praxis', *Journal of Black Studies*, 1998, 29:2, 239; Elise Johnson McDougald, 'The Double Task: The Struggle of Negro Women for Sex and Race Emancipation', *Survey Graphic*, Mar. 1926, 6, cited in Gerda Lerner (ed.), *Black Women in White America*, New York, 1972, p. 171; Greater Manchester Coalition of Disabled People, *A Brief History of Disabled People's Self-Organisation*, Manchester, 2010, pp. 8–10; Claire Bond Potter, 'Taking Back Times Square', *Radical History Review*, 2012, 113, 67–80; Finn Mackay, *Radical Feminism*, Basingstoke, 2015, pp. 71–102; Dworkin, 'Pornography and Grief', p. 291; Freedman, 'Women and Restaurants . . .', 2; Georgina Hickey, 'Barred from the Barroom . . .', *Feminist Studies*, 2008, 34:3, 383.

11 Nick Paumgarten, 'Inside the Cultish Dreamworld of Augusta National', *New Yorker*, 14 Jun. 2019; Andrew D. Linden, 'American Football and the 1970s Women's Movement', *Sport in American History*, 29 May 2014: (both accessed 14 Jul. 2022).

12 Karen P. DePauw, 'The (In)Visibility of DisAbility: Cultural Contexts and "Sporting Bodies"', *Quest*, 1997, 49:4, 416–30.

13 Kathrine Switzer, *Marathon Woman*, New York, 2007, pp. 71, 91–2.

14 Gail Elrick, 'Obituary of Ann Sayer', *LDWA*, 17 Apr. 2020, accessed 14 Jul. 2022.

15 Philippa Velija et al., 'Exclusionary Power in Sports Organisations', *International Review for the Sociology of Sport*, 2012, 49:2, 211–26.

16 Courtney Connley, 'The US Open Awards Men and Women Equal Prize Money . . .', *CNBC*, 11 Sep. 2019; Pete Davies, 'Football: Tough Test for the Team England Forgot', *Independent*, 6 Oct. 1994: (both accessed 14 Jul. 2022).

17 Tabei, *Honouring High Places*, p. 210; Blum, *Annapurna*, pp. xxiv, 3, 71; Grace Lichtenstein, 'Himalayan Scaling Called an Inspiration to Women', *New York Times*, 11 Nov. 1978, 8.

18 Gugglberger, 'Climbing Beyond the Summits', 597–613; Pasang Lhamu Foundation, 'The History: Pasang Lhamu Sherpa', accessed 14 Jul. 2022.

19 'American Guides to Teach Climbing', *Climbing*, 16 May 2007, accessed 14 Jul. 2022.

20 Ralph Ranalli, 'A New Mountain to Climb', *Harvard Kennedy School*, Winter 2022; Sarah Stirling, 'Climbing against Repression: The Afghan Women with High Mountain Dreams', *Summit Magazine*, 7 Oct. 2019: (both accessed 14 Jul. 2022).

21 Bowman, 'Street Harassment', 520; I am grateful to Professor John Spencer for explaining the existing legal mechanisms for prosecuting street harassment.

22 Maya Wolfe-Robinson and Vikram Dodd, 'Institutional Misogyny "Erodes Women's Trust in UK Police"', *Guardian*, 16 Mar. 2021; Anoosh Chakelian, 'Are UK Police Forces Institutionally Misogynistic?', *New Statesman*, 17 March 2021; Kearl, *Unsafe and Harassed*, p. 34: (all accessed 14 Jul. 2022).

23 https://twitter.com/bindelj/status/1371729121370312705?s=20&t=e4KeMA4NI4xMxoKvRiEXZg; Kearl, *Unsafe and Harassed*, p. 34; Lorcan Lovett, 'Yangon Puts "Girl Power" into Green Spaces', *Nikkei Asia* 28 Aug. 2019, (all online sources accessed 14 Jul. 2022). I am very grateful to Anna Livia Cullinan and Susannah Walker (of Make Space for Girls) for sharing their research and telling me about their important work in helping teenage girls to feel more at home in the world.

24 Hannah Peckham et al., 'Male Sex Identified by Global COVID-19 Meta-Analysis as a Risk Factor for Death and ITU Admission', *Nature Communications*, 9 Dec. 2020, 11, 6317; 'Gender and Road Traffic Injuries', *Gender and Health*, Geneva, Jan. 2002, 2; Ivan Cuk et al., 'Sex Differences in Pacing during Half-Marathon and Marathon Race', *Research in Sports Medicine*, 2020, 28:1, 111–20; Matthew P. Buman et al., 'Hitting the Wall in the Marathon . . .', *Psychology of Sport & Exercise*, 2008, 9:2, 177–90.

25 Sunil S. Solomon et al., 'The Impact of HIV and High-Risk Behaviours on the Wives of Married Men Who Have Sex with Men and Injection Drug Users . . .', *Journal of the International AIDS Society*, 2010, 13, S7–S7; Jeff Turner and John Fletcher, 'TI-UP Enquiry: Gender and Road Safety', *TI-UP*, May 2018; Lucy Ellmann, "Why Can't Women Be More Like Men, and Enjoy Failing?', *Independent*, 12 Jan. 1997; https://twitter.com/lukejostins/status/1374011559807176704: (all online sources accessed 15 Jul. 2022). I am grateful to Marina Strinkovsky for pointing out that men's risk-taking directly impacts on women's safety in this way.

26 Hamilton, 'Running While Female'; Kearl, *Unsafe and Harassed*, p. 29.

27 For example, see LAC G21: Cutting from Dorothy Pilley 'Christmas Climbing for Ladies', *Daily Mail*, 22 Dec. 1920.

Index

Page numbers in *italics* indicate illustrations

abolitionists, 93–4
Abrahams, Adolphe, 331
Access to Countryside Act (UK; 1949), 203, 316
Across Patagonia (Dixie), 88
'activewear', 124
Adams, Mary Louise, 161, 241
adolescence, 210–20, 225–6, 293
fear of assault, 217–19
self-consciousness, 216–17
Adventures on the Roof of the World (Le Blond), 306
Aegis Magazine on Ending Violence against Women, 188
Afghanistan, 329, 359–61
Agelasto, Loucia 'Lucy', 309
agoraphobia, 196–7
Aiello, John R., 182
Aiguille du Belvédère, 131
Aiguille du Midi, 134
Aiguille du Tacul, 131, 134
Aiguille du Tour, 131
Aix-les-Bains, France, 75
Akenson, Donald Harman, 47
Algiers, 54
Allbutt, Thomas Clifford, 145–6
Allin, Linda, 279, 281
Alpine Club, 45, 87–91, 93, 153, 173–4, 177, 242, 278, 308, 356, 370
Alpine Club of Williamstown, Massachusetts, 87
Alpine Guide (Ball), 70
Alpine Journal, 87, 134, 135, 138, 236, 312
Alpine Post, 164, 305
Alvares, Leonardo Azevedo Mobilia, 127
Amateur Athletics Union (AAU), 354–5
American Alpine Club, 357–8
American football, 238, 352–3
American Tennis Championship, 335
anaemia, 75
ancient Greece, 3, 193, 226, 349
Anderegg, Peter, 145
Anderson, Ada, 93
Anderson, Dr Tempest, 308
Anderson, Eric, 243
Anderson, Mimi, 108
Andrew, Christopher, 326
Andrews, Kerri, 121
d'Angeville, Henriette, 91, 143
Annapurna I, Nepal, 358
Antelope Island 50K, 111
Anthony, Susan B., 161
Appalachian Mountain Club, 87
Appalachian Trail, 5
'Ascend: Leadership Through Athletics' programme, 359–60
Atalanta, 349
'athleisurewear', 124
Athletes' Coalition, 122
Atkinson, John, 349
Atwater, Tanya, 358*n*
Au Bonheur des Dames (Zola), 256–7
Augusta National golf club, Georgia, 352

Austen, Jane, 79
Australia, 218
Avon (cosmetics company), 356
Ayres, Elizabeth, 118

Bad Homburg, Germany, 54
Badass Mother Runners, 111
  Badass Epic 10K, 111
Baden-Powell, Robert, 259
Badrutt, Caspar, 162
Baedeker, Karl, 70
Baig, Samina, 359
Baker, Colonel Valentine, 151, 247–8, 257
Baker, Ella, 351
Ball, John, 70
Balmat, Jean-Pierre, 44
Balmhorn, Bernese Alps, 85
BAME sportswomen, 5, 95, 214, 215
Bancroft, Effie, 163
bandy (game), 6, 7, 161
Bangladesh, 216
Bannister, Roger, 331
Barr Trail Mountain Race, 111
Bartlett, William Ashmead, 57
baseball, 242–3
'Battle of the Sexes' tennis match, 336
BBC (British Broadcasting Corporation), 110
Beachy Head (Smith), 81
Bell, Gertrude, 234, 317
Benham, Gertrude, 234
Benson, Edward Frederick, 157, 162
Berlin, Germany, 65
Bernard, Anne, 329
Bertheau, Therese, 232
Big Bear Events, 111
Billinghurst, May, 316
Bird, Isabella, 136, 233
Bird, Sue, 110
Black Girls Hike, 42
Blackheath Ladies' Hockey Club, 242
Blatch, Harriet Stanton, 249–50, 315
Bloomer, Amelia, 143
Blum, Arlene, 329, 336, 357–8
Blunt, Wilfrid Scawen, 56
Bly, Nelly, 166
Bob Graham Round, 108
bobsleighing, 163, 240
Boer War (1899–1902), 257
Bonnie Boots, 42
Boston Marathon, 354–5, *355*
Bostonians, The (James), 258
botany, 251–2
de Bourrienne, Louis Antoine Fauvelet, 180
Bowes, Ali, 184
Bowman, Cynthia Grant, 188, 362
boxing, 242, 353–4
Boyd, Robert, 49
Brady, Martha, 214
Brandeis, Louis, 102
Braysher, Ellen Drew, 78
Brevoort, Marguerite 'Meta', 86, 142, 233
Bright Alpine Club, Australia, 87
Brimham Rocks, 276–9, 282
Bristow, Lily, 136, 309
British Astronomical Association, 251
British Blind Sport, 42
British Federation of University Women, 314
British Journal for the Philosophy of Science, 184
British Ladies' Football Club 319
British Mountaineering Council, 107, 334
British Red Cross Society, 322–3
Britten, Benjamin, 341
Brodigan, Ina, 309
Brontë, Charlotte, 317
Brooks, John Ellingham, 157
Bröske, Käthe, 234

Brown, Hannah, 57
Brown, Lyn Mikel, 210–11, 213, 221, 292
Brucks, Otto, 158
Brueger, Alexandra 'Ally', 191–2
Bryce, James, 316
Buet, Chablais Alps, 81–2
Bulpett, William Henry, 162
Burdett-Coutts, Angela, 57–9
Burke, Edmund, 83
Burkeman, Oliver, 185
Burnaby, Frederick Gustavus 'Fred', 52–7, 59, 135, 151, 247
Burnaby, Harry Arthur Gustavus St Vincent, 56–7, 59, 151, 154, 322, 325
Burrill, Mary, 335
Burton, Richard, 157

Caine, Barbara, 58
Cam Houses, 204
Cambridge University, 242–5, *245*, 251, 317, 335
Cambridge University Women's Boat Club, 335
camping, 201–2
Cano, Carolina, 192
Capper, Mabel, 324
Capri, Italy, 157
Captain, Gwendolyn, 318
Carers Stepping Out, 43
Caron, Ernest, 89
Carter, Elizabeth, 79
Carthew, Alice, 309–10
Cavendish Laboratory, Cambridge, 251
Cavendish-Bentinck, Eliza, 48–9, 75
Cavendish-Bentinck, William 'Dartchie', 48–50, 53, 323
Chadwyck-Onyszkiewicz, Alison, 358
chaise-à-porteurs, 75–7, *76*
Chamberlin, Silas, 71
Chamonix, France, 72, *72*
Chamonix Compagniedes Guides, 72
Chandler, Timothy, 257
Chanel, Coco, 313
Charlet, Alphonse, 44
Charlet, Jean, 136
Charteris, Hugo 'Lord Elcho', 157
Chasseurs Alpins, 323
Chicago, USA, 64
childbirth, 75, 123
childcare costs, 125
childhood, 286–8, 366
Cho Oyu, Himalayas, 330–31
Claxton, Kate, 157
Cleveland Way, 22–3, 26, 31–3, 345
Clift, Stephen, 166
Climbers' Club, 242
Club Alpin Française (CAF), 73, 87, 89, 235
clubs and societies, 87–90, 236, 239, 330, 356–7
  exclusion from, 88–90, 254, 352
  ladies-only clubs, 314–15, 356–7
coaching, 125
Cobden, Jane, 308
Coe, Sebastian, 183
Col du Géant, 131
Colden, Jane, 251–2
Cole, Eliza, 71, 73, 82, 142, 145–6
Coleridge, Samuel Taylor, 68, 88
Collier, Mary, 91–2, 94
Collum, Vera, 324
Colvile, Henry and Alice, 55–6, 327
Comparative Political Studies journal, 184
Coniston Coppermines, Lake District, 27
Connochie, Kathleen, 332
Cook, Thomas, 70
Cooky, Cheryl, 110
Coolidge, Willy, 85–6, 88

Cooperative Holidays Association, 334
Cossey, Ada, 309
Cotton, Sir Henry, 239
de Coubertin, Baron Pierre, 8, 15–16, 41, 259–60
'Couch to 5K', 183
Coutts, Thomas, 57
Covid-19, 176–83, 201, 270, 366
  lockdowns, 178–9, 182–4, 227
  social distancing, 180–1
Cowley, Bill, 36, 342–3, 347–8, 351
Coxhead, Elizabeth, 334
Craig, Malcolm, 59
Crawford, Mary E., 320
Creasy, Stella, 362–3
Cresta Run, St Moritz, 6, *6*, *162*, 163, 240
Criado Perez, Caroline, 225
cricket, 237–8, 356–7
Croydon Camera Club, 306
Cullinan, Anna Livia, 365
Cupelin, Auguste, 134, 137
Cupelin, Edouard, 134–8, 148
curling, 161, *161*
Cust, Elizabeth, 79
cycling, 159–61, 239–40, 319
Cycling magazine, 159

Dabbs Jr, James, 182
Daily Express, 326
Daily Mail, 326
Daily Telegraph, 110
Dales Way, 201, 203–4, 223–4
  Dales Way Challenge, 176–7, 273, 275
  Dales Way ultra-marathon, 203
Dalesman magazine, 342–3
Daly, Lady Harriet, 47
Danenberg, Sophia, 5
Darke, Karen, 122
Darwin, Charles, 88
Daughters' Rights, 58
Dauwalter, Courtney, 107
Davis, Cathy 'Cat', 353
Davis, Deirdre, 193
Davos, Switzerland, 74
Davos-Platz (MacMorland), 74
Davy, Dr John, 73–4
Day In, Day Out (Le Blond), 42
De Morgan, Augustus, 294
Degeneration (Nordau), 258–9
Degeneration: A Chapter in Darwinism (Lankester), 258
Delmonico's, New York, 249
Demény, Károly, 158
Dent du Géant, Mont Blanc massif, 137–9
Depression (1929–39), 326
Desailloud, Marie, 81–2
Désir, Alison, 122
Dhanapala, Sam, 113
Dick, Kerr Ladies football team, 246
Dickens, Charles, 57, 83, 85
Dickinson, Anna, 317
Dickinson, Rebecca Kate, 247–8, 257
disability rights, 5, 243, 319, 351
Disabled Ramblers, 42
diversity, 122–3
Dixie, Lady Florence, 88–9, 319
Dod, Lottie, *141*, 160, *162*, 239
Dod, Tony, 7, 160, *161*
domestic labour, 184–6, 261
Donkin, William, 139
Douglas, Lord Francis, 88
Douglas, Mary, 281–2
Douglass, Sarah Mapps, 93–4
Dowie, Ménie Muriel, 317
Doyle, Arthur Conan, 132, 157
Drew, Mary, 117
Dworkin, Andrea, 196, 352
Dyhrenfurth, Hettie, 330

Eaton, Suzanne, 192
Edgeworth, Maria, 276
Edmunds, Sheila, 357

education, 80–81, 242–5, *245*, 250, 251–2
Edwards, Adeline, 306–8, 311
Edwards, Amelia, 70, 78, 81–2, 89, 144, 233, 312
Eliot, George, 54
Eliot, T. S., 158, 167
Ellmann, Lucy, 367
Emerson, Ralph Waldo, 82
Emile (Rousseau), 82
Enclosure Acts, 315–16
endurance sports, 107–9
Engadin valley, 148, 154–8
Engelhörner mountains, 234
England and Wales Cricket Board, 356
Englishwoman's Review, The, 58
Equality Act (UK, 2010), 114
equipment, 72–3, 312–13
d'Este, Beatrice, 159
Everard, Sarah, 248, 363
Everest, 5, 328–9, 357–9
Expédition Féminine au Nepal (1959), 330
Explorers' Club of New York, 88

Fairhall, Neroli, 5
Fane, Violet, 52
Farr, William, 65
Featherhood (Gilmour), 66
Fédération Internationale de Bobsleigh et de Tobogganing, 240
female bodies, 225–6
'female pedestrian' competitions, 92
female role models, 236
Feuerstein, Stubai Alps, 86
First Duty of Women, The (Taylor), 317
Fish, Sue, 363
Fitzgerald, Hermione, Duchess of Leinster, 157
Fletcher, Eliza, 192
Flores, Olivia, 353
Folsom, Charles, 252
'foot races', 92–3
football, 126, 242, 245–6, 299, 324–5, 356–7
Football Association (FA), 242, 245–6, 324, 356–7
Forest Leaves (Harper), 94
Forno Glacier, Bregaglia range, *133*
Forrest, Simon, 166
Forward Suffrage Union, 320
Fox Tuckett, Elizabeth 'Lizzie', 76, 310–12
Fox Tuckett, Francis, 310
Fox Tuckett, Mariana, 41, 76, 310
Franco-Prussian War (1870–71), 257, 259
Frederickson, Megan, 184
freedom of movement, 213–15, 253–6
Freshfield, Jane, 71, 73, 78, 81–2, 147, 233
Freud, Sigmund, 212, 258, 271
Friedrich, Caspar David, 82

Gant, Anita, 318
Garmin, 114, 294
Garner, Bill, 69
Gaskell, Elizabeth, 248
Gatewood, Emma, 5
Gavin, Hector, 65
Gayter, Sharon, 108
General Federation of Women's Clubs, 254
Gentlewoman magazine, 306
German and Austrian Alpine Club, 87
German, Julie, 122
Germany, 92, 259
Gibb, Roberta 'Bobbi', 354
Gibson, Frances, *163*, 164
Gibson, Harry, 164
Gilligan, Carol, 210–11, 213, 221, 292

Gilmour, Charlie, 66
Glaisdale, 348–9
Glass Universe, The (Sobel), 251
Goethe, Johann Wolfgang von, 82
'Golden Age of Alpinism', 67, 69–70
Golden Gate Dirty 30, 113
Goldman, Barry, 12
golf, 238–9, 243, 318, 352
Gooley, Tristan, 290
Gordon Cumming, Constance, 86
Grandchamp, Gail, 353
Grandes Jorasses, 131
Grands Mulets, 44–5, 46, 59
Granite Crags (Gordon Cumming), 86
Granta magazine, 5
Great Central Hotel, Marylebone, 310
Green, Margaret Sophia, 136
Greig, Dale, 355
grief, 12, 23, 36, 66, 297, 339–40, 373–4, 377–8
Griffiths, Kerry, 121
Grosz, Elizabeth, 225
Guide to the Lakes (Wordsworth), 68
guidebooks, 68, 70–71
guides *see* mountain guides

H is for Hawk (Macdonald), 66
Hall, Edward T., 180–81
Hall, Rob, 280
Hallman, Kelly, 212
Hambleton Drove Road, 22, 34
Handbook for Switzerland (Murray), 71, 75
Handbook for Travellers (Baedeker), 70, 71
Hannon, Elizabeth, 184
harassment *see* sexual harassment and violence
Harberton, Lady Florence, 143
Harcourt, Lewis, 319
Hardmoors, 25, 111
  Hardmoors Osmotherley Marathon, 28, 31–4
  Hardmoors trail marathon races, 174–5
Hardwick ,'Nan', 349–51
Hargreaves, Alison, 280
Harper, Frances Ellen Watkins, 94
Harper, Stephen, 330–31
Harvard College, 250
Harvard Law Review, 102
Hatfield, Ada, 309
Havergal, Frances, 78–9
Hawker, Lizzy, 107–8
Hawkins, Alice, 160
Hawkins-Whitshed, Anne Alicia 'Alice', 52, 59, 151–2
Hawkins-Whitshed, St Vincent 'Vin' Bentinck, 50–51, 150
Hayward, Jane (Edith), 325, 327
health, 75, 145–6
  depression, 271
  health tourism, 73–5
  women and, 75, 225, 270–72
Heffernan, Mike, 55
Heggie, Vanessa, 259
Heminsley, Alexandra, 4
Henderson, William, 349
Henie, Sonja, 241
Heron-Maxwell, Frances, 320
Herron, Camille, 108
High Alps in Winter, The (Le Blond), 135
High Life and Towers of Silence (Le Blond), 59–60, 139
hiking, 74, 80, 333–4
Hillary, Edmund, 329
Himalayan Scientific and Mountaineering Expedition (1961), 329
Himalayas, 328–31
Hingston, James, 66
HIV/AIDS, 366
Hlavka, Heather R., 189

Hochschild, Arlie Russell, 184–5
hockey, 242, 318, 319
Hogg, Kerri, 286
Holland, James, 162
Holland, Jeanette, 159
Holmes, Katie, 331
homophobia, 193
homosexuality, 243–4, 258–9
hooks, bell, 193, 254
Hornby, Emily, 78, 89, 141, 145–6, 233, 317
Horton Women's Holiday Centre, 43
Hotel Belvédère, Davos, 149, 151
Hôtel d'Angleterre, Chamonix, 131
Howard Fox, Maria, 309, 310, *311*
Howard University, Washington, DC, 335
Hughes, James Percival, 152
Hutchinson, Horace, 239

Ibrahimi, Freshta, 359–61
ice-skating, 161–2, *162*, 241
If You Fall . . . It's a New Beginning (Darke), 122
Ilkley Moor, Yorkshire, 316
Imboden, Josef, 148, 231–2
Imboden, Roman, 231–2, 305
Independent, 124
India, 192, 196–7, 216–7, 366
Inglis Clark, Jane, 234
'insult races', 92
International Association of Athletics Federations (IAAF), 331
International Himalaya Expeditions (IHE), 330
International Journal of Sports Physiology and Performance, 123
International Women's Running Circuit, 356
Invisible Women (Criado Perez), 225
Ireland, 47–53, 318
Irish Land War (1879–82), 53, 58
Irish National Land League, 53
Irish Women's Franchise League, 318
Isle of Wight Marathon, 355
Italy, 92

Jack, Dana Crowley, 212, 215
Jackson, Margaret, 233, 310
Jackson, Monica, 330
Jackson, William H., 154
Jacobson, Mary, 154
Jahn, Frederick Ludwig, 259
James, Henry, 258
James, Kandy, 217, 219
Japan, 83, 234
Japanese Alpine Club, 88, 242
Jayden, Kate, 108
'Jim Crow' laws (USA), 254, 351
John, Emma, 5
Johnson, Mordecai Wyatt, 335–6
Jugal Himal, Himalayas, 330
Jungfrau mountain, 43, 310, *311*

Kahn, Russ, 125
Karlsbad, Germany, 73
Kearl, Holly, 189, 196, 218, 368–9
Kelly, Emily 'Pat', 314
Kew Gardens, London, 252
Khan, Sameera, 192
Kilimanjaro, 234
Killincarrick, Ireland, 46–7, 50–51, 53
Kim, Chloe, 110
Kinder Scout, Peak District, 316
Kindleberger Hagan, Lisa, 286
King, Billie Jean, 336
King, Emma, 73
Kirk-Greene, Anthony, 238
Klein, Melanie, 340
Knaresborough, North Yorkshire, 25
Knowles, Eric S., 182
Knox, Katherine 'Kittie', 240

Kogan, Claude, 330
Kuebli, Janet, 286
Kulm Hotel, St Moritz, 132, 148, 154–5, 305
Kvikne, Knut, 136
Kvikne, Margaret Sophia Green, 233

Ladies' Alpine Club, 7, 306–15, *311*, 320–21, 323–4, 356
Ladies' Grand Council of the Primrose League, 317
Ladies' Scottish Climbing Club, 330
Lady Killer Peak (Harper), 330–31
Lady's Life in the Rocky Mountains, A (Bird), 136
Lake District Mountain Trial, 332
Lake, Robert, 239
Langseth, Tommy, 281
Lankester, Sir Edwin Ray, 254, 258
Larcom, Lucy, 67
Larisch, Countess Marie, 157–8, 167
Law, William, 294
lawn tennis *see* tennis
Lawrence, Clyde, 280
Le Blond, Aubrey, 305, 324–7, 373–4
Le Blond, Lizzie, 6–8, 15–16, 41–6, *46*, 70, 80, 82, 95, 102, 140, *140*, *141*, *142*, *165*
  Adventures on the Roof of the World, 306
  Anglo-French Luncheon Club, 325
  Aubrey Le Blond, relationship with, 305, 324, 373–4
  bandy, 161
  curling, 161
  cycling, 159–61
  Day In, Day Out, 42
  death, 327–8
  Dent du Géant and, 137–9
  Edouard Cupelin, relationship with, 134–8
  family and childhood, 47–51
  football and, 324–5
  Fred Burnaby, relationship with, 52–7, 59, 135, 151
  health, 59–60, 74, 305–6
  High Alps in Winter, The, 135
  High Life and Towers of Silence, 59–60, 139
  ice-skating, 161–2, 162, 241
  in Engadin / St Moritz, 156–9, 161, 164–5, 167
  in London, 325–6
  information-gathering, 326–7
  John Main, relationship with, 149–52, 154–5
  Ladies' Alpine Club and, 306–14, 321, 323, 326
  lawn tennis, 158
  'manless climbing' and, 314
  motherhood, 56–7, 151–2
  Norway, 232–3
  photography, 6, *6*, 152–4, *153*, 164–5, 167, 374
  public speaking, 306, 322
  retirement from mountaineering, 305
  rowing, 159
  Story of an Alpine Winter, The, 56–7
  tobogganing, 164
  True Tales of Mountain Adventure, 233
  USA and, 325
  Victory Medal, 324
  women's rights and, 320–21
  World War I and, 322–4, 326
Leadville Trail 100 Race, 109
League of American Wheelmen (LAW), 239–40
Leather, Diane, 331
LeBlanc, Mitch, 109
Legendary Races' Cloud City Multi-Stage race, 111
LeGree, Marina, 359
Leman, Jane Margaret, 86

di Leonardo, Micaela, 188
Lewenhaupt, Countess Ida Felicia, 309
Lewis Lloyd, Emmeline, 86, 136
LGBT community, 189
Liberal Women's Suffrage Union, 320
Light, Rob, 237
Linden, Andrew D., 352–3
Lindley, John, 251–2
Ling, Per Henrik, 259
Lister, Anne, 80
Liverpool Daily Post, 315
Liverpool Women's Suffrage Society, 317
Logan, Bev, 111
Lombroso, Cesare, 258
London Marathon, 118
Longman's Magazine, 237
Loon Mountain Race, New Hampshire, 111
Loukaitou-Sideris, Anastasia, 212, 218
Lourdes, France, 75
Lowell, Abbott Lawrence, 251
Lucrezi, Gina, 122
Luelmo, Laura, 192
Lugard, Frederick, 238
Lundberg, Tommy, 127
Lyautey, Hubert, 324, 327
Lyceum Alpine Club *see* Ladies' Alpine Club
Lyceum Club, 307, 310–11
Lyke Wake Club, 342–3
'Lyke Wake Dirge', 35–6, 341–3
Lyke Wake Walk, 35–6, 340–48, 350–51, 367, 371–2
Lyke Wake Walk (Cowley), 342

Macdonald, Helen, 66
Mackie, Bella, 4
MacMorland, Elizabeth, 74
Main, John Frederic, 149–52, 154–6
Make Space for Girls, 364
Manchester Ramblers' Federation, 334
Manchester Wheelers, 239–40
Manthorne, Katherine, 153
Manuel, Simone, 110
MapMyRun, 183
marathon running, 331, 354–5
Marcotte, Vanessa, 191–2
Margherita, Queen of Italy, 310
Married Women's Property Acts (UK), 246
Martinez, Wendy, 192
Marvingt, Marie, 328–9
Marylebone Cricket Club (MCC), 237
Massachusetts Bicycle Club, 239
Mathews, Charles Edward, 69, 87, 242
Matrimonial Causes Acts (UK), 246
Maxfield, Sylvia, 279–80
Mazamas Club, Portland, Oregon, 88
Mazuchelli, Elizabeth Sarah, 59, 86
McAllister, Pam, 193
McAndrew, Beatrice, 323
McCarthy, Helen, 322
McDonnell, Lady Evelyn, 314
McDougald, Elise Johnson, 351
McLaren, Barbara, 164
McLaren, Eva, 320
McNuff, Anna, 4
Meeting at the Crossroads (Brown and Gilligan), 221
Melbourne, Australia, 65
Memsahb im Himalaja (Dyhrenfurth), 330
men and outdoor sport, 119
  male hostility, 83–7, 128, 335
  male sporting advantage, 119–20
  physical deterioration, 257–61
  see also risk
menopause, 114, 123, 296, 299

menstruation, 114, 244, 299
Mer de Glace, Chamonix, 44, 72
Merz, Teresa, 317–18
Meyer, Maud, 317
Middlesmoor, North Yorkshire, 289–91
'milk cures', 74
Miller, Irene, 329
Miller, Madeleine, 146
Milsom, Marjorie, 87, 142, 319
misogynoir, 192
misogyny, 85, 115, 189–97, 260–62, 362–3
  see also sexual harassment and violence
mobile phones, 101–2
Molinaro, Carla, 108
Moncrieff, Alexander, Lord Moncreiff, 239
Mont Blanc, 44–5, 80, 86, 91, 131, 233
Mont Pelvoux, Massif des Ecrins, 234
Mont Perdu, Pyrenees, 80
Monte Rosa, 134–5
Montgomery, Jordan, 287
Moran, Caitlin, 261
More Than a Woman (Moran), 261
Morel, Bénédict Augustin, 258
Morgan, Alex, 110
Morrell, Jemima, 78
Morrell, Ottoline, 156
Morrongiello, Barbara, 286
Mount Everest Committee, 328–9
mountain guides, 91, 136–7, 145
mountaineering, 5, 41–2, 59–60, 67–72, 80, 88, 90–91, 146–7, 358
  attacks and violence, 146
  clothing, 140–43, *141*, 312–13
  criticism of, 144–5
  equipment, 72–3, 312–13
  exclusion of women, 241–2
  'femininity' and, 143–4
  health, 75–8
  Himalayan expeditions and, 328–31, 357–8
  'manless climbing', 314
  photography, 312
  risk aversion, 279–82
  sexism, 139–40, 144–5, 242, 334
  winter mountaineering, 132–4
  women's rights and, 317–21
Mudd, Edith Emily, 308–9
Muir, Laura, 127
Mumbai, India, 192
Mummery, Albert, 85, 135, 137
Mummery, Mary, 233
Murphy, Ashling, 192
Murray, Brian, 157
Murray, John, 71
My Safetipin app, 364
Myanmar, 365

Naismith, William W., 242
Napoleon Bonaparte, 70, 180
National Association of Colored Women's Clubs (NACWC), 318
National Football Museum, 357
National Organization for Women, 352
National Society for Women's Suffrage, 320
Nauright, John, 257
Nepal, 358–9
Nettleton, Louise, 309, 312
New York City, 64
  Central Park, 67
New York Times, 124, 335–6, 358
Nidderdale Way, 273–7, 282–4, 291–2, 297
Nietzsche, Friedrich, 156
Nike, 124
'noise annoyance', 100–101
Nordau, Max, 258
North and South (Gaskell), 248
North York Moors, 22, 26, 35, 174, 341–7, 371
North, Marianne, 78

Norway, 232–3, 241, 326
Norwegian Peak Club, 241
Norwegian Tourist Association, 73
Nugent, Jim, 136
Nunn, Paul, 280
'Nyonin Kinsei', 83

O'Brien, Margaret, 213
O'Neill, Jarrah, 193
Occupy Wall Street protests, 193–4
Oku-Hodaka mountains, 234
Olstead, Riley, 279
Olympic Games, 8, 242–3, 259–60, 262–3, 332, 354–6
  athletes with disabilities, 243
  exclusion of women, 260
  International Olympic Committee, 8
  Tokyo (2020), 110
  Winter Games (1924), 241
'Oner' ultra-marathon, Jurassic coast, 120
Osborne, Carol, 312, 330, 334
Osius, Alison, 280
Osmotherley, North Yorkshire, 22, 26, 35, 37–8, 344
Ottogalli-Mazzacavallo, Cécile, 89
Ouray 100-Mile Endurance Race, 111
Outdoor Industries Association, 121–2
Outward Bound Trust, 42
Oxford University, 240, 245, 251

Paillon, Mary, 234–6, 309–10, 323
Pakistan, 359
Pakistani Women's Climbing Camp, 359
Pal, Bachendri, 5
Pálffy, Countess Paulina von, 158
Pan Duo, 357
Pankhurst, Emmeline, 318
Paradis, Maria, 80, 82, 91, 94
parental attitudes to gender, 286–9
Paris, France, 65
Paris, Jasmin, 108–9, 115
Parks, Rosa, 351
Parminter, Elizabeth, 81–2
Parminter, Jane, 81–2
Parminter, Mary, 81–2
Pasang Lhamu Sherpa, 358–9
Pastime magazine, 158
PATH, 214
Patterson, Inez, 318
Payne-Gaposchkin, Celia, 251
Peck, Annie Smith, 319
pedestrians, behaviour of, 182, 366–7
Pelvic Roar (campaign group), 114
Pennine Way, 32, 108, 203–4
Pennsylvania, USA, 73
Perez, Caroline Criado, 250
Perreau, Henri, 146
'Personal Best' times, 294–5
Peyman, Bradby, 323
Phadke, Shilpa, 192
Philadelphia, USA, 64, 71
photography, 152–3, 312–13
Pigeon, Anna and Ellen, 233–4
Pinnacle Club, 314, 334
Piz Kesch, Albula Alps, 231
Piz Morteratsch, Switzerland, 165, *165*
Plath, Sylvia, 195–6
Plunket, Frederica, 80, 82, 89, 95, 139, 142, 145–7
Pointe Marguerite, Grandes Jorasses, 86
Pointue, Pierre, 44
Porphyry, 225
Potter, Beatrice, 149
Potter, Claire Bond, 352
Power, Sophie, 112–13, *112*
pregnancy, 109, 112–13, 124, 299
Pregnancy Discrimination Act (USA, 1978), 114
Preston Mountaineering Club, 242
Pride and Prejudice (Austen), 79

Priestley, Joseph, 293
privacy, 102, 144
Proctor, Tammy M., 326
proxemics, 180–81
Prudom, Thomas, 349–50
public health, 65–6
public houses, 250
public libraries, 252–3
Public Order Act (1986), 362
public parks, 67, 116, 213–19, 365
  see also public spaces, male domination of
public schools, sports in, 238, 244
public spaces, male domination of, 103, 180–82, 193–4, 196, 210–20, 248–50, 260–62, 298–300, 314–18, 351–2, 356, 364–5
  'separate spheres', 79–80, 185, 260, 298–9
  see also sexual harassment and violence
public toilets, 216–17
public transport, 70–71, 247–8
puerperal mania, 48–50
Pugh, Griffith, 329
Puma North America, 125–6
Punk Panther, 111

'Q angle', 3
Qualification of Women Acts (UK), 246

Race Relations Act (UK, 1976), 353
racewalking, 356
racial segregation, 239–40, 249, 254, 335, 351–2
racism, 193, 243, 351
Radcliffe, Paula, 127
Rae, Mrs John, 52
railways, 247–8
  ladies-only carriages, 315
Rainshadow Running, 111
Ramazani, Vaheed, 256–7
rambling, 64, 67–71, 90, 315–16, 333–4
Ranade, Shilpa, 192
Rational Dress Society, 143
Rehabilitation Act (USA, 1973), 353
Reid, James, 48
Reid, Mandu, 315
Representation of the People Act (1918), 246
Repton, Humphry, 77*n*
restaurants, 248–50, 254
Revíthi, Stamáta, 262–3
Ribblehead, Yorkshire, 202–3
Richards, Rebecca, 93
Richardson, Anna Deborah, 317
Richardson, Sarah Katharine 'Katy', 234–6, 309, 323
Richter, Hugo, 74
Ride to Khiva, A (Burnaby), 52
riding, 73–3
Riggs, Bobby, 336
risk, 267–301, 365–6
  risk aversion, 272–3, 279–82, 366
  risk-taking behaviour, 181, 279–81, 286–7, 293, 365–6
Robins, Elizabeth, 253
Robinson, Jo Ann, 351
rock climbing, 277–9
Rocky Mountains, Colorado, 317
Romilly, Sophia, 86
Roseberry Topping, Yorkshire, 25, 174
Rosewell, Lizzie, 110
Ross, Hannah, 159–60, 240
Rousseau, Jean-Jacques, 82
rowing, 159, 242, 335
Roy-Batty, Violet, 309, 320
Royal and Ancient Golf Club of St Andrews, 239
Royal Geographical Society, 306, 329
Royal Liverpool Golf Club, 239
Royal Photographic Society, 154

Ruc-Sac magazine, 333
Rudolf, Crown Prince of Austria, 157
Rudolph, Emanuel D., 251
rugby, 243
ruling bodies, 236–40
RunEqual, 127
Runner's World, 187
running, 4, 41, 293–5, 332, 349, 354–6
  cross-country running, 126–7
  fell running, 108, 332
  marathon running, 26–7, 107, 118–20, 260, 262, 331, 354–5
  road running, 121, 295
  trail running, 24–5, 41, 131, 295
  ultra-marathons, 26, 107, 119–20
  ultra-running, 26, 107–10
Running While Black (Désir), 122
Rutkiewicz, Wanda, 357

Saleh bin Osman, 157
Salomon WMN half-marathon, Lake Sonoma, California, 111
Salpini, Cara, 125
Salvesen, Øyvind, 281
Samuels, David, 184
San Francisco Call, 240
Sand, George, 143, 235
Sanday, Peggy Reeves, 260–62
Saunderson, Cissy, *163*, 164
Saunderson, Esther, *163*, 164
Saunderson, Lady Rachel, 164*n*
Savile, Frank, 319
Savoiz, Michel, 137
Sayer, Ann, 356
Scherlis, Lily, 180
Schocher, Martin, 148
scientific investigation, 81
Scott, Florence, 332
Scottish Mountaineering Club, 88
Scouting for Boys (Baden-Powell), 259
Scrambles Amongst the Alps (Whymper), 52, 87
Sedan, France, 75
'Self-Transcendence' race, 27
Semple, Jock, 355, *355*
Sen, Sarmistha, 192
'separate spheres', 79–80, 185, 260, 299
Serenade for Tenor, Horn and Strings (Britten) 341
Serious Call to a Devout and Holy Life, A (Law), 294
Serrano, Laura, 353
Sesia-Joch Pass, Zermatt, 234
Sex Discrimination Act (UK, 1975), 353
Sex Disqualification (Removal) Act (1919), 246
sex segregation, 79–80, 85, 120, 162, 216, 248–9, 314–15, 366
sexism in sport, 107–14, 121–8, 139–40, 331–4
sexual harassment and violence, 126, 146, 186–97, 247–8, 253–4, 288, 315, 352, 361–4
  justice system, 188, 362–4
  murder, 126, 191–2, 197, 248, 363, 368
  street harassment, 15, 188–96, 217–19, 262, 355, 362, 368
Shapiro, Mary, 279–80
Sharp, Emma, 93
Shaw, Martha 'Patty', 76–7
Sherwood, Julie, 352–3
shoes, 3–4
Sholes, Charles H., 88
Sia Kangri, Himalayas, 330
Siegel, Suzie, 196
Silk, Susan, 12
Simon, John, 75
Sims, Stacy, 114, 123
Sinclair, James, 312
Singh, Sophia Duleep, 319
skiing, 132
slavery, 254
Slingsby, Alizon, 232
Slingsby, Edith, 232

Slingsby, Eleanor 'Len', 334
Slingsby, William Cecil, 232
Slowe, Lucy Diggs, 318, 335–6
Słupska, Julia, 124
smart watches, 124
Smedley, Constance, 307
Smedley, Ida, 314
Smith Eaton, Cora, 319
Smith Peck, Annie, 143
Smith, Charlotte, 81
Smith, Victoria, 288
'smock-races', 92
Smyth, Ethel, 318
Snowdon, Wales, 79, 84, 106–7, 115–18
  Llanberis Path, 106
  Watkin Path, 116–17
Sobel, Dava, 251
social class, 91–2, 95
Society for the Prevention of Cruelty to Children, 306
Solomon, Sunil, 366
'Souls, The', 156
South Africa, 212, 218
Sparks, Rennie, 105
Spence Watson, Elizabeth, 317
Spine Race, 32, 108–9
Spinks, Nicky, 108
sport, definition of, 236–8
Sport England, 183
sports books, 122–3
sports science, 123, 332
sportswear, 113–14, 123–4, 140–43, *141*, 216, 312–13
spying, 326–7
St Ermin's Court, London, 325–6
St Gotthard Pass, Switzerland, 76
St Helens Ladies football team, 246
St Moritz, 148, 152, 154–8, 161–2, 165–6, 309
  St Moritz Aid Fund, 152, 164, 306
  St Moritz Skating Club, 162, 241
St Moritz Post, 154
Stanley, Henry Morton, 157
Starley & Sutton Company, 159
Stephen, Leslie, 85, 135
Stockholm, Sweden, 159, 218
Stokes, Neil, 182
Stokes, Rose, 124
Stop Street Harassment Campaign (USA), 189, 363–4
Story of an Alpine Winter, The (Le Blond), 56–7
Straton, Isabella, 86, 136, 233
Strava (fitness-tracking platform), 124–5, 183
street harassment *see* sexual harassment and violence
Strutt, Edward Lisle, 158, 314
Stuart, Helen, 114
'Suffragette, The' (Savile), 319
Sutherland, Sydney, 192
Sutton Bank Visitors' Centre, 22
Swale Pope, Rosie, 4
Swanwick, Helena, 253
Sweden, 259
Swiss Alpine Club, 74, 89, 242
Swiss Lawn Tennis Championship, 158
Switzer, Kathrine, 354–6, *355*
Switzerland, 43, 85, 92, 166
Syers, Madge, 162

Tabei, Junko, 5, 329–30, 357
Tairraz, Auguste, 137
Tamkatsuma mountains, Japan, 234
Tanczer, Leonie, 124–5
Taylor, Annie, 309
Taylor, Joanna, 121
Taylor, Mary, 317
Taylor, Susette, 309
technology, 124–5
tennis, 110, 158, 160, 239, 335–6, 357
Terry Fox Run, 369
thermal spas, 73–4
Thomas and Son, London, 313

Thompson, E. P., 316
Thompson, Robert 'Mouseman', 205
Thompson, Simon, 316, 333
Thomson, J. J., 251
Thoreau, Henry David, 66, 82
Three Sisters, Yorkshire, 33
'Throwing Like a Girl' (Young), 29
Tibbetts, Mollie, 192
Tier, Geoff, 280
Times, The, 55, 133
Timperio, Anna, 214
Title IX legislation (USA), 109–10, 353
To The Lighthouse (Woolf), 309
tobogganing, 162–3, *163*, 240
Tobogganing on Crooked Runs (Gibson), 164
Togakushi mountains, Japan, 234
Togethxr, 110
Tomasson, Beatrice, 158
Tonawanda, Jackie, 353
Topham, Harold Ward, 158
tourism, 67, 70–72
Toynbee, Polly, 280
Trail Sisters, 122
trans athletes, 127–8, 193
Trevelyan, Charles, 316
Tribune, 245
Trimiar, Marian 'Tyger', 353
Trivium Racing, North Carolina, 111
True Tales of Mountain Adventure (Le Blond), 233
tuberculosis, 42, 74, 75
Tubman, Harriet, 93
Tuke, John Batty, 49
Turner, Jeff, 366–7
Tynan, Katharine, 51
Tyndall, John, 88

'Ugly Laws' (USA), 254–5
Ultra Trail du Mont Blanc (UTMB), 107, 112–13, *112*
ultra-marathons, 26, 107, 119–20
ultra-running, 26, 107–10
Under Armour, 124
Union of Practical Suffragists, 320
'unisex' equipment, 113–14
United States Hotel, Boston, 249
universities, sports in, 238
University College, London, 251
Unwin, Thomas Fisher, 308
Urania Cottage, London, 57
urbanisation, 64–7
  life expectancy, 65–6
  population, 64–5
Urra Moor, 345

Vail, Eugénie, 309
Van der Stratten, Claudine, 330
Van Slyck, Abigail A., 252
Vera-Gray, Fiona, 195
Vetrano, Karina, 191–2
Vetsera, Baroness Mary, 157
Vichy, France, 73
Victoria, Australia, 65
Victoria, Queen of the United Kingdom, 58
Victoria Magazine, 317
Vienna, Austria, 65
Vignemale, Pyrenees, 80
violence against women *see* sexual harassment and violence
Virginia, USA, 73
Von Aldenburg Bentinck, Countess Charlotte Sophie, 307
Vonen, Nikka, 232
Votes for Women newspaper, 320

Walker Hartley, James, 138
Walker, Lucy, 85–7, 137, 233, 308–10
Walker, Weldy, 243
Walkowitz, Judith, 253
Wallaby Club, Australia, 87
Wallace, Keri, 109

Wanderer Above the Sea of Fog (Friedrich), 82
Wanderlust Women, 42
Warren, Samuel D., 102
Washington Post, 238
Waste Land, The (Eliot), 158, 167
Watkin, Emmeline, 117
Watkin, Sir Edward, 116–17
Watson, Cecil, 162
Watson, Vera, 358
Webb, Hilda, 318
Weeton, Ellen 'Nelly', 83–4, 102
Werther (Goethe), 82
West Highland Way race, 35–6, 99, 174, 177
West, Amanda, 279, 281
Western States 100-Mile Endurance Run, 113
Western, Emily and Lucy, 309
Weston, Frances Emily, 234
Wetherbee, Nellie, 255
Wethered, Joyce, 239
Whymper, Edward, 52, 87
Wilde, Oscar, 258–9
'wilderness camping', 90
Willing, Ava, 164
Wimbledon Lawn Tennis Championships, 110, 160, 239
Winthrop Young, Geoffrey, 334
Wisden Cricketers' Almanack, 237
witches, 348–51
Withington, Eliza, 153
Woman: Man's Equal? (Abrahams), 331
Woman's Labour, The (Collier), 91–2
women and outdoor sport, 107–14, 121–8, 144, 166–7
  endurance sports, 107–9, 119–20
  exclusion of women, 236–46, 255, 331–5, 352–4
  family and, 279–80
  gender earnings gap, 111, 122, 299, 357
  harassment and violence, 126, 146, 186–97, 217–19
  intimidation, 216–17
  lockdown and, 183–4
  male sporting advantage, 119–20
  media coverage, 110
  murder, 191–2, 197
  pregnancy / childbirth, 112–13, 123
  reduction in participation, 214–16, 226–7, 236–7
  risk aversion, 279–82, 366
  safety, 194–5
  sexism, 139–40, 144–5, 242–3, 331–2
  split consciousness, 29–30
  sportswear, 113–14, 123–4, 140–41, 216
  see also individual sports
Women in Sport charity, 215
'Women in the Hills' (WITH) network, 121, 125
Women's Cricket Association, 356
Women's Football Association, 356
Women's Liberal Association, 317
Women's Liberal Federation, 320
Women's Political Council, 351
women's rights, 58–9, 96, 128, 227, 241–50, 256, 261, 272, 317–19, 351–4
  African-American women's rights, 318, 335, 351–2
  'New Woman' ideal, 317
  suffragists, 88, 160, 314, 317–21
Women's Social and Political Union, 161, 318
Women's Sports Foundation, 336
Woolf, Virginia, 85, 309
Wordsworth, William, 82, 91
Workman, Fanny Bullock, 306, 308–11, 319, 320, 329
World Athletics Championships, 120
World War I (1914–18), 322–4
Wright Graham, Hettie, 250

Wuchang Uprising, China, 326
Wynne, Frances, 51–2

yachting, 159
Yamauchi, Mara, 127
Yari mountains, Japan, 234
Yorke, Philip, 79
Yorkshire Dales National Park, 25, 203, 205–8, 273–4
Yorkshire Ramblers' Club, 144
Young Men's Christian Association (YMCA), 259
Young Women's Christian Association (YWCA), 318
Young, Iris Marion, 29, 105, 144, 211, 217
Younghusband, Francis, 329
Yousoufi, Hanifa, 359–61

Zhong, Bao-Liang, 270
Zimmern, Helen, 156
Zola, Emile, 256–7
Zuccotti Park, New York City, 193–4